Memory Systems 1994

Memory Systems 1994

edited by Daniel L. Schacter and Endel Tulving

A Bradford Book
The MIT Press
Cambridge, Massachusetts
London, England

This book was set in Palatino by Asco Trade Typesetting Ltd., Hong Kong, and was printed and bound in the United States of America.

Second printing, 1995

Library of Congress Cataloging-in-Publication Data

Memory systems 1994 / edited by Daniel L. Schacter and Endel Tulving.
    p.   cm.
"A Bradford book."
Includes bibliographical references and index.
ISBN 0-262-19350-7
1. Memory. 2. Animal memory. I. Schacter, Daniel L. II. Tulving, Endel.
BF371.M4678   1994
153.1'2—dc20   93-36582
                                                CIP

Contents

Preface

The history of scientific thinking about memory was for a long time dominated by the tacit assumption that memory is a unitary or monolithic entity. Occasional doubts expressed about the validity of this assumption took the form of philosophical speculations regarding different "kinds" or "forms" of memory, distinguished from one another phenomenologically and sometimes functionally.

During the past two decades, challenges to the assumption of unitary memory have become more numerous, forceful, and concentrated. A growing number of cognitive and behavioral neuroscientists have advanced increasingly detailed hypotheses concerning the nature of and relations among different memory systems. A crucial difference between the older ideas and these more recent proposals is that the current reevaluation of the assumption of unitary memory is based on a rapidly expanding base of experimental and other empirical evidence, as opposed to enlightened intuition or metaphysical analysis.

In late 1990, with the enthusiastic support of Michael Gazzaniga, we invited a number of students of memory to participate in assembling a special issue of the *Journal of Cognitive Neuroscience* concerning multiple memory systems. They are individuals who have contributed significantly to, and have thought carefully about, the classification and organization of memory. The papers that they wrote for the special issue appeared in the summer of 1992. Taken together, the papers in the special issue (a) illustrated the variety of approaches that have been taken to the problem—cognitive, neuropsychological, neurobiological, and computational; (b) furnished an overview of the kinds of evidence brought to bear on the issue of multiple forms of memory; and (c) brought into focus the main theoretical ideas and conceptualizations that have guided the overall enterprise.

The special issue, we believe, took a useful first step toward the next goal for this domain of research—systematizing the study of multiple memory systems. This book represents an attempt to move closer to that goal. We asked contributors to the special issue to revise and expand their earlier papers with a view toward relating their own ideas about memory systems to those of the other contributors. The reasoning underlying this second phase of the project was straightforward: by encouraging integrative thinking about memory systems, we hoped that points of agreement and disagreement could be brought into sharper focus, thereby facilitating future progress in research and theory. We have also added an introductory chapter in which we attempt to place the issue of memory systems in a broad historical context, consider the logic of and criteria for postulating multiple memory systems, and summarize the nature of and relations between the ideas of the various contributors.

Questions concerning the nature and organization of memory systems are fundamental to our understanding of the processes underlying learning and memory in humans and other animals. We hope that the chapters presented here provide a useful summary of the experimental and theoretical accomplishments to date and serve as a guidepost to future investigations of this important scientific problem.

1   What Are the Memory Systems of 1994?

Daniel L. Schacter and Endel Tulving

Imagine that our present civilization develops more or less peacefully and that the world is still intact a thousand years from now. Imagine further that you could visit the future world and bring back with you, among other things, the answer to one crucial question about human memory. What would the question be, and why?... Our question has to do with the subdivisions of human memory. We assume, along with most other students of the subject, that memory is not a monolithic, unitary entity and that what we label memory in fact represents a number of separate but interacting systems. All these systems have a common function: They make possible the utilization of acquired and retained knowledge. It is their differences that are the subject of our crucial question: How can we characterize the various systems that comprise human memory? (Schacter & Tulving, 1982, pp. 33–34)

When we offered the foregoing reflections over a decade ago, we hoped to arouse the interest of contemporary students in an issue that we believed was scientifically important, although it had not been systematically pursued: the nature and number of memory systems. Understanding of this issue seemed to us then vital to, and perhaps a necessary condition of, progress in memory research. It is even more so today. If memory can indeed be fractionated into multiple systems and subsystems that differ fundamentally from one another, then general theoretical proposals and ideas about the nature of memory are not going to be worthwhile; they have to be qualified with respect to particular systems and subsystems. Hence the choice of our crucial question for the imaginary time traveler.

Even a decade ago, various proposals concerning multiple kinds of memory existed. Indeed, the debate concerning short-term versus long-term memory stores that flourished during the 1960s and 1970s had already passed its peak. During the past ten years, however, discussions concerning the nature and number of memory systems have become more pervasive and intense. They now occupy an unprecedented prominence in cognitive, neuropsychological, and neurobiological research. A large body of empirical observations has accumulated, numerous distinctions among memory systems have been proposed, and discussions of the conceptual and metatheoretical issues surrounding the memory-systems enterprise are gathering force.

The general idea that various forms or kinds of memory are in some sense fundamentally different is not without its critics. A number of contemporary students have questioned whether it is necessary or useful to hypothesize such sharp distinctions, preferring instead to retain the notion of a unitary memory that works, or can be used, in many different ways (e.g., Humphreys, Bain, & Pike, 1989; Jacoby, 1984; Masson & MacLeod, 1992; Roediger, Weldon, & Challis, 1989). For the most part, however, a general consensus has emerged among neuropsychologists, neurobiologists, and many cognitive psychologists that some sort of systematic classification of memory is fundamental to our theoretical understanding of mnemonic processes. The important task now is to organize and, if possible, integrate the variety of approaches, techniques, and outcomes of the systems-oriented research to date, and also to coordinate the expected expansion of these pursuits. The time has come to systematize our knowledge and understanding of memory systems.

There are many unresolved issues facing the field today. They include the very concept of memory system, the nature and number of such systems, how to best characterize their mutual relations and interactions, and the appropriate logic for linking empirical observations of memory-task performance with theoretical and conceptual statements about inferred neurocognitive systems. The chapters in this volume take steps toward clarifying these issues by providing a critical assessment of experimental evidence and theoretical ideas concerning memory systems. All of the contributing authors were presented with two different yet related charges. On the one hand, they were asked to produce an integrative summary of their personal views regarding the nature of and relations between memory systems. On the other hand, they were encouraged to compare and contrast their own positions with relevant ideas advanced by the other authors. Our hope was that jointly pursuing these two tasks would lead to a sharpening of key points of agreement and disagreement among the contributors and thereby yield both a useful assessment of the current state of the art in our understanding of memory systems and a heuristic guide to the next phase of research and theorizing.

The main purpose of this chapter is to orient the reader to the major issues and themes discussed in the volume and to describe our own current understanding of some of the main issues that prominently figure in the debate about multiple memory systems. To accomplish this objective, we divide this chapter into four main sections. In the first we sketch some of the historical background to current research and theorizing about memory systems. The second section considers some of the basic conceptual and logical underpinnings of the memory-systems enterprise. Here we discuss the status of such fundamental concepts as multiple memory systems and examine the inferential logic used to relate experimental evidence to theoretical proposals. In the third section we summarize our current understanding of the nature and number of memory systems in light of the ideas expressed by the contributors to the volume. The fourth section revisits issues concerning human versus animal memory systems.

Daniel L. Schacter and Endel Tulving

1 MULTIPLE FORMS OF MEMORY: SOME HISTORICAL PERSPECTIVES

1.1 Early Speculations

Systematic analysis and discussion of multiple forms of memory is, for the most part, a relatively recent development in memory research. In the experimental study of human memory, for example, the issue was first brought into sharp focus by the debate over short-term versus long-term memory that prospered during the 1960s and 1970s (e.g., Atkinson & Shiffrin, 1968; Melton, 1963; Waugh & Norman, 1965). Discussions of multiple long-term memory systems only began in earnest during the mid 1970s, following the introduction of the distinction between episodic and semantic memory (Tulving, 1972). In the study of nonhuman animals, sustained interest in the issue of memory systems was sparked by several seminal publications in the mid 1970s (Gaffan, 1974; Hirsh, 1974; Nadel & O'Keefe, 1974; O'Keefe & Nadel, 1978). Nevertheless, as noted by several contributors to this volume (see especially the chapters by Eichenbaum and Nadel), there are a number of nineteenth- and twentieth-century antecedents to the distinctions among memory systems that have been put forward recently. Historical overviews can be found in Herrmann and Chaffin (1988), Polster, Nadel, and Schacter (1991), Schacter (1987a), and Schacter and Tulving (1982), and we draw on them to develop the present account.

As with many other scientific ideas, it is difficult to specify unambiguously the first articulation of the hypothesis of multiple memory systems. Certainly, distinctions among types of information retained in memory are about as old as theorizing about the nature of memory itself. For example, the basic distinction between memory and knowledge, which represents one of the diagnostic features that distinguish episodic and semantic memory systems, is traceable in some form to the Greek philosophers and is present in the analyses of numerous seventeenth- and eighteenth-century philosophers (see Herrmann & Chaffin, 1988). Similarly, philosophers of this latter period such as G. W. Leibniz and J. F. Herbart distinguished between conscious and unconscious forms of memory (see Schacter, 1987a, for discussion).

What was missing from these early discussions, however, was the idea of multiple memory systems, that is, the idea of different neurocognitive (brain/mind) structures whose physiological workings produced the introspectively apprehensible and objectively identifiable consequences of learning and memory. Early ideas were based on casual observations; they could be readily dismissed by anyone who decided to wield Ockham's razor. In contemporary discussions of memory systems, as we will discuss at greater length in section 3, the tight coupling between psychological and physiological evidence plays a crucial role; neither alone is decisive.

The fact that concern with the neural mechanisms underlying psychological manifestations of memory and knowledge was absent in the earliest thought about different forms of memory is not surprising. On the one hand, there was little understanding of the brain at the time, and thus the neural influence was necessarily absent. On the other hand, the doctrine of associationism held almost universal sway over philosophical and psychological thinking about memory, rendering any kind of physiologizing superfluous. Moreover, the associative doctrine was dominated by the idea that all expressions of memory could be attributed to the functioning of a single associative mechanism, an idea that is still around even today (for discussion, see Anderson & Bower, 1973; Schacter, 1982).

1.2 Nineteenth-Century Perspectives

In considering the historical antecedents of the hypothesis of multiple memory systems, we are interested principally in those theorists who articulated the idea that the acquisition and retrieval of different kinds of information depends on distinct mechanisms characterized by different properties and principles of operation. Our historical investigations indicate that the initial expressions of this approach are found in the writings of two early nineteenth-century French thinkers: Maine de Biran and Francois Joseph Gall.

Marie François Pierre Gonthier de Biran, known professionally as Maine de Biran, was an eminent French philosopher of the day who wrote a number of treatises in the first two decades of the nineteenth century. For our purposes, his most significant work is a monograph published originally in 1804 and entitled "The influence of habit on the faculty of thinking" (Maine de Biran, 1929).

One of his theses was that the development of habit with repetition is accompanied by increasing automaticity of execution and decreasing conscious awareness, so that habits are eventually carried out with "such promptitude and facility that we no longer perceive the voluntary action which directs them and we are absolutely unaware of the source that they have" (1929, p. 73). Though he argued at great length for the importance of habit in understanding human behavior, Maine de Biran recognized that habit is not the basis of all forms of learning and memory. He went on to postulate the existence of three separate kinds of memory that depend on different mechanisms and can be characterized by different properties: mechanical, sensitive, and representative memory. Mechanical memory, he said, is involved in the acquisition of motor and verbal habits and operates largely at a nonconscious level; sensitive memory (sometimes referred to as sensory memory) is involved in acquiring feelings, affects, and fleeting images, and it too frequently operates nonconsciously; representative memory is involved in conscious recollection of ideas and events.

Maine de Biran was quite specific in distinguishing among these three forms of memory: "If signs ['sign' is his term for a motor-response code] are absolutely empty of ideas or separated from every representative effect, from whatever cause this isolation may arise, recall is only a simple repetition of

Daniel L. Schacter and Endel Tulving

movements. I shall call this faculty for it mechanical memory. When the ... recall of the sign is accompanied or immediately followed by the clear appearance of a well circumscribed idea, I shall attribute it to representative memory. If the sign expresses an affective modification, a feeling or even a fantastic image whatsoever, a vague, uncertain concept, which cannot be brought back to sense impressions ..., the recall of the sign ... will belong to sensitive memory" (1929, p. 156).

Maine de Biran argued that mechanical and representative memory serve "two essential but very distinct functions," explicitly noting that "one of these functions can be exercised without the other" (1929, pp. 209, 210). He also argued that sensitive memory differs sharply from representative memory, contending that "the language of sensations and generally of feeling cannot be representative" (1929, p. 164). Although he treated sensitive memory as a third, distinct form of memory, he also acknowledged that "the gradation which separates mechanical memory from sensitive memory is, in certain cases, rather difficult to grasp" (1929, p. 163). Both mechanical and sensitive memory operate without representation and largely unconsciously. And sensitive memory, like mechanical memory, gives rise to habitual forms of behavior; Maine de Biran contended that sensitive memory is the source of "the most deep-seated, obstinate habits, those the causes of which it would be most important to know in order to avert and moderate their terrible influence" (1929, p. 165). The main difference between the two is that mechanical memory is involved primarily in motor learning, whereas sensitive memory operates in the affective domain: "We attribute to sensory memory every term which, deprived of any representative capacity whatsoever, nevertheless excites some more or less obscure or confused feelings" (1929, p. 168). Maine de Biran, then, distinguished among his three forms of memory with respect to the processes and functions that they perform on the one hand and the type of information that they handle on the other. In many ways his ideas have a surprisingly modern ring to them. The second early forerunner of the perspective of multiple memory systems, Franz Joseph Gall, focused exclusively on differences in the type of information handled by different forms of memory. Gall is well known today largely because of his association with phrenology, but recent authors have attempted to disentangle his useful contributions to neuropsychological thinking from the less useful phrenological component of his work (Fodor, 1983; Young, 1990). Gall's arguments for multiple forms of memory emerged as a natural consequence of his argument for what Fodor (1983) has called "vertical" mental faculties: content- or domain-specific modules that operate on particular kinds of information. These vertical faculties can be contrasted with what Fodor has labeled "horizontal" faculties, which cut across content domains, such as unitary faculties of memory, judgment, perception, and so forth. Gall contended that apparently monolithic (horizontal) faculties should be further subdivided into multiple, content specific (vertical) ones: "Perception and memory are only attributes common to the fundamental faculties, but not [among] the fundamental faculties themselves" (1835,

p. 251). Gall divided his faculties according to particular content domains (e.g., music, mathematics) and assumed that each specialized faculty has its own memory. To support this argument, Gall drew heavily on observations of within- and between-individual differences in memory for particular kinds of information. Noting that some individuals have excellent memory for places but not music whereas others exhibit the opposite pattern, Gall contended such differences could not exist if memory constituted a unitary faculty. He expressed the general point clearly: "If perception and memory were fundamental forces, there would be no reason why they should be manifested so very differently, according as they are exercised on different objects. There would be no reason why the same, and, in fact, every individual, should not learn geometry, music, mechanics and arithmetic, with equal facility since their memory would be equally faithful for all these things" (1835, pp. 251–252).

As far as we can ascertain, the ideas put forward by Maine de Biran and Gall failed to generate widespread interest in the multiple forms of memory hypothesis. To be sure, the general proposal that motor memory or habit should be distinguished from recollection of personal experiences can be detected in the later writings of several nineteenth-century authors. They included William Carpenter, who wrote one of the earliest treatises on physiological psychology (1874, pp. 524–525); Ewald Hering, who argued in a well-known 1870 lecture for the existence of an "organic memory" involved in heredity, development, and habit (for discussion of other proponents of this idea, see Schacter, 1982); and William James, who treated memory and habit in separate chapters of his 1890 classic, *Principles of psychology* (see Eichenbaum, this volume). The most extended discussion of the notion that recollection and habit should be viewed as fundamentally different kinds of memory did not appear until the early twentieth-century, when the French philosopher Henri Bergson devoted most of his celebrated monograph *Matter and memory* (1911) to the elaboration of a single idea: "The past survives under two distinct forms: first, in motor mechanisms; secondly, in independent recollections" (p. 87). Maine de Biran and his ideas are nowhere mentioned in Bergson's work, although Ellenberger (1970) has suggested that he influenced Bergson's thinking.

Gall's ideas were elaborated by fellow phrenologists, such as Spurzheim (1834), who also relied on observations of within-individual variations in memory abilities to make the case that each mental faculty has a separate memory: "A person may, therefore, possess an excellent memory of one kind, be very deficient in another, and be without a third entirely" (p. 84). A number of later writers too endorsed this general logic and reiterated the same conclusions (see Bascomb, 1901; Luys, 1887). As was the case with Maine de Biran, Gall's arguments for multiple forms of memory were largely ignored by later students, perhaps because the kind of evidence that he cited to support it could be more parsimoniously interpreted as a consequence of an individual's differing levels of prior knowledge about different subjects. Ladd, for instance, noted that "the diverse forms of memory are chiefly to be ascribed to diverse tastes and habits, and the interest and attention which accompany them" (1909, p. 138; see also, Fodor, 1983, for a similar argument). Although they appear to be the earliest proponents of a nonunitary view of memory, Maine de Biran and Gall were not the only nineteenth-century thinkers to advance the idea forcefully. Around the middle of the century the hypothesis surfaced again, this time supported by a new and powerful kind of empirical evidence: specific impairments of particular types of memory in brain-damaged patients. The first brain scientist to advance a nonunitary memory hypothesis on the basis of neuropsychological evidence was the French physician Paul Broca. His seminal observations on selective loss of expressive linguistic abilities in an otherwise intact patient, referred to as Tan, are usually discussed in the context of research on aphasia and language processing. However, as Rosenfield (1988) has argued, Broca in fact conceptualized Tan's inability to generate language output in terms of damage to a particular kind of memory: "Is it not, after all, a kind of memory, and those who have lost it have lost, not the memory for words, but the memory of the procedures required for articulating words" (Broca, 1861, cited in Rosenfield, 1988, p. 18). Broca elaborated on this idea in relation to language development: "This gradual perfecting of articulated language in children is due to the development of a particular kind of memory which is not a memory for words, but a memory for the movements necessary for articulating words. And this special memory is in no way related to other memories nor to intelligence" (cited in Rosenfield, 1988, p. 20).

A decade after the publication of Broca's pathbreaking paper, the German neurologist Carl Wernicke published his observations of an aphasic condition in which patients had no difficulty producing linguistic output but had severe comprehension problems. As Rosenfield has noted, Wernicke interpreted these symptoms in terms of damage to a special memory center for auditory word representations, a center that was distinct from the memory center damaged in Broca's case. This view was accepted and developed at length by the German physician Ludwig Lichtheim, who contended that "we may call 'centre of auditory images' and 'centre of motor images,' respectively, the parts of the brain where these memories are fixed" (1885, p. 435; see also Rosenfield, 1988, p. 22). Lichtheim applied his view of multiple memory centers to neurological deficits of reading and writing as well. The French psychologist Theodule Ribot too drew on these kinds of observations to argue for the hypothesis of multiple memories in his well known book *Diseases of memory* (1882). Ribot contended that "if, in the normal condition of the organism, the different forms of memory are relatively independent, it is natural that, if in a morbid state one disappears, the others should remain intact" (1882, p. 142). He went on to suggest that verbal memory, visual memory, and auditory memory are all separate from and independent of each other.

In summary, by the close of the nineteenth century, various hypotheses concerning multiple forms of memory had been advanced and discussed. As Polster, Nadel, and Schacter (1991) point out, however, interest in the issue disappeared rather quickly. With the exception of Bergson's (1911) book, it is difficult to find any relevant discussions of multiple forms of memory during the first half of the twentieth century.

1.3 The Modern Era

In the two decades following World War II, a variety of ideas and hypotheses concerning multiple forms of memory began to appear in the literatures on animal and human learning and memory. The earliest and best known of these hypotheses was advanced by Tolman (1948). He attempted to resolve his ongoing debate with Hull (1933) concerning place learning versus response learning by arguing that, as stated in the title of his 1948 paper, "There is more than one kind of learning." Tolman contended that place and response learning depend on different mechanisms, so there is no need to choose one or the other as the sole or exclusive basis of learned performance. As Nadel (1992, this volume) has pointed out, however, Tolman's arguments failed to ignite widespread interest in the issue of multiple forms of learning, perhaps because of a later, influential paper by Restle (1957) that argued forcefully that place and response learning do not differ fundamentally.

The issue was brought into much sharper focus during the 1970s. The decisive impetus for these developments was provided by the discovery of the important role played in memory by brain regions in the medial temporal lobes, including the hippocampus. A key component of this new realization was Scoville and Milner's (1957) description of a young man, known by the initials H.M., who had undergone a complete bilateral resection of the medial temporal lobes for relief of intractable epilepsy. H.M. exhibited a severe and pervasive impairment of his ability to remember recent experiences and acquire new information, even though his overall level of intelligence remained above average and other perceptual and cognitive functions were unaffected. The selective nature of H.M.'s impairment suggested a special role for the medial temporal region in memory. In the search for an appropriate animal model of the kind of brain damage and cognitive impairment that H.M. exhibited, a number of authors advanced the idea that the hippocampus participates in a kind of memory that can be distinguished empirically, functionally, and neuroanatomically from other kinds of memory (e.g., Gaffan, 1974; Hirsh, 1974; Nadel & O'Keefe, 1974; O'Keefe & Nadel, 1978; Olton, Becker, & Handelmann, 1979; Weiskrantz, 1978). The general conclusion that emerged from these early studies was that rats with hippocampal damage exhibit normal learning on certain kinds of memory tasks despite severely impaired performance on other tasks. Particularly influential were the distinctions between taxon versus locale memory (O'Keefe & Nadel, 1978) and working versus reference memory (Olton et al., 1979), which set the stage for the development in the 1980s of related distinctions based on data from studies of nonhuman animals (see Eichenbaum, Fagan, & Cohen, 1986; Mishkin & Petri, 1984; Packard, Hirsh, & White, 1989; Rudy & Sutherland, 1989; Zola-

Morgan & Squire, 1984). The development of these distinctions over the subsequent years and their current status are discussed in the chapters by Eichenbaum, Lynch and Granger, Nadel, Rudy and Sutherland, and Squire.

In the literature on human memory too, a number of distinctions among forms of memory appeared during the postwar years. As noted earlier, the distinction between short-term and long-term memory was diligently pursued during the 1960s and 1970s. Various kinds of experimental and neuropsychological evidence suggested that retention across delays of seconds and minutes is based on a fundamentally different mechanism than is retention across delays of hours, days, and weeks; the most detailed expression of this idea can be found in the well-known model of Atkinson and Shiffrin (1968). Although serious objections to this "modal model" of short-term versus long-term memory were made (see Craik & Lockhart, 1972; Crowder, 1982), the conceptual core of the idea appeared again in a new and more powerful form with the advent of the working-memory model advanced by Baddeley (e.g., Baddeley & Hitch, 1974; see also Baddeley, 1992a, 1992b, this volume).

It is perhaps less well appreciated that a number of distinctions among forms of long-term memory were proposed at around the same time as the distinction short-term versus long-term memory. For example, Reiff and Scheerer (1959) discussed at great length a distinction between remembrances (recollections of contextually specific, personally experienced events) and memoria (general knowledge, skills, and habits), a distinction that had been foreshadowed a decade earlier by Schactel's (1947) distinction between autobiographical memory and practical memory and by Ryle's (1949) philosophical distinction between knowing how and knowing that. The neurologist Nielsen (1958) used observations of dissociations among forms of memory in brain-damaged patients as a basis for offering a conceptually similar distinction between temporal memory and categorical memory. A decade later, Bruner distinguished between "memory with record" (recollection of the "facts we acquire and events we experience in daily life") and "memory without record" ("some process that changes the nature of an organism, changes his skills, or changes the rules by which he operates, but are virtually inaccessible in memory as specific encounters") (1969, p. 254).

None of these distinctions among forms of human long-term memory exerted a major or even detectable effect on the course of research and theorizing. The establishment of the hypothesis of multiple memory systems as a major research focus occurred only by the confluence of three initially unrelated developments from the late 1960s to the early 1980s. First, neuropsychological research during the 1960s and 1970s revealed, quite surprisingly, that severely amnesic patients retain some learning and memory abilities. Studies by Milner and Corkin and colleagues (e.g., Milner, Corkin, & Teuber, 1968) demonstrated normal or near-normal motor-skill learning in the amnesic patient H.M., which allowed them to infer that motor learning depends on a system different from other forms of memory. Experiments by Warrington and Weiskrantz (1968, 1974) showed that amnesics relatively retained their ability to perform on fragment-cued tests of previously encountered verbal and pictorial material, despite their greatly impoverished ability to recognize these materials as previously encountered. The deeper significance of these studies for the ensuing debate on memory systems was not immediately obvious; it became clear only gradually in the course of subsequent research (for the unfolding story of this clarification, see Cohen & Squire, 1980; Graf, Mandler, & Haden, 1982; Graf, Squire, & Mandler, 1984; Jacoby & Dallas, 1981; Mandler, 1980; Polster, Nadel, & Schacter, 1991; Rozin, 1976; Schacter, 1987a; Squire, 1987; Tulving, Schacter, & Stark, 1982; Warrington, 1979; Warrington & Weiskrantz, 1982). But Warrington and Weiskrantz's (1968, 1970, 1974) findings pointed to the possibility that different kinds of memory are differentially susceptible to lesions of the hippocampus and related structures that are typically damaged in amnesic patients.

A second relevant development was the reemergence of the distinction between remembrances and memoria, under the names of episodic and semantic memory, as "two parallel and partially overlapping information processing systems" (Tulving, 1972, p. 401). Although the 1972 paper focused on the heuristic value of the distinction and had little hard evidence to point to in support of the idea, it served to stimulate discussion and debate concerning the usefulness of postulating separate episodic and semantic systems (see Anderson & Ross, 1980; Herrmann & Harwood, 1980; Kinsbourne & Wood, 1975; Schacter & Tulving, 1982; for a review, see Tulving, 1983).

The third development was, to a large extent, a direct consequence of the previous two: studies of normal subjects that revealed striking dissociations between what we would now refer to as explicit and implicit memory tests (Graf & Schacter, 1985; Schacter, 1987a). On explicit memory tests, such as free recall, cued recall, and recognition, subjects engage in conscious or intentional recollection of previously studied information. By contrast, on implicit memory tests, such as identification of briefly flashed words or completion of incomplete word stems and fragments, no reference is made to a prior study episode; subjects simply perform the task as best they can. Memory is inferred from changes in task performance, typically referred to as priming effects, that are attributable to previously studied information. Several studies published during the early 1980s, all of them motivated to some extent by previous observations of amnesic patients and a concern with the distinction between episodic and semantic memory, revealed that priming effects on implicit memory tests could be dissociated experimentally from performance on standard tests of recall and recognition (Graf, Mandler, & Haden, 1982; Jacoby & Dallas, 1981; Graf & Mandler, 1984; Tulving, Schacter, & Stark, 1982). These results, along with a large amount of subsequent work, provided strong support for the idea that brain lesions in amnesic patients and experimental task manipulations in normal healthy subjects divide systems subserving different memory functions along natural fault lines. The next decade witnessed an explosion of research on priming in both normal subjects and amnesic patients (for reviews, see Richardson-Klavehn & Bjork, 1988; Roediger & McDermott,

Daniel L. Schacter and Endel Tulving

1993; Schacter, 1987a; Schacter, Chiu, & Ochsner, 1993; Shimamura, 1986). The question of whether dissociations between priming and explicit memory require that we postulate multiple memory systems or whether they are more parsimoniously viewed in terms of different processes operating within a unitary system has occupied center stage in the development of this research (for discussion, see Hayman & Tulving, 1989; Roediger, 1990; Schacter, 1992b; Witherspoon & Moscovitch, 1989).

The initial development of ideas about memory systems in the human and animal literatures proceeded on largely independent tracks. As research and theorizing progressed, however, the question naturally arose as to the possibility of interrelating, and perhaps even integrating, the fruits of the experimental and theoretical efforts in these two domains (e.g., Cohen & Eichenbaum, 1993; Olton, 1989; Mishkin, Malamut, & Bachevalier, 1984; Schacter, 1985; Squire, 1992b). One of our goals in inviting contributions from researchers who study humans, monkeys, and rats was to assess the extent to which further cross-fertilization between the human and animal domains is feasible, a point to which we will return later in the chapter.

2   CONCEPTUAL AND LOGICAL ISSUES: WHAT ARE SYSTEMS?

In the preceding sections, we have written rather casually about such notions as "multiple forms of memory" and "different memory systems" and have contrasted them with the "unitary memory" view. But what exactly do these terms mean? And how can we distinguish between the unitary-memory and multiple-memory-systems views, or among different kinds of multiple-systems views? What kinds of evidence are relevant to making such distinctions? These are rather thorny issues that lurk just beneath the surface of most discussions of memory systems. They merit commentary and discussion, even if, as it will turn out, they do not have simple answers.

2.1   Memory: Forms, Processes, Tasks, and Expression

Because of uncertainties in the existing literature, it is helpful to begin with a brief discussion of what memory systems are not. Memory systems are not forms of memory or memory processes or memory tasks or expressions of memory. All these terms, of course, are related to the concept of a memory system, but to minimize terminological and conceptual disorder, they need to be distinguished carefully from it. Two sets of concepts have been frequently confused in the past: forms or kinds of memory (or learning, or learning and memory) and memory systems. These concepts are not equivalent. The latter concept includes the former, but the former does not necessarily include the latter. The criteria for naming a new form of memory are not stringent (see Shettleworth, 1993). Thus, one can think of verbal memory, recognition memory, and olfactory memory as different kinds of memory. Distinctions of this sort can help to describe and organize empirical facts. But these kinds of purely descriptive forms of memory do not constitute memory systems. The criteria for systems are more stringent, as we will discuss shortly.

The notion of a memory process too must be distinguished from that of a memory system. A memory process refers to a specific operation carried out in the service of memory performance. Processes such as encoding, rehearsal, activation, retrieval, and the like are constituents of memory systems but are not identical with them (see, for example, Johnson & Chalfonte, this volume). Indeed, there are good reasons to believe that particular memory processes may participate in the operations of more than one memory system, as in the "weak" version of memory systems discussed by Sherry and Schacter (1987, p. 440).

It is also helpful to consider the logical status of the construct of memory task in relation to that of memory system. It is not uncommon for memory tasks to be described in terms that imply an isomorphism between them and the system they are purported to tap, for example, free recall is often referred to as an episodic memory task, pursuit rotor learning as a procedural memory task, and so forth. Although these kinds of expressions frequently constitute relatively harmless terminological conveniences that simply allow researchers to talk about their work, they can be deceptively problematic. First, they tacitly encourage the idea that performance on a particular task relies exclusively on the output of a single system. This assumption may occasionally be justified, but in many cases it is highly likely that more than one system contributes to performance on a particular task (see Eichenbaum, 1992, this volume; Jacoby, 1991; Schacter, this volume; Tulving, 1983). Tasks can be viewed as probes that tap some systems more than others, but they should not be unthinkingly equated with the operation of a single system. A second, related point is that inferences about systems should be based on converging evidence from a variety of tasks that rely on the output of a hypothesized system and should not depend solely on results from a single task (Roediger, 1990; Schacter, 1992b; Tulving, 1983; see also the discussion below). Thus the relation between tasks and systems is many-to-many: a variety of different tasks can tap, to varying degrees, the functioning of different underlying systems and subsystems.

Finally, a frequently made confusion concerns the concepts of explicit and implicit memory (Graf & Schacter, 1985; Schacter, 1987a). References to the explicit memory system and the implicit memory system are not uncommon in the literature. Explicit and implicit memory are not systems. These terms were put forward to describe and characterize expressions of memory: "explicit" refers to intentional or conscious recollection of past episodes, whereas "implicit" refers to unintentional, nonconscious use of previously acquired information. Schacter noted specifically that the implicit/explicit distinction "does not refer to, or imply the existence of, different underlying memory systems" (1987a, p. 501). Thus, according to this formulation, implicit and explicit memory, though psychologically and behaviorally distinguishable forms of memory, could either depend on the same underlying memory system or different underlying systems; the question is open and subject to experimental investigation. (For further discussion, see Schacter, 1990, 1992a, this volume.)

2.2 Defining Memory Systems

One of the earliest references to memory systems as a concept whose domain was eventually to exceed that of a form or kind of learning or memory appeared in the 1972 paper by Tulving. The very first appearance of the term "memory systems" in the title of a paper, as far as we know, was in a 1979 article by Warrington in which she discussed neuropsychological evidence supporting a distinction between short-term and long-term memory systems and between two kinds of long-term memory systems: event memory and semantic memory. By 1982 the quest for understanding memory systems was advanced enough that we felt it appropriate to speculate that the then recently discovered new form of learning now called perceptual priming is based not on episodic or semantic memory but rather on "some other, as yet little understood, memory system" (Tulving, Schacter, & Stark, 1982, p. 341). The concept of a system was only vaguely specified during these early years of the development of the systems approach. It was only when the critics of this approach began asking the question, What does a memory system mean, anyhow? that attempts were made to confront the issue explicitly.

Like any other complex concept, that of memory system can be defined broadly, narrowly, or in between. One broad definition is that it is "a set of correlated processes" (Tulving, 1985, p. 386). The advantage of this and other similar broad definitions lies in their general acceptability and the fact they allow us to ask further, more specific questions. The disadvantage is that they do not direct, guide, or constrain research, or specific questions that researchers may pose, in any way.

A narrower early formulation (Tulving, 1984) proposed that different memory systems are distinguished in terms of

• different behavioral and cognitive functions and the kinds of information and knowledge they process,

• operations according to different laws and principles,

• different neural substrates (neural structures and neural mechanisms),

• differences in the timing of their appearance in phylogenetic and ontogenetic development, and

• differences in the format of represented information (the extent to which the aftereffects of information acquisition represent the past or merely modify future behavior or experience).

Thus a memory system is defined in terms of its brain mechanisms, the kind of information it processes, and the principles of its operation (see also the section entitled "The concept of system" in Tulving, 1985, p. 386).

Sherry and Schacter (1987) approached the concept of memory systems from an evolutionary perspective, proposing that different systems evolve as special adaptations of information storage and retrieval for specific and functionally incompatible purposes. They defined a memory system as "an interaction among acquisition, retention, and retrieval mechanisms that is characterized by certain rules of operation" (p. 440) and suggested that the term multiple memory systems "refers to the idea that two or more systems are characterized by fundamentally different rules of operation" (p. 440). They also included the specification of brain structures as a necessary component of the definition of a system, although, as in Tulving's (1984) case, this is more of a prescriptive than a descriptive declaration. Sherry and Schacter (1987), unlike Tulving (1984), did not include the criterion that different systems must process different kinds of information, a point to which we will return shortly.

More recently, Nadel (1992, this volume) has focused on similar issues in the section of his contributions to this project entitled "What is a system"? He specifies two criteria for distinguishing among systems: computational differences in different neural architectures (approximately corresponding to Sherry and Schacter's "functional incompatibility") and length of time that information is stored in them. Johnson and Chalfonte (this volume) too have compared and contrasted a number of different criteria by which memory systems and subsystems have been distinguished from one another by various investigators.

The early attempts to clarify the concept of a memory system were meant primarily to launch a debate on the complex issues involved. Now that the debate has begun, we will update and elaborate on the ideas that remain valid. Yet because the concept of a memory system is still in its formative stage and will undoubtedly undergo alterations and modifications as research proceeds, our purpose at this time remains largely unchanged: to stimulate relevant discussion. We present our views of the concept of a memory system, we specify criteria by which candidate systems can be adjudged and evaluated for admission into the domain of hypothetical systems, and we propose an organizational table of memory systems as they appear to us now. Reference to the memory systems of 1994 is meant to underscore our expectation that all these ideas will change in the future. How rapidly they will change and in what ways will necessarily depend on the efforts of scientists who decide to join the enterprise.

2.3 Three Criteria of a Learning and Memory System

We specify three broad criteria that we deem useful for identifying different memory systems. These can be used to make decisions about what is and what is not a memory system and about how different systems are related to one another. We expect that whenever reference is made to a putative memory system, these three criteria should be satisfied.

Our current list of the criteria includes class-inclusion operations, properties and relations, and convergent dissociations. These criteria, like everything else in our proposal, are up for grabs, and we expect others to come up with additional criteria or with ideas for improving the suggested ones.

Class-inclusion operations   An intact memory system enables one to perform a very large number of tasks of a particular class or category, regardless of the specific informational contents of the tasks. Thus a short-term ("working") memory system allows the individual to hold any sample of certain kinds of information (e.g., verbal or verbalizable information) in a buffer storage and to perform a variety of cognitive operations on the information (Baddeley, 1992a, this volume). As long as the system is intact, it operates class-inclusively, in the sense that it can process any particular input or information of the specified kind. Another system, episodic memory, enables people to remember past happenings from their own lives even after long retention intervals, a category of tasks beyond the reach of working memory. Episodic memory can be described as the conscious recollection of personally experienced episodes.

If an environmental condition affects the brain in such a fashion that a whole class of memory functions is selectively altered (e.g., eliminated), the alterations can be thought of as a consequence of changes in the operations of a particular system. The brain regions and mechanisms thus involved are crucial neural components of the system. We take the normal waking adult brain as the reference and define changed brain states with respect to it. Brain-state changes may be brought about through a variety of means, including development (in infancy, childhood, and old age), sleep and sleep deprivation, effective hypnosis, emotional trauma, clinically significant depression, ingestion of a drug, other kinds of pharmacological interventions (such as general anaesthesia), disease, injury, and surgically produced lesions. By a "whole class of memory functions" we mean both particular, objectively identifiable memory processes (such as encoding, recoding, rehearsal, consolidation, storage, and retrieval) and particular kinds of processed information (such as perceptual stimuli, referential symbols, and execution of motor acts).

It is important to emphasize that the stipulation of a category, or whole class, of operations must be accompanied by an insistence on selectivity; that is, while specifiable memory functions subserved by a given system are affected by particular changes in the brain state, nonmemory functions, and memory functions subserved by other memory systems, must not be similarly affected. If all cognitive functions are impaired as a result of brain injury or disease, then any whole class of memory operations also is, which thus satisfies the criterion of class inclusiveness. But the lack of selective specificity invalidates the inference that a memory system has thus been identified, because factors operating outside of the memory system in question may be responsible for the observed effects. We recognize, of course, that many contemporary theorists have intentionally blurred the distinction between processing and memory (e.g., Craik, 1983; Kolers & Roediger, 1984; McClel-land & Rumelhart, 1986), and that clean distinctions between memory and nonmemory functions are not always easy or even desirable to draw (for discussion, see Nadel, 1992, this volume; Schacter, 1987b). However, it is well known that memory impairments can exist without global deterioration of cognitive processing—the amnesic syndrome is a clear example—and so we wish to maintain an important role for selectivity when assessing class inclusion in memory systems.

These conditions leave considerable latitude in determining the identity of individual systems and leave open to a large degree the question of how class-inclusive some selective effects must be before we are justified in proposing a candidate system. Nevertheless, they encourage theorists to consider what we think are critical properties of systems, and to this extent they should help to accelerate progress in thinking about systems.

Properties and relations   A memory system must be described in terms of a property list, that is, an enumeration of its features and aspects by which its identity can be determined and its relation to other systems can be specified. For example, the reader may recall that Maine de Biran specified his proposed forms of memory in terms of descriptions of their various properties. Early examples of property lists from the contemporary era can be found in a number of publications, including O'Keefe and Nadel's (1978) description of the properties of taxon and locale systems, Tulving's enumeration of the properties of procedural memory (1983, pp. 8–9) and listing of the "diagnostic features" of episodic and semantic memory (1983, p. 35), and Tulving and Schacter's listing of properties of the perceptual representation system (PRS) (1990, p. 305). Most of the contributors to the present volume too describe and elaborate property lists of hypothesized memory systems.

The properties of any system include rules of operation, kind of information, and neural substrates. In addition, because memory systems presumably evolved as specializations, and hence serve biologically useful functions, the property list of any system should include one or more statements about what the system is for (see, for example, Tulving, 1983, pp. 52–53, for a preliminary attempt). As noted earlier, Sherry and Schacter argued on evolutionary grounds that multiple memory systems evolved because they serve different and functionally incompatible purposes. They write "Evolutionary change and the various adaptations that result could occur within a unitary memory system. The reason, we will argue, that the evolutionary outcome has been multiple memory systems rather than a single system capable of serving many functions is that the memory system that effectively solves some environmental problems may be unworkable as the solution to others. The kind of memory used by birds, for example, to learn the songs that they sing, or humans to learn certain skills, may be incompatible with an effective solution to other memory problems." (1987, p. 443)

Sherry and Schacter went on to suggest that when proposing a new memory system, it is important to consider whether the system performs functions that are incompatible with those performed by other systems. They acknowledged that it is not a straightforward task to determine whether functional incompatibility exists, yet emphasized the importance of including functional considerations in discussions of multiple memory systems. We agree with this emphasis on functional considerations and view it as a natural component of our more general concern with properties and relations of memory systems.

At the present time, because of the relative immaturity of the classification enterprise, most of the items will be included in such property lists on the basis of intuition and informed speculation rather than on the basis of objective rules, and hence the lists may well be rather ill defined and even intolerably vague. This is where we expect time to come to our aid. The clarity of the lists will be enhanced and the rules of the admission of particular properties into lists will be sharpened as research on memory systems proceeds. Also at the present time, the rules of operation of different systems are typically specified solely in psychological terms. One of the future research objectives in classifying learning and memory will be the inclusion of physiological, chemical, and physical mechanisms in the description of the operations of different memory systems. Similar considerations apply to the description of the information that different systems process: even at the level of a highly abstract analysis, indicated by the extreme inclusiveness of such terms as "information" and "processing," our currently available vocabulary is rather primitive and in obvious need of refinement and elaboration.

Our second criterion, then, holds that to suggest a candidate for a new memory system, a person must be able to do two things, among others: list a number of properties of the candidate system, and specify something about the relations among it and already existing (invented or accepted) systems in terms of these properties. Like all other entities in the known universe, the postulated system will share some properties in common with previously proposed entities in its reference class (i.e., other systems) and will differ with respect to others.

Convergent dissociations   Dissociations between task performances that different systems differentially contribute to constitute a necessary condition for the postulating independent systems. Such postulation is clearly not warranted in the absence of such relevant evidence, that is, where there is no empirical basis for thinking that something is fundamentally different about how memory works in two different situations.

A single kind of a dissociation between the performance of two memory tasks is not sufficient for postulating different memory systems. If it were, those critics of multiple-systems views who have expressed alarm at the prospects of mindless proliferation of systems as more and more (and more and more specific) dissociations are observed (e.g., Roediger, Rajaram, &

Srinivas, 1990) would have a valid argument on their side. But no system has ever been proposed on such flimsy grounds, so the critics' concern is ill founded. Memory systems are postulated on the basis of *converging* dissociations: dissociations of different kinds, observed with different tasks, in different populations, and using different techniques (Schacter, 1992b; Tulving, 1983).

Relevant dissociations can be observed in many forms: functional dissociations on tasks alleged to tap different systems, neuropsychological dissociations that involve contrasts between spared and impaired performance in relevant patient populations, or stochastic independence between tasks that are sensitive to the operation of different systems. Ideally, one would like to see dissociations in which multiple tasks that tap the same system are contrasted with multiple tasks that tap different systems (e.g., Roediger, Rajaram, & Srinivas, 1990). We emphasize convergent dissociations as a way of highlighting the point that the case for a particular system is strengthened in proportion to the amount of independent evidence from separate sources that can be marshalled for it, i.e., evidence from multiple tasks, experimental manipulations, patient populations, and so forth.

To the extent that analogies can help to clarify new ideas, it may be worthwhile to mention that we think of memory systems as comparable to such systems as the economic system of a modern state. One can also think of the frequently invoked notion of subsystems of memory as analogous to such systems as the transportation system or communication system. Memory processes can be seen as analogous to components of the larger systems and subsystems, i.e., (constructing) highways in the transportation system or (installing new) telephone cables in the communication system. In other words, in our view, memory systems are large, elaborate, and complex. They have fuzzy boundaries, have overlapping constituent processes, and interact with one another in intricate ways (see Johnson & Chalfonte, this volume). For example, as the transportation system can be used in the service of the communication system and parts of the communication system can be used to transport goods from one location to another, so too, for example, the semantic memory system may provide information about past events, and the episodic system can provide knowledge about the world, although these are not the functions for which they are specialized (see, e.g., Rajaram, 1992; Tulving, 1987).

2.4   Memory Systems versus Subsystems or Forms of Memory

With the three general criteria for memory systems in mind, it is useful to consider next issues pertaining to the notion of a memory subsystem and the related issue of forms or kinds of memory, which we discussed earlier.

The terms "memory system" and "memory subsystem" are sometimes used interchangeably. For example, Johnson and Chalfonte (this volume) use the term "subsystem" very much in the general spirit of our use of the term "system." Other investigators have used "subsystem" within the context of a hierarchical arrangement to indicate a subordinate relation of a subsystem to a system, as in Schacter's (1992a, 1992b, this volume) discussion of the perceptual-representation system and its various subsystems.

Although the question of exactly what is a system and what is a subsystem is still quite fluid and although we do not wish to rigidly insist on any particular usage now, we do think that it is useful at this early stage of analysis to suggest a distinction between a system and a subsystem. Specifically, whereas systems are characterized by different rules of operation, as embodied in property lists and relations, subsystems, we suggest, are distinguished primarily by different kinds of information (subsystems share the principal rules of operations of their superordinate system, but they differ from one another with respect to the kinds of information each one processes) and different brain loci (although subsystems are all instantiated in the neural circuitry that defines their superordinate system, they can occupy distinct loci within the broader network). This general approach is consistent with ideas suggested previously by Sherry and Schacter (1987), who contended that the existence of domain-specific modules or subsystems that handle different kinds of information and have distinct neural bases but operate according to similar rules does not necessitate postulating multiple memory systems. Our view allows us to conceptualize the overall organization of memory in the form of a hierarchy, with systems and subsystems specifiable at different levels. Whereas postulating of full-blown systems requires satisfaction of all three of our major criteria, postulating of subsystems requires satisfaction of the first (class inclusion operations) and third (converging dissociations) but not the second (property lists and relations, with the corresponding emphasis on different rules of operation).

In addition to allowing a principled distinction between systems and subsystems, our criteria also provide a basis for distinguishing between a memory system or subsystem, on the one hand, and a form or kind of memory on the other. As noted earlier, numerous forms of memory have been discussed, and it is easy to confuse the relatively neutral description of a form of memory with a theoretical statement about the existence of an underlying memory system. Consider again the distinction between explicit and implicit memory. As noted earlier, the terms "explicit" and "implicit" memory are descriptive concepts that are concerned with different ways in which memory can be expressed, but it is not uncommon in the literature to see references to the "explicit memory system" and the "implicit memory system." In light of our three criteria, however, it is relatively easy to see that explicit and implicit memory should not be granted the status of memory systems. While one can find evidence of converging dissociations for separating explicit and implicit memory, the explicit/implicit distinction fails the criteria of class inclusion and properties/relations: explicit and implicit memory do not refer to a "whole class of memory functions" that can be characterized by extensive property lists but rather refer to two different ways in which memories can be expressed.

Thus, in light of our criteria, explicit and implicit memory are more properly viewed as forms of memory than memory systems.

Similar considerations apply to the idea that just about any kind of neuropsychological dissociation can be taken as evidence for a new memory system. Roediger (in press), for example, found patients with extremely specific deficits in accessing particular kinds of knowledge (e.g., impaired knowledge of red fruits) and wondered whether such dissociations imply the existence of a "red fruit" memory system. However, these kinds of observations do not meet any of our three criteria and hence are easily excluded as providing evidence for new memory systems. Similarly, Roediger (in press) noted that women typically deliver their second child faster than their first, and he suggested that this reproductive priming might provide evidence for yet another distinct memory system. However, application of our three criteria makes it difficult to sustain this argument: the criterion of class inclusion is not satisfied, there is no sensible list of properties and relations, and the suggestion is not based on converging dissociations. While both of the examples offered by Roediger can be reasonably viewed as evidence for distinct forms of memory, our criteria exclude them as candidates for memory systems.

3 CLASSIFICATION OF MEMORY SYSTEMS

We now provide a brief overview of how the various contributors to this volume have approached the problem of classifying memory systems, and then summarize some of our own views in light of the three criteria of the previous section.

3.1 Studies of Animal Learning and Memory

An international symposium was convened in 1984 in Umea, Sweden, to examine the nature of the gulf between animal learning and human memory and to discuss possible ways of bridging it (Nilsson and Archer, 1985). The attendants, productive practitioners in the fields of animal learning and human memory, agreed that a rift existed and that overcoming it might be beneficial to all concerned. This project, which was an attempt to systematize memory systems, also included representatives of the two research domains of neuropsychological or neuroscientific studies of animal learning and cognitive/neuropsychological investigations of human memory. What the ambassadors of these two domains have in common is the conviction, or at least a desire to believe, that memory is not a unitary entity and that classification of learning and memory constitutes a worthwhile scientific problem.

Ideally, one would like to take advantage of this kind of a consensus among the representatives of two otherwise noninteracting disciplines. And, indeed, there is basic agreement among students of human and animal memory on the existence and importance of multiple memory systems. Nevertheless, the chapters in this volume indicate that we still have some way to go before we

Daniel L. Schacter and Endel Tulving

will possess a classification system that will embrace both animal learning and human memory (for attempts to bridge the gap, see Cohen & Eichenbaum, 1993, and the chapters by Eichenbaum, by Johnson & Chalfonte, and by Squire, this volume). Thus at this time we are obliged to consider classification schemes separately for animal and human research, although it will become apparent that some points of contact between the two literatures are beginning to appear.

Among those who work with animals, a good deal of agreement prevails on at least the broad lines of classification of memory. The predominant multiple-systems orientation is a dichotomy, with the hippocampus and related brain regions providing the line of demarcation. As in Gaffan, 1974, Hirsh, 1974, and Nadel and O'Keefe, 1974, the core idea is that some forms of learning are critically dependent on the hippocampus and related structures, while others are not. This dependence segregates all of memory into two categories, or systems: hippocampus-dependent versus hippocampus-independent (we use the term "hippocampus" here as a shorthand for "hippocampus and related structures" including the entorhinal and perirhinal cortex, fornix, and diencephalic structures such as the thalamic nuclei and mammillary bodies). The systems-oriented theoretical debate in animal learning revolves around how to characterize these two systems, that is, how the hippocampal and nonhippocampal systems express themselves at the level of observable behavior.

Nadel's chapter elaborates the core idea that he and O'Keefe put forward two decades ago: the hippocampus constitutes the basis of a locale system whose primary function is to encode and store spatial information about the environment in a maplike form. By contrast, taxon systems do not depend on the hippocampus and are involved in various kinds of nonspatial learning. Nadel enumerates in some detail the properties and relations of the two types of systems and considers at length the question of whether the hippocampally based system is specifically and exclusively involved in the representation of spatial information.

This latter issue, whether the hippocampally based memory system is defined by its specifically spatial properties, provides a key point of contention for the other dichotomies based on animal research. Eichenbaum argues that the hippocampal-dependent form of memory is a declarative system, defined by relational representations that allow flexible responding in novel situations and permit the organism to compare and contrast different kinds of information. By contrast, the hippocampal-independent form of memory is subserved by various procedural memory systems concerned with rather rigid and inflexible individual representations and responses. In Eichenbaum's view, spatial information constitutes just one type of relational information handled by the declarative system. Shapiro and Olton agree with Eichenbaum that the key characteristic of the hippocampal-dependent system is the formation of relational representations. They further specify a computational mechanism of pattern separation that subserves the generation of relational representations, and they emphasize the importance of this mechanism for a key function of the hippocampal system: reducing susceptibility to associative interference. Shapiro and Olton do not elaborate on the nature of nonhippocampal forms of memory or memory systems, although they indicate clearly that they assume that the latter do exist.

Squire argues for a view, most closely related to that of Eichenbaum, in which a hippocampal-dependent declarative memory system is contrasted with a hippocampal-independent nondeclarative form of memory. Nondeclarative memory, according to Squire, consists of numerous specialized subsystems that support such phenomena as conditioning and skill learning. The critical role of the hippocampal-dependent system is to bind together different kinds of information, and spatial information constitutes one subset of bound representations.

Rudy and Sutherland offer a related dichotomy in which the critical distinction is between a hippocampal-dependent system that computes configural associations and a hippocampal-independent system that computes elemental associations. Elemental associations consist of simple pairwise links between two stimuli (e.g., *a* and *b*), whereas configural associations involve the construction of a higher order, joint representation (e.g., *ab*) that in turn can be linked with other stimuli. The hippocampal-dependent system is a closed memory system effectively shielded from competing irrelevant associations, whereas the hippocampal-independent system is an open system highly susceptible to interference from competing associations.

The strengths and weakness of the foregoing ideas are discussed and compared at length in the chapters by Nadel, Eichenbaum, Shapiro and Olton, Squire, and Rudy and Sutherland; we will not repeat their arguments here. In light of our earlier discussion, however, it is worth noting that the declarative/procedural, declarative/nondeclarative, and locale/taxon distinctions are all in a certain sense asymmetrical. In each dichotomy, the first term refers to a specific memory system with reasonably well characterized functional and neural properties that meet our criteria for a system. The second term, however, is used in a more descriptive sense to a refer to a class or collection of memory functions that share certain features in common but also differ from one another in various ways. This use is most explicit in Squire's invocation of the term "nondeclarative" to refer a variety of disparate memory functions that are tied together by their hypothesized independence from the hippocampal-dependent system, but it is also apparent in the writings of Eichenbaum and Nadel.

We think that it is important to be alert to asymmetries of this kind, because they can complicate the job of classifying memory systems. Thus, although there is a sense in which the distinctions offered by Eichenbaum, Nadel, and Squire are dichotomies, there is another sense in which they are not: the contrast is between a declarative or locale system on the one hand and a number of other systems and/or subsystems on the other. The ambiguity arises because one term of each distinction refers to a specific system, and the other is a descriptive label. The ambiguity could be avoided by offering distinctions that are symmetrical with respect to the level of the terms contrasted: systems should be contrasted with systems, and descriptive concepts contrasted with descriptive concepts. Lynch and Granger offer a rather different approach from that of others concerned with animal learning. They argue that different types of memory—recognition, recency, memory of recent actions, connecting events across space and time—operate in a manner analogous to an assembly line, in which each component can be thought of as a system that makes a unique informational contribution to the gradually evolving memory. The assembly line operates in a serial manner, with the product of higher-level systems including the previously assembled products of lower-level systems. According to Lynch and Granger, the lower-level systems can operate independently of the higher-level systems, but not vice versa.

In summary, the main point of agreement among the students of animal learning and memory represented in this volume is that a memory system that depends on the hippocampal system differs fundamentally from a system that can function independently of the hippocampus. Disagreements exist on the nature of the hippocampal system and on the question of whether the nonhippocampal system can be divided into multiple systems, forms, or subsystems.

3.2 Studies of Human Memory

As we noted in the historical review, the systematic classification of human memory also began with various dichotomies, such as primary or short-term memory versus secondary or long-term memory (Atkinson & Shiffrin, 1968; Waugh & Norman, 1965), and episodic versus semantic memory (Tulving, 1972). In recent years there has been a consistent trend toward organizing various dichotomous classifications into more comprehensive and elaborate classificatory schemes.

Baddeley's chapter on working memory provides an illustration of this trend within the domain of temporary, short-term memory. Baddeley subdivides working memory into three components: the central executive (a limited-capacity workspace that allows one to perform mental computations on a small number of items of information) and two slave memory systems (a phonological loop that allows temporary storage of several items of speech-based information and a visuospatial sketchpad that can hold small amounts of visual and/or spatial information). The fractionation of working memory into multiple components was initially motivated by attempts to account for various kinds of data that were inconsistent with a unitary short-term store of the kind postulated by the modal model (Atkinson & Shiffrin, 1968). As indicated by the material reviewed in Baddeley's chapter, the model that divides working memory into multiple components has proven quite useful in accounting for a variety of experimental results and in generating novel areas of research. Although aspects of the model have evolved and changed over time, the basic architecture has remained intact.

The trend toward fractionation is also evident in the chapters concerned with distinctions among forms of long-term memory. Much of the recent research and discussion concerning multiple memory systems in humans has been motivated by, and pursued within the context of, dissociations between explicit and implicit memory. Squire considers a number of such dissociations in amnesic patients from the standpoint of the declarative/nondeclarative distinction, and he attempts to account for them with the same set of ideas that he applies to the animal literature. Squire argues that preservation of priming, skill learning, and biasing of judgments in amnesic patients are all mediated by nondeclarative forms of memory that can operate independently of the hippocampal-dependent declarative system. Squire also fractionates the general category of nondeclarative memory, arguing that such phenomena as perceptual priming and skill learning depend on distinct and dissociable subsystems. Although Squire uses the declarative/nondeclarative distinction synonymously with the explicit/implicit distinction, it is worth remembering that the term "declarative memory" refers to a specific memory system whereas "explicit memory" is a descriptive label that is mute concerning the memory system or systems that support it. "Nondeclarative memory" is a descriptive term that is in most respects synonymous with "implicit memory." We prefer to use the explicit/implicit contrast for descriptive purposes because the distinction is consistently neutral regarding the nature and number of underlying memory systems, whereas the declarative/nondeclarative distinction mixes levels of description. We refer to the memory systems themselves with terms other than "explicit memory" and "implicit memory" to emphasize the difference between the underlying systems and the kinds of psychological experience that they support.

Schacter's chapter focuses on a system that, he argues, plays a crucial role in supporting priming effects on tests of so-called data-driven implicit memory: the perceptual-representation system (PRS). Based on evidence from cognitive-neuropsychological observations of patients with deficits of word and object processing, Schacter fractionates the PRS into three distinct subsystems: visual word form, auditory word form, and structural description. Each of the subsystems shares critical properties that characterize the superordinate PRS: they operate at a presemantic level, are preserved in amnesic patients, and appear to be cortically based. However, each subsystem handles a different kind of perceptual information and probably has a different cortical locus. The PRS is distinguished from episodic memory (which supports conscious recollection on explicit memory tests) and semantic memory (which supports the acquisition of general knowledge and conceptual priming effects). Schacter also notes recent evidence suggesting that some implicit memory effects may depend on an interaction, at the time of encoding, between PRS and episodic or semantic systems. These observations highlight again the need to separate descriptive concepts (i.e., implicit and explicit memory) from the underlying memory systems themselves.

Moscovitch offers an account of priming that is similar to that of Schacter, inasmuch as he emphasizes the contribution of perceptual modules quite similar to the various PRS subsystems. Moscovitch's approach to episodic memory involves a distinction between two components. He conceives of the hippocampus as a modular system whose domain is consciously apprehended information that supports associative episodic memory, that is, episodic retrieval in which a cue directly evokes or reinstates a previously associated item or context. By contrast, parts of prefrontal cortex, Moscovitch argues, constitute a central system involved in strategic search through episodic memory. Moscovitch also notes, however, that the role of the frontal search system may be quite general, in the sense that it can be involved with different systems of strategic retrieval on both explicit and implicit tests, and may interact with various memory systems.

Johnson and Chalfonte attempt to account for some of the same phenomena that Moscovitch addresses, within a different yet related framework. They distinguish among four major memory systems—two perceptual systems (P-1, P-2) and two reflective systems (R-1, R-2)—and specify the nature of and relations between particular component processes that constitute each of the systems. P-1 is primarily concerned with the representation of relatively low-level perceptual information, whereas P-2 is concerned with objects and their spatial relations. These systems correspond roughly to the PRS discussed by Schacter and the perceptual modules considered by Moscovitch. R-1 is involved in reactivation of previously conscious information, and R-2 is involved in more strategic forms of search and reflection. The distinction between R-1 and R-2 corresponds roughly to the distinction drawn by Moscovitch between a hippocampally based associative-memory module and a more strategic frontal component. Johnson and Chalfonte discuss at length the role that R-1 reactivation processes play in binding together the various features of complex memories. Metcalfe, Mencl, and Cottrell offer a computational analysis of the relations between explicit and implicit memory, focusing on differences between the priming of performance on word-fragment completion and explicit cued recall. They observe that formal models in which elements of an episode are bound together exhibit properties associated with explicit retrieval, whereas models that do not use binding exhibit properties associated with implicit memory (priming). These differences suggest possibly important differences between the kinds of representations used by the system that supports explicit memory (bound or associated assemblies of multiple features or attributes) and the system that supports perceptual priming (individual features or attributes). Differences along these lines are in fact discussed in the chapters by Johnson and Chalfonte, Moscovitch, Schacter, and Squire, which suggests a possibly important point of convergence among multiple-system theorists.

3.3 Five Major Systems of Human Memory

On the basis of the results of the contributors to this volume, the research and theorizing of other investigators (e.g., Warrington, 1979; Weiskrantz, 1987), and our three criteria for postulating memory systems, we present in table 1 a classification of the major systems of human memory as they appear to us in 1994. The five major systems in the table are procedural memory, perceptual-representation memory, semantic memory, working memory, and episodic memory. We have also included, where appropriate, suggested subsystems or subtypes of a particular system. The contributors to this volume discuss at length the evidence for and the nature of these systems, and we will not duplicate their efforts here. A few words of clarification and elaboration are, however, in order.

The first major system is procedural memory. It is a vast category, as yet largely unexplored and unknown. It probably comprises several further major divisions and a large number of rather specific subsystems, only some of which have so far been tentatively identified (e.g., Squire, 1992a, this volume). Procedural memory can be thought of as a "performance-line" system (Hirsh, 1974). It is involved in learning various kinds of behavioral and cognitive skills and algorithms, its productions have no truth values, it does not store representations of external states of the world, it operates at an automatic rather than consciously controlled level, its output is noncognitive, and it can operate independently of the hippocampal structures (Hirsh, 1974; Squire, 1987). Procedural memory is characterized by gradual, incremental learning and appears to be especially well-suited for picking up and dealing with invariances in the environment over time (Sherry & Schacter, 1987). The

Table 1 Major systems of human learning and memory

System	Other terms	Subsystems	Retrieval
Procedural	Nondeclarative	Motor skills Cognitive skills Simple conditioning Simple associative learning	Implicit
Perceptual representation (PRS)	Nondeclarative	Visual word form Auditory word form Structural description	Implicit
Semantic	Generic Factual Knowledge	Spatial Relational	Implicit
Primary	Working	Visual Auditory	Explicit
Episodic	Personal Autobiographical Event memory		Explicit

existence of procedural memory as a category separate from cognitive memory systems is supported by converging dissociations from amnesic patients (e.g., Charness, Milberg, & Alexander, 1988; Cohen & Squire, 1980; Knowlton, Ramus, & Squire, 1992; Moscovitch, 1982), demented patients (e.g., Butters, Heindel, & Salmon, 1990), drug-induced amnesia (Nissen, Knopman, & Schacter, 1987), and normal subjects (e.g., Schwartz & Hashtroudi, 1991). Evidence from studies of patients with Huntington's disease suggests that at least one form of procedural memory, motor-skill learning, depends on the integrity of the basal ganglia (Butters, Heindel, & Salmon, 1990), a conclusion that is supported by research with animals that implicates a corticostriatal circuit in habit learning (Mishkin, Malamut, & Bachevalier, 1984; Packard, Hirsh, & White, 1989).

Because of our present lack of information about the vast terra incognita that we call procedural memory, its most adequate description at the present time probably is by exclusion: procedural memory refers to a system, or systems, concerned with learning and memory functions other than those supported by the other four major systems. Squire's (1992a, this volume) designating procedural memory as "nondeclarative" reflects the same orientation.

One major division within the procedural system likely to appear soon may be drawn along the lines of the distinction between behavior and cognition. Thus, we can distinguish between learning behavioral skills and procedures and learning cognitive skills and procedures. The neural computations that correspond to behavioral-skill learning (e.g., Butters, et al., 1990) necessarily depend on, and are expressed through, the activation of the premotor and motor cortices of the brain, whereas for cognitive procedural learning (e.g., Cohen & Squire, 1980) such activation is optional rather than obligatory.

The four other major systems are concerned with cognition. That is, the final productions of all these systems can be, and frequently are, contemplated by the individual introspectively, in conscious awareness. Any conversion of such a product of memory into overt behavior, even symbolic behavior such as speech or writing, represents an optional postretrieval phenomenon, characterized by considerable flexibility regarding the behavioral expression. Such flexibility is absent in procedural forms of memory. One of the cognitive-memory systems, working memory, differs from others in that it is concerned with temporary holding and processing of information. The other three systems are long-term systems. Working memory is described in Baddeley's chapter (this volume). It consists of three subsystems: a central executive and two slave subsystems: a visuospatial sketchpad and the phonological loop. Working memory represents a more elaborated and sophisticated version of what used to be called short-term memory, or primary memory. It enables one to retain various kinds of information over short periods of time, is critically involved in carrying out numerous kinds of cognitive tasks, and has complex relations with long-term memory systems. As Baddeley notes, the best characterized component of working memory is the auditory or phonological loop system: converging dissociations support its existence and a good deal is known about the kind of information that it handles. There is less evidence for the separate existence of the visual subsystem, and still less for the central executive; correspondingly, little is known about the kinds of information that these subsystems handle, although this situation is beginning to change (see Baddeley, this volume, 1992a, 1992b).

The other three cognitive-memory systems all can hold stored information over longer periods of time in the presence of other interpolated cognitive processes. The PRS and its subsystems are discussed at length elsewhere in this volume by Schacter, and also by Moscovitch and Squire. The system plays an important role in identifying of words and objects, it operates at a presemantic level, and it is typically involved in nonconscious or implicit expressions of memory, such as priming. The argument that the PRS is a distinct system comes from two independent and converging lines of research: memory experiments indicating that perceptual priming can be dissociated from explicit memory in normal subjects, amnesic patients, elderly adults, and drug-induced amnesias (Roediger, 1990; Tulving & Schacter, 1990) and neuro-psychological research on patients with lexical- and object-processing deficits that indicates relative preservation of access to perceptual/structural knowledge under conditions in which access to semantic knowledge is severely impaired (Schacter, 1990). The subsystems suggested in table 1 include the visual-word-form, auditory-word-form, and structural-description subsystems discussed in Schacter's chapter, along with a face-identification subsystem, whose properties and involvement in various priming effects has been discussed by Ellis, Young, and Flude (1990).

The remaining two systems listed in table 1 are semantic memory and episodic memory. Semantic memory makes possible the acquisition and reten-tion of factual information about the world in the broadest sense. The knowl-edge and beliefs about the world that people gain, possess, and use—whether general or specific, concrete or abstract—is critically dependent upon seman-tic systems. The episodic memory system enables individuals to remember happenings they have witnessed in their own personal past, that is, to consciously recollect experienced events as embedded in a matrix of other happenings in subjective time. Episodic memory is assumed to be the most recently evolved system that has grown out of semantic memory through working memory. It shares many properties and capabilities with the semantic system, but as with working memory, it transcends semantic memory in its ability to record, and subsequently to enable conscious recollection of, personal experiences and their temporal relations to one another. Episodic recollections consist of multifeature representations in which numerous differ-ent kinds of information—spatial, temporal, contextual, and so forth—are bound together with the individual's awareness of personal experiences in subjective time. (For more details, see Tulving, 1987, 1991, 1993).

The neuroanatomical location of the semantic and episodic memory sys-tems is uncertain at the present time. But it is possible to conjecture that semantic memory depends on the medial-temporal-lobe regions and that episodic memory depends on as yet unspecified prefrontal-cortical areas. Because episodic memory depends on semantic memory in some of its operations, although not vice versa, it follows that successful functioning of episodic memory also depends on the integrity of the medial-temporal lobes (Tulving, in press).

Evidence for the separation of the semantic and episodic systems is provided by converging dissociations from several sources. Especially relevant are observations that brain-damaged patients as well as older people can acquire factual knowledge indistinguishably from healthy or younger control subjects, while their recollection of the source of such knowledge may be greatly impaired. In extreme cases, patients can acquire new semantic information while totally lacking an ability to recollect any personal experiences from their past (e.g., Hayman, Macdonald, & Tulving, 1993; Tulving, Hayman, & Macdonald, 1991).

We should note that some students of memory systems, including such contributors to this volume as Johnson and Chalfonte and Squire, doubt the need to distinguish between episodic and semantic memory systems. Johnson and Chalfonte, for example, include both episodic and semantic systems in their R-1/R-2 system, and Squire subsumes them under a single declarative system. Such an approach has the advantage of parsimony, and it is consistent with the observation that episodic and semantic memory often seem to be similarly impaired, as in many cases of amnesia. Nonetheless, we think that the reasons for making some form of an episodic/semantic distinction are more compelling than the reasons against making the distinction, and so we incorporate it into our scheme.

4   COMPARATIVE SYSTEMATIZING OF SYSTEMS: ANIMAL AND HUMAN MEMORY REVISITED

Given the hippocampally oriented dichotomies of animal learning and the somewhat more complex scheme of human memory systems, what are the prospects of mapping one onto the other? We noted earlier that fully unifying the two domains awaits future developments, but some kind of mapping is undoubtedly possible. All one needs to do is to identify a single common dimension that applies to both schemes and then align the two schemes along that dimension. Thus, for example, one could propose that the rather primitive procedural memory system corresponds to the primitive system that subserves, say, elemental associations in Rudy and Sutherland's scheme, whereas the more advanced cognitive human memory systems correspond to the more advanced system that makes possible the acquisition of relational and configural associations. The same general rule could be applied to the hippocampal criterion: align hippocampal and nonhippocampal systems in humans with those in other animals.

This latter approach has been argued most forcefully by Squire and his colleagues. Human and animal amnesia are viewed as impairments of declarative memory with (relative) preservation of nondeclarative memory. Declarative memory, in turn, is defined in terms of its vulnerability to hippocampal damage: declarative memory does, whereas nondeclarative memory does not, depend on the hippocampus. In Squire's organizational scheme, therefore, amnesia is defined with respect to hippocampal damage, and animal memory systems are readily mapped onto the human systems along the dimension of declarative versus nondeclarative. Eichenbaum has taken a similar approach and has attempted to develop experimental paradigms for the study of animal memory that allow relatively direct comparison to human memory.

Such mapping of animal memory onto human memory is a necessary prerequisite for the development of animal models of memory. To the extent that the validity of a mapping can be verified, it can be a viable enterprise. But if much of it depends on assumptions, then one needs to be cautious. Different species have evolved to solve problems of survival that are unique to them. There are good reasons to believe that each species evolved learning and memory systems are correspondingly different from those of other species. Thus the differences in the brains of different species render general comparisons, or even comparability, of behavioral and cognitive functions questionable (e.g., Preuss & Goldman-Rakic, 1991a, 1991b). Even within the boundaries of the order of primates, the homologous correspondence of brain regions concerned with higher mental processes has not yet been established and is based largely on assumptions. Learning and memory systems of animals have many features in common with those of humans. It is equally clear that human memory differs in many ways from that of animals. These simple facts suggest to us that animal brain/behavior relations cannot readily be used for the purpose of modeling aspects of human memory that are uniquely human. In any case, we urge caution in cross-species generalization: animal models constructed on invalid assumptions are more likely to confuse than to help.

In addition to the possible noncorrespondence of functional brain regions in humans and other primates, additional problems remain, including the mediating role of language in humans and the absence of such a role in nonverbal animals, and differences in the kinds of tasks and instructions that are given to humans and animals. These problems have been noted in the chapters by Eichenbaum and by Rudy and Sutherland, who nevertheless do highlight several promising points of convergence. We believe that their enthusiasm is justified, but we also wish to point out that there are several important divisions in human learning and memory that are difficult to make in animal learning: the distinction between recognition and recall, the division between behavior and cognition, and the division between explicit and implicit memory, to list a few. Only one of the five human systems in table 1, procedural memory, can be thought of as a behavioral or action system, and relatively little research has been done on it. And no one has yet succeeded in experimentally separating explicit and implicit retrieval in animals, or in conducting a priming experiment on nonhuman animals. Although gains have been made toward unifying

Daniel L. Schacter and Endel Tulving

aspects of animal and human memory (e.g., Squire & Zola-Morgan, 1991), the obstacles to a complete mapping of the two types of memory should not be underestimated. Thus we prefer to deal with the mapping problem by postponing attempts at a solution. We feel that for the time being, at least, we are probably better off developing separate classifications of memory systems for different species. Although there is nothing wrong with gleaning inspiration for one's own thoughts by listening to those working on other species, we should probably not try too hard to pursue what may be, by nature's standards, a largely procrustean enterprise.

5 SUMMARY

Our overview of the memory systems of 1994 is meant to serve three main functions: to present a summary of past achievements, to point out deficiencies and shortcomings in our current understanding of organization of memory, and to inspire others to correct our errors and to improve the account.

We have presented a sketch of the current status of research on memory systems. Although antecedent ideas already appeared early in the nineteenth century, and although the dominant attitude of unitary memory was questioned from time to time, the multiple-memory orientation has become dominant only in the course of the last twenty years or so. Multiple-memory views were engendered by several joint developments, including (a) the discovery that amnesia was a highly selective disorder of memory and that the hippocampal structures play a crucial role in the acquisition of certain kinds of information, (b) the findings of dissociations between tasks representing short-term versus long-term memory, episodic versus semantic memory, and declarative versus procedural memory, and (c) the realization that the operations of many forms of memory, including cognitive memory, are sometimes expressed implicitly rather than explicitly.

We distinguished the concept of a memory system on the one hand from some related notions on the other, notions such as a kind or form of memory, memory process, memory task, and memory expression, as explicit versus implicit. We suggested that particular memory systems be specified in terms of the nature of their rules of operation, the type of information or contents, and the neural pathways and mechanisms subserving them. For a construct to qualify as a memory system, it has to meet at least three criteria: broad, category-based operations within a specifiable domain, a list of its properties that differentiate a given system from other systems, and relevant evidence in the form of converging task-comparison dissociations. Subsystems share with their supersystems the rules and principles of operations but may process different kinds of information and have a different brain localization.

We concluded that at present there is relatively little overlap between memory systems in humans and those in other animals. Systematic classification of nonhuman memory is firmly anchored in the hippocampal structures, yielding a variety of closely related dichotomies consisting of hippocampal versus nonhippocampal systems. Human memory, on the other hand, can be classified into five major categories, plus a number of subcategories. The major human memory systems include procedural memory, the perceptual representation system (PRS), semantic memory, working (short-term) memory, and episodic memory.

ACKNOWLEDGMENTS

Preparation of this chapter was supported by the National Institute of Mental Health, grant RO1 MH45398-01A, and the National Institute of Neurological Disorders and Stroke, grant PO1 NS27950-01A1. We thank Dana Osowiecki for help with preparation of the manuscript.

REFERENCES

Anderson, J. R., & Bower, G. H. (1973). *Human associative memory*. Washington, DC: Winston and Sons.

Anderson, J. R., & Ross, B. H. (1980). Evidence against a semantic-episodic distinction. *Journal of Experimental Psychology: Learning, Memory, and Cognition, 6,* 441–466.

Atkinson, R. C., & Shiffrin, R. M. (1968). Human memory: A proposed system and its control processes. In K. W. Spence & J. T. Spence (Eds.), *The psychology of learning and motivation* (pp. 89–195). New York: Academic Press.

Baddeley, A. D. (1992a). Is working memory working? *Quarterly Journal of Experimental Psychology, 44A,* 1–31.

Baddeley, A. D. (1992b). Working memory. *Science, 255,* 556–559.

Baddeley, A. D., & Hitch, G. J. (1974). Working memory. In G. A. Bower (Ed.), *The psychology of learning and motivation* (Vol. 8, pp. 47–89). New York: Academic Press.

Bascomb, J. (1901). *The science of mind*. New York: G. P. Putnam.

Bergson, H. (1911). *Matter and memory* (N. M. Paul, W. S. Palmer, Trans.). London: Swan Sonnenschein & Co.

Broca, P. (1861). Remarques sur le siège de la faculté du langage articulé, suivies d'une observation d'aphémie. *Bulletin de la Société d'anthropologie, 6,* 330–357.

Bruner, J. S. (1969). Modalities of memory. In G. A. Talland & N. C. Waugh (Eds.), *The pathology of memory*. New York: Academic Press.

Butters, N., Heindel, W. C., & Salmon, D. P. (1990). Dissociation of implicit memory in dementia: Neurological implications. *Bulletin of the Psychonomic Society, 28.*

Carpenter, W. B. (1874). *Principles of mental physiology*. London: John Churchill.

Charness, N., Milberg, W., & Alexander, M. (1988). Teaching an amnesic a complex cognitive skill. *Brain and Cognition, 8,* 253–272.

Cohen, N. J., & Eichenbaum, H. (1993). *Memory, amnesia, and the hippocampus*. Cambridge: MIT Press.

Cohen, N. J., & Squire, L. R. (1980). Preserved learning and retention of pattern analyzing skill in amnesics: Dissociation of knowing how and knowing that. *Science, 210,* 207–210.

Craik, F. I. M. (1983). On the transfer of information from temporary to permanent memory. *Philosophical Transactions of the Royal Society of London, 302,* 341–359.

Craik, F. I. M., & Lockhart, R. S. (1972). Levels of processing: A framework for memory research. *Journal of Verbal Learning and Verbal Behavior, 11,* 671–684.

Crowder, R. G. (1982). The demise of short-term memory. *Acta Psychologia, 50,* 291–323.

Eichenbaum, H. (1992). The hippocampal system and declarative memory in animals. *Journal of Cognitive Neuroscience, 4,* 217–231.

Eichenbaum, H., Fagan, A., & Cohen, N. J. (1986). Normal olfactory discrimination learning set and facilitation of reversal learning after combined and separate lesions of the fornix and amygdala in rats: Implications for preserved learning in amnesia. *Journal of Neuroscience, 6,* 1876–1884.

Ellenberger, H. F. (1970). *The discovery of the unconscious.* New York: Basic Books.

Ellis, A. W., Young, A. W., & Flude, B. M. (1990). Repetition priming and face processing: Priming occurs within the system that responds to the identity of a face. *Quarterly Journal of Experimental Psychology, 42A,* 495–512.

Fodor, J. A. (1983). *The modularity of mind.* Cambridge: MIT Press.

Gaffan, D. (1974). Recognition impaired and association intact in the memory of monkeys after transsection of the fornix. *Journal of Comparative and Physiological Psychology, 86,* 1100–1109.

Gall, F. J. (1835). *The influence of the brain on the form of the head* (W. Lewis, Trans.). Boston: Marsh, Capen & Lyon.

Graf, P., & Mandler, G. (1984). Activation makes words more accessible, but not necessarily more retrievable. *Journal of Verbal Learning and Verbal Behavior, 23,* 553–568.

Graf, P., Mandler, G., & Haden, P. (1982). Simulating amnesic symptoms in normal subjects. *Science, 218,* 1243–1244.

Graf, P., & Schacter, D. L. (1985). Implicit and explicit memory for new associations in normal subjects and amnesic patients. *Journal of Experimental Psychology: Learning, Memory, and Cognition, 11,* 501–518.

Graf, P., Squire, L. R., & Mandler, G. (1984). The information that amnesic patients do not forget. *Journal of Experimental Psychology: Learning, Memory, and Cognition, 10,* 164–178.

Hayman, C. A. G., Macdonald, C. A., & Tulving, E. (1993). The role of repetition and associative interference in new semantic learning in amnesia. *Journal of Cognitive Neuroscience, 5,* 379–389.

Hayman, C. A. G., & Tulving, E. (1989). Is priming in fragment completion based on "traceless" memory system? *Journal of Experimental Psychology: Learning, Memory, and Cognition, 14,* 941–956.

Herrmann, D. J., & Chaffin, R. (1988). *Memory in historical perspective: The literature before Ebbinghaus.* New York: Springer-Verlag.

Herrmann, D. J., & Harwood, J. R. (1980). More evidence for the existence of separate semantic and episodic stores in long-term memory. *Journal of Experimental Psychology: Human Learning and Memory, 6,* 467–478.

Hirsh, R. (1974). The hippocampus and contextual retrieval of information from memory: A theory. *Behavioral Psychology, 12,* 421–444.

Hull, C. L. (1933). *Hypnosis and suggestibility.* New York: Appleton-Century.

Humphreys, M. S., Bain, J. D., & Pike, R. (1989). Different ways to cue a coherent memory system: A theory for episodic, semantic, and procedural tasks. *Psychological Review, 96,* 208–233.

Jacoby, L. L. (1984). Incidental versus intentional retrieval: Remembering and awareness as separate issues. In L. R. Squire & N. Butters (Eds.), *Neuropsychology of memory* (pp. 145–156). New York: Guilford Press.

Jacoby, L. L. (1991). A process dissociation framework: Separating automatic from intentional uses of memory. *Journal of Memory and Language, 30*, 513–541.

Jacoby, L. L., & Dallas, M. (1981). On the relationship between autobiographical memory and perceptual learning. *Journal of Experimental Psychology: General, 110*, 306–340.

James, W. (1890). *The principles of psychology.* New York: Henry Holt.

Kinsbourne, M., & Wood, F. (1975). Short-term memory processes and the amnesic syndrome. In D. Deutsch & J. A. Deutsch (Eds.), *Short-term memory.* New York: Academic Press.

Knowlton, B. J., Ramus, S. J., & Squire, L. R. (1992). Intact artificial grammar learning in amnesia: Dissociation of classification learning and explicit memory for specific instances. *Psychological Science, 3*, 172–179.

Kolers, P. A., & Roediger, H. L. (1984). Prodecures of mind. *Journal of Verbal Learning and Verbal Behavior, 23*, 425–449.

Ladd, G. T. (1909). *Outlines of descriptive psychology.* New York: Charles Scribner's.

Luys, J. B. (1887). *The brain and its function.* New York: D. Appleton.

McClelland, J. L., & Rumelhart, D. E. (1986). *Parallel distributed processing.* Cambridge: MIT Press.

Maine de Biran (1929). *The influence of habit on the faculty of thinking.* Baltimore: Williams & Wilkins. First published in 1804.

Mandler, G. (1980). Recognition: The judgment of previous occurrence. *Psychological Review, 87*, 252–271.

Masson, M. E. J., & MacLeod, C. M. (1992). Re-enacting the route to interpretation: Context dependency in encoding and retrieval. *Journal of Experimental Psychology: General, 121.*

Melton, A. W. (1963). Implications of short-term memory for a general theory of memory. *Journal of Verbal Learning and Verbal Behavior, 2*, 1–21.

Milner, B., Corkin, S., & Teuber, H. L. (1968). Further analysis of the hippocampal amnesic syndrome: Fourteen year follow-up study of H.M. *Neuropsychologia, 6*, 215–234.

Mishkin, M., Malamut, B., & Bachevalier, J. (1984). Memories and habits: Two neural systems. In G. Lynch, J. L. McGaugh, & N. M. Weinberger (Eds.), *The neurobiology of learning and memory.* New York: Guilford Press.

Mishkin, M., & Petri, H. L. (1984). Memories and habits: Some implications for the analysis of learning and retention. In L. Squire & N. Butters (Eds.), *Neuropsychology of memory* New York: Guilford Press.

Moscovitch, M. (1982). Multiple dissociations of function in amnesia. In L. S. Cermak (Eds.), *Human memory and amnesia* (pp. 337–370). Hillsdale, NJ: Erlbaum.

Nadel, L. (1992). Multiple memory systems: What and why. *Journal of Cognitive Neuroscience, 4*, 179–188.

Nadel, L., & O'Keefe, J. (1974). The hippocampus in pieces and patches: An essay on modes of explanation in physiological psychology. In R. Bellairs & E. G. Gray (Eds.), *Essays on the nervous system: A festschrift for Prof. J. Z. Young.* Oxford: Clarendon Press.

Nielsen, J. M. (1958). *Memory and amnesia.* Los Angeles: San Lucas Press.

Nilsson, L.-G., & Archer, T. (Eds.), (1985). *Perspectives in learning and memory*. Hillsdale, NJ: Erlbaum.

Nissen, M. J., Knopman, D. S., & Schacter, D. L. (1987). Neurochemical dissociation of memory systems. *Neurology, 37,* 789–794.

O'Keefe, J., & Nadel, L. (1978). *The hippocampus as a cognitive map*. Oxford: Clarendon Press.

Olton, D. S. (1989). Inferring psychological dissociation from experiment dissociations: The temporal context of episodic memory. In H. L. Roediger & F. I. M. Craik (Eds.), *Varities of memory and consciousness: Essays in honour of Endel Tulving*. Hillsdale, NJ: Erlbaum.

Olton, D. S., Becker, J. T., & Handelmann, G. E. (1979). Hippocampus, space, and memory. *Behaviorial and Brain Sciences, 2,* 313–365.

Packard, M. G., Hirsh, R., & White, N. M. (1989). Differential effects of fornix and caudate nucleus lesions on two radial maze tasks: Evidence for multiple memory systems. *Journal of Neuroscience, 9,* 1465–1472.

Polster, M. R., Nadel, L., & Schacter, D. L. (1991). Cognitive neuroscience analysis of memory: A historical perspective. *Journal of Cognitive Neurosciencd, 3,* 95–116.

Preuss, T. M., & Goldman-Rakic, P. S. (1991a). Ipsilateral cortical connections of granular frontal cortex in the strepsirhine primate Galago, with comparative comments on anthropoid primates. *Journal of Comparative Neurology, 310,* 507–549.

Preuss, T. M., & Goldman-Rakic, P. S. (1991b). Myelo- and cytoarchitecture of the granular frontal cortex and surrounding regions in the strepsirhine primate Galago and the anthropoid primates Macaca. *Journal of Comparative Neurology, 310,* 429–474.

Rajaram, S. (1992). Remembering and Knowing: Two means of access to the personal past. *Memory and Cognition, 21,* 89–102.

Rajaram, S., & Roediger, H. L. (1993). Direct comparison of four implicit memory tests. *Journal of Experimental Psychology: Learning, Memory, and Cognition, 19,* 765–776.

Reiff, R., & Scheerer, M. (1959). *Memory and hypnotic age regression: Developmental aspects of cognitive function explored through hypnosis*. New York: International Universities Press.

Restle, F. (1957). Discrimination of cues in mazes: A resolution of the 'place-vs-response' question. *Psychological Review, 74,* 151–182.

Ribot, T. (1882). *Diseases of memory*. New York: Appleton-Century-Crofts. First published in 1881.

Richardson-Klavehn, A., & Bjork, R. A. (1988). Measures of memory. *Annual Review of Psychology, 36,* 475–543.

Roediger, H. L. (1990). Implicit memory: Retention without remembering. *American Psychologist, 45,* 1043–1056.

Roediger, H. L. (in press). Learning and memory: Progress and challenge. In D. E. Meyer & S. Kornblum (Eds.), *Attention and performance* (Vol. 14). Cambridge: MIT Press.

Roediger, H. L., & McDermott, K. B. (1993). Implicit memory in normal human subjects. In H. Spinnler & F. Boller (Eds.), *Handbook of neuropsychology*. Amsterdam: Elsevier.

Roediger, H. L., Rajaram, S., & Srinivas, K. (1990). Specifying criteria for postulating memory systems. In A. Diamond (Ed.), *The development and neural bases of higher cognitive functions*. New York: New York Academy of Sciences.

Roediger, H. L., Weldon, M. S., & Challis, B. H. (1989). Explaining dissociations between implicit and explicit measures of retention: A processing account. In H. L. I. Roediger & F. I. M. Craik (Eds.), *Varieties of memory and consciousness: Essays in honor of Endel Tulving* (pp. 3–41). Hillsdale, NJ: Erlbaum.

Rosenfield, I. (1988). *Invention of memory.* New York: Basic Books.

Rozin, P. (1976). The psychobiological approach to human memory. In M. R. Rosenzweig & E. L. Bennet (Eds.), *Neural mechanisms of learning and memory.* Cambridge: MIT Press.

Rudy, J. W., & Sutherland, R. J. (1989). The hippocampus is necessary for rats to learn and remember configural discriminations. *Behaviorial Brain Research, 34,* 97–109.

Ryle, G. (1949). *The concept of mind.* London: Hutchinson.

Schactel, E. G. (1947). On memory and childhood amnesia. *Psychiatry, 10,* 1–26.

Schacter, D. L. (1982). *Stranger behind the engram: Theories of memory and the psychology of science.* Hillsdale, NJ: Erlbaum Associates.

Schacter, D. L. (1985). Priming of old and new knowledge in amnesic patients and normal subjects. In D. S. Olfon, E. Gamzu, & S. Corkin (Eds.) *Memory dysfunctions: An integration of animal and human research from preclinical and clinical perspectives* (pp. 44–53), New York: New York Academy of Sciences.

Schacter, D. L. (1987a). Implicit memory: History and current status. *Journal of Experimental Psychology: Learning, Memory, and Cognition, 13,* 501–518.

Schacter, D. L. (1987b). Memory, amnesia, and frontal lobe dysfunction. *Psychobiology, 15,* 21–36.

Schacter, D. L. (1990). Perceptual representation systems and implicit memory: Toward a resolution of the multiple memory systems debate. In A. Diamond (Ed.) *The development and neural bases of higher cognitive functions* (pp. 543–571). New York: New York Academy of Sciences.

Schacter, D. L. (1992a). Priming and multiple memory systems: Perceptual mechanisms of implicit memory. *Journal of Cognitive Neuroscience, 4,* 244–256.

Schacter, D. L. (1992b). Understanding implicit memory: A cognitive neuroscience approach. *American Psychologist, 47,* 559–569.

Schacter, D. L., Chiu, C. Y. P., & Ochsner, K. N. (1993). Implicit memory: A selective review. *Annual Review of Neuroscience, 16,* 159–182.

Schacter, D. L., & Tulving, E. (1982). Memory, amnesia, and the episodic/sementic distinction. In R. L. Isaacson & N. L. Spear (Eds.), *The expression of knowledge* (pp. 33–61). New York: Plenum Press.

Schwartz, B. L., & Hashtroudi, S. (1991). Priming is independent of skill learning. *Journal of Experimental Psychology: Learning, Memory, and Cognition, 17,* 1177–1187.

Scoville, W. B., & Milner, B. (1957). Loss of recent memory after bilateral hippocampal lesions. *Journal of Neurology, Neurosurgery, and Psychiatry, 20,* 11–21.

Sherry, D. F., & Schacter, D. L. (1987). The evolution of multiple memory systems. *Psychological Review, 94,* 439–454.

Shettleworth, S. J. (1993). Varieties of learning and memory in animals. *Journal of Experimental Psychology: Animal Behavior Processes, 19,* 5–14.

Shimamura, A. P. (1986). Priming effects in amnesia: Evidence for a dissociable memory function. *Quarterly Journal of Experimental Psychology, 38A,* 619–644.

Spurzheim, J. G. (1834). *Phrenology: The doctrine of mental phenomena*: Boston: Marsh, Capen and Lyon.

Squire, L. R. (1987). *Memory and brain*. New York: Oxford University Press.

Squire, L. R. (1992a). Declarative and nondeclarative memory: Multiple brain systems supporting learning and memory. *Journal of Cognitive Neuroscience, 99*, 195–231.

Squire, L. R. (1992b). Memory and the hippocampus: A synthesis from findings with rats, monkeys, and humans. *Psychological Review, 99*, 195–231.

Squire, L. R., & Butters, N. (Ed.). (1984). *Neuropsychology of memory*. New York: Guilford Press.

Squire, L. R., Ojemann, J. G., Miezin, F. M., Petersen, S. E., Videen, T. O., & Raichle, M. E. (1992). Activation of the hippocampus in normal humans: A functional anatomical study of memory. *Proceedings of the National Academy of Sciences, 89*, 1837–1841.

Squire, L. R., & Zola-Morgan, M. (1991). The medial temporal lobe memory system. *Science, 253*, 1380–1386.

Tolman, E. C. (1948). Cognitive maps in rats and men. *Psychological Review, 55*, 189–208.

Tulving, E. (1972). Episodic and semantic memory. In E. Tulving & W. Donaldson (Eds.), *Organization of memory*. New York: Academic Press.

Tulving, E. (1983). *Elements of episodic memory*. Oxford: Clarendon Press.

Tulving, E. (1984). Multiple learning and memory systems. In K. m. J. Lagerspetz & P. Niemi (Eds.), *Psychology in the 1990's* (pp. 163–184). Holland: Elsevier.

Tulving, E. (1985). How many memory systems are there? *American Psychologist, 40*, 385–398.

Tulving, E. (1987). Introduction: Multiple memory systems and consciousness. *Human Neurobiology, 6*, 67–80.

Tulving, E. (1991). Concepts of human memory. In L. R. Squire, N. M. Weinberger, G. Lynch, & J. L. McGaugh (Eds.), *Organization and Locus of Change*. New York: Oxford University Press.

Tulving, E. (1993). What is episodic memory? *Current Perspectives in Psychological Science, 2*, 67–70.

Tulving, E. (in press). Organization of memory: Quo vadis? In M. S. Gazzaniga (Ed.), *The cognitive neurosciences*. Cambridge: MIT Press.

Tulving, E., Hayman, C. A. G., & MacDonald, C. (1991). Long-lasting perceptual priming and semantic learning in amnesia: A case experiment. *Journal of Experimental Psychology: Learning, Memory, and Cognition, 17*, 595–617.

Tulving, E., & Schacter, D. L. (1990). Priming and human memory systems. *Science, 247*, 301–306.

Tulving, E., Schacter, D. L., & Stark, H. (1982). Priming effects in word-fragment completion are independent of recognition memory. *Journal of Experimental Psychology: Learning, Memory, and Cognition, 8*, 336–342.

Warrington, E. K. (1979). Neuropsychological evidence for multiple memory systems. In *Brain and mind: Ciba Foundation Symposium* (pp. 153–166). Amsterdam: Excerpta Medica.

Warrington, E. K. (1982). Neuropsychological studies of object recognition. *Philosophical Transactions of the Royal Society of London, 289* (Series B), 15–33.

Warrington, E. K., & Weiskrantz, L. (1968). New method of testing long-term retention with special reference to amnesic patients. *Nature, 217*, 972–974.

Warrington, E. K., & Weiskrantz, L. (1970). Amnesic syndrome: Consolidation or retrieval? *Nature* (London), *217*, 628–630.

Warrington, E. K., & Weiskrantz, L. (1974). The effect of prior learning on subsequent retention in amnesic patients. *Neuropsychologia, 12*, 419–428.

Warrington, E. K., & Weiskrantz, L. (1982). Amnesia: A disconnection syndrome? *Neuropsychologia, 20*, 223–248.

Waugh, N., & Norman, D. (1965). Primary memory. *Psychological Review, 72*, 89–104.

Weiskrantz, L. (1978). Some aspects of visual capacity in monkeys and man following striate cortex lesions. *Archives Italiennes de biologie, 116*, 318–323.

Weiskrantz, L. (1987). Neuroanatomy of memory and amnesia: A case for multiple memory systems. *Human Neurobiology, 6*, 93–105.

Witherspoon, D., & Moscovitch, M. (1989). Stochastic independence between two implicit memory tasks. *Journal of Experimental Psychology: Learning, Memory, and Cognition, 15*, 22–30.

Young, A. W., & De Haan, E. H. F. (1992). Face recognition and awareness after brain injury. In A. D. Milner & M. D. Rugg (Eds.), *The Neuropsychology of Consciousness* (pp. 69–90). San Diego: Academic Press.

Young, R. M. (1990). *Mind, Brain, and Adaptation in the Nineteenth Century*. New York: Oxford University Press.

Zola-Morgan, S., & Squire, L. (1984). Preserved learning in monkeys with medial temporal lesions: Sparing of cognitive skills. *Journal of Neuroscience, 4*, 1072–1085.

2 Multiple Memory Systems: What and Why, an Update

Lynn Nadel

1 INTRODUCTION

How are learning and long-term memory organized? Is there one global memory system responsible for handling many kinds of information, or are there several systems distinguished in terms of the kind of information they handle, the time over which they handle information, and perhaps the brain systems in which they are realized? Almost everywhere one looks these days, one sees variants of the idea of multiple memory systems, but there is considerable vagueness about what defines these systems and why they take the form they do.

The prevalence of the multiple-systems perspective is relatively new. Within modern cognitive psychology, which dates back to the 1950s, the dominant position until recently was that there is but one general long-term memory system. This idea was also common among neuropsychologists concerned with memory, as reflected in their definition of global amnesia as a defect independent of the specific material or modality involved (see, e.g., Squire, 1975). Material- or modality-specific "memory" defects did not count as examples of this view, because they did not reflect impairments in the general memory system.

Earlier this century, several prominent scholars, for example, the philosopher Bergson (1991) and the psychologist Tolman (1949), favored the multiple-systems view, and the particulars of their theories find echoes in some modern-day treatments of the problem. The debate between Hull and Tolman on this issue was part of the very fabric of experimental psychology for more than a decade. Tolman's (1949) view that "there was more than one kind of learning" was successful in convincing many of the existence of "place learning" as well as "response learning" but did not have the effect of shifting the debate concerning how many learning and memory systems there are. The force of Tolman's contribution was unfortunately undercut by Restle's (1957) apparent resolution of the "place versus response" debate. Restle accepted that these two kinds of learning existed but argued that they did not represent fundamentally different things. Instead, he argued, these two kinds of learning merely involved the use of different cues. In this one can see the roots of current confusion: Are there truly separate systems with distinct properties? What does it mean to say there are separate, but interacting, systems? Indeed, just what does one mean by the concept of a system?

2 SOME HISTORY

The modern cognitive-psychological view that there is a single long-term memory system did allow for multiple memory systems, but these systems differed only in terms of their temporal characteristics. Textbooks and articles from the 1960s and 1970s are full of black-box diagrams explaining the relationships between *iconic* memory, *short-term* memory, and *long-term* memory systems, which were thought to handle information for hundreds of milliseconds, tens of seconds, or as long as memory lasts, respectively. Little thought was given to the possibility that there might be some constraint on the kind of information these memory systems could handle. One very prominent reason for this neglect was the almost militantly abiological stance common in cognitive-psychological circles during those years. This was not the only reason, however, since most neuropsychologists also viewed memory this way at that time. Events in four domains—neurobiology, behavioral neuroscience, cognitive neuropsychology, and finally, cognitive psychology itself—contributed to changing this situation.

2.1 Neurobiology

In the field of neurobiology, investigators interested in the neural bases of learning and memory initiated a process of broadening the concept of memory itself. Psychologists had a rather narrow definition of memory, but for neurobiologists, just about anything that looked like more than a strictly transient change qualified for study (see Nadel & Wexler, 1984, for further discussion). This broadened view of what counts as memory has played a major role in the multiple-memory-systems debate. To some extent, there are now thought to be many memory systems because of a willingness to count as memory various phenomena that wouldn't have been so labeled in the past. Perceptual memory or representation systems are an example of this development (see the contributions by Moscovitch, Schacter, Squire, this volume). Years ago many of these would have simply been called perceptual systems, and phenomena like fragment completion and object priming would not have been described as memory effects.[1]

Part of this broadening of the notion of memory includes a genuine change in how we think about memory itself: it is viewed no longer as distinct from information processing but rather as inextricably intertwined with processing. The view that processing and memory storage occur in the same circuits has also emerged from the neurobiological literature, largely because it is hard to imagine how the nervous system could keep these activities entirely separate from one another. One might almost argue that we have now gone too far in this regard: everything the nervous system does could be construed as "memorylike" in some sense, since just about every form of activity in the nervous system leaves some relatively nontransient trace behind. This fact makes even more important the need to sort out the conceptual issues behind the multiple-memory-system debate. It is unlikely that neurobiologists are going to be able to determine which systems are memory systems and which are not. They have already played a major role in helping us understand that memory is something the nervous system is constructed to do most of the time. It must be left to psychologists, biologically oriented or not, as the case may be, to figure out why there are many memory systems and what makes them separate.

2.2 Behavioral Neuroscience

Behavioral neuroscientists made the next major contribution to this evolution. Interpretation of the effects of brain lesions or stimulation depends upon how one views the nature of memory systems. If Tolman was correct in asserting that there were many different learning systems, this would suggest a rather different approach than if Hull (1943) was correct in asserting that learning was a general process. Well before the multiple-systems view began to be explored in the human neuropsychological literature, investigators working with rats concluded that there were indeed multiple learning and memory systems (e.g., Nadel & O'Keefe, 1974; Hirsh, 1974; O'Keefe & Nadel, 1978; Olton et al., 1979).[2]

The story began with attempts to understand what appeared to be a discrepancy between the observed effects of damage in the hippocampal formation in human and nonhuman subjects. While it was clear from work with amnesic patients that the human hippocampus was essential for some, but not all, aspects of learning and memory (Milner, 1962), the dominant view of a single memory system prevented the selective nature of amnesia from being systematically explored for several decades (see Corkin, 1965, 1968, and Kinsbourne & Wood, 1975, for exceptions). For the most part, neuropsychologists working with human subjects accepted the single-system premise and the view that damage to this system to varying degrees accounted for the global amnesia one observed in subjects with various etiologies, whether or not the root cause was a storage defect or a retrieval defect (e.g., Warrington & Weiskrantz, 1968).

Attempts to model the global memory defect of human amnesics in studies with nonhumans were generally unsuccessful: hippocampal lesions did not impair learning on a wide variety of tasks (see O'Keefe & Nadel, 1978, for a review). The conclusion that the rodent hippocampus was doing something radically different than the human hippocampus seemed unacceptable. Either there was something wrong with how we were viewing memory and the human amnestic syndrome, or we were simply not doing the same kinds of things in our studies with human and nonhuman subjects. It is clear now that both of these possibilities were true.[3] Memory and the amnesic syndrome were being viewed too narrowly, and human and nonhuman subjects were being subjected to different kinds of tasks. It is now generally accepted that memory is not a single system and that one can find memory defects of quite diverse nature (see Whitty & Lishman, 1966, for a very early and prescient statement of this). Given this fact, the kind of task one uses to assess memory defects after circumscribed brain lesions is crucial: one will or will not find a "memory" defect depending on where the lesion is and what task is used. All current treatments of the literature turn on an acceptance of these conclusions, although they differ in terms of how they view the task variables important to understanding what the different memory systems are involved in. The now almost universally accepted view that the hippocampus has a selective role in learning and memory took nearly 20 years to unfold.

3   COGNITIVE-MAP THEORY

An important first step in understanding what kind of learning the hippocampal system was essential for was taken by O'Keefe and Dostrovsky (1971) in their study of the behavioral correlates of single neurons in the hippocampus. The discovery of place cells in the hippocampus laid the foundation for the "cognitive map" theory (Nadel & O'Keefe, 1974; O'Keefe & Nadel, 1978), which was based on the central idea that there are multiple learning and memory systems in the brain and that the hippocampus is the core of but one of these. This aspect of our approach has sometimes been overlooked, but it was central to our thinking then and remains so now. In the past 15 years much energy has been devoted to exploring the virtues of the "spatial" theory and various alternatives to it (see Nadel, 1991), but that argument will not be the focus of this chapter. What is worth stressing here is not only the fact that our cognitive-map theory was embodied within a multiple-memory-systems view but that it was a particular kind of theory. It claimed that brain memory systems differed in virtue of the *contents* of the memories they processed, not the length of time for which memories were stored therein. Thus our view differed from the more traditional perspectives of cognitive psychology and the cognitive neuropsychology prevalent at the time, which saw systems as differing primarily in terms of how long information remained within them, not in terms of what kind of information was involved. In this regard, our proposal was consistent with the emerging understanding that processing and memory storage could not easily be separated from one another neurobiologically. It was also consistent with the notion that information in the brain, as distinct from the digital computer, had to be *content-addressable*.

3.1   Cognitive Neuropsychology

Some time after the notion of multiple memory systems took hold among behavioral neuroscientists, cognitive neuropsychologists began to explore the idea in depth (e.g., Cohen & Squire, 1980). Prior to this, O'Keefe and Nadel (1978) tried to apply their cognitive-map concept to an understanding of human amnesia, arguing that in the amnesic syndrome observed after medial-temporal-lobe damage some memory systems are still intact (what we called "taxon" systems) and that a particular kind of memory system (the "locale" system) is disrupted. These suggestions did not trigger as much discussion as our thoughts about rat memory, but it is important to note that they were based on the same ideas: that there are distinct memory systems and that these systems differ in terms of the contents they process. Perhaps most important, our model of both rat and human memory expressed certain views on what it was that made these systems different from one another: speed of acquisition, underlying motivation, persistence, and susceptibility to interference (see O'Keefe & Nadel, 1978, table 2, p. 100). Yet another difference was built into the very names we chose for the systems: the term "locale" was chosen to highlight the fact that spatial information was always a part of what this system processed, while the term "taxon" was chosen to denote the fact that processing within the nonhippocampal systems was based on the taxonomic principles of category inclusion and generalization. This distinction between systems based on categories versus those based on events in particular spatial contexts is likely to be very important in analyzing why there are separate memory systems and what they are separately good for.

Mounting evidence from cognitive neuropsychological investigations of amnesia confirmed the conclusion that there are multiple memory systems (see Squire, 1987; Schacter, 1985), but these studies have generally failed to clarify our understanding of how these systems differ from one another beyond the observed data showing that they are subserved by distinguishable brain systems (see Rudy & Sutherland, 1992, for some discussion of this shortcoming). In fact, much of this work has been largely free of theoretical content, focusing instead on the existence of dissociations in amnesic patients and on the brain structures involved in these dissociated systems in primate models of human amnesia. Distinctions between "declarative" and "procedural" memory or "nondeclarative" memory, for example, have in the past said very little about what distinguishes one system from another or why indeed there should be separate systems. When one turns to the animal work, one is typically at a loss to know what tasks fit into which memory system until after the research has been completed. If damage to the hippocampal system causes a deficit, then declarative memory is involved; if not, then declarative memory is not involved. This has not been a very firm basis for building a theory of multiple memory systems, and it is therefore not surprising that little progress has been made in understanding the nature of the underlying systems and why they exist. This situation may be changing. In several recent articles the original proponents of this view have tried to spell out more clearly what distinguishes declarative memory from other types of memory (Eichenbaum et al., 1992; Eichenbaum, 1992; Squire, 1992a, 1992b). I will discuss these efforts below.

3.2 Cognitive Psychology

Finally, cognitive psychologists have paid attention to these various findings from behavioral neuroscience and cognitive neuropsychology and concluded that there are indeed multiple systems. In fact, it has become increasingly difficult to identify a domain of human memory research that has not been heavily influenced by work in these other areas. This might account for why memory research now provides such an excellent example of the value of cognitive-neuroscientific analyses (Polster, Nadel, & Schacter, 1991). However, with the exception of one very important contribution (Tulving, 1972), cognitive psychologists have to date added little to our understanding of why there should be different systems.

To conclude this brief historical overview, it is generally accepted that there are distinct learning and memory systems across all the subdisciplines focusing on memory. It is not at all clear how to define these systems. My view is that at least some of the work with nonhuman subjects has actually gone further in contributing to this goal than the rather more descriptive work with human subjects. In the next section I will discuss the animal work in somewhat greater detail.

4 PERSPECTIVES ON MULTIPLE MEMORY SYSTEMS FROM RESEARCH WITH ANIMALS

The functions of the hippocampus has largely been the ground on which discussions of the nature of multiple memory systems has been played out in the work with animals, as noted already. Roughly speaking, the notion that the hippocampus is responsible for the kind of cognitive learning Tolman emphasized (especially place learning), while the rest of the brain is responsible for the kind of noncognitive learning Hull emphasized, has been central to most of the early dichotomies in the field (Hirsh, 1974; Nadel & O'Keefe, 1974; O'Keefe & Nadel, 1978; Mishkin, Malamut, & Bachevalier, 1984). Later models have emphasized a rather different distinction: that between simple and configural or relational learning (Sutherland & Rudy, 1989; Cohen & Eichenbaum, 1991).[4] Let us look more closely at these approaches and the use of the declarative/nondeclarative distinction in the primate literature (e.g., Squire & Zola-Morgan, 1988) for what they can tell us about the distinctions among learning and memory systems.

4.1 Locale and Taxon Systems

According to O'Keefe and Nadel (1978), several factors distinguished hippocampally based (locale) learning from nonhippocampally based (taxon) learning. First, locale learning was assumed to be all-or-none and to show rapid acquisition (and extinction), while taxon learning was assumed to be incremental and to show slower acquisition (and extinction). This analysis was somewhat oversimplified in that not all forms of taxon learning (and unlearning) are slow and incremental. For example, learning taste aversions, which does not require the hippocampal locale system (see O'Keefe & Nadel, 1978, table A23, for references), can occur with but a single pairing. Most forms of taxon learning, however, are slow and incremental, and this distinction between a fast-acquisition system and slow-acquisition systems could turn out to be very important in understanding the what and why of multiple systems.

Second, we assumed locale learning to be quite different from taxon learning with regard to the underlying systems of motivation that drive it. We argued that there is a fundamental connection between locale learning and exploration. Indeed, much locale learning occurs during what we would call exploration, or novelty-directed behavior. The "motivation" to acquire information, in the first instance about one's environment, was taken as the force underlying locale learning. The standard motivations—hunger, thirst, and so on—were not considered to be important in this system, though information about the location of food, water, mates, and safety might well be part of what is acquired. Taxon learning, on the other hand, was assumed to be motivated by the traditional forces emphasized by Hull, and therefore to depend on the standard application of reinforcements. One prediction that flowed from this distinction between locale and taxon learning was that animals with hippocampal lesions, because of their absolute dependence on taxon learning systems, would be much more tied to reinforcement contingencies than would intact animals, whose behavior is at least partially determined by curiosity. This prediction has been largely confirmed in a variety of studies (e.g., Devenport & Holloway, 1980).

Third, we assumed that locale learning yields memory representations less prone to interference effects than are those representations formed in the process of taxon learning. We derived this assumption from our sense that memories represented in maplike formats would provide the basis for unique episodes and multiple access routes, while memories stored in categorylike representations (the basis for representing information in taxon systems) would emphasize generalization and similarity among different traces, and hence would be more susceptible to confusions and interference effects. Here again, our thinking was probably oversimplified in that the taxon systems are not all alike, but the basic thrust of the argument seems to hold. The hippocampal system emphasizes what is unique about a memory, and hence functions to separate memory traces on the basis of what distinguishes one from another; the taxon systems generally emphasize what is similar about memories, and hence function to combine memory traces on the basis of how their features overlap. It is hard not to conclude that there are distinct advantages to each of these kinds of systems and that an intelligent organism needs both.

Fourth, we assumed that the maplike representations in the locale system are the basis for generating novel outputs, such as detours in mazes. This ability to generate novel outputs arises from the *flexibility* of the representation, which allows it to be used in novel ways.

The first striking feature of a map is its flexibility. Whereas a route specifies a starting point, a goal, and a particular direction of movement from the former to the latter, a map specifies none of these, either in its construction or its usage. It can be used with equal facility to get from any particular place to any other. Additional flexibility derives from the freedom from specific objects and behaviours. If one path is blocked another can be easily found and followed. (O'Keefe & Nadel, 1978, p. 87)

Fifth and finally, we assumed that the locale system is the basis for providing the context within which context-free information from the taxon systems could be situated.

The general absence of context information chacterizes the memory-storage properties of the taxon systems. Concepts and categories, the look, the feel and the sound of things, the goodness or badness of objects: all these are represented within the taxon systems. What is missing is the spatio-temporal context within which this knowledge was acquired; this is provided by the locale system, where representations from the taxon systems are located within a structure providing such context. Behaviour which can proceed without contextual information, and there is much that belongs to this class, will not require more than intact taxon system. (O'Keefe and Nadel, 1978, p. 100)

This distinction between locale and taxon systems with regard to context is specifically related to the role of the locale system in storing information about space. It is not intended to imply that the hippocampal locale system is integrally involved in all forms of context representations, for example, temporal context or motivational context; this distinguishes our model from the more general context models of Hirsh (1974) and others (Nadel & Willner, 1980; Nadel, Willner, & Kurz, 1985). Several recent studies have begun to explore and confirm this connection between the hippocampus and learning about spatial context (Good & Honey, 1991; Penick & Solomon, 1991).

To summarize, our model postulates separate memory systems and emphasizes several characteristics of these systems that make them distinct. These include the central role of spatial information, the speed with which information can be acquired or changed, the susceptibility to interference, the kinds of motivation underlying information acquisition, the flexibility with which information can be used, and the role of contextual coding. It is our view that each of these distinguishing features needs to be grounded in some empirical domain if it is to have any explanatory or predictive power (see Nadel & O'Keefe, 1974, for further discussion of this point).

4.2 Memories and Habits

What separates our approach from virtually all other approaches to multiple memory systems grounded in animal research is our insistence that these systems are to be distinguished in terms of the kind of information they handle, as we noted above. Thus the other early dichotomy, that between "memories" and "habits," espoused by Hirsh (1974) and then by Mishkin and his colleagues (Mishkin, Malamut, & Bachevalier, 1984; Mishkin & Petri,

1984), did not in any way address the nature of the contents that these memory systems are concerned with. Of central importance in the analyses of these researchers was the fact that the habit systems were concerned with what used to be called S-R learning and the "memory" system was concerned with cognitive learning, which stood outside the S-R framework. This failure to address the potential content-specificity of separate memory modules is, I submit, a serious flaw in this approach. One could go beyond their analyses to consider the possibility that there are many separate S-R systems, each dealing with a different kind of information (much like our varied taxon memory systems), and that there are many "memory" systems, each dealing with a different kind of cognitive learning, but they did not do this, nor would such an approach to cognitive systems fit comfortably with the facts about human amnesia or the effects of hippocampal damage in nonhumans. There are clearly many kinds of cognitive systems, concerned, for example, with learning about faces or language, that do not depend on the neural systems implicated in "memory" by this analysis. Thus it cannot be the "cognitive" nature of a learning task that is important here. Something else must determine why specific brain systems are involved with some, but not other, kinds of learning and memory.

4.3   Complex and Simple Associations: Configural Learning

Another perspective on multiple memory systems in the animal literature on the functions of the hippocampus is associated most recently with Sutherland and Rudy (1989), whose views are closely related to notions proposed earlier by Wickelgren (1979). The central idea in Sutherland and Rudy's proposal is that the hippocampal formation is essential in the formation of configural, as opposed to simple, associations. On this view, place learning is taken as simply the most common, but certainly not the only, form of learning that the hippocampal configural system is engaged in. To translate this notion into terms of the debate about multiple memory systems, the suggestion here is that some learning systems are concerned with associations between simple cues and at least one other learning system, centered on the hippocampus, "enables an animal to disambiguate the significance of an elemental stimulus or cue when the meaning of that cue depends upon its relationship to one or more other cues" (Sutherland & Rudy, 1991, p. 250).

This position has both virtues and faults. A major virtue is that it says something quite specific about the kind of information processing different memory systems are involved in. At least it can generally make unambiguous predictions about experiments before they are run. On the other hand, it has three serious faults, two conceptual, the other empirical. The first conceptual problem may or may not be fatal, but it is to my mind serious. It concerns the extreme difficulty involved in defining what is meant by the term "simple stimulus." According to this hypothesis, the hippocampus is not involved when simple stimuli are to be associated but is involved when configurations must be acquired. But what is a simple stimulus? Is an odor composed of many odorants simple or configural? Is colored light composed of many different wavelengths simple or configural? Perhaps stimulus complexes are configural only when their parts are separated in space? One can see the kinds of difficulties that arise in trying to deal with the deceptively simple problem of defining a simple stimulus. In fact, psychologists and philosophers have failed abysmally in their attempts to define what constitutes a simple stimulus. Will Sutherland and Rudy fare any better? Perhaps, if they would go on to say something about what it means to be simple or configural in neural terms. To my knowledge, they have not done so yet.

The second conceptual problem, which also applies to the newer version of the declarative/nondeclarative distinction, relates to the issue raised before about whether particular dichotomies rest on *process* or *content* distinctions. The configural theory, as well as the "declarative" model (see below), both assume that the hippocampus is essential for acquiring relational or conjunctional information. This concept straddles the fence between process and content. On the one hand, at stake is a specific process, one that conjoins arbitrarily related inputs. On the other hand, it is asserted that a particular kind of information, relational information, is handled by the hippocampus. The crucial point, however, is that *any kind* of relational information is allowed. In fact, this is the key defining feature of both the configural and declarative models that makes them different from the cognitive-map theory. According to all three theories, place information is but one example of the abstract class of relational data that the hippocampus is generally interested in. Thus these theories seem to be modern-day versions of the old-style notion that specific neural circuits can represent various kinds of information. In this case, the constraint is simply that only relational information is allowed, but there appears to be no constraint on what kind of relational information is involved. It is hard to see how this kind of model can accommodate the generally accepted view that information in the brain is *content-addressed* and that specific circuits can only handle specific contents.

These conceptual problems notwithstanding, the configural enterprise might be worth vigorously pursuing were it not for its empirical difficulties. The problem is that there is mounting evidence of exceptions to its claim that all kinds of configural or conditional learning should be rendered deficient by lesions in the hippocampus (e.g., Davidson & Jarrard, 1989, 1992; Jarrard & Davidson, 1991). Most recently, Gallagher and Holland (1992) compared configural learning and spatial learning in the same animals with hippocampal lesions made with ibotenic acid. These rats were severely impaired on a spatial version of the water-maze task, performed at least as well as controls on a nonspatial version of the water maze, and most important, were slightly better than controls on an operant discrimination task previously noted by Sutherland and Rudy (1989) to be a paradigm example of what their theory states the hippocampus should be necessary for. On the face of it, such data indicate that the specifically spatial theory accounts for the data better than the more general configural theory.

4.4 Declarative and Procedural Memory versus Nondeclarative Memory

Let us now consider the distinction between "procedural" and "declarative" information storage (Cohen & Squire, 1980; Squire, 1987), which has been applied to human amnesia as well as to the animal domain (Zola-Morgan & Squire, 1985) and which enjoys a certain amount of attention at present.

Historically, this approach has suffered from a lack of clear definition of just what constitutes each type of learning. There has been some evolution in this program in recent years, involving a deeper understanding of the diverse memory systems and processes covered by the term "procedural." This led some researchers to abandon the term "procedural" in favor of a new term, "nondeclarative" (see, for example, Squire, 1992b, this volume). This new label hardly helps one distinguish between the two systems in a principled fashion. In general, one understands the distinction between declarative and nondeclarative only because it says pretty much what all the other dichotomies say: some systems are involved with stimulus-response or habitlike learning; others are involved with "cognitive" learning.

Declarative memory is taken to involve information about episodes and facts about the world. However, as was pointed out early in the development of this approach (Mackintosh, 1985; Morris, 1984), it is exceedingly difficult, if not impossible, to say *in advance* whether a particular task taps declarative memory or nondeclarative memory. Too often the determination is made after the fact. An example is offered by classical conditioning. On the face of it, this would seem to involve acquisition of a new fact about the world, i.e., to be an example of declarative learning (see Mackintosh, 1985, for a thorough discussion of this point). However, the demonstration that amnesic patients show relatively normal classical conditioning (e.g., Weiskrantz & Warrington, 1979) forces one to conclude the opposite, namely, that classical conditioning involves nondeclarative learning. This sort of ad hoc approach is hardly the basis for a satisfactory theory, nor is it likely to advance our understanding of why there should be multiple systems.

The problem is particularly acute in trying to apply the findings from animal research to humans. In the work of Squire, Zola-Morgan, and their colleagues, a particular task, the delayed nonmatching-to-sample task (DNMS), has played a predominant role in establishing an animal model of amnesia framed around the declarative/nondeclarative distinction (see, for example, Squire, 1992a). In this task, the subject is first shown the sample, which is typically a junk object of some sort. After a delay the subject is shown two junk objects, one of which is the same as the sample, the other of which is new. In the DNMS task, the subject is rewarded for selecting the new object, hence the name "nonmatching to sample."

Squire and his colleagues argue that the hippocampal declarative-memory system is equally concerned with all kinds of information and that there is nothing particularly spatial about its information processing (Cave & Squire, 1991; Squire & Cave, 1991; but see Pickering, 1993).[5] The fact that monkeys with damage to the hippocampal system have defects in an ostensibly non-spatial task such as DNMS has been taken as perhaps the strongest evidence in favor of this position. The studies on which this claim has been based have typically included animals with lesions to several parts of the hippocampal formation. This leaves open the possibility that a "general" declarative-memory system handles information about facts and episodes for the entire medial temporal lobe system but particular parts of that system, such as the hippocampus, play rather more specific roles. If this turns out to be the case, it could provide a basis for reconciling the primate literature and its assumptions about more general memory functions with the rat literature, which has focused on the hippocampus proper and which strongly implicates the function of spatial memory.

Recently Zola-Morgan et al. (1992) presented important data from a study of DNMS learning in monkeys with lesions strictly limited to the hippocampal formation, made by experimentally induced ischemia.[6] In this study, the ischemia-lesioned animals were only mildly impaired in DNMS learning with a delay of 1 minute (see n. 5), a puzzling result in view of Zola-Morgan and colleagues' previous work and the conclusions they drew therefrom. Only when the delay was increased to 10 minutes, *in which case the animals were taken out of the apparatus and returned to their home cage during the intertrial interval*, was a severe deficit seen in the lesioned animals. This deficit could reflect an inability of the animal to recognize the experimental context when returned to it, as much as it could reflect a deficit in nonspatial aspects of DNMS. Whatever the basis of the defect at this longer interval, the important point is that there was little or no defect with delays of up to 1 minute. Ono et al. (1991) have also tested monkeys with ischemic lesions of the hippocampus on a DNMS task. These animals performed normally at 30 seconds but had deficits at 60-second and 5-minute delays. However, these deficits disappeared after a month, at which point the hippocampus-lesioned monkeys performed normally on DNMS with delays of up to 5 minutes (Ono, personal communication).

Because of the central role played by the DNMS results in determining which brain structures are involved in "declarative" memory, these results suggest either that the hippocampus is *not* involved in declarative memory or that declarative memory is an ill-defined concept. The data show that something is quite amiss with the view that the hippocampus itself is a general "declarative" memory structure. The failure to find a severe and lasting deficit in DNMS after hippocampus damage brings the primate literature into line with the rodent literature, which focuses not on "declarative" memory but rather on the virtually total deficit observed in any place-learning task after lesions of any sort in the hippocampus.

Jarrard (1993) recently summarized his own work involving lesions restricted to the hippocampus, made with local injections of ibotenic acid. Essentially, such lesions create large impairments in spatial tasks and contextual learning but have no effect on object recognition, concurrent discrimination, occasion setting, or negative patterning. Retained capacity to learn these particular tasks is important because each of them is taken as a paradigm example of the various theories of hippocampal function that stress its general role rather than peculiarly spatial role. They are all supposed to be declarative tasks, for instance (see Squire, 1992b, this volume; Eichenbaum, 1992, this volume). Occasion setting and negative patterning are assumed to require configural associations (see Rudy & Sutherland, 1992, this volume). On the basis of all his work, Jarrard concludes, "The severe impairment that rats without a hippocampus have in learning about and utilizing spatial information stands in contrast with the spared performance that is found in learning about and handling (even complex) nonspatial information" (in press). Taken together, these data suggest that if there is an all-purpose "declarative" memory system, it must encompass more than the hippocampus itself, it must incorporate such additional areas as the perirhinal cortex, entorhinal cortex, subiculum, and parahippocampal gyrus. Within this view, the hippocampus itself is not seen as a general-purpose memory structure. Any particular part of the system, for example the hippocampus, could easily be concerned with only certain aspects of such memories, for example spatial episodes, as O'Keefe and I have suggested and as Gaffan (1991) has recently argued.

The point here is that the declarative/nondeclarative distinction as it has been spelled out in the past does not seem likely to illuminate our understanding of the nature of multiple memory systems: it is too coarse a cut for that purpose. The declarative system is made up of many parts, each of which might be concerned with quite distinct kinds of information, perhaps some with facts and others with episodes, for example. We already know the same to be true of the nondeclarative "system" (it is really many systems, each concerned with a qualitatively different kind of information).

4.5   Declarative Memory and Representational Flexibility

Neal Cohen, the originator of the idea of declarative memory, and Howard Eichenbaum have recently provided a much richer conceptualization of declarative memory and the role the hippocampus plays in realizing it neurally (e.g., Cohen and Eichenbaum, 1991; Eichenbaum, 1992; Eichenbaum et al., 1988, 1989, 1990, 1992). They have suggested that the hippocampal "declarative" memory system "subserves a peculiarly relational form of representation. This relational property of declarative memory in turn gives rise to the critical property of representational flexibility" (Cohen & Eichenbaum, 1991, p. 266). This notion has one advantage over the declarative model expressed in the early work of Squire and his colleagues: it says something about where some of the properties of the system come from: in this case, the relational mode of neural representation. According to Cohen, Eichenbaum, and colleagues, declarative memory rests on a system of *relational* representations and by virtue of this conveys to behavior *generativity* and the ability to utilize memory to behave adaptively in novel circumstances. Procedural memory, by contrast, is represented in systems that are *dedicated* and *inflexible*. Procedural memories "can be revealed only in the restrictive range of stimuli and context in which [they are] originally acquired" (Eichenbaum, Otto, & Cohen, 1992, p. 4). I agree that relational storage and representational flexibility are important; indeed, this was one of the major points we stressed in comparing "maps" and "routes" and in ascribing some of the properties we did to the hippocampal mapping system (O'Keefe & Nadel, 1978).

In pursuing this notion of declarative memory, Eichenbaum, Stewart, and Morris (1990) investigated the effect of hippocampal system lesions on several different kinds of "place" learning. I must note here the markedly different way in which these authors talk about their tasks in comparison with how O'Keefe and Nadel (1978) talked about the same ideas. Eichenbaum et al. (1990) describe two tasks, both of which they call *place learning*. In one task, rats learned to swim to a place initially defined by a visible platform, always starting from the same location. In the second task, rats learned to swim to a submerged platform, starting from a variety of locations. This latter version is the only one that I would agree involves place learning; the former version is what we have called *cue learning*, and it does not require the hippocampus. Not surprisingly, the rats with fornix lesions could learn the first, cue, version but could not learn the second, place, version. Further, the fornix-lesioned rats that learned the first version were very inflexible in their learning in comparison with control rats. Their performance deteriorated when cues or the starting position were altered. Surprisingly, Eichenbaum and colleagues claim that cognitive-map "theory does not predict differential success or failure by FX rats in versions of this task guided by the same distal spatial cues" (1990, p. 3541).

That the authors could so misconstrue our meaning tells us something important about the difference between cognitive-map theory and the declarative-memory notion as espoused by Cohen and Eichenbaum. First I need briefly to digress. Cognitive-map theory was embedded in a particular view of how mammalian brains are organized and how this organization relates to behavior. O'Keefe and I supposed that discrete areas of the brain are concerned with processing and storing "representations" of various kinds of information. These informational modules provide the raw material out of which behavior is constructed. When we say that an animal engages in *place learning*, we mean that it behaves on the basis of information in the neural representational module concerned with spatial/cognitive maps. *Cue learning* depends on the brain module concerned with information about the features and values of objects and cues in the environment. In other words, our framework consists of content-specific systems.

This is not the case with the notion of declarative memory. The proponents of this view make much of the fact that declarative memory is more than spatial memory. Hence the importance of the claim that nonspatial forms of declarative memory are as much the province of the hippocampus as are spatial forms. The declarative system is treated as a kind of "general purpose" relational network, within which, roughly speaking, the laws of "mass action" and "equipotentiality" might be expected to exist.[7] The problem, as noted above, is that the recent evidence from work with both primates and rats shows very clearly that the hippocampus itself is concerned predominantly with spatial information. Presumably, its neighbors add their own particular pieces of information so that the system as a whole comprises something roughly like declarative memory. There is little to disagree with in this version of declarative theory, within which the hippocampus makes a selective, spatial or episodic contribution to the overall declarative system. This is not a version of declarative theory that its current proponents would likely own up to, although Cohen and Eichenbaum have left room for such a possibility in their most recent writings.

Some general points about declarative memory, as its proponents would have it, are worth making. To start with, if only "declarative" systems can be generative and declarative systems are subserved by the hippocampal formation and its related structures, how do we account for the generativity of language, which does not appear in any simple way to depend on the hippocampal formation, unless, that is, one wants to say that humans with hippocampus damage lose their ability to generate novel sentences? This has not been claimed by declarative theory, though it was hinted at in our speculations about "semantic maps" (O'Keefe & Nadel, 1978). One wonders in what subtle ways the language use of an amnesic patient differs from normal use. Two decades ago I observed E. Warrington interview the same patient in successive years, and I was struck by the generic quality of the patient's sentences and the fact that he responded to certain repeated questions with *exactly* the same word strings a year apart.

Further, it simply cannot be the case that all procedural memories are restricted to the stimuli and context in which they were acquired. Saying that they are is so trivially incorrect (can you play squash on any squash court or only the court you learned on?) that the authors must have had something else in mind. Perhaps they would wish to exclude motor skills from this claim? Unfortunately, they go on to argue that this (incorrectly assumed) restrictiveness demonstrates the *inflexibility* of the procedural system. I would suggest that some representations in the "procedural" systems are inflexible in the way being discussed but some others surely are not.

Another issue concerns the notion of relational representations. The "declarative" system is supposed to involve information about both episodes and facts. These are two rather different kinds of information, although they are clearly related in the sense that we acquire facts about the world as we are experiencing episodes in it. An episode seems inherently "relational," comprising all the diverse "features" of the world that happen to co-occur during some interval of time. To represent an episode, one needs to capture the spatial, temporal, and perhaps causal relations among all these features. Facts, on the other hand, are not inherently relational, at least not in the same way as episodes and events are. "Apples are fruit" is relational in the sense that it expresses the relation between "apple" and "fruit" in some category memory; that is, fruit is a superordinate category, containing apple, among others. Such categories of things and their exemplars could indeed be stored in relational networks, or "semantic spaces," but they would be quite different from the networks in which the truly spatial relations among the contributors to an episode could be represented. Recall what I noted above: there are good reasons to suppose that the brain would have separate systems devoted to distinguishing between possibly similar events on the one hand and devoted to generalizing across the similarities on the other. The former would enable memory of specific episodes; the latter would enable the extraction of elements common across episodes to create concepts.

It is unlikely that the kinds of relations embodied in episodes could be represented in the same kind of network as the kinds of relations embodied in facts and concepts. In cases like these, when computational needs are distinct, optimal solutions involve the use of separate and different networks to handle them. This logic suggests that within any putative "declarative" system handling both episodes and concepts or facts, there will be separate representational devices for these varied kinds of "relational" information. The evidence indicates that the hippocampus proper is specialized for representing spatial aspects (and perhaps, in an indirect way, temporal aspects) of episodes. Its input and output structures—such as the entorhinal cortex, the perirhinal cortex, the subiculum, the parahippocampal gyrus—can all be viewed as playing roles in representing facts, which serve as the bits and pieces out of which episodes are created within the hippocampus.

To summarize, the animal literature on the role of the hippocampal formation has given rise to a variety of ideas about the nature of multiple memory systems. My view is that the first of these, which split systems according to the kind of information they handle, spacial versus nonspatial information, remains the most viable. Other splits, which tend to stress more abstract aspects of what brain systems are doing, put the cart before the horse. Properties such as representational flexibility derive from the kind of system that must necessarily evolve to store environmental spatial information. The need to store spatial information evolutionarily drives the emergence of such a system. It is the specific information processing task that is central here, not the abstractions that can be used to describe such systems.

Let me return briefly to the issue of the role of the hippocampus proper in declarative memory. The following assertions and facts, taken together, lead us to what appears to be a very counterintuitive conclusion: (1) The delayed nonmatching-to-sample (DNMS) task is a signature *declarative* task, as generally agreed by all. (2) The presence or absence of a deficit in DNMS performance after a specific brain lesion indicates whether or not the lesioned area is a critical component of the declarative memory system. (3) Recent studies of performance on this task by both rodents and primates indicate that when damage is restricted to the hippocampus proper, there is either a mild deficit, a transient deficit, or no deficit at all. The inevitable conclusion these assertions and facts lead us to is that *the hippocampus is not a critical component of declarative memory*. This unlikely conclusion must mean that the way in which declarative memory has been defined and how it has been related to neural substrates are fundamentally in error.

To reemphasize what I said earlier, I think the problems are twofold. To start with, declarative memory is ill-defined: rather than being uniform, it is surely composed of several disparate forms of memory. This lack of clarity, when applied to the neurobiological literature, is compounded by the second problem: previous work and writings (my own included) have failed to clearly distinguish between the various components of the hippocampal system. Much of the data from lesion studies, especially in primates, but also in rats (e.g., Mumby et al., 1992), involves the use of lesions that extend beyond the hippocampus itself into such neighboring regions as the entorhinal cortex, the subiculum, the perirhinal cortex, and the parahippocampal gyrus. Many of these studies seem to suggest a "hippocampal" involvement in "declarative" memory. However, what is meant by the term "hippocampal" in this discussion is the problem. The latest work, as discussed above, which limits damage as much as possible to the hippocampus itself, tells a rather different story. Significant deficits on the DNMS task follow damage not in the hippocampus itself but in some of its neighbors. Thus we are all going to have to be much more careful in the future to separate the hippocampus from its neighbors, and perhaps to eschew using the term "hippocampal formation." I recommend that we henceforth use the term "hippocampus-lesioned" to refer to animals with damage restricted to the hippocampus itself: the term "hippocampal" is too ambiguous and has proven to be misleading.

5 WHAT IS A SYSTEM?

Having discussed the sort of information provided by animal studies of multiple memory systems, I am left with several key questions. I have made much of the fact that the reason there are multiple systems has to do with the need to process different kinds of information, and to do different things with this information, in the service of rather specific adaptive goals. I have yet to address perhaps the most central questions of all: Just what do we mean by the notion of a system? When we say that there are two or more systems, what does this mean? Is it enough to say that they are instantiated in different parts of the brain? Such a distinction seems correct, but it is rather uninteresting in and of itself.

I agree with Sherry and Schacter (1987) when they argue that what renders systems distinct from one another in an interesting way must go beyond the mere fact that they are subserved by distinct brain areas. The latter distinction can be, indeed often is, quite trivial, as in the differences between the visual and somesthetic systems. Processing of these two different kinds of information obviously takes place in different brain regions, and "memory" defects limited to each domain can no doubt be demonstrated, but we have little reason to suppose that there is any theoretically important difference between the two. Both are examples of what O'Keefe and I have called taxon systems and what others call implicit or procedural systems. Each is no doubt composed of several levels of memory (or representation), so that in fact a variety of distinctive "memorylike" deficits could be observed with the appropriate sort of brain damage. However, such distinctions, either between sensory domains or within a particular domain, are not in themselves sufficient to mark off truly distinctive memory systems. Something more is needed.

I suggest that there are two kinds of differences that render (memory) systems distinct. First, they might be doing something computationally different within their circuitries, so that these differences demand that the computations involved be carried out in separate circuits if they are to be done most efficiently. To put this another way, different problems the animal must solve can have different requirements in terms of the information-processing strategies they demand, and these different requirements can call for distinct circuitries. This is what Sherry and Schacter (1987) preferred to as "functional incompatibility." Second, systems might differ in terms of the length of time during which information is to be stored within them, which can require rather different underlying mechanisms. These two possibilities are not mutually exclusive, of course.

There is much in common between this position and that staked out by Fodor (1983) in discussing the notion of modularity. According to Fodor, modules are "domain specific, innately specified, hardwired, autonomous, and not assembled" (1983, p. 37). By "domain specific" he meant that modules do not cross content domains, that is, they are restricted to handling a certain sort of content. "Innately specified," "hardwire," and "not assembled" all refer to the idea that a module maps onto some neural "organ" that is specific, localized, and not created through some learning process. Finally, "autonomous" refers to the fact that a module does not share what Fodor referred to as "horizontal resources," such as memory or attentional processes. I take this to be similar to my claim above that what separates modules or systems is the fact that they have distinct processing needs and hence must be based in different neural architectures (see also Moscovitch, 1992, this volume).

6 CONCLUDING SPECULATIONS

The evidence suggests that there are two rather different kinds of memory systems: one concerned with "memory for items, independent of the time or place of their occurrence" and the other with "memory for items or events within a spatio-temporal context" (O'Keefe & Nadel, 1978, p. 381). Why should these two kinds of systems be separate? What is there about these two sorts of memory storage that makes separation necessary, or beneficial?

Consider again the properties I earlier attributed to the taxon and locale systems: taxon systems generalize over similarities and exhibit incremental acquisition and extinction, while the locale system focuses on the unique aspects of an episode and can learn from one trial. This distinction between systems focused on invariances and another system focused on variance was emphasized by Sherry and Schacter (1987), who went on to explore some of the evolutionary bases for such a distinction. I agree with much of what they said, and I will say little more about these issues here. I have recently pointed out (Nadel, 1991) that mounting evidence indicates that the hippocampus is a "spatial module," in the sense discussed by Sherry and Schacter, and that such evidence offers strong support for the spatial, as opposed to more general, theory of hippocampal function.

Instead, I will close by considering why taxon and locale systems should be separate. One obvious reason, discussed by Sherry and Schacter, is that generalization is quite opposed to discrimination. The former requires a system that overlooks differences between inputs, the latter requires a system that does just the opposite. If one thinks about the sorts of computational systems needed to accomplish these opposed goals, it becomes obvious that rather different architectures are required. In this regard, it is important to note that the sparse, distributed nature of hippocampal representations exactly fits what is needed to form memories of unique episodes. As first pointed out by Marr (1971) and then McNaughton (1988; McNaughton & Nadel, 1989), the internal organization of the hippocampus seems perfectly arranged to accentuate even small differences between inputs, and thereby contribute to the goal of storing unique memories.

Another not so obvious reason concerns the distinction between rates of learning that I emphasized in my discussion of taxon and locale systems (section 4.1). This distinction forms the basis for an interesting model of modular memory systems, which we have recently begun to explore (McClelland et al., 1992). Why should there be a fast learning system and a slow learning system, in constant interaction with each other? The basic idea is simple: a long-term memory system containing distributed representations of many items cannot afford to undergo rapid changes in synaptic weights: such rapid changes would destabilize the memory representations previously formed. Thus in such a system incremental learning is essential. However, the information contained in an episode must be rapidly acquired somewhere in the overall system if it is to have any impact at all. A possible solution is to have two interacting systems: one of these rapidly acquires representations of unique events, storing these sparsely so that they do not interfere with one another; the other interacts with this episode system, receiving slowly over time information about certain aspects of episodes. The former system acts as a kind of rapidly formed template, which then serves as the basis for slowly creating long-lasting change in the latter system. In this model, one sees clear parallels to what O'Keefe and I previously said about the cognitive-mapping function of the hippocampus and its interactions with cortical (and perhaps other) memory systems where information is stored without reference to the unique context in which it was initially acquired. The notion of consolidation falls quite naturally out of this approach.[8]

What is exciting about this proposal is that it provides computational reasons for the particular arrangements one sees in long-term memory, offering an explanation for why there should be separate systems and providing a basis for understanding what kinds of information these separate systems are necessarily concerned with. Thus a fast-learning, unique-episode system more or less has to be a spatial memory system in the sense that O'Keefe and I described; that is, episodes by definition include information about the spatial context in which they unfold. Such contextual information is one of the important ways in which one experience can be distinguished from another, which thereby facilitates separate storage and minimal interference. Were the fast-learning system concerned only with facts devoid of their context, it would not have these properties, and hence could not serve the purpose required. Most important, this latest approach to multiple memory systems brings together evidence from many domains and in so doing promises to provide multiple constraints on our thinking about the nature of memory and its many facets.

NOTES

1. We have made progress in understanding the relations between perception and memory by thinking about these systems in terms similar to the explicit/implicit distinction drawn in the memory literature and demonstrating that such manipulations as type of study process, modality shifts, and retention interval have different effects, depending on the task instructions (Roediger, 1990; Schacter, 1987).

2. It is worth commenting here on some issues of historical priority. Tolman deserves the credit for persistently arguing the case that there are multiple learning systems. He did not, however, relate his arguments to the structure of underlying biological substrates. In fact, Lashley's notions of "equipotentiality" and "mass action" were widely viewed within neuropsychology as establishing the opposite case. The issue remained largely unaddressed through the 1960s even though there were indications in work with both human amnesic patients and experimentally lesioned animals that memory could be selectively affected by brain damage. O'Keefe and Dostrovsky's (1971) discovery of the hippocampal "place" cells changed things. Almost immediately O'Keefe and I began working on the "cognitive map" theory, which was a clearly Tolmanian hypothesis in which there were multiple, distinctive learning and memory systems, each subserved by separate neural substrates. In this view, the hippocampus was the core of a system (the *locale* system) storing nonegocentric, i.e., viewer-independent, information about the spatial layout of the environment and was essential to Tolman's place learning. Other brain systems, which we first intended to label *alocale systems* but later changed to *taxon systems*, stored other kinds of information, including spatial information of an egocentric nature. These notions first appeared in published form in a chapter we contributed to a festschrift for J. Z. Young (Nadel & O'Keefe, 1974). Squire's (1992a) statement that Hirsh (1974) was the first to discuss the notion of multiple memory systems in the animal literature is incorrect. Hirsh (1974) and Nadel and O'Keefe (1974) should be jointly credited with first raising this issue in the animal literature.

3. Another factor in this story has become clear: the nature and extent of the lesions are also important. H. M. and other amnesic patients typically had damage to more than just the hippocampus proper. The roles of various additional structures and pathways (such as the amygdala, temporal stalk, subiculum, entorhinal cortex, parahippocampal gyrus, and perirhinal area) are only now being sorted out. Each of these structures apparently contributes something qualitatively different to the overall memory function of what has been called the medial-temporal-lobe system (see, e.g., Murray et al., 1993).

4. Cohen and Eichenbaum (personal communication) have pointed out to me a crucial difference between these two approaches, aside from whether they rely on relational information. In configural theory, the hippocampus serves to create a configured representation that, once created, is a unitary *merged* representation. It has the same properties as any other individual, isolated representation of a simple stimulus. In Cohen and Eichenbaum's hands, these relational representations are *not* configured. Rather, the relations are embodied in the network of connections in which the representations are instantiated. Such representations would demonstrate considerable *flexibility of usage*, a point Cohen and Eichenbaum stress. The configured representations of Rudy and Sutherland do not have this key property.

5. In a recent article Pigott and Milner (1993) have further explored the spatial nature of the defect resulting from hippocampal damage in humans. Right anterior temporal lobectomy caused deficits in memory for the objects in a scene and for the arrangement of filled and unfilled areas within the scene, *but there was no relation between these deficits and the extent of hippocampus removed.* Only when the right temporal lobectomy included extensive removals of the hippocampus were impairments observed in the ability to detect changes in the spatial location of objects. This deficit was one of retention or retrieval, since immediate recognition was unimpaired. The authors conclude that their "finding provides another example of the critical role of the right hippocampus in memory for spatial location" (p. 14). In contrast, the anterior temporal cortex is apparently crucial for the memory of visual patterns and objects. The most recent evidence suggests a double dissociation between object and location memory in the anterior temporal lobe and the hippocampus, respectively.

6. In the article in which I first discussed these data (Nadel, 1992) I unfortunately got a key detail wrong. Animals were not tested at a delay of 3 minutes, as I had stated (p. 184). The failure to find an impairment occurred at a 1 minute delay, and then only in the monkeys with radio-frequency lesions. The monkeys with ischemic lesions had a deficit at 1 minute, but a rather minor one (the lesioned animals still performed at 85 percent correct, well above chance). The basic thrust of my argument in Nadel (1992) is not affected by this change.

7. It is not surprising that the proponents of the declarative model try to explain the results of various studies of the performance of lesioned primates on a delayed nonmatching-to-sample tasu in terms that smack of equipotentiality. In their view, H + + lesions (lesions including the hippocampus plus a lot more) are more damaging than H + lesions, which in turn are more damaging than H lesions, because greater and greater chunks of some homogeneous declarative system are being deleted. This is in direct contrast with our view, which sees each part of the system as contributing some qualitatively unique part. On our view, it is simply not appropriate to lump data together across delay intervals or lesion groups. Matters are rather more subtle than that, as much recent literature demonstrates.

8. Some years ago, at a conference in Irvine, I discussed in some introductory comments an early variant of this model, without the computational trappings or justification. I suggested that the hippocampus and cortex interact with each other in a way that can best be described as a "dialectic." The hippocampus formed a rapid trace, and the cortex formed one more slowly, and the two shaped each other over time. I did not then, and do not now, accept the notion that the hippocampal trace decays over time, dissipating more or less in parallel with the growing strength of the cortical trace. This notion of decay assumes that the hippocampus must

get rid of its episode traces within a reasonable period of time because of storage limitations. I am not yet convinced of this argument, though it must be admitted that the weight of the (as yet circumstantial) evidence supports this view.

REFERENCES

Bergson, H. (1991). *Matter and memory* (N. M. Paul & W. S. Palmer, Trans.). New York: Zone Books. (Original work published in 1908.)

Cave, C. B., & Squire, L. R. (1991). Equivalent impairment of spatial and nonspatial memory following damage to the human hippocampus. *Hippocampus, 1,* 329–340.

Cohen, N. J., & Eichenbaum, H. (1991). The theory that wouldn't die: A critical look at the spatial mapping theory of hippocampal function. *Hippocampus, 1,* 265–268.

Cohen, N. J., & Squire, L. F. (1980). Preserved learning and retention of pattern analyzing skill in amnesia: Dissociation of knowing how and knowing that. *Science, 10,* 207–209.

Corkin, S. (1965). Tactually-guided maze learning in man: Effect of unilateral cortical excision and bilateral hippocampal lesions. *Neuropsychologia, 3,* 339–351.

Corkin, S. (1968). Acquisition of motor skill after bilateral medial temporal lobe excision. *Neuropsychologia, 6,* 255–265.

Davidson, T. L., & Jarrard, L. E. (1989). Retention of concurrent conditional discriminations in rats with ibotenate lesions of the hippocampus. *Psychobiology, 17,* 49–60.

Davidson, T. L., & Jarrard, L. E. (1992). Support for configural association theory: Now you see it, now you don't. *Hippocampus, 2,* 90–91.

Devenport, L. D., & Holloway, F. A. (1980). The rat's resistance to superstition: Role of the hippocampus. *Journal of Comparative and Physiological Psychology, 94,* 691–705.

Eichenbaum, H. (1992). The hippocampal system and declarative memory in animals. *Journal of Cognitive Neuroscience, 4,* 217–231.

Eichenbaum, H., Fagan, A., Mathews, P., & Cohen, N. J. (1988). Hippocampal system dysfunction and odor discrimination learning in rats: Impairment or facilitation depending on representational demands. *Behavioral Neuroscience, 102,* 331–339.

Eichenbaum, H., Mathews, P., & Cohen, N. J. (1989). Further studies of hippocampal representation during odor discrimination learning. *Behavioral Neuroscience, 103,* 1207–1216.

Eichenbaum, H., Otto, T., & Cohen, N. J. (1992). The hippocampus—What does it do? *Behavioral and Neural Biology, 57,* 2–36.

Eichenbaum, H., Stewart, C., & Morris, R. G. M. (1990). Hippocampal representation in spatial learning. *Journal of Neuroscience, 10,* 3531–3542.

Fodor, J. A. (1983). *The modularity of mind: An essay on faculty psychology.* Cambridge: MIT Press.

Gaffan, D. (1991). Spatial organization of episodic memory. *Hippocampus, 1,* 262–264.

Gallagher, M., & Holland, P. C. (1992). Preserved configural learning and spatial learning impairment in rats with hippocampal damage. *Hippocampus, 2,* 81–88.

Good, M., & Honey, R. C. (1991). Conditioning and contextual retrieval in hippocampal rats. *Behavioral Neuroscience, 105,* 499–599.

Hirsh, R. (1974). The hippocampus and contextual retrieval of information from memory: A theory. *Behavioral Biology, 12,* 421–444.

Hull, C. L. (1943). *A behavior system*. New Haven: Yale University Press.

Jarrard, L. E. (1993). On the role of the hippocampus in learning and memory in the rat. *Behavioral and Neural Biology, 60*, 9–26.

Jarrard, L. E., & Davidson, T. L. (1991). On the hippocampus and learned conditional responding: Effects of aspiration versus ibotenate lesions. *Hippocampus, 1*, 107–118.

Kinsbourne, M., & Wood, F. (1975). Short-term memory and the amnesic syndrome. In D. Deutsch & J. A. Deutsch (Eds.), *Short-term memory* (pp. 257–291). New York: Academic Press.

McClelland, J. L., McNaughton, B. L., O'Reilly, R., & Nadel, L. (1992). Complementary role of hippocampus and neocortex in learning and memory. *Society for Neuroscience, 18:* 1216.

Mackintosh, N. J. (1985). Varieties of conditioning. In N. Weinberger, J. McGaugh, & G. Lynch (Eds.), *Memory systems of the brain: Animal and human cognitive processes* (pp. 335–350). New York: Guilford Press.

McNaughton, B. L. (1988). Neural mechanisms for spatial computation and information storage. In L. Nadel, L. A. Cooper, P. Culicover, & R. M. Harnish (Eds.), *Neural connections, mental computation*. Cambridge: MIT Press.

McNaughton, B. L., and Nadel, L. (1989). Hebb-Marr networks and the neurobiological representation of action in space. In M. A. Gluck & D. E. Rumelhart (Eds.), *Neuroscience and connectionist theory*. Hillsdale, NJ: L. Erlbaum.

Marr, D. (1971). A theory of archicortex. *Philosophical Transactions of the Royal Society, 262*, 23–81.

Milner, B. (1962). Les troubles de la memoire accompagnant des lesions hippocampiques bilaterales. In *Physiologie de l'hippocampe*. Paris: Centre National de la Recherche Scientifique.

Mishkin, M., Malamut, B., & Bachevalier, J. (1984). Memories and habits: Two neural systems. In G. Lynch, J. L. McGaugh, & N. M. Weinberger (Eds.), *The neurobiology of learning and memory* (pp. 65–77). New York: Guilford Press.

Mishkin, M., & Petri, H. L. (1984). Memories and habits: Some implications for the analysis of learning and retention. In L. Squire & N. Butters (Eds.), *Neuropsychology of memory*. New York: Guilford Press.

Morris, R. G. M. (1984). Is the distinction between procedural and declarative memory useful with respect to animal models of amnesia? In G. Lynch, J. L. McGaugh, & N. M. Weinberger (Eds.), *The neurobiology of learning and memory* (pp. 119–124). New York: Guilford Press.

Moscovitch, M. (1992). Memory and working-with-memory: A component process model based on modules and central systems. *Journal of Cognitive Neuroscience, 4*, 257–267.

Mumby, D. G., Pinel, J. P. J., & Kornecook, T. J. (1992). Dissociating the effects of hippocampal and amygdalar lesions in rats with a battery of nonspatial memory tasks. *Society for Neuroscience, 18*, 1423.

Murray, E. A., Gaffan, D., & Mishkin, M. (1993). Neural substrates of visual stimulus-stimulus association in rhesus monkeys. *Journal of Neuroscience, 13*, 4549–4561.

Nadel, L. (1991). The hippocampus and space revisited. *Hippocampus, 1*, 221–229.

Nadel, L. (1992). Multiple memory systems: What and why. *Journal of Cognitive Neuroscience, 4*, 179–188.

Nadel, L., & O'Keefe, J. (1974). The hippocampus in pieces and patches: An essay on modes of explanation in physiological psychology. In R. Bellairs and E. G. Gray (Eds.), *Essays on the nervous system: A festschrift for Prof. J. Z. Young* (pp. 367–390). Oxford: Clarendon Press.

Nadel, L., & Wexler, K. (1984). Neurobiology, representations, and memory. In G. Lynch, J. L. McGaugh, & N. M. Weinberger (Eds.), *The neurobiology of learning and memory* (pp. 124–134). New York: Guilford Press.

Nadel, L., & Willner, J. (1980). Context and conditioning: A place for space. *Physiological Psychology, 8,* 218–228.

Nadel, L., Willner, J., & Kurz, E. M. (1985). Cognitive maps and environmental context. In P. Balsam & A. Tomie (Eds.), *Context and learning.* Hillsdale, NJ: L. Erlbaum.

O'Keefe, J. (1991). An allocentric spatial model for the hippocampal cognitive map. *Hippocampus, 1,* 230–235.

O'Keefe, J., & Dostrovsky, J. (1971). The hippocampus as a spatial map: Preliminary evidence from unit activity in the freely-moving rat. *Brain Research, 34,* 171–175.

O'Keefe, J., & Nadel, L. (1978). *The hippocampus as a cognitive map.* Oxford: Clarendon Press.

Olton, D. S., Becker, J. T., & Handelmann, G. E. (1979). Hippocampus, space, and memory. *Behavioral and Brain Sciences, 2,* 313–365.

Ono, T., Tabuchi, E., Nishijo, H., & Tamura, R. (1991). Ischemic neuronal death in monkey hippocampus. *Society for Neuroscience, 17,* 661.

Penick, S., & Solomon, P. R. (1991). Hippocampus, context, and conditioning. *Behavioral Neuroscience, 105,* 611–617.

Pickering, A. D. (1993). The hippocampus and space: Are we flogging a dead (sea-)horse? *Hippocampus, 3,* 113–114.

Pigott, S., & Milner, B. (1993). Memory for different aspects of complex visual scenes after unilateral temporal- or frontal-lobe resection. *Neuropsychologia, 31,* 1–15.

Polster, M. R., Nadel, L., & Schacter, D. L. (1991). Cognitive neuroscience analyses of memory: A historical perspective. *Journal of Cognitive Neuroscience, 3,* 95–116.

Restle, F. (1957). Discrimination of cues in mazes: A resolution of the 'place-vs-response' question. *Psychological Review, 64,* 217–228.

Roediger, H. L. (1990). Implicit memory: Retention without remembering. *American Psychologist, 45,* 1043–1056.

Rudy, J. W., & Sutherland, R. J. (1992). Configural and elemental associations and the memory coherence problem. *Journal of Cognitive Neuroscience, 4,* 208–216.

Schacter, D. L. (1985). Multiple forms of memory in humans and animals. In N. Weinberger, J. McGaugh, & G. Lynch (Eds.), *Memory systems of the brain: Animal and human cognitive processes* (pp. 351–379). New York: Guilford Press.

Schacter, D. L. (1987). Implicit memory: History and current status. *Journal of Experimental Psychology: Learning, Memory, and Cognition, 13,* 501–518.

Schacter, D. L. (1992). Priming and multiple memory systems: Perceptual mechanisms of implicit memory. *Journal of Cognitive Neuroscience, 4,* 244–256.

Sherry, D. F., & Schacter, D. L. (1987). The evolution of multiple memory systems. *Psychological Review, 94,* 439–454.

Squire, L. R. (1975). Short-term memory as a biological entity. In D. Deutsch and J. A. Deutsch (Eds.), *Short-term memory.* New York: Academic Press.

Squire, L. R. (1987). *Memory and brain.* New York: Oxford University Press.

Squire, L. R. (1992a). Memory and the hippocampus: A synthesis from findings with rats, monkeys, and humans. *Psychological Review, 99,* 195–231.

Squire, L. R. (1992b). Declarative and nondeclarative memory: Multiple brain systems supporting learning and memory. *Journal of Cognitive Neuroscience, 4,* 232–243.

Squire, L. R., & Cave, C. B. (1991). The hippocampus, memory, and space. *Hippocampus, 1,* 269–271.

Squire, L. R., & Zola-Morgan, S. (1988). Memory: Brain systems and behavior. *Trends in Neurosciences, 11,* 170–175.

Sutherland, R. J., & Rudy, J. W. (1989). Configural association theory: The role of the hippocampal formation in learning, memory, and amnesia. *Psychobiology, 17,* 129–144.

Sutherland, R. J., & Rudy, J. W. (1991). Exceptions to the rule of space. *Hippocampus, 1,* 250–252.

Tolman, E. C. (1949). There is more than one kind of learning. *Psychological Review, 56,* 144–155.

Tulving, E. (1972). Episodic and semantic memory. In E. Tulving & W. Donaldson (Eds.), *Organization and memory* (pp. 382–403). New York: Academic Press.

Warrington, E. K., & Weiskrantz, L. (1968). Amnesic syndrome: consolidation or retrieval? *Nature, 228,* 628–630.

Weiskrantz, L., & Warrington, E. K. (1979). Conditioning in amnesic patients. *Neuropsychologia, 17,* 187–194.

Whitty, C. M. M., & Lishman, W. A. (1966). Amnesia in cerebral disease. In C. W. M. Whitty & O. L. Zangwill (Eds.), *Amnesia* (pp. 36–76). London: Butterworths.

Wickelgren, W. A. (1979). Chunking and consolidation: A theoretical synthesis of semantic networks, configuring in conditioning, S-R vs cognitive learning, normal forgetting, the amnesic syndrome, and the hippocampal arousal system. *Psychological Review, 86,* 44–60.

Zola-Morgan, S. M., & Squire, L. R. (1985). Complementary approaches to the study of memory: Human amnesia and animal models. In N. M. Weinberger, J. L. McGaugh, & G. Lynch (Eds.), *Memory systems of the brain: Animal and human cognitive processes* (pp. 463–477). New York: Guilford Press.

Zola-Morgan, S. M., Squire, L. R., Rempel, N. L., Clower, R. P., & Amaral, D. G. (1992). Enduring memory impairment in monkeys after ischemic damage to the hippocampus. *Journal of Neuroscience, 12,* 2582–2596.

3 Variations in Synaptic Plasticity and Types of Memory in Corticohippocampal Networks

Gary Lynch and Richard Granger

1 INTRODUCTION

Experience and behavioral research indicate that the brain possesses a memory system with the following properties:

1. A remarkable capacity

2. The ability to encode new information rapidly (within seconds)

3. A capability for forming extremely persistent encodings

4. A requirement of at least several minutes to stabilize (consolidate) newly acquired material

5. An encoding process triggered by electrophysiological patterns of activity occurring during learning

This fifth property is perhaps so obvious that it is rarely discussed. The long-term potentiation (LTP) effect possesses each of these features, as listed below, and accordingly has become a leading candidate for the substrate of certain forms of memory.

1. LTP is synapse specific, in that its induction in one set of contacts on a cell does not disturb other contacts. Theoretical studies indicate that this property can lead to great capacity.

2. Work by Gustafsson and Wigstrom (1990) indicates that LTP begins to develop within 10 seconds and is fully present by 20–30 seconds.

3. Studies carried out in this laboratory showed that the potentiation can persist without detectable change for weeks (Staubli & Lynch, 1987).

4. Like memory, LTP has a vulnerable consolidation phase lasting at least several minutes (Arai, Larson, & Lynch, 1990).

5. Finally, activity patterns known to occur in the brain during learning have a direct relationship with the cellular events that trigger LTP (Larson, Wong, & Lynch, 1986; Larson & Lynch, 1986, 1988, 1989).

The above correspondences between LTP and memory strongly suggest that at least some forms of memory are due to the chemistries responsible for LTP.

Pharmacological experiments have confirmed this prediction. Antagonists of the NMDA receptor, which block LTP, disrupt spatial-memory encoding in rats (Morris, Anderson, Lynch, & Baudry, 1986; Robinson, Crooks, Shinkman, & Gallagher, 1989) and olfactory-memory encoding in rats (Staubli, Thibault, DiLorenzo, & Lynch, 1989), while benzodiazepines, which are potent amnesic agents in humans and animals, suppress development of LTP (del Cerro, Jung, & Lynch, 1992). It is also the case that potentiation appears in synapses along with learning (Roman, Staubli, & Lynch, 1987) and that prior induction of LTP influences the subsequent course of learning (Berger, 1984; Castro, Silbert, McNaughton, & Barnes 1989). Results of these kinds link LTP and particular instances of memory but should not be overgeneralized; the cellular machinery for LTP (e.g., receptors for NMDA [N-methyl-D-aspartate] and AMPA [alpha-amino-3-hydroxy-5-methylisoxazole-4-propionic acid]) is primarily found in telencephalon (Monaghan & Cotman, 1985), but variants of memory are more widely distributed (Kleckner & Dingledine, 1989). Moreover, there are forms of physiologically induced plasticity unrelated to LTP even within the hippocampus (Staubli, Larson, & Lynch 1990; Zalutsky & Nicoll, 1990). Note also that qualitatively distinct forms of memory could incorporate the first three characteristics listed above (capacity, rapid acquisition, stability); LTP could thus be a common encoding process that yields different behavioral consequences, depending on where in brain it is implemented.

There are two ways of exploring the variants of memory to which LTP might make contributions. First, manipulations that influence the induction of potentiation can be tested across a range of behavioral tasks and note taken of when they do and when they do not affect memory formation. This has the advantage of historical precedent: pharmacological intervention may be the most widely used tactic to study the biology of memory. There are difficulties with this approach, however. Selectively influencing LTP induction is problematic: many of the chemistries implicated in the potentiation effect are involved in more routine cellular functions, and the drugs directed at them typically have uncertain specificities. A less apparent set of difficulties arises when considering what behaviors to study and in particular the need for principled reasons to assume that they involve LTP. It is indeed curious that rats are seldom tested on problems involving stable encoding, rapid acquisition, and very large numbers of similar and specified cues. Yet precisely in such presumably commonplace circumstances does one most expect LTP to make its contributions. Related to this point, pharmacological/behavioral studies are largely restricted to attempts at influencing the encoding process; they are not well suited for attempts to detect the characteristics of LTP in the utilization or expression of memory.

A second approach to exploring links between LTP and different varieties of memory is to predict behavior from biology. Three related kinds of information are pertinent to this:

- Variations in the potentiation effect
- The anatomical types of networks in which LTP is found
- The location and hodologies of these networks

Variations of LTP should have correspondences in behavior and by themselves should suggest memory systems with different properties. The architectural design and physiological operating rules of networks dictate function; the presence of LTP in particular types of networks should therefore provide grounds for predictions about the types of memory operations to which potentiation contributes. Computer-modeling studies incorporating the complex rules for LTP induction and the characteristics of expressed potentiation can be used to make such predictions specific. Location too suggests function, as evidenced by the long history of functional neuroanatomy. Accordingly, identifying the sites at which LTP occurs should help distinguish the classes of memory in which it plays a role.

The research program we and our colleagues have been conducting is directed at obtaining information on the three kinds of information listed above. Results so far collected suggest that LTP does participate in definably different forms of memory. While these forms do in some cases resemble categories deduced from behavioral studies, the neurobiological studies point to a different emphasis for general-classification schemes. Specifically, we take the results to indicate that subtypes of memory operate serially, with the stages in this sequence distinguished in part by the amount of time since the last encounter with the object. Thus we propose a serial "assembly line" of specialized functions, each of which adds a unique aspect to the processing of memories. Owing in part to the different longevity of potentiation in different anatomical systems, processing via these serial steps not only adds separate qualities to the resultant memory but also enables "memory for sequence" or "knowing when," i.e., memory of the order in which events occurred in time. In this chapter we review the types of synaptic plasticity found in the successive stages of the olfactory-hippocampal system, discuss the forms of memory that might result from them, and offer a generalized hypothesis regarding the serial operations of memory in cortical networks. We then interpret the effects of lesions on the encoding versus the expression of memory from the perspective of this hypothesis.

2   CORTICOHIPPOCAMPAL NETWORKS

If data on the designs and positions of networks expressing LTP are needed to analyze the types of memory that depend on potentiation, then it will be necessary to define multiregion brain systems that are tractable subjects for physiological-behavioral studies. Since the hippocampus plays a pivotal role in memory, it is reasonable to begin with the pathways leading into, through, and out of this brain structure. Figure 1 is a schematic from the pertinent

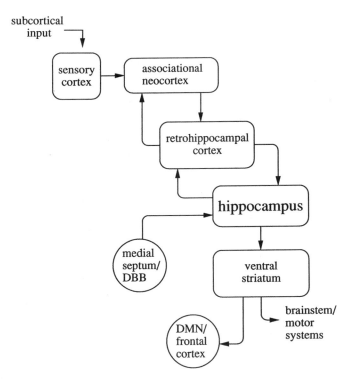

Figure 1 Anatomy of the primary corticohippocampal pathways. Signals from the sensory periphery activate subcortical and primary and secondary sensory cortical regions, traveling eventually to the superficial layers of the retrohippocampal cortex and into hippocampus. The hippocampus is also innervated by the medial septum/diagonal band complex. Efferents from the hippocampus contact the deep layers of retrohippocampal (entorhinal) cortex and extend into the ventral striatum, which in turn gives rise to pathways innervating both hindbrain motor systems and the dorsomedial nucleus of the thalamus and thence to the frontal cortex.

anatomical literature. In this schematic, sensory information travels from subcortical sites to primary and secondary sensory cortices, thence to associational regions, and finally to cortical areas bordering the rhinal fissure. These last regions then innervate the hippocampal formation and ultimately the hippocampus itself. The hippocampus gives rise to fibers that terminate in the deep layers of retrohippocampal (entorhinal) cortex, from which projections to associational cortex arise. It also projects into the ventral striatum, olfactory areas adjacent to it, and diencephalic structures. Finally, the medial-septum/diagonal-band complex provides a small but physiologically important input to the hippocampus. A pathway omitted from the schematic diagram and not discussed in this chapter may nonetheless be of significant interest: the Papez circuit, linking the hippocampus to the mammillary bodies, which in turn project to the anterior thalamus and thence to the retrosplenial agranular cortex and cingulate cortex. This projection enables the hippocampus to be viewed as a peripheral processing device, with its own projections to specific

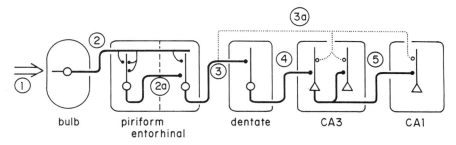

Figure 2 Anatomy of the olfactory corticohippocampal pathway. Axons from the nasal receptors form the olfactory nerve (1), innervating the olfactory bulb, which in turn projects via the lateral olfactory tract (2) to the piriform/entorhinal cortex. The entorhinal cortex and caudal piriform cortex are also contacted by associational fibers (2a) from more rostal regions of the piriform cortex. Cortical efferents form the lateral perforant path (3, 3a), innervating all three hippocampal structures: the dentate gyrus and fields CA3 and CA1. Dentate gyrus granule cells form the mossy fiber projections (4) to CA3, which in turn gives rise to the Schaffer-commissural afferents (5) to field CA1.

thalamic and neocortical regions, as is the case for three major sensory pathways: somatosensory, auditory, and visual.

The hippocampus possesses a number of anatomical features that make it unusually appropriate for studies of plasticity, and most of what we know about LTP comes from work on its connections. The extrahippocampal pathways shown in greatly simplified form in figure 1 are much less accessible for physiological/pharmacological work in situ or in vitro. Indeed, it can be said that much of the descriptive anatomical work needed for such studies has yet to be done. The obvious exception to this is the olfactory-hippocampal circuit. This is composed of a series of well-defined anatomical links, several of which have been characterized physiologically. Accordingly, we turned to this system to ask questions about the forms of potentiation and the types and locations of networks exhibiting LTP.

Figure 2 summarizes the anatomy of the olfactory-hippocampal circuit. We have carried out tests for physiologically induced plasticity in several of the links in this chain, and in all cases but one (see below) we have obtained evidence for LTP by the following criteria: there is induction on stimulation resembling a naturally occurring firing pattern of the circuit; there is synapse specificity; induction is blocked by antagonists of the NMDA receptor; induction depends on changes in intracellular calcium levels; and there is stability over several days. In three of the links, we have also shown LTP to involve a large change in response components mediated by the AMPA subgroup of glutamate receptors, with little if any change in the components produced by NMDA receptors. Cell morphology varies markedly across the links, and there are substantial differences in local circuit organization. Thus it would appear that LTP is a general property of cortical networks and clues as to its contributions to memory are not going to be readily obtained by trying to correlate its occurrence with specific designs. However, as discussed in the following sections, variations in potentiation between elements of the olfactory-hippocampal circuit are apparent and suggestive of particular types of memory operations.

3 POTENTIATION IN THE SUCCESSIVE LINKS OF THE OLFACTORY-HIPPOCAMPAL CIRCUIT

3.1 Input to the Cortex

High-frequency stimulation of the lateral olfactory tract does not normally produce LTP in the bulbar-cortical synapses in layer Ia of the piriform cortex in intact animals (Stripling, Patneau, & Gramlich, 1988; Racine, Milgram, & Hafner, 1983; Roman et al., 1987). However, after rats are trained in a series of two-odor discriminations to the point at which they acquire new discriminations very rapidly, theta-pattern stimulation does elicit robust and stable LTP *when the stimulation is used as a discriminative cue (an electric odor) that the animal learns* (Roman et al., 1987). Apparently, factors associated with past experience and the current environment (i.e., the familiar testing apparatus) combine to allow activity patterns resembling those associated with odor sampling to induce LTP. This behavioral dependency of LTP induction is a unique feature of the first stage of cortical-hippocampal processing.

3.2 Corticocortical Connections

The massive cortical association system generated by the superficial layers of piriform cortex and extending to lateral entorhinal cortex and other areas of olfactory cortex has been studied for LTP only in slices. LTP was readily induced and in no obvious way different from that seen in slices of hippocampus (Kanter & Haberly, 1990; Jung, Larson, & Lynch, 1990). As expected from the in vivo studies, potentiation was considerably more difficult to produce with stimulation of the lateral olfactory tract.

3.3 Corticohippocampal Pathways

The lateral entorhinal cortex, the posterior extension of olfactory cortex, provides a large component of the perforant path, that massive bundle that innervates the dentate gyrus and, to lesser extent, the pyramidal cell fields of the hippocampus proper (Wyss, 1981; Swanson, Wyss, & Cowan, 1978). LTP was discovered in the synapses of the perforant path and dentate gyrus (Bliss & Lomo, 1973) and has been observed in the connections between entorhinal and pyramidal cells as well (Berger, 1984). Potentiation in the dentate gyrus has been reported to decay steadily over a period of several days (Green, McNaughton, & Barnes, 1990; Barnes, 1979). This decremental feature distinguishes it from LTP in the other links of the olfactory-hippocampal circuit.

3.4   Intrahippocampal Connections: Mossy Fibers

The first intrahippocampal pathway is composed of the mossy fibers originating in the granule cells of the dentate gyrus and terminating in the proximal dendrites of the CA3 pyramidal cells. Recent studies have led to the unexpected conclusion that the potentiation produced by high-frequency stimulation of the mossy fibers is not LTP (Zalutsky & Nicoll, 1990; Staubli et al., 1990). That is, mossy-fiber potentiation (MFP) changes the frequency-facilitation characteristics of the synapses, does not require stimulation of NMDA receptors for induction, and indeed is probably not in any regard a postsynaptic effect. If MFP is a purely presynaptic effect, it can be assumed to occur at every synapse along an axon driven to fire at high frequency and hence would lack synapse specificity. Since such a system would quickly saturate if potentiation were stable, we conclude that MFP is a transient effect, with its duration set by the amount of stimulation.

3.5   Intrahippocampal Connections: Associational Projections

LTP elicited by brief episodes of theta stimulation in the connections from field CA3 to field CA1 (i.e., the Schaffer-commissural fibers) can persist without detectable change for weeks (Staubli & Lynch, 1987). Larson and Lynch (1986, 1989) have empirically determined a set of rules describing the relationships between complex patterns of activity of the type likely to occur during behavior and the degree to which synapses potentiate. We assume that these rules hold throughout the olfactory-hippocampal circuit, but this has not been satisfactorily tested. The recent discovery that the nootropic drug aniracetam selectively enhances the function of AMPA receptors (Ito, Tanabe, Khoda, & Sugiyama, 1990) by prolonging the mean open time of their channels (Tang, Shi, Katchman, & Lynch, 1991) has provided a means of probing the status of these receptors before and after induction of LTP. The effects of these compounds on synaptic responses are substantially changed by LTP (Staubli et al., 1990; Staubli, Ambros-Ingerson, & Lynch, 1992; Xiao, Staubli, Kessler, & Lynch, 1991), a result that supports earlier conclusions that LTP modifies the properties of glutamate receptors (see Muller, Joly, & Lynch, 1988). Aniracetam thus can be used as an additional and simple test of whether or not a given example of synaptic facilitation is LTP. It has already been established that mossy fiber potentiation does not affect the actions of the drug (Ito et al., 1990; Staubli, Larson, & Lynch, 1992), which confirms the conclusion that this phenomenon is unrelated to LTP.

3.6   Summary

LTP is not markedly different in the associational/commissural pathways of the hippocampus and the cortex. Induction of LTP in the inputs to the cortex depends on behavior in a way not true for the subsequent links of the olfactory-hippocampal circuit; this may reflect the influence of attention (Roman et al., 1987). Expression of LTP in the inputs to the hippocampus from the cortex seems to differ in terms of stability from its expression in the links that precede and follow them. Finally, the mossy fibers utilize a non-LTP form of plasticity that lacks synapse specificity and is likely to persist only for hours. These variations in plasticity by themselves suggest different types of memory, but this proposal is better considered in the context of the position and internal design of the links in which the variations occur.

4 HYPOTHESIZED MEMORY OPERATIONS OF THE SUCCESSIVE LINKS OF THE OLFACTORY-HIPPOCAMPAL CIRCUIT

4.1 Recognition Memory

Odors are known to activate discrete patches of cells in the olfactory bulb (Moulton, 1976; Harrison & Scott, 1986; Kauer, 1987; 1991; Schneider & Scott, 1983), which project to broad regions of cortex (Mori, 1987; Price, 1973; Haberly, 1985; Haberly & Price, 1977) and hence to overlapping populations of target cells. Such an arrangement is well suited for assembling a unitary response to disparate primary elements, which seems essential to assigning single labels to odors that are complex mixtures (Lynch, 1986). LTP in the cortex should alter the response of the cortex to an odor and hence the signal the cortex sends to the amygdala, hippocampus, and neocortex; in this sense, LTP could provide for a simple form of recognition memory (i.e., a cue has been encountered in the past). The stability of LTP in the cortex would be required for such a function, since recognition memory of odors persists for at least months (Staubli, Fraser, Faraday, & Lynch, 1987).

Simulations incorporating LTP-like plasticity into designs of the bulbar-cortical network generate a much richer type of recognition-memory system. Networks of this type are able to detect known odors when they are masked by stronger signals, an essential operation for the olfactory system (Granger, Ambros-lngerson, Staubli, & Lynch, 1990). Memory in the simulations is also self-organizing, in that learning many cues leads to hierarchical clustering based on similarity. So organized, the network responds by defining the cue in terms of first a broad category of similar cues, then a subcategory, and ultimately a specific odor (Ambros-Ingerson, Granger, & Lynch, 1990). An obvious advantage of such a system is that it allows the cortex, using memory, to make an approximate identification of novel cues or degraded versions of known signals.

4.2 Recency

Upon first inspection, it may seem peculiar that stable potentiation in the cortex would be followed by decremental LTP in connections between the cortex and dentate gyrus. There are no chronic recording studies of the stability of connections between the cortex and pyramidal cells, which, though less dense than the corticodentate projections, are substantial. Hence it is possible that learning leaves stable changes along the entire length of the olfactory-hippocampal circuit via the bypass of the dentate gyrus from the perforant path to the pyramidal cells. Decremental potentiation will result in time-dependent changes in the response of the dentate gyrus to learned cues, and hence will provide a measure of the interval since the last encounter with a particular cue, i.e., a sense of recency. This may have a direct correspondence in memory, albeit memory of a type not widely studied. Humans certainly know whether or not well-known objects were encountered in the past several days; moreover, experiments show an unconscious preference for recently encountered cues (Tulving & Schacter, 1990). Whether animals make similar distinctions, to our knowledge, has not been studied, but the presence of decremental potentiation in the first stage of hippocampal processing suggests that it should be an obvious effect. A sense of recency could be of value in the changing circumstances of natural environments, since it allows the animal to include a confidence factor in its evaluation of cue meaning.

4.3 Memory of Recent Actions

The cortical inputs to the dentate gyrus densely (approximately 90 percent of all synapses) innervate the outer 70 percent of the dendritic field of the granule cells, while the septal and brain stem inputs, although providing some direct input to the granule cells, project most heavily to the infragranular layers of the hilus (figure 3; Wyss, 1981; Swanson et al., 1978). These latter regions contain collections of interneurons as well as the polymorph cells that are innervated by the granule cells and that generate the unusual associational/commissural system of the dentate gyrus (McWilliams & Lynch, 1979). These arrangements suggest a design in which cortical inputs cause the

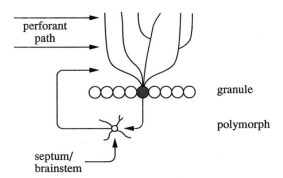

Figure 3 Organization of the dentate gyrus. Perforant path axons from the entorhinal cortex form the primary afferent to the outer 70 percent of the dendritic field of dentate granule cells. Septal and brainstem afferents provide input predominantly to the infragranular layers of the hilus, contacting interneurons and polymorph cells. Polymorphs are contacted by granule cells and in turn generate an associational/commissural system, contacting the granule cells.

Types of Memory in Corticohippocampal Networks

principal cells of the dentate (the granule cells) to discharge, while the subcortical inputs determine whether the positive feedback system from granule cells to polymorph neurons to granule cells will be activated by the response to the cortical afferents (Lynch, 1986; Lynch & Baudry, 1988; see also figure 3). The few chronic recording studies of granule cells support this interpretation (Deadwyler, West, & Lynch, 1979; Deadwyler, West, & Robinson, 1981). The neurons discharge with short latency to learned cues in an auditory go/no-go task but continue firing only if the animals execute an approach response. Thus, well-learned, discrete stimuli drive the granule cells via the perforant path in advance of any movement, but firing lasting for seconds depends on the initiation and performance of a well-learned locomotor behavior. This latter activity occurs in synchrony with the theta rhythm generated by septo-hippocampal inputs and thus presumably reflects a strong influence from the ascending reticular formation and diagonal bands (Rose et al., 1983).

From the above, it is reasonable to conclude that the conditions needed for inducing mossy-fiber potentiation (i.e., long periods of relatively high-frequency activity by the granule cells) obtain when animals are presented with known cues and carry out well-practiced responses to those cues. (This is not to say that these are the only behavioral circumstances that produce MFP; as noted, there are very few chronic recording studies of the dentate gyrus.) If this conclusion is correct, MFP could provide a memory that a response to a particular stimulus has been made earlier. Experiments using odors indicate that rats with lesions to the perforant path have no evident difficulties performing two-cue discriminations (in a go/no-go task) learned before the damage (Staubli et al., 1984). The question thus arises as to the utility of the type of memory hypothesized to be subserved by MFP. One possibility is that it serves to tell the animal that a familiar response to a familiar stimulus was made earlier in the test session. In some circumstances this would be useful, as, for example, in paradigms in which good performance requires the animal not to repeat choices during the session. Note that the MFP would have to be of limited duration to serve this function; otherwise the animal would inappropriately apply information from past to present sessions. This accords with the argument that MFP has a duration ranging from several minutes to a few hours (see above).

4.4 Connecting Events across Space and Time

The intrahippocampal associational/commissural projections (the Schaffer-commissural system) are unu.   ι their density. Axons of the CA3 cells ramify extensively in the CA3 itself as well as in CA1 and provide the great majority of all synapses on the apical and basal dendritic trees of the pyramidal neurons in those fields (Swanson et al., 1978). As a result, CA3 cells are interconnected with each other to a degree that is certainly unusual and perhaps unique for the telencephalon. A likely consequence of a design of this type is self-sustained, recurrent activity. The two major extrinsic inputs to the CA3 region are the mossy fibers and the perforant path. We have proposed that the initial activation of these afferents "selects" a population of CA3 cells and thus sets in motion a cycling pattern of activity; movement-related discharges of the granule cells could provide a kind of driving force that helps to maintain the pattern (Lynch & Granger, 1991). This would provide a reverberating signal to a stimulus-response sequence that remains after the stimulus is gone and while the response continues. In this scheme, arrival of the next extrinsic input would collapse the existing pattern and replace it with transient cell firing or a new pattern.

What role might LTP play in such a system? There are at least three possibilities: (1) Potentiation of connections of the perforant path to CA3 could serve to ensure that a particular subset of cells is used to initiate the recurrent activity and hence to produce a particular pattern. (2) LTP might be needed for reproducible patterns. (3) LTP in the CA3-CA1 projections could link aspects of the pattern set up by an initial stimulus-response combination with the cells stimulated by the next arriving input. This last possibility could be useful in establishing that subsets of cells in CA1 fire when a learned stimulus-response-stimulus sequence has occurred or in essence that the response to a known stimulus results in the consequence expected from past learning. Based on results from chronic recording studies, Ranck (1973) has proposed that activity of CA1 cells provides information about whether behavioral acts produce expected outcomes. The hypothesis advanced here is that this reflects the unusual, intrinsic circuitry of the hippocampus operating to connect events (stimuli) separated by time periods of as much as a few seconds.

4.5 Summary

We propose that the olfactory-hippocampal circuit asks a sequence of questions involving memories that last for many weeks (cortex, CA1 field), days (corticodentate), hours (mossy fibers), and seconds (CA3). These queries require variations of LTP, at least one form of non-LTP plasticity, and a kind of reverberating network. The different anatomical designs of some but not all links are explicitly included in the model. Each step operates on a unique qualitative aspect of a memory, addressing previous encounters with a stimulus, actions involving the stimulus, and cascades from one stimulus to another, mediated by actions taken by the organism. The differential longevity of potentiation in the various serial steps in the pathway place a special emphasis on differential times since the last encounter with the stimulus, which confers a capability for knowing when, and in what order, previous events occurred.

Behavioral studies prompted by this hypothesis are only now being conducted. Preliminary results suggest that rats do form hierarchical recognition memories (Granger et al., 1991), but more rigorous tests are needed. The notions that animals possess a "knowing when" memory based on decremental LTP in the perforant path and that mossy-fiber potentiation provides a record of recent acts have not been explored. As paradigms are developed for testing these specific issues, it should become possible to ask the broader question of whether memory operations in the olfactory-hippocampal circuit follow a fixed order.

5 GENERALIZATIONS FROM THE ANALYSIS OF THE OLFACTORY-HIPPOCAMPAL SYSTEM

5.1 An Assembly-Line Model of Memory Operations

Neuropsychological data on human and animal memory include evidence of tasks that are selectively or differentially impaired by specific treatments, which suggests either distinct forms of memory or distinct memory modules. Behavioral studies also point to qualitatively different memory systems: for instance, some memories are apparently accessible to consciousness, others are not (see Moskovitch, 1992, this volume; Baddeley, 1992, this volume); some memories are acquired quickly, others require extensive training (see Eichenbaum, 1992, this volume). Groupings of these descriptors (susceptibilities to manipulation, psychological qualities) have led many theorists to divide memory into small numbers of categories and relate these to particular anatomical systems. These subsystems presumably interact to give rise to complex emergent behavior, as posited by many researchers, such as Johnson (1992; Johnson & Chalfonte, this volume) and Kosslyn and co-workers (Kosslyn & Shin, 1992; Kosslyn et al., 1990). Figure 4 illustrates two contrasting forms of interaction among memory subsystems. The first (figure 4, top) involves a kind of central processor, of the sort posited by Moscovitch (1992, this volume) and Baddeley (1992, this volume), that receives inputs from several sensory systems and has access to several different pools of memory. The reciprocal connections between the central unit and the memory sites could be used to encode new memory or to activate memories appropriate to particular situations. For instance, a store of permanent memories might be queried for familiarity of an object, in concert with the proposal by Johnson (1992; Johnson & Chalfonte, this volume), and a distinct store of more transient memories may be probed regarding whether the object has been dealt with in the recent past, perhaps in line with the proposal by Baddeley (1992, this volume). This general scheme lends itself naturally to the idea that memories have different properties and can be experimentally dissociated. The system also has the advantage of flexibility, in that the memories called up or the order in which they are used can vary according to the demands of the situation, as critically discussed by Eichenbaum (1992, this volume).

The discussion above of the corticohippocampal pathway suggests a contrasting view, schematically depicted in figure 4, bottom. This view casts the system as an assembly line, with a series of specialists each contributing its

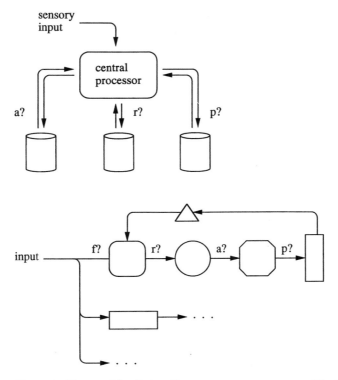

Figure 4 Two models of interactions among memory systems. The top model hypothesizes a central processor receiving inputs from multiple sensory systems and having reciprocal connections to several distinct memory stores, which could be used to encode new memories or to activate memories appropriate to particular situations. (Connection labels correspond to hypothesized categories of memory function, including recent [r?] and permanent [p?] memories and memory for current actions [a?]—see the discussion in the text). The bottom model illustrates the alternative view proposed here: an assembly line of serial specialists, each contributing its unique function to the task of memory processing. In this model, querying a particular type of memory is not on demand but rather arises automatically from the serial arrangements of the circuits in the pathway. This system thus lacks the flexibility found in the central-processor model: the same "questions" (corresponding to the same connection labels as described above) are always asked in the same immutable order during memory processing.

unique function to the overall processing of memories. In this model, querying of a particular type of memory is not voluntary but arises automatically from the serial processing steps in the sequence; moreover, these steps immutably occur in the same order. This system lacks some of thc flexibility found in the central-processor model, in that the same questions are always asked in the same order. It gains speed and allows for parallelism in that several assembly lines could presumably be set in motion at the same time. The plausibility of this generalization from the work on the corticohippocampal system depends on the extent to which ideas derived from the olfactory-hippocampal system can be generalized to other cortical networks and whether the idea can account for memory dissociations. Before turning to these issues (in the next

Types of Memory in Corticohippocampal Networks

section), we might note that the plausibility of the generalized assembly-line hypothesis also depends on how likely it is that the same sequence of questions can be usefully asked across all circumstances by disparate groups of mammals. Put another way, could memory sequences have developed during the early evolution of mammalian telencephalon that retained their utility across the subsequent radiation of the class? This question intrigues us, but it can only be addressed after behavioral tests for the proposed assembly-line operations have been developed.

5.2 Memory Types and Their Dissociation in the Assembly-Line Hypothesis

To apply the results of the olfactory-hippocampal system to cortical memory networks in general and corticohippocampal circuits in particular, we begin with the assumption of an "encephalization of function," due to John Hughlings Jackson (1931; Kennard & Swash, 1989). This holds that the enormous evolutionary growth of neocortex brings a concomitant transferral to neocortex of many functions previously subserved by subcortical structures. For instance, it has been shown that cats with visual cortical lesions are able to perform visual orienting tasks that are impossible for humans with comparable cortical damage; such humans are functionally blind, though the cats apparently are not (Wallace et al., 1989). Thus evolution may bring with it a recasting of function from phylogenetically older circuitry specialized to the task to more generalized circuitry in a way that encompasses (and possibly broadens) these functions. As applied to the discussion here, this assumption leads us to expect that some corticohippocampal contributions to memory prominent in small-brained mammals will be subsumed by corticocortical networks in their large-brained relatives. Encephalized versions of hippocampally derived memory functions may differ somewhat from their initial forms. It is possible, for instance, that the priming effect in humans, typified by (unconscious) retention of a preference for recently learned material (Tulving & Schacter, 1990), arises from a decremental form of memory related to that in the synapses between the perforant path and dentate gyrus. The capacity to expect outcomes of brief cycles of perception/action sequences may, in its encephalized form, give rise to a memory for episodic forms of information (Tulving, 1983). A presumed exception to this rule is the operations attributed to the system comprising the dentate gyrus and mossy fibers: the unique anatomical characteristics found in this system, no replica of which exists elsewhere in telencephalon, are required for it to perform its function (memory for actions in the last several hours).

One of the immediate consequences of seriality in the assembly line is the expectation that late functions can be dissociably removed without affecting early functions but that damage to early functions will also damage late functions. On the basis of the model, then, we predict that the episodic-expectancy system, for instance, could be damaged without affecting other

Gary Lynch and Richard Granger

systems, since this expectancy system occurs late in the sequence of hypothesized memory functions. In contrast, we anticipate that damage to the recency mechanism would bring with it significant processing deficits, since it resides at the input stage to the memory-processing sequence. This leads to the prediction that few if any patients should be observed lacking the recent-memory system alone; rather, such a deficit would be embedded deeply in much more serious and overshadowing cognitive deficits. Similarly, it should be nearly impossible to observe selective deficits to the recognition memory store, which we take to be a component of data memory, since damage to this front-end system would prevent appropriate behavior throughout the rest of the serial chain of processing. Note that this prediction about data memory is to be distinguished from data learning: acquisition of information may well have dependencies beyond those needed for expression or utilization of that information (see below). The dissociability of deficits found with selective brain damage has led naturally to the parsimonious assumption that each observed dissociation may represent a distinct memory channel or pathway (see, e.g., Squire, 1992, this volume). In contrast, we offer the possibility that the dissociations may arise from selective damage to steps in tandem networks operating serially on stimuli to piecewise assemble memories of events.

As mentioned, since the unique anatomy of the system comprising the dentate gyrus and mossy fibers is not replicated elsewhere in telencephalon, we presume that no encephalized version of its purported function (memory for recent acts) will exist. This leads to the prediction that this memory function should remain uniquely vulnerable to hippocampal damage in humans. The expected loss of memory for recent acts might show up as a patient's inability to remember whether he or she recently interacted with a particular object, which is perhaps similar to the type of deficit reported to occur after temporal-lobe damage.

It should be noted that in rats, in contrast to the human examples above, much of the hypothesized functionality is expected to reside solely in the corticohippocampal circuit itself. Thus we expect that in rats, hippocampal damage would destroy memory for recently encountered stimuli, memory for episodic (situation-action) sequences, as well as memory for recent actions. The deficits in spatial-maze performance seen in rats with hippocampal lesions are usually ascribed to a loss of very stable memory about the relationships between distant cues (O'Keefe, 1976) or transient memory about responses made earlier in a testing session (Olton et al., 1979). These deduced memory functions are, from the perspective of our model, specific manifestations of two more generalized operations of hippocampus.

5.3 Learning in the Assembly Line

The discussions above are concerned with the types of memory operations carried out by components of cortical and corticohippocampal networks; they do not address the issue of the contributions of the sequential assembly-line elements to the encoding of different kinds of memory. Two groups of LTP studies are pertinent to this. First, the complex timing rules (i.e., when bursts of activity in one afferent arrive at a target cell relative to those in other afferents) that determine if and how much LTP will be induced in sets of synapses make predictions about what will be learned. Second, the studies on piriform cortex noted above suggest that the initial steps in the assembly line have requirements for LTP induction that are lacking in later stages, and suggest that learning in these studies depends on a constellation of behavioral/environmental variables. To take these suggestions in order, studies using separate, converging inputs have established two theta rules for LTP induction:

• When two inputs are separated by the period of the theta wave (200 milliseconds), bursts to the second input yield LTP, while bursts to the first input do not (Larson & Lynch, 1986; see Larson & Lynch, 1986, 1988, and Mott & Lewis, 1991, for the mechanisms responsible for this rule.

• When multiple, weak inputs converge in an overlapping but asynchronous fashion during theta stimulation, the degree of LTP induced in an input correlates with its order of arrival (i.e., the first input potentiates the most, the last input the least) (Larson & Lynch, 1989).

The first rule (interactions between theta peaks) is well suited for the type of stimulus-response-stimulus sequences proposed to be encoded as expectancies in the field CA1. In particular, if two inputs A and B are separated in time by at least 200 milliseconds, input A will inactivate GABAa inhibition (Mott & Lewis, 1991) in the restricted regions of CA1 experiencing sufficient convergence from the afferent fibers activated by input A. These restricted regions will then be selectively more susceptible to induction of LTP by input B. These induction rules can generate an order-dependent expectancy memory in CA1. If B is followed by A, as it was during training, the individual units encoding the sequence A, B will respond selectively. If the expected B does not occur, no specific target population will selectively respond. Instead, many target units will likely respond but not strongly, since their synapses were not potentiated for this sequence of events. The second rule (interactions within single peaks) has been explored in biophysical simulations, where it results in sequence detecting neurons. That is, given three small inputs a, b, c, the rule adjusts synaptic strength in the order $a > b > c$ and hence may provide for differential responses to different sequences (a, b, c versus c, b, a). Preliminary neurophysiological experiments have confirmed that larger postsynaptic responses are generated by inputs stimulated in the sequence in which they were activated during LTP induction (Granger et al., 1993). Operating together, these two theta rules define the length of a string of elements that can be incorporated into a unitary encoded representation (i.e., as a single cue) and the spacing between cues required for optimal linkages between them. Network simulations show that rule 2 has the additional effect of expanding capacity, in part due to the enhanced orthogonalization of the input cues (see the discussions in Olton & Shapiro, 1992; Shapiro & Olton, this volume). Thus a 1,000-cell network using this rule was able to learn and recognize 10,000 randomly selected words with an error rate of less than 1 percent. Calculations show that networks approaching the size of the CA1 field of the rat hippocampus would have a truly remarkable capacity (Granger et al., 1993).

The second result from the LTP studies that seemingly relates to learning is that potentiation in synapses between the lateral olfactory tract and piriform can only be induced in freely-moving rats with chronically implanted electrodes rats when theta stimulation was used as a discriminative cue for animals having extensive experience with two-odor learning problems (Roman et al., 1987). Since monosynaptic responses were tested in these experiments, we can only conclude that plasticity in the superficial layers of cortex depends on such psychological variables as attention or readiness. These influences have to be mediated by agencies extrinsic to the cortex, of which there are a number of possibilities, including cholinergic input arising from the basal forebrain. Thus, learning in the earliest stages of the assembly line can be strongly influenced by events in the later links operating directly or indirectly on extrinsic inputs to the early stages. The hippocampus with its extensive projections to the basal forebrain seems particularly well situated for such a role; thus, we might imagine that the hippocampus, in addition to encoding certain types of information within its circuitry, uses that information to promote learning of other types of information in prehippocampal steps in the assembly line. Since the subcortical projections of the hippocampus do not appear to be replicated by the neocortex in even large-brained mammals, we assume that this last argument holds for humans as well as laboratory animals. Damage to the hippocampus is widely held to cause anterograde amnesia for data memory in humans, but the arguments outlined here indicate that such effects should be evident in all mammals, and the data on this point are not so clear. Part of the problem may reside in the types of learning tested. An LTP-based recognition-memory system should have rapid acquisition, stability, and enormous capacity. As noted, these properties do not figure prominently in most studies of animal learning. An exception is odor learning in rats: the animals acquire dozens of discriminations, learn new odors in as few as five trials, and show excellent retention months after training (Staubli, Fraser, et al., 1987; Eichenbaum, 1992, this volume). Lesions that sever the connections between the olfactory cortex and the hippocampus blocks this type of learning: lesioned rats seem to acquire new discriminations when trials are given in rapid succession but show little retention when tested one hour later. As expected from the model, the hippocampus itself does not appear to be the repository of the recognition memories, because the animals are not impaired when tested on odors learned before the lesions were made, i.e., they show anterograde but not retrograde amnesia (Staubli et al., 1984). It is noteworthy that the deficit produced by the lesions can be overcome with extensive training; we interpret this to mean either that extrahippocampal systems can eventually organize the extrinsic inputs to olfactory cortex needed for encoding or that learning is occurring in other pathways leading away from the cortex. Studies on the capacity and stability of recognition memory in the absence of the hippocampus would help to discriminate between these possibilities. In any event, these studies support the idea that the hippocampus enables rapid encoding of recognition (data) memory in animals in much the way it does in humans, and they add force to the argument that distinctions must be drawn between the contributions of the links in the assembly line to expression and their contribution to the induction of memory.

5.4   Summary

We suggest that the assembly-line operations deduced for the olfactory-hippocampal system is a common feature of memory processing in cortical networks. In mammals with small neocortices, the later steps of the sequences will be executed by the hippocampus, much as is the case for olfaction; large-brained mammals, however, presumably have encephalized versions of these steps. This allows for elaboration and generalization of recency and expectancy memories, perhaps resulting in the priming and episodic memories reported for humans. The mossy-fiber system is unique to the hippocampus and thus is less likely to be represented in a generalized form in the cortex. These arguments led to a set of predictions about the types of retrograde amnesias likely to be seen in rats and humans after damage to the hippocampus or neocortex. Finally, we used aspects of the LTP effect to make distinctions about the contributions of assembly-line stages, and the hippocampus in particular, to the encoding versus expression of memory.

Among the things lacking in the hypothesis is a prediction about the qualities of behavior and cognition arising from an assembly line using the proposed stages versus other versions of memory interactions. But this issue is perhaps best set aside until further analysis is done on the olfactory-hippocampal system, the model on which the generalized hypothesis rests. Such behavioral and neurobiological work will result in less abstract descriptions of memory operations and, equally important, provide insight into coordinated functioning of assembly lines. We suspect that this information will permit global statements about the nature of cognitive acts based on serial memory processing.

REFERENCES

Ambros-Ingerson, J., Granger, R., & Lynch, G. (1990). Simulation of paleocortex performs hierarchical clustering. *Science, 247,* 1344–1348.

Arai, A., Larson, J., & Lynch, G. (1990). Anoxia reveals a vulnerable period in the development of long-term potentiation. *Brain Research, 511,* 353–357.

Baddeley, A. (1992). Working memory: The interface between memory and cognition. *Journal of Cognitive Neuroscience, 4,* 281–288.

Barnes, C. A. (1979). Memory deficits associated with senescence: A neurophysiological and behavioral study in the rat. *Journal of Comparative Physiology and Psychology, 93,* 74–104.

Berger, T. W. (1984). Long-term potentiation of hippocampal synaptic transmission affects rate of behavioral learning. *Science, 224,* 627–630.

Bliss, T. V. P., & Lomo, T. (1973). Long-lasting potentiation of synaptic transmission in the dentate area of the anaesthetized rabbit following stimulation of the perforant path. *Journal of Physiology* (London), *232,* 334–356.

Castro, C. A., Silbert, L. H., McNaughton, B. L., & Barnes, C. A. (1989). Recovery of spatial learning deficits after decay of electrically induced synaptic enhancement in the hippocampus. *Nature, 342,* 545–548.

Deadwyler, S. A., West, M., & Lynch, G. (1979). Activity of dentate granule cells during learning: Differentiation of perforant path input. *Brain Research, 169,* 29–43.

Deadwyler, S. A., West, M., & Robinson, J. H. (1981). Entorhinal and septal inputs differentially control sensory-evoked responses in rat dentate gyrus. *Science, 211,* 1131–1183.

Del Cerro, S., Jung, M., & Lynch, G. (1992). Benzodiazepines block long-term potentiation in rat hippocampal and piriform cortex slices. *Neuroscience, 49,* 1–6.

Eichenbaum, H. (1992). The hippocampal system and declarative memory in animals. *Journal of Cognitive Neuroscience, 4,* 217–231.

Galfre, G., Howe, S. C., Milstein, C., Butcher, G. W., & Havard, J. C. (1977). Antibodies to major histocompatibility antigens produced by hibrid cell lines. *Nature, 266,* 550–552.

Granger, R., Ambros-Ingerson, J., & Lynch, G. (1989). Derivation of encoding characteristics of layer II cerebral cortex. *Journal of Cognitive Neuroscience, 1,* 61–87.

Granger, R., Ambros-Ingerson, J., Staubli, U., & Lynch, G. (1990). Memorial operation of multiple, interacting stimulated brain structures. In M. Gluck & D. Rumelhard (Eds.), *Neuroscience and connectionist theory* (pp. 95–129). Hillsdale, NJ: Lawrence Erlbaum Associates.

Granger, R., Staubli, U., Powers, H., Ambros-Ingerson, J., & Lynch, G. (1991). Behavioral tests of a prediction from a cortical network simulation. *Psychological Science, 2,* 116–118.

Granger, R., Myers, R., Whelpley, E., & Lynch, G. (1993). Intrinsic and emergent corticohippocampal computation. In M. Baudry and J. Davis (Eds.), *Long-term potentiation* (Vol. 2). Cambridge: MIT Press.

Green, E. J., McNaughton, B. L., & Barnes, C. A. (1990). Exploration-dependent modulation of evoked responses in fascia dentata. *Journal of Neuroscience, 10,* 1455–1471.

Gustafsson, B., & Wigstrom, H. (1990). Long-term potentiation in the CA1 region: Its induction and early temporal development. *Progress in Brain Research, 83,* 223–232.

Haberly, L. B. (1985). Neuronal circuitry in olfactory cortex: Anatomy and functional implications. *Chemical Senses, 10,* 219–238.

Haberly, L. B., & Price, J. L. (1977). The axonal projection of the mitral and tufted cells of the olfactory bulb in the rat. *Brain Research, 129,* 152–157.

Harrison, T. A., & Scot, J. W. (1986). Olfactory bulb responses to odor stimulation: Analysis of response patterns and intensity relationships. *Journal of Neurophysiology, 56,* 1571–1589.

Ito, I., Hidaka, H., & Sugiyama, H. (1991). Effects of KN-62, a specific inhibitor of calcium/calmodulin-dependent k-protein kinase II, on long-term potentiation in the rat hippocampus. *Neuroscience Letters, 121,* 119–121.

Ito, I., Tanabe, S., Khoda, A., & Sugiyama, H. (1990). Allosteric potentiation of quisqualate receptors by a nootropic drug aniracetam. *Journal of physiology, 424,* 533–543.

Jackson, J. H. (1931–1932). *Selected writings of John Hughlings Jackson* (Vols. 1 & 2; J. Taylor, Ed.). London: Hodder and Stoughton.

Johnson, M. K. (1992). MEM: Mechanism of recollection. *Journal of Cognitive Neuroscience, 4,* 268–280.

Jung, M. W., Larson, J., & Lynch, G. (1990). Long-term potentiaton of monosynaptic EPSP's in rat piriform cortex in vitro. *Synapse, 6,* 279–283.

Kanter, E. D., & Haberly, L. B. (1990). NMDA-dependent induction of long-term potentiation in afferent and association fiber systems of piriform cortex in vitro. *Brain Research, 525,* 175–179.

Kauer, J. S. (1987). Coding in the olfactory system. In T. E. Finger (Ed.), *The Neurobiology of Taste and Smell* (pp. 205–231). New York: Wiley.

Kauer, J. S. (1991). Contributions of topography and parallel processing to odor coding in the vertebrate olfactory pathway. *Trends in Neuroscience, 14,* 79–85.

Kennard, D., & Swash, M. (1989). *Hierarchies in Neurology.* London: Springer-Verlag.

Kleckner, N. W., & Dingledine, R. (1989). Selectivity of quinoxalines and kynurenines as antagonists of the glycine site on N-methyl-D-aspartate receptors. *Molecular Pharmacolology, 36,* 430–436.

Kosslyn, S. M., Flynn, R. A., Amsterdam, J. B., & Wang, G. (1990). Components of high-level vision: A cognitive neuroscience analysis and accounts of neurological syndromes. *Cognition, 34,* 203–277.

Kosslyn, S. M., & Shin, L. M. (1992). The status of cognitive neuroscience. *Current Opinion in Neurobiology, 2,* 146–149.

Larson, J., Ambros-Ingerson, J., & Lynch, G. (1991). Sites and mechanisms for expression of long term potentiation. In M. Baudry & J. Davis (Eds.), *Long-term potentiation: A debate of current issues* (pp. 121–139). Cambridge: MIT Press.

Larson, J., & Lynch, G. (1986). Induction of synaptic potentiation in hippocampus by patterned stimulation involves two events. *Science, 232,* 985–988.

Larson, J., & Lynch, G. (1988). Role of N-methyl-D-aspartate receptors in the induction of synaptic potentiation by burst stimulation patterned after the hippocampal theta rhythm. *Brain Research, 441,* 111–118.

Larson, J., & Lynch, G. (1989). Theta pattern stimulation and the induction of LTP: The sequence in which synapses are stimulated determines the degree to which they potentiate. *Brain Research, 489,* 49–58.

Larson, J., & Lynch, G. (1991). A test of the spine resistance hypothesis of LTP expression. *Brain Research, 538,* 347–350.

Larson, J., Wong, D., & Lynch, G. (1986). Patterned stimulation at the theta frequency is optimal for induction of hippocampal long-term potentiation. *Brain Research, 368,* 347–350.

Lynch, G. (1986). *Synapses, circuits, and the beginnings of memory.* Cambridge: MIT Press.

Lynch, G., & Baudry, M. (1988). Structure-function relationships in the organization of memory. In M. Gazzaniga (Ed.), *Perspectives in memory research* (pp. 23–91). Cambridge: MIT Press.

Lynch, G., & Granger, R. (1991). Serial steps in memory processing: Possible clues from studies of plasticity in the olfactory-hippocampal circuit. In H. Eichenbaum & J. Davis (Eds.), *Olfaction as a model system for computational neuroscience.* Cambridge: MIT Press.

McCollum, J., Larson, J., Otto, T., Schottler, F., Granger, R., & Lynch, G. (1991). Short-latency single-unit processing in olfactory cortex. *Journal of Cognitive Neuroscience, 3,* 293–299.

McWilliams, J. R., & Lynch, G. (1979). Terminal proliferation and synaptogenesis following partial deafferentation: The reinnervation of the inner molecular layer of the dentate gyrus following removal of its commissural afferents. *Journal of Comparative Neurolology, 180*(3), 581–615.

Monaghan, D. T., & Cotman, C. W. (1985). Distribution of N-methyl-D-aspartate-sensitive L-[^{3}H]glutamate-binding sites in rat brain. *Journal of Neuroscience, 5,* 2909–2919.

Mori, K. (1987). Membrane and synaptic properties of identified neurons in the olfactory bulb. *Progress in Neurobiology, 29,* 275–320.

Morris, R. G. M., Anderson, E., Lynch, G. S., & Baudry, M. (1986). Selective impairment of learning and blockade of long-term potentiation by an N-methyl-D-aspartate receptor antagonist, AP-5. *Nature, 319,* 774–776.

Moscovitch, M. (1992). Memory and working-with-memory: A component process model based on modules and central systems. *Journal of Cognitive Neuroscience, 4,* 257–267.

Mott, D., & Levis, D. (1991). Facilitation of the induction of LTP by GABA$_B$ receptors. *Science, 252,* 1718–1720.

Moulton, F. N. (1976). Spatial patterning of response to odors in the peripheral olfactory system. *Physiology Review, 56,* 578–593.

Muller, D., Joly, M., & Lynch, G. (1988). Contributions of quisqualate and NMDA receptors to the induction and expression of LTP. *Science, 242,* 1694–1697.

O'Keefe, J. A. (1976). Place units in the hippocampus of the freely moving rat. *Experimental Neurology, 51,* 78–109.

Olton, D. S., Becker, J. T., & Handelmann, G. E. (1979). Hippocampus, space, and memory. *Behaubral and Brain Science, 2,* 313–365.

Olton, D. S., & Shapiro, M. L. (1992). Mnemonic dissociations: The powers of parameters. *Journal of Cognitive Neuroscience, 4,* 200–207.

Price, J. L. (1973). An autoradiographic study of complementary laminar patterns of termination of afferent fibers to the olfactory cortex. *Journal of Comparative Neurology, 150,* 87–108.

Racine, R. J., Milgram, N. W., & Hafner, S. (1983). Long-term potentiation phenomena in the rat limbic forebrain. *Brain Research, 260,* 217–231.

Ranck, J. (1973). Studies on single neurons in dorsal hippocampal formation and septum in unrestrained rats. *Experimental Neurology, 41,* 461–531.

Robinson, G. S., Jr., Crooks, G. B., Jr., Shinkman, P. G., & Gallagher, M. (1989). Behavioral effects of MK-801 mimic deficits associated with hippocampal damage. *Psychobiology, 17,* 156–164.

Roman, F., Staubli, U., & Lynch, G. (1987). Evidence for synaptic potentiation in a cortical network during learning. *Brain Research, 418,* 221–226.

Rose, G., Diamond, D., & Lynch, G. S. (1983). Dentate granule cells in the rat hippocampal formation have the behavioral characteristics of theta neurons. *Brain Research, 266,* 29–37.

Schneider, S. P., & Scott, J. W. (1983). Orthodromic response properties of rat olfactory bulb mitral and tufted cells correlate with their projection patterns. *Journal of Comparative Physiology, 50*, 319–333.

Squire, L. R. (1992). Declarative and nondeclarative memory: Multiple brain systems supporting learning and memory. *Journal of Cognitive Neuroscience, 4*, 232–243.

Staubli, U., Ambros-Ingerson, J. & Lynch, G. (1992). Receptor changes and LTP: An analysis using aniracetam, a drug that reversibly modifies glutamate (AMPA) receptors. *Hippocampus, 2*, 49–57.

Staubli, U., Fraser, D., Faraday, R., & Lynch, G. (1987). Olfaction and the "data" memory system in rats. *Behavioral Neuroscience, 101*, 757–765.

Staubli, U., Ivy, G., and Lynch, G. (1984). Hippocampal denervation causes rapid forgetting of olfactory information in rats. *Proceedings of the National Academy of Sciences, 81*, 5885–5887.

Staubli, U., Larson, J., & Lynch, G. (1990). Mossy fiber potentiation and long-term potentiation involve different expression mechanisms. *Synapse, 5*, 333–335.

Staubli, U., Larson, J., and Lynch, G. (1992). Further evidence that mossy fiber potentiation is expressed by a chance in release variables. *Society for Neuroscience Abstracts, 18*, 1349.

Staubli, U., & Lynch, G. (1987). Stable hippocampal long-term potentiation elicited by "theta" pattern stimulation. *Brain Research 435*, 227–234.

Staubli, U., Thibault, O., DiLorenzo, M., & Lynch, G. (1989). Antagonism of NMDA receptors impairs acquisition but not retention of olfactory memory. *Behavioral Neuroscience, 103*, 54–60.

Stripling, J. S., Patneau, D. K., & Gramlich, C. A. (1988). Selective long-term potentiation in the pyriform cortex. *Brain Research, 441*, 281–291.

Swanson, L. W., Wyss, J. M., & Cowan, W. N. (1978). An autoradiographic study of the organization of intrahippocampal association pathways in the rat. *Journal of Comparative Neurology, 181*, 681–716.

Tang, C., Shi, Q., Katchman, A., Lynch, G. (1991). Modulation of the time course of fast EPSCs and glutamate channel kinetics by aniracetam. *Science, 254*, 288–290.

Thompson, R. F. (1986). The neurobiology of learning and memory. *Science, 233*, 941–947.

Tulving, E. (1983). *Elements of episodic memory.* New York: Oxford University Press.

Tulving, E. & Schacter, D. L. (1990). Priming and human memory systems. *Science, 247*, 301–306.

Wallace, S. F., Rosenquist, A. C., Sprague, J. M. (1989). Recovery from cortical blindness mediated by destruction of nontectotectal fibers in the commissure of the superior colliculus in the cat. *Journal of Comparative Neurology, 234*, 429–450.

Wyss, J. M. (1981). Autoradiographic study of the efferent connections of entorhinal cortex in the rat. *Journal of Comparative Neurology, 199*, 495–512.

Xiao, P., Staubli, U., Kessler, M., Lynch, G. (1991). Selective effects of aniracetam across receptor types and forms of synaptic facilitation in hippocampus. *Hippocampus, 1*, 373–380.

Zalutsky, R. A., & Nicoll, R. A. (1990). Comparison of two forms of long-term potentiation in single hippocampal neurons. *Science, 248*, 1619–1624.

4 Hippocampal Function and Interference

Matthew L. Shapiro and David S. Olton

1 INTRODUCTION

Associative interference can have a profound impact on memory. We propose that a major function of the hippocampus is to reduce associative interference during learning. Normal functioning of the hippocampus is reflected in accurate declarative and episodic (working) memory, and in accurate spatial memory. Neural activity in the normal hippocampus reflects this function, and hippocampal lesions impair it. A computational framework that emphasizes the reduction of interference through the organization and separation of input patterns is proposed as a means of describing the input-output processes that reduce interference. This approach has two potential advantages. First, it brings into the analysis of memory and cognitive mapping a powerful empirical and theoretical variable. Second, it provides a means to integrate diverse theories of hippocampal function into a superordinate conceptual framework that encompasses different approaches and helps to resolve apparent discrepancies in the data.

Humans and animals must remember many different types of information to solve problems and survive. Although one general-purpose memory system could in principle handle all types of memory, in fact, several special-purpose memory systems have evolved to acquire and store different types of information with different types of processes (Hirsh, 1974; O'Keefe & Nadel, 1978; Olton, Becker, & Handelmann, 1979; Packard, Hirsh, & White, 1989; Squire, 1992). Thus simple reflex conditioning (e.g., of the eye blink) requires cerebellar circuitry and is unimpaired by forebrain lesions (e.g., Thompson, 1986), conditioned emotional responses (e.g., conditioned fear) require amygdaloid circuitry (e.g., Phillips & LeDoux, 1992), egocentric, stimulus-response learning (e.g., learning to approach a light) requires the striatum and related circuitry (e.g., Packard et al. 1989), and cognitive or relational learning requires hippocampal circuitry (e.g., Morris, Garrud, Rawlins, & O'Keefe, 1982). These and other learning abilites can be multiply dissociated, which suggests that the different brain systems operate in parallel and independently (Kesner, Bolland, & Dakis, in press; McDonald & White, 1993).

One of the major problems in understanding memory concerns how similar items are stored and retrieved in a way that preserves the identity of individual items without massive interference. The problem of interference can be framed in terms of memory-dependent behaviors, the function of neural circuits, and computation. Our goal here is to explore how neural operations by the hippocampal system may represent and process a unique type of information, and how neural representations and operations on these representations confer the special properties of memory that become subject to interference and lost in amnesia. The approach we take integrates top-down and bottom-up inferences, which provides the maximal constraints for understanding memory processes.

2 TRANSFER EFFECTS

An important fact in mnemonic life is that any information to be remembered is retrieved from or added to a large amount of other information. The influence of this other information on the to-be-remembered information can be enormous, and this provides sufficient variability in performance that evolutionary forces could develop specialized systems to maximize its beneficial effects and minimize its deleterious effects (Sherry & Schacter, 1987).

Many of our experimental procedures are explicitly designed to emphasize the effects of variables manipulated in the experimental design and minimize the effects of other variables. This approach, using relatively simple systems, has been highly productive. However, it inherently ignores many of the possible interactions between the already remembered information and the to-be-remembered information.

These interactions, often described as transfer effects, can be substantial. Positive transfer is the beneficial influence of two sets of information. For example, in a learning set, general principles of performance learned in one set of discriminations can improve performance in subsequent discriminations (Harlow, 1959; Zeldin & Olton, 1986). Reminding an animal of a previously learned association (usually produced by presenting the relevant discriminative stimuli and preventing the relevant response) can reactivate memories and improve performance in the discrimination when it is subsequently presented. The shaping procedures commonly used in every experiment with animals teach procedural rules important for accurate performance in the subsequent test sessions (Olton & Markowska, in press). Increasing the depth of encoding, which is reflected in the number and kinds of associations made with the to-be-remembered information, can facilitate recall of that information (Craik & Lockhardt, 1972). Making conditions for retrieval similar to those for encoding (synergistic ecphory) can improve the accuracy of recall (Tulving, 1983).

Negative transfer, commonly described as interference, can impair memory. In discrimination reversals, learning the initial discrimination can slow down the acquisition of the reverse discrimination, in which the stimulus-response-

Matthew L. Shapiro and David S. Olton

reinforcement contingencies are the opposite of those learned in the original discrimination. Changing contextual stimuli that were present when a discrimination was initially learned (even though these stimuli have no contingent association with reinforcement within the experiment itself) can decrease choice accuracy in the discrimination. In verbal paired associates, learning one response word to a stimulus word can impair the ability to learn a new target word to that stimulus (see the review of studies in Crowder, 1976).

This partial list of interactions between already remembered information and to-be-remembered information demonstrates that interference can have a profound effect on mnemonic accuracy. The next section reviews evidence suggesting that in tasks in which negative transfer from interference is substantial, the hippocampus is active, as reflected in the behavioral correlates of single unit activity, and that hippocampal function is crucial for accurate performance, as reflected in the impairments produced by hippocampal lesions. Consequently, one of the functions of the hippocampus may be to organize to-be-remembered information so that positive transfer, when possible, is maximized, and negative transfer, when present, is minimized.

The term "hippocampal system" refers to the hippocampus and structures related closely to it (figure 1). This terminology is useful for three reasons: (1) It helps to emphasize that the hippocampus functions not as an isolated structure but as part of a larger system that mediates certain mnemonic functions (Jarrard, 1991; Olton, Walker, & Wolf, 1982). (2) The relevant data for the ideas developed here come from both the hippocampus and areas anatomically connected to it. (3) The general idea being proposed here can be emphasized without interference from unnecessary details.

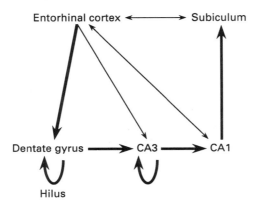

Figure 1 A simplified diagram of the circuitry of the hippocampal system. Information from multimodal association areas in frontal, parietal, and temporal regions converges on the perirhinal and parahippocampal regions, which provide the major input to the entorhinal cortex. The entorhinal cortex provides the major cortical input to the hippocampal formation, which includes the dentate gyrus and the CA3 and CA1 pyramidal layers. The thickness of the arrow reflects the relative importance of the pathway in the system. The circular arrows show recurrent pathways in the dentate and CA3 regions. The recurrent pathway in the dentate gyrus includes a layer of excitatory interneurons in the hilus that interconnect granule cells in the dentate gyrus. The septal area innervates each of these regions.

3 LESIONS OF THE SEPTOHIPPOCAMPAL SYSTEM AND INTERFERENCE

3.1 Delayed Conditional Discrimination

A delayed conditional discrimination may explicitly manipulate interference by presenting stimuli that produce interference and by varying temporal parameters to alter the temporal association of relevant items. Each trial of a delayed conditional discrimination begins with the presentation of one or more stimuli. A delay interval follows, during which the relevant discriminative stimuli are removed. At the end of the delay, two or more response alternatives are provided. The correct response at the end of the trial depends on the stimuli presented at the beginning of the trial. Because the stimuli presented at the beginning of the trial vary from trial to trial, some representation of the stimuli must be present at the end of the trial for the animal to respond correctly.

The amount of interference, as operationally defined by the number of stimuli presented at the beginning of the trial (list length) and the length of the delay interval during which information must be remembered, can have a substantial effect on the performance of normal animals (Wright, Urcuioli, & Sands, 1986). In many cases, lesions to the hippocampal system increase susceptibility to interference. With minimal interference (only a single item to be remembered and a short delay interval), hippocampal system lesions may have little effect. With substantial interference (a large number of stimuli to be remembered, a long delay interval), hippocampal system lesions can produce a substantial impairment (see the review in Squire, 1987).

3.2 Concurrent Discriminations

Concurrent object discriminations can vary the amount of interference by manipulating the number of discriminations to be learned concurrently. There is least interference in a one-pair object discrimination because only that single pair is being learned. Interference can be increased by having several object discriminations learned concurrently. The relevant experiments compared performance in two tasks that differed in the number of discriminations presented during a test session. In each discrimination, one object was correct, and the other was incorrect. The one-pair object discrimination presented only one pair of objects for all trials in a test session. The eight-pair concurrent object discrimination used identical procedures except that eight pairs of objects were presented during each test session. To compare performance in rats and monkeys, the procedures were made as similar as possible (Markowska et al., 1989; Murray et al., 1989; Rothblat & Hayes, 1987). For both rats and monkeys, choice accuracy in the one-pair object discrimination was unaffected or only slightly affected by hippocampal system lesions, whereas choice accuracy in the eight-pair object discrimination was severely compromised (Mahut et

Matthew L. Shapiro and David S. Olton

Table 1 Object discriminations: Hippocampal lesions impair choice accuracy in concurrent discriminations but not one-pair discriminations

Discrimination	Behavioral measure	Controls	Hippocampal lesions
One-pair	% reaching criterion	100	100
	Errors to criterion	68	83
Concurrent	% reaching criterion	71	14
	% correct responses at end of testing	98	70

Note: Data taken from Wible, Shiber, and Olton (1992).

al., 1981; Moss et al., 1981; Olton, Golski, et al., 1991; Wible et al., 1992; see table 1). Many variations of concurrent object discrimination may require the hippocampal system (Aggleton et al., 1992; Rothblat et al., in press).

Although systematic tests of one-pair and concurrent spatial discriminations have not yet been completed in a fashion similar to the experimental designs for object discriminations, the available data suggest that the same pattern of results will occur. (We use the term "spatial" in an empirical sense to indicate a left-right discrimination at a two-choice choice point in a maze. The appropriate experiments have not yet been done to determine the set of discriminative stimuli that mediate this choice.) A one-pair spatial discrimination in a T-maze is taken as the spatial equivalent of a one-pair object discrimination, and a multi-pair spatial discrimination in a more extensive maze is taken as the spatial equivalent of a concurrent object discrimination. Hippocampal system lesions impaired choice accuracy in multi-pair spatial discriminations but not in one-pair spatial discriminations (O'Keefe & Nadel, 1978, pp. 461, 464; Olton, 1989b). A systematic comparison of the effects of hippocampal system lesions in concurrent spatial and object discriminations can provide a good comparison of the effects of interference in these two types of tasks, and may help resolve the apparent discrepancies in the analysis of spatial and nonspatial functions of the hippocampus (Aggleton, 1985; Aggleton et al., 1986, 1992; Barnes, 1988; Becker & Olton, 1980; Cave & Squire, 1991; O'Keefe & Nadel, 1978; Olton, 1989b; Raffaelle & Olton, 1988; Rawlins, 1985; Rudy & Sutherland, 1989; see *Hippocampus, 1*, no. 3 [1991], pp. 221–292, for a recent series of papers on this topic).

In concurrent discriminations, the orderliness of the discriminations may influence the extent to which the hippocampal system is required for normal choice accuracy. A variable order of presentation, as compared to a fixed order, increased the magnitude of the impairment produced by hippocampal system lesions in concurrent discriminations, both spatial and object (Mumby et al., 1991; Olton, Shapiro, & Hulse, 1984; Wible et al., 1992). Increased variability in the order of presentation of the stimuli may increase interference and the importance of the hippocampal system in reducing this interference. Other variables may also be important: the time for consolidation of the memory of each discrimination before a subsequent discrimination disrupts this consolidation, the strengthening of memory from repeated presentations of the same material to be remembered, and the amount of information to be remembered in any given temporal or physical context. Parametric manipulations can include: the number of discriminations, the length of time between trials of the same discrimination, the number of different discriminations following a given discrimination, the consistency of the order of the discriminations, and the number of discriminations given each session. If the hippocampal system normally functions to reduce associative interference, then manipulations that increase interference should increase the magnitude of the deficit produced by hippocampal lesions.

3.3 Discrimination Reversals

Discrimination reversals, as implied by the name, require a new response to be substituted for a previous response to a given stimulus. In the initial discrimination, one response is reinforced in the presence of the discriminative stimulus. In the discrimination reversal, a different response is reinforced in the presence of that stimulus. Consequently, the animal must substitute the new response for the old response. The procedure is similar in experimental design to that for *AB-AD* paired associates, described below.

Hippocampal system lesions impair discrimination reversals, whether spatial or nonspatial—a result consistent with the idea that interference among items to be remembered is an important variable of hippocampal function. Because performance in a discrimination was normal when that discrimination was the first one acquired, but was impaired following previous experience with the reverse discrimination, interference between the two discriminations must be reduced by the hippocampal system (O'Keefe & Nadel, 1978, pp. 463–464; Raffaelle & Olton, 1988).

4 THE HUMAN AMNESIC SYNDROME AND INTERFERENCE

Human amnesic patients have increased sensitivity to interference in many different forms. The patient H.M., who had bilateral removal of the temporal lobes, showed this increased susceptibility in both formal and informal testing. In one of the early observations, he was asked to remember three numbers. When undisturbed, he was able to rehearse and recall the numbers accurately. When interrupted, however, he had no memory for these numbers. Amnesic patients, with widely different etiologies, show a similar pattern of performance on many different tests. General intelligence is normal, whereas memory is severely impaired. Our prediction, a strong one, is that any amnesic patient who has direct damage to the hippocampal system or who has compromised function of the hippocampal system as a result of damage elsewhere will have increased susceptibility to interference (Press, Amaral, & Squire, 1989). Human amnesic patients do show increased susceptibility to interference (Kinsbourne & Winocur, 1980; Mayes et al. 1987; Van der

Linden, Bruyer, Roland, & Schils, 1993; Warrington & Weiskrantz, 1974, 1978; Winocur & Weiskrantz, 1976), and below we review one example of this phenomenon to indicate how the results from human amnesia are consistent with the analysis of the mnemonic effects of hippocampal lesions in animals.

An extensive analysis of the role of associative interference in human amnesia has been provided by Hayman et al. (in press). The amnesic patient K.C. had extensive brain damage. However, his general pattern of performance on cognitive tests was similar to patients whose amnesia results from temporal lobe damage involving the hippocampus (patient H.M.) and from relatively selective damage to the hippocampus itself (patient R.B.) (Zola-Morgan, Squire, & Amaral, 1986). As with other amnesic patients, K.C. had a relatively selective loss of memory; measures of general intelligence, attention, and language comprehension were normal. Consequently, the effects of interference in K.C.'s amnesic syndrome is likely to be relevant to amnesic syndromes produced by hippocampal damage.

The mnemonic task for K.C. was learning to produce a response word when a phrase was presented. Associative interference was manipulated in two ways. First, preexperimental interference was assessed by presenting each stimulus phrase to K.C. and asking him to respond if he thought of an appropriate word or not to respond if he did not think of an appropriate word. Low-interference items were operationally defined as those stimulus phrases for which no response was given. High-interference items were operationally defined as those phrases for which a response was given. The second manipulation of interference was the method of presentation of the stimuli. In the low-interference condition, the response word was presented at the same time as the stimulus phrase, so each stimulus phrase was associated with only a single response word. In the high-interference condition, the stimulus phrase was first presented by itself, K.C. was asked to respond with the response word, and then the correct response word was presented if K.C. made an error. In the high-interference condition, incorrect response words were associated with each stimulus phrase, whereas in the low-interference condition, only the correct response word was associated with the stimulus phrase. The amount of interference significantly affected K.C.'s accuracy. In both low-interference conditions, his memory was better than in the high interference conditions.

This increased sensitivity to interference is common in amnesic syndromes. The *AB-AD* paired associate procedure illustrates this sensitivity. In the first part of the experiment, one response (*B*) is learned to a stimulus (*A*). In the second part of the experiment, a new response (*D*) is learned to the same stimulus. This *AB-AD* procedure is similar to a discrimination reversal used with animals (see previous discussion), and like animals with hippocampal lesions, human amnesic patients have excessive negative transfer (see the reviews in Hayman et al., in press; Kinsbourne & Winocur, 1980; Mayes et al. 1987; Van der Linden et al., 1993; Warrington & Weiskrantz, 1974, 1978; Winocur & Weiskrantz, 1976). Together these data from K.C. and other amnesic patients indicate that the amount of interference has a substantial effect on mnemonic accuracy and that amnesic patients are more susceptible to interference than normal people. Though our model assumes that interference is a factor primarily during encoding, the sources of this interference remain to be completely identified.

5 THE POWER OF PARAMETERS

The emphasis on interference as a variable influencing mnemonic accuracy is an example of the dimensional analysis of memory advocated by Gage et al. (1980), Olton (1989b), and Olton and Shapiro (1992). This dimensional analysis emphasizes the advantages of incorporating parametric manipulations into experimental designs and theories of memory, and it can identify different cognitive variables, operationally defined in terms of the parameters being manipulated, that have a profound impact on the extent to which a brain structure is involved in a mnemonic function (Gage et al., 1980; Olton, 1989b).

Dimensional analysis also points out some important qualifications for any dichotomous analysis of memory that does not include parametric manipulation of task demand for both types of memory being considered in the dichotomy. Double dissociations in a 2 × 2 experimental design (two different lesions, two different tasks) have often been used to infer a dichotomy in the cognitive and neural mechanisms of memory. If a lesion in structure *a* impairs performance in task *x* but not in task *y*, and a lesion in structure *b* produces the complementary pattern of results (an impairment in task *y* but not in task *x*), the dichotomous approach concludes that the mnemonic processes represented in the two tasks must be parallel and independent of each other and that each mnemonic process is selectively mediated by the structure in which the lesion impairs performance in the task that requires that mnemonic process.

Of particular importance in the interpretation of a double dissociation are the conclusions from results indicating that a lesion has no behavioral effect. This absence of an effect with a certain set of parameters is often taken to indicate that the type of memory required for performance of the task is not impaired by the lesion. However, an alternative interpretation is that this type of memory is impaired by the lesion but the experimental parameters were not appropriate to detect this impairment. The only way to distinguish between these two alternative explanations is to manipulate parameters. If the structure is involved in the function, then a lesion-induced behavioral impairment should appear as the magnitude of the task demand for this function is increased. If the structure is not involved in the function, then a lesion-induced behavioral impairment should not appear, regardless of the magnitude of the task demand for this function (Olton, 1989a; Olton & Shapiro, 1992; see Loftus, 1978, 1985, for other variables affecting the interpretation of interactions).

Our emphasis on interference has all of the advantages of a dimensional approach, and suggests one particular dimension that engages hippocampal function. The general predictions of this analysis are clear. The greater the interference in a task, then the more hippocampal function is required, the greater the involvement of hippocampal neural activity, as reflected in behavioral correlates of single-unit activity, and the greater the mnemonic impairment following hippocampal lesions.

6   THE SEPTOHIPPOCAMPAL SYSTEM AND MEMORY

Functional localization in the brain reflects an interaction of both neuroanatomical and neurochemical systems. For a given neurotransmitter system, projections to different neuroanatomical areas may influence different cognitive functions. Consequently, experiments that can provide simultaneous specificity for both neuroanatomical and neurochemical variables ought to provide more detailed information about localization of function than experiments that manipulate only one of these variables at a time (Olton, Golski, et al., 1991; Olton & Pang, 1992). Cholinergic and GABAergic neurons in the septal area terminate on and modulate the activity of neurons in the hippocampal system. Some of the neurobiological mechanisms involved in the mnemonic processes mediated by the hippocampal system have been demonstrated by a series of experiments that have combined direct intraseptal infusion of compounds that alter the activity of neurons in the medial septal area with electrophysiological recording to measure hippocampal theta and long-term potentiation (LTP), in vivo microdialysis to measure release of neurotransmitters in the hippocampus, and behavioral testing to measure mnemonic processes (Balogh, Pang, & Olton, 1991; Givens & Olton, 1990, 1992, 1993; Givens et al., 1991; Golski, et al., 1991; Gorman et al., 1991; Markowska et al., 1991; Olton, Givens, et al., 1992; Wan et al., 1991).

The general pattern of results leads to the following conclusions. In young rats, inhibition of neurons in the medial septal area by microinfusion of scopolamine (a cholinergic antagonist), muscimol (a GABAergic agonist), and B-endorphin (an opioid agonist) disrupted hippocampal electrophysiology as measured by a decrease in the power of theta (rhythmic slow activity), and impaired choice accuracy in recent memory tasks such as continuous spatial alternation in a T-maze and continuous nonmatch-to-sample in an operant box. In old rats that had age-related impairments in memory, theta, and induction of LTP, stimulation of neurons in the medial septal area with oxotremorine, a cholinergic agonist, increased the power of theta, increased the induction of LTP in the dentate gyrus, and improved spatial memory as assessed by performance in a spatial, delayed, conditional discrimination.

Converging evidence comes from behaviorally induced changes in the neurobiological activity of the hippocampal system. Cholinergic activity, as measured by high-affinity choline uptake, differentially increased following experience on a spatial task requiring working memory in comparison with a cued reference memory task in a water maze. The amount of membrane-bound protein kinase C, as measured by the binding of phorbol ester, in certain areas of the hippocampus was decreased by discriminations that required hippocampal function (Golski et al., 1991; Olds et al., 1992; Olton, Golski, et al., 1991; Wenk et al., 1984).

6.1   Mnemonic Correlates of Hippocampal Unit Activity

Mnemonic correlates of hippocampal single unit activity include components of tasks that are highly susceptible to interference. Of particular importance are mnemonic correlates associated with the comparison of discriminative stimuli in a delayed conditional discrimination (see the review in Olton, 1989a). For example, consider the experiment of Wible et al. (1986). They used a nonspatial delayed match-to-sample task with visual stimuli. Each rat was trained to perform the task accurately. Single units were recorded from the CA1 layer of the hippocampus. The most relevant data come from units that were differentially active in the sample phase (when the discriminative stimulus was presented to be remembered for the trial) and the choice phase (when the discriminative stimulus was presented after a response was made). The physical stimuli and the behavior of the rat were identical in both the sample phase and the choice phase; the only difference between the two phases was the mnemonic demand: registration during the sample phase and retrieval during the choice phase. The differential activity of these units demonstrates that the hippocampal system was responding to the mnemonic demands of this task. Furthermore, the mnemonic processes involved in the comparison of stimuli in the choice phase with those in the sample phase are highly susceptible to interference.

Similar mnemonic correlates of hippocampal unit activity occurred in an auditory continuous nonmatch-to-sample task (Sakurai, 1990). CA1 and CA3 units had differential activity on correct nonmatch trials and incorrect match trials (both of which were followed by the same response) and had the same activity on all correct nonmatch trials irrespective of the stimulus presented during that trial. This pattern of unit activity must represent some mnemonic comparison of the stimulus on the present trial and the stimulus on the previous trial, rather than a simple sensory input or motor response. Together the results of these and other studies (see the review in Olton, 1989a) demonstrate that hippocampal units reflect the memory of stimulus/response/reinforcement relationships for a variety of different nonspatial stimuli. These mnemonic correlates occurred in different areas of the hippocampus (CA1 and dentate gyrus) and in response to stimuli in three different modalities (visual, auditory, and olfactory), which provide considerable generality to the conclusion that the hippocampus has a major role in nonspatial as well as spatial memory. (See also Eichenbaum, this volume.)

If the hippocampal system is engaged by mnemonic tasks that require reduction of interference, then manipulating task interference ought to vary

Matthew L. Shapiro and David S. Olton

the activity of these neurons. Relatively little information is available to test this hypothesis directly. However, single units in the hippocampal system of both rats and monkeys have mnemonic correlates in nonspatial tasks, and some of the parameters affecting the activity of these units suggest that interference may have an important influence unit activity (Brown, 1982; Olton, 1989a; Rolls, 1990; Sakurai, 1990; Wible et al., 1986). If the same parametric manipulations of task interference that influence the magnitude of impairment produced by hippocampal lesions also influence the activity of hippocampal system units, then these two lines of evidence would provide strong converging support for the view proposed here.

Together the behavioral and neural analyses suggest that the hippocampal system has electrophysiological mechanisms (theta activity and LTP) and neurochemical mechanisms (the activity of neurons in the medial septal area that project to the hippocampus) that help to reduce the interference that occurs when the task demand for control of interference is high. Tests of this hypothesis require more parametric manipulations of specific variables to determine what kind of interference may be involved.

7 RELATIONAL REPRESENTATIONS AND PATTERN SEPARATION

We propose that the hippocampal system reduces interference during learning by direct pattern separation and by constructing and operating on a hierarchy of relational representations (Damasio et al., 1985; Eichenbaum, 1992, this volume; Eichenbaum & Cohen, 1988), of which spatial representations (O'Keefe & Nadel, 1978) and configural representations (Rudy & Sutherland, 1989, 1992, this volume; Sutherland & Rudy, 1989) are special cases. The idea of encoding and representing relationships among stimuli in relational representations has been considered by Tolman (1948), Hirsh (1974, 1980), O'Keefe and Nadel (1978), Wickelgren (1979), Eichenbaum and Cohen (1988), and Sutherland and Rudy (1989). The theoretical goal of defining relational representations is to form a general and inclusive description of representation and processing that can account for the learning and memory abilities impaired by hippocampal lesions (see Eichenbaum, 1992, this volume). For example, the set of visual angles subtended on the retina by distal objects contains information that can help an animal calculate its location (Zipser, 1985; Shapiro & Hetherington, 1993). In this example, the relationship among the set of angles is crucial, because each angle alone is insufficient to unambiguously define a location.

Our proposal, like others, attempts to link specific aspects of hippocampal anatomy and physiology to specific representations and processes that confer the special properties of memory. We assume that memory storage and retrieval are not veridical, but involve compression and reconstruction of information. We assume that cortical regions distinguish, separate, and categorize sensory information into identifiable stimuli (e.g., Marr, 1971, 1982). The hippocampus rapidly encodes relationships among these stimuli as relational representations, increases differences among relational representations, and links individual relational representations to one another in abstract, multidimensional maps (Hirsh, 1974; O'Keefe & Nadel, 1978; Eichenbaum & Cohen, 1988; Damasio et al., 1985). The rapid encoding of relational representations also serves to compress the huge amount of perceptual data represented in sensory cortical assemblies into a compact code in the hippocampus. Activation of hippocampal assemblies in turn activates cortical regions from medial temporal to occipital cortices that reconstruct perceptual attributes of memories (Damasio, 1993). Hippocampal function is crucial in any situation in which new relational representations must be created. The output from the hippocampus allows these relational representations to be stored (consolidated, e.g., Zola-Morgan & Squire, 1990) across many cortical regions. Below we compare the link between hippocampal function and relational encoding as defined here with other theories of hippocampal function.

Our proposal has three central ideas: First, the relationships among identified stimuli are stored as sets of synaptic weights on groups of single cells in hippocampus. The convergence of many axons from the entorhinal cortex onto single hippocampal neurons and the synaptic plasticity that allows individual synapses to potentiate or depress let hippocampal cells respond to specific combinations of inputs. Thus, hippocampal neurons are *relational cells*. Second, a hierarchical organization of these relational representations is encoded by recurrent connections among relational cells. By encoding relationships among relational cells, the recurrent architecture of the hippocampus can represent hierarchical information as locations within a multidimensional space (O'Keefe & Nadel, 1978). Just as relationships among stimuli (e.g., the sizes of several stimuli in an environment) can encode a location, relationships among locations (e.g. distances among locations) can encode a map of an environment. Third, the hippocampal network operates to directly increase differences among similar input patterns (i.e., it performs *pattern separation*). Because physical space is easy to visualize, we will describe these processes and representations primarily using examples from spatial processing, and we will indicate other types of processing at the end of the next section.

7.1 Conjunctive Encoding Forms Relational Units

Hippocampal pyramidal cells fire when behaving rats or monkeys are in specific locations in spatial environments (O'Keefe & Dostrovsky, 1971; O'Keefe, 1979). The locations in the environment where the cells are most active are called *place fields*. The neurons, or *place cells*, fire with respect to the constellation of distal stimuli in the environment. When the constellation of stimuli is moved (e.g., rotated to positions 90 degrees clockwise with respect to the room), place cells continue to fire in a consistent location relative to the stimuli (O'Keefe & Conway, 1978; O'Keefe & Nadel, 1978). CA1 cells do not respond to a single stimulus, because removing any one stimulus has little effect on place fields. If, however, the spatial *relationship* among the stimuli is altered

Matthew L. Shapiro and David S. Olton

by *interchanging* the stimuli, then the place field is often disrupted (O'Keefe & Conway, 1978; O'Keefe & Nadel, 1978). Thus place cells respond to the relationships among stimuli in the environment.

In our view, relational representations encode specific relationships among sets of identified cues. For example, the set of retinal angles formed by each member of a set of visual cues can define a unique location and provide sufficient input for the defining properties of place cells (figure 2; O'Keefe & Nadel, 1978; Shapiro & Hetherington, 1993; Zipser, 1985, 1986). Neurons in layer II of medial entorhinal cortex (MEC) provide the major cortical input to the hippocampus. If MEC cells respond to quantitative changes in stimulus attributes (e.g., retinal angle of an identified cue), these cells could encode values along a dimension (e.g., distance to that cue). The convergence of MEC axons onto single hippocampal cells, which allows the cells to respond to and encode conjunctions of these values, could in turn specify a multidimensional location (e.g., the conjoint retinal angle of several cues define a two-dimensional location). Because relational items coded with similar inputs in one dimension can be separated by differences in another dimension, storing conjunctions of inputs increases the dimensionality of the representation, which can help separate similar items. The process of conjunctive encoding (Barnes et al., 1990) can account for other patterns of single-unit activity that have been recorded in the hippocampus in many experiments in rats, primates, and humans, e.g., place, face, and word cells (O'Keefe & Dostrovsky, 1971; Ono et al., 1991; Heit, Smith, & Halgren, 1988, 1990; also see below).

The conjunctions that define a unique relational unit are presumably stored rapidly by the same mechanisms that support long-term potentiation (LTP) and long-term depression (LTD) (e.g., Austin, Fortin, & Shapiro, 1990). CA1 cells are estimated to have $\sim$30,000 inputs, yet only 300 of these axons ($\sim$1%) are required to fire a CA1 cell (Andersen, 1990). Conjoint input provides the necessary conditions for inducing LTP in the hippocampus (see Bliss & Lynch, 1986, for a review). Therefore, each CA1 cell can, in principal, participate in many relational representations, each encoded by a small subset of its inputs. This functional architecture is reflected in chronic recording studies showing that individual CA1 units can have several different behavioral correlates in different tasks, even within the same environment (e.g., Wiener, Paul, & Eichenbaum, 1989; Kubie & Ranck, 1983).

7.2   Recurrent Connections Form Hierarchies of Relational Units

We propose that cells within the dentate gyrus or CA3 lamina of the hippocampus interconnect to form *maps*, which compose a second order of relational representations. Thus, interconnected place units form a spatial map of neighboring locations (see O'Keefe & Nadel, 1978, for related arguments). The connections within these lamina (e.g., among dentate gyrus or CA3 neurons) will be enhanced among *functional* neighbors, defined as synaptically connected cells located anatomically across the hippocampus that have similar

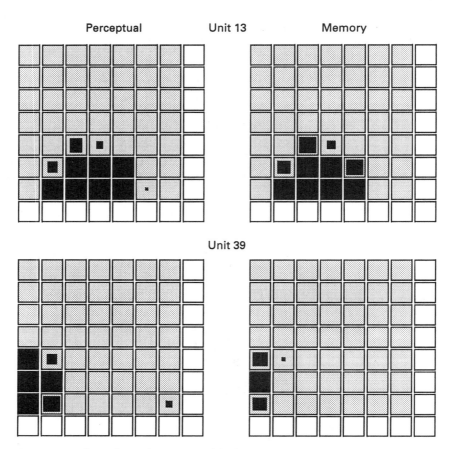

Figure 2 Relational encoding in a model of a recurrent neural network. The model was trained to produce representations of spatial trajectories. After training, these trajectories were reproduced with high accuracy, and the internal representation by single units resembled place fields recorded from hippocampal cells. Input to the units included visual angle inputs and recurrent connections. Even when the visual cues were removed after the first processing step, correct trajectories were reproduced when the network was given a visually defined starting location and a goal, which stimulate spatial working memory performance (see O'Keefe & Speakman, 1987). The figure shows a simulated place field in a model that encoded location as the weighted set of visual angle inputs. The level of activation in each of 64 locations is shown by the size of the black squares. White squares never included feedback. Spatial selectivity was determined by many inputs, so removing any one cue had minor effects (not shown). Perceptual and memory columns show the activation of the unit when all spatial stimuli were included and excluded, respectively, as input. The persistence of place fields in the memory condition was produced by recurrent connections only.

Matthew L. Shapiro and David S. Olton

response properties (e.g., overlapping or neighboring place fields) (Hetherington & Shapiro, 1991; Muller, Kubie, Saypoff, 1991). Appropriately timed pre- and postsynaptic activation of these cells will produce either LTP or LTD of connections from one cell to the other. The strength of connections between two cells encodes the *functional* proximity or distance of the two cells along a given dimension in the map (e.g., spatial proximity). One prediction from this hypothesis is that if functional proximity is encoded by the synaptic strength among CA3 neurons, then pairs of interconnected CA3 cells with overlapping place fields should share stronger synapses than pairs of cells with nonoverlapping place fields (for elaboration of this proposal, see Hetherington & Shapiro, 1993; Muller, Kubie, & Saypoff, 1991). Furthermore, the timing requirements for induction of LTP suggest that animals using consistent spatial paths should develop directional place fields. Because the animal would reliably occupy one position before another, the CA3 cells upstream of, and earlier in the trajectory relative to, the recorded cell would reliably fire before the recorded cell, and not vice versa. If direction is coded by recurrent connections, then learning to perform regular trajectories should produce directional place fields (Hetherington & Shapiro, 1993). Finally, just as one unit can help represent many types of relationships, each unit can serve in many types of maps (Wiener, Paul, & Eichenbaum, 1989).

Third-order relational representations can be formed by more prolonged recurrent activation within maps. The physiological properties of recurrent circuits confer several important properties to maps: the ability to complete patterns (Rolls, 1990), the ability to form active, self sustaining cell assemblies that can act as working memory (e.g., Lynch & Granger, 1992, this volume; Hetherington & Shapiro, 1993), and the ability to activate sequences of assemblies within a map that can represent, e.g., spatial trajectories (Hetherington & Shapiro, 1993). Higher-order relational representations can be formed by recurrent architectures (e.g., the recurrent activation of sequences might encode episodes). Because recurrent networks can, in principle, compute anything (i.e., are Turing equivalent), and the functional capacity of hippocampal circuits is presumably limited, not all of these functions should be expected to be implemented in the structure. Nonetheless, this recurrent architecture provides a mechanism for encoding potentially unlimited hierarchies of relational representations.

7.3   Behavioral Correlates of Hippocampal Neural Activity and Pattern Separation

Recording from single neurons along the processing stream from the entorhinal cortex to the hippocampus to the subiculum (see figure 1) in behaving animals suggests that relational representations are formed and input patterns are separated by the hippocampal system (e.g., Barnes et al., 1990). Neurons in layer II of the medial entorhinal cortex provide the major cortical input to the hippocampus. Although the receptive fields of cells in the medial entorhinal cortex have not yet been extensively analyzed, in rats performing spatial tasks the cells have large and diffuse place fields (Barnes et al., 1990; Quirk et al., 1992). These fields resemble the units in simulations that respond to visual angles of identified cues (Shapiro & Hetherington, 1993; Zipser, 1985, 1986).

In different environments, the locations of place fields recorded from single CA1 or CA3 cells are unpredictable, even if two environments differ only in geometry (e.g., a gray cylinder with a white stripe versus a gray box with a white stripe) (Muller & Kubie, 1987; Quirk et al., 1992). Indeed, a CA1 cell with a robust place field in one of these environments may not fire at all in the other, highly similar environment. In striking contrast to CA1 place fields, cells in the medial entorhinal cortex have fields that tend to change in shape, but not position, in two visually similar environments, so that the radial location of the place field relative to the aforementioned stripe is similar (Quirk et al., 1992). The visual similarity between the two environments is preserved in the medial entorhinal cortex, and the differences in the two environments are increased in CA1. Thus the difference between the medial entorhinal cortex and CA1 is consistent with the proposal that pattern separation is accomplished by hippocampal circuitry. The spatial correlation between the unit responses between the two environments is high in the entorhinal cortex and near zero in CA1. This difference between the medial entorhinal cortex and CA1 provides a strong constraint on computational models of hippocampal function. If pattern separation is a general process of the hippocampus, and is not limited to spatial processing, then similar decorrelations in the activity patterns of the entorhinal cortex and CA1 should be observed in nonspatial modalities, e.g., olfactory tasks. Our prediction is that the correlation of unit responses between similar inputs should be higher in the entorhinal cortex than in CA1.

CA1 axons terminate in a columnar pattern in the subiculum (Amaral & Witter, 1989), where neurons fire in patterns that resemble broadly tuned place fields (Barnes et al., 1990) as well as highly directional place fields (Sharp et al., 1990). The synaptic connection from CA1 to the subiculum supports LTP (Racine, Milgram, & Hafner, 1983), and so hippocampal output can presumably contribute to cortical plasticity and information storage. Others have proposed that the pattern separation and rapid encoding performed by the hippocampus contributes to storing long-term representations in the cortex (e.g., McNaughton & Morris, 1987). We propose that the relational encoding performed in the hippocampus is sufficient to perform both pattern separation and content-addressable information storage. However, more detailed properties of the sensory/behavioral correlates of subicular units must be analyzed before the computational role of hippocampal output can be understood. A preliminary report by Sharp, Ranck, and Muller (1990) describes three types of sensory/behavioral correlates in the subiculum, including sharply tuned place specific cells with strong directional preference (e.g., the cell fires in one location only when the animal's head points north), place-irrelevent direc-

Matthew L. Shapiro and David S. Olton

tional cells, and broadly tuned place cells. The subiculum projects strongly to the postsubiculum, where the majority of cells fire only when the rat faces one direction (so-called head-direction cells) (Taube, Muller, & Ranck, 1990a, 1990b). In the same testing environment, hippocampal CA1 and CA3 cells show no directional preference. Although subicular place fields may appear less specific than hippocampal place fields (Barnes et al., 1990), we propose that appropriate probe tests will reflect the pattern separation computed by the hippocampus, so that changes in the shape of the recording chamber (Quirk et al., 1992) or memory demands will alter firing of subicular cells more than entorhinal cells. Note that the directional place fields recorded in the subiculum and postsubiculum represent relations, and add the new dimension of direction, which should separate similar patterns while also allowing content addressability. Direct projections from the entorhinal cortex to the subiculum make more precise predictions difficult (Witter et al., 1989).

7.4 Local Circuit Mechanisms May Separate Input Patterns in CA1

Local circuit properties in CA1 may contribute to pattern separation to reduce interference among inputs (Martin, Lake, & Shapiro, 1992). Long-term potentiation is typically induced in CA1 by stimulating many presynaptic axons simultaneously and repeatedly, and is typically recorded using either macroelectrodes to record population spikes and excitatory postsynaptic potentials (EPSPs) or intracellular electrodes to measure single cell responses (e.g., Larson & Lynch, 1989; Foster & McNaughton, 1991).

Recording from local groups of discriminated CA1 units before and after tetanic stimulation in anesthetized rats showed that while stimulation produced LTP at the level of population evoked field potentials, the local, single-unit response to Schaffer collateral stimulation was highly variable (Martin et al., 1992). Of several complex-spike units typically recorded simultaneously in each experiment, some units showed evoked firing. Importantly, the stimulation produced different responses within a local group of simultaneously recorded units. Theta burst stimulation (Larson & Lynch, 1989) selectively increased evoked firing rates of some units, decreased others, and left yet others unchanged (Martin et al., 1992). Thus within a local region, inputs powerful enough to produce significant LTP at the population level produced a highly distributed response at the single-cell level. Intracellular recording experiments have also demonstrated that tetanizing stimulation does reduce the EPSP size of a subset of synapses between CA3 and CA1 neurons (Foster & McNaughton, 1991). The decreased responses of some CA1 units recorded extracellularly may be produced by many different mechanisms, including feed-forward and feedback inhibition, as well as monosynaptic long-term depression (Foster & McNaughton, 1991). This result predicts that the correlation among active CA3 neurons would be far greater than the correlation among activated units in CA1, and such decorrelation should separate patterns and reduce interference. The results are consistent with our proposal that circuit properties intrinsic to the hippocampal formation separate input patterns, which may contribute to the computational role of reducing interference among similar inputs to the hippocampus. The results also suggest that experiments using LTP saturation to test the relationship between LTP and learning (e.g., Castro et al., 1989) may be difficult to interpret, because what appears to be asymptotic LTP induction at the population level may not saturate responses at the more local, single unit level.

Manipulations of the septal input to the hippocampus also influence interference among neural representations in the hippocampus (see above). The effects of actetylcholine on hippocampal circuits may provide a mechanism for this. In other cortical areas, acetylcholine suppresses the activation of recurrent pathways, while increasing the response of pyramidal cells to extrinsic inputs (Hasselmo & Bower, 1993). This effect may prevent previously learned patterns from interfering with new learning (Hasselmo & Bower, 1993). Septal stimulation, which releases acetylcholine in the hippocampus, also prolongs the excitability of pyramidal neurons (Krnjevic & Ropert, 1982), which in turn may increase the probability of LTP induction (Hasselmo & Bower, 1993) and conjunctive encoding (Shapiro et al., 1989).

7.5 Nonspatial Relational Encoding

We propose that maps of relational units are not limited to encoding spatial representations but include other relational representations, such as those for faces, words, odors, and other configural stimuli. The crucial assumption here is that hippocampal units encode unique combinations of inputs to define relational units. The shape and hairiness of a head are principal components that activate face units in the anterior inferotemporal cortex (Young & Yamane, 1992). If our proposal is correct and if these units influence activity in the medial entorhinal cortex, then single unit activity in the entorhinal cortex should vary quantitatively along these facial dimensions and in turn should activate hippocampal units to encode and store unique faces. Furthermore, similar faces should activate overlapping populations of hippocampal units, and similarity should be encoded by relatively strong connections among CA3 cells with functionally similar responses. Analogously, the syntactic frame of word strings could define unique verbal items, and interconnected verbal units may form a semantic map as suggested by O'Keefe and Nadel (1978). Single hippocampal units in humans respond to faces and words (Heit, Smith, & Halgren, 1988, 1990). However, the absence of probe tests, such as comparing synonyms to homonyms, kept the structure of the representation from being analyzed. Interconnected olfactory sampling units (Wiener, Paul, & Eichenbaum, 1989) may form a map of odors with similar perceptual or contingent properties. Finally, the mnemonic units in the delayed conditional discriminations coded the relationship between stimuli in the sample phase and those in the choice phase (see our previous discussion).

Other experiments using single-unit data recorded from behaving animals can determine whether neuron activity is directly related to the functions proposed here. As mentioned above, the sensory and behavioral correlates of hippocampal single-unit activity are consistent with the concept of relational cells. A crucial test of the role of recurrent connections in forming hierarchical representations would be to selectively lesion the recurrent pathways in the dentate gyrus or CA3 and test spatial learning. However, the method for performing this type of lesion has yet to be developed. Other properties of recurrent circuits may already be excluded by available evidence. Consider a reverberating model of working memory as an example. In different cortical regions, a small proportion of neurons are active during stimulus presentation and continue to fire during the delay period of delayed conditional discriminations (e.g., Fuster & Jervey, 1981, 1982; Miller & Desimone, 1991; Miyashita & Chang, 1988; Quintana, Yajeya, & Fuster, 1988; Sakurai, 1990). These "delay cells" have the firing properties that could be expected in an active cell assembly for encoding working memory. If the recurrent circuitry of the hippocampus supports reverberatory working-memory representations, then cue-related delay cells should be common in CA3 and perhaps in the dentate gyrus. However, delay cells in working-memory tasks are rare in CA1 and CA3 (Wible et al., 1986; Wiener et al., 1989; O'Keefe & Speakman, 1987), and when present, their activity does not correlate with stimulus presentation or task performance (Otto & Eichenbaum, 1992). These data suggest that reverberatory cell assemblies do not implement a working-memory mechanism in the hippocampus. Other properties of recurrent circuits, such as pattern completion or representation of trajectories, may well be encoded there instead. Working memory may be encoded by other properties of hippocampal circuits, such as decremental LTP (Lynch & Granger, 1992), or by mossy fiber potentiation, which is independent of N-methyl-D-aspartate (NMDA) receptors (Harris & Cotman, 1986). Hippocampal units do fire differently in sample and match phases of delayed discrimination tasks, which suggests that the hippocampus is sensitive to the demand for working memory, especially when interference among items to be remembered is high. This temporal information may be encoded in another form of sequential activation of neural groups within recurrent hippocampal circuits, such as one representing space-time trajectory. Together the physiological and pharmacological data suggest that working memory may be encoded by a mechanism insensitive to NMDA receptor antagonists and is not implemented by Hebbian reverberatory circuits (O'Keefe & Speakman, 1987; Shapiro & Caramanos, 1990; Shapiro & O'Connor, 1992).

8   COMPARISONS WITH OTHER THEORIES

Our approach is similar to the others in this volume because it seeks to explain many of the same basic phenomena, but it is different from the others because it emphasizes two mnemonic processes: reduction of interference and formation of relational representations. This emphasis is important for both empirical and theoretical reasons. Empirically, it encourages experimental designs that parametrically manipulate each relevant variable, rather than having two types of tasks with many differences between them. Theoretically, it identifies two variables that can have a profound effect on mnemonic associations, and any computational model of our approach must explicitly include quantitative settings for each of the critical processes, particularly the amount of interference and the strength and character of relational associations.

The distinction between performance line and contextual retrieval (Hirsh, 1974) is similar to the model proposed here because contextual retrieval emphasizes the importance of hippocampal function to encode and retrieve stimulus relationships and suggests that this mechanism can reduce interference between ongoing behavior and stored information. Further elaboration of the ideas proposed that cognitive maps generated by the hippocampus could provide a powerful, general framework for encoding nonspatial, as well as spatial, structured representations (Hirsh, 1980). Finally, dimensional encoding was proposed as a mechanism for pattern separation (Hirsh, 1990). The theory differs from ours in its emphasis on the role of motivation in behavior and its emphasis on neural modulation as the mechanism for dimensional encoding (Hirsh, 1990).

Distinguishing between vertical and horizontal associations, Wickelgren (1979) proposed that the hippocampus is required for adding new nodes (vertical associations), organized hierarchically, to semantic memory. The emphasis on associative interference as a problem inherent in horizontal associative networks, and on the reduction of interference by encoding combinations of horizontal associations into vertical associations, is similar to our view of the combination of individual representations into relational representations. Finally, the potential power of recursive vertical associations as a mechanism for encoding increasingly complex concepts (Wickelgren, 1979) is similar to our proposal of linked relational representations in high dimensional maps. According to Wickelgren, vertical associations are encoded by recruiting new neurons to represent new vertical associations, a very different mechanism from the one proposed here.

In distinguishing between configural and simple associations, Sutherland and Rudy (1989) also state that the hippocampal system is needed to learn about relationships among stimuli and emphasize the advantages of configural encoding as a general representation scheme that includes, but is not limited to, space. Configural learning tasks, exemplified by negative-patterning tasks, demonstrate that nonspatial learning in rodents can be impaired by hippocampal lesions. The configural-learning view differs from our relational view because in the former, relationships among simple stimuli are considered to be embedded permanently within configurations by the hippocampal system (Sutherland & Rudy, 1989; Rudy & Sutherland, 1992). Thus, learning about new configurations requires the creation of new configural representations; even when simple stimuli are familiar, they cannot be used flexibly in other representations without relearning. Relational representations are more flexible than configural representations.

The distinction between relational and individual representations (Eichenbaum & Cohen, 1988; Eichenbaum, Fagan, Matthews, & Cohen, 1988) is directly related to our same distinction. Relational representations confer special advantages to memory processing, most notably the ability to use simple stimuli flexibly, both within and between specific constellations of stimuli. These constellations can define a configural stimulus. In transfer tests with new stimulus configurations, normal rats immediately use individual stimuli, whereas rats with hippocampal damage require the same number of trials to relearn the new configuration (with familiar individual stimuli) as they did to learn the original stimulus configurations composed of novel stimuli (Eichenbaum et al., 1988). This flexible use of individual stimuli distinguishes relational from configural representations (see Eichenbaum & Cohen, 1988; Cohen & Eichenbaum, in press). We propose that conjunctive encoding provides a mechanism for establishing first-order relational representations, and that recurrent circuitry in the hippocampus provides a mechanism for establishing links among these. As implemented in relational maps, these links among representations provides a mechanism for the flexible use of relational representations.

The distinction between episodic and semantic memory (Tulving, 1983) has been well developed and has many properties associated with it. Some of these are unique to the assessment of memory in humans and are not directly applicable here. However, the variables that influence episodic memory include interference and relations among different stimuli. Furthermore, episodic memory has many similarities to working memory, the type of memory required for correct performance in conditional discriminations, tasks for which the hippocampus is both engaged (single units have mnemonic associations) and required (hippocampal lesions impair choice accuracy). Other characteristics of episodic memory include emphasis on time, place, temporal coding, and dependency on context. All of these are very prone to interference and require relational representations. Our view differs in that it attempts to avoid criteria that can only be assessed with verbal responses in humans, and that it emphasises parametric dimensions relevant to semantic (knowledge-based) as well as episodic memory.

Associations across time (Rawlins, 1985) and temporal parameters have a strong influence on mnemonic functions. Rawlin's and our views are similar, especially with respect to the generality of these influences on nonspatial memory, as well as on spatial memory. This approach has helped to resolve some apparent discrepancies in the effects of hippocampal lesions on choice accuracy in delayed conditional discriminations. Hippocampal lesions impaired performance with a small number of discriminative stimuli, which enhances interference, but had no effect with a large number of discriminative stimuli, which minimizes interference. Consequently, this analysis of temporal factors (see Wright et al., 1986) has identified a set of experimental parameters and mnemonic processes that influence the extent to which the hippocampus is required in mnemonic associations.

The distinction between declarative and nondeclarative memory (Squire, 1992, this volume) was also designed to account primarily for human amnesia. To the extent that declarative memory, which includes memory for facts and events, is highly susceptible to interference from a variety of sources and may be referred to as relational memory (Squire, 1992, p. 232), the ideas presented here are consistent with this theoretical framework. The reference to conscious recollection is not useful in our model, because we seek to extend our analysis of memory to many different animals, and operational definitions to test conscious recollection in animals are very difficult to establish. Another difference is our assumption that interference and relational representations have a significant influence on both declarative and nondeclarative memories. For example, facts and events presented in conditions of low interference are more memorable than these same facts and events presented in conditions of high interference. Some amnesic patients can eventually learn new vocabulary words when taught in restricted contexts (Glisky & Shacter, 1988), and H.M. can perform stylus mazes when path lengths are short (Corkin, 1965; Milner, 1965). In both cases, this fact learning is restricted and inflexible. In our view, the flexibility characteristic of declarative memory derives from its use of relational representations. Although we don't know of any systematic manipulations of interference for tests of nondeclarative memory, our approach predicts an important influence here as well.

The distinction between maps and taxons (O'Keefe & Nadel, 1978; Nadel, 1992, this volume) also includes the role of interference: "Whatever it is the hippocampal system is doing, it is emphasizing that which is unique about a memory, and hence functions to separate memory traces on the basis of what distinguishes one from another" (Nadel, 1992, p. 182). One interpretation of the distinction between maps and taxons has operationalized this differences in terms of the type of stimuli to be remembered, spatial and nonspatial, respectively (see *Hippocampus, 1* (1991), pp. 221–292, for a recent series of papers on this topic). Although the neural systems for spatial and nonspatial stimuli are certainly independent of each other at some points, our approach suggests that this spatial/nonspatial distinction is not a fundamental one for the hippocampal system. Rather, the hippocampus is just as important for reducing interference and coding relational representations among nonspatial stimuli as it is for spatial stimuli. Additionally, the map/taxon distinction incorporates many other variables (rate of learning, type of motivation, etc.) that are not fundamental in our analysis.

The distinction between memory and habits (Mishkin, Malamut, & Bachevalier, 1984) also seeks to identify the variables that determine whether a task does or does not require the hippocampus for normal performance. Many types of habits are acquired in conditions that have low interference, and the lack of importance of the hippocampus in the memory for these habits may reflect this characteristic. However, our analysis assumes that the associations that form cognitive memory or the stimulus-response connections that form habits do not inherently require or bypass, respectively, the hippocampus. Rather, the crucial variables are ones that have to do with the importance of interference and relational representations in these two categories of memory.

The attribute model of memory (Kesner, 1990) suggests that the hippocampus is a crucial component in the neural system underlying spatial and temporal attributes. As illustrated in our discussion of place fields, our own analysis assumes that some of the characteristics of spatial memory involve relational representations, which in turn are mediated by the hippocampal formation. However, accurate memory for nonspatial and nontemporal information can also require reduction of interference and formation of relational representations in some circumstances, and these circumstances will engage the hippocampus for these nonspatial stimuli.

The analysis of the human amnesic syndrome in terms of reversal learning and excessive interference has many similarities to our approach (see our previous discussion of human amnesia). "If two successive tasks share common cues, amnesic subjects are differentially impeded in learning the second task" (Warrington & Weiskrantz, 1978, p. 169). The explicit comparison to a discrimination reversal for animals and the attempt to link together data from animals and humans is also an important point of similarity in the two approaches. Our approach is similar but more specific because it assumes that the hippocampus is crucial in this process and suggests a computational framework for its basis. Warrington and Weiskrantz (1974, 1978) proposed that amnesic patients are unable to constrain competing responses during memory retrieval. In contrast to this view, we propose that interference will be highest during acquisition of information, and that the hippocampus reduces interference during learning. Detailed analysis of the differences in performance of amnesic patients and normal subjects may further constrain descriptions of the exact mechanisms responsible for the interference produced by prior learning.

9   MEMORY, INTERFERENCE, AND HIPPOCAMPAL FUNCTION

Interference can be varied parametrically in a variety of tasks, including the delayed, concurrent, and reversal discriminations described above. In each of these tasks, a mechanism for reducing the similarity among items to be remembered should improve memory performance. Simple matrix memories are highly susceptible to interference, which can arise from attempting to store too many similar items (McNaughton & Morris, 1987), or from storing sequential sets of different items (McClosky & Cohen, 1989). Both pattern separation and the imposition of structure on inputs reduce interference in human memory and in artificial neural networks (e.g., Hetherington & Seidenberg, 1989). We have proposed that hippocampal circuitry performs these two operations. The hippocampus reduces interference among similar stimuli by direct pattern separation and the organization of stimuli into hierarchical, relational representations.

"In the last decade, the interference approach to memory has undergone a very rapid decline. Psychology tends to have a depressingly short memory, and it would be a great pity if the awareness of the very powerful effects of interference were to be lost simply because they tended to be associated with a theoretical approach that became regarded as outmoded and somewhat sterile" (Baddeley, 1990, p. 248).

ACKNOWLEDGMENTS

We thank D. Schacter and E. Tulving for the invitation to participate in this work, E. Tulving and T. Wright for helpful comments and directions for the analysis of interference, R. Hirsch for comments on our original contribution, and M. McCarrick, E. Kelmartin, K. Caramia, and J. Krach for preparing the manuscript.

REFERENCES

Aggleton, J. P. (1985). One-trial object recognition by rats. *Quarterly Journal of Experimental Psychology, 37B,* 279–294.

Aggleton, J. P., Hunt, P. R., & Rawlins, J. N. P. (1986). The effects of hippocampal lesions upon spatial and non-spatial tests of working memory. *Behavioral Brain Research, 19,* 133–146.

Aggleton, J. P., Kentridge, R. W., & Sembi, S. (1992). Lesions of the fornix but not the amygdala impair the acquisition of concurrent discriminations by rats. *Behavioral Brain Research, 48,* 103–112.

Amaral, D. G., & Witter, M. P. (1989). The three-dimensional organization of the hippocampal formation: A review of anatomical data. *Neuroscience, 31,* 571–591.

Andersen P. (1990). Synaptic integration in hippocampal CA1 pyramids. *Progress in Brain Research, 83,* 215–222.

Austin, K. B., Fortin, W. F., & Shapiro, M. L. (1990). Place fields are altered by NMDA antagonist MK-801 during spatial learning. *Society for Neuroscience. Abstracts, 20th Annual Meeting, 16,* 263, no. 113.11.

Baddeley, A. (1990). *Human memory: Theory and practice.* Toronto: Allyn and Bacon.

Balogh, A., Pang, K., & Olton, D. S. (1991). Medial septal area and hippocampal synaptic plasticity: Effects of oxotremorine in aged rats. *Society for Neuroscience, 55*(11), 138.

Barnes, C. A. (1988). Spatial learning and memory processes: The search for their neurobiological mechanisms in the rat. *Trends in Neuroscience, 11,* 163–169.

Barnes, C. A., McNaughton, B. L., Mizumori, S. J., Leonard, B. W., & Lin, L. H. (1990). Comparison of spatial and temporal characteristics of neuronal activity in sequential stages of hippocampal processing. *Progress in Brain Research, 83,* 287–300.

Becker, J. T., & Olton, D. S. (1980). Object discrimination by rats: The role of frontal and hippocampal systems in retention and reversal. *Physiology and Behavior, 24,* 33–38.

Bliss, T. V. P., & Lynch, M. A. (1988). Long term potentiation of synaptic transmission in the hippocampus: Properties and mechanisms. In P. W. Landfield & S. A. Deadwyler (Eds.), *Long-term potentiation: From biophysics to behavior* (pp. 3–72). New York: Alan Liss, Inc.

Brown, M. W. (1982). Effects of context on the response of single units recorded from the hippocampal region of behaviorally trained monkeys. In C. Ajmone Marsan & H. Matthies (Eds.), *Neuronal Plasticity and Memory Formation* (pp. 557–573). New York: Raven Press.

Castro, C. A., Silbert, L. H., McNaughton, B. L., & Barnes, C. A. (1989). Recovery of spatial learning deficits after decay of electrically induced synaptic enhancement in the hippocampus. *Nature, 342,* 545–548.

Cave, C. B., & Squire, L. R. (1991). Equivalent impairment of spatial and nonspatial memory following damage to the human hippocampus. *Hippocampus, 1,* 329–340.

Cohen, N. J., & Eichenbaum, H. B. (1993). *Memory, amnesia, and hippocampal function.* Cambridge: MIT Press.

Corkin, S. (1965). Tactually guided maze learning in man: Effects of unilateral cortical excisions and bilateral hippocampal lesions. *Neuropsychologia, 3,* 339–351.

Craik, F. I. M., & Lockhart, R. S. (1972). Levels of processing a framework for memory research. *Journal of Verbal Larning and Verbal Behavior, 11,* 671–684.

Crowder, R. G. (1976). *Principles of learning and memory.* New York: Lawrence Erlbaum Associates.

Damasio, A. R. (1993). Perception: General concepts. Presented at the Mind-Brain: Sensory Processes conference, Madrid, Spain, November 16.

Damasio, A. R., Eslinger, P. J., Damasio, H., Van Hoesen, G. W., & Cornell, S. (1985). Multi-modal amnesic syndrome following bilateral temporal and basal forebrain damage. *Archives of Neurology, 42,* 252–260.

Eichenbaum, H. (1992). The hippocampal system and declarative memory in animals. *Cognitive Neuroscience, 4,* 217–231.

Eichenbaum, H., & Cohen, N. J. (1988). Representation in the hippocampus: What do hippocampal neurons code? *Trends in Neuroscience, 11,* 244–248.

Foster, T. C., & McNaughton, B. L. (1991). Long-term synaptic enhancement in hippcampal field CA1 is due to increaed quantal size, not quantal content. *Hippocampus, 1,* 79–91.

Fuster, J. M., & Jervey, J. P. (1981). Inferotemporal neurons distinguish and retain behaviorally relevant features of visual stimuli. *Science, 212,* 952–955.

Fuster, J. M., & Jervey, J. P. (1982). Neuronal firing in the inferotemporal cortex of the monkey in a visual memory task. *Journal of Neuroscience, 2,* 361–375.

Gage, F. H., Armstrong, D. R., & Thompson, R. G. (1980). Behavioral kinetics: A method for derivig qualitative and quantitative changes in sensory responsiveness following septal nuclei damage. *Physiology and Behavior, 24,* 479–484.

Givens, B., Markowska, A. L., & Olton, D. S. (1991). Muscarinic activation of the medial septal area: Imporvements in working memory and modulation of hippocampal physiology in aged rats. *Society for Neuroscience, 55*(4), 136.

Givens, B., & Olton, D. S. (1990). Cholinergic and GABAergic modulation of medial septal area: Effect on working memory. *Behavioral Neuroscience, 104,* 849–855.

Givens, B., & Olton, D. S. (1992a). Time-dependent modulation of working memory by the medial septal area: Assessment in a continuous conditional discrimination task. (In preparation.)

Givens, B., & Olton, D. S. (1992b). Working memory and cholinergic autoregulation in the medial septal area. In E. D. Levin, M. W. Decker, & L. Butcher (Eds.), *Neurotransmitter interactions and cognitive functions* (pp. 301–311). Boston: Birkhauser.

Glisky, E. L., & Schacter, D. L. (1988). Long-term retention of computer learning by patients with memory disorders. *Neuropsychologia, 26,* 173–178.

Golski, S., Gorman, L. K., & Olton, D. S. (1991). Behaviorally induced cholinergic activity: Role of associative and nonassociative processes. *Society for Neuroscience, 55*(10), 137.

Gorman, L. K., Pang, K., Givens, B., Kwon, C., & Olton, D. S. (1991). Intraseptal infusion alters acetylcholine release in the hippocampus of the rat. *Society for Neuroscience, 55*(8), 137.

Harlow, H. F. (1959). Learning set and error factor theory. In S. Koch (Ed.), *Psychology: A study of a science* (Vol. 2, pp. 492–537). New York: McGraw-Hill.

Harris, E. W., & Cotman, C. W. (1986). Long-term potentiation of guinea pig mossy fiber responses is not blocked by N-methyl-D-aspartate antagonists. *Neuroscience Letters, 70,* 132–137.

Hasselmo, M. E., & Bower, J. M. (1993). Acetylcholine and memory. *Trends in Neuroscience, 16,* 218–222.

Hayman, C. A. G., Macdonald, C. A., & Tulving, E. (in press). The role of repetition and associative interference in new semantic learning in amnesia. *Neuropsychologia.*

Hebb, D. O. (1949). *The organization of behavior.* New York: Wiley.

Heit, G., Smith, M. E., & Halgren, E. (1988). Neural encoding of individual words and faces by the human hippocampus and amygdala. *Nature, 333,* 773–775.

Heit, G., Smith, M. E., & Halgren, E. (1990). Neuronal activity in the human medial temporal lobe during recognition memory. *Brain, 113,* 1093–1112.

Hetherington, P. A., & Seidenberg, M. S. (1989). Is there "catastrophic interference" in connectionist networks? *Proceedings of the Eleventh Annual Conference of the Cognitive Science Society* (pp. 26–33). Hillsdale, NJ: Lawrence Erlbaum.

Hetherington, P. A., & Shapiro, M. L. (1991). A recurrent PDP model simulates hippocampal place cell activity in goal-directed, sequential behavior. *International Brain Research Organization, Third Annual Meeting,* Montreal, Quebec, August, abstract P25.27, p. 168.

Hetherington, P. A., & Shapiro, M. L. (1993). A simple neural network model simulates hippocampal place fields: II, Computing goal directed trajectories and "memory fields." *Behavioral Neuroscience, 107,* 434–443.

Hirsh, R. (1974). The hippocampus and contextual retrieval of information from memory: A theory. *Behavioral Biology, 12,* 421–444.

Hirsh, R. (1980). The hippocampus, conditional operations, and cognition. *Physiological Psychology, 8,* 175–182.

Hirsh, R. (1990). Modulatory integration: A concept capable of explaining cognitive learning and purposive behavior in physiological terms. *Psychobiology, 18,* 3–15.

Jarrard, L. E. (1991). On the neural bases of the spatial mapping system: Hippocampus versus hippocampal formation. *Hippocampus, 1,* 236–239.

Kesner, R. P. (1990). Learning and memory in rats with an emphasis on the role of the hippocampal formation. In R. Kesner & D. Olton (Eds.), *Neurobiology of comparative cognition* (pp. 179–204). Hillsdale, NJ: Erlbaum.

Kesner, R. P., Bolland, B. L., & Dakis, M. (in press). Memory for spatial locations, motor responses, and objects: Triple dissociation among the hippocampus, caudate nucleus, and extrastriate visual cortex. *Experimental Brain Research, 93,* 462–470.

Kinsbourne, M., & Winocur, G. (1980). Response competition and interference effects in paired-associate learning by Korsakoff amnesics. *Neuropsychologia, 18*(4–5), 541–548.

Krnjevic, K., & Ropert, N. (1982). Electrophysiological and pharmacological characteristics of facilitation of hippocampal population spikes by stimulation of the medial septum. *Neuroscience, 7*, 2165–2183.

Kubie, J. L., & Ranck, J. B. (1983). Sensory-behavioral correlates in individual hippocampus neurons in three situations: Space and context. In W. Seifert (Ed.), *The hippocampus* (Vol. 2, pp. 433–447). New York: Academic Press.

Larson, J., & Lynch, G. (1989). Induction of synaptic potentiation in hippocampus by patterned stimulation involves two events. *Science, 232*, 985–988.

Loftus, G. R. (1978). On interpretation of interactions. *Memory and Cognition, 6*, 312–319.

Loftus, G. R. (1985). Evaluating forgetting curves. *Journal of Experimental Psychology, 11*, 397–406.

Lynch, G., & Granger, R. (1992). Variations in synaptic plasticity and types of memory in corticohippocampal networks. *Journal of Cognitive Neuroscience, 4*, 189–199.

Mahut, H., Moss, M., & Zola-Morgan, S. (1981). Retention deficits after combined hippocampal resections in the monkey. *Neuropsychologica, 19*, 201–225.

McClosky, M., & Cohen, N. J. (1989). Catastrophic interference in connectionist networks: The sequential learning problem. In G. H. Bower (Ed.), *The Psychology of Learning and Motivation* (pp. 109–164). New York: Academic Press.

McDonald, R. J., & White, N. M. (1993). A triple dissociation of memory systems: Hippocampus, amygdala, and dorsal striatum. *Behavioral Neuroscience, 107*(1), 3–22.

McNaughton, B. L., & Morris, R. G. M. (1987). Hippocampal synaptic enhancement and information storage within a distributed memory system. *Trends in Neuroscience, 10*, 408–415.

Markowska, A. L., Caprioli, A., Pang, K., & Olton, D. S. (1991). Blockade of muscarinic receptors in medial septal area or nucleus basalis magnocellularis impairs spatial memory. *Society for Neuroscience, 55*(6), 137.

Markowska, A. L., Olton, D. S., Murray, E. A., & Gaffan, D. (1989). A comparative analysis of the role of the fornix and cingulate cortex in memory: Rats. *Experimental Brain Research, 74*, 255–269.

Marr, D. (1971). Simple memory: A theory for archicortex. *Proceedings of the Royal Society of London*, Series B, Biological, *262*, 23–81.

Marr, D. (1982). *Vision*. San Francisco: W. H. Freeman.

Martin, P. D., Lake, N., & Shapiro, M. L. (1992). Effects of burst stimulation on neighboring single CA1 neurons in rat hippocampus. Society for Neuroscience, 22nd Annual Meeting, Anaheim, CA, October 25–30.

Mayes, A. R., Pickering, A., & Fairbairn, A. (1987). Amnesic sensitivity to proactive interference: Its relationship to priming and the causes of amnesia. *Neuropsychologia, 25*, 211–220.

Miller, E. K., & Desimone, R. (1991). A neural mechanism for working and recognition memory in inferior temporal cortex. *Science, 254*, 1377–1379.

Milner, B. (1965). Visually guided maze learning in man: Effect of bilateral hippocampal, bilateral frontal, and unilateral cerebral lesions. *Neuropsychologia, 3*, 317–338.

Mishkin, M., Malamut, B., & Bachevalier, J. (1984). Memories and habits: Some implications for the analysis of learning and retention. In L. Squire & N. Butters (Eds.), *Neuropsycholgoy of memory* (pp. 287–296). New York: Guilford Press.

Miyashita, Y., & Chang, H. S. (1988). Neuronal correlate of pictorial short-term memory in the primate temporal cortex. *Nature, 331,* 68–70.

Morris, R. G. M., Garrud, P., Rawlins, J. N. P., & O'Keefe, J. (1982). Place navigation impaired in rats with hippocampal lesions. *Nature, 297,* 681–683.

Moss, M., Mahut, H., & Zola-Morgan, S. (1981). Concurrent discrimination learning of monkeys after hippocampal, entorhinal, or fornix lesions. *Journal of Neuroscience, 1,* 227–240.

Muller, R. U., & Kubie, J. L. (1987). The effects of changes in the environment on the spatial firing of hippocampal complex-spike cells. *Journal of Neuroscience, 7,* 1951–1968.

Muller, R. U., Kubie, J. L., & Saypoff, R. (1991). The hippocampus as a cognitive graph (abridged version). *Hippocampus, 1,* 243–246.

Mumby, D. G., Pinel, J. P. J., Hill, M., & Shen, M. J. (1991). Combined lesions of the hippocampus and the amygdala impair concurrent-object-discrimination learning in rats: Evidence on both anterograde and retrograde amnesia. Paper presented at the Third IBRO World Congress of Neuroscience, Montreal, Quebec.

Murray, E. A., Davidson, M., Gaffan, D., Olton, D. S., & Suomi, S. (1989). Effects of fornix transection and cingulate cortical ablation on spatial memory in rhesus monkeys. *Experimental Brain Research, 74,* 173–186.

Nadel, L. (1992). Multiple memory systems: What and why. *Journal of Cognitive Neuroscience, 4,* 179–188.

O'Keefe, J. (1979). A review of the hippocampal place cells. *Progress in Neurobiology, 13,* 419–439.

O'Keefe, J., & Conway, D. H. (1978). Hippocampal place units in the freely-moving rat: Why they fire and where they fire. *Experimental Brain Research, 31,* 573–590.

O'Keefe, J., & Dostrovsky, J. (1971). The hippocampus as a spatial map: Preliminary evidence from unit activity in the freely-moving rat. *Brain Research, 34,* 171–175.

O'Keefe, J., & Nadel, L. (1978). *The hippocampus as a cognitive map.* Oxford: Clarendon Press.

O'Keefe, J., & Speakman, A. (1987). Single unit activity in the rat hippocampus during a spatial memory task. *Experimental Brain Research, 68,* 1–27.

Olds, J. L., Golski, S., McPhie, D. L., Olton, D. S., Mishkin, M., & Alkon, D. L. (1992). Discrimination learning alters the distribution of protein kinase C in the hippocampus of rats. *Journal of Neuroscience, 10,* 3707–3713.

Olton, D. S. (1989a). Mnemonic functions of the hippocampus: Single unit analyses in rats. In V. Chan-Palay & C. Kohler (Eds.), *The hippocampus: New vistas* (pp. 411–424). New York: Alan R. Liss, Inc.

Olton, D. S. (1989b). Dimensional mnemonics. In G. H. Bower (Ed.), *The psychology of learning and motivation* (pp. 1–23). San Diego: Academic Press.

Olton, D. S., Becker, J. T., & Handelmann, G. H. (1979). Hippocampus, space, and memory. *Behavioral and Brain Sciences, 2,* 313–365.

Olton, D. S., Givens, B., Markowska, A. L., Shapiro, M., & Golski, S. (1992). Mnemonic functions of the cholinergic septohippocampal system. In L. R. Squire, N. M. Weinberger, & J. L. McGaugh (Eds.), *Memory: Organization and locus of change* (pp. 250–269). Oxford: Oxford University Press.

Olton, D. S., Golski, S., Mishkin, M., Gorman, L. K., Olds, J. L., & Alkon, D. L. (1991). Behaviorally induced changes in the hippocampus. *Brain Research Reviews, 16,* 206–209.

Olton, D. S., & Markowska, M. L. (in press). Mazes: Their use in delayed conditional discriminations and place discriminations. In F. Von Harren (Ed.), *Methods in behavioral pharmacology.* Amsterdam: Elsevier Science Publishers.

Olton, D. S., & Pang, K. (1992). Interactions of neurotransmitters and neuroanatomy: It's not what you do, it's the place that you do it. In E. D. Levin, M. W. Decker, & L. Butcher (Eds.), *Neurotransmitter interactions and cognitive functions* (pp. 277–286). Boston: Birkhauser.

Olton, D. S., & Shapiro, M. L. (1992). Mnemonic dissociations: The power of parameters. *Journal of Cognitive Neuroscience, 4,* 201–207.

Olton, D. S., Shapiro, M. L., & Hulse, S. H. (1984). Working memory and serial patterns. In H. L. Roitblat, T. G. Bever, & H. S. Terrace (Eds.), *Animal Cognition* (pp. 171–182). Hillsdale, NJ: Lawrence Erlbaum.

Olton, D. S., Walker, J. A., & Wolf, W. A. (1982). A disconnection analysis of hippocampal function. *Brain Research, 233,* 241–253.

Olton, D. S., Wible, C. G., & Markowska, A. (1991). A comparative analysis of the role of the hippocampal system in memory. In H. J. Weingartner & R. G. Lister (Eds.), *Cognitive Neuroscience* (pp. 186–196). New York: Oxford University Press.

Ono, T., Nakamura, K., Fukada, M., & Tamura, R. (1991). Place recognition responses of neurons in monkey hippocampus. *Neuroscience Letters, 121,* 194–198.

Otto, T., & Eichenbaum, H. (1992). Neuronal activity in the hippocampus during delayed non-match to sample performance in rats: Evidence for hippocampal processing in recognition memory. *Hippocampus, 2,* 323–334.

Packard, M. G., Hirsh, R., & White, N. M. (1989). Differential effects of fornix and caudate nucleus lesions on two radial maze tasks: Evidence for multiple memory systems. *Journal of Neuroscience, 9,* 1465–1472.

Phillips, R. G., & LeDoux, J. E. (1992). Differential contribution of amygdala and hippocampus to cued and contextual fear conditioning. *Behavioral Neuroscience, 106,* 274–285.

Press, G. A., Amaral, D. G., & Squire, L. R. (1989). Hippocampal abnormalities in amnesic patients revealed by high-resolution magnetic resonance imaging. *Nature, 341,* 54–57.

Quintana, J., Yajeya, J., & Fuster, J. M. (1988). Prefrontal representation of stimulus attributes during delay tasks: Unit activity in cross-temporal integration of sensory and sensory-motor information. *Brain Research, 474,* 211–221.

Quirk, G. J., Muller, R. U., Kubie, J. L., & Ranck, J. B., Jr. (1992). The positional firing properties of medial entorhinal neurons: Description and comparison with hippocampal place cells. *Journal of Neuroscience, 12,* 1945–1963.

Racine, R. J., Milgram, N. W., & Hafner, S. (1983). Long-term potentiation phenomena in the rat limbic forebrain. *Brain Research, 260,* 217–231.

Raffaelle, K., & Olton, D. S. (1988). Hippocampal and amygdaloid involvement in working memory for nonspatial stimuli. *Behavioral Neuroscience, 102,* 349–355.

Rawlins, J. N. P. (1985). Associations across time: The hippocampus as a temporary memory store. *Behavioral and Brain Sciences, 8,* 479–497.

Rolls, E. (1990). Spatial memory, episodic memory, and neuronal network functions in the hippocampus. In L. R. Squire & E. Lindenlaub (Eds.), *The biology of memory* (pp. 445–470). New York: Schattauer Verlag.

Rothblat, L. A., & Hayes, L. L. (1987). Short-term recognition memory in the rat: Nonmatching with trial-unique junk stimuli. *Behavioral Neuroscience, 101,* 587–590.

Rothblat, L. A., Vnek, N., Gleason, T. C., & Kromer, L. F. (in press). Role of the parahippocampal region in spatial and nonspatial memory: Effects of parahippocampal lesions on rewarded alternation and concurrent object discrimination in the rat. *Behavioral Brain Research*.

Rudy, J. W., & Sutherland, R. J. (1989). The hippocampus is necessary for rats to learn and remember configural discriminations. *Behavioral Brain Research, 34,* 97–109.

Rudy, J. W., & Sutherland, R. J. (1992). Configural and elemental associations and the memory coherence problem. *Journal of Cognitive Neurosceince, 4,* 208–216.

Sakurai, Y. (1990). Hippocampal cells have behavioral correlates during the performance of an auditory working memory task in the rat. *Behavioral Neuroscience, 104,* 253–263.

Shapiro, M. L., & Caramanos, Z. (1990). NMDA antagonist MK-801 impairs acquisition but not performance of spatial memory. *Psychobiology, 2,* 231–243.

Shapiro, M. L., & Hetherington, P. A. (1993). A simple network model simulates hippocampal place fields: Parametric analyses and physiological predictions. *Behavioral Neuroscience, 107,* 34–50.

Shapiro, M. L., & O'Connor, C. (1992). NMDA receptor antagonist MK-801 and spatial memory: Working memory is impaired in an unfamiliar, but not a familiar, environment. *Behavioral Neuroscience, 106*(4), 604–612.

Shapiro, M. L., Simon, D. K., Olton, D. S., Gage, F. H., III, Nilsson, O., & Bjorklund, A. (1989). Intrahippocampal grafts of fetal basal forebrain tissue alter place fields in the hippocampus of rats with fimbria-fornix lesions. *Neuroscience, 32,* 1–18.

Sharp, P. E., Ranck, J. B., Jr., & Muller, R. U. (1990). Direction and location correlates of cell firing in the rat subiculum. *Abstracts: Society for Neuroscience Annual Meeting, 16*(1), 737.

Sherry, D. F., & Schacter, D. L. (1987). The evolution of multiple memory systems. *Psychological Review, 94,* 439–454.

Squire, L. R. (1987). *Memory and brain.* New York: Oxford University Press.

Squire, L. R. (1992). Memory and the hippocampus: A synthesis from findings with rats, monkeys, and humans. *Psychological Review, 99,* 195–231.

Sutherland, R. J., & Rudy, J. W. (1989). Configural association theory: The role of the hippocampal formation in learning, memory, and amnesia. *Psychobiology, 17,* 129–144.

Taube, J. S., Muller, R. U., & Ranck, J. B. (1990a). Head direction cells recorded from the postsubiculum in freely moving rats: I, Description and quantitative analysis *Journal of Neuroscience, 10*(2), 420–435.

Taube, J. S., Muller, R. U., & Ranck, J. B. (1990b). Head-direction cells recorded from the postsubiculum in freely moving rats: II, Effects of environmental manipulations. *Journal of Neuroscience, 10*(2), 436–447.

Thompson, R. F. (1986). The neurobiology of learning and memory. *Science, 233,* 941–947.

Tolman, E. C. (1948). Cognitive maps in rats and men. *Psychological Review, 56,* 144–155.

Tulving, E. (1983). Elements of episodic memory. New York: Oxford University Press.

Van der Linden, M., Bruyer, R., Roland, J., & Schils, J. P. (1993). Proactive interference in patients with amnesia resulting from anterior communicating artery aneurysm. *Journal of Clinical and Experimental Neuropsychology, 15*(4), 525–536.

Wan, R. Q., Givens, B., & Olton, D. S. (1991). Opiod system in the medial septal area: The effect of microinfusion of beta-endorphin on spatial working memory in rats. *Society for Neuroscience, 17*(1), 137, no. 55.7.

Warrington, E. K., & Weiskrantz, L. (1974). The effect of prior learning on subsequent retention in amnesic patients. *Neuropsychologia, 12,* 419–428.

Warrington, E. K., & Weiskrantz, L. (1978). Further analysis of the prior learning effect in amnesic patients. *Neuropsychologia, 16,* 169–177.

Wenk, G. L., Helper, D., & Olton, D. S. (1984). Behavior alters the uptake of (3H)-choline into acetylcholinergic neurons of the nucleus basalis magnocellularis and medial septal area. *Behavioral Brain Research, 13,* 129–138.

Wible, C. G., Findling, R. L., Shapiro, M., Lang, E. J., Crane, S., & Olton, D. S. (1986). Mnemonic correlates of unit activity in the hippocampus. *Brain Research, 399,* 97–110.

Wible, C. G., Shiber, J. R., & Olton, D. S. (1992). Hippocampus, fimbria/fornix, amygdala, and memory: Object discriminations in rats. *Behavioral Neuroscience, 106,* 751–761.

Wickelgren, W. A. (1979). Chunking and consolidation: A theoretical synthesis of semantic networks, configuring in conditioning, normal forgetting, the amnesic syndrome, and the hippocampal arousal system. *Psychological Review, 86,* 44–60.

Wiener, S. I., Paul, C. A., & Eichenbaum, H. (1989). Spatial and behavioral correlates of hippocampal neuronal activity. *Journal of Neuroscience, 9,* 2737–2763.

Winocur, G., & Weiskrantz, L. (1976). An investigation of paired associate learning in amnesic patients. *Neuropsychologia, 14,* 97–110.

Witter, M. P., Groenewegen, H. J., Lopes da Silva, F. H., & Lohman, A. H. M. (1989). Functional organization of the extrinsic and intrinsic circuitry of the parahippocampal region. *Progress in Neurobiology, 33,* 161–253.

Wright, A. A., Urcuioli, P. J., & Sands, S. F. (1986). Proactive interference in animal memory. In D. F. Kendrick, M. E. Rilling, & M. R. Denny (Eds.), *Theories of animal memory* (pp. 101–125). Hillsdale, NJ: Erlbaum.

Young, M. P., & Yamane, S. (1992). Sparse population coding of faces in the inferotemporal cortex. *Science, 256,* 1327–1331.

Zeldin, R. K., & Olton, D. S. (1986). Rats acquire spatial learning sets. *Journal of Experimental Psychology, 12,* 412–419.

Zipser, D. (1985). A computational model of hippocampal place fields *Behavioral Neuroscience, 99,* 1006–1018.

Zipser, D. (1986). Biologically plausible models of place recognition and goal location. In J. L. McClelland & D. E. Rumelhart (Eds.), *Parallel distributed processing* (Vol. 1, pp. 432–470). Cambridge: MIT Press.

Zola-Morgan, S. M., & Squire, L. R. (1990). The primate hippocampal formation: Evidence for a time-limited role in memory storage. *Science, 250,* 288–290.

Zola-Morgan, S. M., Squire, L. R., & Amaral, D. G. (1986). Human amnesia and the medial temporal region: Enduring memory impairment following a bilateral lesion limited to field CA1 of the hippocampus. *Journal of Neuroscience, 6,* 2950–2967.

5 The Memory-Coherence Problem, Configural Associations, and the Hippocampal System

Jerry W. Rudy and Robert J. Sutherland

1 INTRODUCTION

In his last published paper, the eminent neuropsychologist Alexander R. Luria discussed the importance of maintaining a coherent memory for adaptive memory function. In his words, "The single most important factor to this entire process is attempting to make the data presented and retrieved a 'closed system' (i.e., closed to all extraneous and confounding influences except the actual material preserved and coded). Corollary to this objective is avoiding any possibility of converting it over to an 'open system' (i.e., a system that allows one's immediate impressions and/or associations to confound the preservation of coherence and coding of the material) (Luria, 1979, p. 280).

Luria (1979) illustrated the problem by reporting the performance of several brain-injured patients that were read a short fable by Leo Tolstoi and asked to recall it. One patient was read the fable "The Hen with the Golden Eggs": "A peasant had a hen who laid golden eggs. He wanted to become rich at once and killed the hen; but he found nothing. The hen was as all hens are." That patient began the story as follows: "A peasant ... , a small bourgeois who liked money, ... had a hen.... It's very nice to have poultry ... who laid golden eggs.... You know how precious gold is in our time of inflation." Note that each retrieved component of the story generated a series of extraneous associations that would not intrude on the recall of this fable in normal people. So this patient's memory system was unable to maintain a closed system.

Another example of memory coherence is provided by the "crossed associates" paradigm (Humphreys, Bain, & Pike, 1989). In this task, the subject is asked to learn a list of paired associates constructed from strongly related words, but the paired items are counter to the subject's preexperimental history, for example, *spider-blue*, *sky-bank*, and *river-web*. Learning such a list is potentially difficult because of the conflict between the demands of the list and the subject's preexperimental history. Yet the ease with which normal subjects learn such lists suggests that these conflicting associations, e.g., *spider-web*, *sky-blue*, and *river-bank*, have little or no influence on task performance (Slamecka, 1966). Amnesics, however, have difficulty just learning paired associates constructed from unrelated words (Graf & Schacter, 1985; Shimamura & Squire, 1984).

Memory coherence is not confined to humans or verbal tasks. It can also be seen in a variety of problems that can be solved by animals. A compelling example is sometimes called the "transswitching" problem. In a Pavlovian version of the problem, an animal is exposed to two conditioned stimuli, A and B, alternately in two experimental contexts. In context 1 ($C1$), A is paired with the unconditioned stimulus and B is not, $C1[A+/B-]$, but in context 2 ($C2$) the opposite relationship is in effect: B is paired with the unconditioned stimulus and A is not, $C2[A-/B+]$. Maintaining memory coherence is critical because if the animal is to perform correctly to A and B when they are presented in $C1$ (respond to A but not to B), the memory system must be closed to the competing associations established to A and B in $C2$. Animals can readily solve the transswitching problem (e.g., Rescorla, Durlach, & Grau, 1985; Saavadra, 1975), but there is some evidence that animals with damage to the hippocampal system cannot solve problems of this sort (Sutherland, McDonald, Hill, & Rudy, 1989).

These examples make the point that cues available to retrieve task-appropriate memories are often associated with other irrelevant or incompatible memories. Successful performance under such conditions may require a memory system closed to the influence of task-inappropriate memories associated with the cues.

These examples also serve to illustrate a second important point. Retrieval cues still generate memories (or their behavioral indices) even when memory coherence is lost. This result is obvious in Luria's patient, who recalled information irrelevant to the fable. But I should mention that, even though amnesics have difficulty learning paired associates constructed of unrelated words, when asked to respond to the stimulus words with the first thing that comes to mind, they respond like normal people (Graf, Squire, & Mandler, 1984; Shimamura & Squire, 1984). Moreover, animals with damage to the hippocampal system respond to the ambiguous elements of the transswitching problem; they just don't respond in a context-appropriate manner (Rudy & Sutherland, 1989; Sutherland, McDonald, et al., 1989; Sutherland & McDonald, 1990). In the context of the memory-coherence perspective, these aspects of performance indicate how an open memory system functions.

Luria's memory-coherence perspective provides a framework for considering some of the phenomena that have been important in the development of the approach of multiple memory systems (Tulving, 1985) and might help illuminate fundamental differences in the operating characteristics of the systems. This approach recognizes that most retrieval cues used in natural settings and sometimes in the laboratory have multiple associations. Whether these multiple associations matter to adaptive functioning, however, depends on the task requirements. Some task demands can be met by an open system, but others require a closed system.

Jerry W. Rudy and Robert J. Sutherland

This perspective raises several related questions: What is the difference in how retrieval is accomplished by a closed versus an open system? What task demands require a closed system and what demands can be met by an open system? And what neural processes determine when the closed system cannot function?

2 ELEMENTAL AND CONFIGURAL ASSOCIATIONS

We recently put forth a theory directed at understanding the contribution of the hippocampal system (dentate gyrus, CA3, CA1, subiculum cortices, and entorhinal cortex) to learning and memory (Sutherland & Rudy, 1989). In a broader context, it can also address the interrelated questions that emerge from the memory-coherence perspective. We introduce the theory by considering the problem of how retrieval is accomplished when memory exhibits Luria's open versus closed characteristics. The reader should be aware that we are using the word "system" to refer to three different levels of description. The first level is neuroanatomical. At this level we distinguish between hippocampal versus nonhippocampal circuitry. The second is the representational level, within which we distinguish between configural- and elemental-association systems. At a third level, we draw upon Luria's distinction between when memory performance is relatively impervious to interference (closed) and when it is more easily influenced by extraneous associations (open). Note that we attempt to describe relationships among these three levels, but we do not assume isomorphism.

2.1 Elements of the Theory

Like other theorists in the associationist's tradition (e.g., Anderson & Bower, 1973; Rescorla & Wagner, 1972; Spence, 1936), we assume that memory representations for individual events are laid down in an associative network. A target memory is then activated by retrieval cues whose representations are connected with the target memory in the network. The retrieval cues themselves are viewed as a set of independent environmental stimuli or as elements each having some representation in the network. The critical assumptions we then make are about how these cues cooperate or combine to retrieve a target memory. We distinguished between a system that can acquire *elemental associations* and a system that can acquire *configural associations*. This distinction can be appreciated by looking at figure 1 and assuming that the subject previously experienced two stimuli A and B, followed by a third stimulus C.

Elemental associations are illustrated in figure 1, left. As a result of experience, representations of A and B (a and b) each become connected to the representation of C (c). The ability of either A alone or B alone to activate c will be determined by the strength of the a-c and b-c connections, and the ability of A and B together to activate c will be a function of the strength of the combined a-c and b-c connections. This position is no different than what

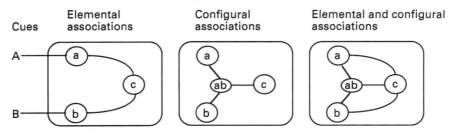

Figure 1 Associations that might result after a subject experienced a stimulus compound composed of two elements, *A* and *B*, followed by a third stimulus, *C*. The left panel shows the set of independent elemental associations that might result, the middle panel shows the configural association representing the conjunction of the *A* and *B* events, and the right panel indicates that a normal adult subject has both elemental and configural associations.

many theorists (e.g, Rescorla & Wagner, 1972) have assumed, beginning with Spence's (1936) classic paper on discrimination learning. So the strengths of the *a-c* and *b-c* connections would sum even if they were established by independent experiences (e.g., Kehoe & Graham, 1988).

A configural association is illustrated in figure 1, center. The key assumption portrayed here is that the subject can construct a representation of the joint occurrence or conjunction of *A* and *B* [*ab*] that also can associate with *c*. Although composed from *a* and *b*, this configural representation is unique and can be discriminated from its constituents (e.g., Kehoe & Gormezano, 1980; Rescorla, 1972; Whitlow & Wagner, 1972).

Memories can be retrieved by both elemental and configural representations. Moreover, as shown in figure 1, connections from the configural representation and its elemental constituents often converge on the target memory appropriate to the task. In such cases, there is no particular advantage to having both elemental and configural associations. This distinction becomes important when the representations of the elements are involved in several associations, only one of which is appropriate to the specific task.

To illustrate this problem, figure 2, top, shows how the transswitching discrimination problem just described, $C1[A+/B-]$ and $C2[A-/B+]$, might be represented in a memory system that only can be cued by elemental associations. Note that the representation of each element, *a* and *b*, and the two contexts, *c*1 and *c*2, have associations with the representation of the unconditioned stimulus (us) and its absence ($\overline{us}$). There is no way for these representations, either acting alone or in algebraic combination (e.g., $c1+a$ or $c2+b$) to sort the *conflicting memories* associated with *a* and *b* and selectively retrieve the memories that satisfy the demands of the task. So it is impossible for a subject having only elemental associations to solve the transswitching problem. In contrast to the conflicting memories activated by elemental associations, configural associations, representing the conjunction of *C1* and *A* [*c*1a], *C1* and *B* [*c*1b], *C2* and *A* [*c*2a], and *C2* and *B* [*c*2b], *selectively* activate the memories appropriate to the task (see figure 2, bottom).

Jerry W. Rudy and Robert J. Sutherland

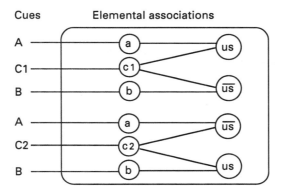

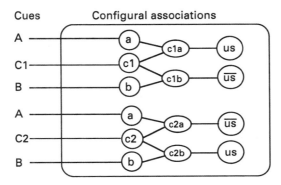

Figure 2   The top panel shows the set of elemental associations that could result when a subject learns the transswitching problem (see text for a description of the problem). Note that each of the elements *c1*, *a*, and *b* become associated with both the unconditioned stimulus present (us) and the unconditioned stimulus absent ($\overline{us}$). So there is no combination of elemental associations that would selectively activate us or $\overline{us}$. The bottom panel shows the set of configural associations that could result: *c1a*, *c1b*, *c2a*, and *c2b*. Note that each configural representation is selectively associated with either us or $\overline{us}$.

2.2   Specifying the Task Demands

A key difference between memory performance that is closed to task-irrelevant associations and memory performance that is open is that the former depends upon the acquisition of configural associations but an open system operates according to the rules of elemental associations. For this position to be useful, however, one has to sort out the various tasks used for studying memory according to whether they can be accomplished by elemental associations or require configural associations. One way to approach this issue is to describe a *continuum of retrieval-cue ambiguity* that represents the degree to which the set of retrieval cues appropriate to a task contains elements that are *only* connected to the task-appropriate target memory. Such a continuum would be anchored on one end by tasks whose retrieval-cue sets contain *no* ambiguous elements and at the other end by tasks whose retrieval-cue sets contain *all* ambiguous elements, each connected with at least two conflicting memories. An elemental-association system can perform tasks that contain no ambiguous retrieval cues, but as the ambiguity of the set of retrieval cues increases, successful task performance increasingly depends on the acquisition of configural associations.

An example of a task with a relatively unambiguous cue set is a Pavlovian discrimination in which one conditioned stimulus, *A*, always is paired with the unconditioned stimulus and another, *B*, never is paired with the unconditioned stimulus. *A*'s representation would be connected only to the representation of the unconditioned stimulus (*a*-us), and *B*'s would be connected only with the representation of no unconditioned stimulus (*b*-$\overline{\text{us}}$). This task could be solved by elemental associations. An example of a task that has a completely ambiguous retrieval-cue set would be the *transswitching* problem previously discussed. Correct performance on this problem requires configural associations, as noted (see figure 2).

Most tasks fall somewhere in the middle on the retrieval-cue ambiguity continuum: the relevant retrieval-cue set contains some elements that are ambiguous and others that are not. One can easily generate Pavlovian discrimination problems that have this characteristic. One example takes the form $AX \rightarrow$ US and $BX \rightarrow$ no US. Note the *A* and *B* elements are unambiguous but the common element *X* is associated with both the US and its absence. Another example is sometimes called the *feature-positive* problem. It has the form $AX \rightarrow$ US and $X \rightarrow$ no US. Again, *X* is involved in two connections (*x*-us and *x*-$\overline{\text{us}}$), but *A* is involved in only one association.

If the subject's preexperimental history is considered, the paired-associates task, often used with people, has a similar property. The subject is instructed to associate pairs of words (e.g., *box-spoon*, *pen-glove*), so when presented the stimulus member of the pair (*box*), the subject is to give the response member (*spoon*). Although each stimulus member of the pair is associated with only one response word in the list, it also has preexperimental associations with other words. If the preexperimental associations of a word are unrelated to the ones established during the experiment, then that word is an ambiguous retrieval cue for other words in the list.

Tasks that fall in the middle of the continuum of retrieval-cue ambiguity are somewhat problematic because in principle the task-appropriate memories can be retrieved by the sum of elemental associations. In the feature-positive discrimination mentioned above, *X* is involved in two associations (*x*-us, *x*-$\overline{\text{us}}$), but *A* is involved in only one (*a*-us). So by summation, the retrieval set *AX* should be more likely to activate the representation of the unconditioned stimulus than should *X* alone. Although intermediate tasks permit an elemental-association solution, the problem is that configural-cue retrieval might still be more adaptive. We do not know much about the variables that encourage the subject to use configural cuing even when it is unnecessary to do so, but there is evidence that they do (see Alvarado & Rudy, 1992).

3 OPENING THE SYSTEM: THE IMPORTANCE OF HIPPOCAMPAL-SYSTEM DYSFUNCTION

The study of organismic variables has played an important role in shaping much contemporary thinking about memory. Such studies usually take the form of comparing how organisms that differ on some dimension (such as age, degree, or location of brain damage) perform on two or more memory tasks. This organism × task analysis (Gollin, 1965; Rudy, 1991) often yields an interaction where, in comparison with the appropriate control, the subject with brain damage is impaired on some memory task but not on others. To account for this pattern of spared and impaired performance, a number of *multiple memory systems* schemes have been proposed (see Squire, 1987, p. 169). To mention just a few examples, there is Graf and Schacter's (1985) distinction between explicit and implicit memory; Squire and Cohen's distinction between declarative and procedural memory (Squire & Cohen, 1984; Squire, 1987); Tulving's (1985) distinction between procedural, semantic, and Episodic memory; and O'Keefe and Nadel's (1978) distinction between taxon and locale systems.

Some of the findings that have generated these taxonomies might be understood as reflecting task demands that can be met by an open system supporting only elemental associations, versus other task demands that require a closed system involving configural associations. The value of this approach can be illustrated by applying it to some of the more prominent findings that have contributed to the multiple-memory-systems approach.

Since Milner's (1959, 1970) classic studies of humans with temporal lobe damage, it has become generally accepted that the hippocampal system plays an important role in learning and memory. Rats, monkeys, and people with damage to this region of the brain show a pattern of spared and impaired performance when tested on a range of tasks that has encouraged a multiple-memory-systems approach (for reviews, see Squire & Cohen, 1984; Squire, 1987; O'Keefe & Nadel, 1978; Sutherland & Rudy, 1989). We proposed the theory of elemental versus configural associations as a way to integrate some of this literature (Sutherland & Rudy, 1989). We suggested that in many instances where animals with damage to the hippocampal system show impaired performance, the tasks that revealed the impairment required configural associations. So in the broader context of Luria's memory-coherence perspective, animals with damage to the hippocampal system have to solve problems with the operating features of an open memory system. We will mention just a couple of examples to illustrate the application of our theory to this literature.

3.1 Application to Animal Studies

Rats with damage to the hippocampal system are severely impaired on some kinds of place-learning tasks. Consider for example, the water-escape task

(Morris, 1981), which requires a rat to find an escape platform located in a circular pool of water. In *place-learning* versions of the task, the animal is required to learn the spatial location of an escape platform that is hidden beneath the surface of the water. To do this the animal needs to learn the location of the platform in relationship to the distal cues located outside of the swimming pool. In a *cued-learning* version, the platform is visible, and all the animal has to learn is to swim directly to it. Normal rats easily solve both problems (Morris, 1981). Animals with damage to the hippocampal system are severely impaired on the place-learning task but have little difficulty in learning to find a visible platform (Morris, Garrud, Rawlins, & O'Keefe, 1982; Sutherland, Kolb, & Whishaw, 1982; Sutherland & Rudy, 1988).

O'Keefe and Nadel (1978) have argued that impaired place learning produced by hippocampal damage reflects the loss of spatial-mapping processes that are the special function of the hippocampal system. However, according to our analysis, place learning is impaired because if an animal is required to find the hidden platform from several starting locations in the pool, then the relation of each distal cue to the platform location is ambiguous. The location of the platform is unambiguous only if the animal can construct a configural representation of the distal cues and its starting location. In contrast, there is nothing ambiguous about the location of the visible platform. So elemental associations are sufficient to guide performance in the cued task.

Other findings from our laboratories provide support for the view that damage to the hippocampal system opens the memory system, because associations involving configural representations are not available to the subject (e.g., Alvarado & Rudy, 1989; Rudy & Sutherland, 1989; Sutherland, McDonald, et al., 1989; Sutherland & McDonald, 1990). For instance, one set of studies examined the effect of damage to the hippocampal system on the acquisition and retention of what is called the *negative-patterning* discrimination problem (Woodbury, 1943). The subject is rewarded for responding when either a light or tone (L+ and T+) is presented but is not rewarded when a compound stimulus composed of the light and tone (LT−) is presented. This problem requires the animal to respond to the tone and light elements but not respond to the tone and light compound. Because the combined associative strengths of the elements presented in a compound can never be less than their individual strengths, elemental associations cannot provide a basis for a differential response. So differential responses critically depend on associations involving configural representations of the conjunction of the tone and light. Animals with damage to the hippocampal system failed to solve the negative patterning problem, and animals that had learned it did not retain the solution after their hippocampal system was damaged. Yet these same animals did learn a discrimination that only required elemental associations. That is to say, they learned to respond in the presence of the light but not to respond in the presence of the tone (Rudy & Sutherland, 1989).

3.2   Application to Human Amnesia

It is important to consider how our position relates to the memory performance of people with damage to the hippocampal system. Patient R.B.,
described by Zola-Morgan, Squire, and Amaral (1986), is the best case of selective damage to the hippocampal system that has been reported. A postmor-
tem histology of R.B. revealed a circumscribed bilateral lesion involving the
entire CA1 field of the hippocampus but very little other pathology. Formal
tests of R.B.'s memory included paired-associate learning with pairs of *unrelated* words, story recall (R.B. was read a short passage of prose and asked to
recall it about 10 minutes later), word recall after twice hearing a list of 10
words, and word recognition 20 minutes after being presented a list of 36
words. Compared to control subjects, R.B. performed poorly on all of these
assessments of his memory.

R.B.'s performance can be understood as reflecting an open memory system, one that cannot support configural associations. The four tasks all use
material (words) with which the subject has an extensive pretest experience,
and so their representations are already embedded in a rich associative network. The subject's basic problem in these tasks is distinguishing between the
newly acquired and *preexisting* memory traces involving the same items. This
problem is obvious for paired-associate learning involving unrelated words
because one element of the retrieval-cue complex (the stimulus member of a
pair) most likely has strong preexperimental associations with other words.
This task is relatively easy for normal subjects because they can construct
configural representations of the context in which the learning occurred and
each stimulus word that can become associated with the appropriate response
word. Configural associations then constrain the retrieval process and isolate
task-appropriate memories from inappropriate memories also associated with
the stimulus words of the pairs. R.B. has a damaged hippocampus and, in our
view, cannot use configural associations. So he is impaired on the paired-
associate learning task.

R.B. performed poorly on the word-recall task for similar reasons. The task
is to recall just those words experienced in the experimental context. In this
task a word to be recalled is both a target memory and a retrieval cue for some
other word in the list. Again, the problem is to prevent interference that
would result if irrelevant preexisting associations involving the list words are
activated. Such activation is reduced in normal subjects, whose memory systems can retrieve information using configural representations of the conjunction of the cues that define the context and the individual words in the
list. R.B.'s memory system cannot support configural associations, so he is
impaired.

Since words and interword relationships are the target memories when the
subject is asked to recall story passages for reasons already mentioned, configural associations should greatly enhance performance on this task. So R.B.

should also be impaired in recalling stories. Word recognition should also be better if the memory system is closed and can support configural associations. The target memories are words, but in this case the subject has to discriminate between words that occur in a specific experimental context and words not experienced in that context. Normal people do this by storing a configural representation of list words and the context during acquisition, which is then activated on the test trial. R.B. can't do this.

To summarize, amnesics like R.B. differ from normal people in how they can combine the available cues at the time of learning and retrieval. Normal people can combine the associative strengths of these cues to activate a target memory, but they also have available unique configural representations of the conjunction of the set of cues present during acquisition, which can constrain the process. We suggest that in the absence of an intact hippocampal system, R.B. can only use linear combinations of retrieval cues.

There is a potential weakness in our analysis of R.B.'s impairments. The tasks we just analyzed must be classified as belonging to the intermediate category on the continuum of retrieval-cue ambiguity, previously described. So elemental associations, together with a linear-combination rule, in principle should permit a solution to these tasks. This being the case, our analysis of R.B. impairments has a distinct post-hoc flavor because, a priori, it is not clear that he should be impaired on these tasks. In fact, we believe that had R.B. been given sufficient training, his performance of these tasks would have approached those of normal people (but obviously by a different route). For example, with enough repetitions, the summed associative strengths of the context cues and stimulus terms of the paired associations tasks would be sufficient to retrieve the correct target response words, even against a background of irrelevant associations.

Some might view our theory as being ambiguous when applied to the above tasks. A virtue of our theory, however, is that it also predicts that there are certain memory problems that cannot be solved by people who, like R.B., have extensive bilateral damage to the hippocampal system. Included in this category of problems are simple variations of commonly used memory tests. For example, suppose that an eight-item list of paired associates is constructed from only four stimulus words (S_1, S_2, S_3, and S_4) and four response words (R_1, R_2, R_3, and R_4), so that each stimulus term is paired with two response terms (e.g., S_1-R_1, S_1-R_2, S_2-R_1, and S_2-R_2). The specific pairs would be presented against one of two distinct contexts or backgrounds, such as on a red card or a blue card. So, for example, the S_1-R_1 and S_2-R_2 pairs are always presented on a red (R) card and the S_1-R_2 and S_2-R_1 pairs are presented on a blue (B) card.

This problem is analogous to the transswitching problem used with animals, described at the beginning of this chapter. There is no elemental-association solution to this problem because both color contexts and all stimulus elements are involved in conflicting associations with the response terms. Yet this problem does allow a configural-association solution. For example, the configural representations of the conjunction of red and S_1 and blue and S_1 would selectively retrieve the correct response, $[RS_1] \rightarrow R_1$ and $[BS_1] \rightarrow R_2$. Normal subjects should learn this list of conflicting associations, but patients with extensive damage to the hippocampal system, like R.B., should find the problem impossible.

Our theoretical analysis also implies that one can construct a similar problem from the same materials that patients like R.B., if given enough trials, can solve. Again, for example, the task would be an eight-item list of paired associates, constructed from two contexts and four stimulus terms. But in this task, there are *eight* response terms. So, again, the four stimulus terms would be paired equally often with two different response terms, but the set $\{S_1\text{-}R_1, S_2\text{-}R_2, S_3\text{-}R_3, S_4\text{-}R_4\}$ would occur only against a red background, and the set $\{S_1\text{-}R_5, S_2\text{-}R_6, S_3\text{-}R_7, S_4\text{-}R_8\}$ would only occur against a blue background. This arrangement permits an elemental-association solution, because, although each stimulus term is involved in two conflicting associations (e.g., $S_1\text{-}R_1$ and $S_1\text{-}R_5$), the two contexts are selectively associated with only one set of the response terms. For example, red occurs only with R_1, R_2, R_3, and R_4. With sufficient training, the two context cues would build up enough associative strength to their respective response terms so that when combined with the stimulus term (e.g., $R + S_1$), the correct response could be differentially retrieved (e.g., R_1 and not R_5).

Reported cases like R.B. are not common. Memory disorders typically result from less circumscribed brain damage, such as that associated with Korsakoff's syndrome or encephalitis. Nevertheless, such amnesics also are impaired on many of the same tasks that we have just discussed in relationship to R.B. (see Squire, 1987; Squire, Shimamura, & Amaral, 1989). We would offer the same explanation of their impairments as we did for R.B.'s. Their memory systems are open because they can no longer support the formation of and retrieval by configural associations.

4 SOME COMMON GROUND

Our position shares important common ground with other views presented in this volume and elsewhere (Wickelgren, 1979). Like many others, we embrace the idea that multiple memory systems underlie the effects of experience on behavior. We also accept as a starting point that some systems can perform their operations in the absence of a normally functioning hippocampal system but that one system depends importantly on a functional hippocampal system to do its job.

Luria's memory-coherence perspective focused on the exceptional ability of normal subjects to function in the face of potential interference and on how brain damage markedly increases susceptibility to interference. We suggested that a primary consequence of the operation of the hippocampal-dependent memory system is that it *reduces interference*. Several contributors to this volume make a similar point. For example, Nadel (1992, this volume), in describing the hippocampal-dependent locale system (O'Keefe & Nadel, 1978), said "Locale learning is assumed to yield memory representations that are less prone to interference effects than are those representations formed in the process of taxon learning" (Nadel, 1992, p. 182). Olton and Shapiro, devoting considerable space to the problem of interference, write, "On the basis of electrophysiological, neurochemical, behavioral, and computational analysis of hippocampal function, we suggest that its major role is the reduction of interference" (1992, p. 200; see also Shapiro and Olton, this volume). The interference problem also has figured prominently in other theories on the role of the hippocampal system in memory (e.g., Hirsh, 1974, 1980; Wickelgren, 1979).

We suggest that the hippocampal system reduces interference by supporting the acquisition of configural associations. In various forms, the idea of a relational representational system that codes for the *co-occurrence* of independent stimulus elements, features, or attributes is important to several other contributions to this volume. A shared ingredient is an appreciation that a system that can store information provided by the conjunction of stimuli has considerable power in reducing interference over a system that cannot. For example, O'Keefe and Nadel's locale system (see Nadel, 1992) provides for the uniqueness of a memory because it stores relational information in a maplike format, where the map is composed of a set of place representations connected together according to the rules that represent distances and directions among them (O'Keefe & Nadel, 1978). Eichenbaum (1992, this volume) also proposed that the hippocampal formation supports a relational-representational system.

Johnson (1992) did not focus specifically on the problem of interference, but she noted that the problem of how cues become compounded, configured, or related is fundamental to understanding the process of *recollecting* autobiographic personal experiences (see also Johnson & Chalfonte, this volume). She devoted much of her effort to characterizing the processes by which such relational units get established. Metcalfe, Cottrell, and Mencl (1992; also Metcalfe et al., this volume) investigated how four different models of computational memory deal with the findings that Hayman and Tulving (1989) generated in their study of explicit and implicit memory tasks. Although Metcalfe et al. (1992) did not use the terms configural and elemental, their conclusions are certainly in keeping with these ideas. They concluded that only the models that "have some inherent mechanism that fuses or glues the elements together" (1992, p. 297) could generate the pattern of results that Hayman and Tulving obtained for their explicit memory task. Models that did not bind the elements together generated the data pattern Hayman and Tulving found with the implicit task. Human amnesics of various etiologies are often characterized as unable to recollect personal experiences (see Squire, 1987, this volume). Moreover, Graf and Schacter (1985) proposed that it is the explicit memory system that is impaired in amnesics, whereas their implicit system(s) is intact.

Here we have a remarkable point of convergence. Theorists concerned with how animals perform in the face of ambiguous retrieval cues, navigate in space, or preserve the uniqueness of a memory emphasize a key role for some form of a configural/relational process in reducing interference. Other theorists point to the importance of a configural or cue-binding process for how people recollect autobiographical experiences and perform on other explicit memory tasks. Such convergence from diverse sources suggest that some fundamental understanding of the operating characteristics of the memory system that depends on the hippocampal formation is at hand. This memory system enables us to construct representations of the joint occurrence of otherwise independent features of the environment. This property is important because it contributes to our success in reducing interference and recollecting our past.

5 WHAT ABOUT FLEXIBILITY?

Several contributors suggested that the hippocampal-dependent system gives memory performance flexibility. Eichenbaum (1992, this volume), for example, in offering a concept of declarative memory that he hopes can be meaningfully applied to animals, uses the term "representational flexibility." Squire (1992, this volume) adopted a similar position in characterizing the human declarative memory system: "Declarative memory is fast, accessible to conscious recollection, and is flexible, i.e., available to multiple response systems" (1992, p. 237). An important common point for both Eichenbaum and Squire is that the hippocampal-dependent system permits stored information to be adaptively applied to *novel* situations. Eichenbaum suggests that representational flexibility "is a quality that permits inferential use of memories in novel situations" (1992, p. 218). Although this is an intuitively appealing idea, we don't think that it is the best way to characterize the system, nor do we think that the supporting data are convincing.

In support of their concept of flexibility, both Eichenbaum and Squire discuss an experiment by Eichenbaum, Mathews, and Cohen (1989). In this study, intact rats and rats with damage to the hippocampal system solved two simultaneous odor discriminations. In one problem (*AB*), odor *A* was the correct (rewarded) stimulus, and *B* was the incorrect stimulus; in the second problem (*CD*), *C* was correct, and *D* was incorrect. After solving the two problems, the subjects were given occasional probe trials with two novel problems: *A* was presented with *D* (*AD*), and *C* was presented with *B* (*CB*). Normal animals transferred correctly to the new problems, they most often chose *A* and *C*. In contrast, the animals with damage to the hippocampal system chose randomly on the probe trials. The transfer performance of controls was interpreted as reflecting the flexible nature of hippocampal-dependent memory, the ability to support transfer to novel problems. Eichenbanm and Squire interpreted the chance behavior of the damaged animals as reflecting the absence of flexibility.

Before the reader accepts Eichenbaum and Squire's interpretation, it should be pointed out that most other theories would predict that animals with hippocampal-system damage *would transfer* their solutions to the *AD* and *CB* probe problems. For example, the elemental association system that, we propose, still functions after damage to the hippocampal system would store a set of independent associations between the elements *A*, *B*, *C*, and *D* and trial outcomes, and choice behavior would then be based on the relative excitatory strengths of the stimulus elements. So *A* and *C* should always be chosen over *B* and *D*. The same could be said for O'Keefe and Nadel's (1978) taxon system and Hirsh's performance system. As best as we can tell, even the hippocampal-independent memory system that Eichenbaum (1992, this volume) described should also support such transfer. On our view, there is a more appropriate interpretation of the data of Eichenbaum et al. (1989).

We suspect that Eichenbaum and Squire may have misinterpreted the data, but to understand a potential source of error, it is necessary to provide more information about the task Eichenbaum et al. (1989) used and how the animals solved the problems. On a choice trial the two odors streamed out of two adjacent ports. A nose poke at the correct port generated a reward; a poke at the incorrect port did not. According to Eichenbaum (1992), normal rats and rats with damage to the hippocampal system solved the original problems differently. Normal animals "consistently approached and sampled one odor port first, then either performed a nose poke there, or approached and sampled the other odor port. In contrast, the animals with damage to the hippocampal system did not preferentially sample a port. They "sampled the entire compound at once" (Eichenbaum, 1992, p. 222).

That animals with damage to the hippocampal system and control animals used different sampling strategies during original learning seriously compromises the value of the novel probe trials. Given the strategy the normal animals used, it is questionable whether the probe trials actually constituted a novel test. On trials when the correct odor appeared at the port that was sampled first, the animal would simply initiate a nose poke and consume the reward. It would not even encounter the other odor, and *no novel combination would be experienced*. On the other hand, the sampling strategy of the animals with damage to the hippocampal system both made the original problems (*AB* and *CD*) more difficult to learn and insured that they would encounter different and novel odor combinations on the probe trials. So the strategy the control animals used minimized their being exposed to novel odor combinations during probe trials, but the strategy used by the animals with damage to the hippocampal system maximized their encountering unfamiliar odor mixtures or blends generated by the new odor combinations. It is difficult to see how these data indicate that the controls have flexible memory representation but animals with damage to the hippocampal system do not. The behavioral differences Eichenbaum et al. (1989) obtained on the probe trials are interpreted more simply as resulting from the different behavioral strategies they learned to solve the original problems. Data supporting the idea that damage to the hippocampal system makes unavailable a flexible memory system that supports inferences will have to come from different memory tasks.

Eichenbaum (1992, this volume) and Squire (1992, this volume) also interpreted an experiment by Eichenbaum, Stewart, and Morris (1990) as providing support for the idea of a flexible memory system. Eichenbaum et al. (1990) trained rats to find a submerged platform in a Morris water task. The unique feature of this experiment was that on each trial, the animals were started from the same location. Under these conditions, the animals with damage to the hippocampal system eventually escaped to the platform as quickly as control animals. The evidence for flexibility in the hippocampal-dependent memories is based on an interpretation of performance on a probe trial when the animals were started from a new location. Normal rats still swam straight to the platform, but animals with damage to the hippocampal system did not. That the control animals went straight to the platform from a *novel* starting point is interpreted as indicating the flexibility of hippocampal-dependent memories. Apparently, only control rats had the ability to apply old knowledge to new situations.

The problem with the Eichenbaum et al. (1990) study is that the probe trial clearly is not a novel transfer task. The subjects were started from only one location during training, but this does not mean that they only learned to approach the platform from that location. The animals' experience is constrained by the experimenter's wishes only at the start location. Once the rat is released it goes wherever it pleases and can learn to approach the platform from many locations. So before one can conclude that the animals in the Eichenbaum et al. (1990) experiment transferred old knowledge to a novel situation, it necessary to restrict *both* the starting location and the animals' swim paths. Sutherland, Chew, Baker, and Linggard (1987) conducted just such an experiment. When their animals were released from a novel starting point, they *did not swim* directly to the platform. They did not show immediate transfer to the new test situation. Sutherland et al. (1987) did, however, obtain the result of Eichenbaum et al. (1990) when they restricted *only* the animals starting location; the animals swam straight to the platform on the test trial. The simplest explanation of these findings is that even though animals are started from only one location, when their swimming behavior is not constrained, they learn to approach the platform from multiple directions. For these animals, a probe trial from a new starting location is novel only from the experimenter's perspective and probably was only measuring old knowledge in the same old situation.

The control animals and animals with damage to the hippocampal system in the Eichenbaum et al. (1990) study certainly acquired different kinds of information. Control animals stored information about *topographical relationships* among many cues. Animals with damage to the hippocampal system stored information about approaching a *particular cue*. Yet, in our opinion, there is absolutely no evidence that the memories themselves differed in flexibility.

We think the hippocampal-dependent memory system does allow for a certain flexibility in behavior, but we would characterize it differently than Eichenbaum (1992, this volume) and Squire (1992, this volume). Eichenbaum and Squire want to have the hippocampal circuitry be the site of a cognitive operation that compares memories. Such mnemonic comparison permits inferences to be reached. In contrast, we think the flexibility afforded by the hippocampal system *resides in the content* that is stored. The hippocampal system supports the acquisition of configural associations, and behavioral flexibility emerges because of the availability of this memory system. It's contribution is seen in many situations, especially when the subject's prior experiences *conflict* with the demands of a new task. A subject with damage to the hippocampal system and who can only learn elemental associations is inflexible because the associative strengths of the independent retrieval cues would have to change. A subject who can use configural associations can be flexible because the configural representation of the retrieval cues appropriate to the new task can be associated uniquely to relevant memory items. Interference from potentially conflicting past experiences is reduced by the distinctiveness of prior versus current configural representations. So subjects appear to be flexible because the interference produced by prior experience is reduced, and learning to solve the new task proceeds more quickly.

6   WHAT ABOUT SPATIAL MAPS?

O'Keefe and Nadel's (1978) spatial-mapping theory of the hippocampal-dependent memory system has been notably successful. The essence of their theory, as noted above, is that the hippocampal formation provides for the acquisition of a particular kind of relational information, spatial relations. This is the fundamental property of their *locale system*. It stores information about environments in a maplike format. The "strong" version of the theory asserts that performance will be impaired *only* on memory tasks that normally are solved by acquiring spatial maps. Their theory gains support from the many reports that rats with damage to the hippocampal system are impaired on the kind of place-learning tasks that fit O'Keefe and Nadel's requirement for needing a locale system (Morris et al., 1982; Okaichi, 1987; Sutherland et al., 1982; O'Keefe et al., 1975; Sutherland & Rudy, 1988).

The finding that animals are impaired on place-learning tasks is consistent with spatial mapping theory. Yet these demonstrations alone do not force one to accept O'Keefe and Nadel's (1978) explanation of the impairment. Their explanation is that damage to the hippocampal formation eliminates an explicitly topographical memory representation of the environment, a kind of relational information that is necessarily spatial. There are other accounts. Spatial mapping could be a specific instance of the *more general* kind of configural representations afforded by hippocampal circuitry. Place learning could be impaired precisely because, viewed alone, the significance of each independent distal cue (its relation to the goal) is ambiguous. The significance of a given cue for guidance necessarily depends on its relationship to some other element of the environment, the animal's starting location, and other distal cues (see McNaughton, 1989).

The fundamental problem with spatial-mapping theory is that it predicts that only tasks that have a spatial-mapping requirement should require a functional hippocampal system. So the weakness in the "strong" theory is revealed by studies that show that animals and people are impaired on tasks that do not appear to be solved by learning a spatial map. For example, recall that patient R.B., who had selective damage to the hippocampus, was impaired in story recall, word recall, paired-associate learning, and recognition memory (Zola-Morgan et al., 1986). It is not apparent how these tasks depend on a memory system that stores only spatial relations. In fact, Nadel (1992) concedes that such data cannot be explained by the "strong" version of the theory. It is the inability of spatial-mapping theory to explain why animals with damage to the hippocampal system are impaired on some nonspatial tasks that motivated configural-association theory (see Sutherland & Rudy, 1989, 1991).

In testing configural theory, we have found additional *nonspatial* tasks on which animals with damage to the hippocampal system are impaired. We already mentioned the *negative-patterning* problem. Impaired performance on this problem has now been found in experiments by Rudy and Sutherland (1989); Sutherland and McDonald (1990); Sutherland, McDonald, et al. (1989); and Sutherland and Palmer (1992). A second example is called the *transverse-patterning* problem (see Alvarado & Rudy, 1989). In this task the animal is required ultimately to solve three simultaneous visual discriminations. In phase 1, the subject has to chose between a black (B) card and a white (W) card, and black is correct. In phase 2, a new problem is introduced. The choice is between a white card and a striped (S) card, and the white card is correct. The third problem is introduced in phase 3. The choice is between the striped card and the black card, and the striped card is correct. Because the significance of each element (B, W, S) is ambiguous, the animal can only solve the three problems given in phase 3 (B+ versus W−, W+ versus S−, S+ versus B−) by constructing a configural representation of the stimulus patterns [BW], [WS], and [SB], but the other two phases of the problem permit an elemental solution. Control animals solved all three phases of the problem, but animals with damage to the hippocampal formation only solved phase 1 (B+ versus W−) and phase 2 (B+ versus W−, W+ versus S−) (Alvarado and Rudy, 1989).

A third example comes from a problem involving a transswitching conditional discrimination (Sutherland, McDonald et al., 1989). In this case, rats had to choose between two stimulus elements, a black goal box and a white goal box. On trials in which the start box was illuminated, black was correct and white was incorrect (B+ versus W−), but on trials when the start box was dark, the significance of the elements was reversed (W+ versus B−). Note there is no elemental solution to this problem, because the significance of the elements is ambiguous. Yet the problem permits a configural-association solution. Again, control animals solved the problem, but animals with damage to the hippocampal formation did not.

These examples do not exhaust the list of findings demonstrating that animals and people with hippocampal damage are impaired on nonspatial memory tasks (see Cave & Squire, 1991), but they do illustrate the kind of data that pose a serious problem for the "strong" form of spatial mapping theory. If there is a compelling argument about why these discrimination problems (and not others on which performance is not impaired by damage to the hippocampal formation) depend upon the operation of a spatial-mapping memory system, it is yet to be made.

Perhaps for this reason, there has been some drift away from the "strong" version of spatial mapping theory. In some of his more recent papers, Nadel (1991, 1992) appears to open the door to the hippocampal formation also being necessary for storing the timing of events and/or storing nonspatial (at least linguistic) information in a relational representation. O'Keefe (1991) has amended his version to allow that normal performance in nonspatial configural/relational memory problems may depend critically on hippocampal circuitry in some situations. We suspect that as Nadel and O'Keefe are forced to deal with the number of *exceptions to the rule of space* that exist and will emerge (Sutherland & Rudy, 1991), they will be forced to drift even farther toward a less restrictive, more general theory about the kind of relational information that the hippocampal formation allows animals to acquire.

7 SOME POTENTIAL PROBLEMS FOR CONFIGURAL THEORY

Many theorists, including ourselves, are becoming persuaded that an important general property of the hippocampal-dependent memory system is that it provides for some form of a configural, relational, cue-binding, or chunking process. Yet Nadel (1992, this volume), after considering two versions of this approach, ours (Sutherland and Rudy, 1989) and Cohen and Eichenbaum's (1991), concluded that they were not worth pursuing. As he put it, "The problem with the configural approach, regardless of whose version of it one discusses, is that what is new about it is seemingly wrong and what is right about it is not new" (Nadel, 1992, p. 185).

Nadel's dismissal of *all* configural/relational theories (except the maplike relational theory of O'Keefe and Nadel, 1978) rests in large part on a reading of the literature that is beginning to emerge to evaluate configural association theory. He refers to several papers that report data appearing to go against the theory (Davidson & Jarrard, 1989; Jarrard & Davidson, 1991; Gallagher & Holland, 1992). In these papers, the authors failed to find differences between animals with damage to the hippocampal system and control animals on tasks they assumed would require the contribution of configural associations. A closer look at these reports, however, suggests that it is premature to abandon a general approach to configural theory.

In two of these experiments (Davidson & Jarrard, 1989; Jarrard & Davidson, 1991), a Pavlovian conditioning problem was constructed so that when two stimuli, B and A, were presented in sequence, the unconditioned stimulus was presented ($B \rightarrow A \rightarrow US$), but when A occurred alone, the unconditioned stimulus was omitted ($A \rightarrow$ no US). Evidence that the animal learned the discrimination is provided if the animal responds to A more when it is preceded by B than when A occurs alone. Animals could use configural associations to solve this problem, but as we pointed out both in response to Jarrard and Davidson (1991) (Rudy & Sutherland, 1992) and in our first paper on configural-association theory (Sutherland & Rudy, 1989), animals can use either elemental associations or configural associations to solve this problem. An elemental-association solution is possible because the animal can associate the B stimulus directly with the unconditioned stimulus. This B-US association can then influence responding to A in at least three ways. One, it can provide a source of excitation that sums with that acquired by A. This would mean that the net excitatory strength of the serial $B \rightarrow A$ compound is greater than that of A alone. Two, as Rescorla (1985) suggests B could acquire the power to lower the threshold value for A's activating the unconditioned-stimulus representation. Three, differential responses in the presence of $B \rightarrow A$, compared to A alone, could be based solely on B's association with the unconditioned stimulus.

Jarrard and Davidson (1991) found no difference between animals with damage to the hippocampal system and control animals on this problem, and they concluded that these data scored against configural-association theory. Note, however, that this result only counts against configural theory if their control animals solved the problem using configural associations. If they solved the problem using elemental associations, then Jarrard and Davidson's data not only do not count against configural theory, they provide support for it. Fortunately, Jarrard and Davidson reported the results of a transfer test that revealed how their animals solved the problem. On the basis of this transfer test, they concluded that their animals *did not use configural associations to solve the problem.* In their words, "Hence it did not appear that the performance of controls or ibotenic rats was based on learning about configural cues" (Jarrard & Davidson, 1991, p. 113). Given this conclusion, we simply cannot understand why either Nadel (1992) or Jarrard and Davidson (1991) offer these data as evidence against configural-association theory. The theory may ultimately be shown to have some problems, but it should not be dismissed for the wrong reasons and especially with data that, if anything, support it.

Gallagher and Holland's (1992) result, however, is another matter. Their task did not have an obvious elemental-association solution. Their animals had to solve an operant discrimination of the following form: N+, LT+, T−, LN−. When either a noise (N) or a light-tone compound (LT) was presented, a rat's bar press was rewarded (+), but when just the tone or the light-noise (LN) compound was presented, the bar press was not rewarded. So the rat should respond on N and LT trials and not respond on T and LN trials.

The individual elements were associated equally often with rewarded non-rewarded outcomes, so the solution to the problem requires a functional configural-association system. Gallagher and Holland found no difference between normal rats and rats with damage to the hippocampal formation induced by ibotenic acid injected into the hippocampus.

The Gallagher and Holland findings certainly go against configural theory. Yet we think that it is premature to dismiss the theory on the basis of their findings. First, one of our laboratories (Alvarado & Rudy, 1993) has found that animals with hippocampal damage were impaired on the Gallagher and Holland problem. But our lesions were made by a different neurotoxin: intrahippocampal injections of kainic acid and cochicine. Second, Sutherland's laboratory (Sutherland & Palmer, 1992) has found that hippocampal damage induced by ibotenic acid (used by Gallagher and Holland) impairs performance on the negative patterning problem: $L+$, $T+$, $LT-$. This problem is similar but not identical to the Gallagher and Holland problem. So at this point it is difficult to assess the implications of Gallagher and Holland's findings for configural theory. Whether the conflicting data are a result of anatomical differences resulting from the two types of lesions or due to some unidentified properties of the tasks still has to be determined.

8   SOME NEW SUPPORT FOR CONFIGURAL THEORY

There are some potential problems for configural theory emerging from experimental tests. Yet other recent findings (Kim & Fanselow 1992; Phillips & LeDoux, 1992; Young, Fanselow, & Bohenek, 1992) strongly suggest that the fundamental configural idea is correct. The relevant findings come from a simple paradigm. Normal rats are placed into a conditioning chamber and several minutes later experience several pairings of a tone and a foot shock. When tested the next day, these rats show a conditioned fear response both to the conditioning environment (context) and the tone, even when the tone is tested in a novel environment (e.g., Kim & Fanselow, 1992; Phillips & LeDoux, 1992). Animals with damage to the hippocampal formation, however, only conditioned to the tone; they *failed* to condition to the context.

These findings support configural-association theory because, as Fanselow (1986, 1990) has argued, to condition to the context, the animal has to construct or synthesize what Pavlov (1962) called a *dynamic stereotype*, or, in our terms, a configural representation of the joint occurrence of the elements that compose the context. (More recently, Fanselow, DeCola, & Young, in press, have used the term "configural" to describe the representation of context.) It is this configural representation that gets associated with shock. Without this representation, the animal does not show fear to the conditioning environment. Conditioning to the tone, however, only requires that its representation gets associated with shock. Such conditioning only requires an elemental association.

Jerry W. Rudy and Robert J. Sutherland

Fanselow's (1990) support for the configural interpretation of the normal animal's conditioning to context is provided by his analysis of what is sometimes called the immediate-shock effect (Fanselow, 1986). If animals are given a single strong shock *immediately* after being placed in the conditioning chambers, they fail to show fear of the conditioning context when tested 24 hours later, but they do show fear if they are in the conditioning chambers for *about 2 minutes* before being shocked. Fanselow suggested that animals in the immediate-shock group failed to condition because they did not have time to construct a configural representation of the conditioning context before the shock occurred. He provided support for this interpretation by showing that if 24 hours prior to conditioning, the animals were exposed to the conditioning context for 2 minutes, they would then condition to context even when shock occurred immediately. Presumably, this 2-minute exposure was sufficient to permit the animals to construct the configural representation of the context needed for conditioning when shock occurred immediately after the animal was placed in the chamber.

We have proposed that the construction of configural representations depends on the hippocampal system. Fanselow (1990) has proposed and given evidence that to condition to the context, rats have to construct a configural representation of the stimulus elements of the conditioning chamber. It follows from these two premises that animals with damage to the hippocampal system would fail to condition to the context. So reports that animals with damage to the hippocampal formation fail to show conditioned fear to the context but do show conditioned fear to a single stimulus element strongly supports our hypothesis and related ideas (e.g., Wickelgren, 1979).

A final caveat is worth noting. A priori, it is possible that associating the *independent elements* of the context with the shock unconditioned stimulus is sufficient to support conditioning to context. So we claim only that the impaired context conditioning shown by animals with damage to the hippocampal system *supports* configural theory, because Fanselow (1990) has provided *independent evidence* that normal animals need to construct or synthesize a dynamic stereotype (or in our language, a configural representation of the elements of the context) in order to condition to the context.

9 CONCLUSION: RELATIONSHIPS TO OTHER THEORIES

We began this essay by considering some of the important empirical findings and theoretical views of interest to contemporary students of learning and memory from the memory coherence perspective borrowed from Luria (1979). Our theoretical position in this context is simple. Normally, memories can be retrieved by either *elemental associations* or by *configural associations*, and configural associations provide a powerful basis for maintaining coherent memory. Our contention is that memory coherence is lost when the hippocampal system is damaged, because it is essential to the normal functioning of the configural-association system. Spared memory performance after damage to the hippocampal system reflects the operations of the elemental-association system.

We end the essay by placing our position in historical context and relating it to some of the other important views. The idea that there is more than one learning and memory system is shared among a number of theorists, but Hirsh (1974) and Nadel and O'Keefe (1974) may be the first to suggest that the approach of a dual memory system can be valuable to understanding learning and memory impairments following brain damage in experimental animals. Hirsh distinguished between what he called *performance-line storage* and *memory* (the latter he linked to the hippocampal formation). Mishkin and his colleagues (Mishkin & Petrie, 1984; Mishkin, Malamut, & Bachevalier, 1984) made a similar distinction between *habits* and *memories*, which are subserved by different neural systems. O'Keefe and Nadel (1978), as noted, distinguished between the *taxon* and *locale* memory systems, which also depend differentially on hippocampal function.

Our conception of an elemental-association system that mediates the learning displayed by animals with damage to the hippocampal system does not differ in any important way from Hirsh's *performance line* and Mishkin's *habit system*. Each of these conceptions have evolved from the learning theories of Thorndike (1898), Spence (1936), and Hull (1942).

We trace our views on the configural-association system and the behavioral consequences of damage to the hippocampal system to the important insights of earlier theorists. In particular, the ideas put forth by Hirsh (1980), Mishkin and Petrie (1984), O'Keefe and Nadel (1978), and Wickelgren (1979) have much in common with our conceptualization. These theorists recognized that in some sense the hippocampal system or limbic system is especially critical to tasks that require solutions where the controlling cues consist of *relationships among the stimulus elements*, as opposed to the elemental associations between a stimulus element and a behavior or reward.

O'Keefe and Nadel's (1978) hippocampal-system-dependent *locale system*, as noted, also stores relational, *albeit exclusively spatial*, information. It allows an animal to acquire maplike representations of its environment. Hirsh (1980) suggested that the hippocampal formation permits animals to perform conditional operations, so that the meaning of the same physical stimulus can vary depending on the presence or absence of some other stimulus. Mishkin and Petrie's (1984) view of the limbic-system-dependent *memory system* is almost identical to our configural-association system. Their memory system stores representations of stimulus configurations that can become associated with representations of affective states, environmental places, or behavioral acts (see Mishkin & Petrie, 1984, p. 288).

Wickelgren's (1979) concept of a hippocampal-system-dependent *vertically associative memory*, as distinct from a horizontally associative memory, can be considered the direct predecessor of both Mishkin and Petrie's memory system and our configural-association system. The important feature of his system is that it allows for the process of chunking. Chunking is "a learning process by which a set of nodes representing constituents (components, attributes, features) of a whole comes to be associated to a new node that, thereby, represents the whole chunk" (Wickelgren, 1979). The node representing a chunk is conceptually similar to our concept of a configural association.

One of the most well-known positions advocating multiple memory systems is the view that distinguishes *declarative* and *nondeclarative* memory systems (see Squire, 1992, this volume; Squire & Cohen, 1984). Declarative memory, but not nondeclarative memory, is thought to depend on the hippocampal system. In addition, "Declarative memory is fast, accessible to conscious recollection, and is flexible, i.e., available to multiple response systems. Nondeclarative memory is nonconcious, and it is less flexible, i.e., it provides limited access to response systems not involved in the original learning" (Squire, 1992, p. 237).

It may be instructive to compare other views with this account. As noted above, flexibility, for Squire (1992, this volume) and Eichenbaum (1992, this volume), results because the hippocampal-dependent declarative memory system supports a cognitive operation that performs a comparison among memories. The concept of *flexibility* is central to Hirsh's (1974) performance-line versus memory-system distinction, Mishkin and Petrie's (1984) habit versus memory-system distinction, and O'Keefe and Nadel's (1978) taxon-system versus locale-system view. Each theorist has one system that is said to provide for more flexible performance than is provided by the other system.

In developing the distinction between an elemental and configural association system (Sutherland & Rudy, 1989), we explicitly did not address the flexibility issue. Yet in section 5 of this chapter, we noted that the hippocampal-dependent configural-association system does allow for a certain flexibility *in responding to cues* not present in the elemental-association system. We suggested that flexibility resides in the content that the configural-association system stores. Configural associations allow animals to show superior transfer (flexibility) because such animals do not have to overcome as much interference from prior learning as would animals that only have an elemental-association system. Our view on the flexibility issue is much in the spirit of Hirsh's (1974) view and the view of O'Keefe and Nadel (1978; see also Nadel, 1992, this volume). Flexibility derives from the relational (configural, contextual, system, spatial) storage content of the system, as opposed to a comparator process (Squire, 1992, this volume; Eichenbaum, 1992, this volume).

The issue of access to *conscious recollection* is fundamental to the distinction between declarative and nondeclarative memory systems. Yet our theory and the theories of Hirsh, Mishkin, and O'Keefe and Nadel are silent on this issue, primarily because the theories were developed in large part to address the nonhuman animal literature. To our knowledge, no one has yet come up with any objective way to infer conscious recollection from the behavior of nonverbal organisms. Nevertheless, animals with damage to the hippocampal system are impaired on some behavioral tasks but perform normally on others. So the distinction between conscious and nonconscious recollection does not add anything to our understanding of these phenomena. It is also not clear that the distinction between conscious and unconscious recollection adds anything to our understanding of why human amnesics are impaired on some tasks, such as paired-associate learning and story recall, but not on others, such priming. This problem emerges, in our view, because Squire and his colleagues have not described the processes that subserve conscious recollection, so one cannot specify in advance what properties of a task will make it depend on conscious recollection. Consequently, despite the disclaimer that "the concept of declarative memory is not locked into circularity around the performance of amnesic patients" (Squire, 1992, p. 233; see also this volume), it still has a distinctive post hoc flavor (for a similar view, see Nadel, 1992, p. 183, this volume).

Thus, there are differences between our theory and those just mentioned. However, it is important to end by noting that there is *basic agreement* among the theorists just mentioned and many others (e.g., Eichenbaum, 1992; Gaffan, 1991; Gage, 1985; Hirsh, 1974, 1980; Nadel, 1992; Nadel & Willner, 1980; Nadel, Willner, & Kurz, 1985). They agree that there are at least two memory systems. One system is hippocampal-system-dependent and is critical for storage of relational information. The other systems do not depend on the hippocampal system and do not store relational information. These shared views should provide a strong foundation for future advances in our understanding of memory.

ACKNOWLEDGMENTS

Research reported in this chapter was supported by NSF grant BNS-9008251 to Jerry W. Rudy and grants from the Natural Science and Engineering Research Council, Medical Research Council of Canada, and University of New Mexico to Robert J. Sutherland. Reprint requests should be sent to Jerry W. Rudy, Department of Psychology, CB-345, University of Colorado, Boulder, Colorado 80309.

REFERENCES

Alvarado, M., & Rudy, J. W. (1989). The transverse patterning problem, configural processes, and the hippocampus. *Society for Neuroscience Abstracts, 15,* 610.

Alvarado, M., & Rudy, J. W. (1992). Some properties of configural learning: An investigation of the transverse patterning problem. *Journal of Experimental Psychology: Animal Behavior Processes, 18,* 145–153.

Alvarado, M., & Rudy, J. W. (1993). Configural theory and the hippocampus: Is lesion type critical? Evidence from four tasks. *Society for Neuroscience Abstracts, 19,* 363.

Anderson, J. R., & Bower, G. H. (1973). *Human associative memory.* Washington, DC: Winston and Sons.

Bachevalier, J., & Mishkin, M. (1984). An early and a late developing system for learning and retention in infant monkey. *Behavioral Neuroscience, 98,* 770–778.

Cave, C. & Squire, L. R. (1991). Intact and long-lasting repetition priming in amnesia. *Journal of Experimental Psychology: Learning, Memory, and Cognition, 18,* 509–520.

Cohen, N. J., & Eichenbaum, H. (1991). The theory that wouldn't die: A critical look at the spatial mapping theory of hippocampal function. *Hippocampus, 1,* 265–268.

Davidson, T. L., & Jarrard, L. E. (1989). Retention of concurrent conditional discriminations in rats with ibotenate lesions of the hippocampus. *Psychobiology, 17,* 49–60.

Eichenbaum, H. (1992). The hippocampal system and declarative memory in animals. *Journal of Cognitive Neuroscience, 4*(3), 217–231.

Eichenbaum, H., Mathews, P., & Cohen, N. J. (1989). Further studies of hippocampal representation during odor discrimination learning. *Behavioral Neuroscience, 103,* 1207–1216.

Eichenbaum, H., Stewart, C., & Morris, R. G. M. (1990). Hippocampal representation in spatial learning. *Journal of Neuroscience, 10,* 331–339.

Fanselow, M. S. (1986). Associative vs. topographical accounts of the immediate shock-freezing deficit in rats: Implications for the response selection rules governing species-specific defensive reactions. *Learning and Motivation, 17,* 16–39.

Fanselow, M. S. (1990). Factors governing one-trial contextual conditioning. *Animal Learning and Behavior, 18,* 264–270.

Fanselow, M. S. (1993). Mechanisms responsible for reduced contextual conditioning with massed unsignaled unconditioned stimuli. *Journal of Experimental Psychology: Animal Behavior Processes, 19,* 121–137.

Fanselow, M. S., DeCola, Joseph P., & Young, Stacey L. (1993). Mechanisms responsible for reduced contextual conditioning with massed unsignaled unconditional stimuli. *Journal of Experimental Psychology: Animal Behavior Processes, 19,* 121–137.

Gaffan, D. (1991). Spatial organization of episodic memory. *Hippocampus, 1,* 262–264.

Gage P. D. (1985). Preserved and impaired information processing systems in human bilateral amnesics and infrahuman analogues: Role of hippocampectomy. *Journal of Mind & Behavior, 4,* 515-552.

Gallagher, M., & Holland, P. C. (1992). Preserved configural learning and spatial learning impairment in rats with hippocampal damage. *Hippocampus, 2,* 81–88.

Gollin, E. S. (1965). A developmental approach to learning and cognition. In L. P. Liptsitt & C. C. Spiker. (Eds.), *Advances in child development and infancy* (Vol. 2). New York: Academic Press.

Graf, P., & Schacter, D. L. (1985). Implicit and explicit memory for new associations in normal and amnesic patients. *Journal of Experimental Psychology: Learning, Memory, and Cognition, 11,* 501–518.

Graf, P., Squire, L. R., & Mandler, G. (1984). The information that amnesic patients do not forget. *Journal of Experimental Psychology: Learning, Memory, and Cognition, 10,* 164–178.

Hayman, C. A. G., & Tulving, E. (1989). Is priming in fragment completion based on a "traceless" memory system? *Journal of Experimental Psychology: Learning, Memory, and Cognition, 15,* 941–956.

Hirsh, R. (1974). The hippocampus and contextual retrieval of information from memory: A theory. *Behavioral Biology, 12,* 421–444.

Hirsh, R. (1980). The hippocampus, conditional operations, and cognition. *Physiological Psychology, 8,* 175–182.

Hull, C. L. (1942). *Principles of behavior.* New York: Appleton-Century-Crofts.

Humphreys, M. S., Bain, J. D., & Pike, R. (1989). Different ways to cue a coherent memory system: A theory for episodic, semantic, and procedural tasks. *Psychological Review, 96,* 208–233.

Jarrard, L. E., & Davidson, T. L. (1991). On the hippocampus and learned conditional responding: Effects of aspiration versus ibotenate lesions. *Hippocampus, 1,* 107–118.

Johnson, M. K. (1992). MEM: Mechanisms of recollection. *Journal of Cognitive Neuroscience, 4(3),* 268–280.

Kehoe, E. J., & Gormezano, I. (1980). Configuration and combination laws in conditioning with compound stimuli. *Psychological Bulletin, 87,* 351–378.

Kehoe, E. J., & and Graham, P. (1988). Summation and configuration: Stimulus compounding and negative patterning in the rabbit. *Journal of Experimental Psychology: Animal Behavior Processes, 14,* 320–333.

Kim, J., & Fanselow, M. S. (1992). Modality-specific retrograde amnesia of fear. *Science, 256,* 675–676.

Luria, A. R. (1979). Neuropsychology of complex forms of memory. In L. Nilsson (Ed.), *Perspectives on memory research: Essays in honor of Uppsala University's 500th anniversary.* Hillsdale, NJ: Erlbaum.

McNaughton, B. L. (1989). Neuronal mechanisms for spatial computation and information storage. In L. Nadel, L. Cooper, P. Culicover, & R. M. Harnish. (Eds.), *Neuronal Connections and Mental Computations,* Cambridge: MIT Press.

Metcalfe, J., Cotterell, G. W., & Mencl, W. E. (1992). Cognitive binding: A computational-modeling analysis of a distinction between implicit and explicit memory. *Journal of Cognitive Neuroscience, 4(3),* 289–298.

Milner, B. (1959). The memory defect in bilateral hippocampal lesions. *Psychiatric Research Reports, 11,* 43–52.

Milner, B. (1970). Memory and the medial temporal regions of the brain. In K. P. Pribram & D. E. Broadbent (Eds.), *Biology of memory.* New York: Academic Press.

Mishkin, M., Malamut, B., & Bachevalier, J. (1984). Memories and habits: Two neural systems. In G. Lynch, J. L. McGaugh, & N. Weinberger (Eds.), *Neurobiology of learning and memory.* New York: Guilford Press.

Mishkin, M., & Petrie, H. L. (1984). Memories and habits: Some implications for the analysis of learning and retention. In L. R. Squire & N. Butters (Eds.), *Neuropsychology of memory,* New York: Guilford Press.

Morris, R. G. M. (1981). Spatial localization does not require the presence of local cues. *Learning and Motivation, 12,* 239–260.

Morris, R. G. M., Garrud, P., Rawlins, J. N. P., & O'Keefe, J. (1982). Place navigation in rats with hippocampal lesions. *Nature, 297,* 681–683.

Nadel, L. (1991). The hippocampus and space revisited. *Hippocampus, 1,* 221–229.

Nadel, L. (1992). Multiple memory systems: What and why. *Journal of Cognitive Neuroscience, 4(3),* 179–188.

Nadel, L., & O'Keefe, J. (1974). The hippocampus in pieces and patches: An essay on modes of explanation in physiological psychology. In R. Bellairs & J. Gray (Eds.), *Essays on the nervous system: A festschrift for Professor J. Z. Young,* Oxford: Clarendon Press.

Nadel, L., & Wilner, J. (1980). Context and conditioning: A place for space. *Physiological Psychology, 8,* 218–228.

Nadel, L., Wilner, J., & Kurz, E. (1985). Cognitive maps and environment context. In P. D. Balsam & A. Tomie (Eds.), *Context and learning*. Hillsdale, NJ: Erlbaum.

Okaichi, H. (1987). Performance and dominant strategies on place and cue tasks following hippocampal lesions in rats. *Psychobiology, 15*, 58–63.

O'Keefe, J. (1991). An allocentric spatial model for the hippcampal cognitive map. *Hippocampus, 1*, 230–235.

O'Keefe, J., & Nadel, L. (1978). *The hippocampus as a cognitive map*. Oxford: Clarendon Press.

O'Keefe, J., Nadel, L., Keightly, S., & Kill, D. (1975). Fornix lesions selectively abolish place learning in the rat. *Experimneal Neurology, 48*, 152–166.

Olton, D. S., & Shapiro, M. L. (1992). Mnemonic dissociations: The power of parameters. *Journal of Cognitive Neuroscience, 4*(3), 200–207.

Overman, W. H. (1990). Performance on traditional matching to sample and object discrimination tasks by 12- to 32-month-old children: A developmental progression. *Annals of the New York Academy of Sciences, 608*, 365–394.

Pavlov, I. (1962). *Essays in psychology and psychiatry*. New York: Citadel.

Phillips, R. G., & LeDoux, J. E. (1992). Differential contribution of amygdala and hippocampus to cued and contextual fear conditioning. *Behavioral Neuroscience, 106*(2), 274–285.

Rescorla, R. A. (1972). "Configural" conditioning in discrete-trial bar pressing. *Journal of Comparative and Physiological Psychology, 79*, 307–317.

Rescorla, R. A. (1985). Inhibition and facilitation. In R. R. Miller & N. E. Spear (Eds.), *Information processing in animals: Conditioned inhibition*. Hillsdale, NJ: Erlbaum.

Rescorla, R. A., Durlach, P. J., & Grau, J. W. (1985). Context learning in Pavlovian conditioning. In P. D. Balsam & A. Tomie (Eds.), *Context and learning*. Hillsdale, NJ: Erlbaum.

Rescorla, R. A., & Wagner, A. W. (1972). A theory of Pavlovian conditioning: Variations in the effectiveness of reinforcement and nonreinforcement. In A. H. Black & W. F. Prokasy (Eds.), *Classical conditioning: Vol. 1. Current research and theory*. New York: Appleton-Century-Crofts.

Rudy, J. W. (1991). Elemental and configural associations, the hippocampus, and development. *Developmental Psychobiology, 24*, 219–236.

Rudy, J. W., & Sutherland, R. J. (1989). The hippocampus is necessary for rats to learn and remember configural discriminations. *Behavioral Brain Research, 34*, 97–109.

Rudy, J. W., & Sutherland, R. J. (1992). Wait a minute, Jarrard and Davidson's data support configural theory. *Hippocampus, 2*, 89.

Saavadra, M. (1975). Pavlovian compound conditioning in the rabbit. *Learning and Motivation, 6*, 314–326.

Schacter, D. L. (1985). Priming of old and new knowledge in amnesic patients and normal subjects. *Annals of New York Academy of Science, 444*, 42–53.

Schacter, D. L., & Moscovitch, M. (1984). Infants, amnesics, and dissociable memory systems. In M. Moscovitch (Eds.), *Infant memory*. New York: Plenum.

Shimamura, A. P., & Squire, L. R. (1984). Paired-associate learning and priming effects in amnesia: A neuropsychological study. *Journal of Experimental Psychology: General, 113*, 556–570.

Slamecka, N. J. (1966). Differentiation versus unlearning of verbal associations. *Journal of Experimental Psychology, 71*, 822–828.

Spence, K. W. (1936). The nature of discrimination learning. *Psychological Review*, 43, 427–449.

Squire, L. R. (1987). *Memory and Brain*. New York: Oxford University Press.

Squire, L. R. (1992). Declarative and nondeclarative memory: Multiple brain systems supporting learning and memory. *Journal of Cognitive Neuroscience*, 4(3), 232–241.

Squire, L. R., & Cohen, N. J. (1984). Human memory and amnesia. In G. Lynch, J. L. McGaugh, & N. M. Weinberger (Eds.), *Neurobiology of learning and memory*. New York: Guilford Press.

Squire, L. R., Shimamura, A. P., & Amaral, D. G. (1989). Memory and the hippocampus. In J. Byrne & W. Berry (Eds.), *Neural models of plasticity*. New York: Academic Press.

Sutherland, R. J., Chew, G. L., Baker, J. C., & Linggard, R. C. (1987). Some limitations on the use of distal cues in place navigation by rats. *Psychobiology*, 15, 48–57.

Sutherland, R. J., Kolb, B., & Whishaw, I. (1982). Spatial mapping: Definitive disruption by hippocampal or medial frontal cortical damage in the rat. *Neuroscience Letters*, 31, 271–276.

Sutherland, R. J., & McDonald, R. J. (1990). Hippocampus, amygdala, and memory deficits in rats. *Behavioral Brain Research*, 37, 97–109.

Sutherland, R. J., McDonald, R. J., Hill, C. R., & Rudy, J. W. (1989). Damage to the hippocampal formation in rats selectively impairs the ability to learn cue relationships. *Behavioral and Neural Biology*, 52, 331–356.

Sutherland, R. J., & Palmer, M. (1992). Impairment in spatial and nonspatial configural tasks after hippocampal (HPC) ibotenate or kainate + colchicine lesions. *Fifth Conference on the Neurobiology of Learning and Memory Abstracts*, Vol. 5, 92.

Sutherland, R. J., & Rudy, J. W. (1988). Place learning in the Morris place navigation task is impaired by damage to the hippocampal formation even if the temporal damands are reduced. *Psychobiology*, 16, 157–163.

Sutherland, R. J., & Rudy, J. W. (1989). Configural association theory: The role of the hippocampal formation in learning, memory, and amnesia. *Psychobiology*, 17, 129–144.

Sutherland, R. J., & Rudy, J. W. (1991). Exceptions to the rule of space. *Hippocampus*, 1, 250–253.

Thorndike, E. L. (1898). Animal intelligence: An experimental study of the associative processes in animals. *Psychological Monographs*, 2(8).

Tulving, E. (1985). How many memory systems are there? *American Psychologist*, 40, 385–398.

Whitlow, J. W., & Wagner, A. R. (1972). Negative patterning in classical conditioning: Summation of response tendencies to isolable and configural components. *Psychonomic Science*, 27, 299–301.

Wickelgren, W. A. (1979). Chunking and consolidation: A theoretical synthesis of semantic networks, configuring, S-R versus cognitive learning, normal forgetting, the amnesic syndrome, and the hippocampal arousal system. *Psychological Review*, 86, 44–60.

Woodbury, C. B. (1943). The learning of stimulus patterns by dogs. *Journal of Comparative and Physiological Psychology*, 35, 20–40.

Young, S. L., Fanselow, M. S., & Bohenek, D. L. (1992). The dorsal hippocampus and contextual fear conditioning. *Society for Neuroscience Abstracts*, 18, 1564.

Zola-Morgan, S., Squire, L. R., & Amaral, D. (1986). Human amnesia and the medial temporal region: Enduring memory impairment following a bilateral lesion limited to the CA1 field of the hippocampus. *Journal of Neuroscience*, 6, 2950–2967.

6

The Hippocampal System and Declarative Memory in Humans and Animals: Experimental Analysis and Historical Origins

Howard Eichenbaum

The notion that there are multiple memory systems has received widespread, if not universal (see Roediger et al., 1989), support among both cognitive psychologists and neuroscientists. It might be said that our progress in delineating the brain's memory systems is one of the incipient success stories in cognitive neuroscience. From the perspective of this discipline, a comprehensive understanding of multiple memory systems requires not only that we confirm there *are* more than one system but also that we *characterize* both the psychological processes and the functional circuitry supporting each identified system. In other words, the ultimate aim of the cognitive-neuroscientific approach is to map each memory system onto a brain system and to account for the defining cognitive processes of each system in terms of its mediating neural pathways, coding schemes, and computational processes.

In this chapter I will offer preliminary evidence toward just such an analysis, specifically with respect to the declarative-memory system. My starting point is quite general and involves a consideration of how we go about characterizing memory systems from the contributions of psychological and neurobiological approaches at successive levels of analysis. The aim of this introductory segment is to set the experimental work of my colleagues and me in the context of other investigations on the cognitive neuroscience of memory described in this book. What then follows is a two-part review of efforts to map one particular memory system, the declarative system, onto one particular brain system, the hippocampal system. In section 2, I will outline our own efforts to identify some essential properties of declarative memory observed in humans, to show how these can be applied to understand the variety of accounts of hippocampal function in animals, and to employ a particular characterization of declarative memory to gain insights into the functional circuitry and coding schemes of the hippocampal system. Then in section 3, I will discuss these observations in light of historical precedents and other current theoretical conceptions of hippocampal function. My overall aim is to provide the preliminary outline of a comprehensive analysis of declarative memory.

1 WHERE THIS CHAPTER FITS IN THIS BOOK

A full understanding of the cognitive neuroscience of memory requires several coordinated levels of analysis, including the identification of component cognitive processes in memory and the distinctions among them, the localization of particular memory processes within specific neural structures and pathways, and the characterization of the neural circuits and coding schemes supporting these processes. All of these levels are represented by chapters in this book. Here I seek to place the topics of this chapter within these levels.

Cognitive analyses serve to define what we mean by "memory" and "memory systems" in terms of constituent psychological processes. For example, Johnson (1992; Johnson & Chalfonte, this volume) focuses on identifiying "functional specifications" of the cognitive mechanisms supporting episodic memory; she has identified multiple levels of memory processing, each responsible for different cognitively defined functions (e.g., rehearsing, retrieving). Analyses of this form are essential for generating a list of memory functions distinguishable in terms of cognitive processes, and they suggest how some of these processes might be related. Such analyses are a necessary first step in the development of testable hypotheses about the organization of a memory system.

However, cognitive analyses do not tell us how the constituent memory processes are separated and organized within the nervous system; this is the business of neuropsychological studies that further distinguish memory processes and assign them to structures and systems within the brain. Through neuropsychological testing, distinct memory processes can be identified by dissociating impaired performance based on one memory process from intact performance based on another in amnesic patients or animals with experimental brain damage (for a review, see Squire et al., 1993). Olton and Shapiro (1992; Shapiro & Olton, this volume) stress the importance of experimental dissociations in amnesic subjects in this phase of memory research, and they focus on parametric explorations in search of the relevant operational dimensions of memory processing. Work cited in their review suggests that, for example, a capacity for holding recent memories and decreasing interference are associated with hippocampal function. Neuropsychological analyses also help localize specific brain structures and pathways essential to fundamental memory processes or systems. For example, there is general agreement that declarative or explicit memory is specifically associated with the hippocampal system; several authors contributing to this volume have argued that this kind of memory reflects conscious recollective processes, as contrasted with implicit memory for aspects of performance, that can be revealed without conscious awareness. Thus we might say that the declarative/explicit memory system can be mapped, at least in part, onto the anatomical system defined by the hippocampus and closely interconnected cortical areas of the medial temporal lobe (Squire & Zola-Morgan, 1991). Nondeclarative or implicit processes, whose independent operation has been strikingly revealed in studies on normal humans and human amnesics, include multiple perceptual and semantic subsystems associated with specific neocortical association areas (see Schacter, 1992, this volume) and a motor-habit or procedural system associated with the neostriatum (Mishkin et al., 1984; see also Moscovitch, 1992, this volume). Other procedural systems have been investigated to a greater extent in animals (see below). In addition, an executive or strategic memory system has been associated with prefrontal cortex (see Baddeley, 1992, this volume; Moscovitch, 1992, this volume; Goldman-Rakic, 1992). This chapter will focus on mapping the declarative memory system onto the neural structures that compose the hippocampal system.

There are two important limitations in the resolution with which we can characterize a memory system using neuropsychological studies of human amnesic patients. First, brain damage due to accidents or disease is rarely limited to the specific brain structures and substructures that must be independently examined to delineate the components of a functional system (for an exception, see Zola-Morgan et al., 1986). So the study of human amnesia can yield at best a crude delineation of the essential neural components of a memory system. Without experimental methods that permit a much more detailed description of functional circuitry, it is impossible to sort out the component subprocesses of each of these systems, and it may be quite impossible to determine how the major memory systems interact, as they surely do. Second, some memory processes are, even in principle, impossible to separate from nonmemory functions through studies of brain damage. This occurs when the same brain structure or system that performs nonmemory processing encodes memories in the form of modifications of its normal processing function. For example, it is widely believed that visual memories are finally stored as modifications of perceptual processing in the highest visual association area, the inferior temporal cortex. Damage to this area results in both a deficit in visual learning and memory and visual agnosia (e.g., Gross, 1973), which makes it impossible to fully sort out the distinct contributions of the inferior temporal cortex to memory and perceptual functions. Sometimes we can distinguish memory and other processing functions by differential activation of brain areas during memory versus nonmemory performance, using state-of-the-art brain imaging techniques in intact subjects (e.g., Squire et al., 1992). However, the resolution of these methods, which is the level of whole brain structures or areas, is not substantially better than that available from studies of brain damage in humans. Valuable as these methods are in defining essential functional contributions and assigning them to brain structures or regions, such methods can give little insight about the underlying circuits and computational processes. Without a degree of resolution that can reveal the coding properties of the relevant computational elements, there is little hope for our desired comprehensive understanding of the circuitry supporting the identified memory processes.

These limitations can be addressed by employing animal models in combinations of neuropsychological studies of the effects of discrete brain damage and electrophysiological studies of the circuitry and coding properties of specific neural structures. One benefit of animals is that they can be employed to study the effects of highly specific, localized brain damage, and thus in principle to identify the constituent components of a memory system in detail. Successful examples of this strategy include mapping the components of the medial-temporal-lobe system in object-recognition memory (Squire & Zola-Morgan, 1991) and mapping the pathways essential to simple forms of emotional conditioning (LeDoux, 1991). Even when such a delineation is impossible with the experimental-lesion technique, as in the case of a brain structure involved in the mixed memory and nonmemory functions described above, differential characterization of memory and nonmemory coding processes is possible through such readily available high-resolution techniques as single neuron recording in active animals. In cases where a compelling animal model of a particular type of memory exists, these studies can, at least in principle, reveal the relevant coding processes and circuit elements subserving that memory system. This chapter focuses directly on this level of analysis, specifically with regard to declarative memory and the hippocampal system.

Before turning to a summary of the work of my colleagues and me, there is a final important caveat regarding the role our work plays among the levels of analysis described here. There is often a critical obstacle to the goal of outlining a memory system across all these levels of analysis, and this obstacle occurs because a full analysis requires a coordinated approach between species. Thus analyses at the cognitive and neuropsychological levels can be performed appropriately in human subjects, but detailed circuit analyses can be accomplished only in animals. The transition from humans to animals may not be a serious problem for simpler forms of learning, where the behavioral phenomenology is identical. However, this transition could be insurmountable for the highest forms of cognition and memory. Thus neurobiologists who study animal models of higher cognitive processes have a problem of demonstrating the very *existence* of complex human memory processes in animals. For example, declarative memory is one of the most interesting and exciting aspects of human memory processes that has been revealed in the first two stages of analysis. To the extent that this kind of memory is defined in terms such as "conscious recollection" and "explicit" expression, however, it relies on forms of mediation nonexistent or unavailable for investigation in animals, which makes it impossible to create an adequate animal model. How one might succeed in creating an appropriate animal model of declarative memory and then study the relevant circuitry and coding schemes is a central topic of the present chapter. To the extent that my arguments are compelling, this exercise may serve to demonstrate that even the most complex aspects of human memory might be understood to exist at each level of cognitive and neural analysis.

2 AN ANIMAL MODEL FOR STUDIES OF THE HIPPOCAMPAL SYSTEM AND DECLARATIVE MEMORY

The work of my colleagues and me seeks to support the notion that the hippocampal system subserves declarative or explicit memory in animals as well as humans, and procedural or implicit memory is accomplished outside the hippocampal system across species. To the extent that the declarative-memory hypothesis can be extended to animals and across the various behavioral paradigms used to study animal learning, our understanding of memory systems would be improved in at least three general ways: First and most obvious, such a view would provide a single characterization of hippocampal function that might bring together the literatures on human and animal memory which have developed along largely separate lines. Even if it turns out that only some properties of hippocampal-dependent memory are shared by humans and animals, knowledge about what properties are and what properties are not shared across species might reveal insights about the evolution of hippocampal function in declarative memory (see Sherry & Schacter, 1987). Second, this extension of such a general view of memory might go far to close gaps between seemingly disparate accounts that have been offered to explain hippocampal function in animals. Currently a variety of hypotheses each advance a separate and competing account of hippocampal-dependent memory based on data from a limited domain of behavioral paradigms. In our view, these theoretical positions reflect different aspects of a single processing function. Third, demonstrating a continuity between hippocampal function in humans and animals would indicate which aspects of human declarative memory can properly be modeled in animals, and thus provide a basis for a wide range of neurobiological studies focused on the circuitry supporting this kind of memory processing (Otto & Eichenbaum, 1992c).

There is, as mentioned above, an important obstacle to pursuing the notion that the hippocampal system supports declarative memory across species: animals, unlike humans, obviously don't express their memories by verbal declaration. How, then, can we evaluate the existence of declarative memory and its possible dependence on the hippocampal system in animals? Our strategy has been to carefully examine characterizations of declarative memory in humans in an effort to identify the properties that can be operationalized for nonverbal species as well as humans. To the extent that such properties can be identified and convincingly discribed as defining qualities of declarative memory, then, at least in principle, appropriate experiments can be developed for testing the hypothesis about declarative memory and the hippocampal system in animals.

In a study of amnesia, Cohen and Squire (1980; see also Squire, 1987) originally characterized declarative memory as a record of everyday facts and events that can be brought to conscious recollection and is typically subject to verbal reflection or other explicit means of expression (Graf & Schacter, 1985).

By contrast, procedural memory is the nonconscious acquisition of a bias or adaptation typically revealed only by implicit measures of performance. These descriptions indeed present a formidable challenge for the study of declarative memory in animals. We do not have the means for monitoring conscious recollection in animals; the very existence of consciousness in animals is a matter of debate (see Eichenbaum, Cohen, et al., 1992a, for an extended discussion of this point with regard to hippocampal function). An assessment of verbal reflection is, of course, out of the question, and it is not otherwise obvious how to assess explicit-memory expression in animals. However, it may in fact be possible if we consider further characterizations that have been offered to distinguish declarative and procedural memory. To the extent that these descriptions do not rely on consciousness or verbal expression, they might be operationalized for experimental analysis in animals.

Cohen (1984) offered descriptions that could be helpful toward this goal. He suggested that "a declarative code permits the ability to *compare and contrast* information from different processes or processing systems; and it enables the ability to *make inferences* from and generalizations across facts derived from multiple processing sources. Such a common declarative code thereby provides the basis for access to facts acquired during the course of experiences and for conscious recollection of the learning experiences themselves" (p. 97, italics added). He characterized procedural learning as the acquisition of specific skills, adaptations, and biases and noted that such "procedural knowledge is tied to and expressible only through activation of the particular processing structures or procedures engaged by the learning tasks" (p. 96). During our development of assessments of declarative and procedural memory, my collaborators and I have exploited two distinctions revealed in these characterizations that may be applicable to animal studies. First, declarative memory is distinguished by its role in comparing and contrasting items in memory; procedural memory involves facilitating particular routines for which no such comparisons are executed. Second, declarative memory is distinguished by its capacity to support inferential use of memories in novel situations; procedural memory supports only alterations in performance that can be characterized as rerunning more smoothly the neural processes involved in the performance.

We have also extended these distinctions in a way that makes contact with the broad literature on hippocampal function in animals, arriving at a proposal for the representational mechanisms that might underlie declarative memory. However, incorporating the accounts of hippocampal function in animals was difficult because of major gaps between theoretical positions on hippocampal function and amnesia in animals. An initial overview of this literature suggests that there is little in common between the above-described characterizations of hippocampal-dependent memory in humans and views on hippocampal function in animals. Thus in animals, it has been suggested, the hippocampal system selectively supports "place learning" (O'Keefe & Nadel, 1978), "contextual encoding" (Hirsh, 1974; see also Winocur & Olds, 1978; Davidson

& Jarrard, 1991), learning of "external context attributes" (Kesner, 1984), "configural association" (Sutherland & Rudy, 1989; Sutherland, Macdonald, et al., 1989), "scene memory" (Gaffan & Harrison, 1989), "memory" (Mishkin et al., 1984), "recognition" (Gaffan, 1974), "working memory" (Olton, Becker et al., 1979; Olton, 1986), and "representational memory" (Thomas & Gash, 1988). Superficially, these proposals seem to have little in common even with each other. Yet I believe that there is a common thread that runs through all of them. Moreover, an accounting of the general properties of hippocampal function shared by these accounts offers some insights about the fundamental mechanisms of declarative memory across species. One set of proposals suggests that the hippocampal system supports the encoding of configurations of cues, like of cues that compose places and scenes and items in context and perhaps configural cues. Another set of proposals suggest that the hippocampal system supports the representation of temporal relations among cues presented sequentially, as required for working memory (as the term is used in the animal literature). Some of these accounts have explicitly suggested that the hippocampal system serves as a comparator of present information with representations of past events (Gray & Rawlins, 1986; Gabriel et al., 1980). Both sets of proposals implicate the hippocampal system in the processing of comparisons among items in memory and the encoding of essential relations among items presented either simultaneously or sequentially.

Based on this general aspect of hippocampal-dependent memory our hypothesis is that the hippocampal system supports a *relational representation* of items in memory (Eichenbaum, Cohen, et al., 1992a; Eichenbaum, Otto, & Cohen, 1992; Cohen & Eichenbaum, 1993). Furthermore, we have suggested that a critical property of the hippocampal-dependent memory system is its *representational flexibility*, a quality that permits inferential use of memories in novel situations. According to this view, the hippocampal system mediates the organization of memories into what may be thought of as a multidimensional memory "space," with particular items in memory as informational nodes in the space and the relevant relations between the items as connectives between informational nodes. In such a memory space, activation of one node results in activation of all sufficiently strongly associated connectives and, consequently, other informational nodes, including ones never directly associated with the originally activated element. Such a process supports the recovery of memories in a variety of contexts outside the learning situation and permits the expression of memories via various pathways of behavioral output. The combination of relational representation (a consequence of processing comparisons among items in memory) and representational flexibility (a quality of relational representation that permits inferential expression of memories) suggests an information-processing scheme that might underlie declarative memory in humans and, indeed, in animals as well. Our conception of memory space coincides with the description of highly interactive parallel distributed networks of the type that simulate performance on an explicit memory test (Metcalfe et al., 1992, this volume).

Conversely, according to our view, hippocampal-independent memories involve *individual representations*; such memories are isolated in that they are encoded only within the brain modules that engage in perceptual or motor processing during learning. These individual representations are *inflexible* in that they can be revealed only through reactivation of those modules within the restrictive range of stimuli and situations in which the original learning occurred. One might expect individual representations to support the acquisition of task procedures habitually performed during training trials; individual representations should also support the acquisition of specific information not requiring comparison and consequent relational representation. These properties share much with such hippocampal-independent acquisition of general procedures previously characterized as "learning along the performance line" (Hirsh, 1974), the acquisition of "rules" (Kesner, 1984), and "habit" formation (Mishkin et al., 1984), and with hippocampal-independent acquisition of individual representations characterized as "simple association" (Sutherland & Rudy, 1989), "taxon learning" (O'Keefe & Nadel, 1978), "association" (Gaffan, 1974), "reference memory" (Olton, Becker, & Handlemann, 1979), and "dispositional memory" (Thomas & Gash, 1988). The inflexibility and specificity of such hippocampal-independent memory representations have been highlighted in previous accounts of preserved learning in amnesia (Schacter, 1985; Saunders & Weiskrantz, 1989; Eichenbaum, Cohen, et al., 1992b). Our conception of the circuitry supporting such performance coincides with a network of separate, noninteracting traces that can simulate performance based on implicit memory (Metcalfe et al., 1992, this volume).

In the following two sections I will consider two approaches by which the above hypothesis can be tested with variants of the discrimination and maze-learning paradigms traditionally employed in studies of animal memory capacities. For each approach I will offer specific predictions, generic tests of those predictions, and some illustrative examples of successful applications. The first approach considers the pattern of impaired and spared learning consequent to hippocampal-system damage. The second considers the nature of memory coding by neural elements in the hippocampus during learned performances by intact animals. Then in section 2.3, I will summarize some of our ongoing efforts to exploit these approaches to gain an understanding of interactions among subcomponents of the hippocampal system and our efforts to bridge the gaps between assessments of memory capacities commonly employed in humans and animals.

2.1 Impaired and Spared Learning Capacities in Animals with Hippocampal Damage: Three Predictions

This account of declarative memory and hippocampal function focuses on the organizational capacities and flexibility of the hippocampal-dependent memory system; the hypothesis is global regarding the types of learning materials that the hippocampal system encodes. An important theoretical consequence of this perspective is that a conventional task analysis of hippocampal function will not be fruitful, because the hippocampal system is involved in all sorts of tasks. In a task analysis, the learning materials are varied and the performance of animals with hippocampal system damage and that of intact animals are compared. The prediction is that animals with hippocampal-system damage will be impaired at learning some tasks and succeed in others, which will reveal which "kind of memory" the hippocampal system supports. Yet according to our view, hippocampal representation involves all manner of experience. Thus my *first prediction* is that the hippocampal system is involved in all tasks and all kinds of learning and memory. This bold prediction suggests that in principle one should be able to identify a declarative representation, and therefore a role for the hippocampus, in virtually any behavioral paradigm that involves learning and memory, including those usually not considered dependent on hippocampal function. On the other hand, in principle, virtually any learning paradigm contains components that involve procedural representations, and indeed, any particular task can be construed as supported entirely by one or more individual representations, which would make performance hippocampal-independent.

These considerations suggest that a task analysis will necessarily lead to mixed and conflicting results. How, then, can one distinguish hippocampal-dependent from hippocampal-independent memory representation? Our view is that one needs to exploit the two fundamental properties of declarative representation, outlined above, in a double-pronged experimental approach. Thus the *second prediction* has two parts corresponding to the two prongs of this approach: (1) animals with hippocampal damage will be selectively or disproportionately impaired in those task variants that emphasize comparison among items; conversely, preserved learning ability is predicted when the task variant encourages separate representations for the items to be remembered, and (2) even when learned performance is apparently normal, animals with hippocampal damage will be impaired when challenged to use their memories in novel situations. In accordance with the first prong of this approach, within any behavioral paradigm one must hold the learning materials constant and either encourage comparing and contrasting items during learning or encourage the encoding of individual items and hinder comparison between them. Specifically, how task parameters should be manipulated to implement these two conditions will vary across experimental paradigms; I provide some illustrative examples below.

The second prong of declarative-memory analysis requires an assessment of the flexibility of acquired memories. This requires testing with a variant of a task successfully learned by animals with hippocampal damage, preferably at the same rate as in normal animals so as to equate quantitative aspects of performance throughout training. As long as the ultimate performance level of amnesic animals is normal, such an analysis is valid. Assessing flexibility involves probing the representation of each animal by asking it to employ the acquired information in a new way, typically in a context where familiar cues have been rearranged in a manner consistent with their original relationships. Again, precisely how this manipulation is accomplished varies across behavioral paradigms, and I provide illustrative examples below.

There is one more issue with regard to the pattern of impaired and spared abilities of animals with hippocampal damage. Some aspects of virtually any behavioral paradigm involve habitual procedures common to all trials and therefore can be supported without relational representation. Thus the *third general prediction* is that such consistent procedures will be normally acquired by animals with hippocampal system damage.

Our investigations of learning and memory in rats with hippocampal damage have focused on two learning paradigms in which normal rats perform exceedingly well: odor-guided discrimination and matching tasks and place-learning tasks. In each case hippocampal function was disrupted either by disconnection of the fornix (a major input-output pathway to subcortical areas) or ablation of the parahippocampal region (the cortical area mediating convergence and communication with the cerebral cortex). Implementing this double-pronged experimental strategy for each paradigm has involved an assessment of learning identical olfactory or spatial materials under task variations that encourage or hinder relational processing and an assessment of flexible use of acquired representations under novel conditions. Consistent with our predictions, in both paradigms we found that rats with hippocampal damage are impaired in learning when the demand for relational representation is high and that they can succeed in learning when the demand for relational representation is low. Furthermore, intact animals can demonstrate their ability to use memories flexibly during probe testing in novel situations, but animals with hippocampal damage can display their learned abilities only in the limited context of a repetition of the learning experience.

The hippocampal system and odor-guided learning   Our initial investigations exploited the excellent learning and memory capacities of rats in learning odor discriminations (Eichenbaum, Fagan, & Cohen, 1986; Eichenbaum, Fagan, et al., 1988; Eichenbaum, Mathews, & Cohen, 1989). The learning ability of intact rats was compared with that of rats with transections of the fornix, a fiber bundle supporting necessary connections of the hippocampus with subcortical structures. We evaluated learning performance in several variations of the paradigm for learning odor discriminations assessing the capacity for relational representation by manipulating the demand for comparison and representation of relations among the identical odor cues (Eichenbaum, Fagan, et al., 1988). In a simultaneous-discrimination task, two odor cues were presented at the same time and in close spatial juxtaposition; the discriminative response required a selection between equivalent left and right choices. Under these training conditions, rats with fornix lesions were severely and persistently impaired on a series of different odor-discrimination problems (figure 1). Alternatively, in a successive-discrimination task, odors were presented separately across trials, which hinders comparison among

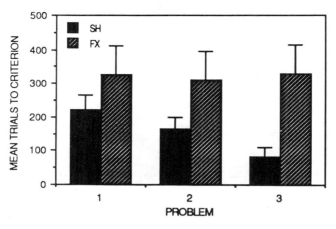

Figure 1 Performance of sham-operated rats (SH) and rats with lesions of the fornix (FX) on a task of simultaneous oder discrimination. (From Eichenbaum, Otto, & Cohen, 1992.)

items, and the response required only completing or discontinuing stimulus sampling, which thus eliminates the response choice. In striking contrast to the preceding results, under these training conditions, rats with fornix lesions were *superior* to normal rats in acquiring the same series of discriminations that they had failed to learn under other task demands (figure 2; see also Eichenbaum, Fagan, & Cohen, 1986; Otto et al., 1991; Staubli et al., 1984). Our interpretation of these findings is that one may observe severe impairment, transient impairment, or even facilitation under different task demands, even with identical stimulus materials. Moreover, the differences in performance by rats with hippocampal damage can be related to the demand for stimulus and response comparison.

To assess the capacity for representational flexibility in normal rats and rats with hippocampal damage, we pursued a follow-up experiment using the simultaneous-discrimination task (Eichenbaum, Mathaws, & Cohen, 1989). Our investigation explored a surprising finding in the results from this training condition: although rats were generally impaired on this task, they succeeded in learning some of the discrimination problems at least as rapidly as normal animals. To understand why they occasionally succeeded and to explore the nature of memory representation when they did succeed, we trained yoked pairs of normal rats and rats with fornix lesions on a series of problems involving simultaneous odor discrimination until the rat with the fornix lesion in each pair had acquired two discriminations within the normal range of scores. We then assessed the flexibility of their representations by challenging them with probe trials composed of familiar odors mispaired in combinations not previously experienced. According to our notion of relational representation, normal animals encode all the odor stimuli presented both within and across trials, using an organized scheme that would support comparisons among odors not previously experienced together. On the other hand, we

The Hippocampal System and Declarative Memory

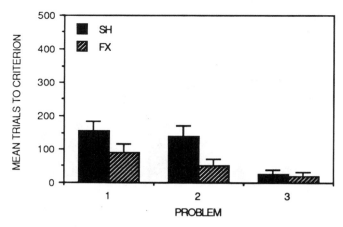

Figure 2 Performance of sham-operated rats (SH) and rats with lesions of the fornix (FX) on a task of successive oder discrimination. (From Eichenbaum, Otto, & Cohen, 1992.)

postulated that the representation systems of rats with hippocampal damage would not support recognition of the separate elements within each compound. To test these predictions, we mixed within a series of trials used in two different instruction problems occasional probe trials composed of a mispaired rewarded odor from one problem and the nonrewarded odor from the other. Both normal rats and rats with fornix lesions continued to perform well on the trials composed of the odor pairings used in instruction trials. Normal rats also performed accurately on the probe trials, but, in striking contrast, rats with fornix lesions performed at chance levels on the probe trials, as if they were presented with novel stimuli (figure 3).

A further analysis focusing on the response latencies (or reaction times) of animals performing the simultaneous discrimination provided additional evidence that the nature of learned odor representations was abnormal in rats with hippocampal damage. This analysis also provided insight into how rats with hippocampal damage succeeded in learning some simultaneous discriminations. We determined that each rat with a fornix lesion had a quantitatively shorter average response latency than each normal rat, even though all rats consistently performed at high accuracy and showed the speed-accuracy tradeoff typical of reaction-time measures. Furthermore, rats with fornix lesions also had an abnormal pattern of reaction times (figure 4). Each normal rat had a bimodal distribution of response latencies, and each of the two modes was associated with one of the positions where the rewarded odor was presented and the response executed. This pattern of reaction times suggests that the rat consistently approached and sampled one odor port first, then either performed a nose-poke there or approached and sampled the other odor port. In contrast, rats with fornix lesions had a unimodal distribution of response latencies, and the pattern of their response latencies was the same, regardless of odor and response positions. Our interpretation of these results

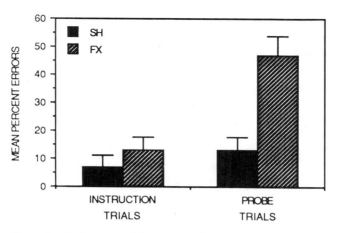

Figure 3 Performance of sham-operated rats (SH) and rats with lesions of the fornix (FX) on probe tests of oder discrimination. (From Eichenbaum, Otto, & Cohen, 1992.)

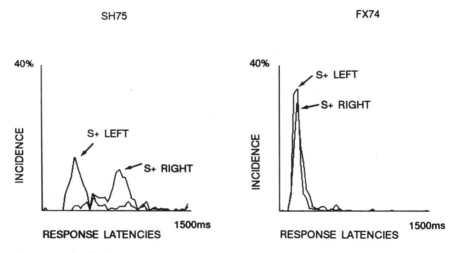

Figure 4 The distributions of response latencies for a sham-operated rat (SH75) and a rat with a fimbria/fornix transection (FX74) on odor-discrimination trials given during overtraining. Performance in these trials was equivalent for the two rats (87 percent and 84 percent correct, respectively). Separate distributions are shown for correct responses when the S+ odor was presented on the rat's left or right. Note the different modes in the distribution of response latencies of the sham-operated rat, depending on where S+ was presented. The response latencies of the FX rat had a single mode, representing latencies more rapid than even the early mode of the sham-operated rat. (From Eichenbaum, Mathews, & Cohen, 1989.)

was that rats with hippocampal damage sample the entire stimulus compound at once, and so require less time to complete the trial. On just those problems where different left-right combinations of the odors were distinguishable, they succeeded in learning an individual association for each odor compound and the appropriate response. Indeed, this account of representational strategies suggests that their performance was inflexible on our probe tests because novel mispairings of odors were perceived as unfamiliar odor compounds.

The hippocampal system and place learning   Perhaps the clearest demonstration of the critical role the hippocampus plays in place learning comes from experiments using the Morris water maze (Morris et al., 1982). The apparatus used in these studies is a large circular swimming pool filled with an opaque water solution and containing an escape platform slightly submerged at a fixed location relative to salient extramaze visual cues. In the standard version of this task, rats are released into the water at different starting points on successive trials—a manipulation that strongly encourages rats to compare views of the positions of extramaze stimuli and the rat's own position across trials. Indeed, it is difficult to imagine how the task could be solved without a representation of spatial relations among cues that disentangles otherwise conflicting associations of the separate views seen from each starting point. To assess the importance of the demand for relational representation in place learning, we compared the performances of intact rats and rats with fornix lesions on the standard variable-start version of this task with a version of the task that eliminated the need to compare views across different starting positions by having the rat start from a constant position on each trial (Eichenbaum, Stewart, & Morris, 1990). Under the variable-start condition, intact animals rapidly learned the place of the platform, demonstrating their memory by escaping with progressively shorter latencies. In contrast, rats with fornix lesions failed to learn the escape locus (figure 5). However, in the constant-start version of the task, rats with fornix lesions learned to escape nearly as rapidly as normal animals (figure 6). To confirm that both sets of rats were using the same extramaze cues to guide performance, we applied the standard "transfer" test developed by Morris (1984), in which the escape platform is removed and the swimming pattern of the rats is observed for a fixed period. Both normal rats and rats with fornix lesions swam near the former location of the platform, which indicates that they could identify the place of escape by the same set of available extramaze cues rather than solely by the approach trajectory.

To assess the flexibility of the memory representations supporting accurate performance on the constant-start version of place learning, we presented rats with different types of probe trials, each involving an alteration of the cues or starting points, intermixed within a series of repetitions of the instruction trial. One of our probe tests demonstrated a particularly striking dissociation between the subject groups. In this test the platform was left in its normal place, but the starting position was moved to various novel locations. When the

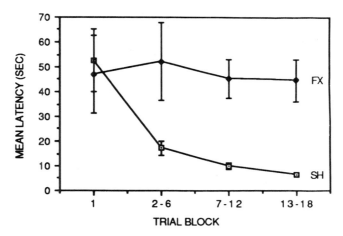

Figure 5 Performance of sham-operated rats (SH) and rats with lesions of the fornix (FX) on a place-learning task with variable starts. (From Eichenbaum, Otto, & Cohen, 1992.)

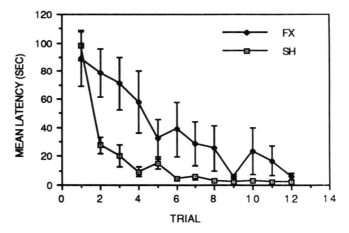

Figure 6 Performance of sham-operated rats (SH) and rats with lesions of the fornix (FX) on a place-learning task with a constant start. (From Eichenbaum, Otto, & Cohen, 1992.)

starting position was the same as that used during instruction trials, both normal rats and rats with fornix lesions had short escape latencies (figure 7). On probe trials, normal rats also swam directly to the platform, regardless of the starting position. In contrast, rats with fornix lesions swam in various directions and subsequently had abnormally long average escape latencies, sometimes never locating the platform (figure 8).

The data from both odor- and place-guided learning confirmed each of our general predictions about the performance of animals with hippocampal damage. First, performance by rats with hippocampal damage may be either impaired or preserved, even when the same odor or place cues are involved across conditions. Second, whether learning was impaired or spared depended on the demand for comparing and contrasting cues in each task, and even

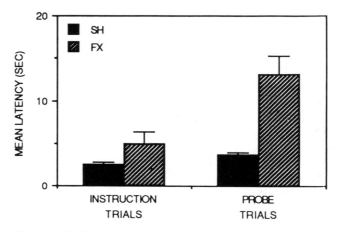

Figure 7 Performance of sham-operated rats (SH) and rats with lesions of the fornix (FX) on probe tests of place learning. (From Eichenbaum, Otto, & Cohen, 1992.)

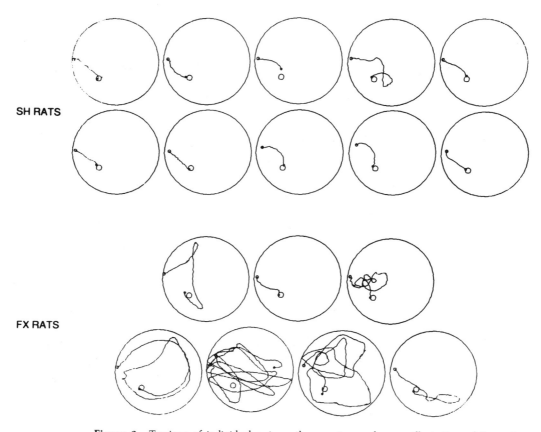

Figure 8 Tracings of individual swim paths superimposed on an illustration of the water maze (large circles). The escape platform location is indicated by the small circles. These data were taken from probe trials in which the swim was begun from a novel starting position (west). The data shown are for each sham-operated rat (SH) and for each rat with a fornix lesion (FX). The starting position during training was south (i.e., at the bottom of each circle). (Adapted from Eichenbaum, Stewart, & Morris, 1990.)

when learning was spared in rats with hippocampal damage, their memory representations were inflexible and could be expressed only in a repetition of the learning event. Third, even in those variants of each paradigm where rats with hippocampal damage were impaired in learning, they readily acquired the necessary instrumental procedures common across all trials, such as waiting for a signal to begin the trial, performing nose-poke responses, and locating the reward-delivery cup in the odor-guided tasks, and developing efficient swimming and search strategies in the place task.

2.2 Aspects of Learned Performance Encoded by Hippocampal Neurons: Three Corresponding Predictions

So far our predictions and experimental tests deal only with the pattern of impaired and spared memory performance after hippocampal damage predicted by the elaborated declarative-memory hypothesis. We can derive additional evidence that supports our account from analyses of single-neuron activity in animals performing the same kinds of learning and memory tasks explored with ablation. The hypothesis suggests a number of predictions about what features of events in learning tasks will be reflected in the activity patterns of hippocampal neurons of intact animals. I have framed these predictions about the behavioral physiology of the hippocampus to parallel those made regarding the pattern of spared and impaired learning capacities in animals with hippocampal damage. In accord with our view of the hippocampal system as involved in memory representation for virtually any kind of learning, the *first prediction* from behavioral physiology is that hippocampal neurons will be activated by the key cues in any behavioral task examined, including during behaviors and in tasks in which no performance impairment is observed after hippocampal damage. As discussed above, our view is that a hippocampal representation is formed during virtually every experience; the experimental conditions determine whether the hippocampal-dependent representation is essential to guide accurate performance or whether the performance demands can be accomplished by an extrahippocampal representation.

The next issue about hippocampal neural activity concerns precisely what aspects of events are represented within hippocampal circuitry. In accord with our view of the hippocampal system as supporting a representation of relevant relations among items necessary for learned performance, the *second prediction* from behavioral physiology is that the activity of single hippocampal neurons will reflect particular conjunctions and configurations of specific items relevant to the behavioral task at hand. Such neural correlates of relational processing might be thought of as the product of activity at specific information nodes and connectives in the hippocampal memory space. The specific nature of the conjunctions or configurations among essential cues reflected by neural activity will vary across tasks depending on the particular types of relationships relevant to accurate performance; these should include both the relevant configurations of items presented simultaneously and the sequence of items presented successively.

Finally, in accord with our view that hippocampal representations do not involve procedural aspects of behavioral performance, the *third prediction* from behavioral physiology is that hippocampal neurons will not fire in relation to simple sensory or motor events.

Evidence concerning these predictions can be derived from various experiments in which the activity of single hippocampal neurons was recorded while rats performed the same sorts of odor-guided and spatial learning and memory tasks described above. I will focus on the results from CA1 pyramidal cells, the principal neurons at the final stage of hippocampal processing.

Coding properties of hippocampal output neurons in rats performing odor-guided learning and memory tasks   We have recorded the activity of hippocampal cells in rats performing in the same odor-discrimination tasks employed in our lesion experiments (Eichenbaum, Kuperstein, et al., 1986; Otto & Eichenbaum, 1992a; Wiener et al., 1989). In each task, we found cells that fired in time-locked sequence to nearly every significant behavioral event. For example, some cells fired as the animal approached the area where odor stimuli were sampled, others fired selectively during odor sampling or response generation, and yet others fired during the retrieval of rewards. In each task, we focused our analyses on a subset of cells that fired selectively when rats sampled the odors and prepared to make the behavioral response. Some of these cells were active throughout the stimulus-sampling period on all types of trials, beginning to fire at the onset of the cues and abruptly ceasing to fire at the onset of the response. Other cells more selectively increased firing at the conjunction or combination of multiple odors presented either in different spatial configurations or temporal sequences. In simultaneous odor discrimination, these cells fired maximally only during sampling of a specific left-right configuration of a particular pair of odors (figure 9A). In successive odor discrimination, these cells fired maximally only during sampling of the rewarded odor when this was preceded by the nonrewarded odor on the previous trial; that is, the firing of these cells depended on a sequence of odor presentations (figure 9B). Thus the activity of a subset of hippocampal output neurons reflects the relevant stimulus relations in each variant of the odor-discrimination paradigm, even in variants of the task in which the hippocampal system is not required for performance.

Finally, we have more recently recorded the activity of hippocampal output neurons while rats performed an odor-guided delayed nonmatch-to-sample task (Otto & Eichenbaum, 1992a). In this task, some cells fired selectively on trials in which the odor cue was a nonmatch, and other cells fired only when the cue was a match; these responses occurred consistently, regardless of the particular odors involved across trials (figure 10). Thus unit activity reflected the outcome of the comparison process, the *relationship* between two odor cues abstracted from the items about which the comparison was based.

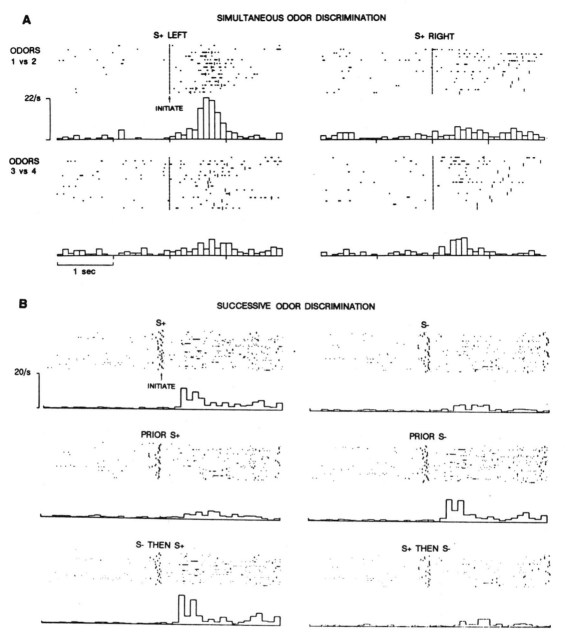

Figure 9 Raster displays and cumulative histograms of spikes from single hippocampal neurons active during stimulus sampling while the rat performed different versions of the odor discrimination task. In the simultaneous-cue task (A), unit activity is time-locked to the trial initiation and onset of odor presentation (adapted from Wiener et al., 1989). The unit response is greatest on trials when the stimulus configuration was odor 1 on the left and odor 2 on the right. In the successive-cue task (B), unit activity is time-locked to the peak of the first inhalation after odor presentation (adapted from Eichenbaum, Kuperstein, et al., 1986). Note that unit activity is time-locked to odor onset. The unit response is larger when the current stimulus is S+ rather than S−, larger when the stimulus on the immediately prior trial was S− rather than S+, and maximal when an S+ trial preceded an S− trial.

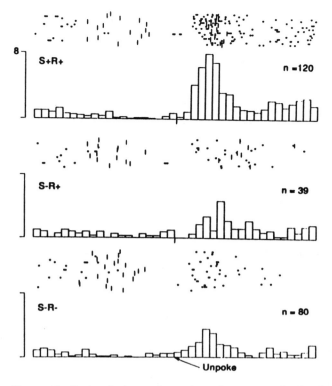

Figure 10 Raster displays and cumulative histograms of spikes from a single hippocampal neuron active during stimulus sampling while the rat performed a continuous delayed nonmatch-to-sample task. Data are synchronized to the animal's withdrawing from the sniff port on all trials. Tic marks to the left of center indicate odor onset; tic marks to the right indicate water-port response. S+R+ = trials with correct go responses on nonmatch trials. S−R+ = trials with incorrect go responses on match trials. S−R− = trials with correct no-go responses on match trials. Note that this cell fired more on nonmatch trials than on match trials, regardless of the behavioral response. (Adapted from Otto & Eichenbaum, 1992a.)

Coding properties of hippocampal output neurons in rats performing spatial tasks. There are no data on hippocampal unit activity in rats performing the Morris water maze, but we have observed the activity of some of the same cells recorded in our odor tasks in a place task similar in cognitive demands to Olton's radial-arm-maze task, another spatial-memory paradigm in which performance depends on hippocampal function (Olton, Becker, & Handlemann, 1979). In addition, there is a wealth of data on the activity of hippocampal neurons in a variety of spatial-learning and other open-field paradigms. The major finding of these studies is that many hippocampal output neurons fire when the rat is in a particular place in the environment as the animal explores a large open field (O'Keefe, 1976, 1979). An example of the so-called "place cell" phenomenon is shown in figure 11. This neuron fired selectively when the rat was approximately at the center of an arena, where it performed a place memory task. As others have observed, the activity of place cells, at least in some circumstances, is also influenced by aspects of spatial movement—such as the animal's speed, direction, and turning angle—which indicates that multiple spatial variables associated with intentional actions may be encoded along with spatial position (figure 11; see Eichenbaum & Cohen, 1988). It is widely accepted that the place-cell phenomenon reflects the representation of relevant positional relations among the distal stimuli that determine the spatial layout of the environment. This suggestion is supported by the finding that place fields move in concert with rotations of salient visual cues (Miller & Best, 1980; Muller, Kubie, & Ranck, 1987; O'Keefe & Speakman, 1987) and that the place fields of some cells "scale" with enlargement of all features of the environment (Muller & Kubie, 1987). In addition, place fields are disrupted only when a large fraction of the cues for spatial orientation are removed (O'Keefe & Conway, 1978; Hill & Best 1981). Even when a critical cue (or cues) is removed, the field may be altered only in the dimension associated with that cue (Muller & Kubie, 1987), and the firing changes are related to behavioral indications of the rat's judgments about its spatial location (O'Keefe & Speakman, 1987).

If there is a common property across the observations on hippocampal neural activity in behaving animals, one reasonable candidate would seem to be that hippocampal neurons encode significant *relations* among cues in all paradigms. This is clearly the case with the place-cell phenomenon and, in our view, is equally apparent in the results showing hippocampal cellular activity associated with nonspatial relations among cues. Our observation of cells whose activity depended on both odor and sniff-port locations in simultaneous odor discrimination is similar in this way to reports of hippocampal neurons that are active in relation to specific conjunctions of cues in other paradigms and species: some cells are specifically active in relation to conjunctions of goal-box color and position in a spatial delayed-response task in rats (Wible et al., 1986) and to conjunctions of two-dimensional patterns and their spatial or temporal positions or to other conditional cues in visual-recognition and delayed-response tasks in monkeys (Brown, 1982; Fuster, 1991; Miyashita et al., 1989; Ono et al., 1991; Rolls et al., 1989; Rolls & O'Mara, 1991; Watanabe & Niki, 1985; Wilson et al., 1987). Our observation of cells whose activity depended on the relationship between current and previous cues in successive odor discrimination and delayed nonmatch-to-sample tasks is similar to Deadwyler and his colleagues' observation of "sequential dependencies" of hippocampal-unit activity across trials in a tone-cued discrimination (Foster et al., 1987) and in rats and monkeys performing delayed matching tasks (Sakurai, 1990; Watanabe & Niki, 1985; Wilson et al., 1987). Collectively, these results indicate that hippocampal neurons encode whatever key relations among cues guide accurate performance on the task at hand.

Finally, it is important to note that the activity of hippocampal neurons is never accounted for by a simple sensory or motor response. With regard to sensory aspects of unit activity, in our studies no cells fired to presentation of a particular stimulus; rather, the cells encoded key relations among the

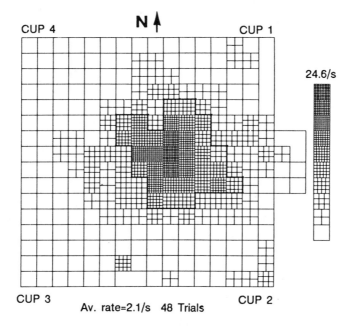

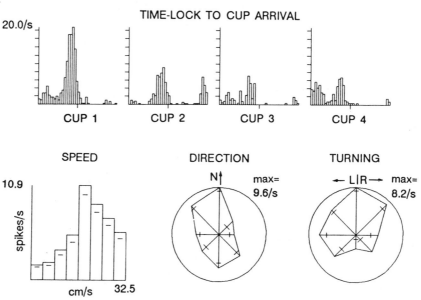

Figure 11 An example of unit activity in relation to spatial variables and goal-directed movements of rats performing a spatial memory task. On each trial of this task a rat begins by moving to the center of the arena (outline shown at top) and then proceeds to one of the corners to receive a water reward. Then the rat must return to the center before each successive approach to a new corner. For each cell, the analysis consists of five things: (1) At the top, a firing-rate map, indicating the firing rate at each pixel and outlining the boundaries of the place field. The firing-rate scale is at the right of the map. This cell had a place field near the center of the arena. (2) At the middle, four histograms showing unit activity time-locked for ±2

cues. With regard to motor aspects of unit activity, in our experiments neural activity was often closely time-locked with a particular behavioral act, but such firing occurred only when the act was associated with a particular stimulus configuration. In perhaps the most direct assessment of motorlike correlates of hippocampal neural activity, Berger and colleagues (1986) demonstrated that many hippocampal cells fire in association with behavioral output in classical-conditioning tasks, but this neural activity occurs only in association with learned behavioral responses, not reflexive movements.

Taken together, data on the functional properties of hippocampal neuronal activity bear out each of the predictions of the declarative-memory hypothesis. First, virtually every significant event in learning tasks is encoded by hippocampal neuronal activity, whether or not conventional assessments of accurate performance in that event, or even in the entire task, depends on hippocampal function. Second, hippocampal neurons encode a variety of relevant relations between perceptually independent cues in every task, including those essential to learned performance. Third, hippocampal neuronal activity does not directly reflect sensory or motor procedures carried out in performing these tasks.

2.3 Bridging the Gaps between Assessments of Animal and Human Memory: Toward a Model of Interactive Components of the Hippocampal System

These observations have allowed us to move beyond paradigms of discrimination and maze learning toward new behavioral tasks designed to demonstrate a continuity between memory assessments used in animals and those commonly used for testing memory in humans. At the same time, our current efforts attempt to go beyond viewing the function of the hippocampal system as a unitary process. We are now investigating how its components may interact to support declarative memory. This recent work has focused on comparing the roles of the parahippocampal region, composed of the perirhinal and entorhinal cortex, and the hippocampal formation itself. These studies involve the development of two behavioral paradigms, paired associate learning and simple recognition memory, tasks in common use on

seconds around the arrival at each reward cup during the same session. The tic mark on the abscissa indicates the arrival time; tic marks on the ordinate are multiples of the average firing rate. This cell fired in a time-locked manner just before arrival at each cup. At the bottom from left to right are the next three items of an analysis. (3) A histogram showing average firing rate at different speeds of movement within each subfield. Lines within the bars indicate standard errors. This cell fired maximally at an intermediate speed. (4) A polar plot showing average firing rate for different directions of movement within the place field. Cross lines indicate standard errors. This cell fired maximally for movement toward north. (5) A polar plot showing average firing rate at different turning directions during movement within the place field. Cross lines again indicate standard errors. Twelve o'clock is straight ahead. This cell fired maximally when the rat moved straight ahead. (From Wiener et al., 1989.)

human subjects. The procedures for each are based on the kinds of odor-discrimination tasks in which normal rats excel, but the task contingencies are modified to reflect the memory demands of assessments of human memory.

The paired-associates task, as typically used for humans, involves studying a list of arbitrarily paired words followed by testing, in which the subject is cued with the first item of each pair and must recall the second item. For rats, we modified the task, using a stimulus modality in which they excel, odors, and using a recognition format that required subjects to distinguish appropriate odor pairings from a large number of foils (Bunsey & Eichenbaum, 1993). Animals were trained to sample a stimulus sequence and then approach a water reward port only when appropriate paired associates were presented; no reward was given for water-port responses to foils. Each stimulus sequence consisted of two brief odor presentations, separated by a period when the airflow was reversed to prevent stimulus blending. The large stimulus set consisted of paired associates odors composed from 8 and 2 different types of foils. One type of foil involved mispairs composed of 48 inappropriate pairings of the same odors, so that distinguishing them from paired associates required learning the arbitrarily assigned relations among items. The other type of foil involved 64 different nonrelational sequences that included one of 4 odors that was never associated with reward; distinguishing these sequences from paired associates did not require relational processing, because they could be identified by single never-rewarded items.

Both intact rats and rats with lesions of the parahippocampal region rapidly learned to distinguish nonrelational pairs. By contrast, while normal rats gradually learned to distinguish correct from inappropriate pairings of odors, rats with parahippocampal lesions failed even with nearly twice as much training as normal rats (figure 12). Examination of the learning patterns of these two groups also reveals qualitative differences in the pattern of performances on these two types of foils. Both groups rapidly acquired appropriate responses to the nonrelational sequences, and normal rats gradually learned to distinguish mispairs, but rats with parahippocampal lesions barely exceeded chance on mispairs. Taken together, these observations indicate a specific deficit in learning the appropriate stimulus relationships.

In tests of simple recognition memory, it has been observed that both amnesic humans and monkeys with hippocampal damage perform well when tested immediately but forget rapidly when the test of retention is delayed. In the recognition of single items, it is certainly possible that explicit recall of studying an item would differentially benefit normal subjects. However, it also seems reasonable that simple recognition ought to be supported by the hippocampal-independent mechanisms of priming and biasing of responses based on representations of individual stimuli. To test this possibility, we developed a test of odor-recognition memory for rats, based on the delayed nonmatch-to-sample task used so successfully in studies of primates (Otto & Eichenbaum, 1992b). The task involves procedures identical to those described earlier, but with the stimuli and contingencies modified for simple

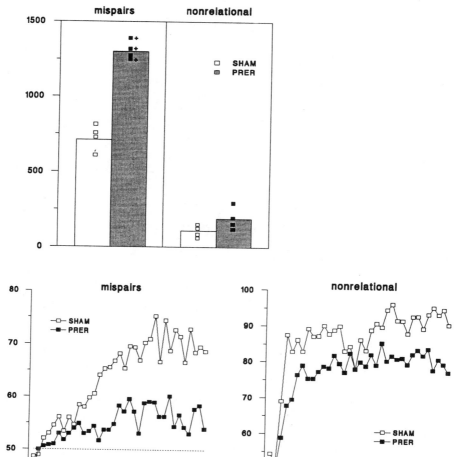

Figure 12 Performance of sham-operated rats (SHAM) and rats with perirhinal-entorhinal lesions (PRER) in distinguishing paired associates from mispairs and from nonrelational sequences. Top: total errors to reach performance criterion on each type of discrimination. Bottom: percent correct on each of the 35 days of testing for paired associates versus mispairs (bottom left) and versus nonrelational sequences (bottom right). Note the poor performance of PRER rats on the mispair discrimination and the relatively spared performance of PRER rats on the nonrelational trials. (From Bunsey & Eichenbaum, 1992.)

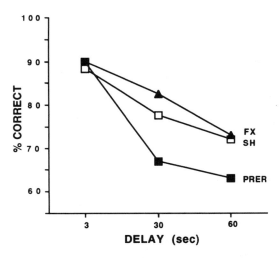

Figure 13 Performance of sham-operated rats (SH), rats with transection of the fornix (FX), and rats with lesions of the perirhinal-entorhinal region (PRER) on the odor-guided continuous delayed nonmatch-to-sample task after varying memory delays. FX rats were unimpaired, and PRER rats performed well at very short delays but demonstrated abnormally rapid forgetting. (Adapted from Otto & Eichenbaum, 1992b.)

recognition testing. In this task, called the continuous delayed nonmatch-to-sample tasks (cDNM), a series of single-odor stimuli were presented on different trials. If the odor was different from (that is, was a nonmatch with) the immediately preceding odor, an appropriate response resulted in reward; if the odor matched that on the previous trial, no reward was available. Rats were initially trained with a short interstimulus delay and then performance was assessed with varying retention delays.

Our findings indicated that normal rats learn this task very readily, performed very well with a short memory delay, and showed gradual memory decay across retention intervals. Rats with damage to the parahippocampal region also readily acquired the cDNM task and performed well at very short intervals, but like monkeys and humans with medial temporal damage, they forgot abnormally rapidly. In contrast, rats with transection of the fornix, a lesion that disrupts hippocampal function but does not interrupt parahippocampal-cortical interactions, had no effect at any delay tested (figure 13). These findings parallel observations on the visual-recognition performance of monkeys (Zola-Morgan et al., 1989; Murray & Mishkin, 1986), which suggests that the parahippocampal region plays a central role in intermediate-term storage of specific individual representations but the hippocampal formation itself is not required for this simple form of recognition memory.

Finally, our recent findings from recordings of hippocampal output cells in rats performing the cDNM task are consistent with these conclusions and shed some light on what contribution the hippocampus itself makes in simple recognition memory (Otto & Eichenbaum, 1992a). We found no cells that fired in a way that indicated encoding of specific information during the memory delay period but found several cells whose activity reflected a comparison of current and past stimuli. For example, the cell whose analysis is presented in figure 10 fired strongly during odor sampling on trials in which a nonmatch stimulus was presented and a correct response made, but it fired much less strongly when a match stimulus was presented, whichever response was made. Note that this pattern was observed across the large number of combinations of stimulus sequences on which these judgments are based. That is, this cell's activity reflected the nonmatch relationship regardless of the specific stimuli that made up particular comparisons. These data indicate that the hippocampus itself does not represent specific memories in this task but encodes comparisons between current cues and representations of previous experiences reflecting the outcome of such relational processing.

Together the data across all the behavioral tasks we have employed suggest that the parahippocampal region, like other components of the hippocampal system, is essential to learning arbitrary relations among stimulus items. In addition, unlike other components of the hippocampal system, the parahippocampal region is essential for retaining information for simple recognition. These observations led us to suggest the following division of processing functions within the hippocampal system (Eichenbaum, Otto, & Cohen, 1994). It seems likely that cortical areas support short-term retention, and these same cortical areas are quite likely the ultimate warehouse for permanent storage of specific items. Within the hippocampal system, the parahippocampal region, through its interactions with the cortex, can support intermediate-term storage of specific items even in the absence of normal hippocampal function. Our findings suggest that the hippocampus contains not specific information about particular items in memory but rather an abstraction of the relationship between the items. These findings suggest that in recognition memory the role of the hippocampus is not to store specific items. Rather its processing that contributes to recognition memory may involve accessing and comparing representations of current sensory experience with items stored earlier at neocortical or parahippocampal cortical areas and detecting similarities and differences in these episodes. This processing is not required for recognition per se but might contribute to recognition and would support more detailed recollections relating successive episodes. The hippocampal formation itself, while not storing representations of individual items, is essential for relational processing and the organization of memories supporting flexible declarative expression across the wide range of stimulus sequences experienced in paired-associate performance, as well as for the inferential use of learned information in discrimination and place learning. Thus we may begin to view the neocortex, the parahippocampal region, and the hippocampus itself as distinct and interactive functional units of the declarative-memory system (for an extended treatment of this point, see Eichenbaum, Otto, & Cohen, 1994).

3 THE HISTORY BEHIND THE DECLARATIVE-MEMORY HYPOTHESIS AND COMPARISON WITH OTHER CONTEMPORARY ACCOUNTS

I now turn back in time to consider the origins of the present formulation of the declarative-memory hypothesis and its relationship to other contemporary views on hippocampal function in memory. The aim of this review is to demonstrate a continuity of thoughts about memory and hippocampal function leading up to the present treatment. This is vital for developing a unified account of the behavioral data on hippocampal function. Such an account reveals the full range of hippocampal involvement across a wide range of performance capacities revealed in various assessments of memory in humans and animals.

I will argue for two central points. First, I intend the present extension of the original declarative/procedural distinction (Cohen & Squire, 1980) to animals not as a "new hippocampal theory" but rather as an attempt to encompass within a single conceptualization the contributions of many previous theoretical perspectives and the broad data base from studies of humans and animals (Eichenbaum, Cohen, et al., 1992a; Cohen & Eichenbaum; 1993). Second, the foundations of this and other contemporary views on hippocampal function can be traced to theoretical formulations about different forms of memory proposed much earlier in this century and before. In relating our account to others represented in this volume, I will begin with a review of the historical origins of these perspectives. Recent reviews by Polster et al. (1991) and Schacter (1987) provide more comprehensive coverage of most of the same material; my summary will focus on the development of the central points incorporated in the view of my colleagues and me. Then I will attempt to relate earlier conceptions of multiple forms of memory to later accounts of the role of the hippocampus in memory in humans (briefly) and animals (more extensively). In this section I will also focus on how each of these contemporary theories of hippocampal function captures some aspects of hippocampal-dependent memory processing but accounts for only a limited portion of the data. Our formulation draws on the common fundamental properties of each of these accounts but suggests a new understanding of the representational distinctions of hippocampal-dependent and hippocampal-independent memory.

3.1 Historical Origins, Antecedents, and Distinguishing Properties of Declarative and Procedural Memory

There are three distinctive properties of declarative memory that bear historical scrutiny here: the role of consciousness in both learning and recollection, the organization of memories according to a relational representation, and representational flexibility exhibited as inferential expression of memories. I will highlight each of these in the following discussion.

In his review of implicit memory, Schacter (1987) made a detailed historical analysis of conceptions about conscious and unconscious forms of memory. He dated the original reference to implicit memory as early as Descartes in 1649 and attributed the first systematic discussion of different types of memory to Maine de Biran's 1804 distinction between multiple forms of memory supported by two distinct "habit" systems and a separate system for "representative memory." The habit systems he described included one for skill learning and another for conditioned emotional responses. Both systems lacked conscious awareness and had a simple, repetitive nature, and these properties contrasted with a strong role for ideational processing in his characterization of representative memory. Although Schacter concluded that Maine de Biran's work had little influence on subsequent thinking, the separation of habit and memory continues in writings later in that century, and the central distinctions in this account are mirrored in today's terminology and categorizations of memory systems.

For example, at the origins of modern experimental psychology, William James's (1890, 1892) writings reflected the widely followed, albeit implicit, separation of unconscious "habits" from conscious "memories." In his treatment of the mechanisms of habits and memory and in his discussion of their practical uses and consequences, James applied characterizations of direct relevance to my account. For example, James defined memory as "the *knowledge* of an event, or fact, of which meantime we have not been thinking, with the *additional consciousness* that we have thought or experienced it before" (James, 1892, p. 154, italics added). Moreover, James captured the essence of our conception of this kind of memory as an organization of items according to a relational representation by characterizing memory in terms of how conscious processing could improve one's recollections: "The one who thinks over his experiences most, and *weaves them into systematic relations with each other*, will be the one with the best memory" (p. 161, italics added). On the other hand, James characterized a habit as a simple, inflexible, and automatic mechanism: "Nothing but a new pathway of discharge formed in the brain, by which certain incoming events ever after tend to escape" (p. 1). He further characterized habits as making our movements simpler, more accurate, and accomplished with less fatigue and as diminishing "the conscious attention with which our acts are performed" (p. 6). James also allowed that habits could guide very complex actions, such as playing well practiced tunes on the piano, by the concatenation of habitual chains. These descriptions clearly capture today's characterizations of procedural learning.

James never explicitly compared habit and memory. Nevertheless, the contrast between his descriptions focusing on the importance of consciousness in memory and its absence in habit could not be more striking (at least it seems so when what he wrote is taken out of context). Schacter (1987) characterized the prevailing view of that era as distinguishing habits and memories in quantitative terms. According to this view, habits simply do not have the strength to reach consciousness; those associations strong enough to reach consciousness we call memories. However, James's descriptions suggest a qualitative distinction between habits and memories in terms of the multiplicity of supporting associations rather than their strength. Complex habits were characterized as a *serial chain* of independent associations, whereas memories were seen as mediated by a *systematic organization* of associations based on various relationships between items. Furthermore, James argued, if indeed our sense of conscious recollection arises out of the associative properties of memory traces, it is not the *strength* of connections but rather their *number and diversity* within a network organization, precisely the properties featured in my account of relational representation. Consistent with this view, James commented that one could improve memory not by attempting to strengthen traces but rather by increasing the number of divergent associations: "All improvement of the memory lies in the line of *elaborating the associates* of each of the several things to be remembered" (James, 1892, p. 163). In a revealing admonition, James advised students not to cram for exams, arguing that "things learned thus in a few hours, on one occasion, for one purpose, cannot possibly have formed many associations with other things in the mind" (p. 162). Cramming produces only the kind of associative chain that characterized James's habits.

In the early half of the twentieth century, the rise of empirical psychology and the ensuing development of stimulus-response (S-R) accounts of memory overwhelmed the attention of investigators and defused most efforts to distinguish different types of learning. Among the most outstanding exceptions to the S-R view were Frederic Bartlett and Edward Tolman, who, in different ways, explored the operating properties of the declarative system as envisioned in the account of my colleagues and me. Bartlett (1932) examined long-term recall of narrative stories that included mythical and surreal characters and events. He found that in retelling such stories, people left out or made more realistic those details that were inconsistent with the conventional social structure and experiences of his subjects. Bartlett proposed that remembering is guided by a systematic mental representation of experiences that he called a *schema*, "an active organization of past reactions." He argued that new information is either encoded in ways consistent with the relevant existing schema or poorly encoded, which accounts respectively for the distortions and omissions in retold mythical stories.

There are two aspects of modern-day work along this theme that are of central relevance to schemes. First, modern investigations on the active nature of schema-based processing emphasizes the *inferential organization* of material to fit the schematic representation (Schacter, 1989a), a property prominent in my conception of declarative processing. Second, Bartlett's notion of a schema shares much in common with current conceptions of "semantic" memory in humans. One extension of this theme of particular importance to this review is Tulving's (1972, 1983, 1985) conception of semantic and episodic memory. According to his account, there is a hierarchy of memory systems, going from procedural memory to semantic memory to episodic memory. Each level is seen as supported by the preceding level, and the levels differ in the degree of associated conscious awareness. Both semantic and episodic memory are viewed as based on an organized network of associations permitting the flexible and inferential expression of knowledge across various situations. The additional defining features of episodic memory involve assigning items a *temporal context* of related events and tagging items as *personal* events. Thus both semantic and episodic memory may be viewed as subdivisions of declarative memory (see Cohen, 1984). However, the distinctions between them will be helpful below toward understanding some of the data on amnesia in animals and humans.

Along with Bartlett's efforts, Tolman's work came to represent the major opposition to the S-R approach that dominated experimental psychology during that period and continues to exert a strong effect today, even on theories of hippocampal function (see below). Tolman (1932, 1948, 1949) distinguished different types of learning and focused on the molar representation of spatial environments by what he called cognitive maps. He distinguished cognitive maps from habits along three lines: the contents of the representation, the role of drives and reinforcements, and representational flexibility. With regard to the structure of cognitive maps, Tolman (1949) emphasized that a *field expectancy* guides the acquisition of knowledge about an environment; he argued that organisms anticipate not only particular stimuli but also "the interconnections or field relationships between such groups of stimuli"(p. 145). With regard to the role of reinforcement, Tolman (1949) distinguished between the Hull's sense of reinforcement as guiding dispositions in various forms of learning and discrimination and the role of reinforcers in "confirming" one's expectancies about the relationship between certain stimuli and their consequences within cognitive representations. With regard to representational flexibility in cognitive maps, Tolman argued that field expectancies made possible the ability to take appropriate short-cuts and roundabout routes. Tolman (1932) explicitly and prominently stated in his account that expectancies can support inferences in altered environments; later (1949) he suggested that a higher level of expectancy representation might support relevant inferences across environments.

In sum, although James, Bartlett, and Tolman each emphasized a different aspect of what appears in my hypothesis and Bartlett only addressed the properties of declarative memory, within the works of these writers are all the essential properties and distinctions of declarative and procedural memory outlined in our account:

• They distinguished between forms of memory according to representational properties, including the potential for different forms of memory for the same materials.

• They conceived of a simpler form of memory based on an individual, stereotyped, and unconscious representation and a more complex organization of memories based on a systematic representation of relevant relations among items.

• Within each account the more complex form of memory supports the recollection of memories and the creative expression of memories in a variety of circumstances outside repetition of the learning situation.

3.2   Contemporary Accounts of Multiple Memory Systems in Humans and Animals Incorporating a Selective Role for the Hippocampus

It has taken a long time for the above notions, proposed well before key discoveries about hippocampal function, to be connected with the cognitive neuroscience of memory. This may be attributed in part to the original description of "global" amnesia consequent to surgical removal of the hippocampal region in the patient H.M. Thus the initial characterizations of memory disorder associated with hippocampal damage extended to all forms of learning, with only a few "exceptions," including the acquisition of motor skills (Corkin, 1968) and perceptual skills (Warrington and Weiskrantz, 1968). It was nearly two decades before most investigators came to view these exceptions as representative of a large domain of learning capacities unaffected in amnesia. When this became apparent in studies on humans, the very properties that distinguished habits and memories were employed to capture most if not all of the properties of impaired and spared capacities of human amnesia. While several new terminologies, in addition to the declarative/procedural distinction, have evolved to characterize these forms of memory, there is a strong consensus on the features of representation that characterize hippocampal-dependent and hippocampal-independent memory in humans (see Johnson, 1990; Squire, 1987; Weiskrantz, 1982).

Such a straightforward coalescence of theoretical and experimental approaches has not characterized our progress in understanding the role of the hippocampal system in animals. After the initial descriptions of H.M., there were several attempts to create an animal model of the severe global anterograde amnesia associated with hippocampal damage. These initial efforts were disappointing in that the range of the learning deficit observed in animals with hippocampal damage was quite limited in comparison with the disorder observed in humans (for a review, see Cohen and Eichenbaum, 1993). This led first to proposals about hippocampal function in animals that were not specifically tied to memory (Kimble, 1968; Douglas, 1967). The investigations of Kimble and Kimble (1970) are particularly relevant here. They analyzed the strategies of rats solving discrimination problems, describing animals with hippocampal lesions as inordinately stubborn in switching from nonproductive to productive strategies. In contemporary studies following the same theme, Devenport and colleagues (1988), noting that rats with hippocampal damage adopt superstitious and stereotyped behaviors with abnormal rapidity, characterized the performances of these rats as showing impoverished behavioral variability during the early stages of learning operant and maze tasks. These observations bear similarities with our account in that we too characterize the behavioral strategies of animals with hippocampal damage as abnormally rigid; this "rigidity" is also manifest in abnormally rapid learning in situations where a highly specific prepotent response is being trained, for example, in our successive odor-discrimination task. The conception of my colleagues and me differs from those of Kimble and Devenport and colleagues in that they attributed the rigidity to inflexibility in *behavioral output*, in contrast to my focus on inflexibility of *memory representations* supported outside the hippocampal system. In our view, the lack of behavioral variability and the abnormally rapid acquisition of superstitious behaviors are consequences of hippocampal-independent conditioning processes, whose influence is more readily exerted in the absence of the sometimes competing objectives of hippocampal-dependent processing.

In the mid and late 1970s three separate theoretical themes developed, each espousing the approach of multiple memory systems and suggesting a selective role for the hippocampus in a distinct higher-order form of memory, versus hippocampal-independent mechanisms for simpler forms of learning (Hirsh, 1974, 1980; O'Keefe & Nadel, 1978; Olton, Becker, & Handlemann, 1979). I will refer to these and succeeding works along these lines as hypotheses suggesting that the hippocampal system mediates cognitive mapping (O'Keefe & Nadel, 1978; Nadel, 1991, 1992), contextual and conditional associations (Hirsh, 1974, 1980; Winocur & Olds, 1978; Sutherland & Rudy, 1989), or working memory (Olton, Becker, & Handlemann, 1979). In an effort to reconcile the differing views expressed by these investigators, I will discuss each account, considering its fundamental properties and origins in learning theory, its strengths and limitations, and how my view has benefitted by and evolved to capture these fundamental properties.

Cognitive mapping   O'Keefe and Nadel's (1978) central contribution was to assign Tolman's cognitive mapping system to the hippocampal system and to interpret the voluminous literature on the behavioral effects of hippocampal damage in animals and O'Keefe's data on the functional correlates of hippocampal neural activity in terms of this hypothesis.

In their analysis of the effects of hippocampal damage on different behavioral tasks, O'Keefe and Nadel concluded that animals with hippocampal damage are severely impaired in many forms of spatial exploration and learning but are impaired on a relatively small number of nonspatial learning tasks. Together with the discovery of hippocampal "place cells," this comparison led them to conclude that hippocampal processing is limited to spatial memory. O'Keefe and Nadel's analysis went well beyond making a simple distinction between spatial and nonspatial learning modalities; they proposed that spatial learning involves the acquisition of cognitive maps that corresponded roughly, if not topographically, to the salient features of the physical environment. They referred to the memory domain supported by the hippocampus as a "locale" system, characterized as maintaining a molar model of space in terms of relations among objects in the environment, as driven by curiosity rather than reinforcement of specific behaviors, and as capable of very rapid learning. In contrast, they proposed that hippocampal-independent learning is supported by a "taxon" system, characterized as mediating dispositions of specific stimuli into categories, as driven by reinforcement of approach and avoidance behaviors, and as involving slow and incremental behavioral adaptations.

Each of the properties of O'Keefe and Nadel's locale and taxon systems be traced directly to Tolman's (1932, 1948, 1949) conceptions about cognitive maps and habits. Thus the form of representation in O'Keefe and Nadel's locale system is very similar to that in Tolman's cognitive maps, which Tolman characterizes as guiding the acquisition of knowledge about an environment defined in terms of the interconnections among various distal stimuli, even to the extent that O'Keefe and Nadel refer to their locale system as a system for "cognitive maps." O'Keefe and Nadel's conception of taxon learning, in which reinforcement mediates category inclusion, shares much with Tolman's (1949) characterization of *cathexes*, in which reinforcement serves to attach positive and negative valences to categories of items. It seems what cathexes were to psychoanalytic theory, prominent in Tolman's period, taxons are to O'Keefe and Nadel's more contemporary ethological perspective. O'Keefe and Nadel explicitly contrasted the rapid acquisition of information into cognitive maps with the incremental learning of taxons; this property was implicit in Tolman's conception of reinforcement as "confirming" knowledge about the world, rather than strengthening habits. (Note, however, that rapid acquisition is not a definitive feature of hippocampal-dependent learning. Various forms of hippocampal-independent learning—e.g., imprinting, conditioned emotional responses, bait-shyness—are also acquired in a single episode.) In addition, Tolman made the capacities for representational flexibility and inferential use of knowledge central among the properties of his cognitive maps. In O'Keefe and Nadel's account, flexibility appears variously as an implicit aspect of mapping, as opposed to route taking, and, in Nadel's (1992) description of cognitive maps, as permitting "multiple access routes." However, O'Keefe and Nadel did not explicitly consider representational flexibility or inference in their consideration of hippocampal function. Finally, although Tolman's writings do not make clear whether his concept of a cognitive map was limited to environmental space, there is no evidence that he intended such a restriction. O'Keefe and Nadel make this restriction explicit.

O'Keefe and Nadel's description of cognitive mapping also shares much with our account of hippocampal-dependent representation, with two exceptions. First, O'Keefe and Nadel restrict the role of the hippocampus to maps of environmental space, whereas our view extends this model to conceptual (or cognitive) space. On this point, our account of the hippocampal system as supporting a "memory space" differs from their view of this system as mediating "spatial memory." Second, We share with Tolman his emphasis on the inferential expression of memories as a defining feature of cognitive maps and differ with O'Keefe and Nadel on this point, either categorically or strongly in emphasis (see Nadel, 1992). A brief reconsideration of our studies of odor- and place-guided learning will serve to emphasize the similarities and differences between our views on these two points.

With regard to O'Keefe and Nadel's restriction to space, it is clear that animals with hippocampal damage are severely impaired on most place-learning tasks, but there are solid examples of impaired nonspatial learning and some examples of spared place learning. An example of findings that exceed O'Keefe and Nadel's account is the pattern of data on odor-guided learning. Our observation of impaired learning in simultaneous odor discrimination versus spared learning in successive odor discrimination after hippocampal damage might be related to the spatially distinct presentation of cues and the requirement of a spatial response in the simultaneous discrimination and the absence of such spatial factors in the successive discrimination. However, three lines of evidence exclude this interpretation: (1) Animals with hippocampal damage are severely impaired on other tasks employing a successive-cue format but lacking a spatial component, e.g., cDNM and paired-associate learning. (2) On the other hand, rats with hippocampal damage are only transiently impaired on an odor-discrimination variant that employs successively presented cues and requires a spatial response—quite arguably a task with greater spatial demands (Eichenbaum, Mathews, & Cohen, 1989). (3) While the simultaneous-discrimination task has a left-right response component, it is not a true place-learning task, since animals need not have attended to the spatial positions of the cues to solve the problem, and indeed animals with hippocampal damage are unimpaired on other forms of simultaneous discrimination with spatially separated cues. In addition, there are several other examples of nonspatial learning and memory in which damage to the hippocampal system results in severe impairment; these include monkeys' performances on tasks of object recognition and discrimination (e.g., Squire & Zola-Morgan, 1991), conditional discrimination (Ross et al., 1984; Daum et al., 1991; Sutherland, Macdonald, et al., 1989), timing (Meck et al., 1984), and a variant of classical conditioning (Moyer et al., 1990). Finally, impairments have been observed when working or representational memory was required but not when reference or dispositional memory sufficed in maze tasks where the spatial demands were the same for both contingencies (Thomas & Gash, 1988; Olton & Papas, 1979). O'Keefe and Nadel's restriction to spatial relations falls short in accounting for each of these observations (see also Cohen & Eichenbaum, 1991, 1993). By contrast, as I will argue below, each of these findings can be interpreted within the framework of the declarative/procedural distinction.

There are also findings indicating that hippocampal processing is not required in all situations where distal spatial cues defining a place are used to guide performance. Rather, as in discrimination learning, what matters is whether the rats are encouraged to use a relational or individual representation of these cues. In our studies on place learning in the Morris water maze, rats with hippocampal damage were trained with identical environmental cues, yet either failed or learned at nearly the normal rate, depending respectively on whether or not they were encouraged to compare and contrast different perspectives of these cues. We have been accused of misinterpreting these data as "showing that the lesioned animals had demonstrated place learning and conclud[ing] that they counted against the cognitive map theory" (O'Keefe, 1991, p. 230). It seems that our interpretation has itself been misinterpreted. As emphasized in our report, animals with hippocampal lesions succeeded in place learning only in the operational sense that they used distal cues, not local ones, to guide their performance. We made it quite clear that animals with hippocampal damage used those cues very differently than normal rats. This was revealed both in the abnormal dependence of animals with hippocampal damage on cues in direct line of view of the escape platform and, even more prominently, in their inability to use any cues effectively to guide navigation from novel starting positions. We found it illuminating that one could produce conditions where animals with hippocampal damage appeared to perform normally on one of the currently most sensitive behavioral tests for hippocampal damage.

Parallel data from a recent study of contextual learning confirm these conclusions in yet another experimental paradigm. After a rat is placed in a novel environment and then exposed to a tone followed by brief foot shock, when the rat is replaced in the experimental chamber where shock occurred it will again freeze and more so when the tone is re-presented. Hippocampal lesions block the acquisition of the context-elicited freezing but spare the conditioned response to the tone (Phillips & LeDoux, 1991; Selden et al., 1991). O'Keefe and Nadel have previously argued that animals with hippocampal damage fail at contextual learning because they cannot remember the place where shock occurred. However, in a variant of this task where no tone is presented prior to the shock, both normal animals and those with hippocampal damage condition strongly to the spatial context (Phillips & LeDoux, 1992). Thus, as in our study with the Morris water maze, the available spatial cues were identical in two versions of a task, yet learning was either spared or severely impaired, depending on how the animal was encouraged to use those cues.

I view data bearing on the capacity of representational flexibility as the most compelling evidence for a distinction in the nature of hippocampal-dependent and hippocampal-independent memory systems. We interpreted the parallel findings from challenge tests on odor discrimination and place learning as indicating that the spared memory representation of animals with hippocampal damage is highly abnormal in form even when it can be successfully used to solve a particular problem. Moreover, the pattern of loss of flexibility and spared performance was consistent with our characterizations of hippocampal-independent memory as a set of isolated individual representations.

Our account of the robust and largely consistent finding of deficits in spatial learning after damage to the hippocampal system is that place learning usually puts a heavy emphasis on relational processing. The use of the Morris water maze, the radial arm maze, and similar paradigms to compare "spatial" versus "visually cued" learning is deceptive; it is *not* equivalent to a comparison between learning guided by visual cues versus, for example, auditory cues. Rather, what is compared in such analyses is learning guided by visual (or other) cues versus that guided by spatial *relationships* among visual (or other) cues. Consistent with our account, place learning is ordinarily a powerful example of relational representation in just the way described above for water-maze learning. Thus I have no argument with the cognitive-mapping theory of hippocampal function except, as proposed by O'Keefe and Nadel, that this view is limited to spatial memory.

Contextual and conditional associations   Combined within this theme are two related proposals: Hirsh's (1974, 1980) contextual-retrieval theory and Sutherland and Rudy's (1989) configural-association theory, both of which can be traced to traditional conditioning theory. Moreover, these proposals share the common motivation of preserving an S-R account of learning in situations that exceed the conventional boundaries of conditioning mechanisms. Specifically, both theories can be construed as attempts to resolve paradoxes in conditioning that occur when cues have ambiguous reinforcement assignments that depend upon their juxtaposition or context, and in both theories the hippocampus is viewed as the central structure mediating the resolution. Hirsh (1974) first confronted this problem by proposing that the hippocampus supports contextual retrieval, the ability to utilize the context in which conditioned cues occur to retrieve the appropriate association. He initially employed this model to explain the deficit, following hippocampal damage, in learning to turn one direction or the other in a T-maze, depending on an imposed motivational context (hunger or thirst). According to this account, choosing a direction to turn was resolved by a hippocampal-dependent mechanism that employed motivational state as a contextual cue for retrieving one of the possible responses. On the other hand, Hirsh characterized the behavior of animals with hippocampal damage as "habit prone," in that they investigate fewer hypotheses and rigidly adopt behaviors associated with reinforcement very early, which is consistent with "everything for which early S-R theorists would have wished" (Hirsh, 1974, p. 439). Contrary to the present characterization of this account as an addendum to conditioning theory, Hirsh considered his proposal about hippocampal-dependent representations as "neo-Tolmanian," although he did not make clear how cue-context interactions are maplike. Hirsh later extended his account to all forms of conditional operations and specifically compared his views with those of O'Keefe and Nadel (1978), arguing that the two accounts differed solely in that "O'Keefe and Nadel hold that logical operations occurring within the hippocampus are applied only to information about space in the literal sense," whereas Hirsh held that "they are applied to problem spaces, in the sense of analytical geometry, of all kinds" (Hirsh, 1980, p. 180). From this perspective, one might consider the contextual-association hypothesis as similar to the cognitive-mapping account. However, as I will discuss below, there is a fundamental distinction (beyond the limitation to literal space) between a system that supports conditional operations and a cognitive map.

More recent findings showing that animals with hippocampal lesions are less influenced by contextual cues than normal animals lend support to Hirsh's account. Thus while the expression of a classically conditioned eye-blink response was found normally to depend on the environmental context of conditioning, animals with hippocampal lesions showed no such context-specificity in retrieval (Penick & Solomon, 1991). Similarly, rats with hippocampal lesions were found deficient in various forms of appetitive conditioning that are normally context-specific (Good & Honey, 1991). In addition, a series of recent experiments on conditioned emotional responses have shown that while intact animals freeze when returned to the environmental context in which a transient conditioned stimulus (CS) previously signaled shock, rats with hippocampal lesions fail to show conditioning to the context (Kim & Fanslow, 1992; Phillips & LeDoux, 1992; Selden et al., 1991). Notably, animals with hippocampal damage show normal strong conditioning to context when the transient CS is omitted, which demonstrates that they are able to process contextual stimuli efficiently. All of these results are consistent with Hirsh's view that animals with hippocampal damage fail to use contextual cues in retrieving associations. However, a separate line of data seems to contradict this conclusion. Using quite different training paradigms, Winocur and Olds (1978) have reported that rats with hippocampal lesions show abnormally *strong* utilization of contextual cues, for example, demonstrating less than normal transfer of a visual discrimination when retested in a novel environmental context and abnormally rapid learning when required to reverse a discrimination in a context different than that used during initial training. They have also observed that the degree to which normal rats show aversion to an environment in which a transient CS was associated with shock is inversely proportional to the probability that the CS predicted the shock but that rats with hippocampal lesions conditioned strongly to contextual cues, regardless of the predictability of the CS. The mixture of findings in a wide range of training paradigms indicates that seemingly idiosyncratic differences in the conditioning stimuli and training procedures can result in either abnormally weak or abnormally strong contextual conditioning in animals with hippocampal damage.

It is far from clear precisely what variables determined the contrasting outcomes across these studies, but some preliminary conclusions can be drawn. First, the contradictory results across studies in which the training environment was the context, combined with the consistent finding that animals with hippocampal damage can process environmental cues when the CS is omitted, indicate that animals with hippocampal damage learn too little, too much, or just the right amount about the spatial environment, depending on other unidentified nonspatial factors. Furthermore, the experiments in which static motivational state was the contextual cue indicate that the role of the hippocampus in contextual learning is not limited to spatial contexts. This pattern of findings falls outside the explanatory power of the view that contextual learning is merely an example of spatial learning. Second, these findings serve to remind us that we cannot simply define contextual stimuli as "background" or "static" cues and then treat them as just another stimulus modality, asking whether this type of cue is used normally by animals with hippocampal damage. As with spatial stimuli, it must be kept in mind that contextual cues are not just another stimulus modality, like visual or auditory stimuli; rather "context" refers to a type of figure-ground relationship between static cues and the designated CS. Moreover, it appears that the nature of the cue-context interaction can vary and can influence behavior in different ways, depending on several perceptual and procedural variables. Third, even though the specific outcome across these studies varied, in each case the hippocampus was shown to play a key role in the representation of cue-context relationships, which is consistent with our view that the hippocampal system serves a broad range of memory organizations.

The historical descendant of Hirsh's proposals regarding hippocampal function in contextual and conditional associations is Sutherland and Rudy's (1989) configural association theory (see also Rudy & Sutherland, 1992, this volume). According to this account, the hippocampus is essential for learning associations of configural stimuli, and the learning of elemental associations occurs independently of the hippocampal system. These investigators, more explicitly than Hirsh, focused on configural association as a resolution to the paradox of an ambiguous reinforcement history. To make their case, Sutherland and Rudy quite rightly selected the negative-patterning problem for fundamental consideration. In this paradigm, two different stimuli are each assigned a positive associative value when presented alone but a negative associative value when presented conjointly. This situation presents a serious challenge to conditioning theory because, according to an S-R account, it is not possible for the combination of two stimuli independently associated with reward to have a net negative association. To resolve the dilemma, Sutherland and Rudy proposed that the hippocampus supports the creation of a configural stimulus, acting as a NAND gate that receives input from the individual cues and yielding a negated output when both cues are present. This output can then be employed as a *unique CS*, a configural cue that is distinct from its constituent elements, used thereafter to support associations with reinforcers in the conventional way. In this way the configural-association account calls not for a wholly new form of memory organization but only for a special mechanism that can convert combinations of ambiguous stimulus presentations into unique representations that can subsequently be employed within the traditional conditioning framework.

The configural-association theory and our relational-representational account are similar in that they both are concerned with how stimuli are combined by hippocampal processing and they both consider spatial memory only a particularly good example of such processing. However, these similarities are superficial, and the two approaches differ in three related and fundamental ways. First, the two accounts differ on the proposed underlying memory structure. Configural associations are an elaboration of S-R conditioning, whereas relational representations are components of a large-scale memory organization, likened to James systematic organization of memories, Tolman's cognitive map, and Bartlett's schema. Second, the two accounts differ on the proposed mechanism for relating cues. Configural associations involve conjoining stimulus elements to create a new and distinct cue, which then operates as the CS in forming a separate association independent of the associations of the stimulus elements. By contrast, a relational network maintains independent representations for stimulus items and events and connects them by the relevant relational linkage in memory space.

Third, and perhaps most important, the two accounts differ in how they mediate flexible performance and in what kinds of flexibility are supported. Configural associations are intended to support responses to cue elements that have ambiguous reinforcement histories; the configural cue serves to disambiguate the situations in which the elements appear. This mechanism will support the ability of the subject to respond in different ways, i.e., flexibly, to the same cue, depending on whether it appears alone or within the configural. There is, however, an important limitation of this kind of flexibility: it extends only to elements and configurals that have reinforcement histories. The configural account makes no prediction on, nor does it support, judgments when the subject is presented with novel configurations of cues. For example, Sutherland and Rudy (1989) suggested that configuring might support performance in the Morris-water-maze task by constructing a unique configural for the elements in scenes viewed from each of the starting locations used in training (customarily, four starting locations are used). The ambiguity that is resolved is important: many of the same visual elements appear in different scenes (i.e., they are in the views from multiple starting points). Configuring could allow the animal to make each scene unique and learn a swim trajectory for each, but what if the rat had to start from a novel location? Memory based on configural cues would be at a loss here. We found that normal rats could indeed navigate from novel starting locations in the water maze, which is consistent with our view that intact animals do not use a configural strategy in this paradigm. Conversely, rats with hippocampal damage performed poorly when required to navigate from novel starting locations, which suggests that they lacked a kind of flexibility that could not, even in principle, be guided by configural associations (Eichenbaum, Stewart, & Morris, 1990).

In contrast to configural associations, relational representations are intended to support performance that can be predicted by any set of links within the network space. These networks are seen to support flexible responses to cue elements with ambiguous histories: in cases like negative patterning, the relational link represents a conditional operation (as per Hirsh, 1980) such that the simultaneous appearance of two elements leads one along a different response path or reinforcement association than either of the elements alone. The representation of the elements experienced in a negative-patterning task is not seen as a set of isolated elemental or configural associations. Rather, representations of the two stimuli are stored within a larger network that includes features of the apparatus and other events surrounding the training experience. Most important, a network of relational representations is seen to do much more than resolve ambiguities of reinforcement history. It supports inferential behavior in new, never-reinforced situations. Thus in the water-maze example the network includes a cognitive map of the spatial relations among the cues around the tank and permits navigation along new routes consistent with the represented spatial relationships, just as O'Keefe and Nadel (1978) would have it. My contention, however, is that the hippocampus supports the construction of similar memory spaces that exceed environmental space, for example, semantic maps, maps of monkeys' associations among various junk objects, maps of rats' associations among odors, etc. The key feature here is that a network representation contains the appropriate indirect links among items never experienced together, which permits the subject to respond in accordance with inferred relationships.

The capacity for inference is central to relational representation and a key distinction between the configural and relational accounts. There are indeed notable examples of situations where rats and monkeys with hippocampal damage actually *resort* to using configurals to solve problems. A particularly striking example involves our findings on simultaneous odor discrimination, where we found that rats with hippocampal damage succeeded by learning an independent association for each pairwise configuration of odor cues. While this representational strategy was satisfactory for learning some of the discrimination problems, it failed to support performance when the stimulus elements were rearranged in novel pairings, which thus demonstrates the inflexibility of configural representations. Saunders and Weiskrantz (1989) made a parallel finding on monkeys performing a conditional discrimination. In this experiment animals were required to discriminate closely juxtaposed object pairs composed of different pairings from the same set of object elements. Monkeys with hippocampal damage succeeded in learning the discrimination but, unlike normal animals, could not demonstrate their knowledge of the appropriate pairings when the object elements were presented separately. On the other hand, other experiments have shown that animals with hippocampal damage sometimes encode the context along with the cues as configurals and then show poor transfer when the context is switched, or perform well when the context switch also involves a switch of reward assignments (Winocur & Olds, 1978; Gaffan & Harrison, 1989). Thus both rats and monkeys with hippocampal damage can succeed in representing stimulus pairs as configurals, but these representations are inadequate to support inferential use of the information about stimulus elements in novel situations.

I see the lack of flexibility as a fatal drawback of the configural-association account, and this limitation is also fatal to any formulation based on conventional conditioning mechanisms that does not allow inferential use of memories. Other accounts proposing an essential role for the hippocampal system in resolving stimulus ambiguities by directing attention to the relevant cues in different contexts (e.g., Schmajuk & Moore, 1988) or by other "interference-reduction" mechanisms (e.g., Olton & Shapiro, 1992, this volume) have the same limitation. My position is that representational flexibility cannot be provided by any mechanism that resolves ambiguity or interference by construing a *special* solution for each stimulus combination, that is, by making a reinforcement assignment for each particular combination of cues experienced. Such solutions can predict unambiguous responses to repetitions of each situation previously encountered and reinforced but fail to address the issue of inferential judgments in novel situations. Indeed, I take this issue to be a key operational distinction that divides memory mechanisms based on reinforcement contingencies, whether the conditioning involves simple, conditional, or configural cues, and truly cognitive accounts.

Working memory   Olton, Becker, and Handlemann (1979) created yet a different formulation of hippocampal function based on Honig's (1978) distinction between working memory and reference memory. The term "working memory" as used in this context differs in meaning from the same term used in characterizations of human memory (see Baddley, 1992, this volume). According to Olton's distinction, "working memory" refers to a representation essential for performance on one trial but "not useful" on subsequent trials of an experimental session. The latter part of this characterization is, importantly, an understatement: in all working-memory tests, memory cues are frequently reused, so a representation based on a cumulative reinforcement history is *counterproductive*. In all of the conventional tests of working memory that reuse cues—including the delayed-response tasks, the alternation task, and the radial-arm-maze task—animals with hippocampal damage are severely impaired. In contrast with "working memory," "reference memory" refers to learned performance based on representations useful across many trials, such as maze tasks in which arms are always or never baited and sensory discrimination tasks; learning these consistent associations is hippocampal-independent. The distinction between working memory and reference memory has been very fruitful in revealing a selective disorder associated with hippocampal damage in animals, but the concept of working memory, as conventionally defined, does not account for the range of the amnesic disorder observed in humans or animals. It may be that the important representational demands of conventional working-memory tasks go beyond whether the stored information is "useful" across trials, which suggests that we must carefully consider the additional representational requirements in working-memory tasks, specifically those associated with the repetitiveness of cues and events across trials.

Howard Eichenbaum

An understanding of the representational demands of working memory tasks requires a clear view of task procedures. Consider, for example, the radial-arm-maze task. The apparatus consists of an elevated maze composed a set of arms radiating from a central platform like spokes on a wheel. On every trial each of the arms is baited and the rat is allowed to retrieve the rewards. In different versions of this paradigm, the maze arms are either identical and performance is guided by the arrangement of distal visual cues surrounding the maze or the arms are covered with different visual and tactile cues that are interchanged between runs so that performance is guided by intramaze cues (Olton, Becker, & Handlemann, 1979). On each trial a well trained rat forages efficiently, visiting each maze arm just once, which indicates that it has remembered arms visited within the course of that trial; this is the working-memory component of the task. It would appear that the representational demands of this sort of task differ from those involved in both cognitive mapping and conditional associations. Olton, Becker, and Handlemann (1979) have provided specific experimental tests comparing predictions of the cognitive-mapping and working-memory perspectives, and they have demonstrated the superiority of the working-memory view in some situations. For example, they found that rats trained preoperatively in a radial-arm-maze task, after hippocampal damage, are selectively impaired in working-memory but not reference-memory components of the task. In addition, they found that rats with hippocampal damage are impaired in performing a working-memory task guided by specific nonspatial cues. Furthermore, they have interpreted other findings, such as the well-described impairment of rats with hippocampal lesions in processing the passage of time (e.g., Meck et al., 1984), within the working-memory framework. As Olton and colleagues have convincingly argued, each of these findings also falls outside the explanatory range of theories based on cognitive mapping and conditional associations.

What are the representational demands of working-memory tasks, and how do they differ from those of cognitive-mapping and conditional-association tasks? As characterized by Olton and colleagues, working memory involves the ability to hold some information "in mind" for a brief period and then use this information and subsequently reject it. However, it is important to consider precisely what must be remembered in these tasks and how representations of more and less recent experiences are related. Let me begin with what working memory and timing have in common. Notably, in both working-memory tasks and timing tasks, the relevant environmental stimuli that guide performance, the maze arms or operant levers, are present throughout the testing session; there is no requirement to remember these stimuli. Rather, what must be remembered during the relevant retention period is the animal's immediately previous interaction with those cues, that is, the most recent behavioral *episode*. In the literature on animals, working memory has been described as a form of episodic memory (Olton, 1984), and indeed this is perhaps a better designation. Although it is not clear whether this kind of memory is fully consistent with the personal nature of human episodic memory (see Tulving, 1985), the key memories in working-memory tasks share much in common with human episodic memory, defined as a record of the events surrounding a particular experience. Viewed in this way, the working-memory hypothesis, like other themes in theories of hippocampal function, can be traced to earlier theoretical accounts based on properties of normal memory (Tulving, 1972; James, 1890). Moreover, interpreting the deficits, on these tasks, associated with hippocampal damage as a loss of episodic-memory capacity aligns the findings on animals with the observation of severe impairment of episodic memory in human amnesia (Schacter & Tulving, 1982; see also Schacter, 1992, this volume; Moscovitch, 1992, this volume) and with viewing episodic memory as one subdivision of declarative memory (Squire, 1992, this volume; Cohen, 1984).

Furthermore, because every behavioral episode is defined by comparisons to earlier and later episodes with the same set of stimuli, the underlying form of episodic memories clearly can be considered to fall under the rubric of relational representation. Neither cognitive mapping nor conditional association includes a mechanism for episodic learning, and episodic memory does indeed demand aspects of relational representation different from those demanded by either cognitive maps or conditional-configural associations. Notably, theorists in both of these camps have stretched their accounts in this direction. Thus both accounts have attempted to incorporate a notion of "temporal context," although these arguments have provided neither a clear understanding of temporal context in terms consistent with the predominant importance of space, in the case of cognitive mapping, nor an indication of mechanisms by which temporal context can act as a conditional CS, in the case of conditional learning (Nadel & Willner, 1980; Nadel, 1992; Sutherland & Rudy, 1989). Admittedly, what is contained in the episodic memories of these tasks is complicated: such memories include perceptual, motor, and affective aspects of the subject's interactions with the cues. Importantly, what distinguishes episodes is the sequence in which events occurred and details that make it unique *relative to other similar past episodes with the same stimuli.* We understand little of how episodes are compared and contrasted, although it seems that such comparisons are strongly encouraged or required for episodic memory judgements. In part, episodes are defined by comparisons with similar previous events; perhaps these comparisons are mediated by some form of "temporal map" that represents both the sequence of like instances and incidental variations of the same fundamental event.

Finally, although the working-memory explanation accounts for an important subset of the findings about hippocampal-dependent memory, there are critical limitations to its applicability. Thus many learning tasks used to reveal impairments after hippocampal damage can be supported by reference memory, that is, learning consistent associations across trials, rather than memory for specific episodes. Examples of such tasks include place learning (e.g., Morris et al., 1982), contextual learning (Phillips & LeDoux, 1991; Selden et al., 1991), and our simultaneous-odor-discrimination task.

3.3 Bridging the Gaps between Theories of Hippocampal Function in Animals and Humans

Each of the three themes discussed above has some important strengths and also some important limitations in accounting for the data most pertinent to other themes (for a more complete review of these comparisons, see Cohen & Eichenbaum, 1993). By identifying the common fundamental features of each account, we can go a long way toward bridging the gaps between theories of hippocampal function in animal and human memory, which would lead to a more comprehensive understanding of declarative memory in animals that is fully compatible with that in humans. The cognitive-mapping account, based explicitly on memory for spatial relations among environmental cues, most fully captures the quality of relational representation in declarative memory; its primary limitation is in O'Keefe and Nadel's restriction to space, which cannot adequately explain the findings on nonspatial tasks, such as the odor-discrimination tasks considered here and many of the behavioral paradigms considered in the contextual, configural, and working-memory accounts described above. The contextual and configural-association accounts focus on how relational representations can resolve ambiguities in the reinforcement history of stimuli, but we should not conclude that this is accomplished by making special exceptions to reinforcement assignments—rather, it is done within an organized network of interactions that include, but are not restricted to, contextual and conditional relations. The working-memory account focuses on episodic memories that highlight variations across repetitions of similar events, by which events may be compared and contrasted within an organization of their temporal relations. Combining these accounts provides a compelling view of the range of dimensions incorporated in the organization of declarative memory. The hippocampal system supports systematic memory organizations based on spatial, contextual, conditional, and episodic relations, and indeed, perhaps all manner of relations.

Representational flexibility and the testability of the declarative-memory hypothesis Each of the main themes based on experimentation on animals address only tangentially the key property of representational flexibility. Importantly, each of the behavioral paradigms central to the above-described accounts contains an *implicit* demand for representational flexibility, such as required for navigation along different routes in most place-learning tasks and for responding differently to the same particular cues in contextual, conditional-learning, and working-memory tasks. But none of these accounts has incorporated the full range of representational flexibility so prevalent in assessments of human memory, more specifically, the ability to express memories across many situations and even in wholly new contexts. Yet it is this property that offers the definitive test of the declarative-memory hypothesis and can provide the closest link to the concept of explicit-memory expression in humans.

Some (e.g., Nadel, 1992) have criticized the declarative-memory hypothesis because it fails to predict in advance the situations where impairment will be observed after hippocampal damage. The basis of such criticisms lies in apparent inconsistencies in data on, for example, odor-discrimination learning and simultaneous versus successive discrimination. Indeed, Kimble and Zack (1967) and, more recently, Reid et al. (1991) have reported normal learning of olfactory discrimination by rats with hippocampal lesions. Of course, we too reported that odor-discrimination learning can proceed at a normal or even supernormal rate in animals with hippocampal damage *under some task conditions* (see above and Eichenbaum, Fagan, & Cohen, 1986; Otto et al., 1991). Staubli et al. (1984) and we (see above) have reported deficits in other conditions. When different conditions could be directly compared, as accomplished above, our formulation provides an accounting of the discrepancies. Also, in apparent contradiction to our findings on odor discrimination, some previous reports (e.g., Kimble, 1963) have indicated impairment on successive visual discrimination and sparing of simultaneous visual discrimination after hippocampal lesions. Yet a reconsideration of these findings also aligns the results with our account. Thus Kimble's successive brightness discrimination, which required subjects to turn in different directions, depending on the color of the maze, can now be viewed as a conditional-discrimination task. On the other hand, his simultaneous brightness discrimination involved widely separated cues and close contiguity of each stimulus with its reinforcement, procedures that encourage individual stimulus representations and hinder stimulus comparisons, unlike our discrimination protocol.

Beyond these particular applications of the declarative-procedural account, it is important to consider that all experiences invoke both declarative and procedural representations. What matters is *not* how the experimenter formally characterizes a task (e.g., as a spatial or nonspatial discrimination, as a simultaneous or successive discrimination) but what representational strategies guide the animal's behavior. Even a seemingly subtle change in the nature of stimulus materials can shift the predominant representation from being largely under the control of one system to being under the control of another. This characterization also applies to the data on monkeys and humans. For example, in human amnesics, performance on verbal-learning tasks may be severely impaired or completely spared, depending on retrieval instructions (e.g., Graf et al., 1984; Moscovitch, 1984). In monkeys with medial-temporal-lobe damage, performance on learning a visual discrimination can be severely impaired or completely spared, depending on whether the cues are three-dimensional objects or two-dimensional patterns (Zola-Morgan & Squire, 1985).

If we can't predict whether impairment will be observed on any particular kind of task, isn't the declarative-procedural hypothesis useless? This is true only if one limits the approach to a conventional comparison among tasks and leaves explaining the variations in results to ad hoc interpretations about how the information was differentially encoded. Our approach suggests that a major shift in how we go about assessing hippocampal function will lead to a clearer understanding of the mixture of behavioral findings. Specifically, implementing the above-described double-pronged approach may go a long way in providing this advance. First, we must develop variations of memory paradigms that offer a differential advantage to either relational or individual representation and demonstrate a selective disorder after hippocampal damage when the relational-processing demands are high. Second, we must assess the nature of successfully acquired representations, focusing on the capacity for flexible expression of memories across a range of circumstances and novel situations, and demonstrate a loss in flexibility after hippocampal damage, even when performance during repetitions of the learning event is quantitatively normal. Under such a strategy the declarative-memory hypothesis can be tested using virtually any behavioral paradigm and any species. Such a shift in experimental perspective is needed to break the impasse in the controversies among the various existing theoretical positions and to reveal the fundamental features of hippocampal-dependent declarative memory common to humans and animals.

3.4   Toward a Cognitive-Neuroscientific Account of Declarative Memory

The above accounting of data from the literatures on human amnesia, on the effects of damage to the hippocampal system in animals, and on the behavioral physiology of the hippocampus provides a preliminary outline for mapping declarative memory onto the hippocampal system. Progress toward this goal can be summarized in terms of the multiple levels of analysis presented at the outset of this chapter. At the cognitive level, considerable data has been accumulated toward characterizing the psychological properties of declarative memory in humans. In addition to the defining characterizations of declarative memory as "conscious" and "explicit," its distinguishing properties include the ability to support comparisons among items in memory and the expression of memories in a variety of contexts, including wholly new situations. These memory capacities can be dissociated from other, contrasting memory abilities in studies of normal humans, human amnesics, and animals with selective brain damage. Furthermore, at the neuropsychological level of analysis, damage to the hippocampal system in humans results in a selective loss of the characteristics of declarative memory, which has enabled us to initially identify the brain system supporting this form of memory.

This chapter has focused on a deeper level of analysis: establishing an animal model of amnesia and detailed studies of the functional components of the hippocampal system and their neural-coding schemes. Much of our effort has been aimed at developing assessments of amnesia that test for properties of declarative memory identified in the studies on humans. Our work has shown that one can demonstrate in animals a capacity for declarative memory defined by two critical properties: *relational representation* (supporting comparisons among items in memory) and *representational flexibility* (permitting the expression of memories in new contexts). Morevover, these studies have confirmed the essential role of the hippocampal system in memory representation supporting these capacities in animals. Furthermore, these particular characterizations of declarative memory associated with the hippocampal system are shared with earlier proposals about hippocampal function in animals, which considerably expands the range of applicable data about the hippocampal system.

Our neuropsychological and electrophysiological investigations on animals have also provided an initial characterization of functional distinctions and flow of information between components of the hippocampal system. Our findings indicate that the parahippocampal region acts as an intermediary between cortical and hippocampal information processing, serving first as a convergence center and temporary storage site for cortical representations bound for the hippocampus and then as a distribution center for sending the output of hippocampal processing back to the cortex. The hippocampus itself interacts extensively with the parahippocampal area and encodes abstract relations among the convergent cortical information represented and stored there, ultimately influencing the nature of cortical representations via outputs sent back to the cortex. This processing serves to organize cortical representations as a memory space that supports the properties of relational representation and representational flexibility. Finally, these preliminary and tentative conclusions about the functional interactions of the cortex and hippocampal system offer a working sketch of the functional circuitry and coding schemes that might support declarative representations. If confirmed and elaborated by additional data, these findings may serve as the beginnings of a cognitive-neuroscientific account of how declarative memory is mediated by the brain.

ACKNOWLEDGMENTS

Preparation of this manuscript was supported in part by the National Institutes of Health, grant NS26402; the National Institute of Aging, grant AG09973; and the Office of Naval Research, grant N0014-91-J-1881. I gratefully acknowledge the work of several collaborators involved in the experiments described herein: Michael Bunsey, Anne Fagan, Pat Mathews, Richard Morris, Jennifer Nagode, Tim Otto, Carolyn Stewart, and Sidney Wiener. The theoretical position articulated here was developed in collaboration with Neal Cohen.

REFERENCES

Baddeley, A. (1992). Working memory: The interface between memory and cognition. *Journal of Cognitive Neuroscience, 4,* 281–288.

Bartlett, F. C. (1932). *Remembering.* London: Cambridge University Press.

Berger, T. W., Berry, S. D., & Thompson, R. F. (1986). Role of the hippocampus in classical conditioning of aversive and appetitive behaviors. In R. L. Isaacson & K. H. Pribram (Eds.), *The hippocampus* (Vol. 4, pp. 203–239). New York: Plenum Press.

Brown, M. W. (1982). Effect of context on the response of single units recorded from the hippocampal region of behaviourally trained monkeys. In C. A. Marsan & H. Matthies (Eds.), *Neuronal plasticity and memory formation* (pp. 557–573). New York: Raven Press.

Bunsey, M., & Eichenbaum, H. (1993). Paired associate learning in rats: Critical involvement of the perirhinal-entorhinal area. *Behavioral Neuroscience*, in press.

Cohen, N. J. (1984). Preserved learning capacity in amnesia: Evidence for multiple memory systems. In N. Butters & L. R. Squire (Eds.), *The neuropsychology of memory* (pp. 83–103). New York: Guilford Press.

Cohen, N. J., & Eichenbaum, H. (1991). The theory that wouldn't die: A critical look at the spatial mapping theory of hippocampal function. *Hippocampus, 1*, 265–268.

Cohen, N. J., & Eichenbaum, H. (1993). *Memory, amnesia, and the hippocampal system*. Cambridge: MIT Press.

Cohen, N. J., & Squire, L. R. (1980). Preserved learning and retention of a pattern-analyzing skill in amnesia: Dissociation of knowing how and knowing that. *Science, 210*, 207–210.

Corkin, S. (1968). Acquisition of a motor skill after bilateral medial temporal lobe excision. *Neuropsychologia, 6*, 225–265.

Daum, I., Channon, S., Polkey, C. E., & Gray, J. A. (1991). Classical conditioning after temporal lobe lesions in man: Impairment in conditional discrimination. *Behavioral Neuroscience, 105*, 396–408.

Davidson, T. L., & Jarrard, L. E. (1991). A role for the hippocampus in the control of ingestive behavior. *Society for Neuroscience Abstracts, 17*, 493.

Devenport, L. D., Hale, R. L., & Stidham, J. A. (1988). Sampling behavior in the radial maze and operant chamber: Role of the hippocampus and prefrontal area. *Behavioral Neuroscience, 102*, 489–498.

Douglas, R. J. (1967). The hippocampus and behavior. *Psychological Bulletin, 67*, 416–442.

Eichenbaum, H., & Cohen, N. J. (1988). Representation in the hippocampus: What do the neurons code? *Trends in Neuroscience, 11*, 244–248.

Eichenbaum, H., Cohen, N. J., Otto, T., & Wible, C. G. (1992a). Memory representation in the hippocampus: Functional domain and functional organization. In L. R. Squire, G. Lynch, N. M. Weinberger, & J. L. McGaugh (Eds.), *Memory: Organization and locus of change* (pp. 163–204). Oxford: Oxford University Press.

Eichenbaum, H., Cohen, N. J., Otto, T., & Wible, C. G. (1992b). A snapshot without the album. *Brain Research Reviews, 16*, 209–215.

Eichenbaum, H., Fagan, A., & Cohen, N. J. (1986). Normal olfactory discrimination learning set and facilitation of reversal learning after combined and separate lesions of the fornix and amygdala in rats: Implications for preserved learning in amnesia. *Journal of Neuroscience, 6*, 1876–1884.

Eichenbaum, H., Fagan, A., Mathews, P., & Cohen, N. J. (1988). Hippocampal system dysfunction and odor discrimination learning in rats: Impairment or facilitation depending on representational demands. *Behavioral Neuroscience, 102*, 3531–3542.

Eichenbaum, H., Kuperstein, M., Fagan, A., & Nagode, J. (1986). Cue-sampling and goal-approach correlates of hippocampal unit activity in rats performing an odor discrimination task. *Journal of Neuroscience, 7*, 716–732.

Eichenbaum, H., Mathews, P., & Cohen, N. J. (1989). Further studies of hippocampal representation during odor discrimination learning. *Behavioral Neuroscience, 103*, 1207–1216.

Eichenbaum, H., Otto, T., & Cohen, N. J. (1994). Two functional components of the hippocampal-memory system. *Behavioral and Brain Sciences,* in press.

Eichenbaum, H., Otto, T., & Cohen, N. J. (1992). The hippocampus—What does it do? *Behavioral and Neural Biology, 57,* 2—36.

Eichenbaum, H., Stewart, C., & Morris, R. G. M. (1990). Hippocampal representation in spatial learning. *Journal of Neuroscience, 10,* 331—339.

Foster, T. C., Christian, E. P., Hampson, R. E., Campbell, K. A., & Deadwyler, S. A. (1987). Sequential dependencies regulate sensory evoked responses of single units in the rat hippocampus. *Brain Research, 40,* 86—96.

Fuster, J. M. (1991). Hippocampal neurons in short term color memory. *Society for Neuroscience Abstracts, 17,* 661.

Gabriel, M., Foster, K., Orona, E., Saltwick, S. E., & Stanton, M. (1980). Neuronal activity of cingulate cortex, anteroventral thalamus, and hippocampal formation in discriminative conditioning: Encoding and extraction of the significance of conditional stimuli. *Progress in Psychobiology and Physiological Psychology, 9,* 125—231.

Gaffan, D. (1974). Recognition impaired and association intact in the memory of monkeys after transection of the fornix. *Journal of Comparative and Physiological Psychology, 86,* 1100—1109.

Gaffan, D., & Harrison, S. (1989). Place memory and scene memory: Effects of fornix transection in the monkey. *Experimental Brain Research, 74,* 202—212.

Goldman-Rakic, P. S. (1992). Working memory and the mind. *Scientific American, 267,* 111—117.

Good, M., & Honey, R. C. (1991). Conditioning and contextual retrieval in hippocampal rats. *Behavioral Neuroscience, 105,* 499—509.

Graf, P., & Schacter, D. L. (1985). Implicit and explicit memory for new associations in normal and amnesic patients. *Journal of Experimental Psychology: Learning, Memory, and Cognition, 11,* 501—518.

Graf, P., Squire, L. R., & Mandler, G. (1984). Amnesic patients perform normally on one kind of memory test for previously presented words. *Journal of Experimental Psychology: Learning, Memory, and Cognition, 10,* 164—178.

Gray, J. A., & Rawlins, J. N. P. (1986). Comparator and buffer memory: An attempt to integrate two models of hippocampal function. In R. L. Isaacson & K. H. Pribram (Eds.), *The hippocampus* (Vol. 4, pp. 159—202). New York: Plenum Press.

Gross, C. G. (1973). Visual functions of the inferotemporal cortex. In R. Jung (Ed.), *Handbook of sensory physiology* (Vol. VII-3B, pp. 451—482). New York: Springer Verlag.

Hill, A. J., & Best, P. J. (1981). Effects of deafness and blindness on the spatial correlates of hippocampal unit activity in the rat. *Experimental Neurology, 74,* 204—217.

Hirsh, R. (1974). The hippocampus and contextual retrieval of information from memory: A theory. *Behavioral Biology, 12,* 421—444.

Hirsh, R. (1980). The hippocampus, conditional operations, and cognition. *Physiological Psychology, 8,* 175—182.

Honig, W. K. (1978). Studies of working memory in the pigeon. In S. H. Hulse, H. Fowler, & W. K. Honig (Eds.), *Cognitive processes in animal behavior,* pp. 211—248. Hillsdale, NJ: Lawrence Erlbaum.

James, W. (1890). *The principles of psychology.* New York: Holt. (1918 edition.)

James, W. (1892). *Psychology: The briefer course.* New York: Harper & Row. (1961 edition.)

Johnson, M. K. (1990). Functional forms of memory. In J. L. McGaugh, N. Weinberger, & G. Lynch (Eds.), *Brain organization and memory: Cells, systems, and circuits* (pp. 106–136). New York: Oxford University Press.

Johnson, M. K. (1992). MEM: Mechanisms of recollection. *Journal of Cognitive Neuroscience, 4*, 268–280.

Kesner, R. P. (1984). The neurobiology of memory: Implicit and explicit assumptions. In J. L. McGaugh, G. Lynch, & N. Weinberger (Eds.), *The neurobiology of learning and memory* (pp. 111–118). New York: Guilford Press.

Kim, J. J., & Fanslow, M. S. (1992). Modality-specific retrograde amnesia of fear. *Science, 256*, 675–677.

Kimble, D. P. (1963). The effects of bilateral hippocampal lesions in rats. *Journal of Comparative and Physiological Psychology, 56*, 273–283.

Kimble, D. P. (1968). Hippocampus and internal inhibition. *Psychological Bulletin, 70*, 285–295.

Kimble, D. P., & Kimble, R. J. (1970). The effect of hippocampal lesions on extinction and "hypothesis" behavior in rats. *Physiology and Behavior, 5*, 735–738.

Kimble, D. P., & Zack, S. (1967). Olfactory discrimination in rats with hippocampal lesions. *Psychonomic Science, 8*, 211–212.

LeDoux, J. (1991). Emotion and the limbic system concept. *Concepts in Neuroscience, 2*, 169–199.

Lynch, G., & Granger, R. (1992). Variations in synaptic plasticity and types of memory in corticohippocampal networks. *Journal of Cognitive Neuroscience, 4*, 189–199.

Meck, W. H., Church, R. M., & Olton, D. S. (1984). Hippocampus, time, and memory. *Behavioral Neuroscience, 98*, 3–22.

Metcalfe, J., Cottrell, G. W., & Mencl, W. E. (1992). Cognitive binding: A computational-modeling analysis of a distinction between implicit and explicit memory. *Journal of Cognitive Neuroscience, 4*, 289–298.

Miller, V. M., & Best, P. J. (1980). Spatial correlates of hippocampal unit activity are altered by lesions of the fornix and entorhinal cortex. *Brain Research, 194*, 311–323.

Mishkin, M., Malamut, B., & Bachevalier, J. (1984). Memories and habits: Two neural systems. In J. L. McGaugh, G. Lynch, & N. M. Weinberger (Eds.), *The neurobiology of learning and memory* (pp. 287–296). New York: Guilford Press.

Miyashita, Y., Rolls, E. T., Cahusac, P. M. B., & Niki, H. (1989). Activity of hippocampal formation neurons in the monkey related to a stimulus association task. *Journal of Neurophysiology, 61*, 669–678.

Morris, R. G. M. (1984). Developments of a water-maze procedure for studying spatial learning in the rat. *Journal of Neuroscience Methods, 11*, 47–60.

Morris, R. G. M., Garrud, P., Rawlins, J. N. P., & O'Keefe, J. (1982). Place navigation impaired in rats with hippocampal lesions. *Nature, 297*, 681–683.

Moscovitch, M. (1984). The sufficient conditions for demonstrating preserved memory in amnesia: A task analysis. In N. Butters & L. R. Squire (Eds.), *The neuropsychology of memory* (pp. 104–114). New York: Guilford Press.

Moscovitch, M. (1992). Memory and working-with-memory: A component process model based on modules and central systems. *Journal of Cognitive Neuroscience, 4*, 257–267.

Moyer, J. R., Deyo, R. A., & Disterhoft, J. F. (1990). Hippocampectomy disrupts trace eyeblink conditioning in rabbits. *Behavioral Neuroscience, 104*, 243–252.

Muller, R. U., & Kubie, J. L. (1987). The effects of changes in the environment on the spatial firing of hippocampal complex-spike cells. *Journal of Neuroscience, 7*, 951–1968.

Muller, R. U., Kubie, J. L., & Ranck, J. B., Jr. (1987). Spatial firing patterns of hippocampal complex spike cells in a fixed environment. *Journal of Neuroscience, 7*, 1935–1950.

Murray, E. A., & Mishkin, M. (1986). Visual recognition in monkeys following rhinal cortical ablations combined with either amygdalectomy or hippocampectomy. *Journal of Neuroscience, 6*, 1991–2003.

Nadel, L. (1991). The hippocampus and space revisited. *Hippocampus, 1*, 221–229.

Nadel, L. (1992). Multiple memory systems: What and why. *Journal of Cognitive Neuroscience, 4*, 179–188.

Nadel, L., & Willner, J. (1980). Context and conditioning: A place for space. *Physiological Psychology, 8*, 218–228.

O'Keefe, J. A. (1976). Place units in the hippocampus of the freely moving rat. *Experimental Neurology, 51*, 78–109.

O'Keefe, J. A. (1979). A review of hippocampal place cells. *Progress in Neurobiology, 13*, 419–439.

O'Keefe, J. (1991). An allocentric spatial model for the hippocampal cognitive map. *Hippocampus, 1*, 230–235.

O'Keefe, J., & Conway, D. H. (1978). Hippocampal place units in the freely moving rat: Why they fire when they fire. *Experimental Brain Research, 31*, 573–590.

O'Keefe, J., & Nadel, L. (1978). *The hippocampus as a cognitive map*. New York: Oxford University Press.

O'Keefe, J., & Speakman, A. (1987). Single unit activity in the rat hippocampus during a spatial memory task. *Experimental Brain Research, 68*, 1–27.

Olton, D. S. (1984). Comparative analyses of episodic memory. *Brain and Behavioral Sciences, 7*, 250–251.

Olton, D. S. (1986). Hippocampal function and memory for temporal context. In R. L. Isaacson & K. H. Pribram (Eds.), *The hippocampus* (Vol. 4). New York: Plenum Press.

Olton, D. S., Becker, J. T., & Handlemann, G. E. (1979). Hippocampus, space, and memory. *Brain and Behavioral Sciences, 2*, 313–365.

Olton, D. S., & Papas, B. C. (1979). Spatial memory and hippocampal function. *Neuropsychologia, 17*, 669–682.

Olton, D. S., & Shapiro, M. L. (1992). Mnemonic dissociations: The power of parameters. *Journal of Cognitive Neuroscience, 4*, 200–207.

Ono, T., Nakamura, K., Fukuda, M., & Tamura, R. (1991). Place recognition responses of neurons in the monkey hippocampus. *Neuroscience Letters, 121*, 194–198.

Otto, T., & Eichenbaum, H. (1992a). Neuronal activity in the hippocampus during delayed non-match to sample performance in rats: Evidence for hippocampal processing in recognition memory. *Hippocampus, 2*, 323–334.

Otto, T., & Eichenbaum, H. (1992b). Complementary roles of orbital prefrontal cortex and the perirhinal-entorhinal cortices in an odor-guided delayed non-matching to sample task. *Behavioral Neuroscience, 106*, 763–776.

Otto, T., & Eichenbaum, H. (1992c). Toward a comprehensive account of hippocampal function: Studies of olfactory learning permit an integration of data across multiple levels of neurobiological analysis. In L. R. Squire & N. Butters (Eds.), *Neuropsychology of Memory* (2nd ed., pp. 415–428). New York: Guilford.

Otto, T., Schottler, F., Staubli, U., Eichenbaum, H., & Lynch, G. (1991). The hippocampus and olfactory discrimination learning: Effects of entorhinal cortex lesions on learning-set acquisition and on odor memory in a successive-cue, go/no-go task. *Behavioral Neuroscience, 105,* 111–119.

Penick, S., & Solomon, P. R. (1991). Hippocampus, context, and conditioning. *Behavioral Neuroscience, 105,* 611–617.

Phillips, R. G., & LeDoux, J. E. (1991). Different contributions of amygdala and hippocampus to cued and contextual fear conditioning. *Behavioral Neuroscience, 106,* 274–285.

Phillips, R. G., & LeDoux, J. E. (1992). Hippocampal lesions interfere with contextual fear conditioning in some but not all procedures: Clues to the nature of context. *Proceedings of the Fifth Conference on the Neurobiology of Learning and Memory.* Abstract no. 89.

Polster, M. R., Nadel, L., & Schacter, D. L. (1991). Cognitive neuroscience analyses of memory: A historical perspective. *Journal of Cognitive Neuroscience, 3,* 95–116.

Reid, I. C., Bannerman, D. M., & Morris, R. G. M. (1991). The role of the hippocampus in olfactory discrimination learning in rats. *Society for Neuroscience Abstracts, 17,* 130.

Roediger, H. L., Weldon, M. S., & Challis, B. H. (1989). Explaining dissociations between implicit and explicit measures of retention: A processing account. In H. L. Roediger & F. I. M. Craik (Eds.), *Varieties of memory and consciousness: Essays in honour of Endel Tulving* (pp. 3–41). Hillsdale, NJ: Erlbaum.

Rolls, E. T., Miyashita, Y., Cahusac, P., Kesner, R. P., Niki, H. D., Feigenbaum, J. D., & Bach, L. (1989). Hippocampal neurons in the monkey with activity related to the place where a stimulus is shown. *Journal of Neuroscience, 9,* 1835–1846.

Rolls, E. T., & O'Mara, S. M. (1991). Are there place cells in the primate hippocampus? *Society for Neuroscience Abstracts, 17,* 1101.

Ross, R. T., Orr, W. B., Holland, P. C., & Berger, T. W. (1984). Hippocampectomy disrupts acquisition and retention of learned conditional responding. *Behavioral Neuroscience, 2,* 211–225.

Rudy, J. W., & Sutherland, R. J. (1992). Configural and elemental associations and the memory coherence problem. *Journal of Cognitive Neuroscience, 4,* 208–216.

Sakurai, Y. (1990). Hippocampal cells have behavioral correlates during performance of an auditory working memory task in the rat. *Behavioral Neuroscience, 104,* 253–263.

Saunders, R. C., & Weiskrantz, L. (1989). The effects of fornix transection and combined fornix transection, mammillary body lesions, and hippocampal ablations on object pair association memory in the rhesus monkey. *Behavioral Brain Research, 35,* 85–94.

Schacter, D. L. (1985). Multiple forms of memory in humans and animals. In N. M. Weinberger, J. L. McGaugh, & G. Lynch (Eds.), *Memory systems of the brain* (pp. 351–380). New York: Guilford Press.

Schacter, D. L. (1987). Implicit memory: History and current status. *Journal of Experimental Psychology: Learning, Memory, and Cognition, 13,* 501–518.

Schacter, D. L. (1989a). Memory. In M. I. Posner (Ed.), *Foundations of cognitive science* (pp. 683–726). Cambridge: MIT Press.

Schacter, D. L. (1989b). On the relation between memory and consciousness. In H. L. Roediger & F. I. M. Craik (Eds.), *Varieties of memory and consciousness: Essays in honour of Endel Tulving* (pp. 355–389). Hillsdale, NJ: Erlbaum.

Schacter, D. L. (1992). Priming and multiple memory systems: Perceptual mechanisms of implicit memory. *Journal of Cognitive Neuroscience, 4,* 232–243.

Schacter, D. L., & Tulving, E. (1982). Memory, amnesia, and the episodic/semantic distinction. In R. L. Isaacson & N. E. Spear (Eds.), *The expression of knowledge.* New York: Plenum Press.

Schmajuk, N. A., & Moore, J. W. (1988). The hippocampus and the classically conditioned nictitating membrane response: A real-time attentional-associative model. *Psychobiology, 16,* 20–35.

Selden, N. R. W., Everitt, B. J., Jarrard, L. E., & Robbins, T. W. (1991). Complementary roles for the amygdala and hippocampus in aversive conditioning to explicit and contextual cues. *Neuroscience, 42,* 335–350.

Sherry, D. F., & Schacter, D. L. (1987). The evolution of multiple memory systems. *Psychological Reviews, 94,* 439–454.

Squire, L. R. (1987). *Memory and Brain.* New York: Oxford University Press.

Squire, L. R. (1992). Declarative and nondeclarative memory: Multiple brain systems supporting learning and memory. *Journal of Cognitive Neuroscience, 4,* 217–231.

Squire, L. R., Knowlton, B., & Musen, G. (1993). The structure and organization of memory. *Annual Review of Psychology, 44,* 453–495.

Squire, L. R., Ojemann, J. G., Miezin, F. M., Petersen, S. E., Videen, T. O., & Raichle, M. E. (1992). Activation of the hippocampus in normal humans: A functional anatomical study of memory. *Proceedings of the National Academy of Sciences, 89,* 1837–1841.

Squire, L. R., & Zola-Morgan, S. (1991). The medial temporal lobe memory system. *Science, 253,* 1380–1386.

Staubli, U., Ivy, G., & Lynch, G. (1984). Hippocampal denervation causes rapid forgetting of olfactory information in rats. *Proceedings of the National Academy of Sciences, 81,* 5885–5887.

Sutherland, R. J., Macdonald, R. J., Hill, C. R., & Rudy, J. W. (1989). Damage to the hippocampal formation in rats selectively impairs the ability to learn cue relationships. *Behavioral and Neural Biology, 52,* 331–356.

Sutherland, R. J., & Rudy, J. W. (1989). Configural association theory: The role of the hippocampal formation in learning, memory, and amnesia. *Psychobiology, 17,* 129–144.

Thomas, G. J., & Gash, D. M. (1988). Differential effects of hippocampal ablations on dispositional and representational memory in the rat. *Behavioral Neuroscience, 102,* 635–642.

Tolman, E. C. (1932). *Purposive behavior in animals and men.* Berkeley: University of California Press. (1951 edition.)

Tolman, E. C. (1948). Cognitive maps in rats and men. *Psychological Review, 55,* 189–208.

Tolman, E. C. (1949). There is more than one kind of learning. *Psychological Review, 56,* 144–155.

Tulving, E. (1972). Episodic and semantic memory. In E. Tulving & W. Donaldson (Eds.), *Organization of memory* (pp. 381–403). New York: Academic Press.

Tulving, E. (1983). *Elements of episodic memory.* Oxford: Clarendon Press.

Tulving, E. (1985). How many memory systems are there? *American Psychologist, 40,* 385–398.

Warrington, E. K., & Weiskrantz, L. (1968). New method for testing long-term retention with special reference to amnesic patients. *Nature, 217,* 972–974.

Watanabe, T., & Niki, H. (1985). Hippocampal unit activity and delayed response in the monkey. *Brain Research, 325,* 241–254.

Weiskrantz, L. (1982). Comparative aspects of studies of amnesia. *Philosophical Transactions of the Royal Society, London, 298,* 97–109.

Wible, C. G., Findling, R. L., Shapiro, M., Lang, E. J., Crane, S., & Olton, D. S. (1986). Mnemonic correlates of unit activity in the hippocampus. *Brain Research, 399,* 97–110.

Wiener, S. I., Paul, C. A., & Eichenbaum, H. (1989). Spatial and behavioral correlates of hippocampal neuronal activity. *Journal of Neuroscience, 9,* 2737–2763.

Wilson, F. A. W., Brown, M. W., & Riches, I. P. (1987). Neuronal activity in the inferomedial temporal of medial temporal lobe origin. In C. D. Woody (Ed.), *Cellular mechanisms of conditioning and behavioral plasticity.* New York: Plenum.

Winocur, G., & Olds, J. (1978). Effects of context manipulation on memory and reversal learning in rats with hippocampal lesions. *Journal of Comparative and Physiological Psychology, 92,* 312–321.

Winocur, G., Rawlins, J. N. P, & Gray, J. A. (1987). The hippocampus and conditioning to contextual cues. *Behavioral Neuroscience, 101,* 617–625.

Zola-Morgan, S., & Squire, L. R. (1985). Medial temporal lesions in monkeys impair memory on a variety of tasks sensitive to human amnesia. *Behavioral Neuroscience, 99,* 22–34.

Zola-Morgan, S., Squire, L. R., & Amaral, D. G. (1986). Human amnesia and the medial temporal lobe region: Enduring memory impairment following a bilateral lesion limited to the filed CA1 of the hippocampus. *Journal of Neuroscience, 9,* 897–912.

Zola-Morgan, S., Squire, L. R., Amaral, D. G., & Suzuki, W. A. (1989). Lesions of perirhinal and parahippocampal cortex that spare the amygdala and hippocampal formation produce severe memory impairment. *Journal of Neuroscience, 9,* 4355–4370.

7 Declarative and Nondeclarative Memory: Multiple Brain Systems Supporting Learning and Memory

Larry R. Squire

The recognition that there are multiple forms of memory developed beginning in the early 1980s, and now only 10 years later a substantial body of experimental data and theoretical material has accumulated. As with any new idea, one can point to historical precedents and anticipations (for reviews, see Hintzman, 1990; Polster, Nadel, & Schacter, 1991; Roediger, 1990; Schacter, 1987; Squire, 1987; Squire, Knowlton, & Musen, 1993; Tulving 1985; Weiskrantz, 1987). One can also identify a few experimental findings in the early 1980s that were especially influential in establishing the idea that memory is not a single mental faculty (Cohen & Squire, 1980; Graf, Squire, & Mandler, 1984; Jacoby & Witherspoon, 1982; Malamut, Saunders, & Mishkin, 1984; Tulving, Schacter, & Stark, 1982; Warrington & Weiskrantz, 1982). In the short time since these experiments were carried out, the topic of multiple forms of memory has become a major theme of memory research. Recent work has focused especially on three fundamental issues: What are the various kinds of memory? What are their characteristics? How is each kind of memory implemented in the organization of brain systems? Following some introductory remarks about terminology, I discuss each of these issues in turn.

1 TERMINOLOGY

1.1 Declarative Memory

Although a variety of terms have been used, one finds striking consistency among them. One kind of memory provides the basis for conscious recollections of facts and events. This is the kind of memory that is usually meant when the terms "memory" and "remembering" are used in ordinary language. "Fact-and-event memory" refers to memory for words, scenes, faces, and stories, and it is assessed by conventional tests of recall and recognition. This kind of memory was termed "declarative" to signify that it can be brought to mind and that its content can be declared (Cohen & Squire, 1980; Cohen, 1984; for its earlier use in psychology, see Anderson, 1976). Other similar terms include *explicit memory* (Schacter, 1987; Schacter, 1992b, this volume), *configural memory* (Rudy & Sutherland, 1992, this volume), and *relational memory* (Eichenbaum, 1992, this volume). *Declarative memory* identifies a biologically real category of memory abilities. Severely amnesic patients fail tasks of recall and recognition (declarative memory), while succeeding as well as normal subjects at many other kinds of memory tasks (see below). Thus, declarative memory depends on the integrity of brain structures and connections in the medial temporal lobe and the diencephalon that are associated with memory functions and that, when damaged, cause amnesia. Within the medial temporal lobe, the important structures are the hippocampal formation (including the hippocampus proper, the dentate gyrus, the subicular complex, and entorhinal cortex), together with the adjacent parahippocampal and perirhinal cortices. The amygdala appears not to be a component of the medial-temporal-lobe memory system. Within the diencephalon, the important structures and connections for declarative memory include the mediodorsal nuclus of the thalamus, the anterior nucleus, the mammillothalamic tract, and the internal medullary lamina (for review, see Zola-Morgan & Squire, 1993).

It should be emphasized that the term "declarative memory" does not derive its meaning only on the basis of what amnesic patients can and cannot learn. That is, the concept of declarative memory is not locked into circularity around the performance of amnesic patients. For example, it is notable that the operating characteristics of declarative memory also distinguish this form of memory from other forms (see sec. 3, below). It is important that distinctions between kinds of memory not rest on dissociations alone and that they be supported by independent sources of evidence (see Roediger, 1990; Sherry & Schacter, 1987; Schacter, 1992a). In this way one can go beyond simply dissociating one component of cognition from another and begin to understand how functions are actually related to each other and how they are organized in the brain.

1.2 Nondeclarative Memory

Declarative memory can be contrasted with a collection of nonconscious memory abilities, all of which are intact in otherwise severely amnesic patients. The term *procedural memory* was originally used to contrast with *declarative memory* (Winograd, 1975; Cohen & Squire, 1980). Whereas the term "procedural" appropriately describes a wide variety of skill-based kinds of learning, certain memory phenomena have also come to light that are clearly not declarative but that are also not well accommodated by the term "procedural." Subsequently, we suggested the broader and more neutral term "nondeclarative" to identify a heterogeneous group of learning abilities that are defined not by any positive feature so much as by the fact that they are not declarative (Squire & Zola-Morgan, 1988). Thus the memory abilities that are not declarative are not of a single type and are not subserved by a single brain system. Whereas "declarative memory" refers to a biologically meaningful category of memory dependent on a specific brain system, nondeclarative memory embraces several kinds of memory and depends on multiple brain systems. The term *implicit memory* (Schacter, 1987) has a meaning similar to "nondeclarative memory."

2 KINDS OF MEMORY: A SUMMARY OF RECENT DATA

Studies with amnesic patients have provided particularly compelling evidence about the kinds of learning that are declarative and nondeclarative. Amnesic patients fail tasks of recall and recognition (tasks that are thought to depend on declarative memory), so that a finding of fully normal performance in this patient group constitutes strong evidence that a task does not depend materially on the strategies of declarative memory. Although this section focuses on findings from amnesic patients, other important information has come from demonstrations of functional dissociations in normal subjects and also from studies of rats and monkeys with surgical damage to the brain structures that, when damaged in humans, cause amnesia.

Nondeclarative memory includes information that is acquired during skill learning (motor skills, perceptual skills, and cognitive skills), habit formation, simple classical conditioning (including some kinds of emotional learning), priming, and other knowledge expressed through performance rather than recollection. Experience can cumulate in behavioral change but without affording conscious access to any previous learning episodes or to any memory content. To be sure, many skill-learning and conditioning paradigms give rise to both declarative and nondeclarative knowledge (Mackintosh, 1985; Willingham, Nissen, & Bullemer, 1989). However, the two kinds of knowledge can arise independently. Some tasks tap primarily what has been acquired declaratively; some tap nondeclarative knowledge; still other tasks measure the contribution of both declarative and nondeclarative knowledge. Figure 1 shows a classification scheme for declarative and nondeclarative memory.

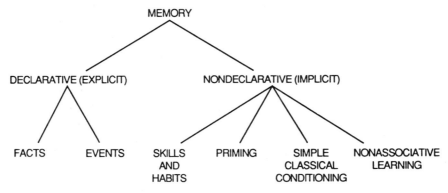

Figure 1 Classification of memory. *Declarative (explicit) memory* refers to conscious recollections of facts and events. *Nondeclarative (implicit) memory* refers to a heterogeneous collection of abilities whereby experience alters behavior nonconsciously without providing access to any memory content. (From Squire & Zola-Morgan, 1991.)

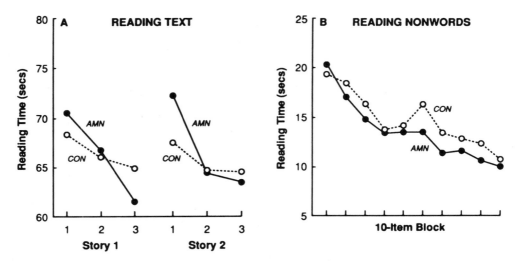

Figure 2 Intact learning by amnesic patients as measured by improved reading times. In both cases, other experiments demonstrated that the learning persists across a 10-minute delay. (A) A text-specific reading skill. Subjects read aloud a story three times in succession and then immediately read a second story three times. (B) Acquisition of a reading skill for novel material. Subjects read aloud a 100-item list consisting of 5 nonwords repeated 20 times each. Amnesic patients improved their reading speed at the same rate as normal subjects. AMN = amnesic patients; CON = control subjects. (From Musen, Shimamura, & Squire, 1990; Musen & Squire, 1991.)

2.1 Skills and Habits

Amnesic patients can acquire a variety of skills at an entirely normal rate. These include motor skills (Brooks & Baddeley, 1976), perceptuomotor skills (Nissen & Bullemer, 1987), perceptual skills (Cohen & Squire, 1980), and cognitive skills (Squire & Frambach, 1990). Studies with speeded reading tasks, among other methods, show that acquired skills can reflect highly specific information about the items that were encountered (Moscovitch, Winocur, & McLachlan, 1986; Musen, Shimamura, & Squire, 1990; figure 2A). Moreover, the skills can be based on novel material (Musen & Squire, 1991; figure 2B).

Skill learning is also intact in monkeys with large lesions of the medial temporal lobe who fail tasks of object recognition (Zola-Morgan & Squire, 1984). For example, monkeys with medial-temporal-lobe lesions succeeded at acquiring an associative habit, specifically, the 24-hour concurrent discrimination task, in which the same 20 object pairs are presented once each day and one object in each pair is always correct (Malamut, Saunders, & Mishkin, 1984). Similarly, rats with damage to the hippocampal system succeeded as well as control animals at a win-stay task, in which specific arms of a radial maze were associated with reward, despite failing a win-shift task in the same apparatus (Packard, Hirsh, & White, 1989).

Recently there has been interest in the possibility that more complex kinds of learning, such as probability learning or artificial-grammar learning, might

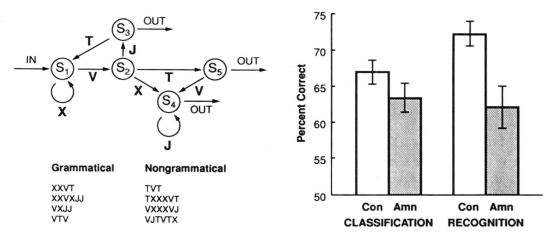

Figure 3 Normal artificial grammar learning by amnesic patients. Left: a finite-state rule system for generating grammatical letter strings. Below the diagram are examples of grammatical letter strings that can be generated by this rule system and nongrammatical letter strings that violate the rule system at one letter position. Right: percent of correct classification judgments and recognition judgments by amnesic patients ($n = 13$) and control subjects ($n = 14$). After studying 23 grammatical letter strings twice each, subjects saw 46 new items (half grammatical and half nongrammatical) and attempted to classify each letter string, or they saw 23 old items and 23 new (nongrammatical) items and decided which ones had been presented. Brackets show standard error of the mean Amn = amnesic patients; Con = control subjects. (From Knowlton, Ramus, & Squire, 1992.)

also depend on nondeclarative memory. In the paradigm for artificial-grammar learning (Reber, 1967), subjects first inspect a group of letter strings that adhere to a finite-state rule system. Subjects are then able to classify new letter strings as either grammatical or nongrammatical at well above chance levels. There has been disagreement as to whether learning to classify successfully reflects implicit (nonconscious) memory or partially developed, imperfect explicit (conscious) memory. Amnesic patients provide a way to decide between these two views. In a recent experiment, amnesic patients were able to classify grammatical and nongrammatical letter strings as well as normal subjects despite impaired recognition memory for the items they had encountered (Knowlton, Ramus, & Squire, 1992; figure 3). Whereas in this study, amnesic patients scored a little below normal subjects (though not significantly so), in a more recent study of artificial-grammar learning, amnesic patients and normal subjects exhibited essentially identical performance: amnesic patients, 59.1 percent correct; normal subjects, 58.3 percent correct (Knowlton & Squire, 1994).

These results argue for the operation of two kinds of memory in artificial-grammar learning. One kind of memory stores declarative information about the specific items that were presented. The second kind of memory stores information nondeclaratively, either by abstracting information from the items in the form of rules or by assembling information from the items as a collection of associations between item features and the grammatical category. Memory for the specific items themselves is not essential for the second kind of learning. What is important is the information that is invariant across many trials. In this sense, artificial-grammar learning resembles skill learning, habit formation, and conditioning.

2.2 Priming

Priming refers to the improved facility for detecting or processing a perceptual object on the basis of recent experience (Shimamura, 1986; Tulving & Schacter, 1990). Contrary to the suggestion from early studies that priming is based on modifying preexisting memory representations (Diamond & Rozin, 1984; Cermak, Talbot, Chandler, & Wolbarst, 1985), priming can involve the acquisition of new information. The important finding is that amnesic patients exhibit fully intact effects of repetition priming, whether the test materials are words, familiar objects, or entirely novel material, such as nonwords, novel objects, or line patterns (Gabrieli, Milberg, Keane, & Corkin, 1990; Haist, Musen, & Squire, 1991; Schacter, Cooper, Tharan, & Rubens, 1991; Musen & Squire, 1992). In one study, perceptual identification of briefly presented words and nonwords was enhanced in amnesic patients and control subjects to a similar extent following a single presentation of the test items (Haist et al., 1991; figure 4). The priming effect for nonwords did not appear to be based on the priming of words that were phonologically or orthographically

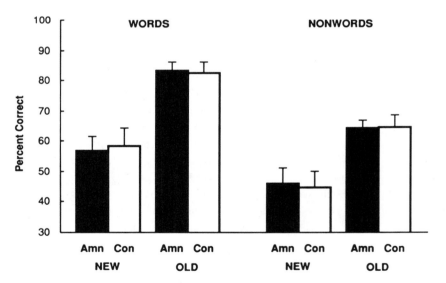

Figure 4 Intact repetition priming in amnesic patients. The graph shows the percent of correct identifications of briefly presented words and nonwords. Old items were presented once prior to the perceptual identification test. The advantage in identifying old items over new items indicates priming. Brackets show standard errors of the mean. Amn = amnesic patients; Con = control subjects. (From Haist, Musen, & Squire, 1991.)

similar to the nonwords, i.e., the priming effect for nonwords was not based on neighborhood effects involving real words. Accordingly, it appears that priming can involve the creation of novel representations and does not reflect simply the activation of preexisting representations. These priming effects can be highly specific in that the magnitude of priming is often diminished by altering the perceptual features of test material (Schacter, 1990; Cave & Squire, 1992).

Priming not only improves the ability to identify stimuli but also alters judgments and preferences that involve the same stimuli. In a recent study, amnesic patients exhibited the same tendency as normal subjects to judge proper names as famous if the names had recently been presented (Squire & McKee, 1992). This facilitatory effect, which was originally studied in normal subjects (Jacoby, Woloshyn, & Kelley, 1989; Neeley & Payne, 1983), was as large for nonfamous names (e.g., "Fritz Bernowski") as for famous names (e.g., "Leon Jaworski"). Specifically, the probability of identifying a famous name as famous increased from 53 percent to 65 percent as a result of a recent encounter with the name, and the probability of identifying a nonfamous name as famous increased from 12 percent to 23 percent.

In some circumstances, priming effects can last a very long time. For example, in normal subjects the response time to name pictures of common objects is lower for several weeks after a single, brief presentation of the pictures (Mitchell & Brown, 1988). Amnesic patients exhibit this facilitatory effect at full strength (Cave & Squire, 1992). In the first of two experiments, amnesic patients exhibited intact priming of picture naming even 7 days after the pictures had been presented (figure 5). In the second experiment, priming in

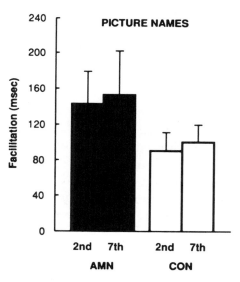

Figure 5 Facilitation of picture naming at 2 days and 7 days after a single presentation. Priming was measured in each case by subtracting the time needed to name 50 new pictures from the time needed to name 50 old pictures. Brackets show standard errors of the mean. AMN = amnesic patients; CON = control subjects. (From Cave & Squire, 1992.)

Declarative and Nondeclarative Memory

both normal subjects and amnesic patients was shown to depend on highly specific visual information as well as on less visual, more conceptual information. Thus, new pictures were named in 1,129 milliseconds, old pictures were named in 996 milliseconds, and pictures that changed from one example to another example of the same item (e.g., two kinds of dogs) were named in 1,051 milliseconds. In contrast to these effects, recognition memory was severely impaired in the amnesic patients, whether assessed by choice accuracy or response time. These results provide the first evidence in amnesic patients of long-lasting priming after a single encounter, which occurs as strongly in the patients as in normal subjects. Nondeclarative memory can apparently support even long-lasting changes in performance following a single encounter. (For a more extensive discussion of priming that is compatible with the perspective on memory systems developed here, see Schacter, 1992b, this volume.)

2.3 Declarative Memory: Recall, Recognition, and Conscious Feelings of Familiarity

Recall and recognition are ordinarily considered to provide two different ways to measure declarative memory. One view is that recall and recognition are closely linked functions and are similarly impaired in amnesia. An alternative view, based on studies of normal subjects, is that recognition is supported in part by priming, i.e., by the fluency with which a subject processes the recognition cue (Mandler, 1980; Jacoby, 1983). On this view, recall depends on declarative memory, and recognition depends on both declarative and nondeclarative memory. Haist, Shimamura, and Squire (1992) recently carried out a test of these two views with amnesic patients. They parametrically tested free recall, forced-choice recognition, and confidence ratings for recognition judgments, which presumably assess conscious feelings of familiarity. They presented 20 different words on 12 separate occasions and tested memory at one of several retention intervals ranging from 15 seconds to 8 weeks. Free recall and forced-choice recognition (together with confidence ratings) were tested 6 times each. If recognition judgments are significantly supported by a nondeclarative process, like priming, that is intact in amnesia, then recognition memory should be disproportionately spared in amnesia in comparison to recall. However, this effect was not observed (figure 6).

The crucial finding was that the recognition judgments of amnesic patients, and the confidence ratings attached to these judgments, were about the same at every retention interval as would have been predicted from the recall scores. These results do not rule out the possibility that priming or other nonconscious processes might sometimes contribute to recognition performance (see Johnston, Hawley, & Elliott, 1991). However, the results do not support the idea that recognition typically draws support from such processes. The results also do not support the suggestion that amnesic patients will make correct recognition choices but then claim they are guessing (Weiskrantz,

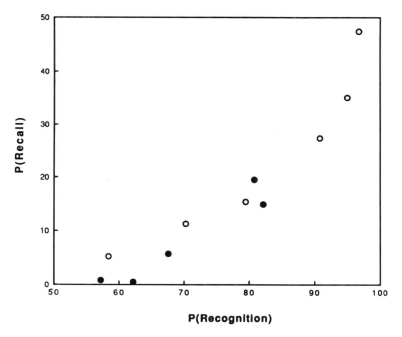

Figure 6 A state-trace plot showing the probability of recall as a function of the probability of recognition. Average scores are plotted for 12 amnesic patients (filled circles) and for 19 control subjects (open circles) at 11 different retention intervals ranging from 15 seconds to 8 weeks. Recall and recognition were tested at the same (variable) retention interval in all 11 cases. The points appear to align themselves along a single monotonically increasing function, which indicates that recall and recognition scores can be expressed as a quantitative change along a single dimension. These results do not support the view that nondeclarative memory significantly supports recognition memory. (From Haist, Shimamura, & Squire, 1992.)

1988). Recall, recognition, and associated feelings of familiarity are related functions of declarative memory and are similarly dependent on the brain system damaged in amnesia. This conclusion about recall and recognition, and their link to declarative memory, is consistent with the idea that recall and recognition processes can also differ from each in other significant ways (see below).

Two earlier studies of amnesic patients came to a different conclusion about recall and recognition on the basis of comparisons at a single performance level (Hirst, Johnson, Phelps, Risse, & Volpe, 1986; Hirst, Johnson, Phelps, & Volpe, 1988). We were unsuccessful at replicating the second of these two studies using the identical experimental design (Haist et al., 1992, experiment 2). Although it is unclear what accounts for the different findings, one possibility is that there are important differences in the patient populations, such as the prevalence of frontal-lobe pathology. In the study by Hirst et al. (1988), three of the six patients had amnesia resulting from a ruptured aneurysm of the anterior communicating artery, a condition known to produce personality change and flatness of affect, i.e., signs of frontal-lobe dysfunction (Damasio,

Graff-Radford, Eslinger, Damasio, & Kassell, 1985). Thus frontal-lobe pathology occurs in some etiologies of amnesia and produces characteristic cognitive impairment in addition to amnesia itself (see Shimamura, Janowsky, & Squire, 1991). Indeed, damage to the frontal lobe can affect recall performance more than recognition (Jetter, Poser, Freeman, & Markowitsch, 1986), perhaps because of deficient search strategies that are more critical for recall than for recognition.

Recent insights about frontal-lobe function can further illuminate the relationship between recall, recognition, and feelings of familiarity. Feelings of familiarity can occur either with or without successful recognition that a stimulus item has been encountered previously. For example, when one recognizes and identifies a familiar person on the street, one ordinarily has feelings of familiarity along with successful recognition. Yet one can also have feelings of familiarity about a person, to the point of being quite sure that he or she is familiar, but at the same time be entirely unable to identify the person or call to mind any facts about the person. It is sometimes supposed that such feelings of familiarity in the absence of recognition are an indication of priming. Thus it has been proposed that recognition performance is constructed out of two separate processes: an activation of the stimulus target through the process of priming, which results in the subjective experience of familiarity, and a search and retrieval process that depends on declarative (explicit) memory (Mandler, 1980, 1986). On this view, the circumstance in which feelings of familiarity occur without successful recognition reflects a dissociation between conscious recollection and priming, i.e., between declarative and nondeclarative memory (for a similar view based on the distinction between remembering and knowing, see Gardiner, 1988; Gardiner & Java, 1990).

Recent work suggests a different way to understand this phenomenon. Specifically, feelings of familiarity not accompanied by full recognition can be viewed as dependent on declarative memory, but declarative memory that is not normal in one important respect. The missing piece has been termed "source memory," i.e., memory for the time and place the information was acquired. Thus when one sees a familiar face but cannot place the face in its proper context, one experiences "source amnesia." The interesting finding is that impairment of source memory is observed in patients with frontal-lobe damage who are not otherwise amnesic (Janowsky, Shimamura, & Squire, 1989). Moreover, impaired source memory, where it has been studied directly, is dissociable from impaired declarative memory (Schacter, Harbluk, & McLactlan, 1984; Shimamura & Squire, 1987), just as remembering (recollecting) is dissociable from knowing (recognizing a stimulus item as familiar without recollecting anything else about it) (Gardiner, 1988).

Accordingly, an interesting possibility is that the dissociation between feelings of familiarity and recollection reflects the special contribution that the frontal lobe makes to recollection (including access to information about context). Thus, such a dissociation might be understood not as a separation

Larry R. Squire

between declarative and nondeclarative memory but as a dissociation within declarative memory itself. Specifically, the dissociation between feelings of familiarity and full contextual recall might reflect a dissociation between a limbic-diencephalic system that supports recognition as well as feelings of familiarity and a frontal-lobe system essential for source memory, including information about context. (For additional information about the role of the frontal lobes when declarative memory depends on implementing strategies and organization processes for encoding or recall, see Moscovitch, 1992, this volume.)

2.4 Learning Novel Associations

The varieties of learning that can be acquired in a normal fashion by amnesic patients might lead one to suppose that nondeclarative memory can support any kind of learning that declarative memory can accomplish. However, consider the case of rapidly acquiring new associations. Normal subjects can quickly memorize new-word pairs declaratively. The hippocampal formation and related structures are specialized for rapidly forming conjunctions between arbitrarily different stimuli. By contrast, nondeclarative memory appears poorly suited for such learning. Nondeclarative memory can support the gradual and cumulative acquisition of new associations, as in classical conditioning, but does not seem well adapted for rapidly acquiring novel associations. This issue has been explored in two different paradigms. The first involves the priming of new associations, which is a robust phenomenon in normal subjects (Graf & Schacter, 1985). Specifically, word-stem-completion priming is greater when the word stem presented at the test is paired with a previously associated word than when the word stem is paired with a new word (e.g., study BELL-CRADLE, test BELL-CRA versus test LAND-CRA). Subsequently, it was found that amnesic patients do not reliably exhibit this effect (Shimamura & Squire, 1989; Mayes & Gooding, 1989; Cermak, Bleich, & Blackford, 1988; Schacter & Graf, 1986), probably because at one crucial step the phenomenon depends critically on declarative memory (see Shimamura & Squire, 1989).

The second paradigm in which learning new associations has been explored involves measures of reading speed (Moscovitch et al., 1986; Musen & Squire, 1993) or perceptual identification (Musen & Squire, 1993). In this case, word pairs are presented for study and then memory is tested by presenting the same word pairs, different word pairs, or the already presented (old) words in new pairings. One expects old-word pairs to be read more rapidly (or identified more accurately) than new-word pairs. In addition, if new associations are formed between the two members of each word pair, then presenting the members of a pair in combination with other old words should break the association. If new associations are formed, recombined word pairs should be treated more like new-word pairs than like old-word pairs. Evidence for learning new associations in a single trial was reported in an initial study involving young, elderly, and memory-impaired subjects (Moscovitch et al., 1986), but the effect was a small one, and it was not demonstrated that it was detectable in the memory-impaired group itself. Subsequently, in three separate experiments involving a reading-speed measure, this effect was not observed in either normal subjects or amnesic patients unless there were multiple learning trials (Musen & Squire, 1993). In a fourth experiment, a small effect was observed using a perceptual-identification method, but only when the results for amnesic patients and control subjects were combined.

In summary, amnesic patients do not readily form new associations between unrelated stimuli. While such an effect might yet be observed under optimal circumstances, it would appear that nondeclarative memory is not specialized for such learning. In contrast, declarative memory is adapted precisely for such learning, i.e., for the rapid acquisition of relational information involving multiple stimuli.

3 CHARACTERISTICS OF DECLARATIVE AND NONDECLARATIVE MEMORY

To what extent can declarative and nondeclarative memory be identified and characterized independently of evidence from functional dissociations in normal subjects and independently of the evidence concerning what amnesic patients can and cannot learn? Declarative memory is fast, accessible to conscious recollection, and flexible, i.e., available to multiple response systems. Nondeclarative memory is nonconscious and less flexible, i.e., it provides limited access to response systems not involved in the original learning. Attempts to account for multiple kinds of memory within a framework of transfer-appropriate processing (Blaxton, 1989; Roediger, 1990) usefully capture this feature of nondeclarative memory. The transfer-appropriate processing approach emphasizes that memory retrieval is successful to the extent that the processing requirements of the study task are similar to the processing requirements of the retrieval task.

Three important experiments in rats and monkeys have demonstrated striking differences in the flexibility of declarative and nondeclarative kinds of memory (Eichenbaum, Mathews, & Cohen, 1989; Eichenbaum, Stewart, & Morris, 1990; Saunders & Weiskrantz, 1989). Indeed, there is a straightforward connection between the constructs of declarative and nondeclarative memory grounded in studies with humans and the kinds of memory studied in rats and monkeys: in both cases, one kind of memory depends on the integrity of the hippocampus and related structures and another kind does not. The studies with experimental animals have as their starting point the finding that animals with hippocampal damage will sometimes learn tasks successfully, albeit at a much slower rate than normal. Subsequent transfer tests then demonstrate that normal animals and the animals with damage to the hippocampal system have acquired different kinds of knowledge. The normal animals have acquired a flexible representation that can be expressed in new ways. For example, in one study of discrimination learning involving two pairs of stimuli (*AB* and *CD*), a high level of performance persisted in the normal animals when the correct stimuli (*A* and *C*) were paired with different incorrect stimuli (i.e., *AD* and *BC*). In contrast, the animals with hippocampal-system damage had apparently acquired conditional associations and could not express their knowledge outside the context in which the knowledge was originally acquired. Performance fell to chance levels when the stimuli were recombined (Eichenbaum, et al., 1989). Other evidence from humans also suggests that nondeclarative memory can be inflexible and hyperspecific (Tulving & Schacter, 1990). These studies show that declarative and nondeclarative memory have different characteristics (also see Eichenbaum, 1992, this volume).

4   MEMORY AND BRAIN SYSTEMS

It has sometimes been suggested that the distinction between kinds of memory is best understood as reflecting the different processes required to access a common underlying engram (Blaxton, 1989; Jacoby, 1988; Masson, 1989; Roediger, 1990). In support of this idea, it could be pointed out that the different kinds of memory (i.e., declarative and nondeclarative memory) can appear to be rather similar to each other. For example, the same word can be produced as verbal output, either as a result of priming or as a result of cued recall, and in both cases the effect can be rather specific to the training conditions. Thus the memories formed in each case can seem to substitute for one another as viewed from a behavioral endpoint. However, the view presented here is that these forms of memory are different in terms of what kind of learning occurs in each case, what is stored as knowledge, and what brain systems are involved. When discussion of the issues is limited to priming, the matter can seem difficult to settle (see Schacter, 1990, 1992a, for a discussion of the so-called processes versus systems debate that focuses on how to account for priming phenomena). In the next section, I suggest that when the discussion is broadened to include skill learning, habit learning, and conditioning, a brain-systems view of multiple memories is more consistent with the biological and psychological facts than a processing view.

4.1   Anatomy of Habit Learning and Conditioning

What is known about the brain systems important for declarative and nondeclarative learning? The evidence is clearest in the case of classical conditioning of reflexes involving the skeletal musculature (Thompson, 1986, 1991). In this case, pathways and connections within the cerebellum are part of the essential circuitry that supports the memory. The hippocampus is not essential. Relevant evidence also comes from tasks in which monkeys learn about visually presented objects. The ability to remember a newly presented visual object so that it can later be selected in a test of recognition memory depends on an interaction between, on the one hand, the visual areas in the neocortex (especially area TE in the inferotemporal cortex) that are important for perception and, on the other hand, the limbic-diencephalic regions essential for transforming perceptions into declarative memories (Mishkin, 1982; Squire & Zola-Morgan, 1991). By contrast, the ability to develop a habit involving the same visual object (e.g., when the object is one of the stimuli in the previously mentioned 24-hour concurrent-discrimination task) requires an interaction between visual areas in the neocortex and the neostriatum (Wang, Aigner, & Mishkin, 1990). A similar distinction between memory and habit learning in terms of the importance of the hippocampal system and the caudate nucleus, respectively, has been elegantly demonstrated in rats (Packard, Hirsch, & White, 1989; Packard & McGaugh, 1992).

One could conceivably argue from these data that the neocortex holds the engram in both the memory and the habit tasks, and that the hippocampal system and the basal ganglia are simply two different routes by which the same information can be expressed in behavior. If so, one could hold that the biological facts just summarized are consistent with a processes view of multiple memories. This scenario presumes that the information expressed in memory tasks and in habit tasks is in fact stored in the neocortex from the first moment that learned behavior is evident. However, there is no evidence to support such an assumption. Single-cell recording in monkeys has identified plasticity in the temporal lobe in one-trial learning tasks, so it is clear that neurons can change their properties quickly in response to a change in the environment (Fuster & Jervey, 1981; Miller, Li, & Desimone, 1991; Riches, Wilson, & Brown, 1991). However, it is not at all clear that this plasticity is related to long-term declarative memory. Instead, altered neuronal activity could reflect short-term (working) memory or priming.

It is consistent with a number of observations about the role of the medial temporal lobe in memory (for a review, see Squire, 1992) to suppose that plasticity related to long-term declarative memory can occur rapidly in the hippocampal system. Neocortical plasticity related to long-term memory may then develop only slowly. Thus, in the case of the interaction between the neocortex and the hippocampal system that supports declarative memory, the plasticity that records the memory may initially exist within the hippocampal system itself and in the connections between this system and the neocortex (Alvarez & Squire, in press). If these ideas are correct, it cannot be the case that a common engram in neocortex serves both declarative memory (through the hippocampal system) and nondeclarative memory (through the basal ganglia).

4.2 Anatomy of Priming

Recent studies also provide some clues about the neural basis of repetition priming and suggest that priming is also best understood as depending on a brain system different from the system supporting declarative memory. First, divided-visual-field studies show that more word-stem-completion priming occurs when word stems are presented to the right cerebral hemisphere (in the left visual field) than to the left cerebral hemisphere (in the right visual field) (Marsolek, Kosslyn, & Squire, 1992). This right-hemisphere advantage occurred if and only if the study words and the test stems were in the same sensory modality and in the same typecase (figure 7A). Thus word priming is sometimes based on form-specific mechanisms that are more effective in the right cerebral hemisphere than in the left.

By contrast, when subjects received cued-recall (i.e., explicit-memory) instructions to the effect that they should try to recall the study words using word stems as cues, cued recall was slightly (though not significantly) better when the word stems were presented to the left hemisphere than to the right (figure 7B). Furthermore, in striking contrast to the priming results for word-stem completion, presenting study words and test stems in the same typecase improved performance only when the stems were presented to the left hemisphere.

These findings make the distinction between priming and declarative memory more specific and concrete. Indeed, the divided-visual-field experiments provide direct evidence about the locus of brain systems supporting declarative and nondeclarative memory. Whereas priming can sometimes be supported more effectively by the right hemisphere than the left, declarative memory need not depend on this same brain organization. Thus word-stem-completion priming and word-stem-cued recall differ with respect to which cerebral hemisphere is most effective in supporting performance. This finding suggests that the same engram does not support performance in both cases. One could argue that memory for recently studied words is represented in a widely distributed network and that one component of this network in the right hemisphere is dominant in supporting priming and that a different component in the left hemisphere is dominant in supporting cued recall. However, on this view, priming and declarative memory cannot depend on the same engram.

One could also suppose that different processes in the left and right hemispheres, important for cued recall and priming respectively, are able to access a common engram. However, such an interpretation conflicts with much biological data and with current perspectives about the locus of memory storage, which emphasize the close relationship between the locus of storage and the locus of the processing systems engaged during the perception, processing, and analysis of material being learned (Mishkin, 1982; Squire, 1987). For example, split-brain studies show that the left and right hemispheres can store separate memories relating to different components or features of the same stimulus (Levy & Trevarthen, 1977).

4.3 Functional Anatomical Studies of Memory and Priming

A recent study using positron emission tomography (PET) provided direct evidence for the importance of the right posterior, extrastriate cortex in word

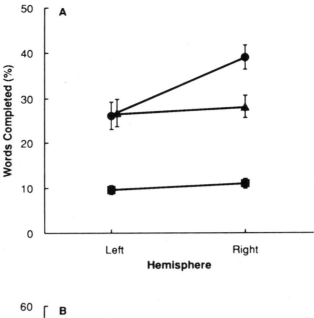

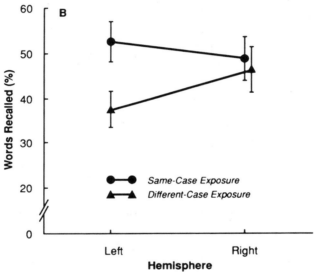

Figure 7 Normal subjects saw words in their central visual field (e.g., "MOTEL" or "motel" and then saw word stems (e.g., "MOT" or "mot") presented briefly in either the left or right visual field, i.e., so that the stems were initially received by the right or left cerebral hemispheres, respectively. Half the word stems were presented in the same typecase as during study, and half were presented in the opposite typecase. (A) Word-stem-completion priming. Subjects were instructed to complete each stem to form the first word that comes to mind. Squares show baseline priming rates, e.g., the probability of completing "MOT" to form "MOTEL" when no words beginning with "MOT" were encountered during study. (B) Cued recall. Subjects were instructed to recall study words using the word stems as cues. Brackets show standard errors of the mean. (From Marsolek, Kosslyn, & Squire, 1992.)

priming (Squire, Ojemann, Miezin, Petersen, Videen, & Raichle, 1992). In this experiment, both study words and test word stems were presented to central visual field and both were presented in uppercase letters. One finding was a significant reduction in cerebral blood flow in a region of the right extrastriate cortex during word-stem-completion priming. The reduction occurred in comparison to a baseline condition in which subjects also completed word stems but priming could not occur because none of the possible word completions had been presented for study. One way to understand the finding of reduced activity during priming is to suppose that for a time after a perceptual stimulus has been presented, less neural activity is required to process the same stimulus. This observation thus suggests a neural account for the key psychological feature of priming: that less information is needed to perceive and identify a stimulus the second time it is presented. A second finding was activation of the right hippocampal region when subjects used word stems as cues to recall the study words. The activation was significantly greater during cued recall than during priming. Reasons why activation was observed in the right but not in the left hippocampal region have been discussed in Marsolek et al., 1992; Squire, Ojemann, et al., 1992; and Marsolek et al., in press.

The PET study strongly endorses the brain-systems view of multiple forms of memory. Word-stem-completion priming can be significantly supported by the early-stage right posterior cortex, which operates prior to the analysis of meaning and prior to the involvement of the hippocampal region and widespread cortical areas that must be engaged for an item to be remembered declaratively, i.e., in relation to the meaning of the item and in relation to the context in which the item was presented. It remains possible that the posterior-cortical locus identified in PET, which is important for form-specific word-stem-completion priming, is one of the critical sites that are bound together by the hippocampal system (Squire & Zola-Morgan, 1991) and that together constitute a declarative memory for a whole event. However, this posterior-cortical locus could not support much declarative knowledge on its own. Indeed, in earlier PET studies (Petersen, Fox, Posner, Mintun, & Raichle, 1988; Petersen, Fox, Snyder, & Raichle, 1990), precisely this region of the right extrastriate cortex was found to be activated by the visual features of words, not their orthographic regularity. Words, nonwords, nonsense letter strings, and letterlike shapes were all effective at activating this locus.

Finally, recent studies of event-related potentials (ERPs) in normal subjects also point to different brain systems for declarative and nondeclarative memory (Paller, 1990; Paller & Kutas, 1992). ERPs related to declarative memory (word recall or recognition) had a different amplitude, latency, and scalp distribution than ERPs related to word-stem completion or perceptual identification. For example, in Paller and Kutas, 1992, the ERP associated with recollection was largest at a latency of 500−800 milliseconds, whereas the ERP associated with priming was largest at a latency of 400−500 milliseconds. The ERP for recollection was dominant at left, anterior electrode placements. The

ERP for priming was dominant at posterior electrode placements. These findings demonstrate that declarative and nondeclarative memory are associated with different neural events at different brain loci.

A left-hemispheric word-form area has been proposed as a locus of word priming (Schacter, 1990; Tulving & Schacter, 1990). The PET findings and the divided-visual-field studies directly indicate that this cannot be a general explanation for repetition priming of words. More likely, the left or right posterior cortex is important according to whether repetition priming is largely form-specific or supported by more abstract mechanisms. For example, some priming is found across sensory modalities, albeit less than within a modality, and cross-modality priming cannot be form-specific. Priming may occur in any of the multiple cortical areas known to be involved in visual processing. Which areas are most important in any particular case should depend on task demands, the characteristics of the test stimuli, and the similarity between study and test stimuli.

4.4 The Hippocampus, Human Amnesia, and Spatial Memory

The work reviewed here comes largely from studies of human amnesic patients and from related studies of an animal model of human amnesia in the monkey. It is important to note that the perspective suggested by this work has many points of contact with the findings from experimental work in rodents (Eichenbaum, 1992, this volume; Nadel, 1992, this volume; Squire, 1992). Here I consider three points that merit special attention: the importance of anatomical rigor, the question of how memory impairment is to be compared across laboratories and across species, and the role of the hippocampus in spatial memory.

Anatomical rigor   Studies of human amnesia and of memory in monkeys have mainly involved behavioral testing following damage to limbic-diencephalic brain structures. An important objective of this work has been to identify the anatomical structures and connections important for declarative memory. A separate tradition of work, pursued especially in the rodent, is directed specifically toward understanding the function of the hippocampus. Thus the objectives of these traditions are somewhat different. While the work with humans and monkeys suggests that the hippocampus is a part of the medial-temporal-lobe memory system, it should be emphasized that it has seldom been possible to study the effects of bilateral damage limited to the hippocampus itself. The most circumscribed lesions studied in monkeys include damage to the hippocampus proper together with the dentate gyrus and the subicular complex (Alvarez-Royo, Clower, Zola-Morgan, & Squire, 1991; Clower, Alvarez-Royo, Zola-Morgan, & Squire, 1991). The best evidence from humans or nonhuman primates linking the hippocampus itself directly to memory functions is probably patient R.B., who developed a moderately severe amnesic syndrome following global ischemia (Zola-Morgan, Squire, & Amaral, 1986). R.B. was subsequently found to have bilateral lesions limited to the CA1 region of the hippocampus (for further discussion and other evidence against the idea that more widespread neuronal dysfunction occurred, see Zola-Morgan, Squire, Rempel, Clower, & Amaral, 1992).

The best opportunity for studying the behavioral effects of lesions restricted to the hippocampus is found in the rat, where it is now possible to produce fiber-sparing, ibotenate lesions of the hippocampus proper (see Jarrard, 1993). Many studies of rodents have involved lesions produced with different techniques that either damage the dentate gyrus or the subiculum in addition to hippocampus or that, in addition to the hippocampus, damage the fiber tracts that connect the subicular complex to other brain regions. Now that improvements in technique permit the components of the hippocampal formation to be separately damaged (at least in the rat), it is especially important to be precise and specific about what exactly has been damaged. One should be cautious about placing studies of patients or monkeys with large lesions of the hippocampal formation (i.e., hippocampus, dentate gyrus, subicular complex, and entorhinal cortex) into the same conceptual framework as studies of rats with restricted hippocampal lesions.

One useful direction of study would be to carry out studies of rats using a select group of tasks to explore systematically the effects of damage to structures and connections within the hippocampal region. In the monkey, the severity of memory impairment is known to be related to the extent of damage within the medial-temporal-lobe memory system (Zola-Morgan, Squire, & Ramus, in press). Damage limited to the hippocampus proper, dentate gyrus, and subicular complex (the H lesion) produces mild memory impairment. When this lesion is extended ventrally to include the parahippocampal gyrus and the posterior entorhinal cortex (the H^+ lesion), a moderate memory impairment is produced. Finally, when the H^+ lesion is extended forward to include the anterior entorhinal cortex and the perirhinal cortex (the H^{++} lesion), a severe memory impairment occurs. Thus in the monkey, quantitative differences in the severity of memory impairment result from variations in the locus and extent of damage in the medial temporal lobe. It should also be fruitful to search for qualitative differences in the contributions of these regions to memory function. In such a venture, it will be important to be precise about which anatomical areas are being studied.

Comparing behavioral deficits   When an animal is impaired on a behavioral task, it is difficult to relate the impairment to other impairments exhibited on other tasks and to know how severely affected an animal "really is" (e.g., if a human had the same impairment, how disabled would he or she be?). For example, monkeys with H lesions (bilateral lesions of the hippocampus proper, dentate gyrus, and subiculum) were impaired on the delayed-nonmatching-to-sample task, a standard task for testing recognition memory in the monkey, when the delays were extended to 10 minutes and 40 minutes (Clower et al., 1991). This deficit is mild compared to the deficit exhibited following larger lesions in the medial temporal lobe, but the findings provide no basis for concluding that the deficit is mild in any absolute sense. Moreover, one cannot conclude that animals with H lesions have fully intact memory functions at the shorter delays tested (15 seconds and 60 seconds, not 3 minutes as stated by Nadel, 1992), simply because no impairment on one task (delayed nonmatching to sample) was observed at these delays. Short delays on this task might not tax memory to a sufficient extent. On the other hand, a 10-minute delay is especially demanding. First, the delay is a long one; second, the animals are removed from the testing room and returned to their home cages during the delay interval. Interpolation of distracting events during the retention interval impairs memory in monkeys (Zola-Morgan & Squire, 1985). Thus the 10-minute delay provides a particularly challenging test of memory.

It is therefore appropriate to conclude that H lesions in monkeys produce a memory deficit and that the deficit is overall less severe than what is observed following larger lesions. However, it is not correct to conclude on the basis of one task that animals have a normal capacity for retaining information up to a 10-minute retention interval. Failures to find behavioral deficits following restricted hippocampal lesions in the rat (Jarrard, 1993) can be similarly difficult to interpret. Parametric variations in the radial maze task, i.e., variations in the number of training trials given preoperatively and in the number of maze arms used, can cause rats with ibotenate lesions of the dorsal hippocampus to range from entirely unimpaired to severely impaired in their ability to learn (Davis & Volpe, 1990).

Spatial memory and the hippocampus   One robust observation is that animals with lesions of the hippocampus or related structures have severe deficits in spatial memory tasks (O'Keefe & Nadel, 1978; Nadel, 1992, this volume). It is also true that rats with fimbria-fornix lesions or damage to other components of the hippocampal formation are impaired on a variety of nonspatial tasks, including simple odor-discrimination tasks (Eichenbaum, Fagen, Mathews, & Cohen, 1988), timing tasks (Meck, Church, & Olton, 1984), and some tasks of configural learning (Rudy & Sutherland, 1989, 1992, this volume; but see Whishaw & Tomie, 1991; Gallagher & Holland, 1992; Davidson, McKernan, & Jarrard, 1993). Notably, rats with lesions to the hippocampal formation were also impaired on an object-recognition task modeled after the trial-unique, delayed nonmatching-to-sample task for monkeys (Mumby, Pinel, & Kornecook, 1992). It may be important that in this case all training and testing occurred after surgery. According to the parametric studies of Davis and Volpe (1990), a task should be most sensitive to hippocampal damage when no preoperative training is given.

Despite this array of behavioral deficits following damage to the hippocampal formation, some favor the view that the primary deficit after hippocampal lesions is a deficit in spatial memory (Nadel, 1992, this volume; Gaffan, 1992; Jarrard, 1993). There are at least two reasons why this view seems plausible. First, it has been suggested that some so-called nonspatial memory tasks can be reinterpreted and that the tasks actually contain a critical spatial component (Nadel, 1992, this volume; Gaffan, 1992). Second, following damage to the hippocampal formation, the deficit exhibited on spatial memory tasks is usually quite severe, whereas impairment on nonspatial memory tasks is often quite modest. These findings have been taken to mean that the hippocampus, if not exclusively spatial in its functions, is disproportionally concerned with spatial memory.

At the present time, experimental support for this hypothesis of hippocampal function is weak. One difficulty is that, as discussed above, studies differ in the locus of damage, and it is not entirely clear which lesions provide the appropriate test for the spatial-memory view. Nadel (1992, this volume) refers sometimes to the hippocampus and sometimes to the hippocampal system when discussing spatial functions, and Gaffan (1992) suggests that a fornix transsection in the monkey provides a useful way to study the presumed spatial functions of the hippocampus. If structures within the medial temporal lobe do make qualitatively different contributions to memory functions, the anatomical descriptions of the lesions used to dissect function must be precise.

A second difficulty is that differences in the severity of impairment exhibited by lesioned animals on spatial and nonspatial tasks can reflect differences in how difficult the tasks are for normal animals. Spatial tasks are usually recall-like in that performance occurs in the absence of any external differences in the familiarity of the environment. In contrast, many nonspatial tasks, such as object recognition, depend on the ability to distinguish a novel cue from a familiar one. For normal humans, recall and recognition tasks are strikingly different in difficulty. An amnesic patient who fails altogether at free recall or paired-associate learning (cued recall) can often perform much better on multiple-choice recognition tasks (albeit not normally and not disproportionately better than would be expected from the free-recall scores). Accordingly, if one administered a free-recall test to an amnesic patient, one would conclude that the patient had a severe memory deficit. Alternatively, if one administered a multiple-choice recognition test to the same patient, one might conclude that only a modest deficit was present. This conclusion would be inappropriate. For normal subjects and amnesic patients, a quantitative comparison of free recall and recognition was carried out across virtually the full extent of the forgetting curves, i.e., from 15 seconds to 8 weeks. The results suggested that the impairment exhibited by the amnesic patients on the two tests was just what it should be in comparison with the performance of normal subjects on the same two tests (Haist, Shimamura, & Squire, 1992; figure 6 above). The two levels of impaired performance reflect the simple fact that normal subjects also find the two tests very different in difficulty.

This same issue needs to be addressed experimentally in the case of spatial memory. Does a rat with a hippocampal lesion perform worse on a spatial task than would be expected on the basis of how difficult the spatial task is in comparison to a nonspatial task? Such a comparison has not been done for the rat using two tasks known to depend on the hippocampal formation. For the monkey, a relevant study has been done. A bilateral lesion of the posterior medial temporal lobe impaired spatial memory, whereas a lesion of the anterior medial temporal lobe did not (Parkinson, Murray, & Mishkin, 1988). The two lesions appeared to have little effect on a nonspatial task (delayed matching to sample, 10-second delays), perhaps because the matching task was presented in a way that did not challenge memory very much. The lesion to the posterior medial temporal lobe damaged the hippocampus proper, dentate gyrus, subicular complex, posterior entorhinal cortex, and parahippocampal cortex. Further studies could determine whether this spatial deficit is indeed disproportionately severe in comparison with impairments in nonspatial memory, and if so, whether the deficit depends on hippocampal damage per se or on damage to adjacent cortex. It is worth noting that anatomical considerations provide a basis for supposing that impairment of spatial memory might result when the parahippocampal cortex is damaged, but not when damage occurs to the perirhinal cortex, entorhinal cortex, or hippocampus proper (Zola-Morgan & Squire, 1993). Finally, in humans with damage to the hippocampal formation, no evidence for a disproportionally large impairment of spatial memory was found (Cave & Squire, 1991). Amnesic patients were equivalently impaired on a test of free recall for object names, a test of recognition memory for object names, and a test of memory for object locations.

5 CONCLUSION

During the past few years, a considerable amount of new information has become available about different forms of memory. Data from amnesic patients, as well as from normal subjects and experimental animals, have expanded and redefined the category of nondeclarative memory. Nondeclarative memory is now understood to include highly specific perceptual-skill learning, win-stay habit learning, artificial-grammar learning, and priming of novel material. At the same time, studies of normal human subjects using new neuroimaging technology and event-related potentials, and studies of animals with selective lesions, have affirmed the biological reality of multiple memory systems. Organisms have available to them multiple ways of benefiting from experience and acquiring knowledge. In most situations, more than one memory system will be engaged. These memory systems have different operating characteristics, acquire different kinds of knowledge, and depend on different brain structures and connections for their operation.

A final comment is in order about "processing" views of multiple forms of memory. When any idea about the function of a complex device is stated very abstractly, it can be difficult to know what evidence would count for or against it, and even whether it can be properly tested. The discussion of multiple memories cast in the language of processing functions is rather abstract, and it has focused mostly on priming. It is therefore not entirely clear that a processing approach and a brain-systems framework are mutually exclusive (also see Schacter, 1992a). What is clear is that multiple forms of memory are supported by separate brain systems and have different characteristics. While there is surely interaction between the systems, a feature emphasized within the processing approach (Jacoby, 1988), a brain-systems framework provides the most complete and satisfying account of memory. To understand the organization of a complex problem like memory, it will be essential to combine the strategies of cognitive psychology with those of neuroscience. "It is not usually advantageous to have one hand tied behind one's back when tackling a very difficult job" (Crick, 1988, p. 150).

ACKNOWLEDGMENTS

Supported by the Medical Research Service of the Department of Veterans Affairs; The National Institute of Mental Health (NIMH), grant MH 24600; the Office of Naval Research; and the McKnight Foundation.

REFERENCES

Alvarez, P., & Squire, L. R. (in press). Memory consolidation and the medial temporal lobe: A simple network model. *Proceedings of the National Academy of Sciences.*

Alvarez-Royo, P., Clower, R. P., Zola-Morgan, S., & Squire, L. R. (1991). Stereotaxic lesions of the hippocampus in monkeys: Determination of surgical coordinates and analysis of lesions using magnetic resonance imaging. *Journal of Neuroscience Methods, 38,* 223–232.

Anderson, J. R. (1976). *Language, memory, and thought.* Hillsdale, NJ: Lawrence Erlbaum Associates.

Blaxton, T. A. (1989). Investigating dissociations among memory systems: Support for a transfer appropriate processing framework. *Journal of Experimental Psychology: Learning, Memory, and Cognition, 15,* 657–668.

Brooks, D. N., & Baddeley, A. (1976). What can amnesic patients learn? *Neuropsychologia, 14,* 111–122.

Cave, C., & Squire, L. R. (1991). Equivalent impairment of spatial and nonspatial memory following damage to the human hippocampus. *Hippocampus, 1,* 329–340.

Cave, C., & Squire, L. R. (1992). Intact and long-lasting repetition priming in amnesia. *Journal of Experimental Psychology: Learning, Memory, and Cognition, 18,* 509–520.

Cermak, L. S., Bleich, R. P., & Blackford, S. P. (1988). Deficits in implicit retention of new associates by alcoholic Korsakoff patients. *Brain and Cognition, 1,* 145–156.

Cermak, L. S., Talbot, N., Chandler, K., & Wolbarst, L. R. (1985). The perceptual priming phenomenon in amnesia. *Neuropsychologia, 23,* 615–622.

Clower, R. P., Alvarez-Royo, P., Zola-Morgan, S., & Squire, L. R. (1991). Recognition memory impairment in monkeys with selective hippocampal lesions. *Society for Neuroscience Abstracts, 17,* 338.

Cohen, N. J. (1984). Preserved learning capacity in amnesia: Evidence for multiple memory systems. In L. R. Squire & N. Butters (Eds.), *Neuropsychology of memory* (pp. 83–103). New York: Guilford Press.

Cohen, N. J., & Squire, L. R. (1980). Preserved learning and retention of pattern analyzing skill in amnesia: Dissociation of knowing how and knowing that. *Science, 210*, 207–209.

Crick, F. (1988). *What mad pursuit*. New York: Basic Books.

Damasio, A. R., Graff-Radford, N. E., Eslinger, P. J., Damasio, H., & Kassell, N. (1985). Amnesia following basal forebrain lesions. *Archives of Neurology, 42*, 263–271.

Davidson, T. L., McKernan, M. G., & Jarrard, L. E. (1993). Hippocampal lesions do not impair negative patterning: A challenge to configural association theory. *Behavioral Neuroscience, 107*, 227–234.

Davis, H. P., & Volpe, B. T. (1990). Memory performance after ischemic or neurotoxin damage of the hippocampus. In L. R. Squire & E. Lindenlaub (Eds.), *The biology of memory*. Stuttgart: F. K. Schattauer Verlag.

Diamond, R., & Rozin, P. (1984). Activation of existing memories in anterograde amnesia. *Journal of Abnormal Psychology, 93*, 98–105.

Eichenbaum, H. (1992). The hippocampal system and declarative memory in animals. *Journal of Cognitive Neuroscience, 4*, 217–231.

Eichenbaum, H., Fagan, A., Mathews, P., & Cohen, N. (1988). Hippocampal system dysfunction and odor discrimination learning in rats: Impairment or facilitation depending on representational demands. *Behavioral Neuroscience, 102*, 331–339.

Eichenbaum, H., Mathews, P., & Cohen, N. J. (1989). Further studies of hippocampal representation during odor discrimination learning. *Behavioral Neuroscience, 103*, 1207–1216.

Eichenbaum, H., Stewart, C., & Morris, R. G. M. (1990). Hippocampal representation in place learning. *Journal of Neuroscience, 10*, 3531–3542.

Fuster, J. M., & Jervey, J. P. (1981). Inferotemporal neurons distinguish and retain behaviorally relevant features of visual stimuli. *Science, 212*, 952–955.

Gabrieli, J. D. E., Milberg, W., Keane, M. M., & Corkin, S. (1990). Intact priming of patterns despite impaired memory. *Neuropsychologia, 28*, 417–427.

Gaffan, D. (1992). The role of the hippocampus-fornix-mammillary system in episodic memory. In L. R. Squire and N. Butters (Eds.), *Neuropsychology of memory*, 2nd ed. (pp. 336–346). New York: Guilford Press.

Gallagher, M., & Holland, P. C. (1992). Preserved configural learning and spatial learning impairment in rats with hippocampal damage. *Hippocampus, 2*, 81–88.

Gardiner, J. M. (1988). Functional aspects of recollective experience. *Memory & Cognition, 16*, 309–313.

Gardiner, J. M., & Java, R. I. (1990). Recollective experience in word and nonword recognition. *Memory & Cognition, 18*, 23–30.

Graf, P., & Schacter, D. L. (1985). Implicit and explicit memory for new associations in normal and amnesic subjects. *Journal of Experimental Psychology: Learning, Memory, and Cognition, 11*, 501–518.

Graf, P., Squire, L. R., & Mandler, G. (1984). The information that amnesic patients do not forget. *Journal of Experimental Psychology: Learning, Memory, and Cognition, 10*, 164–178.

Haist, F., Musen, G., & Squire, L. R. (1991). Intact priming of words and nonwords in amnesia. *Psychobiology, 19*, 275–285.

Haist, F., Shimamura, A. P., & Squire, L. R. (1992). On the relationship between recall and recognition memory. *Journal of Experimental Psychology: Learning, Memory, and Cognition, 18,* 691–702.

Hintzman, D. (1990). Human learning and memory: Connections and dissociations. *Annual Review of Psychology, 41,* 109–139.

Hirst, W., Johnson, M. K., Phelps, E. A., Risse, G., & Volpe, B. T. (1986). Recognition and recall in amnesics. *Journal of Experimental Psychology: Learning, Memory, and Cognition, 12,* 445–451.

Hirst, W., Johnson, M. K., Phelps, E. A., & Volpe, B. T. (1988). More on recognition and recall in amnesics. *Journal of Experimental Psychology: Learning, Memory, and Cognition, 14,* 758–762.

Jacoby, L. L. (1983). Remembering the data: Analyzing interactive processes in reading. *Journal of Verbal Learning and Verbal Behavior, 22,* 485–508.

Jacoby, L. L. (1988). Memory observed and memory unobserved. In U. Neisser & E. Winograd (Eds.), *Remembering reconsidered* (pp. 145–177). New York: Cambridge University Press.

Jacoby, L. L., Woloshyn, V., & Kelley, C. (1989). Becoming famous without being recognized: Unconscious influences of memory produced by dividing attention. *Journal of Experimental Psychology: General, 118,* 115–125.

Jacoby, L. L., & Witherspoon, D. (1982). Remembering without awareness. *Canadian Journal of Psychology, 32,* 300–324.

Janowsky, J., Shimamura, A. P., & Squire, L. R. (1989). Source memory impairment in patients with frontal lobe lesions. *Neuropsychologia, 27,* 1043–1056.

Jarrard, L. E. (1993). On the role of the hippocampus in learning and memory in the rat. *Behavioural and Neural Biology, 60,* 9–26.

Jetter, W., Poser, U., Freeman, R. B., Jr., & Markowitsch, J. H. (1986). A verbal long term memory deficit in frontal lobe damaged patients. *Cortex, 22,* 229–242.

Johnston, W. A., Hawley, K. J., & Elliott, M. G. (1991). Contribution of perceptual fluency to recognition judgments. *Journal of Experimental Psychology: Learning, Memory, and Cognition, 17,* 210–223.

Knowlton, B. J., Ramus, S. J., & Squire, L. R. (1992). Intact artificial grammar learning in amnesia: Dissociation of classification learning and explicit memory for specific instances. *Psychological Science, 3,* 172–179.

Knowlton, B. J., & Squire, L. R. (1994). The information acquired during artificial grammar learning: Item similarity vs. grammaticality. *Journal of Experimental Psychology: Learning, Memory, and Cognition, 20,* 79–91.

Levy, J., & Trevarthen, C. (1977). Perceptual, semantic, and phonetic aspects of elementary language processes in split-brain patients. *Brain, 100,* 105–118.

Mackintosh, N. J. (1985). Varieties of conditioning. In N. M. Weinberger, G. Lynch, & J. McGaugh (Eds.), *Memory systems of the brain* (pp. 335–350). New York: Guilford Press.

Malamut, B. L., Saunders, R. C., & Mishkin, M. (1984). Monkeys with combined amygdalo-hippocampal lesions succeed in object discrimination learning despite 24-hour intertrial intervals. *Behavioral Neuroscience, 98,* 759–769.

Mandler, G. (1980). Recognizing: The judgment of previous occurrence. *Psychological Review, 87,* 252–271.

Mandler, G. (1986). Memory: Conscious and unconscious. In P. Solomon, G. R. Goethals, C. M. Kelly, & B. R. Stephens (Eds.) *Memory—An interdisciplinary approach.* New York: Springer-Verlag.

Marsolek, C. J., Kosslyn, S. M., & Squire, L. R. (1992). Form-specific visual priming in the right cerebral hemisphere. *Journal of Experimental Psychology: Learning, Memory, and Cognition, 18,* 492–508.

Marsolek, C. J., Squire, L. R., Kosslyn, S. M., & Lulenski, M. E. (in press). Form-specific explicit and implicit memory in the right cerebral hemisphere. *Neuropsychology.*

Masson, M. E. J. (1989). Fluent reprocessing as an implicit expression of memory for experience. In S. Lewandowsky, J. C. Dunn, & K. Kirsner (Eds.), *Implicit Memory: Theoretical Issues* (pp. 123–138). Hillsdale, NJ: Lawrence Erlbaum Associates.

Mayes, A. R., & Gooding, P. (1989). Enhancement of word completion priming in amnesics by cuing with previously novel associates. *Neuropsychologia, 27,* 1057–1072.

Meck, W. H., Church, R. M., & Olton, D. S. (1984). Hippocampus, time, and memory. *Behavioral Neuroscience, 98,* 3–22.

Miller, E. K., Li, L., & Desimone, R. (1991). A neural mechanism for working and recognition memory in inferior temporal cortex. *Science, 254,* 1377–1379.

Mishkin, M. (1982). A memory system in the monkey. *Philosophical Transactions of the Royal Society of London,* series B, *298,* 85–92.

Mitchell, D. B., & Brown, A. S. (1988). Persistent repetition priming in picture naming and its dissociation from recognition memory. *Journal of Experimental Psychology: Learning, Memory, and Cognition, 14,* 213–222.

Moscovitch, M. (1992). Memory and working-with-memory: A component process model based on modules and central systems. *Journal of Cognitive Neuroscience, 4,* 257–267.

Moscovitch, M., Winocur, G., & McLachlan, D. (1986). Memory as assessed by recognition and reading time in normal and memory-impaired people with Alzheimer's disease and other neurological disorders. *Journal of Experimental Psychology: General, 115,* 331–347.

Mumby, D. G., Pinel, J. P. J., & Kornecook, T. J. (1992). Dissociating the effects of hippocampal and amygdalar lesions in rats with a battery of nonspatial memory tasks. *Society for Neuroscience Abstracts,* 1423.

Musen, G., Shimamura, A. P., & Squire, L. R. (1990). Intact text-specific reading skill in amnesia. *Journal of Experimental Psychology: Learning, Memory, and Cognition, 6,* 1068–1076.

Musen, G., & Squire, L. R. (1991). Normal acquisition of novel verbal information in amnesia. *Journal of Experimental Psychology: Learning, Memory, and Cognition, 17,* 1095–1104.

Musen, G., & Squire, L. R. (1992). Nonverbal priming in amnesia. *Memory and Cognition, 20,* 441–448.

Musen, G., & Squire, L. R. (1993). On the implicit learning of novel associations by amnesic patients and normal subjects. *Neuropsychology, 7,* 119–135.

Nadel, L. (1992). Multiple memory systems: What and why. *Journal of Cognitive Neuroscience, 4,* 179–188.

Neeley, J. H., & Payne, D. G. (1983). A direct comparison of recognition failure rates for recallable names in episodic and semantic memory tests. *Memory and Cognition, 11,* 161–171.

Nissen, M. J., & Bullemer, P. (1987). Attentional requirements of learning: Evidence from performance measures. *Cognitive Psychology, 19,* 1–32.

O'Keefe, J., & Nadel, L. (1978). *The hippocampus as a cognitive map.* London: Oxford University Press.

Packard, M. G., Hirsh, R., & White, N. M. (1989). Differential effects of fornix and caudate nucleus lesions on two radial maze tasks: Evidence for multiple memory systems. *Journal of Neuroscience, 9,* 1465–1472.

Packard, M. G., & McGaugh, J. L. (1992). Double dissociation of fornix and caudate nucleus lesions on acquisition of two water maze tasks: Further evidence for multiple memory systems. *Behavioral Neuroscience, 106,* 439–446.

Paller, K. A. (1990). Recall and stem-completion priming have different electrophysiological correlates and are modified differentially by directed forgetting. *Journal of Experimental Psychology: Learning, Memory, and Cognition, 16,* 1021–1032.

Paller, K. A., & Kutas, M. (1992). Brain potentials during memory retrieval provide neurophysiological support for the distinction between conscious recollection and priming. *Journal of Cognitive Neuroscience, 4,* 375–391.

Parkinson, J. K., Murray, E., & Mishkin, M. (1988). A selective mnemonic role for the hippocampus in monkeys: Memory for the location of objects. *Journal of Neuroscience, 8,* 4159–4167.

Petersen, S. E., Fox, P. T., Posner, M. I., Mintun, M., & Raichle, M. E. (1988). Positron emission tomographic studies of the cortical anatomy of single-word processing. *Nature, 331,* 585–589.

Petersen, S. E., Fox, P. T., Snyder, A. Z., & Raichle, M. E. (1990). Activation of extrastriate and frontal cortical areas by visual words and word-like stimuli. *Science, 249,* 1041–1044.

Polster, M., Nadel, L., & Schacter, D. (1991). Cognitive neuroscience analysis of memory: A historical perspective. *Journal of Cognitive Neuroscience, 3,* 95–116.

Reber, A. S. (1967). Implicit learning of artificial grammars. *Journal of Verbal Learning and Verbal Behavior, 6,* 855–863.

Riches, I. P., Wilson, F. A. W., & Brown, M. W. (1991). The effects of visual stimulation and memory on neurons of the hippocampal formation and the neighboring parahippocampal gyrus and inferior temporal cortex of the primate. *Journal of Neuroscience, 11,* 1763–1979.

Roediger, H. (1990). Implicit memory: Retention without remembering. *American Psychologist, 45,* 1043–1056.

Rudy, J. W., & Sutherland, R. J. (1989). The hippocampal formation is necessary for rats to learn and remember configural discriminations. *Behavorial Brain Research, 34,* 97–109.

Rudy, J. W., & Sutherland, R. J. (1992). Configural and elemental associations and the memory coherence problem. *Journal of Cognitive Neuroscience, 4,* 208–216.

Saunders, R. C., & Weiskrantz, L. (1989). The effects of fornix transection and combined fornix transection, mammillary body lesions, and hippocampal ablations on object-pair association memory in the rhesus monkey. *Behavioral Brain Research, 35,* 85–94.

Schacter, D. (1987). Implicit memory: History and current status. *Journal of Experimental Psychology: Learning, Memory, and Cognition, 13,* 501–518.

Schacter, D. L. (1990). Perceptual representation systems and implicit memory: Toward a resolution of the multiple memory systems debate. In A. Diamond (Ed.), *Development and neural bases of higher cognitive functions,* Annals of the New York Academy of Sciences (Vol. 608, pp. 543–571). New York: New York Academy of Sciences.

Schacter, D. L. (1992a). Understanding implicit memory: A cognitive neuroscience approach. *American Psychologist, 47,* 559–569.

Schacter, D. L. (1992b). Priming and multiple memory systems: Perceptual mechanisms of implicit memory. *Journal of Cognitive Neuroscience, 4,* 244–256.

Schacter, D. L., Cooper, L. A., Tharan, M., & Rubens, A. B. (1991). Preserved priming of novel objects in patients with memory disorders. *Journal of Cognitive Neuroscience, 3*, 118–131.

Schacter, D. L., & Graf, P. (1986). Preserved learning in amnesic patients: Perspectives from research on direct priming. *Journal of Clinical and Experimental Neuropsychiatry, 8*, 727–743.

Schacter, D. L., Harbluk, J. L., & McLachlan, D. R. (1984). Retrieval without recollection: An experimental analysis of source amnesia. *Journal of Verbal Learning and Verbal Behavior, 23*, 593–611.

Sherry, D. F., & Schacter, D. L. (1987). The evolution of multiple memory systems. *Psychological Review, 94*, 439–454.

Shimamura, A. P. (1986). Priming effects in amnesia: Evidence for a dissociable memory function. *Quarterly Journal of Experimental Psychology, 38A*, 619–644.

Shimamura, A. P., Janowsky, J. S., & Squire, L. R. (1991). What is the role of frontal lobe damage in amnesic disorders? In H. S. Levin, H. M. Eisenberg, & A. L. Benton (Eds.), *Frontal lobe function and dysfunction* (pp. 173–195). New York: Oxford University Press.

Shimamura, A. P., & Squire, L. R. (1987). A neuropsychological study of fact memory and source amnesia. *Journal of Experimental Psychology: Learning, Memory, and Cognition, 13*, 464–473.

Shimamura, A. P., & Squire, L. R. (1989). Impaired priming of new associations in amnesia. *Journal of Experimental Psychology: Learning, Memory, and Cognition, 15*, 721–728.

Squire, L. R. (1987). Memory and brain. New York: Oxford University Press.

Squire, L. R. (1992). Memory and the hippocampus: A synthesis from findings with rats, monkeys, and humans. *Psychological Review, 99*, 195–231.

Squire, L. R., & Frambach, M. (1990). Cognitive skill learning in amnesia. *Psychobiology, 18*, 109–117.

Squire, L. R., Knowlton, B., & Musen, G. (1993). The structure and organization of memory. *Annual Review of Psychology, 44*, 453–495.

Squire, L. R., & McKee, R. (1992). The influence of prior events on cognitive judgments in amnesia. *Journal of Experimental Psychology: Learning, Memory, and Cognition, 18*, 1837–1841.

Squire, L. R., Ojemann, J. G., Miezin, F. M., Petersen, S. E., Videen, T. O., & Raichle, M. E. (1992). Activation of the hippocampus in normal humans: A functional anatomical study of memory. *Proceedings of the National Academy of Sciences, U.S.A., 89*, 1837–1841.

Squire, L. R., & Zola-Morgan, S. (1988). Memory: Brain systems and behavior. *Trends in Neurosciences, 11*, 170–175.

Squire, L. R., & Zola-Morgan, M. (1991). The medial temporal lobe memory system. *Science, 253*, 1380–1386.

Thompson, R. F. (1986). The neurobiology of learning and memory. *Science, 233*, 941–947.

Thompson, R. F. (1991). Neural mechanisms of classical conditioning in mammals. In J. R. Krebs and G. Horn (Eds.), *Behavioural and neural aspects of learning and memory* (pp. 63–72). Oxford: Clarendon Press.

Tulving, E. (1985). How many memory systems are there? *American Psychologist, 40*, 385–398.

Tulving, E., & Schacter, D. L. (1990). Priming and human memory systems. *Science, 247*, 301–306.

Tulving, E., Schacter, D. L., & Stark, H. A. (1982). Priming effects in word-fragment completion are independent of recognition memory. *Journal of Experimental Psychology: Learning, Memory, and Cognition, 8*, 336–342.

Wang, J., Aigner, T., & Mishkin, M. (1990). Effects of neostriatal lesions on visual habit formation of rhesus monkeys. *Society for Neuroscience, 16*, 617.

Warrington, E. K., & Weiskrantz, L. (1982). Amnesia: A disconnection syndrome. *Neuropsychologia, 20*, 233–248.

Weiskrantz, L. (1987). Neuroanatomy of memory and amnesia: A case for multiple memory systems. *Human Neurobiology, 6*, 93–105.

Weiskrantz, L. (1988). Some contributions of neuropsychology of vision and memory to the problem of consciousness. In A. Marcel & E. Bisiach (Eds.), *Consciousness and contemporary science* (pp. 183–189). New York: Oxford University Press.

Whishaw, I. Q., & Tomie, J. (1991). Simple, conditional, and configural learning using tactile and olfactory cues is spared in hippocampus rats: Implications for hippocampal function. *Behavioral Neuroscience, 105*, 787–797.

Willingham, D. B., Nissen, M. J., & Bullemer, P. (1989). On the development of procedural knowledge. *Journal of Experimental Psychology: Learning, Memory, and Cognition, 15*, 1047–1060.

Winograd, T. (1975). Frame representations and the declarative-procedural controversy. In D. Bobrow & A. Collins (Eds.), *Representation and understanding: Studies in cognitive science* (pp. 185–210). New York: Academic Press.

Zola-Morgan, S., & Squire, L. R. (1984). Preserved learning in monkeys with medial temporal lesions: Sparing of motor and cognitive skills. *Journal of Neuroscience, 4*, 1072–1085.

Zola-Morgan, S., & Squire, L. R. (1985). Medial temporal lesions in monkeys impair memory on a variety of tasks sensitive to human amnesia. *Behavioral Neuroscience, 99*, 22–34.

Zola-Morgan, S., & Squire, L. R. (1993). The neuroanatomy of amnesia. *Annual Review of Neuroscience, 16*, 547–563.

Zola-Morgan, S., Squire, L. R., & Amaral, D. G. (1986). Human amnesia and the medial temporal region: Enduring memory impairment following a bilateral lesion limited to field CA1 of the hippocampus. *Journal of Neuroscience, 6*, 2950–2967.

Zola-Morgan, S., Squire, L. R., & Ramus, S. J. (in press). Severity of memory impairment in monkeys as a function of the locus and extent of damage within the medial temporal lobe memory system. *Hippocampus*.

Zola-Morgan, S., Squire, L. R., Rempel, N., Clower, R., & Amaral, D. G. (1992). Enduring memory impairment in monkeys after ischemic damage to the hippocampus. *Journal of Neuroscience, 12*, 2582–2596.

8 Priming and Multiple Memory Systems: Perceptual Mechanisms of Implicit Memory

Daniel L. Schacter

During the past 25 years, questions concerning the nature and number of memory systems have been at the forefront of cognitive, neuropsychological, and neurobiological research (for a historical overview, see Polster, Nadel, & Schacter, 1991). In the study of human memory, a key line of evidence for multiple memory systems has been provided by investigations concerned with the descriptive distinction between *explicit* and *implicit* forms of memory (Graf & Schacter, 1985; Schacter, 1987). Explicit memory refers to intentional or conscious recollection of prior experiences, as assessed in the laboratory by traditional tests of recall or recognition; implicit memory, by contrast, refers to changes in performance or behavior, produced by prior experiences, on tests that do not require any intentional or conscious recollection of those experiences. The distinction between explicit and implicit memory is similar to distinctions between *memory with awareness* versus *memory without awareness* (Jacoby & Witherspoon, 1982), *declarative memory* versus *nondeclarative memory* (Squire, 1992a), and *direct memory* versus *indirect memory* (Johnson & Hasher, 1987). However, these distinctions appear less frequently in the literature than the explicit/implicit distinction, and there are various reasons to prefer the explicit/implicit contrast over alternative terms (Roediger, 1990a).

The explicit/implicit distinction is a *descriptive* one that contrasts two different ways in which memory for previous experience can be expressed; it does not refer to, or necessarily imply the existence of, distinct underlying memory systems. However, interest in the relation between explicit and implicit forms of memory has been sparked by demonstrations of striking dissociations between the two that do indeed suggest that different underlying systems are involved in explicit and implicit memory. Thus, for example, it has been known for many years that amnesic patients exhibit robust and sometimes normal learning of various perceptual, motor, and cognitive skills, despite impaired or absent explicit memory for having acquired them (e.g., Cohen & Squire, 1980; Milner, Corkin, & Teuber, 1968). Amnesic patients can also exhibit the effects of classical conditioning, despite poor explicit memory (Daum, Channon, & Canavar, 1989; Weiskrantz & Warrington, 1979), and they can acquire knowledge needed to perform complex computer-related tasks, despite the absence of any recollection for having previously performed the tasks (Glisky, Schacter, & Tulving, 1986; Glisky & Schacter, 1987, 1988, 1989).

Perhaps the most intensively studied form of implicit memory has come to be known as repetition or direct *priming*: the facilitated identification of perceptual objects from reduced cues as a consequence of a specific prior exposure to an object (e.g., Tulving & Schacter, 1990). Priming can be thought of as a form of implicit memory in the sense that it can occur independently of any conscious or explicit recollection of a previous encounter with a stimulus. Thus amnesic patients can show entirely normal priming as a consequence of a recent encounter with a word or object, despite impaired or even absent explicit memory for the word or object, and studies of nonamnesic, normal subjects have shown that various experimental manipulations affect priming and explicit memory in different and even opposite ways (for reviews, see Richardson-Klavehn & Bjork, 1988; Roediger & McDermott, 1993; Schacter, 1987; Schacter, Chiu, & Ochsner, 1993; Shimamura, 1986). These and other observations indicate that the kind of information about a recently encountered word or object that supports priming is quite different from the kind of information that supports explicit recollection for an encounter with the word or object. Moreover, priming has also been dissociated from skill learning: studies of dementia indicate that patients with Alzheimer's disease show impaired priming and intact motor skill learning, whereas patients with Huntington's disease show the opposite pattern (e.g., Butters, Heindel, & Salmon, 1990). A number of investigators have further argued that priming is the expression of a neurocognitive systems that differs functionally and neuroanatomically from the neurocognitive systems that supports explicit remembering and skill learning (Cohen, 1984; Schacter, 1985, 1990; Butters et al., 1990; Squire, 1987, 1992b; Tulving, 1985; Tulving & Schacter, 1990).

This chapter examines in some detail one such proposal, namely, that priming reflects, to a very large extent, the operations of a perceptual representation system (PRS) that can function independently of the episodic or declarative memory system, which supports explicit memory (Schacter, 1990, 1992; Tulving & Schacter, 1990). The PRS refers to a class of domain-specific subsystems that process and represent information about the form and structure, but not the meaning and other associative properties, of words and objects. The construct of the PRS is broadly similar to systems and subsystems that have been proposed and discussed by other contributors to this volume: Moscovitch's input modules; Johnson and Chalfonte's perceptual subsystem; Metcalfe, Cottrell, and Menzl's quasi memory (see also Hayman & Tulving, 1989); and certain kinds of memory subsumed under Squire's nondeclarative memory and Eichenbaum's procedural memory.

The chapter will delineate and evaluate characteristics of, and evidence for, three PRS susbsytems: visual word form, structural description, and auditory word form. Although they probably do not constitute an exhaustive list of PRS subsystems, various kinds of evidence about them is available, including data from priming studies. The three subsystems all share common features:

they operate at a *presemantic* level, that is, at a level of processing that does not involve access to the meanings of words or objects; they are involved in *nonconscious* expressions of memory for previous experiences; and they all likely depend on *cortical* mechanisms. The subsystems differ with respect to the kind of information that they handle. After discussing pertinent issues and results at some length, I will conclude by considering similarities and differences between my framework and other pertinent views put forward in this volume, with respect to four main issues: alternative conceptualizations of PRS subsystems, the relation between perceptual and conceptual forms of priming, memory systems in humans versus animals, and the meaning and implications of the terms "systems" and "subsystems" for theoretical endeavors.

1 PRS SUBSYSTEMS AND PRIMING

1.1 The Visual-Word-Form System

The term "visual-word-form system" was first used by Warrington and Shallice (1980) in the context of their research on patients suffering from a type of reading impairment known as letter-by-letter reading. Warrington and Shallice proposed that the deficit in at least some of these patients could be attributed to a breakdown of the system that represents information about the visual and orthographic form of words. Evidence that such a system operates at a presemantic level is provided by studies that have focused on brain-damaged patients who maintain relatively intact abilities to read words yet exhibit little or no understanding of them (see Sartori, Masterson, & Job, 1987; Schwartz, Saffran, & Marin, 1980). Importantly, such patients can read words with irregular spellings, which indicates that they can gain access to the representations in the word-form system (see Schacter, 1990, for further elaboration). Data from neuroimaging studies using positron emission tomography (PET) suggest that the visual-form system is based in regions of the extrastriate occipital cortex and is neuroanatomically distinct from brain regions subserving semantic processing (e.g., Petersen et al., 1989).

Several lines of evidence have led to the proposal that the visual-word-form system subserves priming effects on so-called data-driven, or perceptual, implicit memory tasks, such as *stem* or *fragment completion*, where subjects provide the first word that comes to mind in response to three-letter stems or graphemic fragments, and *perceptual* or *word identification*, where subjects attempt to identify briefly presented words. One such line of evidence is that amnesic patients show normal priming of familiar words and word pairs on completion, identification, and similar tasks (Cermak, Chandler, & Wolbarst, 1985; Graf, Squire, & Mandler, 1984; Moscovitch, 1982; Schacter, 1985; Shimamura & Squire, 1984; Tulving, Hayman, & MacDonald, 1991; Warrington & Weiskrantz, 1974). These results are consistent with the proposal that visual-word priming is mediated by a perceptual system in the posterior cortical regions because the critical sites of brain damage in amnesic patients typically involve the limbic system and medial-temporal-lobe structures; the posterior cortex is spared in the amnesic syndrome (e.g., Rozin, 1976; Scoville & Milner, 1957; Squire, 1992b; Weiskrantz, 1985).

Further evidence from the study of amnesia that bears on this idea has been provided by studies that have examined whether amnesic patients show intact priming of novel word forms, that is, nonwords (e.g., "numdy") that do not have preexisting memory representations. Such effects, which have been shown in normal subjects (e.g., Feustel, Shiffrin, & Salasoo, 1983; Rueckl, 1990), provide evidence against the idea that priming is mediated simply by the activation of preexisting representations and instead suggest the creation of a novel perceptual representation by the word-form system (Schacter, 1990). Accordingly, if priming of verbal items in amnesic patients is indeed mediated by an intact word-form system, such patients should show priming for nonwords as well as familiar words. Although several studies have reported impaired or absent priming of nonwords in some amnesic patients, i.e., Korsakoff patients and demented subjects (Cermak et al., 1985; Diamond & Rozin, 1984; Smith & Oscar-Berman, 1990), recent research has provided clear evidence that non-Korsakoff amnesics, and even some Korsakoff patients, can show normal or near-normal priming of nonwords under appropriate experimental conditions (see Cermak et al., 1991; Gabrieli & Keane, 1988; Gordon, 1988; Haist, Musen, & Squire, 1991; Musen & Squire, 1990; for detailed review, see Bowers & Schacter, 1993). Thus the weight of evidence is consistent with the proposition that a spared visual-word-form system supports priming in amnesic patients.

A second line of evidence that bears on the hypothesis of a word-form system has been provided by experiments examining the effects of semantic versus nonsemantic study tasks on priming and explicit memory. Since the initiation of research in the levels-of-processing framework during the 1970s, it has been known that explicit recall and recognition of a list of target words is much higher following semantic study tasks (e.g., judging the meaning of a word) than nonsemantic study tasks (e.g., counting the number of vowels and consonants in a word) (Craik & Tulving, 1975). Many studies that have been done since have shown that the same manipulations have little or no effect on priming in such data-driven implicit tests as stem completion (Bowers & Schacter, 1990; Graf & Mandler, 1984), fragment completion (Roediger et al., 1992), and perceptual identification (Jacoby & Dallas, 1981).

The foregoing findings are important because they provide support for the idea that priming is a presemantic phenomenon: if visual-word priming depends on a form-based system that does not represent the meaning of a word, then it makes sense that semantic study tasks that improve explicit memory do not confer the same benefit on priming. In this connection it is therefore worth noting that under some conditions the magnitude of visual-word priming is increased significantly by semantic study over nonsemantic study (e.g., Bowers & Schacter, 1990; Challis & Brodbeck, 1992). However, results from Bowers and Schacter's experiments suggest strongly that when such effects are observed, they can be attributed to the use of explicit memory strategies by subjects who have caught on to the relation between the implicit task and the study list. Through the use of a postexperimental questionnaire, Bowers and Schacter determined that subjects who exhibited awareness of the relation between the completion test and the study list showed higher completion rates following semantic study over nonsemantic study, whereas subjects who remained unaware of the study-test relation showed equivalent priming following the two study sessions.

Recent neuroimaging studies using positron emission tomography (PET) provide a third type of evidence that bears on the PRS account and that also relates to the foregoing considerations concerning "contamination" of priming by explicit retrieval. PET studies provide estimates of local neuronal activities associated with particular cognitive or memory demands. Squire, Ojemann, Miezin, Petersen, Videen, and Raichle (1992) reported that priming of visual stem-completion performance is associated with a significant reduction of blood flow in right extrastriate occipital cortex. Given the involvement of this brain region with high-level visual processing, their finding provides general support for the PRS view. It suggests that visual priming may make it easier for the PRS mechanisms involved with visual word form representation to extract visual information from the test cue or to generate the target item. In addition, however, Squire et al. also found that priming was associated with significant activation in the right hippocampus. Because the hippocampus is generally thought to be associated with explicit memory and Squire et al. observed hippocampal activation in an experimental condition that required explicit retrieval, this observation is not consistent with the PRS account.

There are strong reasons to believe, however, that the hippocampal activation observed by Squire et al. was produced by explicit-memory contamination, much like that documented by Bowers and Schacter (1990). The magnitude of the priming effects reported by Squire et al. were unusually large—approximately twice as large as priming effects typically observed in stem-completion priming studies—and only slightly lower than the levels of explicit memory that Squire et al. reported. This apparent explicit-contamination effect, noted by the authors, is likely attributable to the fact that Squire et al. provided subjects with two exposures to a short study list and used a semantic study task that promoted elaborative encoding. Under these conditions, it is highly likely that subjects either intentionally or unintentionally remembered study list items on the nominally implicit stem-completion test.

My colleagues and I have recently completed a PET study that provides strong support for the foregoing suggestions (Schacter, Albert, Alpert, Rafferty, & Rausch, in preparation). To avoid explicit contamination, we gave subjects only a single exposure to the study list and used a nonsemantic encoding task (counting the number of **T** junctions in a word) that yields significant priming effects together with low levels of explicit memory. We expected that the use of this shallow encoding task would eliminate the hippocampal increase, but not the occipital decrease, reported by Squire et al.

Results confirmed these predictions. We observed significant priming following the T-junction-encoding task, but the overall levels were much lower than those in the study by Squire et al. Most important, analysis of the PET data revealed a highly significant decrease in right extrastriate occipital cortex (Brodman area 19) and no hint of activation in the hippocampus. These findings support the idea that the PRS is critical to visual priming on the stem completion test, whereas the hippocampus is not. Note also, however, that the right occipital region most strongly implicated in visual priming by these PET data differs from the primarily left-hemisphere regions associated with visual word-form processing in other PET studies (see Howard, Patterson, Wise, Brown, Friston, Weiller, & Frackowiak, 1992; Petersen, Fox, Snyder, & Raichle, 1990). We did indeed observe some rather small priming-related left-occipital decreases, and other PET studies have also shown left-occipital decreases (Buckner, Petersen, Ojemann, Miezin, Squire, & Raichle, submitted), but this point remains to be resolved in future studies.

A fourth line of evidence bearing on the nature of the system that subserves visual-word priming comes from experiments in which perceptual attributes of target items are changed between study and test. The argument here is that if a visually based system plays a major role in priming, then the magnitude of the effect should be reduced when relevant perceptual attributes are changed between study and test. Various manipulations have been used to evaluate this proposal, and a range of experimental outcomes have been observed, including findings that study-to-test changes in perceptual attributes of target items either reduce or eliminate priming (for reviews and discussions, see Kirsner, Dunn, & Standen, 1989; Roediger, Weldon, & Challis, 1989; Schacter, 1990; Schacter, Chiu, & Ochsner, 1993a). For my present purposes, I focus on the theoretical implications of results from two types of stimulus transformations: modality shifts and changes in the format of target words.

Experiments that have examined effects of modality shifts (e.g., target words are presented auditorily and tested visually) have yielded a relatively consistent pattern of results: priming on completion, identification, and similar tasks is always reduced, and sometimes eliminated, by study-test modality shifts (Graf, Shimamura, & Squire, 1985; Jacoby & Dallas, 1981; Clarke & Morton, 1983; Kirsner & Smith, 1974; Morton, 1979; Roediger & Blaxton, 1987). The observed reduction in priming as a consequence of a modality shift supports the hypothesis of a visual-word-form system. However, the fact that significant cross-modal priming is typically observed, particularly with stem- and fragment-completion tests, suggests that word priming is not based entirely on visual/perceptual processes, a point that I will elaborate on later.

The question of whether visual-word priming is affected by study-test changes in the specific format of target items (e.g., typefont, upper/lower case) is theoretically of great interest: if priming is reduced or eliminated by alterations in perceptual format, we have evidence that the system underlying visual-word priming computes highly specific perceptual representations of the particular word tokens encountered on a study list; if priming in unaffected by such changes, we have evidence that the system operates at a more abstract level. Moreover, comparative analysis of which perceptual features do and do not impair priming when changed between study and test could provide rather precise information concerning the representational properties of the system underlying priming. A great deal of experimental effort has been devoted to this issue, and it has yielded a rather mixed pattern of results. On the one hand, a number of studies have provided evidence that transformations of typefont, case, and orthographic structure can have a significant impact on priming (e.g., Gardiner, 1988; Jacoby & Hayman, 1987; Hayman & Tulving, 1989; Roediger & Blaxton, 1987; Scarborough, Cortese, & Scarborough, 1977; Whittlesea, 1990). On the other hand, however, other studies have failed to obtain effects of similar manipulations (e.g., Carr, Brown, & Charalambous, 1989; Clarke & Morton, 1983; Tardif & Craik, 1989).

Although some of the conflicting results may be attributable to subtle aspects of experimental procedures (Carr et al., 1989; Whittlesea, 1990), recent studies have helped to clarify matters by elucidating, within the same experimental situation, conditions under which study-to-test transformations of perceptual features do and do not impair priming. Thus Graf and Ryan (1990) found that study-to-test changes in typefont reduced priming on a word identification test when the study task required subjects to focus on perceptual features of words but not when the study task focused on word meaning (see also, Jacoby, Levy, & Steinbach, 1992). Marsolek, Kosslyn, and Squire (1992) found that changing the case of target words between study and test reduced stem-completion priming when test stems were presented to the right hemisphere, via the left visual field, but not when test stems were presented to the left hemisphere, via the right visual field (see Squire, 1992a, this volume, for further discussion).

These findings indicate that a visual encounter with a word does not necessarily or inevitably create a highly specific and novel of representation of it in the word-form system, but they also indicate that specific perceptual representations are created under appropriate conditions. Graf and Ryan's (1990) data suggest that the system creates novel perceptual representations only when initial processing focuses on visual characteristics of a word, and perhaps only when unusual typefonts are encountered. The data of Marsolek, Kosslyn, & Squire (1992) suggest that this effect may depend on right-hemisphere involvement; that is, the right hemisphere may constitute the substrate of the novel perceptual representations that produce format-specific priming effects. Marsolek et al. have further suggested that it is necessary to fractionate what they called the visual-form system into two further subsystems: a left-hemisphere subsystem that computes abstract visual form representations (i.e., it produces one output for many inputs) and a right-hemisphere subsystem that computes perceptually specific form representations (i.e., it produces a single output for a particular input). I will return to this point later in the chapter.

Two further pertinent findings are worth noting. In a PET study Buckner et al. (submitted) examined visual stem-completion priming under conditions in which the case of words was changed between study and test (from lowercase to uppercase). They found occipital decreases similar to those described earlier by Squire et al. (1992) and Schacter et al. (in preparation). However, they found no evidence for hippocampal activation, even though they used the same semantic-encoding task employed by Squire et al. (1992), who, as noted earlier, observed hippocampal activity when the case of words was the same at study and test. These observations raise the possibility that case-specific priming may be based on an episodic memory trace whose encoding and/or retrieval depends in some way on the hippocampus.

Further evidence that case-specific priming may depend on some of the same processes that ordinarily underly explicit memory is provided by recent observations concerning amnesic patients. Kinoshita and Wayland (1993) found that on a test of word-fragment completion, Korsakoff patients showed similar amounts of priming, regardless of whether the typography of target items (handwritten or typed) was the same or different at study and test; control subjects, by contrast, showed significantly more priming in the same-typography condition than in the different-typography condition. Interpretation of this study is not entirely straightforward, however, because no explicit memory tests were used. Thus we cannot exclude the possibility that the specificity effects observed in control subjects are attributable to the use of voluntary, intentional retrieval processes, processes not available to amnesic patients. Nevertheless, the data do suggest that some aspects of priming may be impaired in at least some amnesic patients. I will elaborate on the theoretical implications of this point when I later consider analogous results from a recent experiment concerning auditory priming in amnesic patients.

1.2   The Structural-Description System

The term *structural description* refers to a representation of relations among parts of an object that specifies the global form and structure of the object (Sutherland, 1968; Winston, 1975). Several investigators have argued that structural descriptions are computed by a specific brain system, termed the *structural-description system* by Riddoch and Humphreys (1987), that does not handle semantic-level information about the associative and functional properties of objects (cf., Kosslyn, Flynn, Amsterdam, & Wang, 1990; Riddoch & Humphreys, 1987; Warrington, 1975, 1982). My colleagues and I have suggested that the structural-description system can be viewed as a PRS subsystem involved in the various priming effects observed in the domain of visual-object processing (e.g., Schacter, 1990, 1992; Schacter, Cooper, & Delaney, 1990; Tulving & Schacter, 1990). As with the visual-word-form system, evidence that the structural-description system operates at a presemantic level has been provided in the first instance by neuropsychological studies of brain-damaged patients. Specifically, a number of investigators have described patients who have severe deficits in gaining access to semantic information about visual objects but exhibit relatively intact access to perceptual/structural knowledge of the same objects (e.g., Riddoch & Humphreys, 1987; Sartori & Job, 1988; Warrington & Taylor, 1978). Such patients perform quite poorly when required to name pictured objects, when tested for functional knowledge of what a visual object is used for, and when queried regarding associative knowledge of where an object is typically encountered. But they perform relatively well when given tests that tap knowledge of object structure, such matching different views of common objects or distinguishing between real and nonsense objects.

There has been a good deal less work on visual-object priming than on visual-word priming, but as with the visual-word-form system, three main kinds of evidence implicate the structural-description system as a major substrate of priming: spared implicit memory in amnesic patients, invariance of priming across semantic versus nonsemantic manipulations of the study task, and the effects of study-to-test transformations of various stimulus properties. I will first consider each type of evidence in the context of an experimental paradigm that my colleagues and I developed to test the hypothesis of a structural-description system and then briefly note pertinent data from other, related implicit-memory tasks.

The paradigm that we have developed for examining priming of structural descriptions makes use of two-dimensional line drawings that depict unfamiliar three-dimensional visual objects (see figure 1). Although all of the objects are novel, half of them are structurally possible—they could exist in three-dimensional form—whereas the other half are structurally impossible—they contain surface and edge violations that would prohibit them from existing in three-dimensions (see Schacter, Cooper, & Delaney, 1990, for more details on the objects). In a typical experiment, subjects initially study a list of possible and impossible objects by making various kinds of judgments about them and then are given an *object-decision test* to assess priming or a yes/no recognition test to assess explicit memory. For the object-decision test, previously studied and nonstudied objects are presented quite briefly (e.g., 50–100 milliseconds), one at a time, and subjects decide whether they are possible or impossible. Our reasoning is that making the possible/impossible object decision requires access to information about the three-dimensional structure of an object, and that to the extent that subjects have acquired information about object structures during the study trial, object decisions should be more accurate for previously studied objects than for nonstudied objects. In an initial experiment we observed significant priming on the object-decision task following a study task that requires analysis of global object structure but not following a study task that focuses attention on local object features (Schacter, Cooper, & Delaney, 1990). Moreover, we observed a priming effect for structurally possible objects but not for structurally impossible objects. Our failure to observe priming for impossible objects has been replicated many times and may indicate that it is difficult to form an internal representation of the global structure

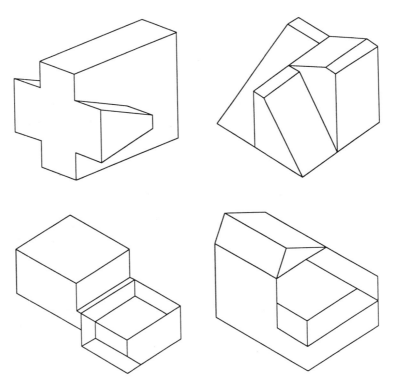

Figure 1 A sample of drawings used in experiments on implicit and explicit memory for novel objects. The drawings in the upper row depict *possible* objects that could exist in three-dimensional form. The drawings in the lower row depict *impossible* objects containing structural violations that would prohibit them from actually existing in three-dimensional form.

of an impossible object (see Schacter, Cooper, & Delaney, 1990; Schacter, Cooper, Delaney, Peterson, & Tharan, 1991).

The foregoing findings are consistent with the idea that priming on the object-decision task is supported by newly formed structural descriptions of previously studied objects. Evidence that the priming effect reflects the operation of a presemantic structural-description system distinct from episodic memory is provided by experiments in which we have compared encoding tasks that require processing of object structure (e.g., deciding whether an object faces primarily to the left or to the right) with encoding tasks that require processing of semantic and functional properties of objects. Figure 2 displays the results of two such experiments. The left panel depicts priming and recognition scores following a structural-encoding task (left/right judgment) and an elaborative-encoding task that taps subjects' semantic knowledge of real-world objects (they are required to generate a verbal label of a common object that each drawing reminds them of most). A striking cross-over interaction was observed (Schacter, Cooper, & Delaney, 1990): explicit recognition was much higher following elaborative than structural encoding, whereas the opposite pattern was found for object decision. Indeed, the ela-

Daniel L. Schacter

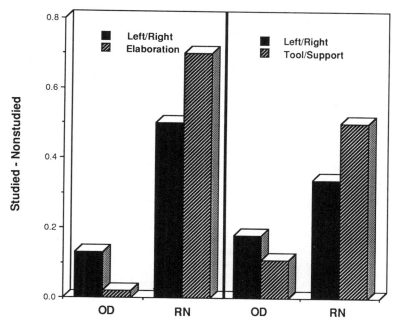

Figure 2 A summary of two experiments examining object-decision (OD) priming and recognition (RN) memory using the possible and impossible figures presented in figure 1. Only data for possible objects are shown, because no priming of impossible objects was observed in either experiment. The left panel presents results from an experiment by Schacter, Cooper, and Delaney (1990) in which subjects in the study session either judged whether the object faces primarily to the left or to the right or generated the name of a real-world object that the target reminded them of most. The figure presents priming scores from the object-decision task that were computed by subtracting the proportion of nonstudied possible objects classified correctly from the proportion of studied possible objects classified correctly, and corrected-recognition scores that were computed by subtracting "yes" responses to nonstudied objects (i.e., false alarms) from "yes" responses to studied objects (hits). The right panel presents priming and corrected-recognition scores from an experiment in which subjects performed either the left/right study task or a functional encoding task in which they judged whether an object would be best used as a tool or for support (Schacter & Cooper, 1993).

borative task failed to produce significant priming on the object-decision task, a finding probably attributable to the fact that subjects often based their elaborations on local, two-dimensional features of target objects. The right panel shows a similar crossover interaction from an experiment in which the left/right encoding task was compared to a functional encoding task in which subjects decided whether target objects could be best used as a tool or for support (Schacter & Cooper, 1993). The functional-encoding task did, however, produce some priming, probably because making the decision about function requires some analysis of structure.

These results are entirely consistent with the idea that object-decision priming depends on a presemantic system dedicated to the analysis and representation of object structure and does not involve information about the semantic and functional properties of objects. We have also found that object-decision priming was spared in a group of amnesic patients who showed poor explicit memory for the objects on a recognition test (Schacter, Cooper, Tharan, & Rubens, 1991). This finding suggests that the priming effect, and the structural-description system that supports it, are not critically dependent on the limbic structures typically damaged in amnesic patients.

Further information regarding the functional properties and possible neuroanatomical basis of the structural-description system is provided by experiments in which we examined the effects on priming of changing the size, reflection, and picture-plane orientation of target objects between study and test. The results of these experiments are relatively clear cut (for a review, see Cooper & Schacter, 1992). On the one hand, study-to-test changes in size and left/right reflection of objects have no effect on priming, despite producing an impairment of recognition memory (Cooper, Schacter, Ballesteros, & Moore, 1992). On the other hand, changing the picture-plane orientation of target objects by 120, 180, or 240 degrees from a standard orientation eliminates priming and also reduces recognition memory substantially (Cooper, Schacter, & Moore, 1991). Consistent with these observations, size-independent priming has been observed in amnesic patients on the object-decision task (Schacter, Cooper, & Treadwell, 1993). This pattern of results suggests that the structural-description system computes object representations that do *not* include information about size or left-right reflection but *do* include information that specifies the relation between the parts of an object on the one hand and its principal axis and frame of reference on the other (Cooper et al., 1991; Cooper, Schacter, Bellesteros, & Moore, 1992).

Data from other studies on priming of nonverbal information provide converging evidence on the foregoing points. Evidence for the presemantic nature of priming has been obtained on implicit tests that involve completing fragments of familiar pictures with the first object that comes to mind (Schacter, Delaney, & Merikle, 1990) and identifying novel dot patterns (Musen, 1991). Spared priming of novel dot patterns has also been documented in amnesic patients (Gabrielli, Milberg, Keane, & Corkin, 1990; Musen & Squire, 1992). And invariance of priming across study-to-test changes in size and reflection has been documented in a picture-naming paradigm, both in normal subjects (Biederman & Cooper, 1992) and amnesic patients (Cave & Squire, 1992).

Although relatively little information is available concerning the exact neural locus of the structural-description system, the findings on size- and reflection-invariant priming have led to the proposal that regions of the inferior temporal cortex may be involved (Biederman & Cooper, 1991; Cooper, Schacter, Ballesteros, & Moore, 1992; Schacter, Cooper, Tharan, & Rubens, 1991). This idea is based to a large extent on findings from single-cell recordings and brain lesions in nonhuman primates indicating that inferior temporal regions are involved in the computation of size- and reflection-invariant representations of objects (for a review, see Plaut & Farah, 1990). It is possible, of course, that the precise neuroanatomical locus of this system differs in monkey and man, but the human data on this point are not conclusive. Studies using PET imaging should help to clarify the matter, and we are in the process of completing such a study with the possible/impossible-object-decision task.

1.3 The Auditory-Word-Form System

The great majority of research on priming and implicit memory has focused on visual paradigms and processes; there has been relatively little investigation of, or theorizing about, implicit memory in the auditory domain (see Schacter & Church, 1992, for a review). Nevertheless, neuropsychological evidence on auditory-processing deficits has revealed a form/semantic dissociation similar in kind to those discussed in previous sections, and this implies that there is a presemantic auditory subsystem of the PRS. Specifically, patients have been identified who exhibit severe deficits in understanding spoken language together with relatively intact abilities to repeat and write auditorily presented words and sentences. In cases of *word-meaning deafness*, the semantic deficit is modality specific; patients show relatively spared comprehension of visual inputs (e.g., Kohn & Friedman, 1986). In cases of *transcortical sensory aphasia*, comprehension is impaired in both the auditory and visual modalities (e.g., Coslett, Roeltgen, Rothi, & Heilman, 1987). By contrast, patients characterized by *pure-word deafness* exhibit selective deficits in repeating spoken words (e.g., Metz-Lutz & Dahl, 1984). Taken together, these observations point toward the existence of a presemantic auditory-word-form system dedicated to processing and representing acoustic/phonological information, but not semantic information, about spoken words (Ellis & Young, 1988). PET studies suggest that regions of the posterior temporoparietal cortex may be involved in encoding phonological word forms (Petersen et al., 1989).

Relatively little work has been done to link the auditory-word-form system with priming effects observed on auditory implicit tests, but some data are available concerning two of the key issues discussed in previous sections: invariance of priming as a function of semantic versus nonsemantic encoding processes and the effects of study-to-test changes in perceptual attributes of targets on the magnitude of priming.

Several recent experiments from our laboratory have provide evidence supporting the idea that auditory priming depends on a presemantic system. In studies with college students, we have examined auditory priming on two tests quite similar to the perceptual, or data-driven, implicit memory tasks used previously in the visual domain: auditory-word identification and auditory-stem completion (Schacter & Church, 1992). In the former task, subjects hear previously studied and nonstudied words masked by white noise and attempt to identify them; in the latter task, subjects hear the initial syllable of studied and nonstudied words and respond with the first word that pops into mind (the syllable stimulus is created by editing a whole word utterance on a Macintosh computer system). To investigate whether priming on these tasks depends on semantic-level processes, during the study phase of the experiment subjects heard a series of spoken words and either performed a semantic encoding task (e.g., rating the number of meanings associated with the word) or a nonsemantic encoding task (e.g., rating the clarity with which the speaker enunciated the word). Implicit and explicit memory were tested after brief delays of several minutes. A series of five experiments yielded a consistent pattern of results: explicit memory was considerably higher following semantic rather than nonsemantic encoding tasks, whereas the magnitude of priming on identification and completion tasks was either less affected or entirely unaffected by the manipulation of the study task.

Further evidence for the hypothesis that auditory priming reflects the operation of a presemantic system is provided by a recent study in which we assessed priming in a case of word-meaning deafness (Schacter, McGlynn, Milberg, & Church, 1993). The patient, J.P., suffered a large stroke-induced lesion within the distribution of the left middle cerebral artery that affected primarily the anterior portions of Wernicke's area, largely sparing the posterior temporoparietal cortex. He has great difficulty understanding spoken words. For example, J.P. exhibits a severe impairment on the auditory comprehension subtests of the Boston Diagnostic Aphasia Examination, whereas he shows only mild deficits on subtests that assess repetition of spoken words, writing to dictation, or comprehension of visual input. If, as we have suggested, priming on a task such as auditory word identification is mediated by a presemantic system, then J.P. should show robust priming despite his semantic impairment. Using the identification-in-noise task from Schacter and Church (1992), we indeed observed intact priming in J.P. relative to four matched control subjects (figure 3). In a follow-up experiment, we observed a similar pattern of results on a different auditory identification task in which words were degraded by removing selected frequencies with a low-pass filter (Schacter, McGlynn, Milberg, & Church, 1993).

While the foregoing results support the idea that auditory priming need not involve access to semantic representations, they do not indicate what kinds of processes and representations are involved in this phenomenon. Evidence that priming is based largely on an auditory *perceptual* system is provided by experiments on study/test modality shifts: when target words are studied visually, priming on the tasks of auditory-word identification (Ellis, 1982; Jackson & Morton, 1984) and stem completion (Bassilli, Smith, & MacLeod, 1989) is reduced significantly relative to auditory-study conditions. Since a modality-specific auditory system plays a key role in priming, an important question concerns the nature of this system: is auditory priming based on acoustic features of spoken input that are specific to a particular speaker, or is it based on more abstract phonological representations that do not include speaker-specific perceptual information?

This issue was addressed initially in experiments by Jackson and Morton (1984), who examined priming on the auditory-identification test when target

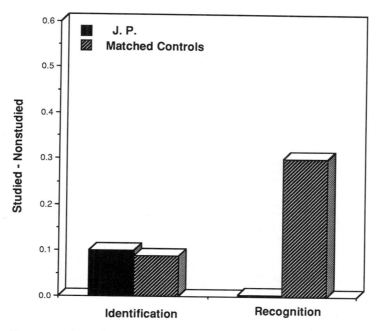

Figure 3 The results of an experiment that examined priming of auditory-word identification and explicit recognition memory in a patient with word-meaning deafness (J.P.) and four matched controls (Schacter, McGlynn, Milberg, & Church, 1993). The figure presents priming scores from the auditory identification task, which were computed by subtracting the proportion of nonstudied words identified correctly from the proportion of studied words identified correctly, and corrected recognition scores, which were computed by subtracting "yes" responses to nonstudied words from "yes" responses to studied words. J.P.'s corrected recognition score was zero.

words were spoken by the same voice at study and test, and when they were spoken by different voices (male or female) at study and test. They observed priming effects of comparable magnitude in the same- and different-voice conditions and argued on this basis that priming depends entirely on abstract (but modality-specific) representations of invariant phonological features of spoken words. In experiments discussed earlier, Schacter and Church (1992) also found nonsignificant effects of study-to-test changes in the speaker's voice on priming of auditory identification. In fact, Schacter and Church observed voice-invariant priming even following nonsemantic study tasks that focused subjects' attention on characteristics of the speaker's voice (see also Graf & Ryan, 1990).

While the foregoing results are consistent with the idea that auditory priming depends on a system that represents abstract phonological word forms, it is also possible that the absence of voice-change effects in the Jackson and Morton (1984) and Schacter and Church (1992) experiments reflects idiosyncratic features of the auditory-identification test used in these experiments. Specifically, Schacter and Church suggested that the use of white noise on the identification test may have interfered with processing those components of

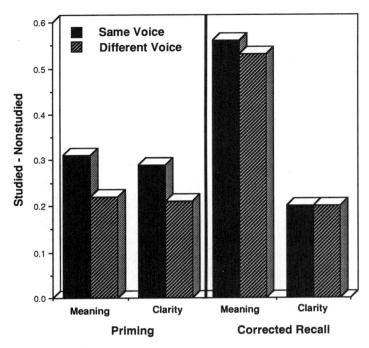

Figure 4 The results of an experiment that examined priming of auditory stem completion and explicit cued recall following word-meaning and voice-clarity encoding tasks (Schacter & Church, 1992). Target words were spoken in the same voice or a different voice at study and test. The figure presents priming scores and corrected recall scores computed by subtracting the proportion of nonstudied target words that subjects provided from the proportion of studied target words that they provided.

the acoustic waveform that provide voice information. Consistent with this suggestion, when we examined the effect of changing the speaker's voice on priming of the auditory stem-completion task, which does not involve the use of white noise, significant voice-change effects were observed in each of two experiments. Data from one of those experiments, presented in figure 4, show that priming was lower in the different-voice condition than in the same-voice condition following both semantic and nonsemantic encoding tasks. The voice change had no effect on explicit memory, whereas semantic versus nonsemantic study affected explicit memory but not priming. To ascertain that the presence/absence of white noise is the crucial factor determining whether or not voice changes affect priming, we performed an additional experiment with auditory stem completion that was identical in all respects to the previous one except for one change: stems were masked by white noise. Under these conditions, we observed significant priming but no effect of voice change (Schacter and Church, 1992).

The foregoing data indicate that priming of auditory stem completion is influenced by study-to-test changes in the speaker's gender. In a series of more recent experiments, Church and Schacter (1994) demonstrated that study-to-test changes within a single speaker's voice influence priming of auditory stem completion and also of auditory identification of words degraded with a low-pass filter. For example, in one experiment the emotional intonation of the speaker's voice was varied: target words were spoken in the same emotional intonation at study and test (e.g., angry-angry), or they were spoken in different emotional intonations (e.g., angry-happy). Priming of filter identication was significantly higher in the same-intonation condition than in the different-intonation condition, whereas explicit memory for the words was not significantly affected by the intonation manipulation. Even more impressive, subsequent experiments revealed that priming of both filter identification and stem completion is sensitive to relatively small study-to-test changes in the fundamental frequency of a single speaker's voice: more priming was observed when the fundamental frequency was the same at study and test than when it was either raised or lowered by about 10 percent between study and test (by a computer algorithm). The fundamental frequency of a speaker's voice is the major determinant of pitch and must be represented at a relatively early stage in acoustic processing (e.g., Zatorre, 1988). Importantly, however, study-to-test changes in the intensity of the acoustic waveform, that is, the loudness of the speaker's voice, had no effect on priming. Thus Church and Schacter's (1994) experiments indicate that priming depends specifically on pitch information.

The overall pattern of results from the Schacter and Church (1992) and Church and Schacter (1994) studies is similar to that observed in studies of visual-word priming: priming is influenced by changes in perceptual features of target words in some experimental conditions but not in others. The crucial issue for present purposes concerns the theoretical implications of such observations for understanding the kind of subsystem that subserves auditory priming. Schacter and Church (1992) speculated that the left- and right-hemisphere subsystems subserve abstract and perceptually specific components of auditory priming, respectively. Their reasoning is relatively straightforward and turns on three kinds of observations. First, a number of investigators have argued that the left hemisphere represents exclusively abstract or categorical phonological information, whereas the right hemisphere represents perceptually specific "acoustic gestalts," including information about the speaker's voice (Gazzaniga, 1975; Lieberman, 1982; Mann & Lieberman, 1983; Zaidel, 1985). Second, several types of empirical evidence link the right hemisphere with access to voice information: patients with right-hemisphere lesions have voice-recognition impairments (e.g., Van Lancker & Kreiman, 1987) and difficulties in processing voice prosody (e.g., Ross, 1981); patients with right-hemisphere lesions involving Heschl's gyrus have special problems performing the computations necessary for extracting fundamental-frequency information from the acoustic waveform (Zatorre, 1988); and studies of normal subjects using dichotic-listening techniques have shown a left-ear (i.e., right-hemisphere) advantage for processing intonational contours (e.g., Blumstein & Cooper, 1974). Third, evidence from split-brain patients indicates that the right hemisphere is greatly impaired—more than the left—when required to process spoken words presented in background noise (Zaidel, 1978).

Since voice-change effects in auditory priming appear to depend on the presence or absence of white noise and the right hemisphere represents voice information and is especially affected by background noise, it is possible that voice-change effects are not observed when target items are masked by noise, because a right-hemisphere subsystem has been effectively excluded from contributing to task performance. Stated slightly differently, auditory priming may depend both on a left-hemisphere subsytem that represents abstract phonological information and a right-hemisphere subsystem that represents voice-specific acoustic information. When both subsytems can contribute to implicit-task performance (i.e., if no white noise is used), voice-change effects will be observed, but when only the left-hemisphere subsystem can contribute (i.e., if white noise eliminates right-hemisphere contributions), voice-change effects will not be observed. The general idea that two lateralized subsystems are involved in auditory priming is quite similar to an idea offered by Marsolek et al. (1992) to account for the finding that perceptually specific effects were observed in visual-word priming when test stems were presented to the right hemisphere, whereas abstract priming was observed when stems were presented to the left hemisphere.

I must emphasize, of course, that Schacter and Church's argument for right-hemisphere involvement in voice-specific priming is based entirely on indirect evidence and hence must be treated cautiously. To test this hypothesis more directly, we have recently initiated experiments that use dichotic listening techniques to examine voice-change effects on priming. A large body of literature indicates that with dichotic presentation, verbal stimuli presented to the right ear (i.e., left hemisphere) are more accurately reported than are verbal stimuli presented to the left ear (e.g., Bryden, 1988; Wexler, 1988), and as noted earlier, there is some evidence that voice information is processed more efficiently by the left ear (Blumstein & Cooper, 1974). Accordingly, we hypothesized that priming effects would be reduced by study-to-test changes in the speaker's voice when test stimuli were presented to the left ear but not when they were presented to the right ear. In an initial experiment (Schacter, Aminoff, & Church, 1992), subjects first made clarity-of-enunciation judgments concerning a series of words spoken by male or female voices. They were then given a dichotic version of the auditory-stem-completion task: stems representing studied or nonstudied target words were presented to either the left or right ear, a nontarget distractor stem was presented to the opposite ear (to inhibit the hemisphere ipsilateral to the target stimulus), and subjects were instructed to respond with the first word that came to mind in response to the stem presented to either the left ear or the right ear (left-ear and right-ear presentations were ordered randomly for individual subjects, and they were cued to the appropriate ear on each test trial). Results of the experiment were clear-cut: for right-ear (i.e., left-hemisphere) presentations, significant and virtually identical amounts of priming were observed in same- and different-voice conditions; for left-ear (i.e., right-hemisphere) presentations, significant priming was observed in the same-voice condition and no priming was found in the different-voice condition. A follow-up experiment yielded a similar, but not quite as clear-cut, pattern of results.

In view of the fact that data from dichotic-listening experiments sometimes vary across procedures and subject populations, these observation must be treated cautiously, pending additional investigations under a variety of experimental conditions. Nevertheless, they are consistent with the idea that voice-specific and voice-nonspecific components of auditory priming may depend on differential contributions from the two hemispheres.

An alternative and perhaps complementary way of thinking about the relations between components of auditory priming is suggested by recent work that we have conducted with amnesic patients. In an initial experiment, we examined auditory priming in a mixed group of Korsakoff and non-Korsakoff amnesic patients (Schacter, Church, & Treadwell, 1994). In the auditory-identification test and the semantic/nonsemantic study tasks developed by Schacter and Church (1992, experiment 2), amnesics exhibited normal priming effects: their overall level of priming was indistinguishable from that of control subjects, and, like controls, patients' priming scores were similar after semantic and nonsemantic study and were virtually identical under the same- and different-voice conditions.

In a subsequent set of experiments, we examined whether amnesic patients would exhibit voice-specific priming under conditions in which normal control subjects are known to show such effects. Patients and controls heard a list of familiar words spoken by male and female speakers and were then given a low-pass-filter identification test for studied and nonstudied words; half of the studied words were spoken in the same voice as during the study phase, and half were spoken in a different voice (from among the set of speakers used for presenting the list of words). The key result is a significant interaction between subject group and speaker's voice: control subjects exhibited significantly more priming in the same-voice condition than in the different-voice condition, whereas amnesic patients exhibited nonsignificantly less priming in the same-voice condition than in the different-voice condition (Schacter, Church, & Bolton, in press).

Why did amnesic patients fail to exhibit voice-specific priming? One possibility is that this effect depends on the use of intentional, explicit retrieval strategies, strategies available to control subjects but not to amesic patients. Thus the control subjects may have converted the nominally implicit test of filter identification into a functionally explicit test of episodic memory. This possibility seems unlikely, however, for two reasons. First, the control subjects did not exhibit voice-specific effects when given a test of explicit recognition; if the effect had indeed been based on explicit retrieval, one would have expected to observe it on an explicit test. Second, previous research with college students has shown that the magnitude of voice-specific priming on the filter identification test is the same after nonsemantic-encoding tasks that produce low levels of explicit memory as after semantic-encoding tasks that produce high levels of explicit memory (Church & Schacter, 1994).

An alternative possibility is that voice-specific priming, while a genuine implicit-memory phenomenon, depends on the formation of specific links between a target word and a speaker's voice at the time of study; this binding process may require involvement of the hippocampus and related structures, which are damaged in amnesic patients. Thus amnesics are unable to perform the necessary binding and hence do not exhibit voice-specific priming. Similar ideas can be applied to Kinoshita and Wayland's (1993) finding, noted earlier, that Korsakoff patients failed to exhibit perceptual-specificity effects on a test of visual-fragment completion; perhaps the amnesics failed to bind the specific typography with a more abstract visual representation of the target word. We are currently exploring the implications of this binding hypothesis with additional experiments on voice-specific priming in amnesic patients.

Although the foregoing data and hypotheses should be treated as merely suggestive, pending further investigation, there is one potentially important theoretical implication that I ought to note: Some perceptual-specificity effects in priming may involve an interaction or collaboration between the PRS and episodic (or semantic) memory system. Thus, for example, it is possible that auditory-word-form information and acoustic (e.g., voice) information are computed by separate PRS subsystems, as suggested earlier. However, for an arbitrary word form and a particular speaker's voice to be bound into a single representation at the time of encoding, an additional system may be required. As Squire (1992a, 1992b, this volume), among others, has argued, the hippocampal system seems to be particularly well suited for computing such arbitrary conjunctions. The results from PET studies of priming discussed earlier (Buckner et al., submitted; Schacter et al., in preparation; Squire et al., 1992) are certainly consistent with the idea that the hippocampus plays some role in perceptually specific priming and no role in more abstract forms of perceptual priming. Whatever the merit of this particular proposal, this general line of argument suggests that it is now time to turn our attention to understanding interactions between the PRS and other memory systems with a view toward understanding how certain kinds of implicit-memory phenomena may emerge from such interactions.

2 CONCLUDING COMMENTS

To conclude this chapter, I will consider four general issues in the context of other contributions to this volume: perceptual versus conceptual forms of priming, the fractionation of perceptual subsystems, the relation between implicit and explicit memory, and relations between the notion of a system and a subsystem.

2.1 Perceptual versus Conceptual Priming

This chapter has focused on the contributions of presemantic perceptual sub-systems to priming on data-driven implicit-memory tests in the visual and auditory domains. However, it can be questioned whether the entire priming effect on such tasks can be attributed to perceptual processes. As noted earlier, experiments examining the effects of study-to-test modality shifts have reported reduced priming in cross-modality conditions relative to within-modality conditions but have still generally documented significant cross-modal effects; priming is rarely eliminated by a modality shift (for reviews, see Kirsner, Dunn, & Standen, 1989; Roediger & Blaxton, 1987). Some authors have assumed that the existence of cross-modal priming necessarily implies that semantic or conceptual processes are involved in priming (e.g., Hirshman et al., 1990; Keane et al., 1991). For example, Keane et al. (1991) have argued that the existence of significant cross-modal priming on the stem-completion task indicates that a lexical/semantic system plays a role in stem-completion priming. If their reasoning is correct, it will be necessary to qualify the statement that priming on stem completion (and other tasks that include a significant cross-modal component) is mediated entirely by subsystems that operate at a presemantic level (see also Masson and MacLeod, 1992).

There are, however, some grounds for questioning the conclusion that cross-modal priming necessarily implies that semantic-level processes are involved. Kirsner et al. (1989), for instance, have suggested two alternative sources of cross-modal priming on visual implicit tests: phonological representations and amodal "production records" (i.e., motor programs involved in response production) activated by an auditory presentation. Their own review of the literature led Kirsner et al. to favor the production-record hypothesis. Similarly, McClelland and Pring (1991) provided evidence supporting the hypothesis that cross-modal effects on the priming of auditory-stem completion are attributable to phonological processes. Whether or not these ideas about the basis of cross-modal priming are ultimately correct, they underscore the point that the presence of cross-modal priming need not imply that conceptual or semantic processes are involved. Nevertheless, it is clear that priming can be observed on tasks that involve semantic processing, such as answering general-knowledge questions or producing category instances in response to a category label. The magnitude of priming on such tasks is increased by semantic study relative to nonsemantic study (Hamann, 1990) and can be dissociated from perceptually based priming (Blaxton, 1989). These kinds of observations indicate that conceptual priming is based on processes different from perceptual priming (Blaxton, 1989; Roediger, 1990a; Tulving & Schacter, 1990), processes that occur outside of the PRS, although the precise locus of these effects has not been well specified.

The nature of conceptual priming is also relevant to questions concerning the priming of new associations. In nearly all of the experiments discussed in this chapter, target materials consisted of individual words or objects. However, evidence also exists indicating that novel associations between unrelated words can influence performance on such implicit tests as word-stem completion. To investigate priming of novel associations, Graf and Schacter (1985, 1987; Schacter & Graf, 1986a, 1989) developed a paradigm in which subjects were initially exposed to a pair of unrelated words (e.g., *window-reason*), and were then given a stem completion test in which half of the target words were presented in the *same context* as during study (e.g., *window-rea_____*) and half were presented in a *different* context (e.g., *officer-rea_____*). To the extent that more priming is observed in the same-context condition than in the different-context condition, it can be said that priming is influenced by the novel association between the unrelated words established during the study trial. Graf and Schacter's experiments have provided extensive evidence for this pattern of results.

There are, however, some key differences between priming of new associations on the one hand and priming of individual words and objects on the other. First, priming of new associations on the stem-completion task appears to require some semantic processing (Graf & Schacter, 1985; Schacter & Graf, 1986a; but see also Micco & Masson, 1991). Second, priming of new associations is not consistently preserved in severely amnesic patients (Mayes & Gooding, 1989; Schacter & Graf, 1986b; Shimamura & Squire, 1989). As pointed out by Schacter, Cooper, Tharan, and Rubens (1991) and by Squire (1992a, this volume), these observations suggest that priming of novel associations is not a presemantic phenomenon and thus does not depend exclusively on the activity of the same perceptual subsystems that support priming of individual words and objects.

It is possible that priming of new associations depends on some of the same (poorly specified) processes that subserve the conceptual priming of individual words. One reasonable hypothesis is that both conceptual priming with familiar items and priming of new associations with novel pairs depend on a semantic memory system. Because acquisition of new semantic knowledge likely depends to some extent on the integrity of the hippocampus and related structures, which are impaired in amnesia (Schacter & Tulving, this volume; Squire, 1992a, this volume), it makes sense that priming of new associations on the stem-completion task is impaired in amnesic patients.

One reason that it is important to understand priming of new associations is that this phenomenon might provide a link to some of the findings and ideas on forms of memory that have been developed in the animal literature. For example, Rudy and Sutherland's (1992) analysis of simple versus configural associations, which is based on studies of normal and lesioned rats, holds that amnesic patients can form and retain simple but not configural associations. To support this view, they cited Graf and Schacter's (1985) results on preserved priming of new associations in amnesic patients and argue that the kind of association tapped by the stem-completion task conforms to their definition of a simple association. As indicated earlier, however, subsequent analyses and research indicated that patients with severe amnesia do not consistently exhibit priming of novel associations; the effects observed by Graf and Schacter (1985) seem to occur largely in patients with relatively mild memory disorders. Thus to the extent that Rudy and Sutherland contend that normal priming of new associations by amnesics on a stem-completion task supports their view, the full spectrum of data available on amnesia and priming of new associations is not entirely consistent with their position.

2.2   Fractionating Perceptual Subsystems

This chapter has focused on three PRS subsystems: visual word form, structural description, and auditory word form. In each case, a putative subsystem was postulated on the basis of neuropsychological observations concerning patients who exhibit form/semantic dissociations within a particular domain, and the role of that subsystem in priming was inferred from patterns of effects of various experimental and subject variables. The fact that the PRS account is supported by converging evidence from independent research domains is an important strength of this general approach (see Schacter, 1992). I also considered results that support a further fractionation of the visual- and auditory-word-form systems into lateralized subsystems: a left-hemisphere component that operates on abstract (but modality-specific) word-form information and a right-hemisphere component that operates on highly specific visual or auditory perceptual information. Experimental evidence supporting the idea that such lateralized subsystems contribute differentially to priming in the visual and auditory domains is still rather scanty and will require further replication and examination. Nonethless, it is worth emphasizing that there is converging evidence for lateralized subsystems of the kind postulated on the basis of the priming results. In the visual domain, recent PET data are consistent with the idea that left posterior regions are involved in processing abstract orthographic information, whereas right posterior regions are involved in processing specific perceptual features of words and nonwords (Petersen, Fox, Snyder, & Raichle, 1990). And in the auditory domain, several kinds of evidence discussed earlier suggest the existence of auditory subsystems that operate on abstract and specific information.

If we accept for the moment the idea that lateralized perceptual subsystems contribute to priming, questions arise concerning the nature of their relation to the three subsystems that have been the focus of this chapter: Is it necessary to fractionate the visual-word-form, structural-description, and auditory-word-form systems into left-hemipshere and right-hemisphere subsystems, which would yield a total of six distinct PRS subsystems? Or is it more useful to think in terms of a visual-form system and an auditory-form system that can each be fractionated into left- and right-hemisphere components, which would yield four basic PRS subsystems? Although we cannot provide conclusive answers to these questions at this early stage of research and theorizing, they raise fundamental problems that will require careful analysis. As pointed out by Schacter (1990) and Moscovitch (1992, this volume), it is likely that progress in thinking about such questions with respect to implicit memory will be facilitated by considering them in relation to debates in cognitive neuropsychology concerning the nature and number of visual- and auditory-recognition systems (e.g., Farah, 1990; Humphreys & Riddoch, 1987; Ellis & Young, 1988).

Progress in understanding the foregoing issues will probably depend on elucidating further the extent to which, and the sense in which, perceptual priming is "hyperspecific" (Hayman & Tulving, 1989; Schacter, 1985)—an issue discussed by a number of contributors to this volume (Eichenbaum, 1992, this volume; Moscovitch, 1992, this volume; Squire, 1992a, this volume). Hyperspecificty refers to the observation that in some conditions the knowledge expressed by implicit or nondeclarative systems exhibits greater inflexibility and rigidity than does the knowledge expressed by explicit or declarative systems. With respect to priming, evidence for hyperspecificity is obtained when changing a perceptual attribute of a target between study and test, or between two tests (Hayman & Tulving, 1989), impairs priming more than explicit memory. As pointed out earlier, a variety of experiments have reported evidence of hyperspecific priming (Hayman & Tulving, 1989; Roediger & Blaxton, 1987; Schacter & Church, 1992), but other experiments have delineated conditions under which priming does not exhibit perceptual hyperspecificty; that is, changing various attributes of target stimuli between study and test has no effect on priming (Carr et al., 1989; Cooper, Schacter, Ballesteros, & Moore, 1992; Schacter & Church, 1992). Thus, as Moscovitch (1992, this volume) rightly points out, priming is not hyperspecific in the sense that changing *any* perceptual attribute necessarily or inevitably reduces the magnitude of a priming effect.

The fractionation of the PRS into abstract and form-specific subsystems represents one possible approach to understanding the presence and absence of hyperspecific priming in different experimental situations (Marsolek et al., 1992; Schacter & Church, 1992; Squire, 1992a, this volume). That is, hyperspecific priming may be observed under experimental conditions in which a form-specific subsystem (possibly right-hemisphere-lateralized) plays a dominant role in performance, whereas nonspecific priming may be observed under conditions in which an abstract subsystem (possibly left-hemisphere-lateralized) plays a dominant role in performance. A related idea, suggested earlier, is that PRS subsystems (perhaps lateralized) represent different kinds of perceptual attributes and that binding them together requires the involvement of the hippocampal system. On this view, hyperspecificity of priming emerges from an interaction between the PRS and episodic or semantic systems.

The issue of hyperspecificity is also important because it plays a significant role in conceptualizations of nondeclarative or procedural memory in animals (Eichenbaum, 1992, this volume; Squire, 1992a, this volume). Dramatic demonstrations that the knowledge acquired by amnesic rats is highly inflexible, summarized by Eichenbaum (1992, this volume), suggest a possible link to priming and other manifestations of implicit memory in humans (see Butters, Glisky, & Schacter, 1993; Glisky, Schacter, & Tulving, 1986). However, the question of whether the mechanisms of hyperspecific priming in humans are manifestations of, or even related to, mechanisms of hyperspecificity in amnesic rats is wide open. Although the surface resemblances between the two phenomena are suggestive, the fact that they arise in profoundly different organisms and experimental situations suggests the need for approaching such comparisons cautiously (see Schacter and Tulving, this volume). Indeed, it is worth emphasizing that we are uncertain whether an experimental analogue of human perceptual priming exists in animals. The kinds of tasks that amnesic animals can learn tend to involve slow, incremental acquisition of habits and skills over numerous trials, whereas those that they cannot learn often involve memory for single-trial events (see the chapters in this volume by Eichenbaum, Nadel, Rudy & Sutherland, Shapiro & Olton, and Squire); it is not clear that a kind of learning that corresponds neatly to perceptual priming has been demonstrated.

2.3 Relation between Implicit and Explicit Memory

This chapter has focused on the nature and composition of the PRS; it has paid relatively little attention to the relation between the implicit expressions of memory supported by the PRS and the the explicit expressions of memory supported by an episodic system. My own general approach to the matter is relatively straightforward: the outputs of PRS subsystems can serve as inputs to episodic memory. As noted earlier and as argued by several other contributors to this volume (see, for instance, the chapters by Metcalfe et al., Moscovitch, and Squire), a key function of the episodic system is to bind together perceptual with other kinds of information (e.g., semantic, contextual) and thereby allow subsequent recall or recognition of multiattribute events. Whether or not the outputs of particular PRS subsystems are "selected" for representation in the episodic trace likely depends on a variety of factors that guide encoding processes at any particular moment.

This general orientation leaves many questions unanswered. For example, in light of my earlier suggestion that some perceptual specificity effects in priming may involve binding of representations computed by subsystems within the PRS, a natural question concerns the nature of and relations between binding operations that support implicit and explicit expressions of memory. Similarly, it is also important to ask whether the outputs of PRS subsystems have relatively direct access to the episodic system or whether they must be resolved first (or in parallel) by the semantic system, where they are related to preexisting concepts and associative relations. If the output of PRS subsystems is indeed represented in the episodic system, does this imply that explicit remembering, which depends heavily on the episodic system, should be sensitive to changes in perceptual attributes of target items between study and test? Although explicit remembering can be sensitive to perceptual alterations of target stimuli, it often is not (e.g., Schacter & Church, 1992). Church and I have argued that this outcome is attributable to the fact that conceptual factors typically dominate performance on explicit tests, which thereby obscures the potential influence of perceptual information (Church & Schacter, in press; Schacter & Church, 1992). And indeed, there is some evidence that when explicit tests specifically require access to perceptual information, they exhibit the kind of perceptual sensitivity more often observed with implicit tests (e.g., Blaxton, 1989). But it seems clear that our understanding of this fundamental issue is quite rudimentary and badly in need of further illumination.

Recent PET data provide some suggestive clues on this point. As I noted earlier, Buckner et al. (submitted) found that hippocampal activation was associated with perceptually specific priming effects on a stem-completion test after semantic encoding—the hippocampus was activated in a same-case condition but not in a different-case condition. Schacter et al. (in preparation) found no hippocampal activation in a same-case condition after nonsemantic encoding. Taken together, these findings suggest that the hippocampus may be activated when a rich or strong episodic memory trace has been established (by semantic encoding) and when a matching perceptual cue is provided (as in the same-case condition). This activation may be a largely involuntary process; that is, the hippocampus may be largely involved in what I have previously termed involuntary explicit memory (Schacter, 1987). As Moscovitch (1992, this volume) argues, the hippocampus operates on a modular, automatic basis, and thus does not play a major role in voluntary, intentional retrieval. Further evidence on this point is provided by Buckner et al.'s failure to observe hippocampal activation in a different-case condition even when subjects were given explicit memory instructions; that is, although subjects were intentionally thinking back to the list, no hippocampal activation was observed in the presence of different-case cues. Similarly, no hippocampal activation was observed on an explicit (visual) cued-recall test after auditory study (Buckner et al., submitted). Although these negative findings might reflect the difficulty of detecting hippocampal activation with PET, significant hippocampal activation was observed on an explicit cued-recall test in the same-case condition (Squire et al., 1992). These findings lead me to speculate that the critical condition for activating the hippocampus is not the act of voluntary or intentional retrieval but rather the overlap between a richly bound episodic trace and a perceptually matching cue; when these conditions are met, the hippocampus automatically outputs a specific match. Importantly, Buckner et al. observed that areas in right prefrontal cortex were activated on the explicit cued-recall test in both same-case and different-case conditions and after auditory input. Tulving, Kapur, Craik, Moscovitch, & Houle (in press) have observed that right prefrontal activation is consistently associated with intentional, explicit retrieval in a variety of PET studies, including their own. This kind of intentional retrieval appears to be largely indifferent to the degree of perceptual match between study and test. Thus, perceptual specificity in explicit memory may be attributable to involuntary activation of the hippocampus, which may also be the source of many perceptual specificity effects in priming.

A question related to the foregoing ones concerns whether explicit retrieval can be based on the output of PRS subsystems without the involvement of a separate episodic system. For example, Johnson (1992) has described two perceptual subsystems, P-1 and P-2, that are broadly similar to the PRS subsystems described in this chapter (see also Johnson & Chalfonte, this volume). But in Johnson's scheme, P-1 and P-2 can be involved in either implicit or explicit expressions of memory, whereas I have argued that the PRS alone does not support explicit recollection. One way to address the question would be to examine the performance of amnesic patients on explicit tests that require, for instance, recognition of perceptual attributes of target items. If the outputs of PRS subsystems alone are not sufficient to support performance on explicit tests, amnesic patients should perform poorly in appropriate test situations (given that amnesic patients are indeed characterized by an intact PRS and an impaired episodic system). If, however, PRS subsystems can directly contribute to performance on explicit tests, then amnesic patients should perform relatively well when given tests that tap explicit recognition of perceptual aspects of target stimuli. Systematic investigations of this issue are sorely needed.

2.4 Systems and Subsystems

Questions concerning relations among PRS subsystems raise a more general issue concerning the use of the terms "system" and "subsystem" in discussions of the PRS and multiple memory systems more generally. Throughout this chapter and elsewhere, I have referred to a perceptual representation *system* and to visual-word-form, structural-description, and auditory-word-form *subsystems*. I use the latter term to reflect the idea that each of the subsystems perform distinct input-output computations within a particular domain. For example, the kinds of modality-specific computations performed by the visual- and auditory-word-form subsystems, and the memory representations they create, must differ from one another because of fundamental differences in the nature of visual and acoustic inputs to these subsystems. Similarly, as noted earlier, the case for postulating lateralized subsystems rests on the notion that the computations performed by abstract (left-hemisphere) and specific (right-hemisphere) perceptual subsystems are functionally incompatible with one another (Marsolek et al., 1992; Sherry & Schacter, 1987). In view of these considerations, one could argue that it is more accurate to refer simply to perceptual representation *systems* than to invoke a monolithic perceptual representation *system*. Indeed, Baddeley (1992, this volume) raised questions about Tulving and Schacter's (1990) use of the term "perceptual representation system," pointing out that neuropsychological evidence (discussed earlier in this chapter) indicates the need for further fractionation among perceptual subsystems.

I agree with Baddelely (1992, this volume) and have previously used the terms "perceptual representation systems" and "perceptual representation system" interchangeably (Schacter, 1990), and the theoretical spirit of this chapter and elsewhere is entirely consistent with this useage. The main reason for invoking the term "perceptual representation system" is to emphasize the notion that all of the various subsystems are tied together by common properties and rules of operations: they are cortically based, operate at a presemantic level on domain-specific perceptual information, and support nonconscious expressions of memory. Thus the term "subsystem" is used to refer to a neurally instantiated input-output unit that operates on certain kinds of information, whereas the term "system" is used at a more abstract level of description to refer to common features of a class of subsystems. Schacter and Tulving (this volume) elaborate on this distinction between a memory system and a memory subsystem. And as Schacter and Tulving point out, careful consideration of the ways in which these and related concepts are used can help to insure that our rather modest understanding of memory systems in 1994 will be deepened and broadened in the coming years.

ACKNOWLEDGMENTS

Supported by the National Institute of Mental Health, grant RO1 MH45398-01A3; the National Institute of Neurological Disorders and Stroke, grant PO1 NS27950-01A1; and the National Institute on Aging, grant RO1 AG08441. I thank Dana Osowiecki and Kimberly Nelson for help with preparating the manuscript.

REFERENCES

Baddeley, A. (1992). Working memory: The interface between memory and cognition. *Journal of Cognitive Neuroscience, 4,* 281–288.

Bassilli, J. N., Smith, M. C., & MacLeod, C. M. (1989). Auditory and visual word stem completion: Separating data-driven and conceptually-driven processes. *Quarterly Journal of Experimental Psychology, 41A,* 439–453.

Biederman, I., & Cooper, E. E. (1991). Evidence for complete translational and reflectional invariance in visual object priming. *Perception, 20,* 585–593.

Biederman, I., & Cooper, E. E. (1992). Size invariance in visual object priming. *Journal of Experimental Psychology: Human Perception and Performance, 18,* 121–133.

Blaxton, T. A. (1989). Investigating dissociations among memory measures: Support for a transfer appropriate processing framework. *Journal of Experimental Psychology: Learning, Memory, and Cognition, 15,* 657–668.

Blumstein, S., & Cooper, W. E. (1974). Hemispheric processing of intonation contours. *Cortex, 10,* 146–158.

Bowers, J. S., & Schacter, D. L. (1990). Implicit memory and test awareness. *Journal of Experimental Psychology: Learning, Memory, and Cognition, 16,* 404–416.

Bowers, J. S., & Schacter, D. L. (1993). Priming of novel information in amnesia: Issues and data. In P. Graf & M. E. J. Masson (Eds.), *Implicit memory: New directions in cognition, neuropsychology, and development,* pp. 303–326. New York: Academic Press.

Bryden, M. P. (1988). An overview of the dichotic listening procedure and its relation to cerebral organization. In K. Hugdahl (Ed.) *Handbook of dichotic listening: Theory, methods, and research* (pp. 1–43). London: John Wiley and Sons.

Buckner, R. L., Petersen, S. E., Ojemann, J. G., Miezin, F. M., Squire, L. R., & Raichle, M. E. (submitted). Functional anatomical studies of explicit and implicit memory retrieval tasks.

Butters, M. A., Glisky, E. L., & Schacter, D. L. (1993). Transfer of new learning in memory-impaired patients. *Journal of Clinical and Experimental Neuropsychology, 15,* 219–230.

Butters, N., Heindel, W. C., & Salmon, D. P. (1990). Dissociation of implicit memory in dementia: Neurological implications. *Bulletin of the Psychonomic Society, 28,* 359–366.

Carr, T. H., Brown, J. S., & Charalambous, A. (1989). Repetition and reading: Perceptual encoding mechanisms are very abstract but not very interactive. *Journal of Experimental Psychology: Learning, Memory, and Cognition, 15,* 763–778.

Cave, C. B., & Squire, L. R. (1992). Intact and long-lasting repetition priming in amnesia. *Journal of Experimental Psychology: Learning, Memory, and Cognition, 18,* 509–520.

Cermak, L. S., Chandler, K., & Wolbarst, L. R. (1985). The perceptual priming phenomenon in amnesia. *Neuropsychologia, 23,* 615–622.

Cermak, L. S., Verfaellie, M., Milberg, W., Letourneau, L., & Blackford, S. (1991). A further analysis of perceptual identification priming in alcoholic Korsakoff patients. *Neuropsychologia, 29,* 725–736.

Challis, B. H., & Brodbeck, D. R. (1992). Level of processing affects priming in word fragment completion. *Journal of Experimental Psychology: Learning, Memory, and Cognition, 18,* 595–607.

Church, B. A., & Schacter, D. L. (1994). Perceptual specificity of auditory priming: Implicit memory for voice intonation and fundamental frequency. *Journal of Experimental Psychology: Learning, Memory, and Cognition, 20,* 521–533.

Clarke, R., & Morton, J. (1983). Cross modality facilitation in tachistoscopic word recognition. *Quarterly Journal of Experimental Psychology, 35A,* 79–96.

Cohen, N. J. (1984). Preserved learning in amnesia: Evidence for multiple memory systems. In L. R. Squire & N. Butters (Eds.), *Neuropsychology of memory* (pp. 83–103). New York: Guilford Press.

Cohen, N. J., & Squire, L. R. (1980). Preserved learning and retention of pattern analyzing skill in amnesics: Dissociation of knowing how and knowing that. *Science, 210,* 207–210.

Cooper, L. A., & Schacter, D. L. (1992). Dissociations between structural and episodic representations of visual objects. *Current Directions in Psychological Science, 1,* 141–146.

Cooper, L. A., Schacter, D. L., Ballesteros, S., & Moore, C. (1992). Priming and recognition of transformed three-dimensional objects: Effects of size and reflection. *Journal of Experimental Psychology: Learning, Memory, and Cognition, 18,* 43–57.

Cooper, L. A., Schacter, D. L., & Moore, C. (1991). Orientation affects both structural and episodic representations of 3-D objects. Paper presented to the Annual Meeting of the Psychonomic Society, San Francisco.

Coslett, H. B., Roeltgen, D. P., Rothi, L. G., & Heilman, K. M. (1987). Transcortical sensory aphasia: Evidence for subtypes. *Brain and Language, 32,* 362–378.

Craik, F. I. M., & Tulving, E. (1975). Depth of processing and the retention of words in episodic memory. *Journal of Experimental Psychology: General, 104,* 268–294.

Daum, I., Channon, S., & Canavar, A. (1989). Classical conditioning in patients with severe memory problems. *Journal of Neurology, and Neurosurgery, and Psychiatry, 52,* 47–51.

Diamond, R., & Rozin, P. (1984). Activation of existing memories in anterograde amnesia. *Journal of Abnormal Psychology, 93,* 98–105.

Eichenbaum, H. (1992). The hippocampal system and declarative memory in animals. *Journal of Cognitive Neuroscience, 4,* 217–231.

Ellis, A. W. (1982). Modality-specific repetition priming of auditory word recognition. *Current Psychological Research, 2,* 123–128.

Ellis, A. W., & Young, A. W. (1988). *Human cognitive neuropsychology.* London: Erlbaum.

Farah, M. J. (1990). *Visual agnosia.* Cambridge: MIT Press.

Feustel, T. C., Shiffrin, R. M., & Salasoo, A. (1983). Episodic and lexical contributions to the repetition effect in word identification. *Journal of Experimental Psychology: General, 112,* 309–346.

Gabrieli, J. D. E., & Keane, M. M. (1988). Priming in the patient H.M.: New findings and a theory of intact and impaired priming in patients with memory disorders. *Society for Neuroscience Abstracts, 14,* 1290.

Gabrieli, J. D. E., Milberg, W., Keane, M. M., & Corkin, S. (1990). Intact priming of patterns despite impaired memory. *Neuropsychologia, 28,* 417–428.

Gardiner, J. M. (1988). Generation and priming effects in word-fragment completion. *Journal of Experimental Psychology: Learning, Memory, and Cognition, 14,* 495–501.

Gazzaniga, M. S. (1975). Partial commissurotomy and cerebral localization of function. In K. J. Zulch, O. Creutzfeldt, & G. G. Galbraith (Eds.), *Cerebral Localization* (pp. 133–139). New York: Springer-Verlag.

Glisky, E. L., & Schacter, D. L. (1987). Acquisition of domain-specific knowledge in organic amnesia: Training for computer-related work. *Neuropsychologia, 25,* 893–906.

Glisky, E. L., & Schacter, D. L. (1988). Long-term retention of computer learning by patients with memory disorders. *Neuropsychologia, 26,* 173–178.

Glisky, E. L., & Schacter, D. L. (1989). Extending the limits of complex learning in organic amnesia: Computer training in a vocational domain. *Neuropsychologia, 27,* 107–120.

Glisky, E. L., Schacter, D. L., & Tulving, E. (1986). Computer learning by memory-impaired patients: Acquisition and retention of complex knowledge. *Neuropsychologia, 24,* 313–328.

Gordon, B. (1988). Preserved learning of novel information in amnesia: Evidence for multiple memory systems. *Cognition, 7,* 257–282.

Graf, P., & Mandler, G. (1984). Activation makes words more accessible, but not necessarily more retrievable. *Journal of Verbal Learning and Verbal Behavior, 23,* 553–568.

Graf, P., & Ryan, L. (1990). Transfer-appropriate processing for implicit and explicit memory. *Journal of Experimental Psychology: Learning, Memory, and Cognition, 16,* 978–992.

Graf, P., & Schacter, D. L. (1985). Implicit and explicit memory for new associations in normal and amnesic patients. *Journal of Experimental Psychology: Learning, Memory, and Cognition, 11,* 501–518.

Graf, P., & Schacter, D. L. (1987). Selective effects of interference on implicit and explicit memory for new associations. *Journal of Experimental Psychology: Learning, Memory, and Cognition, 13,* 45–53.

Graf, P., Shimamura, A. P., & Squire, L. R. (1985). Priming across modalities and priming across category levels: Extending the domain of preserved functioning in amnesia. *Journal of Experimental Psychology: Learning, Memory, and Cognition, 11,* 385–395.

Graf, P., Squire, L. R., & Mandler, G. (1984). The information that amnesic patients do not forget. *Journal of Experimental Psychology: Learning, Memory, and Cognition, 10,* 164–178.

Haist, F., Musen, G., & Squire, L. R. (1991). Intact priming of words and nonwords in amnesia. *Psychobiology, 19,* 275–285.

Hamann, S. B. (1990). Level of processing effects in conceptually driven implicit tasks. *Journal of Experimental Psychology: Learning, Memory, and Cognition, 16,* 970–977.

Hayman, C. A. G., & Tulving, E. (1989). Contingent dissociation between recognition and fragment completion: The method of triangulation. *Journal of Experimental Psychology: Learning, Memory, and Cognition, 15,* 228–240.

Hirshman, E., Snodgrass, J. G., Mindes, J., & Feenan, K. (1990). Conceptual priming in fragment completion. *Journal of Experimental Psychology: Learning, Memory, and Cognition, 16,* 634–647.

Howard, D., Patterson, K., Wise, R., Brown, W. D., Friston, K., Weiller, C., & Frackowiak, R. (1992). The cortical localization of the lexicons. *Brain, 115,* 1769–1782.

Humphreys, G. W., & Riddoch, M. J. (1987). *Visual object processing: A cognitive neuropsychological approach.* London: Erlbaum.

Jackson, A., & Morton, J. (1984). Facilitation of auditory word recognition. *Memory and Cognition, 12,* 568–574.

Jacoby, L. L., & Dallas, M. (1981). On the relationship between autobiographical memory and perceptual learning. *Journal of Experimental Psychology: General, 110,* 306–340.

Jacoby, L. L., & Hayman, C. A. G. (1987). Specific visual transfer in word identification. *Journal of Experimental Psychology: Learning, Memory, and Cognition, 13,* 456–463.

Jacoby, L. L., Levy, B. A., & Steinbach, K. (1992). Episodic transfer and automaticity: Integration of data-driven and conceptually-driven processing in rereading. *Journal of Experimental Psychology: Learning, Memory, and Cognition, 18,* 15–24.

Jacoby, L. L., & Witherspoon, D. (1982). Remembering without awareness. *Canadian Journal of Psychology, 36,* 300–324.

Johnson, M. K. (1992). MEM: Mechanisms of recollection. *Journal of Cognitive Neuroscience, 4,* 268–280.

Johnson, M. K., & Hasher, L. (1987). Human learning and memory. *Annual Review of Psychology, 38,* 631–668.

Keane, M. M., Gabrieli, J. D. E., Fennema, A. C., Growdon, J. H., & Corkin, S. (1991). Evidence for a dissociation between perceptual and conceptual priming in Alzheimer's disease. *Behavioral Neuroscience, 105,* 326–342.

Kinoshita, S., & Wayland, S. V. (1993). Effects of surface features on word-fragment completion in amnesic subjects. *American Journal of Psychology, 106,* 67–80.

Kirsner, K., Dunn, J. C., & Standen, P. (1989). Domain-specific resources in word recognition. In S. Lewandowsky, J. C. Dunn, & K. Kirsner (Eds.), *Implicit memory: Theoretical issues* (pp. 99–122). Hillsdale, NJ: Erlbaum.

Kirsner, K., & Smith, M. C. (1974). Modality effects in word identification. *Memory and Cognition, 2,* 637–640.

Kohn, S. E., & Friedman, R. B. (1986). Word-meaning deafness: A phonological-semantic dissociation. *Cognitive Neuropsychology, 3,* 291–308.

Kosslyn, S. M., Flynn, R. A., Amsterdam, J. B., & Wang, G. (1990). Components of high-level vision: A cognitive neuroscience analysis and accounts of neurological syndromes. *Cognition, 34,* 203–277.

Lieberman, A. M. (1982). On finding that speech is special. *American Psychologist, 37,* 148–167.

McClelland, A. G. R., & Pring, L. (1991). An investigation of cross-modality effects in implicit and explicit memory. *Quarterly Journal of Experimental Psychology, 43A,* 19–33.

Mann, V. A., & Lieberman, A. M. (1983). Some differences between phonetic and auditory modes of perception. *Cognition, 14,* 211–235.

Marsolek, C. J., Kosslyn, S. M., & Squire, L. R. (1992). Form specific visual priming in the right cerebral hemisphere. *Journal of Experimental Psychology: Learning, Memory, and Cognition, 18,* 492–508.

Masson, M. E. J., & MacLeod, C. M. (1992). Re-enacting the route to interpretation: Context dependency in encoding and retrieval. *Journal of Experimental Psychology: General, 121,* 145–176.

Mayes, A. R., & Gooding, P. (1989). Enhancement of word completion priming in amnesics by cueing with previously novel associates. *Neuropsychologia, 27,* 1057–1072.

Metcalfe, J., Cottrell, G. W., & Mencl, W. E. (1992). Cognitive binding: A computational-modeling analysis of a distinction between implicit and explicit memory. *Journal of Cognitive Neuroscience, 4,* 289–298.

Metz-Lutz, M. N., & Dahl, E. (1984). Analysis of word comprehension in a case of pure word deafness. *Brain and Language,* 13–25.

Micco, A., & Masson, M. E. J. (1991). Implicit memory for new associations: An interactive process approach. *Journal of Experimental Psychology: Learning, Memory, and Cognition, 17,* 1105–1123.

Milner, B., Corkin, S., & Teuber, H. L. (1968). Further analysis of the hippocampal amnesic syndrome: Fourteen year follow-up study of H.M. *Neuropsychologia, 6,* 215–234.

Morton, J. (1979). Facilitation in word recognition: Experiments causing change in the logogen model. In P. A. Kolers, M. E. Wrolstad, & H. Bouma (Eds.), *Processing models of visible language* (pp. 259–268). New York: Plenum.

Moscovitch, M. (1982). Multiple dissociations of function in amnesia. In L. S. Cermak (Eds.), *Human memory and amnesia* (pp. 337–370). Hillsdale, NJ: Erlbaum.

Moscovitch, M. (1992). Memory and working-with-memory: A component process model based on modules and central systems. *Journal of Cognitive Neuroscience, 4,* 257–267.

Musen, G. (1991). Effects of verbal labeling and exposure duration on implicit memory for visual patterns. *Journal of Experimental Psychology: Learning, Memory, and Cognition, 17,* 954–962.

Musen, G., & Squire, L. R. (1990). *Pseudoword priming in amnesic patients.* Paper presented to the Annual Meeting of the Psychonomic Society, New Orleans, November.

Musen, G., & Squire, L. R. (1992). Nonverbal priming in amnesia. *Memory and Cognition, 20,* 441–448.

Petersen, S. E., Fox, P. T., Posner, M. I., Mintun, M. A., & Raichle, M. E. (1989). Positron emission tomographic studies of the processing of single words. *Journal of Cognitive Neuroscience, 1,* 153–170.

Petersen, S. E., Fox, P. T., Synder, A. Z., & Raichle, M. E. (1990). Activation of extrastriate and frontal cortical areas by visual words and word-like stimuli. *Science, 249,* 1041–1044.

Plaut, D. C., & Farah, M. J. (1990). Visual object representation: Interpreting neurophysiological data within a computational framework. *Journal of Cognitive Neuroscience, 2,* 320–343.

Polster, M. R., Nadel, L., & Schacter, D. L. (1991). Cognitive neuroscience analyses of memory: A historical perspective. *Journal of Cognitive Neuroscience, 3,* 95–116.

Richardson-Klavehn, A., & Bjork, R. A. (1988). Measures of memory. *Annual Review of Psychology, 36,* 475–543.

Riddoch, M. J., & Humphreys, G. W. (1987). Visual object processing in optic aphasia: A case of semantic access agnosia. *Cognitive Neuropsychology, 4,* 131–186.

Roediger, H. L. (1990a). Implicit memory: Retention without remembering. *American Psychologist, 45,* 1043–1056.

Roediger, H. L. (1990b). Implicit memory: A commentary. *Bulletin of the Psychonomic Society, 28,* 373–380.

Roediger, H. L., & Blaxton, T. A. (1987). Effects of varying modality, surface features, and retention interval on priming in word fragment completion. *Memory and Cognition, 15,* 379–388.

Roediger, H. L., & McDermott, K. B. (1993). Implicit memory in normal human subjects. In H. Spinnler & F. Boller (Eds.) *Handbook of Neuropsychology* (Vol. 8). Amstserdam: Elsevier.

Roediger, H. L., Weldon, M. S., & Challis, B. H. (1989). Explaining dissociations between implicit and explicit measures of retention: A processing account. In H. L.Roediger & F. I. M. Craik (Eds.), *Varieties of memory and consciousness: Essays in honor of Endel Tulving* (pp. 3–41). Hillsdale, NJ: Erlbaum.

Roediger, H. L., Weldon, M. S., Stadler, M. L., & Riegler, G. L. (1992). Direct comparison of two implicit memory tests: word fragment and word stem completion. *Journal of Experimental Psychology: Learning, Memory and Cognition, 18,* 1251–1269.

Ross, E. D. (1981). The aprosodias: Functional-anatomic organization of the affective compontents of language in the right hemisphere. *Archives of Neurology, 38,* 561–569.

Rozin, P. (1976). The psychobiological approach to human memory. In M. R. Rosenzweig & E. L. Bennet (Eds.), *Neural mechanisms of learning and memory.* Cambridge: MIT Press.

Rudy, J. W., & Sutherland, R. J. (1992). Configural and elemental associations and the memory coherence problem. *Journal of Cognitive Neuroscience, 4,* 208–216.

Rueckl, J. G. (1990). Similarity effects in word and pseudoword repetition priming. *Journal of Experimental Psychology: Learning, Memory, and Cognition, 16,* 374–391.

Sartori, G., & Job, R. (1988). The oyster with four legs: A neuropsychological study on the interaction of visual and semantic information. *Cognitive Neuropsychology, 5,* 105–132.

Sartori, G., Masterson, J., & Job, R. (1987). Direct-route reading and the locus of lexical decision. In M. Coltheart, G. Sartori, & R. Job (Eds.), *The cognitive neurospychology of language* (pp. 59–78). London: Erlbaum.

Scarborough, D. L., Cortese, C., & Scarborough, H. S. (1977). Frequency and repetition effects in lexical memory. *Journal of Experimental Psychology: Human Perception and Performance, 3,* 1–17.

Schacter, D. L. (1985). Priming of old and new knowledge in amnesic patients and normal subjects. In D. Olton, S. Corkin, & E. Gamzu (Eds.) *Memory dysfunctions: an integration of animal and human research from preclinical and clinical perspectives,* Annals of the New York Academy of Sciences, no. 444, 44–53.

Schacter, D. L. (1987). Implicit memory: History and current status. *Journal of Experimental Psychology: Learning, Memory, and Cognition, 13*, 501–518.

Schacter, D. L. (1990). Perceptual representation systems and implicit memory: Toward a resolution of the multiple memory systems debate. In A. Diamond (Ed.) *The development and neural bases of higher cognitive functions*, Annals of the New York Academy of Sciences, no. 608 (pp. 543–571).

Schacter, D. L. (1992). Understanding implicit memory: A cognitive neuroscience approach. *American Psychologist, 47*, 559–569.

Schacter, D. L., Albert, M. S., Alpert, N. M., Rafferty, B. P., & Rauch, S. L. (in preparation). A positron emission tomography study of stem completion priming.

Schacter, D. L., Aminoff, A., & Church, B. A. (1992). [A dichotic listening study of voice-specific priming in auditory stem completion]. Unpublished data.

Schacter, D. L., Bowers, J., & Booker, J. (1989). Intention, awareness, and implicit memory: The retrieval intentionality criterion. In S. Lewandowsky, J. C. Dunn, & K. Kirsner (Eds.), *Implicit memory: Theoretical issues*. Hillsdale, NJ: Erlbaum.

Schacter, D. L., Chiu, C. Y. P., & Ochsner, K. N. (1993). Implicit memory: A selective review. *Annual Review of Neuroscience, 16*, 159–182.

Schacter, D. L., & Church, B. (1992). Auditory priming: Implicit and explicit memory for words and voices. *Journal of Experimental Psychology: Learning, Memory, and Cognition, 18*, 915–930.

Schacter, D. L., Church, B. A., & Bolton, E. (in press). Implicit memory in amnesic patients: Impairment of voice-specific priming. *Psychological Science*.

Schacter, D. L., Church, B. A., & Treadwell, J. (1994). Implicit memory in amnesic patients: Evidence for spared auditory priming. *Psychological Science, 5*, 20–25.

Schacter, D. L., & Cooper, L. A. (1993). Implicit and explicit memory for novel visual objects: Structure and function. *Journal of Experimental Psychology: Learning, Memory, and Cognition, 19*, 988–1003.

Schacter, D. L., Cooper, L. A., & Delaney, S. M. (1990). Implicit memory for unfamiliar objects depends on access to structural descriptions. *Journal of Experimental Psychology: General, 119*, 5–24.

Schacter, D. L., Cooper, L. A., Delaney, S. M., Peterson, M. A., & Tharan, M. (1991). Implicit memory for possible and impossible objects: Constraints on the construction of structural descriptions. *Journal of Experimental Psychology: Learning, Memory, and Cognition, 17*, 3–19.

Schacter, D. L., Cooper, L. A., Tharan, M., & Rubens, A. B. (1991). Preserved priming of novel objects in patients with memory disorders. *Journal of Cognitive Neuroscience, 3*, 118–131.

Schacter, D. L., Cooper, L. A., & Treadwell, J. (1993). Preserved priming of novel objects across size transformation in amnesic patients. *Psychological Science, 4*, 331–335.

Schacter, D. L., Delaney, S. M., & Merikle, E. P. (1990). Priming of nonverbal information and the nature of implicit memory. In G. H. Bower (Ed.), *The psychology of learning and motivation* (pp. 83–123) New York: Academic Press.

Schacter, D. L., & Graf, P. (1986a). Effects of elaborative processing on implicit and explicit memory for new associations. *Journal of Experimental Psychology: Learning, Memory, and Cognition, 12*, 432–444.

Schacter, D. L., & Graf, P. (1986b). Preserved learning in amnesic patients: Perspectives on research from direct priming. *Journal of Clinical and Experimental Neuropsychology, 8*, 727–743.

Schacter, D. L., & Graf, P. (1989). Modality specificity of implicit memory for new associations. *Journal of Experimental Psychology: Learning, Memory, and Cognition, 15*, 3–12.

Schacter, D. L., McGlynn, S. M., Milberg, W. P., & Church, B. A. (1993). Spared priming despite impaired comprehension: Implicit memory in a case of word meaning deafness. *Neuropsychology, 7*, 107–118.

Schwartz, M. F., Saffran, E. M., & Marin, O. S. M. (1980). Fractionating the reading process in dementia: Evidence for word specific print-to-sound associations. In M. Coltheart, K. Patterson, & J. C. Marshall (Eds.), *Deep dyslexia* (pp. 259–269). London: Routledge and Kegan Paul.

Scoville, W. B., & Milner, B. (1957). Loss of recent memory after bilateral hippocampal lesions. *Journal of Neurology and Neurosurgery and Psychiatry, 20*, 11–21.

Sherry, D. F., & Schacter, D. L. (1987). The evolution of multiple memory systems. *Psychological Review, 94*, 439–454.

Shimamura, A. P. (1986). Priming effects in amnesia: Evidence for a dissociable memory function. *Quarterly Journal of Experimental Psychology, 38A*, 619–644.

Shimamura, A. P., & Squire, L. R. (1984). Paired-associate learning and priming effects in amnesia: A neuropsychological approach. *Journal of Experimental Psychology: General, 113*, 556–570.

Shimamura, A. P., & Squire, L. R. (1989). Impaired priming of new associations in amnesia. *Journal of Experimental Psychology: Learning, Memory, and Cognition, 15*, 721–728.

Smith, M. E., & Oscar-Berman, M. (1990). Repetition priming of words and pseudowords in divided attention and amnesia. *Journal of Experimental Psychology: Learning, Memory, and Cognition, 16*, 1033–1042.

Squire, L. R. (1987). *Memory and brain.* New York: Oxford University Press.

Squire, L. R. (1992a). Declarative and nondeclarative memory: Multiple brain systems supporting learning and memory. *Journal of Cognitive Neuroscience, 99*, 195–231.

Squire, L. R. (1992b). Memory and the hippocampus: A synthesis from findings with rats, monkeys, and humans. *Psychological Review, 99*, 195–231.

Squire, L. R., Ojemann, J. G., Miezin, F. M., Petersen, S. E., Videen, T. O., & Raichle, M. E. (1992). Activation of the hippocampus in normal humans: A functional anatomical study. *Proceedings of the National Academy of Sciences, 89*, 1837–1841.

Sutherland, N. S. (1968). Outline of a theory of pattern recognition in animal and man. *Proceedings of the Royal Society of London, B171*, 297–317.

Tardif, T., & Craik, F. I. M. (1989). Reading a week later: Perceptual and conceptual factors. *Journal of Memory and Language, 28*, 107–125.

Tulving, E. (1985). How many memory systems are there? *American Psychologist, 40*, 385–398.

Tulving, E., Hayman, C. A. G., & MacDonald, C. (1991). Long-lasting perceptual priming and semantic learning in amnesia: A case experiment. *Journal of Experimental Psychology: Learning, Memory, and Cognition, 17*, 595–617.

Tulving, E., Kapur, S., Craik, F. I. M., Moscovitch, M., & Houle, S. (1994). Hemispheric encoding/retrieval asymmetry in episodic memory: Positron emission tomography findings. *Proceedings of the National Academy of Sciences, 91*, 2016–2020.

Tulving, E., & Schacter, D. L. (1990). Priming and human memory systems. *Science, 247*, 301–306.

Van Lancker, D., & Kreiman, J. (1987). Voice discrimination and recognition are separate abilities. *Neuropsychologia, 25*, 829–834.

Warrington, E. K. (1975). The selective impairment of semantic memory. *Quarterly Journal of Experimental Psychology, 27*, 635–657.

Warrington, E. K. (1982). Neuropsychological studies of object recognition. *Philosophical Transactions of the Royal Society of London, 289* (Series B), 15–33.

Warrington, E. K., & Shallice, T. (1980). Word-form dyslexia. *Brain, 30*, 99–112.

Warrington, E. K., & Taylor, A. M. (1978). Two categorical stages of object recognition. *Perception, 7*, 695–705.

Warrington, E. K., & Weiskrantz, L. (1974). The effect of prior learning on subsequent retention in amnesic patients. *Neuropsychologia, 12*, 419–428.

Weiskrantz, L. (1985). On issues and theories of the human amnesic syndrome. In N. M. Weinberger, J. L. McGaugh, & G. Lynch (Eds.), *Memory systems of the human brain: Animal and human cognitive processes* (pp. 380–415). New York: Guilford Press.

Weiskrantz, L., & Warrington, E. K. (1979). Conditioning in amnesic patients. *Neuropsychologia, 17*, 187–194.

Wexler, B. E. (1988). Dichotic presentation as a method for single hemisphere stimulation studies. In K. Hugdahl (Ed.), *Handbook of dichotic listening: Theory, methods, and research* (pp. 85–115). London: John Wiley & Sons.

Whittlesea, B. W. A. (1990). Perceptual encoding mechanisms are tricky but may be very interactive: Comment on Carr, Brown, and Charalambous (1989). *Journal of Experimental Psychology: Learning, Memory, and Cognition, 16*, 727–730.

Winston, P. H. (1975). Learning structural descriptions from examples. In P. H. Winston (Ed.), *The psychology of computer vision* (pp. 157–209). New York: McGraw-Hill.

Zaidel, E. (1978). Concepts of cerebral dominance in the split brain. In P. A. Buser & A. Rougel-Buser (Eds.), *Cerebral correlates of conscious experience* (pp. 263–284). Amsterdam: Elsevier.

Zaidel, E. (1985). Language in the right hemisphere. In D. F. Benson & E. Zaidel (Eds.), *The dual brain: Hemispheric specialization in humans* (pp. 205–231). New York: Guilford Press.

Zatorre, R. J. (1988). Pitch perception of complex tones and human temporal-lobe function. *Journal of the Acoustical Society of America, 84*, 566–572.

9 Memory and Working with Memory: Evaluation of a Component Process Model and Comparisons with Other Models

Morris Moscovitch

Memory is not unitary but depends on the operation of potentially independent, but typically interactive, components. One of the jobs of a cognitive neuropsychologist is to identify these components and indicate how they interact with each other. Although we are far from being able to specify these components with the precision we would like, either functionally or structurally, there is sufficient information to tempt many of us to sketch the outlines of what we think a complete model might be like. I offer my version of such a model. A more detailed account appears in Moscovitch (1989, 1992a, 1992b) and Moscovitch and Umiltà (1991).

The model I sketch has four essential components, each of which mediates processes that dominate performance on four different types of memory tests: (1) a nonfrontal neocortical component made up of various perceptual and "semantic" modules that mediate performance on item-specific, implicit (indirect) tests of memory; (2) a basal-ganglia component that mediates performance on sensorimotor procedural tests of memory; (3) a medial-temporal/hippocampal component, *which also is modular*, that mediates encoding, storage, and retrieval on explicit-episodic-memory tests that are *associative/cue-dependent*; (4) a central-system frontal-lobe component that "works with memory" and mediates performance on *strategic* explicit and rule-based explicit tests. After sketching the model, I will discuss some of its implications and compare it with other models from the human and animal literature.

1 MODULES AND CENTRAL SYSTEMS

A distinguishing feature of this memory model is that its basic principles are derived from Fodor's (1983) notion that modules and central systems are the constituents of the mind (and brain). Carlo Umiltà and I proposed a modified version of Fodor's ideas that retained its core assumptions and suggested how Fodor's criteria of modularity can be translated to the neuropsychological level (Moscovitch and Umiltà, 1990, 1991).

Modules are computational devices that have propositional content and satisfy all of the following three criteria: domain specificity, informational encapsulation or cognitive impenetrability, and shallow output. *Domain speci-ficity* entails that the type of information modules accept for processing is restricted or circumscribed. At the neuropsychological level, it must be shown that damage to a particular region or system, the structural embodiment of the module, leads to deficient processing in the purported domain with relative sparing of function in other domains. This condition is not sufficient by itself, since central-system structures can also be localized to circumscribed regions. *Informational encapsulation* implies that modules resist the effects of higher-order knowledge on processing and are cognitively impenetrable to probes of their content and operation. Only the module's shallow output is available for conscious inspection. Neuropsychologically, this criterion is satisfied if the processes mediated by a module are unaffected by gross intellectual decline caused by degeneration or focal damage to structures other than the module itself. For example, patients with generalized dementia caused by Alzheimer's disease fail to understand even simple words or appreciate the function of objects, but they can still read relatively well (Schwartz, Saffran, & Marin, 1980) and have a good three-dimensional representation of objects (Chertkow & Bub, 1990; Moscovitch & Umiltà, 1990; Warrington & Taylor, 1978). Informational encapsulation is also satisfied by evidence of a domain-specific deficit, despite preserved intellectual functions and semantic knowledge about material in the affected domain. Patients with associative agnosia may not recognize an object visually but can provide detailed semantic informa-tion about the object when given its name. Yet the patient may not be able to use this knowledge to identify the object visually (Behrmann, Winocur, Moscovitch, 1992; Moscovitch & Umiltà, 1990; Riddoch & Humphreys, 1987). *Shallow output* is output that has no meaning beyond the value assigned to it by the module; interlevel representations that led to the shallow output are not available for conscious inspection. The neuropsychological correlate of this criterion is evidence of normal domain-specific performance without any ability to interpret semantically the information pertaining to that domain. Here too patients with associative agnosia or dementia are the paradigmatic cases. Though such patients retain the ability to process objects, faces, and words at a structural, presemantic level, they cannot assign any meaning to the structural information they have computed (Bauer, 1984; Chertkow & Bub, 1990; Moscovitch & Umiltà, 1990, 1991; Tranel & Damasio, 1985; Warrington & Taylor, 1978).

Thus a module, no matter how complex its inner workings, is essentially a stupid, closed computational device that delivers its shallow output to inter-pretative *central systems*, where meaning and relevance are assigned. *None of the criteria of modularity apply to central systems* (but see Moscovitch & Umiltà, 1990, for some provisos). Unlike modules, central systems integrate informa-tion from superficially dissimilar domains and are open to top-down influ-ences. The output of central systems is deep or meaningful, and the inter-level representations that give rise to the final output may be available to consciousness.

I will argue that memory, like perception, consists of the operation of modules and central systems. Although no memory test is likely to be process-pure (Jacoby, 1991), performance on some tests can be considered to be mediated primarily by modules, whereas performance on others depends more on central systems. Before considering which tests are modular and which are not, it is necessary first to classify memory tests into various types.

2 CLASSIFICATION OF MEMORY TESTS

Task analysis and evidence of preserved memory abilities in amnesic patients (Moscovitch, 1984) suggests that it is possible to distinguish between two broad classes of memory tests: explicit and implicit (Graf & Schacter, 1985). Explicit tests require conscious recollection of past events, whereas on implicit tests, memory for the past is inferred from changes in performance with experience or practice. To be implicit, a test must also be highly structured, so that the goal of the task and the means to achieve it are apparent and available to the subject (Moscovitch, 1984). When an implicit test does not meet the latter criteria, the amnesic patient shows no evidence of preserved learning even though conscious recollection may not be involved (Nissen, Willingham, & Hartman, 1989).

Implicit and explicit tests can each be further subdivided into at least two subtypes (see table 1). For implicit tests, the two are procedural and item-specific tests. *Procedural tests* are those that assess learning and retention of general sensory-motor skills, procedures, or rules. *Item-specific* tests, on the other hand, assess memory for a particular item, such as a certain word, face, or object, by seeing the effect that initial presentation of the item has on the accuracy or speed of identification of the item when it is repeated. The benefit gained is known as the *repetition priming effect*.

The two subtypes of explicit tests are associative/cue-dependent and strategic. *Associative* episodic memory tests are those in which the cue is sufficient for retrieval. When given the cue "Have your read *War and Peace*?" or "Have your seen *Gone with the Wind*? the answer automatically pops into mind as surely as the word "night" pops into mind to the semantic cue "day." For *strategic* tests, the cue does not automatically elicit the target memory but only provides the starting point of a memory search that has elements in common with problem solving. Such strategic processes can be initiated by questions that require the reinstatement of a particular spatial and temporal context, such as "What did you do two weekends ago?"

Few if any tests are made up of only a single component. The classificatory scheme suggests ideal prototypes against which impure tests can be compared and thus provides a crude framework for fractionating a test into its component parts.

Table 1 Classification of implicit and explicit tests

	Type of test					
	Implicit				Explicit	
	Item-specific		Procedural			
	Perceptual	Conceptual	Sensorimotor	Ordered/rule-based	Associative	Strategic
Characterization	Identification or classification of particular stimuli based on sensory cues	Generation, production, or classification of targets in response to conceptual or semantic cues	Acquisition and improvement of motor or sensory skills	Learning to solve problems with rules or organized response contingencies	Conscious recollection of episodes in which the cue is sufficient for retrieval	Conscious recollection of episodes in which extracue strategic factors are critical
Some variables and factors that influence performance	Perceptual variables (e.g., modality, representational format), retention interval	Semantic variables (e.g., levels of processing), number of presentations, proactive interference, attention (?)	Number of trials, feedback	Number of trials, feedback, hierarchical organization, monitoring	Semantic variables (e.g., levels of processing), retention interval, stimulus duration and repetition, interference, attention	Organizational variables (e.g., clustering), attention, cognitive resources
Typical tests used to assess memory	Identification of fragmented words or pictures (e.g., fragment completion or perceptual identification)	Generation of exemplars of category cues	Pursuit rotor, mirror drawing, reading transformed script	Tower of Hanoi	Simple recognition or cued recall	Free recall (particularly of categorized lists), memory for temporal order, conditional associative learning
Probable neural substrate	Perceptual input modules (representational systems) in the posterior neocortex	Interpretative multimodal central systems in the lateral temporal, parietal, and possibly frontal, lobes	Basal ganglia, cerebellum	Dorsolateral and midlateral frontal lobes	Hippocampus and related limbic structures in the medial temporal lobes and diencephalon	Dorsolateral and ventromedial frontal lobes, cingulate cortex

3   A NEUROPSYCHOLOGICAL MODEL OF MEMORY

3.1   Item-Specific Implicit Tests

Reactivation of perceptual and semantic records   Memory begins with registering information in cortical modules that pick up and transform stimulus events into presemantic structural representations. The output of these modules is delivered to central-system structures for early semantic interpretation. The input modules and interpretative central systems, which are presumed to be located in the posterior and midlateral neocortex, are modified by the information they process, which thereby becomes, respectively, a *perceptual* and *semantic record* (Kirsner & Dunn, 1985) of the processing activity. The altered neuronal circuitry that underlies the records preserves information about the stimulating event and enables subsequently related events to be processed and identified more quickly. Reactivation of perceptual and semantic records is the basis for *perceptual* and *conceptual repetition-priming effects*, which are at the heart of item-specific implicit tests of memory. The term *engram* is reserved for the informational content of these records.

Registration: The rapid formation of records   I propose that the term *registration* or *recording* be used to refer to the neocortical process involved in forming the perceptual records or engrams that support performance on item-specific implicit tests. By designating these processes with special terms, I indicate that they are different, at least at the functional level, from other processes involved in forming long-term memory traces, for which the generic term *consolidation* has traditionally been used.

Perceptual input modules and perceptual repetition priming   In accordance with the criterion of *domain specificity*, perceptual input modules restrict their operation to a specific domain. Since they are *informationally encapsulated*, their operation is not affected by higher-order semantic information, nor are their workings and informational content accessible to conscious inspection. By the criterion of *shallow output*, the information that perceptual input modules deliver is restricted to presemantic structural descriptions within the specific domain of the module. Carlo Umiltà and I (Moscovitch & Umiltà, 1990, 1991) identified a few systems that can qualify as perceptual modules: the visual-word-form system (Warrington & Shallice, 1980), a visual-object or structural-description system (Riddoch & Humphreys, 1987; Warrington & Taylor, 1978), a face-recognition system (Bruce & Young, 1986), and a phonological-word-form system (Schacter, 1992) or speech module (Liberman & Mattingly, 1989). From the properties of modules, it follows that the perceptual record formed in each module also contains domain-specific, presemantic, structural information about the stimulus that gave rise to it.

Anatomical localization Structures in the posterior neocortex are presumed to be the locus of the perceptual input modules mediating repetition-priming effects. There is both negative and positive evidence implicating these structures. The negative evidence is that the medial temporal lobes and related limbic structures in the diencephalon, which are crucial for performance on explicit tests of memory, are not necessary for normal performance on implicit tests. Repetition-priming effects are well-preserved in amnesic patients with damage to these structures (for reviews, see Moscovitch, Vriezen, & Goshen-Gottstein, 1993; Shimamura, 1986; Squire, 1992, this volume). Similarly, demented patients whose pathology spares the sensory or parasensory areas of the posterior neocortex perform normally on perceptual item-specific implicit tests (see Moscovitch et al., 1993), just as they can read and identify objects at a presemantic perceptual level (Chertkow & Bub, 1990; Schwartz, Saffran, & Marin, 1980). In short, to the extent that their input modules are intact, amnesic and demented patients show normal perceptual-repetition effects.

Suggestive positive evidence for the localization of perceptual input modules to the posterior neocortex comes from studies of patients with domain-specific agnosias and from PET scan studies in normal people. Umiltà and I (Moscovitch & Umiltà, 1990) distinguished between two types of agnosic patients: those whose input modules are damaged and those whose modules are intact but whose shallow outputs are inaccessible to interpretative central systems (see also Schacter, McAndrews, & Moscovitch, 1988). These patients correspond to apperceptive and associative agnosics, respectively (Lissauer, 1890). Patients in the former group include individuals with damage to the word-form system in the left occipitotemporal region (Warrington & Shallice, 1980), the face-recognition system in the right lingual, fusiform, and para-hippocampal gyrus (Sergent & Signoret 1992), the object-recognition system in the left and right temporoparietal region (McCarthy & Warrington, 1990; Warrington & Taylor, 1978), and phonological-word-form system in the left superior temporal region (Kohn & Friedman, 1986; Saffran & Marin, 1977).

As yet only with respect to face-recognition has it been established firmly that damage to the critical region impairs face-recognition on both explicit and implicit tests of knowledge (see reviews in Bruyer, 1991; Sergent & Signoret, 1992; Young, 1994). Such patients also show no repetition-priming effects for faces (Newcombe, Young, & de Haan, 1989; Sergent & Signoret, 1992). On the other hand, prosopagnosic patients whose damage spares the crucial region can respond differentially to familiar and unfamiliar faces on implicit tests (de Haan, Bauer, & Greve, 1992) and also show normal repetition-priming effects (de Haan, Young, & Newcombe, 1987; Greve & Bauer, 1990). Similarly, dyslexic patients who show evidence of an intact word-form system, as indicated on implicit tests of reading, also show preserved repetition-priming effect for words (Schacter, Rapcsak, Rubens, Tharan,

& Laguna, 1990). Thus, as predicted by Moscovitch & Umiltà (1990, 1991), if the module is sufficiently well-preserved to support performance on *implicit*, domain-specific perceptual tests of knowledge, then it will also support performance on perceptual repetition-priming tests.

Functional neuroimaging studies of perceptual priming are a potential valuable source of evidence. As yet only one report has been published, but its findings, though broadly consistent with the view presented here, are somewhat puzzling (see my discussion in section 4.1).

3.2 Conceptual Repetition Effects and Semantic Records

What distinguishes conceptual from perceptual item-specific tests is that the target is not repeated at test, even in degraded form, but rather is elicited by semantic cues, such as a related word or a question. Because conceptual repetition-priming effects, unlike perceptual ones, are influenced by semantic variables, it is unlikely that conceptual repetition effects are mediated by presemantic input modules. I suggest that they are mediated by central systems, which interpret the shallow output of perceptual modules and store a *semantic* record of their activity or representations (see Tulving and Schacter, 1990, for similar views). Accordingly, performance on conceptual implicit tests should not be sensitive to either modality or format but should be affected by level-of-processing manipulations. In general, these predictions have been confirmed (for reviews, see Blaxton, 1989; Roediger, 1990; Roediger & McDermott, 1993). As yet it is not clear whether attention at encoding is a necessary component. If conceptual repetition-priming effects can be preserved when material is presented under anaesthesia, as some studies have indicated (see Kihlstrom & Couture, 1992), then this suggests that establishing semantic records can occur automatically (see Moscovitch & Umiltà, 1990, for a discussion on derived versus associative semantics).

Damage to the hippocampal component alone spares conceptual repetition-priming effects. Amnesic patients, though severely impaired on explicit tests, can show normal conceptual repetition effects (Gardner, Boller, Moreines, & Butters, 1973; McAndrews, Glisky, & Schacter, 1987; Tulving, Hayman, & Macdonald, 1991; Winocur & Weiskrantz, 1976), though more studies are needed to confirm the generality of these observations.

Because they are mediated by interpretative central-system structures, conceptual, repetition-priming effects are reduced or absent in demented patients with Alzheimer's disease (Butters, Heindel, & Salmon, 1990). Blaxton (1992) reports a similar pattern of impaired conceptual, but preserved perceptual, repetition effects in patients with unilateral temporal lobectomies. Because gross intellectual decline is not typical in these patients, her findings, if replicated, would suggest that the anterior, lateral temporal cortex is necessary for storing semantic records but not for interpreting information semantically. The studies on patients with Alzheimer's disease suggest that other regions of the temporal and parietal association cortex may be important. Future work on patients with focal lesions and on functional neuroimaging in normal people should help specify the crucial areas.

3.3 The Hippocampal Component: A Module for Episodic, Associative Memory

The hippocampal component consists of a variety of structures in the medial temporal lobes and diencephalon that form a circuit. In addition to the hippocampus, these structures include the parahippocampal gyrus, the entorhinal and perirhinal cortices, the mammilary bodies and dorsomedial nucleus of the thalamus, the cingulate cortex, and the fornix. Amnesia in humans is associated with bilateral damage to any one of these structures, except for the fornix and cingulate, for which the evidence is equivocal (Squire, 1987).

The input modules and central systems deliver their output to working memory (Baddeley, 1986), whose content is accessible to consciousness (see Moscovitch & Umiltà, 1990, 1991, for a discussion of working memory and consciousness), and to procedural systems that can affect behavior but whose operation cannot be inspected consciously. Consciously apprehended information is necessarily picked up by the hippocampal component (see figure 1).

The hippocampal component is thus a module whose specific domain is consciously apprehended information. *To the extent that an event does not receive full conscious attention, it is not processed by the hippocampal component.* Using reciprocal pathways that connect the hippocampus to the cortex, the hippocampus binds or integrates the engrams of the modules and central systems

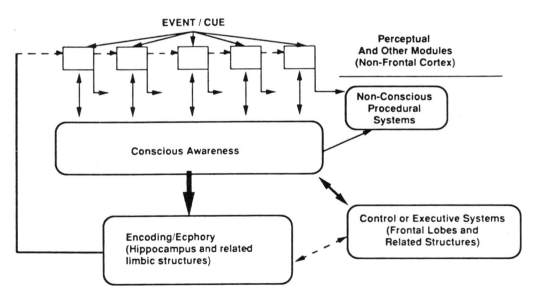

Figure 1 A sketch of the interaction of modules and central-system structures in a neuropsychological model of memory (from Moscovitch, 1989).

whose output contributed to the conscious experience as well as those elements that make the experience conscious. In this way "consciousness" is bound by the hippocampal formation to other aspects of the event. The resulting collection of bound engrams constitutes a *memory trace*, which is encoded as a file entry or index within the hippocampal component (Teyler & Di Scenna, 1986).

To recollect a recent event consciously, a memory trace must be reactivated either directly or via the hippocampal component. This occurs when an external cue or internally generated cue automatically interacts with a memory trace, a process called *ecphory* by Semon, who also coined the term *engram* (1921; cited in Schacter, Eich, & Tulving, 1978). The product of that interaction is delivered to consciousness or, simply put, is made conscious.

Once initiated, ecphoric processes are rapid, obligatory, informationally encapsulated, and cognitively impenetrable. The same is true of the initial formation and encoding of memory traces. We are aware only of the input to the hippocampal component and the shallow output from it. Thus we remember countless daily events without intending to remember them: memories may pop into mind, much as preattentive perceptual stimuli pop out of their background.

This analogy of memory with perception is appropriate insofar as aspects of both are modular. Just as it would be maladaptive to have a perceptual system that is too much under our control and subject to our motivations and expectations, so it would not be useful to have a memory system that relies on our intentions to remember. Because most often we do not know in advance what is worth committing to memory, it is important to have a system capable of encoding and storing information automatically, as a natural consequence of apprehending the material consciously. Moreover, because events unfold at their own pace, most of them would not be encoded by the time we can determine that they were worth remembering.

The central idea of levels-of-processing theory (Craik & Lockhart, 1972), that remembering is a natural by-product of cognition, follows directly from this view that the hippocampal component is modular. According to the levels-of-processing framework, what determines what is remembered is not the intention to remember as such but the extent to which events are attended and information from them is processed to a deep level and properly organized. Paying close attention to the target and encoding it semantically makes it distinctive and makes its memory traces more easily retrievable (Moscovitch & Craik, 1976). Once events are fully apprehended in consciousness, they are obligatorily picked up and encoded by the hippocampus. Conversely, without a hippocampal component, no lasting memory traces can be formed and recovered, no matter how deeply the information is processed (Cermak, 1982; Cermak & Reale, 1978).

An additional benefit of an automatic hippocampal component is that it does not draw cognitive resources away from other activities. If committing something to memory always required additional effort beyond that involved in apprehending the relevant information, it would lead to a peculiar tradeoff: resources allocated to attention and comprehension would be unavailable for memory and vice versa. We would remember well only those items that were processed poorly, an unacceptable and counterfactual condition.

The cost of being modular is that the hippocampal component lacks the intelligence for self-organization, strategic intervention, and monitoring. Events are encoded only by simple contiguity and by associations that memory traces form with each other and with cues. The hippocampal component responds reflexively to cues; it cannot conduct a memory search if cues are initially ineffective or monitor the ecphoric output to determine whether the recovered memories are veridical or even plausible. In other words, its output is shallow, in the sense that it is not interpreted properly in relation to other memories; that is, the output cannot be related to a spatial and temporal context with respect to other events. I call this latter context *organizational* or *historical*, in contrast with the hippocampal component's *associative* context, which is the multimodal spatial and temporal background within which the target is embedded and that constitutes an event. The job of organizing the input, verifying the shallow output, and placing it in a proper historical context is left to pre- and postecphoric, extrahippocampal processes probably mediated by the frontal lobes. Because its organization and retrieval method is associative and cue-dependent, I refer to the hippocampal component as an associative/episodic-memory component, a term that also describes the explicit memory tests mediated by it.

3.4 The Frontal Lobes: Central Systems and Strategic Explicit Tests

The prefrontal cortex is a large, heterogeneous structure consisting of a number of distinct areas, each with its own projections to and from other brain regions and each having presumably different functions (Pandya & Barnes, 1987). It has been appreciated for some time that lesions to the dorsolateral and orbital regions of the prefrontal cortex produce different deficits (Milner, 1964). More recently, evidence has been accumulating that the functions of other, smaller regions can also be distinguished one from another (Goldman-Rakic, 1987; Petrides, 1989).

Despite the evidence for localization of function among regions of prefrontal cortex, Umiltà and I argued that they are central-system structures that contribute to performance on strategic explicit tests of memory (Moscovitch & Umiltà, 1990, 1991). The frontal lobes are prototypical organizational structures crucial for selecting and implementing encoding strategies that organize the input to the hippocampal component and the output from it, for evaluating that shallow output and determining its correct temporal sequence and spatial context with respect to other events, and for using the resulting information to guide further mnemonic searches, direct thought, or plan future action. In short, the frontal lobes are necessary for converting remembering from a stupid reflexive act triggered by a cue to an intelligent, reflective, goal-directed activity under voluntary control. When you try to place a person that looks familiar or to determine where you were during the last week of July, the appropriate memory does not emerge automatically but must be ferreted out, often laboriously, by retrieval strategies.

Memory disorders following frontal lesions are not related to deficits in storage and retention, which are hippocampal functions. Instead, they are associated with impaired organizational and strategic processes. As befits a central-system structure, for which the criterion of domain specificity does not apply, the frontal lobes' function with respect to memory is similar to its function in other domains. The frontal lobes organize the raw material made available by other modules and central systems. The frontal lobes' representations are available to conscious inspection, and the output is deep. If the hippocampal circuit can be considered to consist of raw-memory structures, then the frontal lobes are "working-with-memory" structures that operate on the input to the hippocampal component and the output from it. Winocur and I (Moscovitch & Winocur, 1992a) prefer this term to the superficially similar term *working memory* (Baddeley, 1992, this volume) because the latter is too theoretically loaded: use of it implies endorsing aspects of a working-memory theory in the human and nonhuman literature that may not only be incompatible with each other (see, for example, how the term is used by Olton et al., 1979) but may be wrong or inappropriate when applied to frontal-lobe functions (Moscovitch & Umiltà, 1990, 1991). If we restrict our consideration only to the functions of the central executive in working memory, my conception of working-with-memory structures is very closely related to Baddeley's (1992, this volume) and to the various reflective subsystems proposed by Johnson (1992; see also Johnson & Chalfonte, this volume).

3.5 Procedural Implicit Tests

Of the various types of tests discussed so far, procedural implicit tests are the most heterogeneous, consisting of a large variety of subtypes that do not have obvious components in common. The tests range from mastering a motor skill (e.g., a pursuit rotor), to acquisition of general perceptual skills (reading geometrically transformed script), to learning and applying the rules necessary to solve intellectual puzzles like the Tower of Hanoi. Even classical conditioning of skeletal responses may be a subtype of procedural implicit tests of memory. To make the procedural implicit tests more amenable to analysis, I will use the term to refer to only two subtypes: (a) acquisition and retention of sensorimotor skills, (b) implicit learning and application of rules.

Sensorimotor skills   The model I have developed is not directly applicable to the domain of sensorimotor skills, because its main concern is with encoding sensory input. Nonetheless, the same principle may apply: acquisition and retention results from modification of the very structures involved in performing the task. Just as perceptual structures are modified by the act of perceiving so as to form perceptual records of their activity, so motor structures involved in programming are altered so as to leave behind a *sensorimotor record*. Reactivation of sensorimotor records accounts for performance on implicit sensorimotor tests of memory.

Two predictions follow from this assertion: insofar as the tests are truly implicit (Moscovitch, 1984), acquisition and retention of sensorimotor skills should be normal in amnesic and demented patients with intact sensorimotor structures; deficits should be observed only in patients with damage to sensorimotor structures, regardless of how well preserved their intellect is.

Both predictions are confirmed by the neuropsychological evidence. Acquisition and retention of sensorimotor skills, such as mirror drawing and the pursuit rotor, is normal in the amnesic patient H.M., who had bilateral surgical excision of the medial temporal lobes (Corkin, 1968; Milner, 1966), in patients with lesions to other portions of the hippocampal circuit, and in demented patients with Alzheimer's disease (Butters, Heindel, & Salmon, 1990). Learning a general perceptual skill, such as reading geometrically transformed script, is also preserved in these patients (Butters et al., 1990; Cohen, 1984; Moscovitch, Winocur, & McLachlan, 1986).

By contrast, deficits on the same sensorimotor implicit tests have been noted in patients with Huntington's or Parkinson's disease, which are degenerative disorders associated with damage to the basal ganglia, structures that are part of the extrapyramidal motor system (Butters et al., 1990). The same patients, however, perform normally on perceptual, item-specific implicit tests, which suggests that the deficit concerns only the formation of sensorimotor records or programs.

Rule learning   Amnesic patients can learn and apply mathematical rules, such as the Fibonacci rule (Kinsbourne & Wood, 1975) or the rules for deriving square roots of two-digit numbers (Charness, Milberg, & Alexander, 1988). Amnesic patients with lesions restricted to cortical or diencephalic parts of the hippocampal circuit may also normally acquire and retain recursive rules necessary for solving puzzles like the various versions of the Tower of Hanoi (Cohen, 1984; Moscovitch, Osimani, Wortzman, & Freedman, 1990; Saint-Cyr, Taylor, & Lang, 1988). Amnesic patients can even learn to write simple computer programs (Glisky, Schacter, & Tulving, 1986).

Implicit derivation and application of rules that require planning and monitoring of responses are dependent on the frontal lobes. The Tower of Hanoi is such a goal-directed task. Predictably, patients with focal frontal lesions have difficulty with it (Shallice, 1982), as do patients with frontal dysfunction that accompanies degenerative diseases of the basal ganglia (Butters et al., 1990; Saint-Cyr et al., 1988). The difficulty that Korsakoff patients have in solving Tower of Hanoi problems is attributable more to their impaired frontal-lobe functions than to their amnesia (Joyce & Robbins, 1991). Korsakoff patients, however, may not be deficient at learning mathematical rules (Kinsbourne & Wood, 1975) if they do not have to be derived and their application provides little opportunity to diverge from the goal-directed path (Moscovitch, 1984).

Independence of procedural and item-specific implicit tests   The evidence from studies of patients with neurological disorders indicates that performance on many implicit procedural tests is independent of performance on implicit perceptual or conceptual item-specific tests. Studies of normal people support these conclusions. Using an anagram-solving task, McAndrews and I (1990) showed that studying a target and learning a solution rule without awareness contributed additively to the speed and accuracy of solving anagrams. More recently, Schwartz and Hashtroudi (1991) showed that the general perceptual skill involved in learning to read perceptually degraded letters affected perceptual identification of words independently of whether the target item was studied.

4   IMPLICATIONS OF THE MODEL AND COMPARISON WITH OTHER MODELS AND FRAMEWORKS

In the following sections, I will explore some of the implications of the model I presented, determine how consistent they are with the available evidence, and, where evidence is lacking, suggest studies that could provide useful information. I will compare the model with others and discuss ways in which the various models can be evaluated.

4.1   Perceptual Item-Specific Tests: Implications

The hypothesis that long-lasting effects of repetition priming result from the reactivation of perceptual records in perceptual-input modules accounts for a variety of findings.

Modality   Repetition-priming effects are modality-specific if input from different modalities activate modules that operate in different domains. Thus repetition-priming effects for written and spoken words are diminished if they are presented in different modalities at study and test (Roediger, 1990; Schacter, 1992; Tulving & Schacter, 1990), because there are separate input modules for spoken and written words. I should note that the crucial factor in the model, however, is not modality per se but domain specificity. If the domain of the module includes information that crosses modalities, then strong cross-modal repetition priming should be observed for some material. A possible candidate is the perceptual-speech module whose domain, according to some theorists, is the speech gesture—not a particular set of acoustic features but the intended gesture that the wave form conveys (Liberman and Mattingly, 1989). This means that the same information can be conveyed not only through sound but also through vision, as in lip reading (McGurk & MacDonald, 1976). Thus the effects of cross-modal repetition priming might be observed for vocal (auditory) and lip-reading (visual) speech (Campbell, Landis, & Regard, 1986), since both are encoded by a single speech module.

Format Even when stimuli are presented in the same modality, the effects of repetition priming are diminished if the stimuli are represented in different representational formats at study and test. Priming from pictures to words (and vice versa) is very weak (Roediger, 1990; Roediger & McDermott, 1993), as would be expected if separate modules exist for pictures and words.

The results are more complicated when stimuli are in the same format but different tokens of the same item are presented at study and test. For line drawings of real and novel objects, if crucial features are visible, the effects of repetition priming are maintained between study and test across transformations of size, reflection, orientation, and foreshortening (Biederman & Cooper, 1991, 1992; Cooper, Biederman, & Hummel, 1992; Cooper, Schacter, Ballesteros, & Moore, 1992; Jolicoeur, 1985; Jolicoeur & Milliken, 1989). Changing exemplars between study and test, say from one kind of dress or airplane to another that looks quite different, reduces the repetition-priming effect substantially. Similarly, in tests of lexical decision, naming, and perceptual identification, changes in surface features of written words, such as font and color, have little effect on repetition priming (Carr, Brown, & Charalambous, 1989). On the other hand changes in the language in which the word is written greatly reduces repetition effects (Kirsner & Dunn, 1985). These findings are consistent with the hypothesis that input modules and their perceptual records store information about particular objects rather than generic objects (a particular dog or dress rather than protypical ones, as Fodor, 1983, assumed) and about their invariant properties rather than their surface features. The effects of repetition priming can thus tolerate changes in surface features so long as the structurally invariant properties of the stimulus are similar at study and at test.

Evidence from other studies, however, is contradictory. On tests of visual-word-stem or visual-word-fragment completion, changes in surface features reduce repetition-priming effects (Hayman & Tulving, 1989). Changes in voice and other acoustic features have similar effects on auditory versions of word-stem completion (Schacter, 1992, this volume). Presenting different degraded versions of the same line drawing at study and at test also reduces repetition effects in comparison with the condition in which identical versions are presented on both occasions (Snodgrass & Feenan, 1990; Srinivas, 1993).

On the basis of these latter findings, a number of investigators have proposed that repetition-priming effects are *hyperspecific*, in the sense that the stored representations are accessible through highly specific cues, so that any alteration, even in sensory features, is likely to lead to diminished repetition effects (Roediger, 1990; Squire, 1992, this volume; Tulving & Schacter, 1990). The available evidence, however, suggests that extreme hyperspecificity may be peculiar to studies in which the stimuli are fragmented or degraded. As a result, the gestalt of the target is broken, making it difficult to recover a structural description of it. Under such conditions, more precise, specific information is needed to reactivate the perceptual record of the target than when a stimulus is presented intact.

A related explanation is that the processes involved in cleaning up the degraded stimulus are separate from those involved in forming or reactivating a perceptual record (Schwartz & Hashtroudi, 1991; Snodgrass, 1989). McAndrews and Moscovitch (1990) and Schwartz and Hashtroudi; (1991) showed that the two components make independent contributions to the repetition-priming effect (see Moscovitch et al., 1994, for an extended discussion).

A third possibility, suggested by Squire (1992, this volume) and Schacter (1992, this volume), is that hyperspecificity of repetition effects, at least for words, is mediated by right-hemisphere input modules whose perceptual records store information about sensory features. Their suggestion is based on evidence from tachistoscopic (Marsolek, Kosslyn, & Squire, 1992), dichotic-listening (Zaidel, 1985), and PET studies (Squire et al., 1992) that format-specific repetition effects for words show involvement of the right, but not the left, hemisphere. These sensory-sensitive right-hemispheric modules are the mates of corresponding left-hemisphere visual-word-form and phonological-word-form modules that code information about graphemic and phonological features of words, respectively. The evidence for corresponding, but different, left and right modules is consistent with studies of left- and right-hemisphere reading (Coltheart, 1980; Coslett & Saffran, 1989; Moscovitch, 1976, 1981; Patterson, Vargha-Khadem, & Polkey, 1989; Rabinowicz & Moscovitch, 1984; Zaidel & Peters, 1981) and speech perception (see the references in Schacter, 1992, this volume).

An interpretation that combines aspects of the last two proposals is that the right hemisphere specializes in cleaning up degraded perceptual input and delivers the decoded message to input modules. It is the reactivation of these right-hemisphere processes that accounts for a right-hemisphere effect on format-sensitive tests of repetition priming.

Another alternative, suggested by a study by Kinoshita and Wayland (1993), is that the sensitivity to low-level sensory featuers observed on some implicit tests may result from their contamination by explicit-memory processes. They found that only normal people, not amnesic patients, benefitted from having word fragments repeated in the same font, as compared to a different font, at study and at test.

Levels of processing   Because perceptual records are presemantic and because modules are informationally encapsulated, the depth to which a stimulus is processed should have no influence on repetition-priming effects. In contrast to explicit tests of memory, where information to deep semantic levels enhances performance considerably, levels-of-processing manipulations have only a small effect on implicit perceptual tests in normal people (for reviews, see Roediger & McDermott, 1993; Schacter, 1992; this volume). This residual but consistent effect of level of processing is probably caused by contamination of ostensibly implicit tests by explicit retrieval strategies. In normal people unaware that their memory is being tested, even small levels-of-processing effects are eliminated (Bowers & Schacter, 1990; but see Graf, Squire, & Mandler, 1984, for amnesia, and Howard, Fry, & Brune, 1991).

Attention and consciousness   The uptake of information by input modules is obligatory and requires minimal attention or cognitive resources (see the discussion in Moscovitch & Umiltà, 1990, on different types of modules). Consequently, manipulation of attention and even of conscious awareness at the time of encoding should have much less effect on performance on implicit tests of memory than on explicit tests. The mere uptake of information by the module is sufficient to modify it and leave a perceptual record of the stimulating event. This prediction is confirmed by evidence of substantial and long-lasting perceptual repetition effects in studies in which the stimulus is so degraded that the subject is often not aware of it and his explicit recognition of it is no better than chance (Merikle & Reingold, 1991; for a summary of studies, see Moscovitch & Bentin, 1993). Similarly, engaging attention by having subjects perform a demanding concurrent task at study has relatively little influence on performance on perceptual implicit tests but marked influence on performance on explicit tests (Eich, 1984; Jacoby, Woloshyn, & Kelley, 1989; Parkin, Reid, & Russo, 1990). Most impressive of all are a number of reports that repetition priming can be observed for items that are picked up even while the individual is anaesthetized (Kihlstrom, Schacter, Cork, Hurt, & Behr, 1990; Kihlstrom & Conture, 1992; Bonke, Fitch, & Millar, 1990).

Interference and speed of acquisition   These two properties, though not derivable from notions of modularity, may also be crucial features of perceptual repetition priming. Registration is rapid and can occur in the first trial. A single brief exposure to the stimulus may be sufficient to produce asymptotic performance on tests of perceptual repetition priming (Challis & Sidhu, 1993; Schacter et al., 1991), though some studies have reported that multiple presentations can improve performance (Bentin & Moscovitch, 1988; Rueckl, 1990). The effects of perceptual repetition priming are not very susceptible to interference (Graf & Schacter, 1987), though additional studies are needed to confirm this finding. I will discuss these aspects of repetition priming more fully below.

4.2   Perceptual Item-Specific Tests: Comparison with Human Models

The framework I proposed to account for performance on item-specific perceptual and conceptual tests of memory has much in common with the proposals advanced by Squire (1992, this volume) to explain repetition priming and by Johnson (1992; Johnson & Chalfonte, this volume) to explain perceptual learning. Squire suggests that repetition-priming effects are mediated by neocortical structures involved in picking up, decoding, and storing presemantic stimulus information. His proposal that repetition-priming effects are likely mediated by the right-hemisphere goes farther than I am willing to venture at the moment. Johnson's approach is a more functional, process-oriented one than mine, though clear similarities are discernable between her perceptual subprocess P-1 and P-2 and the processes that Umiltà and I presume to be mediated by perceptual-input modules and first-order interpretative central systems (Moscovitch & Umiltà, 1990, 1991). The primary difference between our view and hers is that the separate perceptual modules we propose are distinguished from each other on the basis of informational content, with different modules for written and spoken words, faces, objects, voices, and so on. Her distinctions concern processes that in principle can cut across these various representations. Aside from the question of whether she has correctly identified the appropriate subprocesses (many of them sound too much like a description of what the subject does, e.g., placing, identifying, tracking), it may be that what determines the representational content of the module are the distinctive subprocesses that constitute its operation (see Farah, 1994). Repetition-priming effects occur because these processes are reiterated more quickly with repetition. It remains to be seen whether a processing account or representational account, or some combination of the two, best describes repetition-priming effects.

My idea that perceptual repetition-priming effects are mediated by a perceptual input modules most closely resembles Schacter's (1992, this volume) idea that they are mediated by a presemantic perceptual representation system (PRS). Both the PRS and perceptual-input modules are domain-specific and presemantic. One might even venture that the other criteria of modularity (informational encapsulation and shallow output) are implicitly assumed to apply to the PRS, though Schacter may prefer to maintain a more neutral, pragmatic stance in this regard. My commitment to a more principled notion of modularity allows me to place memory into a broad, unifying framework of modules and central systems, from which I can derive organizational principles about episodic memory as well as repetition priming.

In another sense, the component-process framework I have advanced is more flexible than Schacter's PRS. According to my framework, the magnitude of repetition-priming effects depends on the overlap between the components enlisted at study and those recruited at test (Moscovitch et al., 1986; Witherspoon & Moscovitch, 1989). Although reactivation of perceptual or semantic records may be crucial, the overall effect of repetition priming depends as well on the contribution of processes involved in gaining access to the record, as well as subsequent decision and response processes following reactivation of the record. Consideration of all the components is necessary to help account for the independence observed among different repetition-priming tests within the same domain, such as between fragment completion and perceptual identification (Witherspoon & Moscovitch, 1989), or even between different fragments of the same word (Hayman & Tulving, 1989).

Last, it may be worth reiterating that *not* all implicit tests of memory implicate the input modules or the PRS, as Baddeley (1992, this volume) seems to assume. Tulving and Schacter (1990), Schacter (1992, this volume), and I (1992a, this volume) have distinguished between perceptual and conceptual repetition effects. Beyond this, I have also indicated that some implicit tests are best conceived as procedural, of which various subtypes exist and which are mediated by neural components that differ from those involved in item-specific tests (see also Squire, 1992, this volume; Butters et al., 1990).

4.3 Perceptual Item-Specific Tests: Comparison with Animal Models

Reserachers working on animal models of hippocampal function were the first to promote the idea that there are at least two distinct memory systems: one that involves the hippocampus and related structures and another that is extrahippocampal (see Nadel, 1992, this volume). Their theoretical and research program was so successful that there is now hardly anyone conducting research on animals who would dispute their general claim. (This is in marked contrast with the current state of affairs in studies of normal human memory.) As the essays on animal models in this volume illustrate, what is at issue now is how best to describe the properties, operation, and function of the different memory systems.

In discussing the nonhippocampal memory system, many of these authors assert or assume that there is a close correspondence between animal and human models (Eichenbaum, 1992, this volume; Lynch & Granger, 1992, this volume; Nadel, 1992, this volume; Rudy & Sutherland, 1992, this volume; Squire, 1992, this volume). In particular, they draw comparisons between the spared memory abilities of animals with hippocampal damage and the performance of amnesic and normal people on perceptual repetition-priming tests. The implication in making these comparisons is that the preserved memory capacities of the rat and monkey are mediated by the same functional and structural systems that mediate repetition-priming effects in humans.

Although it is appealing for all kinds of reasons to hold this position, a number of important discrepancies between animal and human studies give one pause. Because the presumed or hoped-for similarities are discussed at length by some (Rudy & Sutherland, 1992, pp. 213–215; Squire, 1992, pp. 238–240) or noted briefly by others (Eichenbaum, 1992, this volume; Lynch & Granger, 1992, this volume; Nadel, 1992, this volume), I will not dwell on them here. Instead, I will focus on some of the inconsistencies.

Interference Nadel (1992, this volume) and especially Olton and Shapiro (1992; Shapiro & Olton, this volume) note that the hippocampus is necessary for reducing interference in memory. According to them, memory representations not mediated by the hippocampus are therefore much more prone to interference than those that are mediated by it. An extensive literature on learning and memory in rats and monkeys with hippocampal lesions generally supports this assertion.

On the basis of the implied correspondence between animal and human models of memory, one might infer that repetition-priming effects are much more susceptible to interference than explicit tests of memory, since only the latter are mediated by the hippocampus. The evidence on this point is contradictory but potentially revealing.

Tests of A-B, A-C paired-associate (negative-transfer) learning have been used to compare the effects of interference on implicit and explicit memory. In one set of studies, subjects learned a set of highly related words, A-B (e.g., *soldier-battle*) and then studied another similar set, A-C (e.g., *soldier-army*). Their memory for the A-C list was then tested. In the explicit version of the test, subjects had to try to recall the second member of the A-C pair when presented with the first, whereas in the implicit version they merely had to respond with the first word that came to mind. In normal people, interference from the A-B list was greater in the implicit version than in the explicit version (Mayes, Pickering, & Fairbairn, 1987; Winocur & Moscovitch, in press). High levels of interference on the explicit version were found only in amnesic people and people with left temporal lobectomy (see table 2).

Graf and Schacter (1987) combined the stem-completion technique with the negative-transfer paradigm. They had subjects study two sets of unrelated word pairs, A-B followed by A-C. Memory for the A-C association was then tested by presenting the first number of the pair and the initial three-letter stem of the second member. In the implicit version, subjects completed the stem with the first word that came to mind, whereas in the explicit version they attempted to complete it with the word they remembered as being associated with the first member. In contrast to other negative-transfer studies, interference was greater in the explicit version than in the implicit version.

Contrary to the view derived from animal models, these studies indicate that susceptibility to interference is not a universal characteristic of performance

Table 2 Mean response words recalled (maximum = 12) from the A-C or A-B list of associations on an explicit or implicit test of negative transfer

| | Memory test | | | | | | |
| | Explicit | | | | | Implicit | |
List	Young	Old	R temp	L temp	Amnesic	Young	Old
(N)	(12)	(12)	(12)	(7)	(5)	(12)	(12)
A-C	9.8	9.0	10.6	7.4	3.5	3.8	2.9
A-B	1.6	2.1	0.3	2.7	6.5	4.3	4.8

Note: Subjects were normal young and old people, patients with right temporal (R temp) or left temporal (L temp) lobectomies, and amnesic patients.

on tests of memory not mediated by the hippocampus. As an implicit test of memory, stem completion is considered to be primarily perceptual, whereas the related association test is conceptual. One possible conclusion is that perceptual implicit tests are relatively immune to interference, whereas conceptual ones are especially susceptible. More studies are clearly needed to test the generality of this observation and to examine the effects of interference on procedural implicit tests about which almost nothing is known. Whatever the outcome of these studies, it is evident that there is no simple correspondence with respect to interference between nonhippocampal memory in animals and performance on implicit memory tests in humans. No common set of principles can be applied to all of them, as some animal-memory models imply by considering nonhippocampal memory systems as a unit governed by common principles or rules. A similar point can be made concerning the speed with which memories are acquired.

Speed of acquisition Nadel (1992, p. 182, this volume), in distinguishing between locale and taxon learning, considers the speed with which information is acquired to be a distinguishing characteristic of the two systems. Learning is all or none, and acquisition and extinction are rapid, in the hippocampally based locale system, whereas learning is incremental, and acquisition and extinction are slower in the nonhippocampally based taxon system. Although he concedes that not all forms of taxon learning are slow, the distinction between a fast and a slow system is central to his analysis and those of other investigators building computational models of memory (see Nadel, 1992, p. 186). Squire (1992, this volume) makes a similar point regarding the formation of new associations (see below).

Although Nadel did not specifically consider performance on perceptual implicit tests as a type of taxon learning, such performance does demonstrate nonhippocampal learning. Indeed, as I noted earlier, perceptual implicit tests have become the prototypical test of nonhippocampal learning in the human-memory literature. It is of interest to know, therefore, whether it satisfies Nadel's criterion that nonhippocampal learning (acquisition of information) is incremental and slow.

A number of studies on repetition priming for words and for line drawings of common objects, and of novel, meaningless forms, have shown that a single brief presentation is sufficient to produce a long-lasting priming effect (for reviews, see Moscovitch, Vriezen, & Goshen-Gottstein, 1993; Moscovitch, Goshen-Gottstein, & Vriezen, 1994; Roediger & McDermott, 1993). Moreover, increasing the duration of exposure or the number of presentations typically has little effect on repetition priming (Challis and Sidhu, 1993; Schacter et al., 1991), except perhaps when nonsense words (Musen & Squire, 1991) and novel faces (Bentin & Moscovitch, 1988) were used. On the other hand, these variables have a marked beneficial effect on explicit tests of memory, which are presumed to be hippocampally based. Contrary to Nadel, these studies indicate, therefore, that registration, the formation of perceptual records, can be rapid and nonincremental and can occur without the participation of the hippocampus.

4.4 Learning versus Registration: A Difference between Animal and Human Studies of Nonhippocampal Memory

The most likely explanation for the lack of correspondence between tests of nonhippocampally mediated memory in animals and tests of repetition priming in humans is that the two types of tests measure different things. Tests of repetition priming measure registration, i.e., the formation of rapid perceptual records. The individual is never asked to learn anything actively or to form new associations. If associations are formed, or registered, they are purely perceptual (see section 4.5). At the phenomenological level, the individual believes that he or she is merely perceiving or identifying a stimulus, such as a word or picture. Sometimes this activity is accompanied by the sense that some perceptions are more fluent (Jacoby, 1983), clearer, or longer (Witherspoon & Allen, 1985) than others and that some words or pictures come more easily to mind, though many subjects are not aware even of this.

By contrast, in the vast majority of animal studies, the animals have to learn to attach some significance to the stimulus and associate it with a response (but see Lynch & Granger, 1992, p. 191). As yet there are few animal studies, if any, designed to test registration independently of learning. Though this type of rapid acquisition and retention of perceptual (and perhaps semantic) information very likely also occurs in animals, no techniques have been devised to let the experimenter know that their perception of a stimulus or event improves with repetition.

In principle, it should not be difficult to demonstrate registration, especially in monkeys. Rather than have the animals learn an association between a particular response and a target stimulus, have the animal emit an already established response in the context of a perceptual-judgment task. One possible procedure is to train a monkey to choose the clearer of two degraded stimuli. Having been trained, the monkey could then view a series of stimuli that are not degraded. This is the study phase. Later, during the test phase, previously studied stimuli are paired with unstudied stimuli, but both are now equally degraded. As in training, the monkey has to choose the one that appears less degraded. If perception is influenced by previous exposure to one of the stimuli, monkeys, like humans, should choose the previously studied stimulus as being the clearer of the two. A similar procedure may be used with smell in rats, though choosing on the basis of intensity, saturation, or even pleasantness would replace clarity.

Something like this has been tried with rats by Winocur (1990) and by Fleming and Winocur (personal communication). They exposed rats to a novel smell at study. In Winocur's study, the smell was that of a new food on the breath of a rat with which the experimental animal interacted socially. When later the experimental rats were exposed to two new foods, they chose to eat the one that carried the same smell that they had encountered earlier. Rats with hippocampal lesions could *register* the information rapidly and also showed the same preference as control rats when tested a day later. Their retention, however, was not as good, which indicates that there may also be a hippocampal component to this process. In another study, Fleming and Winocur (personal communication) exposed female parturient rats to pups for one hour, an exposure that is sufficient to elicit nonhormonally mediated maternal behavior as long as ten days later. Rats whose hippocampus was lesioned either before or after the initial exposure behaved no differently from normal rats.

These studies indicate that it is possible to demonstrate rapid, nonincremental acquisition of perceptual information in animals with hippocampal lesions. They also suggest, contrary to Nadel, that the rapid acquisition of taste aversions may be not an exception but the rule for all types of nonhippocampally based perceptual learning if the rat or monkey already has a repertoire that can readily reveal the information it has registered (Lynch & Granger, 1992, this volume).

The corollary to this hypothesis is that the slow, incremental learning that is observed results from nonhippocampal processes other than those that are not strictly perceptual. I suggest two candidates. One is that what is slow and incremental is the formation of nonhippocampally based stimulus-response associations, not the registration of stimulus input. These associations may be mediated by cortical-neostriatal networks, as others have suggested (Mishkin & Appenzeler, 1987; Packard & White, 1991; Squire, 1992, this volume). They also have their counterpart in humans' relatively slow, incremental acquisition of sensorimotor procedural tasks (Moscovitch, 1992a, this volume, 1992b). As in rats and monkeys, damage to neostriatal structures, particularly the caudate, impairs performance on these tasks (Butters et al., 1990).

Another candidate for slow, incremental learning may be the creation of modules, rather than the formation of perceptual records in preexisting modules. In a critique of Fodor's ideas on modularity, Umiltà and I proposed that there might be three types of modules, the third type being experientially assembled (Moscovitch & Umiltà, 1990). The creation of this type of module, we believe, involves a long and protracted process. The word-form system is one such module. Although the creation of new modules in an experiment is unlikely, it remains a candidate for a nonhippocampal learning process, at least in real life and possibly in the laboratory.

4.5 Learning New Associations between Stimuli: Repetition Priming for Novel Pairs of Items Is Perceptual

This brings us to the question of whether perceptual-input modules can support the formation of new associations between arbitrarily different stimuli. Nadel (1992, this volume) and Squire (1992, this volume) have asserted that "nondeclarative [nonhippocampally based] memory can support the gradual and cumulative acquisition of new associations, as in classical conditioning, but does not seem well adapted for acquiring novel associations rapidly" (Squire, 1992, p. 237). Though there is some truth to this assertion, it needs to be qualified.

Perceptual-input modules and perceptual-representation systems are conceived as dealing with single items or units: a word, an object, a face. Little consideration is given in theories as to whether perceptual-input modules can form perceptual records of conjoined stimuli. If the stimuli are from the same domain, there is no compelling theoretical reason why newly associated items might not be retained as domain-specific perceptual records in the way single items are. The question is therefore an empirical one: Is there evidence of perceptual repetition-priming effects for new associations?

Previous attempts to find *associative repetition-priming* effects have yielded inconclusive results in studies of both normal and amnesic people (see reviews in Lewandowsky, Kirsner, & Bainbridge, 1989; Moscovitch, Goshen-Gottstein, & Vriezen, 1994; Moscovitch, Vriezen, & Goshen-Gottstein, 1993). Even on the most reliable of the tests, word-stem completion, modality-specific associative priming effects were not found in many severely amnesic patients (Cermak, Bleich, & Blackford, 1988; Graf & Schacter, 1985; Mayes & Gooding, 1989; Schacter & Graf, 1986; Shimamura & Squire, 1989) nor in normal people who were truly unaware of the relation between study and test pairs (Bowers & Schacter, 1990, but see Howard et al., 1991). Overall, these studies suggest that associative priming in stem completion has an explicit-memory component mediated by the hippocampus and related structures.

Speeded reading may be a better implicit test of memory than stem completion because its rapid pace may not allow the intrusion of explicit retrieval strategies. Using speeded reading, Moscovitch et al. (1986) had subjects study pairs of radomly associated words and at test had the subjects read lists of studied pairs, new pairs, or old words in new pairings. All items were slightly visually degraded at test to slow down reading speed and allow the priming effect to emerge. We found that reading speed was fastest for the studied pairs when the results from amnesic patients and normal people were combined, which indicates that repetition-priming effects can be found for newly formed associations. We obtained a similar but even stronger result using sentences in which words could be interchanged to produce, at test, sentences that contained old words in new combinations (recombined sentences). Reading speed was faster for the old, intact sentences than for recombined sentences. Light and LaVoie (1993) also found that one or two trials were sufficient to produce associative repetition priming in the word-pair task in normal young and old people, but Musen and Squire (1993) needed to give several learning trials to obtain comparable results. It should be noted that Musen and Squire's scoring and testing procedures differed somewhat from those of Moscovitch et al. and that they never attempted to replicate the sentence

Table 3 Reaction time to make lexical decisions about pairs of newly associated words in the intact, recombined, and control conditions

	Condition		
Modality	Intact	Recombined	Control
Same	860	924	987
Different	907	917	1,019

Note: Study and test pairs were presented in the same or a different modality.

Table 4 Reaction time in milliseconds to make lexical decisions about pairs of newly associated words in the intact, recombined, and control conditions

	Condition		
Encoding	Intact	Recombined	Control
Elaborate	918	971	1,063
Shallow	916	947	998

Note: Encoding at study was elaborate or shallow.

study, which produced the stronger effect (but see Musen & Squire, 1991, for a comparable study with comparable results). In a subsequent experiment using perceptual identification as the measure, Musen and Squire (1993) did find a weak associative-priming effect but, again, only when the results from amnesic and normal control subjects were combined.

The partial successes of the previous studies and the indication that priming of new associations may be perceptual prompted Goshen-Gottstein and me (1992) to design a new procedure for obtaining reliable effects from associative repetition priming. As before, subjects studied simultaneously presented written pairs of randomly associated words. At test, old pairs, new pairs, and recombined pairs were again presented simultaneously and subjects had to indicate whether both members of each pair were words. On negative trials, at least one member of the pair was a pronounceable, but meaningless, letter string.

This modified lexical-decision task produced reliable effects from associative repetition priming in normal people (see table 3). Changing modalities from auditory to visual between study and test eliminated the repetition-priming effect, which indicates that it was likely mediated by domain-specific perceptual-input modules. Also, the effect was almost as great with shallow as with deep levels of processing at study (see table 4). Rueckl and Marsolek (personal communication) found similar results with the same procedure. Using this procedure, we have also obtained preliminary evidence of repetition effects in amnesic patients with confirmed bilateral medial-temporal-lobe lesions and in patients with right or left temporal lobectomies that included large hippocampal excisions.

These results thus suggest that perceptual input modules or the PRS can support the rapid formation of new, but domain-specific, associations without hippocampal involvement. Being represented as domain-specific perceptual records, these new associations have the same status as other perceptual records. They cannot be conjured up voluntarily as new memories but only elicited as percepts by perceptually similar input. In short, they are data-driven. They lack the mnemonic attributes of hippocampally mediated associations that we can recollect consciously. Because they are consciously accessible, we can represent them across modalities and manipulate them to serve our needs. I therefore agree with Eichenbaum (1992, this volume) that the hippocampus is necessary for the formation of flexible mnemonic associations that are not strictly bound to perceptual records and that contain information that can be integrated across domains.

4.6 The Hippocampal Module: Implications and Comparisons with Other Models

The idea that the hippocampus is a module that satisfies the same criteria as perceptual input modules implies that a component of conscious recollection is no more intelligent or under voluntary control than perception. Thus at the core of conscious, episodic memory lies an associative memory component that is informationally encapsulated (cognitively impenetrable) and for which encoding and retrieval are obligatory and not under voluntary control. This claim alone is sufficient to distinguish my proposal from most other models dealing with human memory (Johnson, 1992; Johnson & Chalfonte, this volume; Squire, 1992, this volume; Baddeley, 1992, this volume), which do not differentiate clearly between strategic and associative processes in memory.

The existence of an associative memory module is, however, compatible with animal and neural-network models of memory and the hippocampus, which are associative and content-addressable (Eichenbaum, 1992, this volume; Lynch & Granger, 1992, this volume; Metcalfe, Cottrell, & Mencl, 1992; Metcalfe, Menel, & Cottrell, this volume; Rudy & Sutherland, 1992, this volume; Squire, 1992, this volume; Teyler & Di Scenna, 1986). At issue is what kind of information is encoded, stored, and retrieved by this associative module and how these memory functions are implemented.

Is hippocampally based memory spatial, conscious, or both? Anatomical and conceptual issues   According to Nadel (1992, this volume), the hippocampus is specialized for dealing with spatial information. All the other investigators, however, consider the spatial-memory function of the hippocampus as only a particular instantiation of its much broader function, which is to bind separate representations of stimuli into relational or configural associations. My view (Moscovitch & Umiltà, 1990, 1991; Moscovitch, 1992a, 1992b) is that the hippocampus and its related structures encode any information derived from input that is consciously apprehended, in the sense that it receives full attention. Because I make no distinction between spatial information and other types of information, my view is closer to that of the other authors than to Nadel's.

It may be possible to reconcile the two views if anatomical considerations are taken into account. The hippocampal complex consists of a number of related structures that include the fimbria, fornix, entorhinal and perirhinal cortex, subiculum, and parahippocampal gyrus. It is becoming increasingly evident that damage to these structures have different effects on memory (Lynch & Granger, 1992; Nadel, 1992, this volume; Squire, 1992, this volume), though there is far from universal agreement on how best to characterize these differences. It may prove to be the case that damage to some structures are associated with spatial memory loss and damage to others with loss of nonspatial relational memory.

Research on humans may be relevant in this regard. Consistent with the specialized functions of the cerebral hemispheres in humans, only damage to the right hippocampal region is associated with spatial memory loss (Pigott & Milner, 1993; Smith, 1989; Smith & Milner, 1981, 1989). Left-hippocampal lesions are associated with loss of memory for verbal material, which indicates that the hippocampus can in principle mediate memory for nonspatial information (Milner, 1974, but see the discussions by O'Keefe, 1985, and O'Keefe & Nadel, 1978, on this point). In the region of the right hippocampus, anterior, medial lesions exacerbate the spatial deficits found after lesions to the temporal lobe (Smith, 1989) but to obtain a severe topographical-memory loss, the damage must include the right, posterior parahippocampal gyrus and subiculum (DeRenzi, 1982, chap. 8; Habib & Sirigu, 1987; Van Der Linden & Seron, 1987). Indeed, damage to that region may produce a selective loss of spatial memory with little effect on nonspatial functions. The deficit seems also to pertain to newly acquired spatial information, with old information being relatively preserved. More research on the effects of selective damage to different portions of the hippocampal complex in humans and in other animals is needed to adjudicate among the various hypotheses regarding the function of this region.

A tantalizing possibility is that consciousness and space are closely linked, in the sense that our conscious awareness always has a spatial component (Nadel, 1992, this volume; O'Keefe, 1985). Space is the medium in which all events occur. In this sense, space provides the context for the events we experience phenomenologically. If the hippocampus obligatorily processes all events of which we are conscious, as I have proposed, it must of necessity handle spatial information. To speculate further, it may be that structures involved in processing spatial information provide the primordial substrate for consciousness.

Recovered consciousness: A proposal to explain why conscious recollection is associated with hippocampal memories Before continuing to discuss the relation between consciousness and memory, I should indicate what sense of the word "consciousness" I wish to employ. In this context, I use the word "consciousness" in the ordinary-language sense of being conscious of something. This sense of consciousness is interchangeable with phenomenological awareness. With regard to memory, it means that the individual is aware of a memory rather than a percept or a thought. In the context of an experiment, the individual is aware of having a memory of a stimulus that he or she perceives or recalls, i.e., that was experienced before.

The general concensus that emerges from these chapters is that the hippocampus (and related structures) binds together the neural elements that make up our experience of an event into a multimodal, permanent memory trace. What is up for discussion concerns the nature of the content of that trace: is it spatial, relational, abstract, and so on? What has been neglected in this discussion, and what I wish to emphasize, is the relation of consciousness to memory. According to my model, the hippocampal component picks up only information that is consciously apprehended. The hippocampal component thus binds the neural elements that mediate the information that constitutes conscious experience. This includes the collection of records or engrams of the modules and central systems whose output form the content of conscious experiences as well as the elements that make experience conscious. In this way, consciousness is bound by the hippocampal component along with other aspects of an experienced event and becomes an intrinsic property of the memory trace.

At the neurophysiological level, one can think of collections of neurons or cell assemblies whose firing patterns determine the different properties of an event we experience: its color, form, texture, spatial relations, and so on. Insofar as conscious awareness is a quality of our experience, it too must have neural correlates that interact with other cell assemblies or are part of them. This network of cell assemblies, including the neural correlates of consciousness, are bound together in the memory trace.

When the memory trace is reactivated at retrieval, consciousness is recovered along with other aspects of the experienced event. This is just another aspect of the encoding-specificity principle (Tulving, 1983). *Consciousness in, consciousness out.*

It is the recovery of a trace imbued with consciousness that makes it feel familiar and immediately recognizable as something previously experienced. This *recovered consciousness* is the signal that distinguishes a memory trace from thoughts and perceptions (which involve *on-line consciousness*) and is at the core of conscious recolleciton. With respect to remembering, and perhaps with respect to no other function, consciousness is an inherent property of the very thing we apprehend.

I think this type of conscious awareness is primitive; it is something that enables an organism to experience an event rather than merely to live through it or react to it. For example, it is what underlies the difference between true sight and "blindsight" (caused by cortical lesions that leave the individual blind in terms of felt experience but nonetheless able to respond to visual stimuli of which he or she claims to be unaware) or between other forms of explicit and implicit knowledge (Schacter et al., 1988). Because it is primitive, I think that nonhuman mammals, and perhaps other species, possess this type of conscious awareness, and it enables them to recognize a memory as such. (For further discussion, see Moscovitch, 1994; O'Keefe, 1985.)

Organizational and historical contexts   Because the hippocampus is associative and modular, the information handled by it is ordered according to principles of similarity and simple spatial and temporal contiguity. The hippocampus lacks the capacity for true temporal organization, in which events occurring over widely spaced intervals can be related to each other either sequentially or with respect to an overarching theme. Lynch and Granger (1992, this volume) propose that the hippocampus is necessary for connecting events across space and time, but they are concerned with time intervals that span only a few seconds, well within the realm of simple temporal contiguity but far short of the range of our capacity for temporal ordering.

Lynch and Granger's reference to recency memory and recency mechanisms as crucial components of the hippocampal complex is puzzling. I am assuming that they are referring to memory for recently occurring events or stimuli rather than to a mechanism for determining which events are the most recent. There is good evidence that the latter function, and temporal ordering in general, is affected by frontal rather than hippocampal damage (Milner, Petrides, & Smith, 1985; Shimamura, Janowsky, & Squire, 1991; Vriezen & Moscovitch, 1990). Patients who are poor at making recency judgements can indeed show relatively well preserved memory for recently occurring events; they just cannot remember their order.

Cohesion and consolidation: The formation and preservation of long-term memory traces   The term *consolidation* has traditionally referred to any process involved in making long-term memory traces resistant to disruption by amnestic agents. Just as it is important to distinguish between *registration* and other processes involved in the formation of long-term memories, so it is important to distinguish between two types of consolidation processes, both of which involve the hippocampus. The first type is rapid and involves the formation of long-term memory traces by the hippocampus. I refer to this process as *cohesion* because it involves hippocampal binding of elements into a memory trace. Once bound, a slower process ensues that makes the memory trace permanent. This second process, which is *consolidation* proper, probably involves tonic input to the hippocampus. It is assumed to be complete when explicit memory for an event can survive disruption by amnestic agents. With this as the marker, consolidation has been estimated to take up to three years in humans (Milner, 1966; Squire & Cohen, 1982), weeks in monkeys (Zola-Morgan & Squire, 1990), and days in rats (Winocur, 1990). Once memory traces are fully consolidated, access to them can be gained via an extra-hippocampal route, perhaps involving the frontal lobes (Kopelman, 1989).

The appropriate marker for the time course of cohesion, the formation of hippocampally mediated memories, is their susceptibility to memory loss following temporary disruption or inactivation of hippocampal processes, not hippocampal destruction. Temporary hippocampal disruption can be achieved by electroconvulsive shock, inhibition of protein synthesis, blockage of relevant neurotransmitters, and electrical stimulation. In studies using such methods, the designated procedure is applied at different intervals after the learning episode, and the subject is tested once the effects of the procedure have dissipated. With this as the measure, the estimation of cohesion time is typically on the order of seconds to minutes (for reviews, see Milner, 1970; Squire, 1987). Permanent memory loss for events that occurred at longer intervals is usually associated with extreme trauma, such as severe concussion or coma, which can cause hippocampal damage.

The rapid time course of cohesion is consistent with findings from studies of normal human memory that immediate free recall is mediated by a long-term memory component that must have been rapidly formed. The contribution of this long-term component is revealed, among other ways, in the primacy portion of the serial-position curve. This portion is greatly diminished in amnesia (Baddeley & Warrington, 1970) and in patients with left hippocampal lesions (Moscovitch, 1982), which suggests that the primacy effect is hippocampally mediated.

4.7   The Frontal Lobes and Strategic Tests of Memory: Implications and Comparison with Other Models

Without the frontal lobes, performance on *strategic, explicit,* and perhaps some *implicit* tests of memory is impaired (Milner et al., 1985; Moscovitch & Winocur, 1992a, 1992b; Petrides, 1989; Schacter, 1987; Shimamura et al., 1991). These tests include judgment of frequency of occurrence, self-ordered pointing, conditional associative learning, memory for temporal order, different types of delayed response that use a small, repeated set of items, and perhaps release from proactive inhibition. Consistent with my hypothesis, the tests are performed poorly not because the target event is forgotten, as is the case following hippocampal lesions on the very same tasks, but because organization at encoding and strategic search and monitoring at retrieval is deficient in frontal patients. Even recall (Incissa della Rochetta, 1986; Mayes, 1988) and recognition (Delbecq-Derouesné, Beauvois, & Shallice, 1990) are impaired if strategic processes are involved.

As central-system structures, the frontal lobes do not restrict their operation to a specific domain. Memory impairment associated with frontal damage is accompanied by deficits in other domains such as problem solving and attention (Milner, 1964; Stuss & Benson, 1986). One also sees an ordering deficit on temporal memory tasks when frontal patients recount well-rehearsed scripts of daily-life situations (Godbout, & Doyon, 1992) or reconstruct a motor sequence (Kolb & Milner, 1981). Even on memory tests, strategic impairment encompasses recent and remote memories (Moscovitch, 1989; Shimamura et al, 1991), and extends, as well, to information in semantic memory (see Moscovitch, 1992a, 1992b; Moscovitch & Winocur, 1992a, for details).

Memory without organizational or historical context is seen most clearly in confabulation. This disorder is almost always associated with lesions to the medial frontal lobes as well as basal forebrain structures caused by aneurysms of the anterior communicating artery. The behavior of confabulating patients is instructive because it suggests what remembering is like when it relies only on the shallow output from the hippocampal system (Moscovitch, 1989). Confabulations are usually not pure fabrications but often consist of accurately remembered elements of one event combined with those of another without regard to their internal consistency or even plausibility. Sometimes entire events are recalled but placed in an inappropriate context. Temporal order is grossly impaired, even for salient events separated by decades.

As expected, recognition memory in these patients is relatively spared in comparison with recall, which involves strategic, presumably frontally based retrieval processes, in addition to the hippocampal associative retrieval processes that suffices for most recognition tests (Moscovitch, 1989; Parkin et al., 1988; see also Parkin et al., 1993, for a case with similar frontal-system deficits but without confabulation). Recall performance can be improved if the cues that specify the target item are strong enough so that strategic processes need not be invoked (Delbecq-Derouesné, Beauvois, & Shallice, 1990; Parkin et al., 1993). Similarly, recognition can become impaired if performance depends on selecting target items from related interfering material that evokes associative (hippocampal) memories of their own (Delbecq-Desrouesné et al., 1990; Parkin et al., 1993).

Multiple frontal systems   As I noted at the outset, the frontal lobes are not unitary but consist of a variety of subsystems, each presumably with different central-system functions. Although distinct neuroanatomical and functional regions have been isolated, it is still difficult to determine what global function to assign to them. Johnson's (1992; Johnson & Chalfonte, this volume) proposal of a variety of different reflective subsystems, as well as supervisory and executive functions, provides a useful framework for research on the frontal lobes. Such research would help determine whether her processing subsystems correspond to similar neuroanatomical subsystems in the prefrontal cortex or whether each is best viewed as a cognitive process that draws on a variety of frontal subsystems for its operation.

4.8   Cognitive Resources: Cortical Modules and the Frontal and Hippocampal Components

Because modules, including the hippocampal component, process information automatically, they are likely to require fewer cognitive resources for their

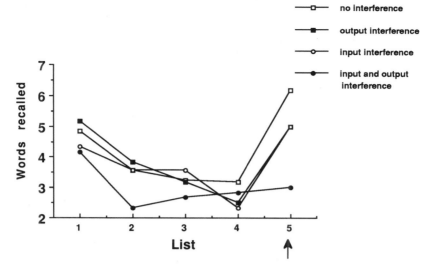

Figure 2 Release from proactive inhibition (PI). The graph shows number of words that college students recalled (of a possible twelve) per trial in various interference conditions. PI was built up on trials 1–4 and released on trial 5. Any word that is recalled within seven items of its presentation is assumed to come from primary or short-term memory, whereas all others are assumed to be recovered from secondary or long-term memory (Tulving & Colotla, 1970).

operation than would strategic central systems (see Moscovitch & Umiltà, 1990, 1991, on the interaction of central systems with a limited-capacity central processor). Interference by a concurrent task at test should be greater for memory tests sensitive to frontal damage than for tests sensitive to hippocampal damage. (Interference at study may affect both types of tests, since it disrupts organization and, if severe enough, may prevent information from being fully available to consciousness so that the hippocampus will not pick it up.)

To test directly the hypothesis of retrieval interference, we designed experiments that compared the effects of concurrent interference on "hippocampal" tests with those on "frontal" tests. The tests were administered either without interference or with interference at study, at test, or on both occasions. The interfering task was sequential tapping of the fingers in the order index, ring, middle, and small.

The tests we chose were Craik and Birtwistle's (1971) version of release from proactive inhibition and the California Verbal Learning Test (CVLT) (see Moscovitch, 1992a, 1992b, in press, for details). Concurrent interference at study and test, but at neither alone, had the predicted effect on both tests: failure to release from proactive inhibition and lower recall and clustering on all the trials on the CVLT (figures 2 and 3). Not affected by interference were the number of words recalled on the first trial in release from proactive inhibition and the improvement with repetition on the CVLT, both of which are presumed to depend on intact hippocampal functions.

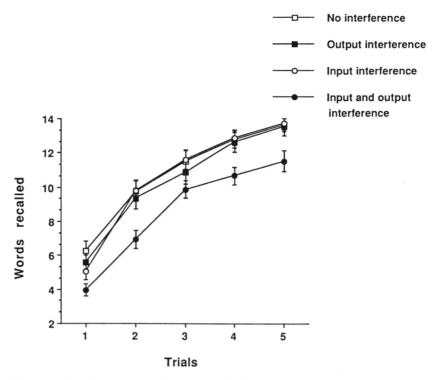

Figure 3 Recall of categorized lists. The graph shows number of words that college students recalled per trial in various interference conditions from categorized lists of the California Verbal Learning Test.

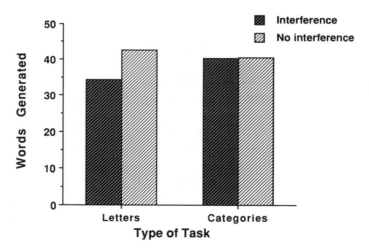

Figure 4 The average number of words subjects generated in 1 minute in a letter (phonemic) and category fluency task with, and without, a concurrent interfering task.

Because the frontal lobes are central-system structures, it was expected that concurrent interference would also affect performance on frontal tests in other domains. As predicted, sequential finger tapping led to a reduction of about 25 percent on a semantic memory test, letter fluency, which is sensitive to left frontal damage, but to less than a 5 percent reduction on category fluency, which is more sensitive to left temporal damage (figure 4).

Although other interpretations of the concurrent-interference studies are possible, the results are encouraging and support the hypothesis that strategic retrieval processes mediated by the frontal lobes are resource-demanding, whereas ecphoric hippocampal processes require less effort by comparison.

5 CONCLUSIONS

A major portion of this chapter was devoted to identifying the components involved in memory and remembering. Dissociation experiments on neurological patients and on normal people provided the main source of evidence for isolating the components and understanding their function. Given my emphasis on dissociations, it is easy to lose sight of the fact that these components, though isolable in principle, are typically highly interrelated. The function of the components is determined not only by their internal organization but also by their network of connections to other components. The interrelatedness of the various components specified in the model helps explain why memory tests (and memory in real-life situations) are not likely to be process (or component) pure when administered to people who are neurologically intact. Performance will depend on the interplay of components and the processes they mediate. By specifying the processes mediated by the various components, the information they represent, and some of the interactions possible among them, I hope that the neuropsychological model I proposed will prove useful in analyzing memory at both the structural and process level in people with normal or impaired memory.

ACKNOWLEDGMENTS

This work benefitted a great deal from many discussions with colleagues and students, and from their papers. I thank Marlene Behrmann, Gus Craik, Jonathan Gottstein, Stephan Hamann, Larry Jacoby, Margaret Keane, Brenda Milner, Lynn Nadel, Paul Rozin, Dan Schacter, Ann Triesman, Endel Tulving, Carlo Umiltà, Ellen Vriezen, and Gordon Winocur. Of these, Umiltà's and Winocur's influence was most extensive, as my references to our collaborative efforts attest. I want also to single out Brenda Milner for special thanks. She may be surprised (I hope pleasantly) to learn that she contributed more than she was aware to the ideas that informed this theoretical paper. Twenty years of conversation have had their effect. Preparation of this paper and some of the work reported in it was supported by grants from the Medical Research Council of Canada, the Natural Science and Engineering Research Council of Canada, and by a Research Associateship from the Ontario Mental Health Foundation.

REFERENCES

Baddeley, A. D. (1986). *Working memory.* Oxford: Oxford University Press.

Baddeley, A. D. (1992). Working memory: The interface between memory and cognition. *Journal of Cognitive Neuroscience, 4,* 281–288.

Baddeley, A. D., & Warrington, E. K. (1970). Amnesia and the distinction between long- and short-term memory. *Journal of Verbal Learning and Verbal Behavior, 9,* 176–189.

Bauer, R. M. (1984). Autonomic recognition of names and faces in prosopagnosia: A neuropsychological application of the guilty-knowledge test. *Neuropsychologia, 22,* 457–469.

Behrmann, M., Winocur, G., & Moscovitch, M. (1992). Dissociation between mental imagery and object recognition in a brain-damaged patient. *Nature, 359,* 636–637.

Bentin, S., & Moscovitch, M. (1988). The time course of repetition effects for words and unfamiliar faces. *Journal of Experiemental Psychology: General, 117,* 148–160.

Biederman, I., & Cooper, E. E. (1991). Evidence for complete translational and reflectional invariance in visual object priming. *Perception, 20,* 585–593.

Biederman, I., & Cooper, E. E. (1992). Size invariance in visual-object priming. *Journal of Experimental Psychology: Human Perception and Performance, 18,* 121–133.

Blaxton, T. A. (1989). Investigating dissociations among memory measures: Support for a transfer appropriate processing framework. *Journal of Experimental Psychology: Learning, Memory, and Cognition, 15,* 657–668.

Blaxton, T. A. (1992). Dissociations among memory measures in both normal and memory impaired subjects: Evidence for a processing account of memory. *Memory and Cognition, 20,* 549–562.

Bonke, B., Fitch, W., & Millar, K. (Eds.) (1990). *Memory and awareness in anaesthesia.* Amsterdam: Swets and Zeitlinger.

Bowers, J. S., & Schacter, D. L. (1990). Implicit memory and awareness. *Journal of Experimental Psychology: Learning, Memory, and Cognition, 16,* 404–416.

Bruce, V., & Young, A. (1986). Understanding face recognition. *British Journal of Psychology, 77,* 305–327.

Bruyer, R. (1991). Covert face recognition in prosopagnosia: A review. *Brain and Cognition, 15,* 223–235.

Butters, N., Heindel, W. C., & Salmon, D. P. (1990). Dissociation of implicit memory in dementia: Neurological implications. *Bulletin of the Psychonomic Society, 28,* 359–366.

Campbell, R., Landis, T., & Regard, M. (1986). Face recognition and lip reading: A neuropsychological dissociation. *Brain, 109,* 509–521.

Carr, T. H., Brown, J. S., & Charalambous, A. (1989). Repetition and reading: Perceptual encoding mechanisms are very abstract but not very interactive. *Journal of Experimental Psychology: Learning, Memory, and Cognition, 15,* 763–779.

Cermak, L. S. (1982). The long and short of it in amnesia. In L. S. Cermak (Ed.), *Human memory and amnesia.* Hillsdale, NJ: Erlbaum.

Cermak, L. S., Bleich, R. P., & Blackford, M. (1988). Deficits in the implicit retention of new associations by alcoholic Korsakoff patients. *Brain and Cognition, 7,* 145–156.

Cermak, L. S., & Reale, L. (1978). Depth of processing and retention of words by alcoholic Korsakoff patients. *Journal of Experimental Psychology: Human Learning and Memory, 4,* 165–174.

Challis, B. H., & Sidhu, R. (1993). Massed repetition has a dissociative effect on implicit and explicit measures of memory. *Journal of Experimental Psychology: Learning, Memory, and Cognition, 19*, 115–127.

Charness, N., Milberg, W., & Alexander, M. (1988). Teaching an amnesic a complex cognitive skill. *Brain and Cognition, 8*, 253–272.

Chertkow, H., & Bub, D. (1990). Semantic memory loss in dementia of the Alzheimer type. In M. F. Schwartz (Ed.) *Modular deficits in dementia*. Cambridge: MIT Press.

Cohen, N. J. (1984). Preserved learning capacity in amnesia: Evidence for multiple memory systems. In L. R. Squire & N. Butters (Eds.), *Neuropsychology of memory* (pp. 83–103). New York: Guilford Press.

Coltheart, M. (1980). Deep dyslexia: A right hemispheric hypothesis. In M. Coltheart, K. Patterson, & J. C. Marshall (Eds.), *Deep dyslexia*. London: Routledge and Kegan Paul.

Cooper, E. E., Biederman, I., & Hummel, J. E. (1992). Metric invariance in object recognition. A review and further evidence. *Canadian Journal of Psychology, 46*, 191–214.

Cooper, L. A., Schacter, D. L., Ballesteros, S., & Moore, C. (1992). Priming and recognition of transformed three dimensional objects: Effects of size and reflectance. *Journal of Experimental Psychology: Learning, Memory, and Cognition, 18*, 43–57.

Corkin, S. (1968). Acquisition of motor skill after bilateral medial temporal-lobe excision. *Neuropsychologia, 6*, 255–266.

Coslett, B., & Saffran, E. M. (1989). Evidence of preserved reading in pure alexia. *Brain, 112*, 327–359.

Craik, F. I. M., & Birtwistle, J. (1971). Proactive inhibition in free recall. *Journal of Experimental Psychology, 91*, 120–123.

Craik, F. I. M. & Lockhart, R. S. (1972). Levels of processing: A framework for memory research. *Journal of Verbal Learning and Verbal Behavior, 11*, 671–684.

De Haan, E. H. F., Bauer, R. N., & Greve, K. W. (1992). Behavioral and physiological evidence for covert face recognition in a prosopragnosic patient. *Cortex, 28*, 77–96.

De Hann, E. H. F., Young, A., & Newcombe, F. (1987). Face recognition without awareness. *Cognitive Neuropsychology, 4*, 385–415.

Delbecq-Derouesné, J., Beauvois, M. F., & Shallice, T. (1990). Preserved recall versus impaired recognition: A case study. *Brain, 113*, 1045–1074.

DeRenzi, E. (1982). *Disorders of space exploration and cognition*. New York: John Wiley and Sons.

Eich, E. (1984). Memory for unattended events: Remembering with and without awareness. *Memory and Cognition, 12*, 105–111.

Eichenbaum, H. (1992). The hippocampal system and declarative memory in animals. *Journal of Cognitive Neuroscience, 4*, 217–231.

Farah, M. J. (1994). Visual perception and visual awareness after brain damage: A tutorial overview. In C. Umiltà and M. Moscovitch (Eds.) *Attention and performance*, vol. 15, *Conscious and nonconscious information processing*. Cambridge: MIT Press.

Fodor, J. (1983). *The modularity of mind*. Cambridge: MIT Press.

Gardner, H., Boller, F., Moreines, J., & Butters, N. (1973). Retrieving information from Korsakoff patients: Effects of categorical cues and reference to the task. *Cortex, 9*, 165–175.

Glisky, E. L., Schacter, D. L., & Tulving, E. (1986). Computer learning by memory-impaired patients: Acquisition and retention of complex knowledge. *Neuropsychologia, 24*, 313–328.

Godbout, L., & Doyon, J. (1992). Schematic representations of knowledge after frontal or posterior lesions. Paper presented at the Canadian Society for Brain, Behaviour, and Cognitive Science, Laval University, Quebec City, Canada.

Goldman-Rakic, P. S. (1987). Circuitry of primate prefrontal cortex and regulation of behavior by representational memory. In F. Plum (Ed.), *Handbook of physiology—The nervous system* (Vol. 5). Bethesda, MD: American Physiological Society.

Goshen-Gottstein, Y., & Moscovitch, M. (1992). *Repetition priming effects for newly-formed and pre-existing associations.* Paper presented at the Psychonomic Society, St. Louis, MO.

Graf, P., & Schacter, D. L. (1985). Implicit and explicit memory for new associations in normal and amnesic subjects. *Journal of Experimental Psychology: Learning, Memory, and Cognition, 11,* 501–518.

Graf, P., & Schacter, D. L. (1987). Selective effects of interference on implicit and explicit memory for new associations. *Journal of Experimental Psychology: Learning, Memory, and Cognition, 13,* 45–53.

Graf, P., Shimamura, A. P., & Squire, L. R. (1985). Priming across modalities and priming across category levels: Extending the domain of preserved functioning in amnesia. *Journal of Experimental Psychology: Learning Memory and Cognition, 11,* 385–395.

Graf, P., Squire, L. R., & Mandler, G. (1984). The information that amnesic patients do not forget. *Journal of Experimental Psychology: Learning, Memory, and Cognition, 10,* 164–178.

Greve, K. W., & Bauer, R. M. (1990). Implicit learning of new faces in prosopagnoisa: An application of the mere-exposure paradigm. *Neuropsychologia, 28,* 1035–1042.

Habib, M., & Sirigu, A. (1987). Pure topographical disorientation: A definition and anatomical basis. *Cortex, 23,* 73–85.

Hayman, C. A. G., & Tulving, E. (1989). Contingent dissociation between recognition and fragment completion: The method of triangulation. *Journal of Experimental Psychology: Learning, Memory, and Cognition, 15,* 228–240.

Howard, D. V., Fry, A. F. & Brune, C. M. (1991). Aging and memory for new associations: Direct versus indirect measures. *Journal of Experimental Psychology: Learning, Memory, and Cognition, 17,* 779–792.

Incissa della Rochetta, A. (1986). Classification and recall of pictures after unilateral frontal or temporal lobectomy. *Cortex, 22,* 189–211.

Jacoby, L. L. (1983). Perceptual enhancement: Persistent effects of an experience. *Journal of Experimental Psychology: Learning, Memory, and Cognition, 9,* 21–38.

Jacoby, L. L. (1991). A process dissociation framework: Separating automatic and intentional uses of memory. *Journal of Memory and Language, 30,* 513–541.

Jacoby, L. L., Woloshyn, V., & Kelley, C. M. (1989). Becoming famous without being recognized: Unconscious influences of memory produced by dividing attention. *Journal of Experimental Psychology: General, 118,* 115–125.

Johnson, M. K. (1992). MEM: Mechanisms of recollection. *Journal of Cognitive Neuroscience, 4,* 268–280.

Jolicoeur, P. (1985). The time to name disoriented natural objects. *Memory and Cognition, 13,* 289–303.

Jolicoeur, P., & Milliken, B. (1989). Identification of disorientated objects: Effects of context of prior presentation. *Journal of Experimental Psychology: Learning, Memory, and Cognition, 15,* 200–210.

Joyce, E. M. & Robbins, T. W. (1991). Frontal lobe function in Korsakoff and non-Korsakoff alcoholics: planning and spatial working memory. *Neuropsychologia, 29*, 709–724.

Kihlstrom, J. F., & Couture, L. J. (1992). Awareness and information processing in general anaesthesia. *Journal of Psychopharmacology, 6*, 410–417.

Kihlstrom, J. F., Schacter, D. L., Cork, R. C., Hurt, C. A., & Behr, S. E. (1990). Implicit memory following surgical anaesthesia. *Psychological Science, 1*, 303–306.

Kinoshita, S., & Wayland, S. V. (1993). Effects of surface features on word fragment completion on amnesic subjects. *American Journal of Psychology, 106*, 67–80.

Kinsbourne, M. & Wood, F. (1975). Short-term memory processes and the amnesic syndrome. In D. Deutsch & J. A. Deutsch (Eds.), *Short-term memory.* New York: Academic Press.

Kirsner, K., & Dunn, D. (1985). The perceptual record: A common factor in repetition priming and attribute retention. In M. I. Posner & O. S. M. Marin (Eds.), *Attention and Performance* (vol. 11, pp. 547–566). Hillsdale, NJ: Lawrence Erlbaum.

Kohn, S. E., & Friedman, R. B. (1986). Word-meaning deafness: A phonological-semantic dissociation. *Cognitive Neuropsychology, 3*, 291–308.

Kolb, B., & Milner, B. (1981). Performance of complex arm and facial movements after focal brain lesions. *Neuropsychologia, 19*, 505–514.

Kopelman, M. D. (1989). Remote and autobiographical memory, temporal context memory, and frontal atrophy in Korsakoff and Alzheimer patients. *Neuropsychologia, 27*, 437–460.

Lewandowsky, S., Kirsner, K., & Bainbridge, V. (1989). Context effects in implicit memory: A sense-specific account. In S. Lewandowsky, J. C. Dunn, & K. Kirsner (Eds.) *Implicit memory: Theoretical issues.* Hillsdale, NJ: Erlbaum.

Liberman, A. M., & Mattingly, I. G. (1989). A specialization for speech perception. *Science, 243*, 489–494.

Light, L. L., & LaVoie, D. (1993). Direct and indirect measures of memory in old age. In M E. J. Masson, & P. Graf (Eds.), *Implicit memory: New directions in cognition, development, and neuropsychology.* Hillsdale, NJ: Erlbaum.

Lissauer, H. (1890). Ein Fallvon Seelenblindheit nebsteinem Beitrag zur Theoric derselben. *Archiv für Psychiatrie, 21*, 222–270. (English translation: M. Jackson (1988), Lissauer on agosia. *Cognitive Neuropsychology, 5*, 155–192).

Lynch, G., & Granger, R. (1992). Variations in synaptic plasticity and types of memory in corticohippocampal networks. *Journal of Cognitive Neuroscience, 4*, 189–199.

McAndrews, M. P., Glisky, E. L., & Schacter, D. L. (1987). When priming persists: Long-lasting implicit memory for a single episode in amnesic patients. *Neuropsychologia, 25*, 497–506.

McAndrews, M. P., & Moscovitch, M. (1990). Transfer effects in implicit tests of memory. *Journal of Experimental Psychology: Learning, Memory, and Cognition, 16*, 772–788.

McCarthy, R. A., & Warrington, E. K. (1990). *Cognitive neuropsychology: A clinical introduction.* New York: Academic Press.

McGurk, H., & MacDonald, J. (1976). Hearing lips and seeing voices. *Nature, 264*, 746–748.

Marsolek, C. J., Kosslyn, S. M., & Squire, L. R. (1992). Form specific visual priming in the right cerebral hemisphere. *Journal of Experimental Psychology: Learning, Memory, and Cognition, 18*, 492–508.

Mayes, A. R. (1988). *Human organic memory disorders.* Cambridge: Cambridge University Press.

Mayes, A. R., & Gooding, P. (1989). Enhancement of word completion priming in amnesics by cueing with previously novel associates. *Neuropsychologia, 27,* 1057–1872.

Mayes, A. R., Pickering, A. D., & Fairbairn, A. (1987). Amnesic sensitivity to proactive interference: Its relationship to priming and the causes of amnesia. *Neuropsychologia, 25,* 211–220.

Merikle, P. M., & Reingold, E. M. (1991). Comparing direct (explicit) and indirect (implicit) measures to study unconscious memory. *Journal of Experimental Psychology: Learning, Memory, and Cognition, 17,* 224–233.

Metcalfe, J., Cottrell, G. W., & Mencel, W. E. (1992). Cognitive binding: A computational-modeling analysis of a distinction between implicit and explicit memory. *Journal of Cognitive Neuroscience, 4,* 289–298.

Milner, B. (1964). Some effects of frontal lobectomy in man. In J. M. Warren and K. Akert (Eds.), *The frontal granular cortex and behavior* (pp. 313–331). New York: McGraw-Hill.

Milner, B. (1966). Amnesia following operation on the temporal lobe. In C. W. M. Whitty and O. L. Zangwill (Eds.) *Amnesia.* London: Butterworth.

Milner, P. (1970). *Physiological psychology.* New York: Holt, Rinehart, and Winston.

Milner, B. (1974). Hemispheric specialization: Scope and limits. In F. Schmitt & F. Worden (Eds.) *The Neurosciences: Third Study Program.* Cambridge: MIT Press.

Milner, B., Petrides, M., & Smith, M. L. (1985). Frontal lobes and the temporal organization of memory. *Human Neurobiology, 4,* 137–142.

Mishkin, M., & Appenzeler, T. (1987). The anatomy of memory. *Scientific American, 256,* 80–89.

Moscovitch, M. (1976). On the representation of language in the right hemisphere of right-handed people. *Brain and Language, 3,* 47–71.

Moscovitch, M. (1981). Right-hemisphere language. *Topics in Language Disorders, 1,* 41–61.

Moscovitch, M. (1982). Multiple dissociations of function in amnesia. In L. S. Cermak (Ed.), *Human memory and amnesia.* Hillsdale, NJ: Lawrence Erlbaum.

Moscovitch, M. (1984). The sufficient conditions for demonstrating preserved memory in amnesia: A task analysis. In N. Butters & L. R. Squire (Eds.), *The neuropsychology of memory.* New York: Guildford Press.

Moscovitch, M. (1989). Confabulation and the frontal system: Strategic vs. associative retrieval in neuropsychological theories of memory. In H. L. Roediger III & F. I. M. Craik (Eds.), *Varieties of memory and consciousness: Essays in honor of Endel Tulving.* Hillsdale, NJ: Lawrence Erlbaum.

Moscovitch, M. (1992a). Memory and working-with-memory: A component process model based on modules and central systems. *Journal of Cognitive Neuroscience, 4,* 257–267.

Moscovitch, M. (1992b). A neuropsychological model of memory and consciousness. In L. R. Squire & N. Butters (Eds.) *The neuropsychology of memory* (2nd ed.). New York: Guilford Press.

Moscovitch, M. (1994). Models of consciousness and memory. In M. S. Gazzaniga et al. (Eds.), *The cognitive neurosciences.* Cambridge, MA: MIT Press.

Moscovitch, M. (in press). The effects of concurrent interference on retrieval from memory: The role of the frontal and medial temporal lobes. *Neuropsychology.*

Moscovitch, M., Goshen-Gottstein, Y., & Vriezen, E. (1994). Memory without conscious recollection: A tutorial review from a neuropsychological perspective. In C. Umiltà & M. Moscovitch (Eds.) *Attention and Performance,* vol. 15, *Conscious and nonconscious information processing.* Cambridge: MIT Press.

Moscovitch, M., & Bentin, S. (1993). The fate of repetition effects when recognition approaches chance. *Journal of Experimental Psychology: Learning, Memory, and Cognition, 19,* 148–158.

Moscovitch, M., & Craik, F. I. M. (1976). Depth of processing, retrieval cues, and uniqueness of encoding as factors in recall. *Journal of Verbal Learning and Verbal Behavior, 15,* 447–458.

Moscovitch, M., Osimani, A., Wortzman, G., & Freedman, M. (1990). The dorsomedial nucleus of the thalamus, frontal-lobe function, and memory: A case report. *Journal of Clinical and Experimental Neuropsychology, 12,* 87. (Abstract.)

Moscovitch, M., & Umiltà, C. (1990). Modularity and neuropsychology: Implications for the organization of attention and memory in normal and brain-damaged people. In M. E. Schwartz (Ed.), *Modular processes in dementia.* Cambridge: MIT Press.

Moscovitch, M., & Umiltà, C. (1991). Conscious and nonconscious aspects of memory: A neuropsychological framework of modules and central systems. In R. G. Lister & H. J. Weingartner (Eds.), *Perspectives in Cognitive Neuroscience.* Oxford: Oxford University Press.

Moscovitch, M., Vriezen, E., & Goshen-Gottstein, Y. (1993). Implicit tests of memory in patients with focal lesions and degenerative brain disorders. In H. Spinnler & F. Boller (Eds.) *Handbook of Neuropsychology* (Vol. 8). Amsterdam: Elsevier.

Moscovitch, M., & Winocur, G. (1992a). The neuropsychology of memory and aging. In T. A. Salthouse and F. I. M. Craik (Eds.) *The handbook of aging and cognition.* Hillsdale, NJ: Erlbaum.

Moscovitch, M., & Winocur, G. (1992b). Frontal lobes and memory. In L. R. Squire (Ed.) *The encyclopedia of learning and memory: Neuropsychology.* New York: Macmillan and Co.

Moscovitch, M., Winocur, G., & McLachlan, D. (1986). Memory as assessed by recognition and reading time in normal and memory impaired people with Alzheimer's disease and other neurological disorders. *Journal of Experimental Psychology: General, 115,* 331–347.

Musen, G., & Squire, L. R. (1991). Normal acquisition of novel information in amnesia. *Journal of Experimental Psychology: Learning, Memory, and Cognition, 17,* 1095–1104.

Musen, G., & Squire, L. R. (1993). On the implicit learning of novel associations by amnesic patients and normal subjects. *Neuropsychology, 7,* 119–135.

Nadel, L. (1992). Multiple memory systems: What and why. *Journal of Cognitive Neuroscience, 4,* 179–188.

Newcombe, F., Young, A. W., & de Haan, E. H. F. (1989). Prosopagnosia and object agnosia without covert recognition. *Neuropsychologia, 27,* 179–191.

Nissen, M. J., Willingham, D., & Hartman, M. (1989). Explicit and implicit remembering: When is learning preserved in amnesia? *Neuropsychologia, 27,* 341–352.

O'Keefe, J. (1985). Is consciousness the gateway to the hippocampal cognitive map: A speculative essay on the neural basis of mind. In D. Oakley (Ed.), *Brain and mind.* London: Methuen.

O'Keefe, J., & Nadel, L. (1978). *The hippocampus as a cognitive map.* Oxford: Clarendon Press.

Olton, D. S., Becker, J. T., & Handelman, G. E. (1979). Hippocampus, space, and memory. *Behavioral and Brain Sciences, 2,* 313–365.

Olton, D. S., & Shapiro, M. L. (1992). Mnemonic dissociations: The powers of parameters. *Journal of Cognitive Neuroscience, 4,* 200–207.

Packard, M. G. & White, N. M. (1991). Dissociation of hippocampus and caudate nucleus memory systems by post-training intracerebral injection of dopamine agonists. *Behavioral Neuroscience, 105,* 73–84.

Pandya, D., & Barnes, C. L. (1987). Architecture and connections of the frontal lobe. In E. Perecman (Ed.), *The frontal lobes revisited*. New York: IRBN Press.

Parkin, A. J., Dunn, J. C., Lee, C., O'Hara, P. F., & Nussbaum, L. (1993). Neuropsychological sequelae of Wernicke's encephalopathy in a 20-year-old woman: Selective impairment of a frontal memory system. *Brain and Cognition, 21*, 1−19.

Parkin, A. J., Leng, N. R. C., Stanhope, N., & Smith, A. P. (1988). Memory loss following ruptured aneurysm of the anterior communicating artery. *Brain and Cognition, 7*, 231−243.

Parkin, A. J., Reid, T., & Russo, R. (1990). On the differential nature of implicit and explicit memory. *Memory and Cognition, 18*, 307−314.

Patterson, K., Vargha-Khadem, F., & Polkey, C. E. (1989). Reading with one hemisphere. *Brain, 112*, 39−63.

Petrides, M. (1989). Frontal lobes and memory. In F. Boller and J. Grafman (Eds.), *Handbook of neuropsychology* (Vol. 3). North Holland: Elsevier Science Publishers B.V. (Biomedical Division).

Pigott, S., & Milner, B. (1993). Memory for different aspects of complex visual scenes after unilateral temporal- or frontal-lobe resection. *Neuropsychologia, 31*, 1−16.

Rabinowicz, B., & Moscovitch, M. (1984). Evidence for right hemisphere language. *Cognitive Neuropsychology, 1*, 343−350.

Riddoch, M. J., & Humphreys, G. W. (1987). Visual object processing in optic aphasia: A case of semantic access agnosia. *Cognitive Neuropsychology, 4*, 131−186.

Roediger, H. L. (1990). Implicit memory: Retention without remembering. *American Psychologist, 45*, 1043−1056.

Roediger, H. L., & McDermott, K. B. (1993). Implicit memory in normal human subjects. In H. Spinnler & F. Boller (Eds.), *Handbook of neuropsychology* (Vol. 8). Amsterdam: Elsevier.

Rudy, J. W., & Sutherland, R. J. (1992). Configural and elemental associations and the memory coherence problem. *Journal of Cognitive Neuroscience, 4*, 208−216.

Rueckl, J. G. (1990). Similarity effects in word and pseudoword repetition priming. *Journal of Experimental Psychology: Learning, Memory, and Cognition, 16*, 374−391.

Saffran, E. M., & Marin, O. S. M. (1977). Reading without phonology: Evidence from aphasia. *Quarterly Journal Experimental Psychology, 29*, 515−525.

Saint-Cyr, J. A., Taylor, A., & Lang, A. (1988). Procedural learning and neostriatal dysfunction in man. *Brain, 111*, 941−959.

Schacter, D. L. (1987). Memory, amnesia, and frontal lobe dysfunction. *Psychology, 15*, 21−36.

Schacter, D. L. (1992). Priming and multiple memory systems: Perceptual mechanisms of implicit memory. *Journal of Cognitive Neuroscience, 4*, 244−256.

Schacter, D. L., Cooper, L. A., Delaney, S. M., Peterson, M. A., & Tharan, M. (1991). Implicit memory for possible and impossible objects: constraints on the construction of structural descriptions. *Journal of Experimental Psychology: Learning, Memory, and Cognition, 17*, 3−19.

Schacter, D. L., Eich, J. E., & Tulving, E. (1978). Richard Semon's theory of memory. *Journal of Verbal Learning and Verbal Behavior, 17*, 721−743.

Schacter, D. L., & Graf, P. (1986). Preserved learning in amnesic patients: Perspectives on research from direct priming. *Journal of Clinical Experimental Neuropsychology, 8*, 727−743.

Schacter, D. L., McAndrews, M. P., & Moscovitch, M. (1988). Access to consciousness: Dissociations between implicit and explicit knowledge in neuropsychological syndromes. In L. Weiskrantz (Ed.) *Thought without language*. Oxford: Oxford University Press.

Schacter, D. L., Rapcsak, S., Rubens, A. B., Tharan, M., & Laguna, J. (1990). Priming effects in a letter-by-letter reader depend upon access to the word form system. *Neuropsychologia, 28,* 1079–1094.

Schwartz, B. L. & Hashtroudi, S. (1991). Priming is independent of skill learning. *Journal of Experimental Psychology: Learning, Memory, and Cognition, 17,* 1177–1188.

Schwartz, M. F. Saffran, E. M., & Marin, O. S. M. (1980). Fractionating the reading process in dementia: Evidence for word-specific print-to-sound associations. In M. Coltheart, K. E. Patterson, & J. C. Marschall (Eds.), *Deep dyslexia.* London: Routledge and Kegan Paul.

Sergent, J., & Signoret, J.-L. (1992). Functional and anatomical decomposition of face processing: Evidence from prosopagnosia and PET study of normal subjects. *Philosophical Transactions of the Royal Society of London, B335,* 55–62.

Shallice, T. (1982). Specific impairments of planning. *Philosophical Transactions of the Royal Society of London, B298,* 199–209.

Shimamura, A. P. (1986). Priming effects in amnesia: Evidence for a dissociable memory function. *Quarterly Journal of Experimental Psychology, 38A,* 619–644.

Shimamura, A. P., Janowsky, J. S., & Squire, L. R. (1991). What is the role of frontal lobe damage in memory disorders? In H. D. Levin, H. M. Eisenberg, & A. L. Benton (Eds.), *Frontal lobe functioning and dysfunction* (pp. 173–195). New York: Oxford University Press.

Shimamura, A. P., & Squire, L. R. (1989). Impaired priming of new associations in amnesia. *Journal of Experimental Psychology: Learning, Memory, and Cognition, 15,* 721–728.

Smith, M. L. (1989). Memory disorders associated with temporal-lobe lesion. In L. R. Squire (Ed.) *Handbook of Neuropsychology* (Vol. 3). Amsterdam: Elsevier.

Smith, M. L., & Milner, B. (1981). The role of the right hippocampus in the recall of spatial location. *Neuropsychologia, 19,* 781–795.

Smith, M. L., & Milner, B. (1989). Right hippocampal impairment in the recall of spatial location: Encoding deficit or rapid forgetting? *Neuropsychologia, 27,* 71–81.

Snodgrass, J. G. (1989). Sources of learning in the picture fragment completion task. In S. Lewandowsky, J. C. Dunn, & K. Kirsner (Eds.), *Implicit memory: Theoretical issues.* Hillsdale, NJ: Erlbaum.

Snodgrass, J. G., & Feenan, K. (1990). Priming effects in picture fragment completion: Support for the perceptual closure hypothesis. *Journal of Experimental Psychology: General, 119,* 276–296.

Squire, L. R. (1987). *Memory and brain.* New York: Oxford University Press.

Squire, L. R. (1992). Declarative and nondeclarative memory: Multiple brain systems supporting learning and memory. *Journal of Cognitive Neuroscience, 4,* 232–243.

Squire, L. R., & Cohen, N. (1982). Remote memory, retrograde amnesia, and the neuropsychology of memory. In L. S. Cermak (Ed.), *Human memory and amnesia* (pp. 275–303). Hillsdale, NJ: Erlbaum.

Squire, L. R., Ojemann, J., Miezin, F., Petersen, S., Videen, T., & Raichle, M. (1992). Activation of the hippocampus in normal humans: A functional anatomical study of memory. *Proceedings of the National Academy of Sciences, 89,* 1837–1841.

Srinivas, K. (1993). Perceptual specificity in nonverbal priming. *Journal of Experimental Psychology: Learning, Memory, and Cognition, 19,* 582–602.

Stuss, D. T. & Benson, D. F. (1986). The frontal lobes. New York: Raven Press.

Teyler, T. J., & Di Scenna, P. (1986). The hippocampal memory indexing theory. *Behavioral Neuroscience, 100,* 147–154.

Tranel, D., & Damasio, A. R. (1985). Knowledge without awareness: An automatic index of facial recognition by prosopagnosics. *Science, 228,* 1453–1454.

Tulving, E. (1983). *Elements of episodic memory.* Oxford: Oxford University Press.

Tulving, E., & Colotla, V. (1970). Free recall of trilingual lists. *Cognitive Psychology, 1,* 86–98.

Tulving, E., Hayman, C. A. G., & Macdonald, C. (1991). Long-lasting perceptual priming and semantic learning in amnesia: A case experiment. *Journal of Experimental Psychology: Learning, Memory, and Cognition, 17,* 595–617.

Tulving, E., & Schacter, D. L. (1990). Priming and human memory systems. *Science, 247,* 301–306.

Van Der Linden, M., & Seron, X. (1987). In P. Ellen & C. Thinus-Blanc (Eds.), *Cognitive processes and spatial orientation in animal and man.* Dordrecht: Martinus Nijhof Publications.

Vriezen, E., & Moscovitch, M. (1990). Temporal ordering and conditional associative learning in Parkinson's disease. *Neuropsychologia, 28,* 1283–1294.

Warrington, E. K., & Shallice, T. (1980). Word-form dyslexia. *Brain, 30,* 99–112.

Warrington, E. K., & Taylor, A. M. (1978). Two categorical stages of object recognition. *Perception, 7,* 695–705.

Winocur, G. (1990). Anterograde and retrograde amnesia in rats with dorsal hippocampal or dorsomedial thalamic lesions. *Behavioral Brain Research, 38,* 145–154.

Winocur, G., & Moscovitch, M. (in press). The effects of unilateral temporal and frontal lobe lesions on *A-B, A-C* learning: Evidence of heightened interference in conceptual repetition priming. *Brain and Cognition.*

Winocur, G., & Weiskrantz, L. (1976). An investigation of paired-associate learning in amnesic patients. *Neuropsychologia, 14,* 97–110.

Witherspoon, D., & Allen, L. G. (1985). The effects of prior presentation on temporal judgments in a perceptual identification task. *Memory and Cognition, 13,* 101–111.

Witherspoon, D., & Moscovitch, M. (1989). Independence of the repetition effects between word fragment completion and perceptual identification. *Journal of Experimental Psychology: Learning, Memory, and Cognition, 15,* 22–30.

Young, A. (1994). Conscious and nonconscious recognition of familiar faces. In C. Umiltà & M. Moscovitch (Eds.) *Attention and performance,* vol. 5, *Conscious and nonconscious information processing.* Cambridge: MIT Press.

Zaidel, E. (1985). Language in the right hemisphere. In D. F. Benson & E. Zaidel (Eds.), *The dual brain: Hemispheric specialization in humans* (pp. 205–231). New York: Guildford Press.

Zaidel, E., & Peters, A. M. (1981). Phonologic encoding and ideographic reading by the disconnected right hemisphere: Two case studies. *Brain and Language, 14,* 205–234.

Zola-Morgan, S. M., & Squire, L. R. (1990). The primate hippocampal formation: Evidence for a time-limited role in memory storage. *Science, 250,* 288–290.

10 Binding Complex Memories: The Role of Reactivation and the Hippocampus

Marcia K. Johnson and Barbara L. Chalfonte

We briefly outline a general cognitive framework called a multiple-entry, modular memory system (MEM). MEM is an attempt to sketch a cognitive architecture that takes into account the wide range of functions memory serves (Johnson, 1983). MEM is one way of summarizing many of the findings and theoretical ideas about attention, perception, and memory that have been generated over the last 100 years of empirical research. As the framework has evolved, we have found it increasingly useful for thinking about many fundamental issues in cognition including dissociations among memory measures (Johnson, 1983), amnesia (Johnson, 1983, 1990, 1991; Johnson & Hirst, 1991, 1993), confabulation (Johnson, 1991), source monitoring (Johnson, Hashtroudi, & Lindsay, 1993), the relation between memory and emotion (Johnson & Multhaup, 1992), and aspects of consciousness (Johnson & Reeder, in press).

This chapter and Johnson (1992) explore in some detail a particular component process of the MEM framework: *reactivation*. We set for ourselves a simple exercise: what might be the consequences for learning and memory of disruption in this one component process of MEM? We argue that reactivation is critical for binding together aspects of complex memories and for maintaining complex memories over time. Furthermore, we consider evidence implicating the hippocampus (and/or related structures) in this central cognitive function.[1] Although not all component processes of MEM are represented in all species (indeed, MEM provides some preliminary hypotheses about the evolution of subsystems; see Johnson & Hirst, 1993), we assume that reactivation is normally operative in rodents as well as humans and other primates. Thus we consider the potential role of reactivation in understanding not only findings from human amnesics but also findings from controlled lesion studies with animals.

We compare and contrast an impairment in reactivation with other explanations of memory deficits (see the articles in the July 1992 issue of *Journal of Cognitive Neuroscience*). We emphasize that reactivation is a component in a process analysis of memory function, and we compare subsystems defined in terms of processes with alternative subsystem accounts of memory. Finally, we consider some general conceptual issues raised by efforts to define subsystems of memory. Among other things, we suggest that any particular subsystem involves a number of structures and circuits and that an architecture in which subsystems interact reflects a balance between efficiency and flexibility.

1 THE MULTIPLE-ENTRY, MODULAR MEMORY SYSTEM AND REACTIVATION

We begin with an overview of MEM (Johnson, 1990, 1992; Johnson & Hirst, 1993). We then more specifically identify the role of *reactivation* within MEM.

1.1 The Multiple-Entry, Modular Memory System

Memory is a record of the operations of cognitive processes. Different environmental demands and personal goals recruit combinations of these component cognitive processes, which results in such diverse memory phemonena as classical conditioning and autobiographical recall. A useful architecture of memory would specify the nature of the component processes underlying memory and the relations among them. We have proposed one such architecture, a multiple-entry, modular memory system, or MEM (Johnson, 1983, 1990, 1991; Johnson & Hirst, 1991, 1993; Johnson & Multhaup, 1992). Within MEM, component processes are organized into subsystems, which gives memory a modular quality. Here, "modularity" is not used in the same sense of "modularity" proposed by Fodor (1983) and adopted by others (e.g., Moscovitch & Umiltà, 1990; Schacter, 1989); that is, the subsystems in MEM are not "encapsulated." MEM's organization permits subsystems to work independently but allows interactions among them as well.

MEM's subsystems reflect a number of fundamental distinctions among types of cognitive processes. First is the distinction between processes initiated by perceptual stimuli and processes that are more centrally generated. This distinction between what we call "perception" and "reflection" arises repeatedly in theoretical discussions of memory and cognition (Craik, 1986; Goldman-Rakic, 1987; Johnson & Raye, 1981; Lindsay & Norman, 1977; Locke, 1959), although various versions of the distinction do not always divide up cognition in exactly the same way (see Johnson & Hirst, 1993). Second, among perceptual processes, some processes support learning without necessarily producing the phenomenal experience of objects and events, while other processes are more essential for creating such a phenomenal world (Johnson, 1983). For example, the processes that allow you to learn to reach for an object are not the same as those that allow you to identify what the object is (e.g., Jeannerod, 1986). In MEM, the P-1 subsystem is largely responsible for the first type of perceptual processing, and the P-2 subsystem is largely responsible for the second type of perceptual processing. Third, among reflective processes too, there seem to be two fundamental types:

Marcia K. Johnson and Barbara L. Chalfonte

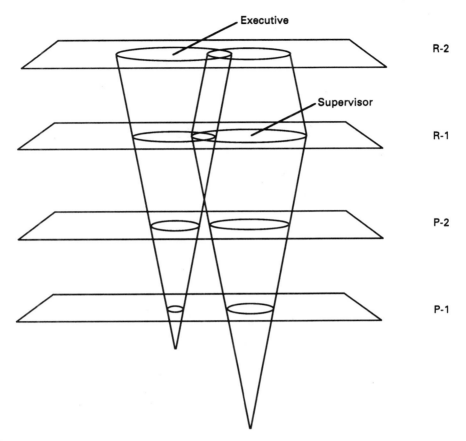

Figure 1 A multiple-entry, modular memory system consisting of two reflective subsystems, R-1 and R-2, and two perceptual subsystems, P-1 and P-2. Reflective and perceptual subsystems can interact through control and monitoring processes (the supervisor and executive processes of R-1 and R-2 respectively), which have relatively greater access to and control over reflective subsystems than perceptual subsystems. (Adapted from Johnson, 1991).

those that can be recruited to express and satisfy relatively simple self-generated goals or agendas and those that communicate or negotiate between multiple goals or agendas (compare Shallice, 1988). In MEM, reflective processes are organized into two subsystems, R-1 and R-2. R-1 and R-2 can each function alone, but they can also function interactively, which gives rise to reflection with a recursive or self-communicative quality.

With these three general distinctions as background, consider figures 1 and 2, which show a schematic representation of the proposed component processes of each of MEM's subsystems and their configuration. The proposed components are derived from and attempt to integrate a variety of theoretical ideas and findings from work on perception, attention, and learning and memory. The minimal requirements for a flexible P-1 subsystem capable of learning are four component processes:

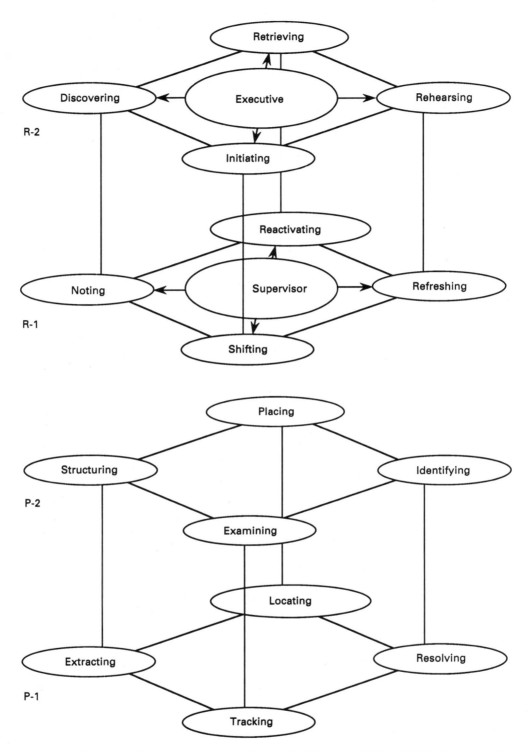

Figure 2 Component processes of R-1 and R-2 (top) and of P-1 and P-2 (bottom). (Adapted from Johnson, 1991).

Marcia K. Johnson and Barbara L. Chalfonte

- Mechanisms for *locating* stimuli, for instance, from abrupt changes in illumination (Posner & Peterson, 1990; Weiskrantz, 1986; Yantis & Johnson, 1990).

- Mechanisms for *resolving* a perceptual array into basic perceptual units by, for example, identifying edges (Marr, 1982), decomposing it into geons (e.g., Biederman, 1987), recovering primitives (Treisman, 1986), or deriving structural descriptions (Riddock & Humphreys, 1987; Schacter, 1992).

- Mechanism for *tracking* stimuli in motion (e.g., Kowler & Martins, 1982; Pylyshyn, 1989).

- Mechanisms for *extracting* invariants from perceptual arrays, e.g., texture gradients, flow patterns, horizon ratios (Gibson, 1950).

These P-1 processes are involved in the acquisition of many types of perceptual-motor skills and often can be tapped with priming procedures.

The minimal computational requirements for a P-2 subsystem capable of learning from phenomenal experience of objects and events are these:

- Mechanisms for *identifying* objects and events, that is, mechanisms by which combined perceptual primitives or integrated geons or computed structural descriptions yield a sense of what something may be or is (e.g., Biederman, 1987).

- Mechanisms for *placing* objects or events in spatial relation to one another, for example, knowing that the dog is closer to the car than to the house. Evidence from a variety of sources indicates that *placing* and *identifying* should be considered the result of different component processes (e.g., Mishkin, Ungerleider, & Macko, 1983). Furthermore, it may be that certain types of agnosias result from a disruption in the interaction between *placing* and *identifying*, producing a jumble of separately identified features (e.g., Luria, 1966).

- Mechanisms for *examining* or perceptually investigating one or many aspects of a stimulus array. That is, perception involves active observers who examine stimulus arrays, which changes the mental pattern that is most active (Hochberg, 1970; Peterson & Hochberg, 1983). Interactions between the component processes of *identifying* and *examining* provide a mechanism for testing perceptual hypotheses, for schema-guided perception (e.g., Hochberg, 1970; Palmer, 1975).

- Mechanisms for *structuring* or abstracting a pattern of organization across a temporally or spatially extended stimulus, e.g., mechanisms for extracting syntax from sentences or melodic structures from notes (Fodor, Bever, & Garrett, 1974; Krumhansl, 1990).

Working in combination, these P-2 component processes give rise to a rich phenomenal world of objects and events, some of which seem novel and some familiar and which together make up the meaningful environment we experience and remember.

In contrast to perceptual processes, reflective processes are important for internally generating and manipulating information. That is, they allow mental experience to take place without perceptual input. The computational requirements for an R-1 subsystem capable of minimal reflective functions are the following:

- A mechanism for *reactivating* currently inactive information.
- A mechanism for *refreshing* that prolongs ongoing activation.
- A mechanism for *shifting* or changing perspective to activate alternative aspects of stimuli.
- A mechanism for *noting* or identifying relations among activated information.

Working together, these component processes permit such "higher level" functions as identifying and establishing connections among objects or events, even when they are spatially or temporally discontinuous, by creating cognitive contiguity, e.g., the organization involved in free-recall learning (Tulving, 1962).

The R-2 subsystem permits even greater degrees of planning and complexity in reflective operations. R-2 consists of more strategic versions of the processes that make up the R-1 subsystem, namely, mechanisms for (1) *retrieving*, (2) *rehearsing*, (3) *initiating*, and (4) *discovering*. The component processes represented by R-2 can best be understood in relation to the analogous operations of R-1. For example, *noting* can compute overlapping relations from associations activated by two items (e.g., "dog" and "cat" both activate "animal"), whereas *discovering* finds relations that are less direct, for example relations that depend on other relations, as in computing analogies (e.g., Gentner, 1988). Prior related information might be *reactivated* in a relatively nonstrategic manner in response to noting a particular relationship among currently activated information (e.g., Faries & Reiser, 1988); in contrast, prior information would be *retrieved* in a strategic and deliberate manner in response to generating a specific memory cue for yourself in order to remember specific information (Baddeley, 1982; Reiser, 1986). *Refreshing* simply prolongs ongoing activation, whereas *rehearsing* cycles information in a self-generated format (e.g., via verbal or visuospatial representations) in order to remember it or use it in some other way (Baddeley, 1986). *Shifting* produces a change in activation by increasing activation of weakly activated aspects of stimuli, as when one shifts activation from the idea that a fire is hot to the idea that it is bright; in contrast, *initiating* produces a change in perspective by strategically looking for ways to activate unactivated aspects of information, for example, separately listing the items available in a problem-solving task in order to escape the mind-set established by the current activation pattern (Glucksberg & Weisberg, 1966).

Component processes of reflection can be recruited and organized in MEM by reflective *agendas* (e.g., the goal to construct a hypothesis about binding in memory). Agendas include the control and monitoring described, for example, by Miller, Galanter, and Pribram (1960), Nelson and Narens (1990), and Stuss

Marcia K. Johnson and Barbara L. Chalfonte

and Benson (1986). In figure 1, reflective agendas are shown as cones passing through the planes representing the different subsystems. To distinguish R-1 and R-2, we collectively refer to R-1 agendas as *supervisor* processes and R-2 agendas as *executive* processes. The procedures represented by the concept of *agenda* are composed of component processes in MEM as applied to particular data structures. Agendas are mechanisms for two important functions: they are programs or recipes of component processes for accomplishing simple and complex cognitive actions, and they provide a means by which reflective and perceptual processes can interact (as represented by the cones in figure 1). For example, the reflective agenda to build a house can activate the perceptual schema that allows you to find a hammer in a visually cluttered environment. Further, agendas may also serve to temporarily group or bind perceptually and reflectively processed information (Johnson, 1992).

The engagement of any of the component processes of MEM constitutes attention. Moreover, it is easy to see that within MEM attention is not simply a matter of quantitative variations along a single dimension. The attention instantiated in *locating* is different from the attention instantiated in *initiating*, for example, although both may illustrate the concept of attention in a general way. Similarly, MEM makes clear that although cognition varies in amount of effort or control (Hasher & Zacks, 1979; Norman & Shallice, 1986; Posner & Snyder, 1975; Shiffrin & Schneider, 1977), such effort or control probably does not vary along a single dimension. In MEM, the phenomenology of effort or control arises from which component processes are recruited and how many are needed for a given task (e.g., R-2 processes yield a greater sense of control than do P-1 processes). Similarly, in MEM, consciousness is not represented as a separate component of the architecture (as, for example, in Schacter's, 1989, DICE model); rather, different types of consciousness arise from the operation of various component processes (Johnson & Hirst, 1993; Johnson & Reeder, in press). For example, the type of self-consciousness that arises when R-2 monitors and controls the operation of R-1 is different than the type of consciousness that arises when R-1 monitors and controls P-2 (Johnson & Reeder, in press; compare Stuss, 1991).

In short, MEM is a process-based cognitive architecture that distinguishes between the processing of externally derived information and the processing of internally generated information; also included are mechanisms for the control and monitoring of, as well as the interaction between, these types of processing. The four hypothesized subsystems represent cognitive processes available to an intact adult human. Development from infancy to adulthood and breakdowns from overload, stress, and organic brain damage are presumed to reflect the architecture. We hypothesize that the four subsystems have evolved in the order P-1, P-2, R-1, R-2 and that they represent increasingly complex variations on several themes: respectively, identifying and keeping active the objects of perception and thought (*resolving, identifying, refreshing, rehearsing*), changing the activation the system experiences (*tracking, examining, shifting, initiating*), organizing relations across time or events (*extracting, structuring, noting, discovering*), and situating or going back to earlier objects of perception and thought (*locating, placing, reactivating, retrieving*). A comparative study of learning and memory should thus find commonalities between the proposed subsystems and component processes for different species, although how the specific themes are played out will likely vary somewhat across species.

1.2 Reactivation as a Component Process of MEM

A detailed consideration of all MEM's component processes is beyond the scope of this chapter. Here we will primarily consider the component processes involved in R-1, with special reference to *reactivating*. Our primary goal is to clarify the role that such a component process plays in learning and memory. Because there is no common agreement in the literature about the meanings of terms such as "reactivating," "retrieving," and so forth, it may help to highlight the differences among *reactivating* and other component processes in MEM with which it might be confused.

Activation occurs as a consequence of perceptual or reflective processes. Activation of a particular representation or pattern within a network presumably dissipates quickly if no further processing occurs. *Refreshing, rehearsing, reactivating*, and *retrieving* are qualitatively distinct proposed mechanisms by which activation can be sustained or revived. *Refreshing* is a process by which activation can be prolonged. In effect, refreshing extends the life of an already activated representation or pattern, allowing it to bridge brief gaps between activation patterns. *Rehearsing* includes processes by which self-generated codes for activated information are produced and recycled, usually with the intent to keep information highly available in a reportable format. Typically, rehearsing bridges much longer gaps than does refreshing (as in rehearsing a telephone number) and gives rise to a stronger phenomenal sense of holding something in mind. It is possible for an item to be refreshed (i.e., kept active through its relation to an ongoing agenda) without being intentionally rehearsed.

In contrast to *refreshing* and *rehearsing*, *reactivating* and *retrieving* are processes that operate on information that is no longer active; they are mechanisms by which information is brought back. *Reactivating* often takes place through a fortuitous combination of agendas and cues. For example, a previous pattern may recur from the concurrent activation of agendas and cues that were previously active together. *Retrieving* requires an additional step: the search for and self-presentation of cues that are not currently active. For example, if you are asked, "What were the exciting papers at the conference last November?" the combination of the agenda to remember and the cues "conference" and "November" might reactivate memories of papers you saw at the conference. If these cues are not sufficient, you might engage in additional processes of *retrieving*. For example, you might try to remember the topic of the conference and think about people who might have been there

Marcia K. Johnson and Barbara L. Chalfonte

in order to cue yourself about what was said. Or you might try listing the people to whom you might have subsequently described the conference in order to cue memory for your report about the papers. In other words, both *reactivating* and *retrieving* require summation of cues to revive activation, but *retrieving* involves a more active self-generation of potential cues that does *reactivating*. A major assumption of the MEM framework is that exploring distinctions such as these, as opposed to grouping a number of processes under a single label such as "retrieval," will be useful for understanding memory development, memory disruption, and other memory phenomena.

Consider this illustration of how a subset of MEM's component processes (those from R-1) might work together in learning to recall a list of randomly selected words: An *agenda* to find a connection between the concepts "passion" and "politics" might *shift* activation around the data structures representing each concept until a relation is *noted* (e.g., both concepts may involve attempts to persuade). In this case, because of the temporally contiguous activation of the agenda, the concepts, and the noted relation, the agenda will now have some capacity to *reactivate* this information in the future. For example, the subsequent presentation of another concept with "persuasion" as part of its activation pattern (e.g., "advertisement") in the presence of this agenda will likely result in the reactivation of the previously noted relation between "passion" and "politics," which will thus strengthen the relation among the associated concepts and lay the groundwork for additional reactivations and a bound, organizational unit involving all three concepts.

Reactivation refers, then, to internally generated repetitions derived from reflective processes. This form of repetition can be contrasted with externally generated, or perceptually derived, repetitions. To help distinguish the two types of repetition, we refer to representations of external stimuli as *reinstatements* (e.g., when an item or relation is presented again by the experimenter). Both reactivation and reinstatement have the capacity to increase the probability that various features of an experience will become bound together and to increase the strength between bound elements. Although some learning and memory can occur without reflective reactivation (e.g., through single presentations or repeated reinstatements), reflective reactivation is crucial for normal memory in a wide range of learning and memory tasks across a wide range of species. Here we illustrate how fundamental this process is by considering the consequences of disrupting it. Our main thesis is that reactivation is crucial for binding information into new relations when essential elements are temporally, spatially, or cognitively discontinuous. For example, if *A* and *B* overlap temporally, they may be bound without reactivation. However, to bind information *A* and subsequently occurring information *C* requires reactivation of *A* in the presence of *C* to provide cognitive contiguity; this cannot be accomplished if reactivation is disrupted. Furthermore, even cotemporal bindings (e.g., between *A* and *B*) miss opportunities for being maintained or strengthened if they cannot be reactivated on subsequent occasions. Reactivation therefore serves a dual role: *to promote opportunities for binding and to strengthen existing relations.* The more a particular behavioral task or reflective agenda recruits reactivation (in either capacity) under normal circumstances, the worse the memory deficit should be if reactivation is disrupted as a consequence of brain damage or experimental procedures (e.g., distraction).

The following sections propose that the array of deficits seen in hippocampally lesioned animals and in human amnesia patients arises from a reactivation deficit. Reactivation can be disrupted in several ways: the reactivation process itself can be disrupted, a link between reactivation and another process or a particular content domain may be impaired, or the relationship between an agenda and the process of reactivation can be disrupted. The basis for the disruption of reactivation is not crucial for the arguments we make here. In whatever manner reactivation is disrupted, the resulting general pattern should be similar, although the underlying mechanisms may be different. In what follows, we do not assume that reactivating operates exactly the same across species. For example, the conditions and the temporal parameters that distinguish *reactivating* from *refreshing* or *retrieving* may be different for different species. Thus, we are claiming not that the evidence reviewed here provides an unambiguous definition of reactivation but rather that a notion such as reactivation can help clarify relations among diverse memory phenomena. In short, we consider whether the varied reports of memory deficits in hippocampally lesioned animals and amnesic patients can be understood and unified by using reactivation as a central explanatory concept.

2   ANIMAL HIPPOCAMPAL LESIONS AND REACTIVATION

The hippocampus has been implicated in learning and memory across a range of species. We will review several studies demonstrating memory deficits observed in animals with hippocampal lesions and attempt to understand the findings by applying the reactivation framework proposed here. Further, we will describe several studies that, as a group, are difficult to understand within any one model of hippocampal functioning but that can be parsimoniously understood by using the reactivation component of the MEM framework. Several models have been proposed that describe the functional role of the hippocampus in memory. These include models that posit that the hippocampus is important for encoding and recollecting spatial information (Nadel, 1992; O'Keefe & Nadel, 1978), temporally discontinuous information (Moore, 1979; Rawlins, 1985; Solomon, 1980), configural associations (Rudy & Sutherland, 1992; Sutherland & Rudy, 1989), or contextual information (Hirsh, 1974; Mayes, Meudell, & Pickering, 1985); for supporting working memory (Olton, 1986) or declarative memory (Eichenbaum, 1992; Squire, 1987); or for selecting information or decreasing interference (e.g., Moore & Stickney, 1980; Rudy & Sutherland, 1992; Winocur, Rawlins, & Gray, 1987). Despite these diverse characterizations of the role of the hippocampus in memory, we suggest that there is commonality underlying these approaches. Two common themes cutting across various theories have been noted by Eichenbaum

(1992): the fundamental role of relational representations and the ability to use such memories in novel situations. We believe there is yet another useful level of abstraction to be made: reactivation at encoding allows relational associations to be developed among incoming stimuli or with prior information; reactivation at retrieval allows for flexibility by calling up prior information in novel situations.

Latent inhibition observed in normal animals illustrates the role of reactivation in learning. In this paradigm, the experimental group is preexposed to an unpaired conditioned stimulus (CS) several times a day for several days, while the control group receives no preexposure. In the second phase, both groups receive normal pairings of conditioned stimuli and unconditioned stimuli (UCS). Animals preexposed to the CS demonstrate significantly fewer responses to the CS than do animals in the control group, which thus demonstrates latent inhibition (Lubow & Moore, 1959). We hypothesize that reactivation is important to latent inhibition in the following manner: Animals that were preexposed to the CS reactivate this information in the pairing phase, noting that there was no pairing with a UCS during the preexposure period. This inconsistent information about the cue value of the UCS slows down learning of the pairings. If reactivation is in fact crucial to latent inhibition, we would not expect to see latent inhibition in animals with hippocampal lesions. This is in fact the case (Kaye & Pearce, 1987a, 1987b; Solomon & Moore, 1975). Preexposed animals with hippocampal lesions do not demonstrate latent inhibition relative to hippocampally lesioned animals that were not preexposed. This is not simply due to an overall decrease in responding rates; hippocampally lesioned animals that had no preexposure to the CS responded at the same rate as control animals (Solomon & Moore, 1975).

It has been well established that simple classical conditioning is normal in animals with hippocampal lesions (Berger & Orr, 1983; Ross, Orr, Holland, & Berger, 1984; Schmaltz & Theios, 1972; Solomon & Moore, 1975; Solomon, Solomon, Vander-Schaaf, & Perry, 1983), and preliminary evidence suggests this may also be the case in humans with brain lesions that include the hippocampus (Daum, Channon, & Canavan, 1989; Daum, Channon, Polkey, & Gray, 1991; Weiskrantz & Warrington, 1979; Woodruff-Pak & Corkin, 1991). We suggest this is true because reactivation is not required for acquisition of a simple conditioned response. When the CS and UCS are paired, onset of the CS typically occurs during the UCS, and the offsets of the CS and UCS occur simultaneously (the CS and UCS are time-locked), so reactivation is not required for successful pairing. Consider, however, a case where a temporal lag is introduced between the CS and UCS. Reactivation of the CS information would then be required for successful pairing of the CS and UCS. In the trace conditioning paradigm, such a lag is introduced between the CS and UCS. Control animals are not affected by this manipulation, while hippocampally lesioned animals are impaired in acquiring conditioned responses (James, Hardiman, & Yeo, 1987; Moyer, Deyo, & Disterhoft, 1990; Port, Romano, Steinmetz, Mikhail, & Patterson, 1986; Solomon, Vander-Schaaf, Thompson,

& Weisz, 1986). This simple difference between standard conditioning (also termed "delay conditioning") and trace conditioning cannot be understood by employing ideas of hippocampal function that stress spatial information (O'Keefe & Nadel, 1978), configural information (Sutherland & Rudy, 1989), or the ability to compare and contrast information (Eichenbaum, 1992). A view that considers the hippocampus crucial when there are relatively long temporal lags (e.g., Moore, 1979; Rawlins, 1985; Solomon, 1980) could be used to understand both latent inhibition, which requires information from the preexposure phase to be available in a later pairing phase, and trace conditioning, where CS information must be available later when the UCS information becomes available. However, an advantage of the hypothesis of a reactivation deficit is that it can also be invoked in nontemporal paradigms, in which a temporal view would not apply. In such cases where conditions for temporal contiguity are met, however, reactivation is necessary for cognitive contiguity and to promote opportunities for binding information together. We describe such a paradigm next.

Phillips and LeDoux (1992a) investigated standard conditioning of fear to both central cues and environmental contexts in normal animals and in animals with hippocampal or amygdala lesions. We will concentrate on their results from normal controls and hippocampally lesioned animals. In normal animals, fear can be conditioned both to a tone cue and to the context of the experimental chamber. Further, conditioning to the tone cue occurs prior to conditioning to the context, although both the cue and the context are present simultaneously with the aversive UCS (Phillips & LeDoux, 1992a). We suggest that animals are at first more likely to note and associate the relationship between the salient, time-locked CS and the aversive UCS. Subsequently, the UCS information may be *reactivated* and associated with the available context information. If this characterization is correct, we would expect normal fear conditioning to the tone in animals with hippocampal lesions. Contrariwise, if conditioning to the context requires reactivation of the UCS information, we would not expect normal conditioning to the context. This pattern was indeed observed (Phillips & LeDoux, 1992a).

Although contextual notions of hippocampal functioning (e.g., Hirsh, 1974) would also have predicted such an outcome, the contextual hypothesis does not predict that hippocampally lesioned animals could condition to context in the absence of a time-locked CS. This prediction (Johnson, 1992) does fall out of a reactivation characterization, however. If a time-locked CS is not present during a UCS, then context should be able to be directly associated with the UCS because animals have the opportunity to *note* the contiguity between context and UCS without competition from an actively noted relation between CS and UCS. Thus, under these circumstances, conditioning to context can occur without reactivation. Consistent with this prediction, preliminary data (Phillips & LeDoux, 1992b) indicate that both intact and hippocampally lesioned rats show a conditioned freezing response to the environmental context when there is no CS. In fact, the time course of conditioning to the context under these conditions is equivalent to the time course of conditioning to the CS when there is both a CS and context. The pattern of conditioning to context in hippocampally lesioned animals is normal when reactivation is not required. However, these same animals do not condition to context when UCS information must be reactivated to associate the information. A contextual characterization cannot readily account for the pattern of preserved conditioning to context under certain conditions and disrupted conditioning to context under others. Furthermore, such a characterization cannot readily account for the pattern of preserved classical conditioning and disrupted trace conditioning. Similarly, although a temporal view of hippocampal functioning can account for the standard-delay and trace-conditioning data, applying this view to the fear-conditioning data would not be appropriate, because both the tone cue and the context are present when the UCS is presented in this paradigm. In contrast, the reactivation view can account for all data from the paradigms presented thus far.

Lastly, consider two studies that lead to seemingly opposing conclusions about the encoding of conditional associations and the effect of changing contexts between acquisition and testing phases for hippocampally lesioned animals. In a study by Eichenbaum, Mathews, and Cohen (1989), both sham-operated and fornix-lesioned animals learned an odor discrimination task involving two pairs of two odors ($A+B-$ and $C+D-$). When the correct odors ($A+$ and $C+$) were subsequently paired with different odors ($A+D-$ and $C+B-$ for example), sham-operated controls continued to perform the discrimination at a level equivalent to that for the old pairings, while the fornix-lesioned animals now performed at chance. These data seem to suggest that hippocampal animals can learn only conditional associations and that content information (A and C) cannot be expressed in the absence of its contextual information (A plus B and C plus D).

Before settling on this interpretation, consider the following study as well. Penick and Solomon (1991) trained normal controls and hippocampally lesioned animals in a standard classical conditioning task in one of two contexts (A or B). When contexts were changed after animals reached learning criterion in the first context (i.e., animals trained in A were tested in B and vice versa), conditioned responses decreased for normal controls but not for hippocampally lesioned animals. When the context remained the same, both groups continued to perform at the established criterion rate. From this study we might conclude that hippocampally lesioned animals *cannot* make conditional associations and that content information (the link between CS and UCS) is expressed *independently* of contextual information. This is precisely the opposite conclusion from that suggested by the data of Eichenbaum et al. (1989). None of the current prominent views of hippocampal functioning predict both of these opposing patterns of results. We suggest that a process analysis of these paradigms, including an attempt to understand where reactivation is crucial, indicates that the reactivation explanation can account for both of these outcomes.

In the Eichenbaum et al. (1989) task, animals were given, for example, *A* plus *B* to encode at acquisition and were then presented with *A* plus *D* at test. Presented with *A* plus *D*, normal animals can reactivate the *A* plus *B* information at test and note that the *A* information is consistent between the phases and respond correctly. Presented with *A* plus *D*, hippocampal animals cannot reactivate the *A* plus *B* information, however; they simply do not respond to *A* plus *D*, for which they have never been rewarded previously. Reactivation is necessary at test in this paradigm.

In the Penick and Solomon (1991) task, as in the Phillips and LeDoux (1992a) study, classical conditioning initially occurs to the salient, time-locked CS-UCS pair. UCS information is then reactivated and paired with the context. Hippocampally lesioned animals cannot accomplish this pairing, because it requires reactivation. Thus because the context has been changed between phases, it is now a poor cue for the normal animals, and their conditioned-response rate decreases. However, when the context is changed for the lesioned animals, there is no relevant difference to be noted, because contextual information was never acquired, so there is no concomitant decrease in their conditioned-response rate. Reactivation is necessary at encoding to establish the UCS-context association in this paradigm.

A similar process analysis, with specific reference to reactivation, can be used to understand the performance, on classic memory tasks, of primates with lesions that include the hippocampus (the amygdala is often additionally lesioned in many of the studies reviewed here) relative to normal controls. Here we will focus on performance of the tasks of delayed retention of object discrimination and a delayed nonmatch to the sample.

In delayed retention of object discrimination, an animal chooses one object of a pair that is baited with a food reward. After an intertrial interval of 15 seconds, the same pair is presented again. Each day 20 trials are given until subjects are able to correctly choose the baited object in 9 of 10 consecutive trials. After a 48-hour delay, 20 test trials are administered. If a reactivation deficit is induced by a bilateral hippocampus-amygdala (HA) lesion, then animals lesioned prior to learning should show poor retention relative to intact controls. Zola-Morgan and Squire (1985) found that performance on the object discrimination task after a 48-hour retention interval was significantly poorer in HA-lesioned animals than for control animals. This deficit is presumably due to the inability of the lesioned animals to reactivate the prior object-discrimination information during the testing trials that occur 48 hours after initial training.

Another task in which HA-lesioned animals typically show deficits is the delayed nonmatch-to-sample task. In this task, a single object baited with a food reward is presented to the animal. After a short delay (typically 8 to 10 seconds), two objects—the previously presented object and a novel object— are presented to the animal. The natural response of the animal, to choose the novel object, is rewarded. Twenty trials, all using new object pairs, with an

Marcia K. Johnson and Barbara L. Chalfonte

intertrial interval of 30 seconds, are presented daily until the animal achieves the criterion performance. Mishkin (1978) and Zola-Morgan and Squire (1985) have shown that animals with HA lesions are impaired in acquiring the criterion performance relative to normal animals. After all animals reach criterion performance in the training trials, test trials are administered in which the delay between the object-presentation phase and the pair-presentation phase is increased from 8 seconds to either 15, 30, 60, or 120 seconds. Retention of the object information is increasingly impaired for the HA-lesioned animals as the delay between the trial phases increases (Mishkin, 1978; Zola-Morgan & Squire, 1984; Zola-Morgan & Squire, 1985). Increasingly longer delays, whether they occur between trials or between phases of a single trial, should increase the likelihood that reactivating information will be necessary for successful performance (e.g., with increasing delays the animal is more likely to be distracted by other stimuli). Acquiring the task requires the reactivation of previous trials during new trials to compare and note the behavior needed to receive the reward. Since the intertrial interval is 30 seconds in this task, reactivation is likely necessary to acquire cross-trial information. Thus it is difficult for lesioned animals to acquire the nonmatch-to-sample task. During the test trials, increasing the delay between trial phases increases the need to reactivate information about the previously seen object when the animal must choose the novel object. Again, this is difficult for lesioned animals. Adding a distracting task while increasing the delay simply amplifies this deficit (Zola-Morgan & Squire, 1985). Performance by lesioned primates on a delayed match-to-sample task (Malamut, Saunders, & Mishkin, 1984) is analogous to that on a delayed nonmatch-to-sample task; the main difference between these tasks is that the total number of trials to acquire the delayed match-to-sample task is approximately three times greater for both the control and lesion groups. The same argument for a reactivation deficit in the delayed nonmatch-to-sample task holds for the delayed match-to-sample task.

From the animal literature, it appears that characterizing the performance of hippocampally lesioned animals as reflecting disrupted spatial, temporal, or contextual memory is inadequate. As an alternative, we suggest that a process analysis focused on whether reactivation is involved at encoding, retrieval, or both can provide a more comprehensive account of the behavior and memory deficits in hippocampal animals. We do not suggest that reactivation is the only function of the hippocampus, and we suspect that hippocampal lesions represent only one method of disrupting reactivation processes. Since behavior in humans and animals with diencephalic lesions overlaps significantly with that stemming from hippocampal lesions, diencephalic lesions may represent another method by which reactivation processes are disrupted. In short, in this section we conclude that associative learning or binding can occur with hippocampal lesions if multiple features are simultaneously available (especially with repeated external reinstatements) or when simply *refreshing* information is sufficient to bridge temporal, spatial, or cognitive gaps between important features or stimuli of a task (i.e., when cognitive contiguity has not been interrupted). However, when reactivation is necessary at encoding, testing, or both phases, a memory deficit will be observed in proportion to the degree that reactivation is necessary for successful completion of the task.

3 HUMAN AMNESIA AND REACTIVATION

In this section we will show how the reactivation-deficit framework can also be used to understand amnesic deficits in human memory tasks. (For the most part, the patients studied have medial temporal or diencephalic damage, but other areas may be damaged as well.) We begin with human memory tasks that overlap with those reviewed in the previous section (conditioning and delayed nonmatch-to-sample tasks) and additionally consider performance on recall and recognition tasks and memory for autobiographical events. As with the animal studies reviewed earlier, we expect that human memory will be disrupted to the degree that reactivation is necessary during the encoding and/or testing phases of a given memory task.

3.1 Tasks from the Animal Literature

The literature addressing classical conditioning in human amnesic patients is currently very limited. Weiskrantz and Warrington (1979) found that two amnesic patients (one Korsakoff, one postencephalic) were able to acquire a conditioned eye-blink response to an airpuff and to retain that response across 10-minute and 24-hour delays. Despite the acquisition of the conditioned response, only one patient was able to verbalize any component of the task episode when questioned. Daum, Channon, and Canavan (1989) also found that three amnesic patients with bilateral temporal-lobe damage demonstrated an initial conditioned eye-blink response and increasing frequency of conditioned responses in a time course typically reported for normal subjects. However, neither of these studies included normal controls. Recently, Woodruff-Pak and Corkin (1991) assessed the abilities of H.M. and a healthy, age-matched control subject to acquire a conditioned eye-blink response. H.M. acquired the eye-blink response after 473 trials, while the control subject acquired the response after 316 trials. Throughout the experiment, H.M. could neither recognize nor recall the conditioning procedure. Woodruff-Pak and Corkin concluded that H.M. was able to successfully acquire the conditioned response, although the rate of acquisition may have been somewhat slowed because of long-term dilatin treatment for seizure control. Similarly, Daum, Channon, Polkey, and Gray (1991) tested the ability of both amnesics and normal controls to acquire a conditioned eye-blink response. They tested four groups: patients with unilateral right temporal lobectomies, left temporal lobectomies, frontal lobectomies (all lesions for intractable epilepsy), and normal controls. There were no differences among these groups in the time course of their first conditioned response. However, significantly fewer subjects in the temporal lobectomy groups reported being aware of the conditioning procedure than did those in the frontal lobectomy group and the normal control group.

Daum et al. (1991) also investigated the performance of these groups on a conditional discrimination task. In reinforced trials, a colored light (e.g., red) was followed by a tone and then an airpuff; in unreinforced trials, a different colored light (e.g., green) was followed by a tone but no airpuff. Both the normal control group and the frontal-lobectomy group were able to acquire this conditional discrimination. However, the temporal-lobectomy groups showed an equivalent level of conditioned responses to both the reinforced and unreinforced lights; that is, they did not learn the conditional discrimination. We assume that it is helpful in learning such conditional discriminations to be able to reactivate information from previous trials during a given trial in order to compare and note which lights have been reinforced. The inability to reactivate prior trial information makes it difficult for a conditional-discrimination response to develop.

The studies by Daum et al. (1991) and Woodruff-Pak and Corkin (1991) are currently the only studies that demonstrate both intact and impaired conditioned responses in amnesic patients relative to controls. However, Disterhoft (1992), together with his colleagues, are currently investigating performance by both amnesics and controls in the delayed- and trace-conditioning paradigms. We would expect relatively normal performance by amnesic patients both in the delayed-conditioning paradigm and in the trace-conditioning paradigm with a very short trace interval. However, as the trace interval increases or distraction is introduced, which thereby increases the requirements for reactivation of prior information, we would expect the performance of the amnesics to become significantly poorer than that of normal controls.

We can also look at the performance of amnesic patients on memory tasks on which primates with hippocampal lesions are impaired. In the same delayed-retention object-discrimination task described previously for primates, both Korsakoff amnesics and alcoholic controls successfully learned to choose a baited object from a single pair of objects (Squire, Zola-Morgan, & Chen, 1988). Following a 1- or 10-day delay, memory performance on this task was evaluated. Korsakoff patients performed significantly more poorly than controls after both the 1- and 10-day delays. If we assume that reactivation of the previously learned discrimination is necessary at test, we can understand this result as a reactivation deficit on the part of the Korsakoff patients. Korsakoff amnesics have difficulty reactivating information and therefore perform significantly more poorly than the alcoholic controls. The HA-lesioned primates and Korsakoff amnesic patients demonstrated parallel deficits on this task.

We can similarly understand human performance on the delayed nonmatch-to-sample task (Squire et al., 1988) and the delayed match-to-sample task (Oscar-Berman and Bonner, 1985). To use the delayed nonmatch-to-sample study as an example (the delayed match-to-sample study parallels this study in subject population, methods, and results), Korsakoff amnesics and alcoholic controls were first presented with a penny-baited object. After a 5-second delay, subjects saw a pair of objects, one of which was the previously viewed object; here the novel object was baited with a penny and subjects were to choose the novel object. A new pair was used for each trial, and the intertrial interval was 5 to 10 seconds. Trials continued until the learning criterion was reached. Following this, test trials were administered, where the delay between phases was 5, 15, or 60 seconds. Half of the 15- and 60-second delays were filled with a distractor task. We expect behavior in humans to be similar to that in primates; that is, as the delay between phases increases, we expect that the need to reactivate information about the first-viewed object will increase and amnesics will show a concomitant deficit in performance relative to controls. Adding a distractor task during the delay should serve to magnify the deficit. Squire et al. (1988) found that amnesic patients were significantly poorer than controls after all delays and that performance did not decline further as a function of delay length. Further, the distractor task added during the delay decreased performance to the same degree after both 15- and 60-second delay durations. Neither increasing delay nor increasing delay and introducing a distractor led to a decrement in the control performance. The impairment demonstrated in the Korsakoff amnesic patients is more severe than that predicted by a reactivation deficit alone. We expect that damage in Korsakoff patients, relative to that in unilateral- or bilateral-temporal-lobectomy patients, leads to other deficits in addition to a reactivation deficit (e.g., inability to maintain a set or an agenda). Such processing deficits in addition to a reactivation deficit should further impair performance on memory tasks.

It is clear that humans are impaired on tasks in which other animals also demonstrate memory deficits. Preliminary data for intact classical conditioning in humans parallel the animal data, while difficulties in conditioning paradigms that call for reactivation of information for successful performance also appear to be similar. Further, performance by amnesic patients on tests designed for primates indicates findings analogous to the primate data.

3.2 Recall and Recognition Tasks

We now apply the notion of a reactivation deficit to tasks in which observed impairments have provided the benchmarks for human amnesia: recall and recognition. The most salient symptoms of anterograde amnesia are the dramatic disruptions in recall and recognition of information and events experienced subsequent to the onset of the amnesia. As we discuss in this section, *reactivation* plays a fundamental role in normal recall and recognition both in providing the cognitive contiguity necessary for binding together information and in strengthening such relations. Thus a deficit in this component process of the memory system could produce severe impairments in recall and recognition, such as those found in amnesic patients.

Marcia K. Johnson and Barbara L. Chalfonte

Theoretical ideas about recall repeatedly highlight the importance of relational processing, as for example, in work illustrating the benefits of interactive imagery and mnemonics (e.g., Bugelski, Kidd, & Segmen, 1968; Paivio, 1969; Wollen, Weber, & Lowry, 1972), organization (e.g., Mandler, 1967; Miller, 1956; Tulving, 1962), comprehension (e.g., Bransford & Johnson, 1972; Dooling & Lachman, 1971), and schemas, scripts, and story grammars (e.g., Rabinowitz & Mandler, 1983; Schank & Abelson, 1977; Thorndyke, 1977). Most theorists agree that one reason relational processing is powerful is because at acquisition it sets up the structures among cues that are necessary for later recall (e.g., Tulving & Pearlstone, 1966; Seamon & Chumbley, 1977). Reactivation is essential for developing new cue structures among unrelated elements and strengthening relational bindings important for recall.

To take the hypothetical example given earlier of the subject engaged in free recall, the activation of "passion" in the context of the item "politics" allowed the subject to bind these items together via the noted relation of "persuasion." The later activation of the concept of "persuasion" by the item "advertisement" (in the context of the agenda to continue organizing the list) reactivated "passion" and "politics." This reactivation had two consequences: it allowed the binding of a new item to items that occurred some time previously, and it strengthened the earlier binding of "passion" and "politics" to the same organizational unit. Thus some ideas, such as "persuasion," come to function as recall cues for other ideas, such as "passion," "politics," and "advertisement."

In contrast to recall, where the subject must come up with the target items on the test, in a typical recognition experiment the targets are presented along with distractor items, and the subject's task is to identify (or recognize) which came from the target list. Again, having engaged in elaborative processing that sets up relational bindings among items on the list or between list items and extralist cues (e.g., schemas, semantic knowledge) helps recognition, although the effects here are often less dramatic than typically found for recall. Theories differ in how they conceptualize the mechanisms underlying the effects of elaborative or relational activity on recognition. One proposal is that when a subject sees the test item, they may engage in a "retrieval check" (Atkinson & Juola, 1972; Mandler & Boeck, 1974). According to this idea, the subject may attempt to recall a list via recall mechanisms, such as those described above that capitalize on relational information; finding an item via a recall process would be sufficient evidence for "recognizing" that the item was from the target list. To use the same example as above, for the test item "politics," the subject would use the activated cue "persuasion" to recall items from the persuasion category. If "politics" appeared in this set of recall items, it would be recognized. Another idea is that relational processing at acquisition increases the chances that the activation prompted by the item at test will include source-specifying information (e.g., color, spatial location, etc.), which is taken as evidence for recognition (Johnson, Hashtroudi, & Lindsay, 1993; Raye, 1976). For example, noting where on a screen an item occurred will help bind item and location. Later activation of this location information when the item is presented could, because of its specificity, be used as evidence that the item occurred on the acquisition list. In this way, elaboration might help subjects "consciously recollect" the specific episode of the presentation of the item (Jacoby, 1991). Another possibility is that the rapidity of activation of elaborative information could alone be taken as a cue that the item has been seen and acted on before (Raye, 1976). Whatever the underlying mechanisms by which elaborative or relational processing aids recognition, it is readily apparent that reactivation plays a crucial role, because it is instrumental for creating occasions for noting relations, for strengthening relational binding through subsequent reactivations, and for making useful information available at test. Disrupted recognition might therefore result from relational processing deficits as a consequence of disrupted reactivation.

Although the potential impact of relational processing on recognition is incorporated into most recognition models, most models emphasize the role of nonrelational, item-specific familiarity responses in old/new recognition. Again, theories vary in what they assume to underlie this familiarity response. For example, Underwood (1972) suggested that the mnemonic representation of an item builds up frequency increments whenever the item occurs; this frequency information yields the familiarity response that produces recognition (see also Atkinson & Juola, 1974). Underwood explicitly noted that not only external presentations but also covert occurrences of items increase their familiarity value. (In terms of MEM, covert occurrences are a result of *refreshing, rehearsing, reactivating,* and *retrieving.*) In the language of several recent models for recognition, one could say that such covert occurrences add episodes to memory that figure into "echo intensity" (Hintzman, 1988), add to the "global familiarity" computed from degree of total activation (Gillund & Shiffrin, 1984), increase intraitem integration (Mandler, 1980), or add to processing "fluency" (Jacoby, 1991).[2] In any event, anything that would decrease the frequency of reflectively generated reactivations should also produce a disruption in recognition when such reactivations play a central role in the normal case of recognition. It is clear, then, that a reactivation deficit could impair recognition memory, both by disrupting the accrual of information that subserves familiarity (here including frequency increments, echo intensity, global familiarity, item integration, and fluency) and by eliminating the binding opportunities that subserve the ability to recollect specific featural and relational information, which is also important for recognition.

Thus there are a number of variations on the general theme that normal recognition can be based either on a response to undifferentiated information (e.g., "familiarity" with no sense of an item's specific features) (Johnson et al., 1993) or on more specific characteristics of complex memories, such as perceptual detail, spatial location, semantic relations among concepts, and so forth (i.e., information that could be used to infer sources). This raises the question of whether subjects with memory disorders are equally impaired in using familiarity and in using the other bases of recognition. Several investigators have suggested that old/new recognition judgments based on familiarity

Marcia K. Johnson and Barbara L. Chalfonte

alone may be preserved in amnesia, whereas judgments about source are impaired (Cermak & Verfaellie, 1992; Verfaellie & Treadwell, 1993; Weinstein, 1987). For example, Weinstein found quite similar levels of recognition for amnesics and controls when the original processing at acquisition had been directed toward perceptual characteristics of the items (counting the number of black objects in a sequence of colored objects, such as an orange rabbit, a black umbrella, and a pink train) and the distractors on the test were new items in unfamiliar colors (a green goat). In contrast, when the distractors were constructed to elicit familiarity responses based on semantic knowledge (green pepper), the amnesics showed a significant recognition deficit relative to controls. Weinstein suggested that the amnesics could use differential familiarity of targets and distractors as a basis for recognition decisions in the first condition but had difficulty in the second condition sorting out the source of their familiarity responses. Consistent with this interpretation, the fact that amnesics have difficulty separating items that are familiar from day 1 from those familiar from day 2 (Huppert and Piercy, 1976) suggests that they experience familiarity responses to previously encountered stimuli but cannot identify the source of the familiarity. Verfaellie and Treadwell make a similar point in interpreting their study (1993). Prior to the test phase, subjects saw some items as anagrams, read others, and heard still others. Subjects were then tested under two conditions: say "yes" to all old items (whether heard, seen as an anagram, or read) and "no" to new items; or say "yes" only to items that had been heard and "no" to new items, anagram items, and read items. Whereas control subjects decreased "yes" responses to anagrams and read items in the second condition relative to the first, amnesics were equally likely to say "yes" to anagrams and read items in the two conditions. Again, the results suggest that amnesics experience familiarity responses but have difficulty identifying the source of the familiarity. Taken together, these various studies suggest that the processes that newly bind specific, relational, or featural information are disrupted in amnesia. If so, a disruption in reactivation should particularly disadvantage relational information, which is in greatest need of strengthening.

Although reactivation affects both recall and recognition, an important difference between them is that recall characteristically depends more on reactivation than does recognition. For preexperimentally unrelated items, such as words or pictures, normal recognition is often excellent after a single presentation, whereas recall is generally quite poor (Shepard, 1967). That is, a single presentation appears to set up a representation that is easily activated by another presentation of the same stimulus (i.e., by *reinstatement*) but is surprisingly difficult to access through reflective processes (i.e., by *reactivation*). At the same time, recognition generally improves with additional presentations that do *not* allow for reactivation and reflective processing of the material, whereas recall may not (Tulving, 1966). This is because familiarity, supported to some degree by *reinstatement*, is a good basis for recognition (given that the distractors are not too similar to the targets or do not have any other basis for familiarity) but is not particularly good for recall. Reflectively generated cue structures, which depend on *reactivation*, are more likely to be needed in recall.

If amnesics suffer from a reactivation deficit and if recall typically depends more on reactivation than does recognition, we would expect to see variations in amnesic performance on recognition and recall tests that can be traced to variations in reactivation requirements. Although we need better tests of this proposition, several findings in the literature are consistent with it. Complex or abstract pictures, which are difficult to label verbally, are likely to receive relatively more perceptual than reflective processing; in particular, they may undergo few reflective reactivations (e.g., Loftus, 1974). If reactivation does not play much of a role in how control subjects process such pictures, amnesics should do relatively well. A number of studies of complex picture recognition (summarized in Johnson & Kim, 1985) indicate that amnesics seem to do quite well. For example, in a study conducted by Johnson and Kim (1985), subjects saw each of several abstract "paintings" (each composed of three of five possible colors) either 1, 5, or 10 times. On a forced-choice recognition test, amnesics' performance improved as a function of frequency of presentation, as did normal subjects' performance. Furthermore, on an additional recognition test administered 20 days later, the amnesics' recognition rate for items seen 10 times was 78 percent, versus 86 percent for controls. These findings suggest that amnesics, like controls, build up familiarity over repeated presentations, which will support recognition as a function of perceptual reinstatements after substantial intervals (see also Huppert & Piercy, 1982).

One can capitalize on this intact aspect of amnesic processing to equate the recognition performance of amnesics and controls by giving amnesics more presentations of material than controls. Alternatively, one can attempt to limit the self-initiated reactivations and elaborations in normal subjects by presenting material more quickly to normal subjects than to amnesics (see Huppert & Piercy, 1977). By combining both techniques, Hirst, Johnson, Phelps, and Volpe (1988) actually found superior recognition for unrelated words in amnesics than controls: the recognition rate for amnesics, who saw a list twice at a rate of 5,000 milliseconds per item was 85 percent, versus 77 percent for controls, who saw the list once at 500 milliseconds per item. The subjects in the study by Hirst et al. were tested for recall of the list items as well. Amnesics recalled about 7 percent of the words, whereas controls recalled about 16 percent (see also Hirst, Johnson, Kim, Phelps, Risse, & Volpe, 1986). The fact that recall was relatively more disrupted than recognition is consistent with our argument that recall depends more on reactivation and that reactivation is disrupted in amnesia. However, this general line of reasoning does not depend on amnesics invariably showing disproportionate disruption in recall as compared with recognition. Because both recall and recognition recruit various processes depending on the situation, it may be that under certain conditions recall and recognition tasks may *not* differentially draw on

Marcia K. Johnson and Barbara L. Chalfonte

reactivation processes (see Johnson et al., 1993; Verfaellie & Treadwell, 1993). Under such circumstances, amnesics should show equal deficits in recall and recognition (e.g., Haist, Shimamura, & Squire, 1992).

Although profoundly memory-impaired subjects can be brought up to relatively high performance levels on recognition by adding presentation trials, it is almost impossible to bring them up to such levels of recall using the same strategy. Presumably, the extreme difficulty amnesics have in recall tasks arises because additional reinstatements alone are insufficient to establish and strengthen appropriate cue structures and their relations, which are normally established by reflectively guided reactivations. Consequently, the various elements of experience do not become bound into complex, coherent, voluntarily accessible representations (see Hirst, 1989).

In suggesting that amnesics have a disruption in reactivation processes, are we simply postulating a "retrieval" deficit theory of amnesia? The usual objection to the idea that anterograde amnesia involves a retrieval deficit is that anterograde amnesics do not necessarily have difficulty retrieving everything: they may be able to retrieve semantic knowledge and autobiographical information encoded prior to the onset of amnesia (e.g., Hirst, 1982; Shimamura, 1989). However, this critique does not take into account two considerations. First, the state of learned information is not necessarily the same for recently acquired information and information that has survived the test of time and interference. That is, the preonset events represented in memory are probably not exactly like the postonset events that are not remembered. As discussed above, preonset events (and knowledge) have likely benefited from prior reactivations and other organizational processes that improve their chances of being revived relative to newly acquired events and information. Second, there is more than one type of retrieval from memory. Retrieval can be prompted or controlled by external cues, such as the retrieval involved in priming, the retrieval involved in familiarity-based recognition, or the retrieval involved in highly overlearned information, as when someone asks your name and you reply. Even these kinds of retrieval, all prompted by external cueing, are not necessarily alike. More important, these kinds of retrieval all differ from the retrieval that is not controlled by external cues but is prompted by reflective processes. Retrieval can be prompted or controlled by internal cues, as when subjects attempt to recall items without benefit of cues in a free-recall task. Here internal cues are set by agendas and strategic plans or are self-initiated cues, as opposed to external cues, which are set by information presented in reinstatements. In MEM, we begin to differentiate various kinds of reflective retrieval by distinguishing among *refreshing, reactivating, rehearsing,* and *retrieving* (see Johnson, 1990, 1992; Johnson & Hirst, 1993) and further postulate *reactivating* as what is specifically disrupted in amnesia.[3] By postulating a reactivation deficit, we are also postulating that deficits will be observed not only at test but also in learning and maintaining information. If reactivation cannot be recruited to provide the cognitive contiguity necessary for binding aspects of memory together, then complex cue structures will not be properly encoded. If reactivation cannot be recruited to provide the strengthening of reinstatement-generated relations, then relations will not be properly maintained. Thus postulating a deficit in the MEM component process of reactivation is an encoding, maintenance, *and* retrieval account of amnesia.

3.3 Recollection of Autobiographical Events

For the most part, cognitive theories of recall and recognition have been based on empirical studies of normal subjects learning and remembering relatively simple lists or stories. However, studies of memory for naturally occurring autobiographical events, or relatively complex laboratory simulations of autobiographical events, also indicate the importance of reactivation in personal memory. For example, Rubin and Kozin (1984) found that people's more vivid memories were also those they reported having talked about more often. In an extended study of her own memory, Linton (1978) recorded daily events in her life (e.g., "I had coffee with Jeff before his colloquium presentation, and we talked about his research") over a period of years. She regularly tested her memory for such events, and one notable finding was that reactivating memories by cueing them on test trials markedly improved their retention on subsequent tests (see also Allen, Mahler, & Estes, 1969; Hogan & Kintsch, 1971; Landauer & Bjork, 1978). Furthermore, previous reactivations had greater effects on earlier memories; that is, the effect of reactivations was not necessarily seen until much later. In studies conducted in our lab, Aurora Suengas (Suengas & Johnson, 1988) had subjects engage in various "mini-events," such as visiting a computer lab, making a clay pot, and having coffee and cookies. Using cues to control which memories were reactivated, she subsequently had subjects think about some events but not others. Subjects later rated the subjective qualities of their memories, such as the perceptual and spatial detail or the emotional characteristics, for the various events. Their ratings indicated that thinking about events maintained subjective qualities over time more than not thinking about events. Characteristics such as perceptual detail and the spatial relations among objects and people give memory its episodic quality; such details are what distinguish autobiographical memories from more abstract "semantic" memory (Johnson, 1988). Mental rehearsal or reactivation of unique, one-time autobiographical events may be the single most important determinant of which personal memories survive to become part of our autobiographical narrative. An amnesic who cannot think back to earlier events after even only a few minutes cannot make use of reactivation in maintaining the qualitative details necessary for event memory (Johnson, 1988).

As we have noted (Johnson, 1992), there are undoubtedly large individual differences in the amount of reactivation of event memories that people normally engage in or the types of memories to which reactivations are directed. Similarly, there are likely circumstances that generally tend to lower (or raise) the frequency of such reactivations. For example, chronic stress, lung disease, abuse of alcohol or other drugs, and other conditions that influence cognitive functioning might reduce the frequency of naturally occurring reactivations, either because of a direct reduction of cognitive functioning or because of a reduction in the social interactions likely to prompt autobiographical remindings. If so, such individuals should have fewer well-consolidated autobiographical event memories and should therefore be at greater risk for retrograde amnesia in the event of brain damage. Thus some of the temporal gradient that retrograde amnesia often shows, with greater deficits for pre-onset memories closer in time to the onset of amnesia than for memories from longer ago, may actually be produced by a "progressive anterograde amnesia," which, with time, increasingly disrupts reactivation of events and information, as often observed in alcoholic Korsakof patients (Butters & Albert, 1982).

Reactivation is crucial in many tasks for encoding and developing cue structures, for maintaining relations, and for retrieving information. This component process is important for promoting cognitive contiguity and for spanning temporal, spatial, or cognitive lags where other processes are insufficient. We have argued that reactivation is important not only for tasks typically considered "declarative" or "explicit" memory tests (i.e., verbally mediated recall and recognition) but also for tasks, such as classical conditioning, that are not considered declarative or explicit. We also expect deficits in procedural, or skill-based, tasks when there is a reactivation component to the task (Phelps, 1989). Further, if a priming paradigm requires reactivation, then performance on that task should also be impaired. The point here is that the categorizing complex tasks into such dichotomies as procedural/declarative or implicit/explicit does not clearly delineate which tasks will be impaired in amnesia and which will not. Instead, a process analysis of individual tasks is required to predict and understand where memory impairments will be observed. This point begins to highlight the differences in memory deficits as conceptualized within the MEM framework and as conceptualized in other subsystem memory models. We will further explore these differences in the next two sections.

4 MEMORY SUBSYSTEMS IN THE MULTIPLE-ENTRY, MODULAR MEMORY SYSTEM

We have described how reactivation might play a role in a variety of tasks, contributing to, for example, latent inhibition in classical conditioning, performance on delayed nonmatch-to-sample tasks, familiarity in recognition, organization in recall, and maintenance of the qualitative details characteristic of memory for autobiographical events. Disruption in this one component process of mental activity has far-ranging consequences for memory. How does this view of memory deficits as resulting from a disrupted component process compare with views positing a disrupted memory subsystem, such as a disrupted declarative, spatial, or episodic subsystem (e.g., Cohen & Squire, 1980; Nadel, 1992; Schacter, 1992; Squire, 1992; Tulving, 1983)?

Most subsystem models of memory rest on dichotomous distinctions based on broadly defined task content or task categories, such as episodic/semantic (Tulving, 1972, 1983), procedural/declarative (Cohen, 1984; Cohen & Squire, 1980), taxon/locale (O'Keefe & Nadel, 1978), and habit/memory (Hirsh, 1974; Mishkin, Malamut, & Bachevalier, 1984). Johnson's (1983, 1990) initial description of MEM (which posited three subsystems: two perceptual and one reflective) also adopted a relatively broad dichotomy in terms of perceptual and reflective processes, based on Johnson and Raye's earlier distinction between perceptually derived and internally generated information (Johnson & Raye, 1981; Johnson, Taylor, & Raye, 1977). However, MEM differed from many dichotomies in that the basis of the distinctions among the three proposed subsystems was along types of *processing requirements* of tasks rather than classifications between tasks. The MEM framework has evolved to encompass four interacting subsystems, each comprising a specific set of component processes (Johnson, 1992; Johnson & Hirst, 1993).

To understand how subsystems are defined in MEM, consider what is meant by "system" and what the goals are in making distinctions between systems. The homeostatic system of the human body is an example of what can be meant by "subsystems." The system of the human body is made up of such interacting subsystems as the respiratory, circulatory, and central nervous systems. Each subsystem is further made up of component processes; for example, the respiratory (sub)system includes processes for taking in air, cleaning air, and exchanging carbon dioxide for oxygen. Here, a system is a functional unit with interacting interdependent subunits and processes that markedly expand the functional capability of the system as a whole. A subsystem is simply a secondary or subordinate system, which means that it too consists of interacting, interdependent subunits. This same use of "system" can be seen in the MEM framework in the four interacting subsystems (P-1, P-2, R-1, and R-2) making up the memory system and in the specific sets of component processes making up each of the memory subsystems.

The conceptual use of subsystems seen in MEM, which allows for (or even requires) interactions among subsystems, might be characterized as the "weak" view of systems described by Sherry and Schacter (1987). However, distinguishing between the "strong" view, in which components within subsystems can interact but subsystems themselves do not, and the "weak" view seems more appropriate for subsystem memory models that identify subsystems with distinctions among task *content* than for those that define subsystems in terms of *processing* components. In our view, many tasks performed by adult humans recruit processes from most, if not all, subsystems for successful completion. Some tasks, such as perceptual identification or word recognition, will recruit more perceptual processes from P-1 and P-2, but these processes in turn are likely to activate reflective processes to set up cue structures or strengthen relations between current information and prior related instances. Other tasks, such as recall or free association, access relatively more reflective processing from R-1 and R-2, but these processes also activate some perceptual processes when, for example, examining the environment for potential recall cues. The coherence of processes within subsystems increases efficiency, but the interaction of processes across subsystems promotes flexibility and increases the complexity of the tasks that can be accomplished. Further, a system based on task-processing requirements avoids the potential danger of proliferating subsystems presumed to operate by entirely different principles, as experienced by content-based subsystem memory models (Johnson and Hirst, 1993). As Johnson and Hirst (1993) note, the MEM framework does not require unique subsystems with different operating principles for face, language, or spatial memory, for example. That is, the processing subsystems posited in MEM should be replicated across content domains.

In the psychologically defined functional subsystems of MEM, the components are seen as working together for purposes that can be defined in mental and behavioral terms (e.g., to reason, to find food). Behaviors vary greatly in the cognitive complexity they represent, and we have no way to estimate the relative roles of evolutionary pressures and accidental factors in producing variations in complexity of cognition and memory across species. But in any event, we assume that the architecture of human cognition and memory reflects something of our evolutionary history. In figure 1, eliminating subsystems from the top to the bottom would in each case leave intact a viable organism with considerable learning capacity. For example, if we build up from the bottom of figure 1, a fully functioning organism with only a P-1 subsystem should be able to engage in a variety of learning, for example, by connecting incoming stimuli to motor responses. An organism with an additional P-2 subsystem should be able to attach responses differentially to recognized individuals, objects, and locations. Adding in an R-1 subsystem would permit comparing and connecting events across time and the expression of intention and control. Adding in an R-2 subsystem would allow the discovery of relations among many internally generated representations. To give more concrete examples, P-1 processes might be sufficient for acquiring skill at chasing prey, but P-2 processes are needed to recognize a familiar environment. R-1 processes are important for considering whether the current environment is preferable to yesterday's environment, but R-2 processes are needed to contrast one's own idea about the relative desirability of two environments with someone else's idea.

These examples are only to give some flavor of the types of activities each subsystem adds to the cognitive repertoire. The descriptions should not be taken as subsystem labels. For example, we do not want to say that the P-1 subsystem is *for* associating stimuli with motor movements, because associating certain motor movements with stimuli may be greatly helped by activities of subsystems higher than P-1 (e.g., when one learns a new dance, it may be useful to have a reflectively based representation of the overall structure and theme of the piece). Conversely, P-1 may participate in memory feats that are not entirely motor-based, as when starting to dial a phone number helps you remember the names of the digits.

A second crucial point is that functionally important cognition within subsystems typically requires the joint action of several component processes. For example, getting more skilled at chasing prey likely involves *locating, resolving, extracting,* and *tracking*; learning to critically evaluate empirical evidence likely involves *rehearsing, initiating, retrieving,* and *discovering*. Thus the overall architecture of MEM represents two features of cognition that are evident across species: the capacity of certain cognitive components to work easily together to support functionally important behaviors and also the expansion of functionally important behaviors, resulting from the addition of new, smoothly interacting sets of components. The architectu. also reflects such ideas as that interactions are more easily accomplished among component processes from adjacent than nonadjacent subsystems, that recursive reflection (e.g., thinking about thinking) can be accomplished with only two interacting subsystems as long as each has the capacity for control and monitoring (thus R-1 and R-2 resolve the "homunculus" problem), and that component processes going up the vertical edges of the cubes in figure 2 may represent variations on computational themes or provide some clue about the evolutionary history or structural basis of successively evolving components (Johnson & Hirst, 1993).

To understand the cognitive requirements of tasks, we have suggested a process analysis of tasks rather than categorizing tasks according to their content. We believe that comparing radically different tasks, such as perceptual identification and recall, can take us only so far in analyzing component processes of cognition. To tease apart the action of component processes, we have to pay more attention to the detailed requirements of superficially similar tasks. Different theorists have been able to use largely the same data to support different theoretical frameworks because processing requirements tend to be unequally distributed across tasks (e.g., perceptual and skill tasks draw largely on P-1 and P-2 processes, and recall on R-1 and R-2 processes), though the correlation between type of task and type of processing requirements is not perfect. In addition to advocating a processing analysis, we have also posited that a deficit in a single component process within a subsystem can account for a wide range of memory impairments. This notion is more specific than the suggestion that impairments in memory are a result of deficits in particular memory subsystems (e.g., Cohen & Squire, 1980; Nadel, 1992; Schacter, 1992; Squire, 1992; Tulving, 1983). What has been the basis for taking subsystems as the unit of disruption? The main basis for making these distinctions has come from single and double dissociations of task performance in both amnesic and normal subjects (e.g., Schacter, 1989). However, single and double dissociations can also be taken as evidence for disrupted processes, especially when dissociations occur across proposed subsystems (e.g., Blaxton, 1992, although see Dunn & Kirsner, 1988, for problems in using dissociations as evidence for multiple subsystems or processes). In MEM, we do not think that each of the four postulated subsystems breaks down in an all-or-none fashion. Rather, each subsystem could break down in several ways, just as the respiratory (sub)system could break down in multiple ways from problems with the diaphragm or the alveoli. Here we have focused on a disruption in *reactivating*, a single component within a subsystem, with consequences for many memory tasks.

Although we have focused on reactivation, most memory tasks require the participation of a number of component processes, and the more complex the task, the more complex combinations of component processes are necessary. Consequently, especially for more complex tasks, there should be a number of ways to disrupt their performance. For example, organization often involves not only *reactivating* information but also *shifting* from one aspect of meaning to another for the same item, *noting* relations, or *refreshing* information. While hippocampal damage may primarily affect reactivating, we expect that damage to other areas, such as the frontal lobes, primarily affects some of these other component processes (e.g., shifting, noting). All of MEM's component processes are necessary for normal adult human memory, so we should see different patterns of memory disruption, depending on the locus of the brain damage and the information tested. Thus we expect that even if reactivating were intact, brain damage that affected some of these other processes should show up when processing demands for normal performance are high. Consistent with this, patients with frontal lobe lesions do relatively well on tests that require relatively few organizational processes, such as *shifting* and *noting*, but show disruption on tasks requiring relatively more of these processes (Moscovitch, 1989; Shimamura, Janowsky, & Squire, 1991; Smith & Milner, 1984).

As this example suggests, MEM subsystems are not confined to single structures in the brain (e.g., R-1 is not *in* the hippocampus). Rather, subsystems involve brain circuits that cross neuroanatomically defined regions. Similarly, component processes within subsystems may also involve circuits that cross neuroanatomically defined regions (e.g., a neocortex to hippocampus to neocortex circuit). Thus, although we have proposed that the hippocampus is central for *reactivating*, it is important to remember that to reactivate, the hippocampus operates in combination with various other brain structures (e.g., those subserving activated agendas, those subserving the representations to be reactivated). Furthermore, we assume that these component processes and subsystems operate in a "distributed" fashion. For example, within the hippocampus, reactivation mechanisms are evidently replicated: unilateral hippocampal damage appears to disrupt reactivation of verbal information more than visual information or vice versa. Likewise, different areas of the frontal lobes may be important for shifting or noting different types of information. With increasingly sensitive cognitive tests and better characterizations of corresponding brain damage, it should become useful to make finer and finer distinctions among areas within specific brain regions, such as the hippo-campus and frontal lobes. At the same time, we expect to see common pro-cessing components, as represented in MEM, across distinctions that reflect input modality (auditory, visual), form (pictures, words), and content (faces, animals).

In sum, the subsystems of MEM contrast with the subsystems of many other memory models in that they provide a means of analyzing task-processing requirements rather than a means of distinguishing task content. Furthermore, MEM differs in the characterization of memory deficits: rather than positing a disruption of an entire subsystem, we posit a disrupted compo-nent process within a subsystem, which can lead to impairments of encoding, maintenance, and retrieval. When we eventually map MEM subsystems and component processes to brain regions, we expect that some, if not all, will be supported by circuits that may cross anatomically distinct brain regions. Trac-ing out these processing circuits is a great challenge and represents an oppor-tunity to merge insights about processing derived from cognitive analyses with insights about structure derived from neurobiology.

5 CONCLUSIONS

An important goal of this book is to bring together and consider similarities and differences among subsystem approaches to memory. To distinguish be-tween subsystems within a particular memory model, one can use any one (or many) of several criteria. For example, one might use biological interrelated-ness as a criterion: we see this in Squire's (1992) model, in which the hippo-campus and associated cortical regions are especially important for declarative memory, as opposed to nondeclarative memory, and in Moscovitch's (1992) model, in which the hippocampus is important for explicit, episodic, associa-tive memories and the basal ganglia are important for procedural memories. In contrast, one might use computational similarity as a criterion for defining a subsystem: Rudy and Sutherland (1992) highlight a subsystem important for creating configural memories, as opposed to creating elemental memories. Another criterion for positing subsystems is the content of memories, such as speech-based information versus visuospatial information (Baddeley, 1992) or spatial information versus nonspatial information (Nadel, 1992). Clearly these criteria are not exclusive of one another: biologically based subsystems can be computationally distinct and computationally distinct subsystems can be bio-logically distinct. Rather, the situation is that a particular type of criterion tends to be used preferentially within particular models.

A useful by-product of the different criteria employed for defining subsys-tems is that work from different laboratories highlights different aspects of memory. Thus, categorizing memory tasks as implicit versus explicit (e.g., Metcalfe, Cottrell, & Mencl, 1992; Schacter, 1992) has emphasized the impor-tance of awareness and its relationship to memory. Again, categorizing tasks as declarative versus procedural (e.g., Cohen & Squire, 1980) has highlighted voluntary access versus skill acquisition. Similarly, categorizing memories as perceptual versus reflective (e.g., Johnson, 1990, 1992; Johnson & Hirst, 1993) emphasizes the important distinction between externally derived and internally generated components of the acquisition, maintenance, and retrieval of memories. Problems with some of these dichotomies have been discussed elsewhere (Johnson & Hirst, in press; Shimamura, 1989; Squire, 1987).

Problems aside, however, the various proposals about amnesia based on these categories do characterize different important manifestations of what we believe is a common *processing* disruption. For example, declarative, episodic, spatial, explicit, and relational memory all require binding together enough information to differentiate similar representations. We have tried to show how this binding of potentially differentiating featural information is greatly facilitated by reactivation processes that operate both within a session (e.g., when a subject becomes momentarily distracted and then thinks back to recent events or information) and over longer intervals (e.g., when one thinks about what happened yesterday). That is, reactivation is important for noting relations, creating declarative access through structured cues or through self-generated practice, and keeping alive episodic detail, for example. In short, positing a reactivation deficit provides a common processing account of these various characterizations of memory impairments in amnesia.

Researchers proposing subsystems intend for the subsystems to be more than useful alternative categories of description; they hope to capture a structural or functional architecture of the mind/brain that can sensibly organize as much existing data as possible and predict new data. MEM attempts a schematic representation of interactive interdependent functionality. Each of MEM's subsystems consists of sets of component processes that continually work interactively to accomplish functionally important tasks. The organization of component processes into subsystems (as opposed to an undifferentiated collection of components) creates coherence and efficiency in processing routines that call on components within a subsystem. Segregation among components created by subsystem "boundaries" reduces interference among processes and increases our capacity for multitasking (*tracking* a tennis ball and simultaneously *discovering* an opponents' strategy). The capacity for interaction between subsystems, especially under the control of executive and supervisory agendas, allows us access to useful information across subsystems, as, for example, when a reflectively *noted* relation calls up appropriate perceptual *structuring* processes. At this point in development, MEM's architecture attempts to reflect this functional analysis of memory and to suggest a vocabulary for beginning to describe differences in task-processing requirements.

In sum, we have proposed that a single process within a memory subsystem, namely *reactivation*, is important for both binding together and strengthening aspects of memory. These consequences of reactivation are, in turn, important for the encoding, maintenance, and retrieval phases of many memory tasks across a wide range of species. Hippocampal damage appears to be one means by which disruptions in reactivation may occur in humans specifically and animals more generally. Disruption of a single component process can have consequences that are profound for all of memory, cutting across subsystem distinctions made in other memory models.

ACKNOWLEDGMENTS

Preparation of this paper was supported by the National Institute of Aging, grants AG09744 and AG09253, and by grant 11RG-91-123 from the Alzheimer's Association. We also thank Greg Clark, Carol Raye, Tracey Shors, as well as Chad Dodson and John Reeder of the 1992–1993 Princeton Cognition Lab, for helpful discussions of and comments on an earlier draft.

NOTES

1. Throughout this chapter, "hippocampus" means "hippocampus and/or related structures." As pointed out by most investigators in this area, experimental lesions of the hippocampus may vary in size and are sometimes not confined to the hippocampus. Lesion variability is, of course, an even bigger problem in the study of amnesics.

2. In fact, some theorists propose that the effect of elaboration is no different than the effect of repetition: elaboration has its effect by adding to an item's overall level of familiarity by increasing the covert frequency of occurrence of any item entering a relationship with another item (Shaughnessy & Underwood, 1973) or by increasing the number of links contributing to the total amount of activation, which is assessed for familiarity (Gillund & Shiffrin, 1984).

3. Component processes may build on each other. For example, the potential success of *retrieving* will be influenced by prior successful *reactivations*.

REFERENCES

Allen, G. A., Mahler, W. A., & Estes, W. K. (1969). Effects of recall tests on long-term retention of paired associates. *Journal of Verbal Learning and Verbal Behavior, 8*, 463–470.

Atkinson, R. C., & Juola, J. F. (1972). Search and decision processes in recognition memory. Stanford University, Institute for Mathematical Studies in the Social Sciences, Psychology, and Education Series, technical report 194.

Atkinson, R. C., & Juola, J. F. (1974). Search and decision processes in recognition memory. In D. H. Krantz, R. C. Atkinson, R. D. Luce, & P. Suppes (Eds.), *Contemporary developments in mathematical psychology* (pp. 243–293). San Francisco: Freeman.

Baddeley, A. (1982). Amnesia: A minimal model and interpretation. In L. S. Cermak (Ed.), *Human memory and amnesia* (pp. 305–336). Hillsdale, NJ: Erlbaum.

Baddeley, A. (1986). *Working memory.* Oxford psychology series, no. 11. Oxford: Oxford University Press.

Baddeley, A. (1992). Working memory: The interface between memory and cognition. *Journal of Cognitive Neuroscience, 4*, 281–288.

Berger, T. W., & Orr, W. B. (1983). Hippocampectomy selectively disrupts discrimination reversal conditioning of the rabbit nictitating membrane response. *Behavioural Brain Research, 8*, 49–68.

Biederman, I. (1987). Recognition by components: A theory of human image understanding. *Psychological Review, 94*, 115–147.

Blaxton, T. A. (1992). Dissociations among memory measures in memory-impaired subjects: Evidence for a processing account of memory. *Memory and Cognition, 20,* 549–562.

Bransford, J. D., & Johnson, M. K. (1972). Contextual prerequisites for understanding: Some investigations of comprehension and recall. *Journal of Verbal Learning and Verbal Behavior, 11,* 717–726.

Bugeleski, B. R., Kidd, E., & Segmen, J. (1968). Image as a mediator in one-trial paired-associate learning. *Journal of Experimental Psychology, 76,* 69–73.

Butters, N., & Albert, M. S. (1982). Processes underlying failures to recall remote events. In L. S. Cermak (Ed.), *Human memory and amnesia* (pp. 257–274). Hillsdale, NJ: Erlbaum.

Cermak, L. S., & Verfaellie, M. (1992). The role of fluency in the implicit and explicit task performance of amnesic patients. In L. R. Squire & N. Butters (Eds.), *Neuropsychology of memory* (2nd ed., pp. 36–45). New York: Guilford Press.

Cohen, N. J. (1984). Preserved learning capacity in amnesia: Evidence for multiple memory systems. In L. R. Squire & N. Butters (Eds.), *Neuropsychology of memory* (pp. 83–103). New York: Guilford Press.

Cohen, N. J., & Squire, L. R. (1980). Preserved learning and retention of pattern-analyzing skill in amnesia: Dissociation of knowing how and knowing that. *Science, 210,* 207–210.

Craik, F. I. M. (1986). A functional account of age differences in memory. In F. Klix & H. Hagendorf (Eds.), *Human memory and cognitive capabilities* (pp. 409–422). Amsterdam: North-Holland.

Daum, I., Channon, S., & Canavan, A. G. M. (1989). Classical conditioning in patients with severe memory problems. *Journal of Neurology, Neurosurgery, and Psychiatry, 52,* 47–51.

Daum, I., Channon, S., Polkey, C. E., & Gray, J. A. (1991). Classical conditioning after temporal lobe lesions in man: Impairment in conditional discrimination. *Behavioral Neuroscience, 105,* 396–408.

Disterhoft, J. (1992). Colloquium given at the Memory Disorders Research Center, Boston University School of Medicine and Boston Department of Veterans Affairs, Boston, December.

Dooling, D. J., & Lachman, R. (1971). Effects of comprehension on retention of prose. *Journal of Experimental Psychology, 88,* 216–222.

Dunn, J. C., & Kirsner, K. (1988). Discovering functionally independent mental processes: The principle of reversed association. *Psychological Review, 95,* 91–101.

Eichenbaum, H. (1992). The hippocampal system and declarative memory in animals. *Journal of Cognitive Neuroscience, 4,* 217–231.

Eichenbaum, H., Mathews, P., & Cohen, N. J. (1989). Further studies of hippocampal representation during odor discrimination learning. *Behavioral Neuroscience, 103,* 1207–1216.

Faries, J. M., & Reiser, B. J. (1988). Access and use of previous solutions in a problem solving situation. In J. Kolodner (Ed.), *Proceedings of the Tenth Annual Conference of the Cognitive Science Society* (pp. 433–439). San Mateo, CA: Morgan Kaufmann Publishers.

Fodor, J. A. (1983). *The Modularity of mind: An essay on faculty psychology.* Cambridge: MIT Press.

Fodor, J. A., Bever, T. G., & Garrett, M. F. (1974). *The psychology of language: An introduction to psycholinguistics and generative grammar.* New York: McGraw-Hill.

Gentner, D. (1988). Analogical inference and analogical access. In A. Prieditis (Ed.), *Analogica* (pp. 63–88). Los Altos, CA: Morgan Kaufmann.

Gibson, J. J. (1950). *The perception of the visual world.* Boston: Houghton-Mifflin.

Gillund, G., & Shiffrin, R. M. (1984). A retrieval model for both recognition and recall. *Psychological Review, 91,* 1–67.

Glucksberg, S., & Weisberg, R. W. (1966). Verbal behavior and problem solving: Some effects of labeling in a functional fixedness problem. *Journal of Experimental Psychology, 71,* 659–664.

Goldman-Rakic, P. S. (1987). Circuitry of primate prefrontal cortex and the regulation of behavior by representational memory. In F. Plum (Ed.), *Handbook of physiology: Sec. 1. The nervous system: Vol. 5. Higher functions of the brain* (pp. 373–417). Bethesda, MD: American Psychological Association.

Haist, F., Shimamura, A. P., & Squire, L. R. (1992). On the relationship between recall and recognition memory. *Journal of Experimental Psychology: Learning, Memory, and Cognition, 18,* 691–702.

Hasher, L., & Zacks, R. T. (1979). Automatic and effortful processes in memory. *Journal of Experimental Psychology, 108,* 356–388.

Hintzman, D. L. (1988). Judgments of frequency and recognition memory in a multiple-trace memory model. *Psychological Review, 95,* 528–551.

Hirsh, R. (1974). The hippocampus and contextual retrieval of information from memory: A theory. *Behavioral Biology, 12,* 421–444.

Hirst, W. (1982). The amnesic syndrome: Descriptions and explanations. *Psychological Bulletin, 91,* 435–460.

Hirst, W. (1989). On consciousness, recall, recognition, and the architecture of memory. In S. Lewandowsky, J. C. Dunn, & K. Kirsner (Eds.), *Implicit memory* (pp. 33–46). Hillsdale, NJ: Lawrence Erlbaum.

Hirst, W., Johnson, M. K., Kim, J. K., Phelps, E. A., Risse, G., & Volpe, B. T. (1986). Recognition and recall in amnesics. *Journal of Experimental Psychology: Learning, Memory, and Cognition, 12,* 445–451.

Hirst, W., Johnson, M. K., Phelps, E. A., & Volpe, B. T. (1988). More on recognition and recall in amnesics. *Journal of Experimental Psychology: Learning, Memory, and Cognition, 14,* 758–762.

Hochberg, J. E. (1970). Attention, organization, and consciousness. In D. I. Mostofsky (Ed.), *Attention: Contemporary theory and analysis* (pp. 99–124). New York: Appleton-Century-Crofts.

Hogan, R. M., & Kintsch, W. (1971). Differential effects of study and test trials on long-term recognition and recall. *Journal of Verbal Learning and Verbal Behavior, 10,* 562–567.

Huppert, F. A., & Piercy, M. (1976). Recognition memory in amnesic patients: Effect of temporal context and familiarity of material. *Cortex, 12,* 3–20.

Huppert, F. A., & Piercy, M. (1977). Recognition memory in amnesic patients: A defect of acquisition? *Neuropsychologia, 15,* 643–652.

Huppert, F. A., & Piercy, M. (1982). In search of the functional locus of amnesic syndromes. In L. S. Cermak (Ed.), *Human memory and amnesia* (pp. 123–137). Hillsdale, NJ: Erlbaum.

Jacoby, L. L. (1991). A process dissociation framework: Separating automatic from intentional uses of memory. *Journal of Memory and Language, 30,* 513–541.

James, G. O., Hardiman, M. J., & Yeo, C. H. (1987). Hippocampal lesions and trace conditioning in the rabbit. *Behavioural Brain Research, 23,* 109–116.

Jeannerod, M. (1986). Mechanisms of visuomotor coordination: A study in normal and brain-damaged subjects. *Neuropsychologia, 24,* 41–78.

Johnson, M. K. (1983). A multiple-entry, modular memory system. In G. H. Bower (Ed.), *The psychology of learning and motivation* (Vol. 17, pp. 81–123). New York: Academic Press.

Johnson, M. K. (1988). Discriminating the origin of information. In T. F. Oltmanns & B. A. Maher (Eds.), *Delusional beliefs: Theoretical and empirical perspectives* (pp. 34–65). New York: Wiley.

Johnson, M. K. (1990). Functional forms of human memory. In J. L. McGaugh, N. M. Weinberger, & G. Lynch (Eds.), *Brain organization and memory: Cells, systems, and circuits* (pp. 106–134). New York: Oxford University Press.

Johnson, M. K. (1991). Reality monitoring: Evidence from confabulation in organic brain disease patients. In G. P. Prigatano & D. L. Schacter (Eds.), *Awareness of deficit after brain injury* (pp. 176–197). New York: Oxford University Press.

Johnson, M. K. (1992). MEM: Mechanisms of recollection. *Journal of Cognitive Neuroscience, 4,* 268–280.

Johnson, M. K., Hashtroudi, S., & Lindsay, D. S. (1993). Source monitoring. *Psychological Bulletin, 114,* 3–28.

Johnson, M. K., & Hirst, W. (1991). Processing subsystems of memory. In R. G. Lister & H. J. Weingartner (Eds.), *Perspectives on cognitive neuroscience* (pp. 197–217). New York: Oxford University Press.

Johnson, M. K., & Hirst, W. (1993). MEM: Memory subsystems as processes. In A. F. Collins, S. E. Gathercole, M. A. Conway, & P. E. Morris (Eds.), *Theories of memory* (pp. 241–286). East Sussex, England: Erlbaum.

Johnson, M. K., & Kim, J. K. (1985). Recognition of pictures by alcoholic Korsakoff patients. *Bulletin of the Psychonomic Society, 23,* 456–458.

Johnson, M. K., & Multhaup, K. S. (1992). Emotion and MEM. In S.-A. Christianson (Ed.), *The handbook of emotion and memory: Current research and theory* (pp. 33–66). Hillsdale, NJ: Erlbaum.

Johnson, M. K., & Raye, C. L. (1981). Reality monitoring. *Psychological Review, 88,* 67–85.

Johnson, M. K., & Reeder, J. A. (in press). Consciousness as metaprocessing. In J. Cohen & J. Schooler (Eds.), *Approaches to the question of consciousness.* Hillsdale, NJ: Erlbaum.

Johnson, M. K., Taylor, T. H., & Raye, C. L. (1977). Fact and fantasy: The effects of internally generating events on the apparent frequency of externally generated events. *Memory and Cognition, 5,* 116–122.

Kaye, H., & Pearce, J. M. (1987a). Hippocampal lesions attenuate latent inhibition of a CS and of a neutral stimulus. *Psychobiology, 15,* 293–299.

Kaye, H., & Pearce, J. M. (1987b). Hippocampal lesions attenuate latent inhibition and the decline of the orienting response in rats. *Quarterly Journal of Experimental Psychology: Comparative and Physiological Psychology, 39B,* 107–125.

Kowler, E., & Martins, A. J. (1982). Eye movements of preschool children. *Science, 215,* 997–999.

Krumhansl, C. L. (1990). *Cognitive foundations of musical pitch.* New York: Oxford University Press.

Landauer, T. K., & Bjork, R. A. (1978). Optimum rehearsal patterns and name learning. In M. M. Gruneberg, P. E. Morris, & R. N. Sykes (Eds.), *Practical aspects of memory* (pp. 625–632). New York: Academic Press.

Lindsay, P. H., & Norman, D. A. (1977). *Human information processing* (2nd ed.). New York: Academic Press.

Linton, M. (1978). Real world memories after six years: An in vivo study of very long-term memory. In M. M. Gruneberg, P. E. Morris, & R. N. Sykes (Eds.), *Practical aspects of memory* (pp. 3–24). New York: Academic Press.

Locke, J. (1959). *An essay concerning human understanding*. Annotated by A. C. Fraser. New York: Dover Publications. (First published in 1690.)

Loftus, G. R. (1974). Acquisition of information from rapidly presented verbal and nonverbal stimuli. *Memory and Cognition, 2*, 545–548.

Lubow, R. E., & Moore, A. U. (1959). Latent inhibition: The effect of nonreinforced pre-exposure to the conditional stimulus. *Journal of Comparative and Physiological Psychology, 52*, 415–419.

Luria, A. R. (1966). *Higher cortical functions in man*. New York: Basic Books.

Malamut, B. L., Saunders, R. C., & Mishkin, M. (1984). Monkeys with combined amygdalo-hippocampal lesions succeed in object discrimination learning despite 24-hour intertrial intervals. *Behavioral Neuroscience, 98*, 759–769.

Mandler, G. (1967). Organization and memory. In K. W. Spence & J. T. Spence (Eds.), *The Psychology of Learning and Motivation* (Vol. 1, pp. 327–372). New York: Academic Press.

Mandler, G. (1980). Recognizing: The judgment of previous occurrence. *Psychological Review, 87*, 252–271.

Mandler, G., & Boeck, W. J. (1974). Retrieval processes in recognition. *Memory and Cognition, 2*, 613–615.

Marr, D. (1982). *Vision*. San Francisco: W. H. Freeman.

Mayes, A. R., Meudell, P. R., & Pickering, A. (1985). Is organic amnesia caused by a selective deficit in remembering contextual information? *Cortex, 21*, 167–202.

Metcalfe, J., Cottrell, G. W., & Mencl, W. E. (1992). Cognitive binding: A computational-modeling analysis of a distinction between implicit and explicit memory. *Journal of Cognitive Neuroscience, 4*, 289–298.

Miller, G. A. (1956). The magical number, seven plus or minus two: Some limits on our capacity for processing information. *Psychological Review, 63*, 81–97.

Miller, G. A., Galanter, E., & Pribram, K. A. (1960). *Plans and the structure of behavior*. New York: Holt, Rhinehart & Winston.

Mishkin, M. (1978). Memory in monkeys severely impaired by combined but not by separate removal of amygdala and hippocampus. *Nature, 273*, 297–298.

Mishkin, M., Malamut, B., & Bachevalier, J. (1984). Memories and habits: Two neural systems. In G. Lynch, J. L. McGaugh, & N. M. Weinberger (Eds.), *Neurobiology of learning and memory* (pp. 65–77). New York: Guilford Press.

Mishkin, M., Ungerleider, L. G., & Macko, K. A. (1983). Object vision and spatial vision: Two central pathways. *Trends in Neuroscience, 6*, 414–417.

Moore, J. W. (1979). Information processing in space-time by the hippocampus. *Physiological Psychology, 7*, 224–232.

Moore, J. W., & Stickney, K. J. (1980). Formation of attentional-associative networks in real time: Role of the hippocampus and implications for conditioning. *Physiological Psychology, 8*, 207–217.

Moscovitch, M. (1989). Confabulation and the frontal systems: Strategic versus associative retrieval in neuropsychological theories of memory. In H. L. Roediger III & F. I. M. Craik (Eds.), *Varieties of memory and consciousness: Essays in honour of Endel Tulving* (pp. 133–160). Hillsdale, NJ: Erlbaum.

Moscovitch, M. (1992). Memory and working-with-memory: A component process model based on modules and central systems. *Journal of Cognitive Neuroscience, 4,* 257–267.

Moscovitch, M., & Umiltà, C. (1990). Modularity and neuropsychology: Implications for the organization of attention and memory in normal and brain-damaged people. In M. E. Schwartz (Ed.), *Modular processes in dementia.* Cambridge: MIT Press.

Moyer, J. R., Deyo, R. A., & Disterhoft, J. F. (1990). Hippocampectomy disrupts trace eye-blink conditioning in rabbits. *Behavioral Neuroscience, 104,* 243–252.

Nadel, L. (1992). Multiple memory systems: What and why. *Journal of Cognitive Neuroscience, 4,* 179–188.

Nelson, T. O., & Narens, L. (1990). Metamemory: A theoretical framework and some new findings. In G. H. Bower (Ed.), *The psychology of learning and motivation* (Vol. 26, pp. 125–173). New York: Academic Press.

Norman, D. A., & Shallice, T. (1986). Attention to action: Willed and automatic control of behavior. In R. J. Davidson, G. E. Schwartz, & D. Shapiro (Eds.), *Consciousness and self-regulation* (pp. 1–18). New York: Plenum Press.

O'Keefe, J., & Nadel, L. (1978). *The hippocampus as a cognitive map.* Oxford: Clarendon Press.

Olton, D. S. (1986). Hippocampal function and memory for temporal context. In R. L. Isaacson & K. H. Pribram (Eds.), *The hippocampus* (Vol. 4, pp. 281–298). New York: Plenum Press.

Oscar-Berman, M., & Bonner, R. T. (1985). Matching- and delayed-matching-to-sample performance as measures of visual processing, selective attention, and memory in aging and alcoholic individuals. *Neuropsychologia, 23,* 639–651.

Paivio, A. (1969). Mental imagery in associative learning and memory. *Psychological Review, 76,* 241–263.

Palmer, S. E. (1975). The effects of contextual scenes on the identification of objects. *Memory and Cognition, 3,* 519–526.

Penick, S., & Solomon, P. R. (1991). Hippocampus, context, and conditioning. *Behavioral Neuroscience, 105,* 611–617.

Peterson, M. A., & Hochberg, J. (1983). Opposed-set measurement procedure: A quantitative analysis of the role of local cues and intention in form perception. *Journal of Experimental Psychology: Human Perception and Performance, 9,* 183–193.

Phelps, E. A. (1989). *Cognitive skill learning in amnesics.* Unpublished doctoral dissertation, Princeton University.

Phillips, R. G., & LeDoux, J. E. (1992a). Differential contribution of amygdala and hippocampus to cued and contextual fear conditioning. *Behavioral Neuroscience, 106,* 274–285.

Phillips, R. G., & LeDoux, J. E. (1992b). Hippocampal lesions interfere with contextual fear conditioning in some but not all procedures: Clues to the nature of context. Paper presented at the Fifth Conference on the Neurobiology of Learning and Memory, Irvine, CA, October.

Port, R. L., Romano, A. G., Steinmetz, J. E., Mikhail, A. A., & Patterson, M. M. (1986). Retention and acquistion of classical trace conditioned responses by rabbits with hippocampal lesions. *Behavioral Neuroscience, 100,* 745–752.

Posner, M. I., & Petersen, S. E. (1990). The attention system of the human brain. In W. M. Cowan (Ed.). *Annual review of neuroscience* (Vol. 13, pp. 25–42). Palo Alto, CA: Annual Reviews Inc.

Posner, M. I., & Snyder, C. R. R. (1975). Attention and cognitive control. In R. L. Solso (Ed.). *Information processing and cognition: The Loyola Symposium* (pp. 55–85). Hillsdale, NJ: Erlbaum.

Pylyshyn, Z. (1989). The role of location indexes in spatial perception: A sketch of the FINST spatial-index model. *Cognition, 32,* 65–97.

Rabinowitz, M., & Mandler, J. M. (1983). Organization and information retrieval. *Journal of Experimental Psychology: Learning, Memory, and Cognition, 9,* 430–439.

Rawlins, J. N. P. (1985). Associations across time: The hippocampus as a temporary memory store. *The Behavioral and Brain Sciences, 8,* 479–496.

Raye, C. L. (1976). Recognition: Frequency or organization? *American Journal of Psychology, 89,* 645–658.

Reiser, B. J. (1986). The encoding and retrieval of memories of real-world experiences. In J. A. Galambos, R. P. Abelson, & J. B. Black (Eds.), *Knowledge structures* (pp. 71–99). Hillsdale, NJ: Erlbaum.

Riddoch, M. J., & Humphreys, G. W. (1987). Visual object processing in optic aphasia: A case of semantic access agnosia. *Cognitive Neuropsychology, 4,* 131–186.

Ross, R. T., Orr, W. B., Holland, P. C., & Berger, T. W. (1984). Hippocampectomy disrupts acquistion and retention of learned conditional responding. *Behavioral Neuroscience, 98,* 211–225.

Rubin, D. C., & Kozin, M. (1984). Vivid memories. *Cognition, 16,* 81–95.

Rudy, J. W., & Sutherland, R. J. (1992). Configural and elemental associations and the memory coherence problem. *Journal of Cognitive Neuroscience, 4,* 208–216.

Schacter, D. L. (1989). On the relation between memory and consciousness: Dissociable interactions and conscious experience. In H. L. Roediger III & F. I. M. Craik (Eds.), *Varieties of memory and consciousness: Essays in honour of Endel Tulving* (pp. 355–389). Hillsdale, NJ: Erlbaum.

Schacter, D. L. (1992). Priming and multiple memory systems: Perceptual mechanisms of implicit memory. *Journal of Cognitive Neuroscience, 4,* 244–256.

Schank, R. C., & Abelson, R. P. (1977). *Scripts, plans, goals, and understanding.* Hillsdale, NJ: Erlbaum.

Schmaltz, L. W., & Theios, J. (1972). Acquisition and extinction of a classically conditioned response in hippocampectomized rabbits (*Oryctolagus cuniculus*). *Journal of Comparative and Physiological Psychology, 79,* 328–333.

Seamon, J. G., & Chumbley, J. I. (1977). Retrieval processes for serial order information. *Memory and Cognition, 5,* 709–715.

Shallice, T. (1988). *From neuropsychology to mental structure.* New York: Cambridge University Press.

Shaughnessy, J. J., & Underwood, B. J. (1973). The retention of frequency information for categorized lists. *Journal of Verbal Learning and Verbal Behavior, 12,* 99–107.

Shepard, R. N. (1967). Recognition memory for words, sentences, and pictures. *Journal of Verbal Learning and Verbal Behavior, 6,* 156–163.

Sherry, D. F., & Schacter, D. L. (1987). The evolution of multiple memory systems. *Psychological Review, 94,* 439–454.

Shiffrin, R. M., & Schneider, W. (1977). Controlled and automatic human information processing: II. Perceptual learning, automatic attending, and a general theory. *Psychological Review, 84*, 127–190.

Shimamura, A. P. (1989). Disorders of memory: The cognitive science perspective. In F. Boller & J. Grafman (Eds.), *Handbook of neuropsychology* (Vol. 3, pp. 35–73). Amsterdam: Elsevier Press.

Shimamura, A. P., Janowsky, J. S., & Squire, L. R. (1991). What is the role of frontal lobe damage in memory disorder? In H. S. Levin, H. M. Eisenberg, & A. L. Benton (Eds.), *Frontal lobe function and injury* (pp. 173–195). New York: Oxford University Press.

Smith, M. L., & Milner, B. (1984). Differential effects of frontal-lobe lesions on cognitive estimation and spatial memory. *Neuropsychologia, 22*, 697–705.

Solomon, P. R. (1980). A time and place for everything? Temporal processing views of hippocampal function with special reference to attention. *Physiological Psychology, 8*, 254–261.

Solomon, P. R., & Moore, J. W. (1975). Latent inhibition and stimulus generalization of the classically conditioned nictitating membrane response in rabbits (*Orytolagus cuniculus*) following dorsal hippocampal ablation. *Journal of Comparative and Physiological Psychology, 89*, 1192–1203.

Solomon, P. R., Solomon, S. D., Vander Schaaf, E., & Perry, H. E. (1983). Altered activity in the hippocampus is more detrimental to classical conditioning than removing the structure. *Science, 220*, 329–331.

Solomon, P. R., Vander Schaaf, E. R., Thompson, R. F., & Weisz, D. J. (1986). Hippocampus and trace conditioning of the rabbit's classically conditioned nictitating membrane response. *Behavioral Neuroscience, 100*, 729–744.

Squire, L. R. (1987). *Memory and brain*. New York: Oxford University Press.

Squire, L. R. (1992). Declarative and nondeclarative memory: Multiple brain systems supporting learning and memory. *Journal of Cognitive Neuroscience, 4*, 232–243.

Squire, L. R., Zola-Morgan, S., & Chen, K. S. (1988). Human amnesia and animal models of amnesia: Performance of amnesic patients on tests designed for the monkey. *Behavioral Neuroscience, 102*, 210–221.

Stuss, D. T. (1991). Self, awareness, and the frontal lobes: A neuropsychological perspective. In J. Strauss, & G. R. Goethals (Eds.), *The self: Interdisciplinary approaches* (pp. 255–278). New York: Springer-Verlag.

Stuss, D. T., & Benson, D. F. (1986). *The frontal lobes*. New York: Raven Press.

Suengas, A. G., & Johnson, M. K. (1988). Qualitative effects of rehearsal on memories for perceived and imagined complex events. *Journal of Experimental Psychology: General, 117*, 377–389.

Sutherland, R. J., & Rudy, J. W. (1989). Configural association theory: The role of the hippocampal formation in learning, memory, and amnesia. *Psychobiology, 17*, 129–144.

Thorndyke, P. W. (1977). Cognitive structures in comprehension and memory of narrative discourse. *Cognitive Psychology, 9*, 77–110.

Treisman, A. (1986). Features and objects in visual processing. *Scientific American, 255*(5), 114B–125.

Tulving, E. (1962). Subjective organization in free recall of "unrelated" words. *Psychological Review, 69*, 344–354.

Tulving, E. (1966). Subjective organization and effects of repetition in multi-trial free-recall learning. *Journal of Verbal Learning and Verbal Behavior, 5*, 193–197.

Tulving, E. (1972). Episodic and semantic memory. In E. Tulving & W. Donaldson (Eds.), *Organization of memory* (pp. 381–403). New York: Academic Press.

Tulving, E. (1983). *Elements of episodic memory*. Oxford: Clarendon Press.

Tulving, E., & Pearlstone, Z. (1966). Availability versus accessibility of information in memory for words. *Journal of Verbal Learning and Verbal Behavior, 5,* 381–391.

Underwood, B. J. (1972). Word recognition memory and frequency information. *Journal of Experimental Psychology, 94,* 276–283.

Verfaellie, M., & Treadwell, J. R. (1993). The status of recognition memory in amnesia. *Neuropsychology, 7,* 5–13.

Weinstein, A. (1987). Preserved recognition memory in amnesia. Unpublished doctoral dissertation, State University of New York at Stony Brook.

Weiskrantz, L. (1986). *Blindsight*. Oxford: Clarendon Press.

Weiskrantz, L., & Warrington, E. K. (1979). Conditioning in amnesic patients. *Neuropsychologia, 17,* 187–194.

Winocur, G., Rawlins, J. N. P., & Gray, J. A. (1987). The hippocampus and conditioning to contextual cues. *Behavioral Neuroscience, 101,* 617–625.

Wollen, K. A., Weber, A., & Lowry, D. H. (1972). Bizarreness versus interaction of mental images as determinants of learning. *Cognitive Psychology, 3,* 518–523.

Woodruff-Pak, D. S., & Corkin, S. (1991). Successful eyeblink classical conditioning in H.M. *Society of Neuroscience Abstracts, 17,* 5–8.

Yantis, S., & Johnson, D. N. (1990). Mechanisms of attentional priority. *Journal of Experimental Psychology: Human Perception and Performance, 16,* 812–825.

Zola-Morgan, S., & Squire, L. R. (1984). Preserved learning in monkeys with medial temporal lesions: Sparing of motor and cognitive skills. *Journal of Neuroscience, 4,* 1072–1085.

Zola-Morgan, S., & Squire, L. R. (1985). Medial temporal lesions in monkeys impair memory on a variety of tasks sensitive to human amnesia. *Behavioral Neuroscience, 99,* 22–34.

11 Working Memory: The Interface between Memory and Cognition

Alan Baddeley

"Working memory" may be defined as the system for the temporary maintenance and manipulation of information, necessary for the performance of such complex cognitive activities as comprehension, learning and reasoning. Used in this sense, the terms refers to an area of research that may or may not prove to be dependent on a single coherent system. I propose such a system within a broad and relatively speculative overview of human memory that emphasizes the putative role of working memory. This is followed by a brief account of a particular model of working memory and a more detailed discussion of the way in which the various subcomponents of the model relate to other aspects of memory and cognition.

1 HUMAN MEMORY: A SPECULATIVE OVERVIEW

I assume that memory, along with other cognitive capacities, has evolved to allow the organism to cope with a complex but structured world. The world is never entirely predictable, but it has sufficient regularity to make it advantageous for the organism to use the past to predict the future, that is, to make use of learning and memory.

1.1 Working Memory and Perception

Before learning can take place, an organism must be able to perceive the world and take advantage of the fact that the information from the range of sensory channels is likely to be correlated. Objects not only have visual and spatial characteristics but are likely also to have associated tactile features and quite possibly to have a characteristic smell and taste. It seems likely that perceiving and integrating these various sources of information would benefit from at least a temporary form of storage, to allow both for extended processing and also for the fact that the evidence from the various channels may not always be available simultaneously. Indeed, in some cases, such as the subsequent taste of an orange or the sound emitted by a cat, information on one channel, such as vision, may arrive substantially before that of others. It can be argued that this capacity to integrate sensory information requires some form of working memory, particularly if the system is one that actively attempts to build up information about a perceived object. Furthermore, it can also be argued that conscious awareness provides a convenient way of simultaneously representing such diverse streams of information about a common object, although it is almost certainly not the only way (see Baddeley, 1992a, 1992b, 1993, for discussions).

1.2 Aspects of Learning

While a working memory system that coordinates information from a number of sources is likely to aid perceptual organization of the world, it would not necessarily benefit from experience. Hence, it would not form concepts such as would be necessary to recognize a cat as such, nor would it allow one to learn that cats tend to hiss rather than to bark. More important perhaps, it would not allow one to know whether cats were dangerous or, indeed, to recognize one's own cat or, of course, to remember whether it had already been fed or not. It is now widely accepted that long-term memory is not a simple unitary system, although there is considerably less agreement as to how it should be conceptualized (Richardson-Klavehn & Bjork, 1988).

There are two major dimensions along which researchers have proposed to dichotomize long-term memory, one being the distinction between *semantic* and *episodic* memory, while the other uses a rather broader range of terminology of which the distinction between *implicit* and *explicit* memory is one of the most widely adopted. "Semantic memory" is the term applied by Endel Tulving to the storage of information about the world, the name of the capital of France or the chemical formula for salt, for example. Episodic memory, on the other hand, refers to the recollection of a personally experienced event. In its earlier formulations, the theoretical emphasis tended to be on the basic separability of the underlying systems (Tulving, 1972). Later developments have tended rather to emphasize the more phenomenological aspects of episodic memory, which is assumed to be associated with the *conscious recollection* of an earlier episode (Tulving, 1983).

The distinction between implicit and explicit memory, which is also sometimes described as a distinction between procedural and declarative or direct and indirect memory, has developed more recently to reflect the observation that certain types or aspects of (implicit) memory appear to differ markedly from the pattern of function typically observed in laboratory studies of (explicit) learning and memory. Such traditional studies are typically concerned with the subject's explicit capacity to recall or recognize material; they show that performance is a function of such variables as the depth of processing of the material, its meaningfulness, and its degree of active organization.

In contrast, measures of implicit or indirect memory are able to reveal other aspects of learning that appear to be insensitive to depth of processing and much less influenced by strategies and organizational variables. This latter type of learning also tends to be relatively intact in a wide range of neuro-psychological patients who typically have impairment in explicit declarative or directly tested memory. While there is considerable agreement as to the existence and importance of such distinctions, there is considerably less agreement as to the best way of theoretically interpreting this rich and rapidly growing research area. Broadly speaking, proponents fall into two categories. The first attempts to explain the data as reflecting different aspects of a unitary memory system (e.g., Jacoby, Baker, & Brooks, 1989; Roediger, 1990) and typically concentrates on data from normal subjects. On the other hand, those who argue for two or possibly more separate memory systems (e.g., Squire & Zola-Morgan, 1988; Tulving & Schacter, 1990) are typically concerned to account for both normal and neuropsychological evidence. As will become clear, my own views tend to be of this kind.

Since the world is to some extent a predictable place, it makes sense for the organism to be able to capitalize on such predictability, to learn, for example, that food of one kind is typically found in one location, water in another, while a third may be associated with danger. The organism will also find it advantageous to be able to acquire novel skills, allowing hunting to be carried out more effectively or, in the case of humans, allowing language to develop. At a more basic level, there may be advantages to priming, whereby the operation of a particular cognitive process may facilitate the subsequent operation of that process (positive priming) or may cause it to be inhibited (negative priming). While these various forms of learning may employ different underlying neural systems, they tend to have in common the fact that they can in principle be acquired by a gradual accumulation of experience. Such learning of the varied probabilities of events can readily be simulated with connectionist networks that employ one of a range of possible learning algorithms (Rumelhart, 1991).

1.3 Episodic Memory

The limitation of such basic accumulative learning processes, however, is that they do not allow the organism to select one specific episode from the agglomeration of prior experience. For this a different form of associative learning is required (Rumelhart, 1991), which I suggest corresponds to episodic memory. If the organism is to retrieve a specific episode, it must have a means of specifying that episode. The most likely mechanism would seem to be via the use of context. I assume that the episodic-learning mechanism is capable of rapidly forming links between stimuli experienced at the same time. Such a link allows one such experience to evoke another. Hence, if I met Charlie and Gladys together at the Green Dragon Pub, then meeting Charlie is likely to remind me of both Gladys and the pub.

Clearly, the extent of such retrieval needs to be limited. Otherwise, the regulars at the Green Dragon, on entering the pub, would be overcome by a bombardment of memories of everyone they had ever met there, which would potentially cause serious interference with the main purpose of their visit. The study of the utilization and operation of such retrieval cues has, of course, formed one of the most active and successful areas of recent memory research (Tulving, 1983).

I assume that this process of retrieval from episodic memory makes a representation of an earlier episode accessible to working memory, which allows the central executive component of working memory to reflect on its implications and choose an appropriate action. Suppose that I had chatted with Gladys and been told that Charlie always went to that particular pub on Tuesday evenings. Then recollection of that experience would be rather useful if I wanted to make sure that I meet him. In contrast, a learning mechanism that simply strengthened the association between Charlie and the pub would be much less helpful.

1.4   Predicting the Future

So far I have discussed the role of memory as providing information about the past. However, the principal value of such information is for the light it throws on the future, and here again working memory becomes crucial in two ways. First, it provides a system for representing the past in a way that allows the organism to reflect on it and actively choose a further action, rather than simply to respond to the highest probability. Second, it offers the ability to set up and utilize models to predict the future. Johnson-Laird (1983) has argued that mental models play an important role in comprehension, thinking, and problem solving. In cases such as the problem of trying to meet Charlie, the model of his visiting the pub every week is so simple as to hardly constitute thinking, but it does, of course, involve most of the elements of problem solving: identifying the problem, retrieving the relevant information, setting up a simple model, and extrapolating to the solution of going to the pub on Tuesday.

I assume therefore, that episodic memory relies on a rather special kind of learning capable of associating arbitrary events that happen to be present at the same time in conscious awareness. This allows the recollection of individual episodes and the use of such episodes to plan future behavior, again through the operation of working memory.

Semantic memory, in this framework, is assumed to result from the accumulation of many episodes. Whereas the recollection of an individual episode requires differentiating it from other experiences, more generic semantic recall does not require the separation of the many experiences that come together to build up this aspect of knowledge. If one thinks of experiences as being piled one on top of the other, then episodic memory requires more or less accurate access to the residue of a single experience, whereas semantic memory is analogous to viewing the pile of experiences from above and abstracting what the various instances have in common.

1.5 Amnesia

Amnesic patients have a deflcit in the episodic-learning system, a problem that creates difficulties in adding to existing semantic memory. Hence they are typically unable to update their semantic memory: they are unaware of who is the current U.S. president and are not able to keep up with current developments in sport or to follow the plot of a play. They may however, still be able to retrieve old information from semantic memory, since this has already been laid down. In short, I opt for a learning, rather than retrieval, interpretation of the classic amnesic syndrome, while not, of course, denying that brain damage may also cause retrieval deficits in some cases.

I assume that the mechanism impaired in amnesia is not necessary for implicit or procedural learning, since this is typically preserved in most patients. This does not, of course, imply that implicit learning forms a unitary system; it is sufficient to assume that all implicit learning tasks have in common the fact that they do *not* need to rely on episodic learning. Indeed, it seems highly unlikely that classical conditioning, perceptual priming, pursuit tracking, and the acquisition of logical rules, such as the Fibonacci series, all depend on a single unitary system, despite the fact that all are preserved in amnesic patients (Richardson-Klavehn & Bjork, 1988; Squire & Zola-Morgan, 1988).

I have a similar problem in accepting the proposal, made by Tulving and Schacter (1990), that perceptual priming represents the operation of a single system, apparently extending across modalities and across processing levels. The neuropsychological evidence alone seems to argue, for separate perceptual processing modules for visual and auditory processing, which themselves appear to be fractionable into separable subsystems. Priming refers to a particular experimental paradigm that happens to be useful for detecting the persisting aftereffects of earlier processing. The fact that it can be used in broadly analogous ways within different perceptual systems is, of course, important, but referring to the assumed underlying process as a single system seems unnecessary and potentially rather misleading.

If the many implicit and procedural tasks that have been studied do indeed reflect different processes and subsystems, then one might expect to find differential disruption and preservation of aspects of this form of learning in neuropsychological patients, and such data are indeed beginning to appear (Butters, Heindel, & Salmon, 1990).

2 A MODEL OF WORKING MEMORY

The overview of human memory just given assigns an important and central role to working memory. This next section gives a brief account of a preliminary model of a working memory system that might play such a role. I give more detailed descriptions elsewhere (Baddeley, 1986, 1992a, 1992b, 1993).

The model evolved from the modal model of the 1960s, which assumed a short-term store that acts as a working-memory system. The most influential version of the modal model, that of Atkinson and Shiffrin (1968), assumed a unitary short-term store of limited capacity responsible for a range of memory phenomena, including memory span and the recency effect in free recall. This limited capacity memory store was also assumed to be essential for both learning and retrieval. The model received initial support from neuropsychological evidence that indicated a double dissociation between long- and short-term storage deflcits (Baddeley & Warrington, 1970; Shallice & Warrington, 1970). However, the modal model also encountered problems in dealing with the neuropsychological evidence. Patients with grossly defective short-term storage appeared to show normal long-term learning and, indeed, exhibited none of the gross cognitive impairment that one might have expected from an impairment in the functioning of an all-important working memory system (Shallice & Warrington, 1970).

Baddeley and Hitch (1974) investigated this issue through a series of experiments in which a deficit in short-term memory was simulated by requiring subjects to rehearse a sequence of digits while performing simultaneous reasoning, comprehension, and learning tasks. Since we assumed that the digit sequences filled the working memory system to capacity, we predicted that performance on the concurrent cognitive tasks would be markedly impaired. Across the range of tasks, a similar pattern of results occurred: the concurrent requirement to remember digit sequences clearly impaired cognitive performance, but the degree of disruption was far from catastrophic.

To account for these and other results, Baddeley and Hitch proposed to abandon the idea of a single, unitary working-memory system, proposing instead a tripartite model. This assumed an attentional controller, termed the *central executive*, aided by two active slave systems, the *articulatory* or *phonological loop* (which maintains speech-based information) and the *visuospatial scratchpad* or *sketchpad* (which is capable of holding and manipulating visuospatial information). Patients with defective memory span for digits were assumed to have an impairment in the functioning of the phonological loop, but since the central executive and sketchpad were assumed to be unimpaired, they were still able to learn and did not show any overwhelming problems in everyday cognition. The deficits they did show were broadly consistent with our proposed model of the phonological loop, as described below (Vallar & Baddeley, 1984).

2.1 The Phonological Loop

I assume that the phonological loop has two components: a brief speech-based store that holds a memory trace, which fades within approximately two seconds, coupled with an articulatory control process. This process, which resembles subvocal rehearsal, is capable of maintaining the material in the phonological store by a recycling process, and in addition it is able to feed information into the store by a process of subvocalization. One final assumption is that auditory spoken information gains automatic and obligatory access to the store.

This simple model is able to account for a relatively rich array of laboratory findings. The *phonological similarity effect*, whereby memory span for similar sounding items (such as the letters *B, C, G, V, T*) is smaller than for dissimilar items (*F, W, Y, K, R*), is interpreted as reflecting the fact that the store is speech-based. Similar items have fewer distinctive features, and hence are more susceptible to trace decay (Baddeley, 1966b; Conrad & Hull, 1964). The phonological memory trace can also be disrupted by the *irrelevant-speech effect*, whereby the presentation of unattended spoken material disrupts recall (Colle & Welsh, 1976; Salamé & Baddeley, 1982. Such material is assumed to obtain obligatory access to the phonological store, which corrupts the memory trace and leads to impaired performance.

Evidence for the articulatory control process comes from the *word length effect*, whereby memory span for long words is poorer than that for short words (Baddeley, Thomson, & Buchanan, 1975). This is assumed to occur because subjects rehearse in real time, and long words take longer to recycle, which allows a greater degree of trace decay to occur before the next rehearsal cycle. Subvocal rehearsal can be prevented by *articulatory suppression*, requiring the subject to utter some irrelevant sound. This prevents the material being rehearsed and also interferes with any attempt to encode visual material by subvocalization. Articulatory suppression thus forces the subject to abandon phonological storage of visually presented material, which reduces the level of performance and also abolishes any effect of phonological similarity or irrelevant speech. Suppression also removes the effect of word length, in this case whether the presentation is auditory or visual, since the word-length effect relies on subvocalization (Baddeley, Lewis, & Vallar, 1984).

Vallar and Baddeley (1984) studied a patient, P.V., with a very pure deficit of short-term phonological memory and found a pattern of results consistent with the assumption of a defective short-term phonological store. This pattern has subsequently been shown to be characteristic of such patients (see Vallar & Shallice, 1990, for a review).

While the phonological loop model gives a reasonably good account of the performance of both normal subjects and neuropsychological patients on a range of memory span tasks, the question remained as to the functional role of this subsystem. There is some evidence to suggest that it plays a role in speech comprehension, although most patients with short-term memory deficits are only impaired on processing relatively complex sentences (Vallar & Shallice, 1990).

This finding is open to at least two interpretations. One possibility is that the system is used only as an optional backup mechanism for dealing with particularly demanding materials. The other possibility is that sufficient phonological storage is preserved in most patients to allow an experienced user of the language to cope with most sentences. Typically, although such subjects have a digit span of only one or two items, their span for structured sentential material tends to be six or seven words, which may provide a sufficiently wide mnemonic "window" to allow comprehension of all but very complex material. A third possibility, that the phonological loop is not necessary for comprehension, is advocated by Butterworth, Campbell, and Howard (1986), who report the case of a subject with a developmental impairment in short-term memory but apparently without comprehension problems. Interpretation of this case, however, remains controversial (see Howard & Butterworth, 1989; Vallar & Baddeley, 1989).

Baddeley, Papagno, and Vallar (1988) suggested that an important function of the phonological loop might be to facilitate long-term phonological learning. They demonstrated that patient P.V., with a very pure short-term phonological memory deficit, showed normal paired-associate learning for pairs of meaningful words, together with a severely impaired capacity to learn the novel words, needed to acquire items of Russian vocabulary. Subsequent work using normal subjects showed that articulatory suppression (Papagno, Valentine, & Baddeley, 1991) and the effects of length and phonological similarity (Papagno & Vallar, 1992) disrupted the acquisition of novel phonological material substantially more than meaningful paired-associate learning, results that reinforce the conclusion that the phonological loop is particularly important for the acquisition of novel vocabulary.

If the phonological loop has evolved principally for the acquisition of language, then the failure to find major impairments in everyday functioning in patients with deficits of short-term memory becomes readily understandable, since they have already acquired a language and typically would not be required to learn a new language following their brain damage. One might, however, expect deficits in the phonological store to be particularly problematic in children. This possibility was explored by Gathercole and Baddeley (1990a) in a sample of children who had a specific language disability involving a combination of normal or above-average nonverbal intelligence, coupled with a delay of at least two years in language development. The children did indeed prove to have a particularly marked impairment in the capacity to repeat material, whether assessed by conventional memory-span measures or in terms of their capacity for repeating nonwords of varying length.

Gathercole and Baddeley (1989) argued that nonword repetition provides a better estimate of phonological storage than digit span, since it does not rely on knowledge of digits or other lexical items and is functionally more similar to the material involved in learning new vocabulary than the strings of unrelated lexical units that constitute the standard memory span procedure. Nonword repetition proved to be the best predictor of vocabulary acquisition in children tested over a range of ages between four and eight years, and for the four-year-olds at least, a cross-lagged correlation suggested that good nonword repetition leads to good vocabulary, rather than the reverse.

Service (1989) showed in a study of Finnish children that their capacity for learning English was better predicted by their capacity for nonword repetition than by any of a range of other cognitive measures, while Gathercole and Baddeley (1990b) showed in a simulated vocabulary learning task that children who were low in nonword-repetition skills performed more poorly than highly skilled children of equal nonverbal intelligence.

This pattern of results not only argues for an important role of the phonological loop in language acquisition but also casts new light on the question of the role of short-term and working memory in long-term learning. The fact that patients with short-term storage deficits appeared to show normal long-term learning in studies such as that of Shallice and Warrington (1970) had previously seemed to rule out short-term storage as a necessary stage in long-term learning. The observation that such patients have a specific deficit in working memory that is clearly linked to a parallel deficit in long-term learning reopens this question. In addition, there is parallel evidence for the importance of both the visuospatial sketchpad and the central executive components of working memory in long-term learning, as we will see below.

2.2 The Visuospatial Sketchpad

I assume that the visuospatial sketchpad also involves a brief store, together with control processes responsible for registering visuospatial information and for refreshing it by rehearsal. There is, however, rather less evidence as to the nature of this encode and refresh mechanism, and nothing equivalent to the word length effect in phonological memory has so far been discovered. However, storage may be disrupted both by visually presented irrelevant items, such as pictures or even patches of color (Logie, 1986), and by concurrent spatial processing. Such disruption may occur in the absence of visual input, as Baddeley and Lieberman (1980) demonstrated using blindfolded subjects: their capacity to take advantage of a visual imagery mnemonic was disrupted by a requirement to track a moving sound source.

The two types of interference, pattern-based and spatial, may be associated with separate subcomponents of the sketchpad. Farah (1988) presents evidence for this from studies of both normal subjects and neuropsychological patients that use both memory and psychophysiological measures, and argues for the anatomical and functional separation of the pattern-based and spatial components of visual short-term memory. The pattern-based system appears to be particularly dependent on the occipital lobes, while the spatial component appears to depend more on parietal processing. Subsequent work by Goldman-Rakic based on single cell recording in awake monkeys performing a visual short-term memory task suggests that there may also be a frontal lobe involvement, which may possibly be associated with the executive control of visual memory (Goldman-Rakic, 1988; Kojima & Goldman-Rakic, 1984).

As in the case of the phonological loop, there is evidence that the sketchpad is involved in long-term memory. Baddeley and Lieberman (1980) showed that a concurrent visuospatial tracking task disrupted the verbal learning of subjects using a spatial imagery mnemonic, while having no effect on their capacity for learning an equivalent list by rote rehearsal. Similarly, Logie (1986) found that presenting such visual material as color patches or pictures, which the subject was instructed to ignore, interfered with verbal paired-associate learning based on a visual pegword mnemonic, while again having little or no effect on learning by verbal rote rehearsal.

2.3   The Central Executive

The central executive is the most important but least well understood component of working memory. It was initially neglected on the grounds that the peripheral slave systems offered more tractable problems but has subsequently begun to attract considerably more research. Baddeley (1986) proposed to use Norman and Shallice's (1980) model of attentional control as a working hypothesis for the central executive. This model assumes that action can be controlled at either of two levels: by the operation of a series of existing schemata or via the supervisory attentional system, which takes control when novel tasks are involved or when existing habits have to be overridden, for example when danger threatens. A detailed account of the model is presented by Shallice and Burgess (1993), while its application to working memory is discussed by Baddeley (1993).

Shallice's principal concern is to provide a model of the very characteristic pattern of deficits shown by certain patients with bilateral damage to the frontal lobes. Such patients show marked problems in planning and in attentional control, sometimes perseverating on a single response, while in other situations they appear to be captured by whatever stimulus they encounter. Shallice argues that the frontal lobes are necessary for the operation of the supervisory attentional system. In its absence, patients may become locked into an existing schema or, conversely, have their attention captured by any available triggering stimulus.

Within the working memory framework, Baddeley has used Shallice's model to explain existing data on the limited capacity for random generation. When subjects are asked to produce a random string of items, such as letters of the alphabet, they are capable of performing the task well, provided the required rate is slow. As they speed up, however, they become progressively more biased in letter frequency and more stereotyped, producing sequences from the alphabet such as *P, Q, R* and *R, S, T* and familiar acronyms such as *USA* and *BBC* (Baddeley, 1966a). The requirement to perform a concurrent task also decreases randomness. The capacity for random generation tends to be associated with overall intelligence and to decline with age.

While the data in this area are highly consistent and clear, they did not prove easy to interpret. However, Norman and Shallice's (1980) model offers the following clear explanation: The task of retrieving a sequence of letters in random order places the subject in a conflict situation. The names of letters of the alphabet are readily retrievable by reciting the alphabet, but this clearly infringes the requirement to be random. Consequently, the subject must continually attempt to develop new retrieval strategies while avoiding existing alphabetic stereotypes and avoiding the danger of any strategy becoming automated. The capacity of the supervisory system to function in this way is therefore directly challenged, with the randomness of the output providing an indication of its capacity. When used as a secondary task, random generation proves to be very disruptive of such executive processes as those involved in assessing a chess position and choosing an optimal next move (Baddeley, 1993).

A good deal of recent work on the analysis of executive processes has been concerned with a study of patients with frontal lobe damage. In a typical study, patients with known frontal lesions might be required to perform a wide range of tasks that are expected to test different executive functions. The hope is to find one or two tasks that best characterize this deficit and that might then throw light on the nature of the underlying executive processes. In practice, such studies tend not to produce evidence pointing to certain crucial tasks. Typically, the studies find very considerable variability among subjects in terms of both the nature and severity of their impairment, which suggests a constellation of subprocesses rather than a single controlling module (Duncan, 1993; Shallice, 1993). Given the size and complexity of the frontal lobes and the richness of their connection with other parts of the brain, such results are perhaps not surprising. They suggest, however, that the central executive itself will need to be fractionated into a number of separable executive processes.

Given the probable complexity of the central executive, one approach is to attempt to isolate particular functions assumed, on a priori grounds, to be an important feature of the executive and to design tasks that will measure these capacities. One example of this is given in the attempt to test the hypothesis that patients suffering from Alzheimer's Disease show a particularly marked impairment in the functioning of the central executive (Spinnler et al., 1988).

The working-memory model assumes that one very important function of the executive is to coordinate information from separate subsystems. This was studied by combining pursuit tracking, which is assumed to load the sketchpad, with concurrent digit span, expected to make heavy demands on the phonological loop. Tracking speed and the length of the digit sequence were adjusted to give an equivalent level of performance in three groups: patients suffering from Alzheimer's disease, normal elderly subjects, and young controls. Subjects were then required to perform the two tasks simultaneously.

While the normal elderly were no more impaired than the young by the requirement to coordinate two tasks, the Alzheimer patients showed a marked deterioration in performance, which supports the view that their executive capacity was seriously impaired (Baddeley, Logie, Bressi, Della Sala, & Spinnler, 1986). In a subsequent longitudinal study, patients suffering from Alzheimer's Disease showed a steady deterioration in their capacity to combine tasks as the disease progressed, in contrast to their performance on the individual tasks, which remained relatively stable (Baddeley, Bressi, Della Sala, Logie, & Spinnler, 1991).

This latter approach has something in common with that adopted by Daneman and Carpenter (1980, 1983), who define working memory as the capacity to simultaneously store and process information. They have devised a number of tasks that combine storage and processing and have shown that performance on these tasks correlates with important cognitive skills such as language comprehension and reading, with subjects who are low in working memory capacity having difficulty in coping with complex material, such as that presented by garden path sentences or by texts requiring inference for their comprehension (Daneman & Carpenter, 1980, 1983).

While Daneman and Carpenter would not explicitly adopt the particular model of working memory just described, they do not deny the existence of more peripheral systems, such as the phonological loop. Their work, however, concentrates on the more executive aspects of working memory, typically using individual differences as a tool for analyzing the role of working memory in such complex cognitive skills as comprehension and reasoning. Such an emphasis on individual differences has the further advantage of linking up with more traditional psychometric approaches. This appears to be meeting with some success, since measures of working memory appear to correlate very highly with performance on a range of reasoning tasks that have traditionally been used for measuring intelligence (Kyllonen & Christal, 1990).

In conclusion, while the concept of working memory has its roots in the more traditional and constrained concept of short-term memory, it appears to be successfully developing into a much broader model of the crucial interface between memory and cognition.

3 EPILOGUE

How does the concept of working memory relate to the proposals elsewhere in this volume? In the case of the first few chapters, I suspect that the answer is that there is rather little common ground. Simple organisms such as aplysia may be ideal for working out the basic neurochemical and electrophysiological processes involved in learning, but it is doubtful that aplysia has very much in the way of a working memory.

In the case of many of the remaining chapters, the links are much more straightforward. In particular, my own speculations about the fractionation of human learning and memory systems seem to resemble rather closely those of most of my colleagues, and in particular the structure proposed by Squire. I have already discussed the way in which working memory integrates with such a structure, and consideration of the various relevant chapters suggests few problems in integrating my own views with that of others. However, compatibility does not, of course, imply identity. Different investigators, starting from evidence derived from different basic paradigms, come up with systems that emphasize different aspects. The chapter by Squire concerns itself with the neurobiological basis of learning, providing a useful bridge between human and animal work. Where our approaches cover similar ground, we are in broad agreement. My own work, however, is heavily influenced by memory for material coded in terms of language, which is not, of course, a topic that one would expect to be very adequately developed in studies based on animals. Schacter has chosen in his chapter to emphasize implicit learning, a topic that so far has not featured strongly in studies of working memory, although this may be changing with the proposal that the recency effect may be based on a combination of implicit learning with an explicit retrieval strategy (Baddeley & Hitch, 1993). Johnson's chapter emphasizes her interest in the phenomenology of memory, which provides a framework that allows the representation of some relatively subtle differences in the rememberer's evaluation of the evidence on which a recall or recognition response is based. I find such a framework intriguing but would have some difficulty knowing exactly how to map it onto a simple model such as my own.

There are clear similarities between my own views and those expressed by Moscovitch, but there are also differences. These stem principally from the fact that Moscovitch uses localization within the brain to provide his underlying theoretical structure, whereas my own view is that, while localization is an interesting question, it is unlikely to provide a sufficiently rich or readily verified structure for anything as complex as human memory. In particular, although I believe there is considerable evidence for an association between the frontal lobes and executive control, I resist the popular tendency to confound the two by referring to patients with executive problems as "frontal." Executive processes are complex, and the frontal lobes large and poorly understood. I am far from convinced that there is an exact correlation between the two, and I believe that confounding the frontal lobes with executive control has been harmful in the past (see Baddeley & Wilson, 1988, for a discussion of this point).

Moscovitch explicitly avoids using the term "working memory," preferring to use "working with memory." The implication here would seem to be that the system concerned is involved only with manipulating memory and not with nonmnemonic cognitive processing. I would certainly disagree with this (Baddeley, 1993). On the other hand, I sympathize with the desire to avoid using a term that might appear to imply unshared theoretical assumptions. One way of signaling this is to differentiate between general working memory and specific models of working memory (Baddeley, 1986). Unfortunately, this suggested distinction has not met with much enthusiasm, so the problem remains. Yet I am not happy with the solution proposed by Moscovitch, since it implies the need to proliferate systems. Are we likely to come across "working with language" or "working with space" or "working with numbers" all as different systems? There must be a better solution.

Finally, I welcome the introduction of computational modeling techniques into the field, as illustrated in the chapter by Metcalfe, Mencl, and Cottrell. While simple qualitative conceptual models have proved very useful, one eventually reaches a point at which some form of detailed and preferably quantitative model is necessary if the concepts are to develop. I believe that we have already reached this point in analyzing the phonological loop component of working memory. We are currently attempting to explore ways of modeling this system, which at first sight appears to be simple but which incorporates such basic challenges as those of modeling serial order and hierarchical clustering. I suggest that the phonological loop combines the advantages of being relatively complex while at the same time being empirically well explored and hence providing considerable constraints for any potential model (Baddeley, Papagno, & Norris, 1991).

REFERENCES

Atkinson, R. C., & Shiffrin, R. M. (1968). Human memory: A proposed system and its control processes. In K. W. Spence (Ed.), *The psychology of learning and motivation: Advances in research and theory* (Vol. 2, pp. 89–195). New York: Academic Press.

Baddeley, A. D. (1966a). The capacity for generating information by randomization. *Quarterly Journal of Experimental Psychology, 18,* 119–129.

Baddeley, A. D. (1966b). Short-term memory for word sequences as a function of acoustic, semantic, and formal similarity. *Quarterly Journal of Experimental Psychology, 18,* 362–365.

Baddeley, A. D. (1986). *Working memory.* Oxford: Oxford University Press.

Baddeley, A. D. (1992a). Is working memory working? *Quarterly Journal of Experimental Psychology, 44A,* 1–31.

Baddeley, A. D. (1992b). Working memory. *Science, 255,* 556–559.

Baddeley, A. D. (1993). Working memory or working attention? In A. Baddeley & L. Weiskrantz (Eds.), *Attention: Selection, awareness and control. A tribute to Donald Broadbent.* Oxford: Oxford University Press.

Baddeley, A. D., Bressi, S., Della Sala, S., Logie, R., & Spinnler, H. (1991). The decline of working memory in Alzheimer's disease: A longitudinal study. *Brain, 114,* 2521–2542.

Baddeley, A. D., & Hitch, G. (1974). Working memory. In G. A. Bower (Ed.), *The psychology of learning and motivation* (Vol. 8, pp. 47–89) New York: Academic Press.

Baddeley, A. D., & Hitch, G. J. (1993). The recency effect: Implicit learning with explicit retrieval? *Memory and Cognition.*

Baddeley, A. D., Lewis, V. J., & Vallar, G. (1984). Exploring the articulatory loop. *Quarterly Journal of Experimental Psychology, 36,* 233–252.

Baddeley, A. D., & Lieberman, K. (1980). Spatial working memory. In R. S. Nickerson (Ed.), *Attention and performance, VIII* (pp. 521–539) Hillsdale, NJ: Lawrence Erlbaum Associates.

Baddeley, A. D., Logie, R., Bressi, S., Della Sala, S., & Spinnler, H. (1986). Dementia and working memory. *Quarterly Journal of Experimental Psychology, 38A,* 603–618.

Baddeley, A. D., Papagno, C., & Norris, D. (1991). Phonological memory and serial order: A sandwich for TODAM. In W. E. Hockley & S. Lewandowsky (Eds.), *Relating theory and data: Essays on human memory in honor of Bennet B. Murdock* (pp. 175–194) Hillsdale, NJ: Lawrence Erlbaum Associates.

Baddeley, A. D., Papagno, C., & Vallar, G. (1988). When long-term learning depends on short-term storage. *Journal of Memory and Language, 27,* 586–595.

Baddeley, A. D., Thomson, N., & Buchanan, M. (1975). Word length and the structure of short-term memory. *Journal of Verbal Learning and Verbal Behavior, 14,* 575–589.

Baddeley, A. D., & Warrington, E. K. (1970). Amnesia and the distinction between long- and short-term memory. *Journal of Verbal Learning and Verbal Behavior, 9,* 176–189.

Baddeley, A. D., & Wilson, B. (1988). Frontal amnesia and the dysexecutive syndrome. *Brain and Cognition, 7,* 212–230.

Butters, N., Heindel, W. C., & Salmon, D. P. (1990). Dissociation of implicit memory in dementia: Neurological implications. *Bulletin of the Psychonomic Society, 28,* 359–366.

Butterworth, B., Campbell, R., & Howard, D. (1986). The uses of short-term memory: A case study. *Quarterly Journal of Experimental Psychology, 38A,* 705–738.

Colle, H. A., & Welsh, A. (1976). Acoustic masking in primary memory. *Journal of Verbal Learning and Verbal Behavior, 15,* 17–32.

Conrad, R., & Hull, A. J. (1964). Information, acoustic confusion, and memory span. *British Journal of Psychology, 55,* 429–432.

Daneman, M., & Carpenter, P. A. (1980). Individual differences in working memory and reading. *Journal of Verbal Learning and Verbal Behavior, 19,* 450–466.

Daneman, M., & Carpenter, P. A. (1983). Individual differences in integrating information between and within sentences. *Journal of Experimental Psychology: Learning, Memory, and Cognition, 9,* 561–584.

Duncan, J. (1993). Selection of input and goal in the control of behaviour. In A. D. Baddeley & L. Weiskrantz (Eds.), *Attention: Selection, awareness, and control. A tribute to Donald Broadbent.* Oxford: Oxford University Press.

Farah, M. J. (1988). Is visual memory really visual? Overlooked evidence from neuropsychology. *Psychological Review, 95,* 307–317.

Gathercole, S., & Baddeley, A. D. (1989). Evaluation of the role of phonological STM in the development of vocabulary in children: A longitudinal study. *Journal of Memory and Language, 28,* 200–213.

Gathercole, S., & Baddeley, A. D. (1990a). Phonological memory deflcits in language-disordered children: Is there a causal connection? *Journal of Memory and Language, 29,* 336–360.

Gathercole, S., & Baddeley, A. D. (1990b). The role of phonological memory in vocabulary acquisition: A study of young children learning new names. *British Journal of Psychology, 81,* 439–454.

Goldman-Rakic, P. W. (1988). Topography of cognition: Parallel distributed networks in primate association cortex. *Annual Review of Neuroscience, 11,* 137–156.

Howard, D., & Butterworth, B. (1989). Short-term memory and sentence comprehension: A reply to Vallar & Baddeley, 1987. *Cognitive Neuropsychology, 6,* 455–463.

Jacoby, L. L., Baker, J. G., & Brooks, L. R. (1989). Episodic effects on picture identification: Implications for theories of concept learning and theories of memory. *Journal of Experimental Psychology: Learning Memory, and Cognition, 15,* 275–281.

Johnson-Laird, P. N. (1983). *Mental models.* Cambridge: Cambridge University Press.

Kojima, S., & Goldman-Rakic, P. S. (1984). Functional analysis of spatially discriminative neurons in prefrontal cortex of rhesus monkey. *Brain Research, 291,* 229–240.

Kyllonen, P. C., & Christal, R. E. (1990). Reasoning ability is (little more than) working-memory capacity?! *Intelligence, 14,* 389–433.

Logie, R. H. (1986). Visuo-spatial processing in working memory. *Quarterly Journal of Experimental Psychology, 38A*, 229–247.

Morris, R. G., & Baddeley, A. D. (1988). Primary and working memory functioning in Alzheimer-type dementia. *Journal of Clinical and Experimental Neuropsychology, 10*, 279–296.

Norman, D. A., & Shallice, T. (1980). Attention to action: Willed and automatic control of behavior. University of California at San Diego, Center for Human Information Processing, report 99.

Papagno, C., Valentine, T., & Baddeley, A. D. (1991). Phonological short-term memory and foreign language vocabulary learning. *Journal of Memory and Language, 30*, 331–347.

Papagno, C., & Vallar, G. (1992). Phonological short-term memory and the learning of novel words: The effect of phonological similarity and item length. *Quarterly Journal of Experimental Psychology, 44A*, 47–67.

Richardson-Klavehn, A., & Bjork, R. A. (1988). Measures of memory. *Annual Review of Psychology, 39*, 475–543.

Roediger, H. L. (1980). Implicit memory: Retention without remembering. *American Psychologist, 45*, 1043–1056.

Rumelhart, D. E. (1991). Paper on the computational modeling of human memory presented at the First International Memory Conference, Lancaster, England.

Salamé, P., & Baddeley, A. D. (1982). Disruption of short-term memory by unattended speech: Implications for the structure of working memory. *Journal of Verbal Learning and Verbal Behavior, 21*, 150–164.

Service, E. (1989). Phonological coding in working memory and foreign-language learning. University of Helsinki, General Psychology Monographs, No. B9.

Shallice, T. (1993). Neuropsychological investigation of supervisory processes. In A. Baddeley & L. Weiskrantz (Eds.), *Attention: Selection, Awareness, and Control. A Tribute to Donald Broadbent.* Oxford: Oxford University Press.

Shallice, T., & Burgess, P. (1993). Supervisory control of action and thought selection. In A. D. Baddeley & L. Weiskrantz (Eds.), *Attention: Selection, awareness, and control.* Oxford: Clarendon Press.

Shallice, T., & Warrington, E. K. (1970). Independent functioning of verbal memory stores: A neuropsychological study. *Quarterly Journal of Experimental Psychhology, 22*, 261–273.

Spinnler, H., Della Sala, S., Bandera, R., & Baddeley, A. D. (1988). Dementia, aging, and the structure of human memory. *Cognitive Neuropsychology, 5*, 193–211.

Squire, L. R., & Zola-Morgan, S. (1988). Memory: Brain systems and behavior. *Trends in Neurosciences, 11*, 170–175.

Tulving, E. (1972). Episodic and semantic memory. In E. Tulving & W. Donaldson (Eds.), *Organization of memory* (pp. 381–403). New York: Academic Press.

Tulving, E. (1983). *Elements of episodic memory.* Oxford: Oxford University Press.

Tulving, E., & Schacter, D. L. (1990). Priming and human memory systems. *Science, 247*, 301–306.

Vallar, G., & Baddeley, A. D. (1982). Short-term forgetting and the articulatory loop. *Quarterly Journal of Experimental Psychology, 34*, 53–60.

Vallar, G., & Baddeley, A. D. (1984). Fractionation of working memory. Neuropsychological evidence for a phonological short-term store. *Journal of Verbal Learning and Verbal Behavior, 23,* 151–161.

Vallar, G., & Baddeley, A. D. (1989). Developmental disorders of verbal short-term memory and their relation to sentence comprehension: A reply to Howard and Butterworth. *Cognitive Neuropsychology, 6,* 465–473.

Vallar, G., & Shallice, T. (Eds.) (1990). *Neuropsychological impairments of short-term memory.* Cambridge: Cambridge University Press.

12 Cognitive Binding

Janet Metcalfe, W. E. Mencl, and Garrison W. Cottrell

A number of modeling investigations have recently sought to extract common principles among seemingly diverse models. The investigators then relate these principles, rather than just the individual models, to human results. If a variety of models with different detailed characteristics and modes of functioning share some common characteristics, if these characteristics cause the models to produce the same pattern of data, regardless of the other differences among them, and if this pattern also appears in the human memory data, then we might well conclude that the pattern in the human data is attributable to the characteristics that link the models. Humphreys, Pike, Bain, and Tehan's (1989) work, in which they isolate the characteristic of parallel or global matching in recognition retrieval in a variety of otherwise very different recognition models—for example those of Murdock (1982), Raaijmakers and Shiffrin (1981), and Hintzman (1986)—provides a nice example of this productive and informative use of mathematical and computational models of memory.

The use of different but converging models to extract underlying principles of human memory relates closely to the strategy employed in our research. We pushed this strategy a little bit further, though. It appears likely that different memory systems may operate via distinguishably different operations and principles (see Sherry & Schacter, 1987, for example). We therefore investigated the commonalities among the results of classes of model investigations in an effort to isolate these separable principles. The logic is simple: if one group of models exhibits the pattern of data shown experimentally by one memory system and another shows the pattern exhibited by a different system, then the commonalities among models of the first type can be used to characterize principles of the first system and to distinguish these principles from the principles of the second system (which are given by the commonalities of the second group of models).

Our aim, then, is not primarily taxonomical. The arguments for different systems have been made elsewhere, including the other chapters of this volume. We will review some aspects of these, but by and large we shall simply accept that the dissociations in the data of others are sufficiently compelling to warrant the conclusion that there exist different memory systems. Our effort here is directed at building on those distinctions, using a computational modeling analysis to begin to extract and understand the mode of operation and function of those differing systems.

The paradigms we explore here are interesting for another reason as well. The pattern of data in one of the tasks we investigate, the implicit-memory task, while consistent, has also been theoretically problematic. Explicit-memory tasks have tended to be linked by a dependence relation, whereas implicit tasks have been found to be independent of one another. The independence relations within the implicit-memory data have been difficult to interpret. Models, being simpler and more readily understood than the complex human systems themselves, can be used in an effort to disentangle and explain results that are not immediately comprehensible. The models investigated here are directed towards providing some indication of what the dependence/independence results might mean about human memory.

The particular implicit and explicit tasks we investigated—repeated fragment completion and fragment-cued recall—are straightforward from the perspective of network models. One of the strong points of interactive network models is that they are capable of specifying, in detail, a mechanism whereby pattern or fragment completion can be enacted. Thus, doing the task poses no problem for any of the models we will consider. This ability to do the task itself would, of course, seem to be a prerequisite for explanatory models aimed at determining the implications of the microstructure of the mechanism. Other kinds of models specifying transition probabilities from stage to stage or tree structures of processing, such as multinomial models (see Batchelder & Rieffer, 1990, for some interesting examples) contribute in other ways, for example, by allowing us to tease apart different macrocognitive processes and components. But these models are less well suited for the kind of microanalysis of the mechanisms used to dissect the patterns of results studied here.

Of course, even if a model is able to enact the basic task, this does not imply that the methods and mechanisms used to do so are the same as those used by people. Optimization of task performance is often taken as a standard by which to assess models and as an assumption about human performance. But there is reason for eschewing the notion of optimality as criterial for biological/psychological models. The brain structures under study may have evolved to optimize some sort of performance, but it is not at all clear that the situation for which the brain evolved is isomorphic to the one that we choose to study in each and every laboratory task. It is implausible, for example, to imagine that our brain networks evolved specifically to maximize efficiency and performance on a verbal-fragment-completion task. So, although notions of optimality and efficiency may be important in other domains (such as in computer science, where solving a problem as efficiently as possible may be critical), they seem questionable in psychological models. Instead, an adequate psychological model is one that enacts the task in the same way that people do, at least to a first approximation. Thus the entire pattern of the human data—including errors, dependencies, and other characteristics of human

Janet Metcalfe, W. E. Mencl, and Garrison W. Cottrell

performance—are important in allowing modelers to construct successive approximations to the human system. Since the two seemingly identical tasks investigated here—both requiring that the missing parts of a word be filled in—result in different patterns of contingencies in the data, we use these different data patterns, in conjunction with models that can produce such differences, in an effort to understand the human systems that give rise to them.

1 BACKGROUND: DIFFERENT MEMORY SYSTEMS?

A number of theorists have proposed that there may be (at least) two functionally distinct memory, systems sometimes called *episodic* or true memory and *semantic* or quasi memory, that may be differentially tapped by explicit and implicit tasks. Nadel (1992) calls these two systems *locale* (stressing that the spatial, and possibly temporal, parameters of the situation are important) and *taxon* (indicating that the system is categorical or taxonomic rather than necessarily linked to a particular time and/or place), respectively. Squire (1992) calls them *declarative* and *nondeclarative*. Hirsh (1974) uses the terms *memory* and *habits*. The explicit/episodic/locale/"memory"/declarative/true memory system appears anatomically to correspond to the hippocampal system, with perhaps diencephalic and frontal involvement as well. The semantic/implicit/taxon/"habit"/quasimemory system is not so well localized but certainly involves other cortical areas. Despite differences, there is some convergence, though certainly not perfect agreement, about what is meant by the two hypothetical systems. The system underlying explicit memory is assumed to store events that have places and times and personal meaning to the individual (they occurred specifically to him or her and are not just knowledge about the world). It may be anatomically circumscribed and thus susceptible to certain kinds of amnesia. And it requires conscious recollective processes for encoding and retrieval. The system underlying implicit memory may show some plasticity, and in particular, priming effects may manifest themselves, but there need be no conscious recollection associated with this system, or with implicit remembering.

The evidence for these two systems or kinds of processes stems from several sources. One source of evidence, as Richardson-Klavehn and Bjork (1988) note in their review, consists of studies in which two tasks, one purportedly explicit and one implicit, are dissociated, or differentially affected by certain variables. For example, a number of researchers have found that such variables as level of processing and whether a subject generates or reads a word influences explicit tasks like recall and recognition but has no differential effect on implicit tasks like lexical decision and stem or fragment completion (Jacoby & Dallas, 1981; Graf, Mandler, & Haden, 1982).

The second line of evidence comes from studies with amnesic patients. The finding that explicit tasks are selectively impaired in amnesics when their performance is compared to that of normal or matched control patients, while performance on implicit tasks is spared, is often cited as the strongest possible evidence for separable systems. In one such finding, amnesics who show impairment on cued recall and recognition of certain presented target words nevertheless show normal priming on such tasks as fragment completion, stem completion, and lexical decision as a result of having been exposed to these words. The sparing of certain memory functions in the presence of profound impairment of others suggests multiple systems. Shimamura (1986), Hirst (1982), and Schacter (1987) have provided extensive reviews of these results.

The third line of evidence (and the one we will model shortly) stems from studies investigating the stochastic dependence or independence among explicit and implicit tasks. It is well known that the two classic explicit tasks, recognition and recall, show dependence of the following form. Suppose one were given a series of cue-target pairs to study, such as "One can sometimes eat it but never sit upon it: CACTUS," where the cue is given in lowercase and the target in uppercase letters. Then in a recognition test, one is asked to circle all the target words (the word CACTUS included among them). Following the recognition test, one is given the cue and asked to recall the target. Dependence is measured in terms of whether the recall of the target on the first test is (or is not) related to recognition of the same target on the second but different test. One might expect, a priori, that if one recalled a particular item and then a minute or two later one were asked to recognize it, one surely would be able to do so, that is, that there should be a very strong dependency relation. Such dependency relations between recall and recognition are usually not as strong as one might suppose but are nevertheless consistent and systematic, despite a wide range of experimental variables. Indeed, a relation has been found in 278 experimental conditions so far (see Nilsson & Gardiner, 1991, for a review). The probability of recall is greater if the subject recognized the target than it was had the subject failed to recognize the target. This dependency relation between the two tasks has sometimes been taken as evidence that they are enacted by the same system.

Conversely, independence among tasks was at first taken as evidence that the two tasks are enacted by different systems. Tulving, Schacter, and Stark (1982) showed subjects a long list of words. After a one-day or seven-day retention interval, subjects were asked for recognition and fragment completion of the studied words. The experimental results showed independence between the two tasks. This independence was interpreted as indicating that the tasks were enacted by different systems. It turns out that this interpretation is too simple (see Hayman & Tulving, 1989a).

The problem with this seemingly parsimonious and compelling interpretation is that if the standard explicit-memory tasks show a dependence relation because they are processed by the same system, by the same reasoning there should be dependence among the implicit-memory tasks as well. Unfortunately, different implicit-memory tasks fail to show dependence among themselves. Witherspoon and Moscovitch (1989), for example, found that two implicit-memory tasks, word identification and word-fragment completion,

Janet Metcalfe, W. E. Mencl, and Garrison W. Cottrell

even though both are presumably enacted by the same system, were independent of one another. They pointed out that it seems implausible to postulate a completely different memory system for each and every memory task found to be independent of one another. We share Witherspoon and Moscovitch's reservations about having to postulate a separate system for each and every test shown to be independent of some other. Even so, we are left in a quandary about what dependence and independence mean.

This dilemma was taken to its logical extreme by Hayman and Tulving (1989a), who conducted repeated fragment-completion tests or fragment-cued recall tests with exactly the same task and targets using only different parts of the same words as cues. In this case, then, the materials and even the task itself, providing a whole word that filled in the missing letters of the cue, were the same in the implicit and explicit cases. In the explicit-memory version of the tasks, they found dependence, but in the implicit-version, they found independence. The idea that independence means that the two "tasks" (producing the same word under the same instructional set but with different fragments) are attributable to different memory systems is absurd.

But if dependence does not indicate that the tasks are enacted in the same systems, and independence in different systems, then we need to reexamine what it is that these relations do indicate. This is especially important because these differences in the dependency relations correspond to other dissociations across tasks that provide rather nice evidence that there are different systems. In general, a dependency relation occurs in explicit tasks, whereas independence is found in tasks that, on other grounds, we would label implicit-memory tasks.

Roediger, Weldon, and Challis (1989) have suggested that the transfer-appropriate-processing view may be called for. This approach relies on a careful assessment of the compatibility relations between encoding and test, and analyses of the processes involved. This analysis, however, is conducted at a verbal level, and the processes, operations, and structures needed for enacting the implicit and explicit tasks—recognition, fragment completion, lexical decision, and so on—are not detailed. Since the transfer-appropriate-processing view is not actually implemented in a working system, it is premature to conclude whether or not such a view is isomorphic with the systems view. Roediger, Weldon, and Challis note that the systems view and the transfer-appropriate-processing view may not, in fact, be at odds with one another: "We must admit that there is no inherent reason that an approach specifying both memory systems and something like processing modes or procedures cannot be partially correct. Neural structures require processing for their operation, and procedures must be carried out by the brain. A theory specifying both structural bases and processing assumptions is needed (Anderson, 1978), but those presently on the scene emphasize either structure to the relative neglect of processing assumptions (the systems approach) or processing assumptions to the relative neglect of structure (our own approach)" (1989, p. 36).

We agree that one needs to specify the systems, structures, and processes involved in the tasks at hand, and we think that the cleanest and most informative way to do this is to implement working models of the tasks under study. There are a number of interesting models at hand that could be put to such a task, even though these models typically have not been used to explain the data on implicit and explicit memory. However, this seems to us to be an ideal situation for such models, and so in the pages that follow, we report some results of this modeling exploration. Before describing the models and their application to the implicit/explicit distinction, we provide a few more details about the paradigm and the experimental results.

2   THE EXPERIMENTAL PARADIGM

Hayman and Tulving (1989a) investigated the dependency relations in fragment completion and fragment-cued recall in a series of four experiments. Typically, subjects were presented a sequence of words in a study list containing some words, such as AARDVARK, that would later be the primed targets. Later subjects were given one of two tests: an *implicit* test, in which they were asked to complete fragments, such as _AR_VA_ _, or a cued-recall (i.e., *explicit*) test, in which they were asked to recall the word from the list that contained the letters _AR_VA_ _. In both cases, there was a second test in which the subject was either given the same fragment a second time or a different mirror-image fragment. So, for example, the mirror-image fragment for *aardvark* would be: A_ _D_ _RK.

In the control cases, in which the exact same fragments were used on the second test no matter what the instructions to the subjects were, there was strong dependence between the first and second test. This makes sense. If the tests are exactly the same, then the only difference should be due to the noise of testing itself, including possible interfering effects of intervening items and possible priming effects due to the first test.

A number of researchers (Shimamura, 1985) have pointed up potential problems with the repeated-testing methodology, as well as some solutions (Flexser, 1981; Hayman & Tulving, 1989b). To circumvent these problems, Hayman and Tulving (1989a) used a method of testing called the "reduction method" (Watkins & Todres, 1978), which compares a control list not involving repeated testing with the conditionalized list. It is designed to offset the effects of repeated testing. In the formal modeling, such a remedy for the priming effects due to the test situation will, of course, not be needed, since we need not alter the models when testing them.

Hayman and Tulving's (1989a) results were as follows: (1) In both the implicit and the explicit memory tasks, when the exact same fragment was repeated, there was dependence between the two tests. This result is predicted by all models of memory, and it would be cause for considerable concern had this not been the case. (2) In the different-fragment condition there was dependence in the case of the explicit-memory task. (3) In the different-fragment

Janet Metcalfe, W. E. Mencl, and Garrison W. Cottrell

condition in the implicit-memory task, the results of the two tests were independent of one another. The challenge, then, is to say what kinds of systems give rise to the dependence seen in the explicit task and what kinds of systems can produce the independence seen in the implicit task.

3 POTENTIAL BIASES COMMON TO ALL MODELS

There are a number of factors that induce a positive or a negative dependency relation, regardless of the model used to study these relations. In this first modeling section, therefore, we outline some of these general representational constraints common to the models we investigated. In all of the models explored, items were represented as multidimensional vectors, or sets of features. The fragments were made by taking subsets of the elements of those vectors as the cues and reconstructing the remainder of the vector in the manner specified by the model under study. The distributional constraints of the features varied somewhat from model to model. Nevertheless, there are certain characteristics of this representation that can be analyzed separately from the network structures that link and store the representations (which vary greatly across models). In this first section, then, we look at the implications of some of the representational assumptions one might make in determining plausible vector-based representations and at some of the pits we could (and usually did) fall into in our explorations.

3.1 Positive Correlation Due to Overlapping Features in the Two Fragments

If the same item or the identical subset of features is used as the retrieval cue (fragment) in the two tests, then it is straightforward to see that the two tests will show a dependence relation. If the trace is fixed between test 1 and test 2 and there is no interference as a result of the interval between tests, then in all of the models the first test is identical to the second, and so the results should and will be identical, which results in maximal dependence. But even if there is some random fluctuation due to, say, intervening materials and/or to spontaneous fluctuation of elements, positive dependency should still result. If the random fluctuation is serving to modulate the dependency and if introducing a delay increases such random fluctuation, then we should expect to see less dependency with a delay. All of the models that we investigated will produce such effects.

It is unlikely, though, that such differences as could have affected the magnitude of the dependency relations had much, if anything, to do with the critical data contrasting implicit and explicit memory in Hayman and Tulving's (1989a) study. First, the data did show a strong dependency relation in both fragment completion and fragment-cued recall when identical cues were used twice. This dependency relation (expected by all models) was less than perfect, which indicates some noise in the system attributable, presumably, to the intervening completions. This effect is reassuring but does not mitigate the fact that there was a considerable difference in the dependency relation between the implicit and explicit task when nonidentical cues were given for the target items and identical cues were not repeated.

Our modeling investigations showed (with all models) that just as a perfect dependency relation was necessarily induced when all of the features in the cue vectors were identical and there was no change in the testing conditions, so too a dependency relation was introduced when any subset of the features within a cue was identical from test 1 to test 2. The magnitude of the dependency relation depended on the proportion of overlapping features. At first we drew the features randomly with replacement to be in the first or the second fragment, mistakenly thinking that this was an unbiased way to assign features to fragments. Consider the case where .5 of the features are in fragment 1 and .5 are in fragment 2. If these are randomly selected without respect for one another, we would expect that the two fragments will have $.5 \times .5 = .25$ features in common. The common subset of features induces a positive correlation. We found that with this coding scheme for the fragments, all of the models we tested showed positive dependence. To circumvent this problem of feature overlap necessarily inducing a positive correlation, we eventually settled on a scheme of making the features in the two fragments mutually exclusive. If there is no overlap among the features in the two fragments to artifactually induce a correlation, then the intrinsic characteristics of the model should be more obvious.

The fragments used in Hayman and Tulving's (1989a) experiments were not precisely mutually exclusive. It would probably be impossible to construct materials that met this constraint. So while some fragments were strictly complementary, such as _ _HL_A and DA_ _I_, others showed some letter overlap (which the models would realize as feature overlap) such as _A_ _AC and _ _NI_C. We would expect this overlap in the experiment to induce a small positive dependency from test 1 to test 2. However, since the overlap was identical in the implicit and explicit tasks—indeed, all of the materials were identical—we would expect that the dependency relation, so induced, would also be identical. Since it was not, we must seek elsewhere for the reason for the difference in the dependencies in the explicit and implicit tasks.

3.2 Information Content in the Two Linked Fragments Directed at a Single Target

If a model was inherently independent under fragment completion, then that independence was expected to show up when the fragments were mutually exclusive. If the mechanisms or connections in the model itself induced some dependency, then this too should be manifested. In the models we investigated, the number of elements in the vectors representing these items was typically assumed to be fixed. We thought at first that a fair way to assign features to fragments was by going through the item, feature by feature,

Janet Metcalfe, W. E. Mencl, and Garrison W. Cottrell

flipping a computer-generated fair coin for each feature. If a feature was assigned to one fragment, the other fragment was given a value of 0 on that feature. Interestingly, though, especially when the number of features in the vector is small, this procedure results in a negative dependency between the two fragments.

The problem results from the considerable variability in flipping the coin (and in the underlying information content of each feature). If one fragment accidentally gets 60 percent, rather than 50 percent of the features, then the other fragment necessarily gets only 40 percent. Thus better fragments, i.e., those had an above average number of features, were necessarily linked to worse fragments, and this produces a negative correlation a priori. The MINERVA and back propagation models, under some parameter values, actually demonstrated a negative dependence relation under these conditions. Because the correlation or lack thereof was due to idiosyncrasies of the coding rather than to the intrinsic characteristics of the model, we decided that this scheme was not a fair test of the models. The solution that we employed was simply to allow exactly half of the features to contribute to fragment 1 and half to fragment 2. The exact proportion is not crucial, but the lack of variability, which will induce the negative tradeoff, is.

It is not obvious that this negative tradeoff is necessarily a problem in the experiments, but it is also not obvious that it is not. One can imagine that with items that do not have fixed length, a certain number of letters can be assigned to fragment 1, and there can be the same, more, or fewer than average number of letters left for fragment 2. So with less constrained materials than fixed-length vectors, the problem of a necessary negative tradeoff attributable to letter selection may not be problematic. But since we did not take any steps to check whether this was or was not a confounding factor, we cannot claim that it did not contribute to the observed data.

In spite of the potential negative dependency due to letter sampling, we concluded that this factor could not be responsible for the main results of interest in the experiments. The materials were the same in the implicit and explicit task, and so if there had been an accidentally induced negative dependency, it should have shown up equally in both the implicit and explicit tasks. Since the dependency data were different, we felt compelled to seek an explanation elsewhere.

3.3 Variability in the Strength of the Encoding between the List Words

A positive correlation between two fragments directed at the same target will be induced if the vectors for the various words in the study list are each assigned different weighting factors. This could occur experimentally if people's attention fluctuated somewhat during list presentation, remaining constant within item but varying across items. It is entirely possible that subjects pay better attention to some items than to others, which would cause all of the features of those attended items to be stronger than those of the unattended or less attended items. Items that were retrievable with one cue would then also tend to be retrievable with another, and a positive dependency would be observed.

An alternative variable with the same effect would be if some of the items were simply easier than others. A range on the ease or difficulty of the items would be expected to induce a positive correlation. Suppose that a few of the words shown on the list were simply unknown to the subject, for example. These items should be difficult to access, regardless of which cue was used to attempt the retrieval. Alternatively, very easy items, such as the subject's name, might be very easy to access, regardless of the cue. These overall differences in difficulty, attention, and rate of learning will induce a positive dependency.

Within the paradigm that studies recognition failure of recallable words, the dependency relation found between recognition and recall has sometimes been explained by recourse to this differential weighting/learning/attention. So, for example, the MINERVA model has been shown to produce a positive correlation rather readily by allowing some pairs of items to be stronger than other pairs of items. The difficulty with this explanation is that it is not a necessary assumption. It is easy to imagine cases where attention to the first item could be high and attention to the second item in a pair could be low. Thus there is an ad hoc quality to the explanation, especially across a broad range of data.

Whether this hypothesis is or is not viable as a factor that induces a positive correlation in the data may be open to debate, but certainly there is no debate that one can set up experimental conditions that would increase the variability across items. For example, Schwartz (unpublished study conducted in Metcalfe's lab) has varied the presentation rate within lists of pairs of items. This manipulation increases dependency. Hintzman and Hartry (1991) have provided similar experimental manipulations that increase and decrease dependency. We may, thus, entertain the possibility that such variability contributes to observed dependency even when it is not specifically manipulated in the experimental paradigm under scrutiny. We acknowledge this possibility, and since it is open to test, anticipate further experimental studies.

However, in the present situation, since the encoding stage was the same for what would later become the implicit task, as compared to the explicit task, even if attention or learning rate or item difficulty were important, it still could not account for the differences in dependency found between the two conditions of interest.

3.4 Divided Attention within Items

It is possible to construct a plausible conjecture about attention that would have just the opposite effect to that of the induced positive correlation sug-

Janet Metcalfe, W. E. Mencl, and Garrison W. Cottrell

gested in the last paragraph. Items in the lists in question are presented at the time of study at a fixed rate. During that fixed time period, the subject presumably must distribute his or her limited quanta of attention over the various aspects of the complex stimulus. It is possible to argue that to the extent that some aspect of the stimulus is well processed, other aspects of the stimulus will necessarily be poorly processed. Since there is high variability in weighting/learning/attention within item, a negative dependency should result in the contingency data. Variation of attention or learning within each item, combined with uniform attention allocation across items, should conspire to produce a negative correlation. Variation in attention across items, coupled with uniformly distributed attention within items, should produce a positive correlation. We do not really know which of these cases, if either, applied in the experiment. Since one could argue for either or both, in the simulations that follow we chose to keep variability both within and across items constant so as to induce neither a positive nor a negative correlation.

3.5 Summary of the Critiques Suggesting That either Positive or Negative Dependency Is Somehow Artifactually Built into the Representations

We acknowledge that any or all of the above mentioned representational biases that would induce correlations one way or the other could be at work. Presumably, these could be manipulated, and presumably they could be expected to vary from experiment to experiment. Within a single experiment with a circumscribed set of materials, we cannot conclusively rule out these factors as being potentially important. The observation that saves us from despair about the plethora of artifactual explanations for a positive, negative, or null dependency is that in Hayman and Tulving's (1989a) experiment any such qualifying factor applied equally to both the implicit and the explicit task. The materials were the same in the two tasks; the two complementary fragments were the same; and the encoding conditions were the same. And yet differences in dependency were nevertheless uncovered.

Below we thus explore the possibility that the observed differences are not attributable to confounding factors but instead are due to real differences in the underlying cognitive systems used to carry out the implicit and explicit tasks.

4 THE MODELS

In all of the models outlined in this section, we chose representations that were unbiased. Thus any observed positive or negative dependencies that resulted were attributable to the manner in which the model at hand processed the information, rather than to built-in biases in the representations.

4.1 The CHARM Model

The CHARM (composite holographic associative-recall recognition memory) model was originally designed to address the question of how people associate, store, and retrieve events in episodic/explicit memory (Metcalfe, 1991, 1993; Metcalfe Eich, 1985). Items, represented as multidimensional vectors, are associated by the operation of convolution and are stored by being added into a composite memory trace, itself a vector, along with other such convolved pairs of items. In the simulation described below the items are autoassociated. At time of retrieval, the cue vector is correlated with the composite memory trace. This produces a vector, which is identified by being matched to every item in a lexicon. The best-matching item, so long as that item exceeds a lower criterion of goodness-of-match, is considered to be the item generated. An overview of the model is shown in figure 1.

Method We constructed a lexicon of 100 vectors, each consisting of 63 features, which were numbers randomly sampled from a truncated normal distribution centered around a value of 0. Because of this sampling procedure, the items in the lexicon were statistically independent of one another and could be said to be psychological entities like unrelated words. The first 12 items of the lexicon were autoassociated, by the operation of convolution, and added into the composite memory trace.

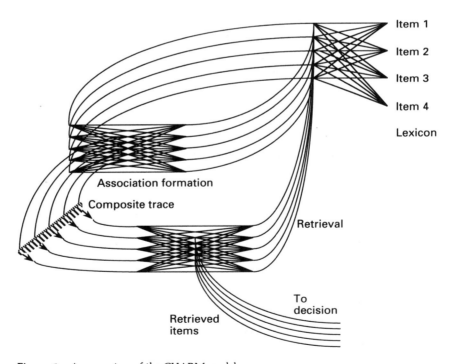

Figure 1 An overview of the CHARM model.

Janet Metcalfe, W. E. Mencl, and Garrison W. Cottrell

The first cue was constructed for each of the 12 items by selecting the first 31 features to be the cue and coding the remainder as zeros. These fragments were correlated with the composite memory trace, and the retrieved item was matched to every item in the lexicon by taking the dot product to each. The criterion for saying that the resonance between the retrieved item and the highest resonating lexical item was good enough for retrieval to be said to have occurred was varied from 0 to .2, .4, .6, .8, to 1. The item that had the highest dot product, so long as it was above the criterion for that particular run, was said to be the item given as the completion of the fragment. For the second test, the fragment cues were the last 31 features in the item, with the other elements being coded as zeros.

Whether the simulation produced the correct result to the first and/or second fragment was tabulated in a 2 × 2 contingency table, from which the simple and conditional probabilities were computed. Each treatment combination was run through 1,000 independent runs, so the data points are each based on 12,000 observations.

Results   The results are plotted in figure 2, which shows the conditional probability of correct completion of fragment 2, given correct completion of

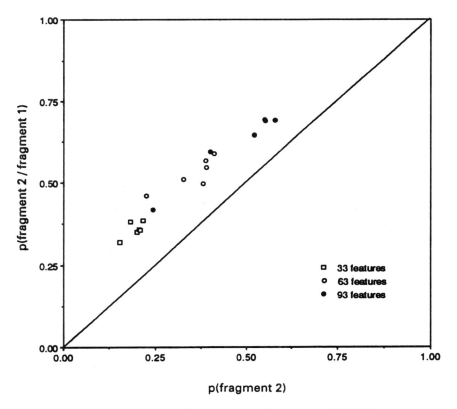

Figure 2   The dependence relation between repeated fragments in CHARM.

fragment 1, on the ordinate, plotted against the simple probability of correct completion of fragment 1 on the abscissa. The diagonal indicates independence; anything above the diagonal indicates a positive dependence; points falling below the diagonal indicate a negative dependence. As can be seen from the figure, the model produced a considerable amount of dependence. Dependence was also produced in the experimental situation, but only under explicit conditions, i.e., when subjects were told to complete the fragment with a just-studied word from the list.

Discussion The reason that the CHARM model, under autoassociation, predicts dependence on the two tasks is that every feature is linked to every other feature by the associative operation. When any feature is given as a cue or part of a cue at the time of retrieval, it provokes signal terms from *all* the features in the initial representation, proportional to the absolute value of the cue feature. Since any feature produces a degraded representation of all of the features for an item, a correlation among features is necessarily built into the autoassociative model.

The basis of this correlation is the fact that the encoding is distributed in CHARM, in that every feature is linked to all other features. (The operation of convolution itself spreads or smears the values of the features in this distributed manner.) So we should find that other models that share or partially share this kind of interactive representational coding such that some or all of the features are linked, bound, or connected to all of the other features should also share a dependence relation under conditions of repeated fragment completion, even in the case of mutually exclusive fragments. A particularly clear case is given by the competitive-learning model.

4.2 The Competitive-Learning Model

The origins of the competitive-learning procedure go back to work by von der Malsberg (1973) and work summarized in Grossberg (1987). Rumelhart and Zipser's (1986) version is used in the simulations reported here. At heart, this type of model consists of at least two layers of units connected by modifiable weight links (see figure 3). When a pattern of input units at the first layer is activated, units in the next layer compete for the privilege of responding to that particular pattern by inhibiting other units in the layer from becoming activated. Only the winning unit is allowed to modify its links, and does so in a manner which makes it increasingly more responsive to that particular input pattern.

Method We implemented a competitive-learning model that consisted of two layers of units, an input layer and a category layer, completely interconnected by feed-forward connections. The weights of these connections were initially set to values selected randomly from a uniform distribution between 0 and 1 and normalized so that the sum of all weights feeding into each

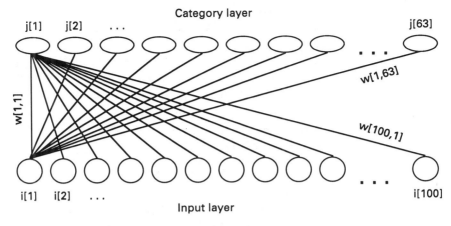

Figure 3 An overview of the competitive-learning model.

category unit was 1. These weights were subsequently modified through training. The model consisted of 100 input units and 63 category units. The 63 input items each contained 100 binary features and were created at random; each feature had an equal probability of being assigned either a 1 or a 0.

On each training trial, the network was presented with a randomly selected (whole) item from the item set, i.e., the item's pattern of features was activated at the input level. The category units computed a weighted sum of this activation based on the connection strengths. The weights were modified according to the competitive learning algorithm of Rumelhart and Zipser (1986):

$$\Delta w_{i,j} = g(c_{i,k}/n_k) - g(w_{i,j}) \tag{1}$$

Here $w_{i,j}$ is the weight link connecting input unit i to hidden unit j, and g is the learning rate. The value of $c_{i,k}$ is 1 if, in stimulus pattern k, input unit i is active, and it is 0 otherwise. Finally, n_k is the total number of active input units in stimulus pattern k.

Strong lateral inhibition operated at the category layer, so that only the most highly activated category unit was allowed to learn. Only the connections that fed to the category unit with the highest activation level (the "winner") were modified: weights to active input units were strengthened, and weights to inactive input units were weakened. The extent of this modification is determined by the value of g, which was set to 0.2 in these simulations. In addition, the activation of each category unit in the simulations reported below was multiplied by a unit-specific parameter of sensitivity, also set initially to a random value selected from a uniform distribution between 0 and 1. On each training trial, the sensitivity of the winning unit was reduced by a factor of 0.05, and the sensitivities of all losing units were increased (equivalently) by a factor necessary to keep the overall amount of sensitivity in the system constant.

To test whether the network had learned to classify the whole items, each item was presented in the same manner as for training, except that no weight modifications were allowed. A given item was deemed to be correctly identified upon presentation if the winning unit did not win the competition for any other pattern, i.e., if it responded exclusively to that particular item. When the network passed a performance level of 66 percent correct on all the items, it was tested for fragment completion.

The first 50 features of each item were present in the first fragment of that item, and features 51 through 100 were assigned a value of 0. Similarly, the second 50 features of each item were present in the second fragment of that item, while features 1 through 50 were assigned 0. Upon presentation of each fragment, the winning category unit was noted. A correct completion was tallied if this unit was the same one that coded exclusively for the whole item from which the fragment was constructed. An incorrect completion was recorded otherwise (i.e., if a different category unit responded most strongly to the fragment). The results from the two exclusive fragments of each of the 63 items were tabulated in a 2×2 contingency table, from which the results presented in figure 4 were computed. The entire procedure was replicated 100 times, giving 100 simulation data points, each based upon 63 observations.

Results As is shown in figure 4, the probability of correctly completing the second fragment was dependent on the successful completion of the first. The probability of successful completion of the second fragment, given successful completion of the first, was higher than the probability of completing the second overall.

Discussion The competitive-learning algorithm forces *all* of the weights that connect a winning category unit to active input units to be strengthened, and so these weights are linked or bound together. They all rise (or fall) together (though not necessarily by the same quantity). This has two implications. First, it makes the winning category unit more likely to win the competition the next time that same pattern is presented. This is what allows category units to become dedicated to a single input pattern. Indeed, it is at the heart of competitive learning. Second, it produces the dependency seen here with the mutually exclusive fragments. This is because a dedicated category unit that responds most strongly to one specific pattern will also respond strongly to both of the mutually exclusive fragments of that pattern, since *all* connecting weights used by the pattern as a whole have been strengthened together.

4.3 An Autoassociative Back-Propagation Model

In this section, we explore a particular nonlinear model: the back propagation autoassociator (Rumelhart, Hinton, & Williams, 1986; Cottrell, Munro, &

Janet Metcalfe, W. E. Mencl, and Garrison W. Cottrell

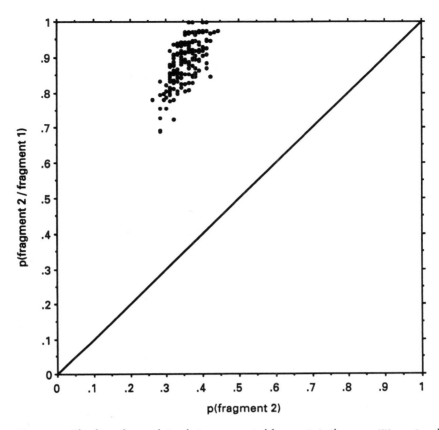

Figure 4 The dependence relation between repeated fragments in the competitive network.

Zipser, 1989; see figure 5). The autoassociative network is trained to reproduce the input pattern at the output layer. In so doing, it must represent the input as a pattern of activation at the hidden layer. The particular representation used depends on the weights on the links. Thus, learning in such networks corresponds to setting these weights. The weights are learned via an error-correction procedure known as the generalized delta rule (Rumelhart, Hinton, & Williams, 1986). Activity is propagated as follows. First, the units of the network compute a weighted sum of the activities of the units in the previous layer:

$$\text{net input}_i = \sum_{j=1}^{N} w_{i,j} \cdot \text{activation}_j \qquad (2)$$

Here activation$_j$ = input$_j$, where j is an input and $w_{i,j}$ is the weight from unit j to unit i. Next, a nonlinear "squashing" function is applied to obtain the unit's activity level:

$$\text{activation}_j = 2/(1 + e^{-\text{net input}_j}) - 1 \qquad (3)$$

The network is initialized with small random weights. Training proceeds by

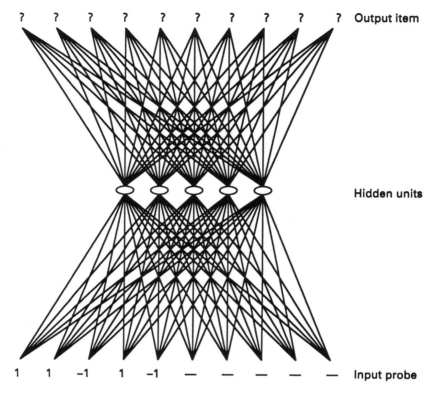

? ? ? ? ? ? ? ? ? ? Output item

Hidden units

1 1 −1 1 −1 — — — — — Input probe

Figure 5 An overview of an autoassociative back-propagation model.

presenting input vectors, propagating activity through the network according to the equations above, and producing an activity vector at the output level. This is compared to a desired output vector, the "teaching signal," and an error is computed. The weights are then changed so as to reduce the error at the output level. The particular form of the weight changing rule is the following:

$$\Delta w_{i,j} = -h \cdot \delta_i \cdot \text{activation}_j \tag{4}$$

Here h is a learning rate, δ_i is the error in the output attributable to unit i, and activation$_j$ is as above. Thus the weights are set according to the correlation between the error attributable to the unit at one end and the activity of the unit at the other end. When this equation is applied to the input-to-hidden weights, the activation$_j$ terms are simply the features of the input pattern, and the δ_i terms are the errors of the hidden units. Thus at the input level, features of the input will be associated with a particular unit at the hidden layer in proportion to the error of that unit on that pattern. To determine whether a particular output is a hit or not, a lexicon of patterns was used. The criterion for whether an output pattern matched a lexical item was that the output vector be within half of the distance from that lexical item to the closest other lexical item in the set.

Janet Metcalfe, W. E. Mencl, and Garrison W. Cottrell

Method   For each trial of the model, a lexicon of 100 vectors, each comprising 64 features, was constructed. The features were determined by a fair coin flip to be either -1 or 1. Thus the items were statistically independent of one another. The model had 50 hidden units, and a learning rate (h) of 0.1 was used. All 100 lexical items were presented to the model, with the desired output patterns (the teaching signal) being identical to the input patterns. The patterns were presented to the model one at a time, the error was computed, and the weights were changed on every presentation. Each simulation run consisted of 10 passes (or epochs) through all 100 patterns.

Two mutually exclusive fragments for each pattern were constructed so that the first 32 features were included in the fragments for test 1 and the second 32 were included in the fragments for test 2. These fragments were presented to the trained network without changing the weights. Using the criterion described above, we recorded a hit if the output pattern was within the proper radius of the lexical item from which the fragment was derived. Each trial of 100 new patterns and new random initial weights was repeated 100 times, which resulted in 10,000 unique observations.

Results   The results from the two tests were tabulated in a 2×2 contingency table, from which the simple and conditional probabilities were computed. As shown in figure 6, the model exhibits a pattern of positive dependence.

Discussion   With the back-propagation model, the individual features of the patterns are linked, internally, via the storage rule. As expressed in equation 4, weights from the features (of the same sign) of a pattern will tend to rise or fall together proportionally to the error of the hidden unit. That is, the d_i term is shared among all the weight changes to a particular unit. Thus if one feature tends to turn on a hidden unit, so will another feature from the same pattern. So the hidden units bind the features of a pattern together. Similarly, at the hidden-to-output level, hidden units correlated with the error of an output unit will change their weights to that output unit together, so all of the hidden units responsive to an input pattern will be bound together for that output feature.

4.4   A Noninteractive Separate-Trace Model: MINERVA

MINERVA (Hintzman, 1986, 1987) is a multiple-trace model of human memory (see figure 7). In MINERVA everything—traces and features within traces—is separate, and as such, the model is noninteractive. This makes it a particularly instructive model by way of contrast to the three previous models.

Each event is stored as a vector of n features in a separate trace in secondary long-term memory (SM). Each feature is represented as $+1$, -1, or 0. During encoding, each feature of the event vector is stored in SM with

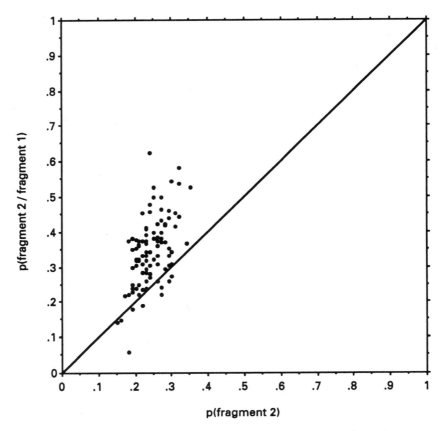

Figure 6 The dependence relation between repeated fragments in the back-propagation model.

probability L, the learning rate. If a feature is not stored, 0 is stored as that feature in the SM trace.

Retrieval is simulated by resonating a retrieval cue with all SM traces. This produces a single composite echo vector. Since this echo is not the same as the original patterns, nor even as the SM traces themselves, it is necessary to store all the complete patterns in a lexicon somewhere outside SM. Upon presentation of a probe, all SM traces (including the missing parts not given in the retrieval environment) are activated to an extent determined by their similarity to the probe. This similarity, S, is determined by a method similar to that used when computing a Pearson correlation, except that features that have a value of 0 in both the trace and the probe do not contribute:

$$S_i = \sum_{j=1}^{N} P_j \cdot T_{i,j} / N_r \tag{5}$$

Here P_j is the value of feature j in the probe, $T_{i,j}$ is the value of feature j in

Janet Metcalfe, W. E. Mencl, and Garrison W. Cottrell

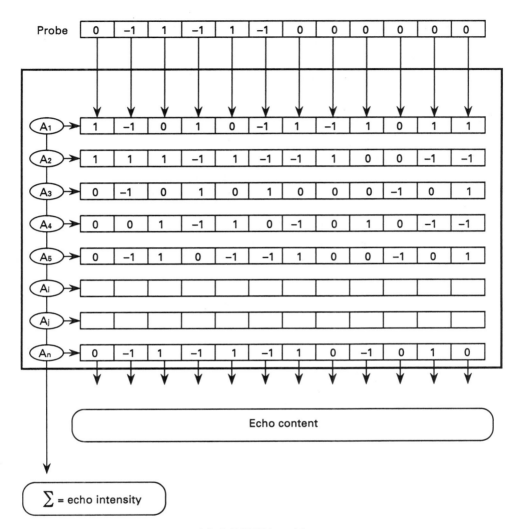

Figure 7 An overview of the MINERVA model.

trace i, and N_r is the number of features that are either 1 or −1 in either the trace or the probe. The similarity value is then used to compute the activation of each trace:

$$A_i = S_i^3 \tag{6}$$

Each trace, weighted by its activation value, is summed into the echo vector. The echo is then matched to every item in a lexicon, and the best match (determined by computing a true Pearson correlation) is said to be the item produced. A modification of the method Hintzman (1987) used for the task of recall can also be used for the task of fragment completion, as illustrated in the simulations that follow.

Method We created a lexicon of 200 items (vectors), each with 20 features, with each feature having an equal probability of being either $+1$, -1, or 0, following the representational coding used by Hintzman (1987). With a learning rate (L) of 0.2, 0.6, or 1.0, 100 these patterns were stored in SM.

The model was tested on 2 mutually exclusive fragments of each pattern, with an equal number of features in each fragment. The first 10 features of the original pattern were assigned to the first fragment of that pattern, while features 11 through 20 were assigned to the second fragment. Features of the original pattern that were not present in the fragment were designated as 0. Each fragment was presented as a probe, which was compared to the 100 stored vectors in SM, and the complete resulting echo was correlated with each of the 200 patterns in the lexicon. If the pattern giving the highest correlation was the same one used to generate the fragment, then a correct completion was tallied. This procedure was replicated 50 times, and the simple and conditional probabilities of successful completion were computed bidirectionally (i.e., both p(fragment 2/fragment 1) and p(fragment 1/fragment 2) for each pair of fragments). Thus each of the 100 (50 × 2) data points in figure 8 is based on 100 simulated observations.

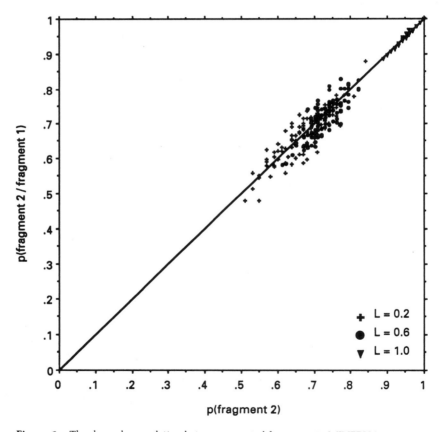

Figure 8 The dependence relation between repeated fragments in MINERVA.

Janet Metcalfe, W. E. Mencl, and Garrison W. Cottrell

Results As is shown in figure 8, MINERVA produces independence. This is just the right pattern of dependency to account for the implicit-memory data.

5 DISCUSSION

The three distributed/interactive models produce the dependence results, as shown in the explicit-memory data, whereas the noninteractive separate-trace model MINERVA produces the independence results, as shown in the implicit-memory data. The critical difference between the two kinds of models is that those producing dependence have some inherent mechanism that fuses or glues the elements together in the items processed. The separate-trace model does not have this characteristic. In this model the features are simply lined up in a vector, but no operation or modification alters any of them or the connections to them (at storage) as a function of the values of the others. They are inert with respect to one another, noninteracting, and as a result, the features within the separate-trace model maintain their functional (and statistical) independence. The models that glue, fuse, or bind together the diverse elements of the events presented to them to form a coherent whole produce the dependence findings shown by human subjects under explicit-memory instructions. The models that do not so bind the features together show independence, as is shown in the human implicit-memory data.

Much discussion has been devoted to the idea that a crucial distinction between explicit and the implicit memory tasks is the role played by consciousness, or attention. The episodic system is assumed to require consciousness and to be distinguished from nonepisodic (or quasi memory) system on this basis. But we may still ask, What does conscious attention do? What is the functional difference between systems that do or do not require it? If we subscribe to the idea that the involvement of consciousness is a distinguishing characteristic of the two systems (and that the models exhibit an essential functional distinction), then we may say that conscious attention is a prerequisite for what distinguishes the models: the binding function.

Within a somewhat different research framework, Treisman and Gelade (1980) also see consciousness or attention as a necessary gateway to the true memory system, although certainly some processing can be done without it. According to Treisman's view, prior to focused attention, the various features in the perceptual world are free-floating rather than integrated—the supporting evidence being the discovery of *illusory conjunctions*. For example, given a blue circle and a red square presented very quickly, a person might report seeing a red circle. The role of conscious attention, then, is to fuse the elements in an event together correctly.

We did not set out to find a connection between the dependence and independence data on fragment completion from Hayman and Tulving's (1989a) lab and the work of Treisman and her colleagues on illusory conjunctions. Nevertheless, the manner in which the models explain the implicit-memory and explicit-memory data makes sense in terms of these other ideas and offers support for them. As we have shown, what the distributed models (accounting for the explicit-memory data) do that the separate-trace model (accounting for the implicit-memory data) does not do is to fuse the episodically presented features of events together to form a cohesive whole, a whole in which the parts will and do, if tested, exhibit interdependence.

6 CONCLUSION

The idea that explicit/episodic memory is distinguishable from implicit memory on the basis of how tightly bound up or interconnected the particular parts of the representation are has considerable intuitive appeal. What makes an episode a unique happening is presumably not just that the characteristics or features striking the observer are experienced, possibly in a helter-skelter manner, but rather that the concatenation or co-occurence of these various features at a certain time and in a certain space is perceived and remembered as a particular, unique configuration (see Johnson, 1992). Episodic events are not mere free fragments but at the core have this unique quality of coherent co-occurrence, a quality preserved by binding these elements together in memory. One might then expect that memory for a particular episodic event, as opposed to semantic or taxonomic knowledge, would rely heavily on the temporal co-occurence of particular attributes in a certain configuration. In spite of the intuitive appeal of this notion of binding as necessary to construct an event as a unique happening in memory, we nevertheless found it remarkable that evidence for this proposition could be found in the empirical data on the dependency relations among features. While this idea has, we believe, tremendous appeal ex post facto, it was hard to imagine in advance what kinds of data might even potentially be brought to bear upon it. After we have gone through the modeling exercise, the dependency relations found in the data from fragment completion now seem relevant in an obvious way. It is also encouraging that the core constraints of a converging group of computational models, despite many secondary differences, provide such straightforward and easily analyzed support for a very elegant notion: that a crucial characteristic distinguishing the explicit memory system from that underlying implicit memory is this special memory-binding function, which serves to coalesce the separate parts of an event into a cohesive and memorable whole.

REFERENCES

Anderson, J. R. (1978). Arguments concerning representations for mental imagery. *Psychological Review*, 85, 249–277.

Batchelder, W. H., & Rieffer, D. M. (1990). Multinomial processing models of source monitoring. *Psychological Review*, 97, 548–564.

Cottrell, G., Munro, P., & Zipser, D. (1989). Image compression by back propagation: An example of extensional programming. In Noel Sharkey (Ed.), *Models of cognition: A review of cognitive science* (Vol 1). Norwood: Ablex.

Flexser, A. J. (1981). Homogenizing the 2 × 2 contingency table: A method for removing dependencies due to subject and item differences. *Psychological Review, 88,* 327–339.

Graf, P., Mandler, G., & Haden, P. (1982). Simulating amnesic symptoms in normal subjects. *Science, 218,* 1243–1244.

Grossberg, S. (1987). Competitive learning: From interactive activation to adaptive resonance. *Cognitive Science, 11,* 23–63.

Hayman, C. A. G., & Tulving, E. (1989a). Is priming in fragment completion based on a "traceless" memory system? *Journal of Experimental Psychology: Learning, Memory, and Cognition, 15,* 941–956.

Hayman, C. A. G., & Tulving, E. (1989b). Contingent dissociation between recognition and fragment completion: The method of triangulation. *Journal of Experimental Psychology: Learning, Memory, and Cognition, 15,* 228–240.

Hintzman, D. L. (1986). "Schema abstraction" in a multiple-trace memory model. *Psychological Review, 93,* 411–428.

Hintzman, D. L. (1987). Recognition and recall in MINERVA2: Analysis of the "recognition-failure" paradigm. In P. Morris (Ed.), *Modeling cognition* (pp. 215–229). New York: Wiley.

Hintzman, D. L., & Hartry, A. L. (1991). Item effects in recognition and fragment completion: Contingency relations vary for different subsets of words. *Journal of Experimental Psychology: Learning, Memory, and Cognition, 16,* 955–969.

Hirsh, R. (1974). The hippocampus and contextual retrieval of information from memory: A theory. *Behavioral Biology, 12,* 421–444.

Hirst, W. (1982). The amnesic syndrome: Descriptions and explanations. *Psychological Bulletin, 91,* 435–460.

Humphreys, M. S., Pike, R., Bain, J. D., & Tehan, G. (1989). Global matching: A comparison of the SAM, MINERVA, Matrix, and TODAM models. *Journal of Mathematical Psychology, 33,* 36–67.

Jacoby, L. L., & Dallas, M. (1981). On the relationship between autobiographical memory and perceptual learning. *Journal of Experimental Psychology: General, 110,* 306–340.

Johnson, M. K. (1992). MEM: Mechanisms of recollection, *Journal of Cognitive Neuroscience, 4,* 268–280.

Metcalfe, J. (1991). Recognition failure and the composite memory trace in CHARM. *Psychological Review, 98,* 529–553.

Metcalfe, J. (1993). Monitoring and control in a composite holographic associative recall model (CHARM): Implications for Korsakoff amnesia. *Psychological Review, 100,* 3–22.

Metcalfe Eich, J. (1985). Levels of processing, encoding specificity, elaboration, and CHARM. *Psychological Review, 92,* 1–38.

Murdock, B. B. (1982). A theory of storage and retrieval of item and associative information. *Psychological Review, 91,* 281–294.

Nadel, L. (1992). Multiple memory systems: What and why. *Journal of Cognitive Neuroscience, 4,* 179–188.

Nilsson, L.-G., & Gardiner, J. M. (1991). Memory theory and boundary conditions of the Tulving-Wiseman law. In W. E. Hockley & S. Lewandowsky (Eds.), *Relating theory and data: Essays on human memory in honor of Bennet B. Murdock* (pp. 57–74). Hillsdale, NJ: Erlbaum.

Raaijmakers, J. G., & Shiffrin, R. M. (1981). Search of associative memory. *Psychological Review, 88*, 93–134.

Richardson-Klavehn, A., & Bjork, R. A. (1988). Measures of memory. *Annual Review of Psychology, 39*, 475–543.

Roediger, H. L., III, Weldon, M. S., & Challis, B. H. (1989). Explaining dissociations between implicit and explicit measures of retention: A processing account. In H. L. Roediger III & F. I. M. Craik (Eds.), *Varieties of memory and consciousness: Essays in Honour of Endel Tulving* (pp. 3–41). Hillsdale, NJ: Erlbaum.

Rumelhart, D. E., Hinton, G. E., & Williams, R. J. (1986). Learning representations by back-propagating errors. *Nature, 323*, 533–536.

Rumelhart, D. E., & Zipser, D. (1986). Feature discovery by competitive learning. In D. E. Rumelhart, J. L. McClelland, & the PDP Research Group, *Parallel distributed processing: Explorations in the microstructure of cognition* (Vol. 1, pp. 151–193). Cambridge: MIT Press.

Schacter, D. L. (1987). Implicit memory: History and current status. *Journal of Experimental Psychology: Learning, Memory, and Cognition, 13*, 501–518.

Sherry, D. F., & Schacter, D. L. (1987). The evolution of multiple memory systems. *Psychological Review, 94*, 439–454.

Shimamura, A. P. (1985). Problems with the finding of stochastic independence as evidence for the independence of cognitive processes. *Bulletin of the Psychonomic Society, 23*, 506–508.

Shimamura, A. P. (1986). Priming effects in amnesia: Evidence for a dissociable memory function. *Quarterly Journal of Experimental Psychology, 38A*, 619–644.

Squire, L. R. (1992). Declarative and nondeclarative memory: Multiple brain systems supporting learning and memory, *Journal of Cognitive Neuroscience, 4*, 232–243.

Treisman, A., & Gelade, G. (1980). A feature-integration theory of attention. *Cognitive Psychology, 12*, 97–136.

Tulving, E. (1986). What kind of hypothesis is the distinction between episodic and semantic memory? *Journal of Experimental Psychology: Learning, Memory, and Cognition, 12*, 307–311.

Tulving, E., Schacter, D. L., & Stark, H. A. (1982). Priming effects in word fragment completion are independent of recognition memory. *Journal of Experimental Psychology: Learning, Memory, and Cognition, 8*, 336–342.

Von der Malsberg, C. (1973). Self-organizing of orientation sensitive cells in the striate cortex. *Kybernetic, 14*, 85–100.

Watkins, M. J., & Todres, A. K. (1978). On the relation between recall and recognition. *Journal of Verbal Learning and Verbal Behavior, 17*, 621–633.

Witherspoon, D., & Moscovitch, M. (1989). Stochastic independence between two implicit memory tasks. *Journal of Experimental Psychology: Learning, Memory, and Cognition, 15*, 22–30.

Contributors

Alan Baddeley is Director of the Medical Research Council Applied Psychology Unit in Cambridge, and Professor of Cognitive Psychology at Cambridge University. His interests extend across the psychology and neuropsychology of human memory, with a particular emphasis on short-term or working memory. He is author of *The psychology of memory* (Basic Books, 1976), *Your memory: A user's guide* (Penguin, 1983; rev. ed., 1993), *Working memory* (Oxford University Press, 1986), *Human memory: Theory and practice* (Allen & Bacon, 1990), and coauthor (with S. Gathercole) of *Working memory and language* (Lawrence Erlbaum Associates, 1993).

Barbara L. Chalfonte is a graduate student in cognitive psychology at Princeton University. She received an M.S. in psychology from McMaster University and was a member of the Technical Staff of Bell Communications Research. Her current research explores how features such as shape, color, and location become bound together in memory and probes potential disruptions in feature coding and binding in amnesia and aging.

Garrison W. Cottrell is Associate Professor of Computer Science at the University of California at San Diego. His interests are in computational modeling, image processing, face recognition, and psycholinguistics. He is coeditor of *Lexical ambiguity resolution: Perspectives from psycholinguistic and artificial intelligence* (Morgan Kaufman, 1988).

Howard Eichenbaum is Professor at the Center for Behavioral Neuroscience at the State University of New York at Stony Brook. He is coauthor, with Neal J. Cohen, of *Memory, amnesia, and the hippocampal system* (MIT Press, 1993). His research focuses on the nature of memory processing mediated by the hippocampus and related brain structures.

Richard Granger is Professor at the University of California at Irvine, with appointments in the Center for the Neurobiology of Learning and Memory and the Computer Science Department. His work in behavioral and computational neuroscience focuses on simulation and mathematical analysis of induction and expression rules for synaptic long-term potentiation (Ambros-Ingerson et al., *Science* 247 [1990]: 1344), differential functional properties of distinct forms of plasticity in different anatomical regions of the telencephalon (Lynch and Granger, *Journal of Cognitive Neuroscience* 4 [1992]: 189), and behavioral and physiological predictions based on these analyses (Granger et al., *Psychological Science* 2 [1991]: 116; Granger et al., *Synapse* 15 [1993]: 326).

Marcia K. Johnson is Professor of Psychology at Princeton University. Her laboratory group studies human memory and considers such issues as source monitoring (e.g., how memories for actual and imagined events are discriminated), memory disorders, dissociations among memory measures, the binding of features into complex memories, the relation between emotion and cognition, and the nature of consciousness.

Gary Lynch is Professor above Scale in the Center for the Neurobiology of Learning and Memory at the University of California at Irvine. He is the author of nearly 400 publications in the field of neuroscience. His current research involves how particular patterns of activity in brain circuits produce lasting changes in the strength of synaptic connections (Larson and Lynch, *Science* 232 [1986]: 985), specific modifications to the glutamate receptor that underlie these synaptic changes (Vanderklish et al., *Synapse* 12 [1992]: 333; Ambros-Ingerson and Lynch, *Proceedings of the National Academy of Science* 90 [1993]: 7903), the relationship of these changes to the encoding, organization, and utilization of memory (Granger and Lynch, *Current Opinion in Neurobiology* 1 [1991]: 209), and recently discovered links between the encoding machinery and the development of neuropathology (Peterson et al., *Neuroscience Letters* 121 [1991]: 239).

W. E. Mencl is a Ph.D. candidate at Dartmouth College. His interests are in computational modeling and music cognition.

Janet Metcalfe is Professor of Psychology and Cognitive Neuroscience at Dartmouth College. Her research focuses on human memory, problem solving, and metacognition, including work on face recognition, eyewitness testimony, insight processes, and monitoring and control deficits. She has proposed a computational model of human explicit memory called the CHARM model. She and Arthur Shimamura have recently edited *Metacognition: Knowing about knowing* (MIT Press, 1994).

Morris Moscovitch is Professor of Psychology at Erindale College, University of Toronto, and Research Consultant at the Rotman Research Institute and Department of Psychology of the Baycrest Centre for Geriatric Care in Toronto. His research is on hemispheric specialization, and memory and attention in normal and brain-damaged people. His recent interest in modularity and consciousness, which is evident in his chapter in this book, prompted him and Carlo Umiltà to organize a conference and edit a book based on the proceedings. The book is *Attention and performance*, vol. 15, *Conscious and nonconscious information processing* (MIT Press, 1994).

Lynn Nadel is Professor and Chair of the Psychology Department at the University of Arizona in Tucson. He is coauthor of *The hippocampus as a cognitive map* (Oxford University Press, 1978) and coeditor of a number of books on computational neuroscience and complex systems, on the one hand, and Down Syndrome and Alzheimer's

Disease, on the other. His research interests include the hippocampus, spatial cognition and memory, and developmental disabilities involving hippocampal dysfunction.

David S. Olton was Professor of Psychology at the Johns Hopkins University. His research examined the neural mechanisms of memory. In particular, his work has investigated the role of the hippocampal system in normal memory and in animal models of human amnesia. He died on February 1, 1994.

Jerry W. Rudy is Professor of Psychology at the University of Colorado. His research interests are in learning and memory processes. His current work focuses on memory development in animals.

Daniel L. Schacter is Professor of Psychology at Harvard University and is affiliated with the Department of Neurology at Massachusetts General Hospital. His research interests center on cognitive and neuropsychological aspects of implicit and explicit memory. He is the author of *Stranger behind the engram: Theories of memory and the psychology of science* (Lawrence Erlbaum Associates, 1982).

Matthew L. Shapiro is Assistant Professor of Psychology at McGill University. His research concentrates on the physiology of memory. His work has examined neural information processing in the hippocampus, using pharmacological and computational modeling techniques.

Larry R. Squire is Professor of Psychiatry and Neurosciences at the University of California School of Medicine, San Diego, and Research Career Scientist at the Veterans Administration Medical Center, San Diego. He received his Ph.D. from the Massachusetts Institute of Technology. His research investigates the organization and neurological foundations of memory. He is the author of *Memory and brain* (Oxford University Press, 1987) and more than 200 scientific articles. He is a member of the National Academy of Sciences, is a recipient of the 1993 Charles A. Dana Award for Pioneering Achievement in Health, and is currently President of the Society for Neuroscience (1993–1994).

Robert J. Sutherland is Associate Professor of Psychology and Physiology at the University of New Mexico in Albuquerque. His primary research interests are in the organization of memory systems in the mammalian forebrain and in the relationship between the mechanisms of synaptic plasticity and memory.

Endel Tulving, F.R.S., is Tanenbaum Chair in Cognitive Neuroscience at the Rotman Research Institute of Baycrest Centre, Toronto, Canada. He taught previously at the University of Toronto and Yale University. He has spent all of his professional life pursuing riddles and puzzles in the domain of human memory.

Index